pic - Mountain High Resort

CONTENTS 2001

Visit, www.worldsnowboardguide.com
for details on,
Accommodation Directory - Avalanche Call - Backcountry Guide - Rider services
Job Seekers Guide - Language Guide - Ride Time Guide - Summer Ride Guide.

WSG would like to give a massive thanks to Gerard Houllier and all the players at Liverpool Football Club who's first class efforts made completing this book a real pleasure. Much of the work for this edition was slotted in between some great matches and final games (mind you it was also done with a lot of lager and some major hangovers after each final).

Liverpool - winners of the Worthington Cup against Birmingham was a testing one, but still a result is a result.

Liverpool - winners of the FA Cup against Arsenal was in the end a richly deserved prize thanks to golden boy Michale Owen (weep dear Arsenal weep).

Liverpool - winners of the UEFA Cup against Alaves was a truly magical and historic game of football and not one for the faint harted. Nail biting stuff followed by a major booze up, a major hangover and subsequently the loss of three days work. But not all was lost as you now have this book in you're hands to read.

(guess someone around here is a Liverpool fan then!)

Lyndsey D' resistance is futile

World Snowboard Guide 2002
ISBN 1-900916-10-X
Written and Compiled by : TONY BROWN
Layout and Design by: TONY BROWN

Edited by: CAROL ROBERTSON

Published by: ICE PUBLISHING
45 CORROUR RD, AVIEMORE,
INVERNESS-SHIRE, PH22 1SS.
tel & fax ++44 (0)1479 810 362
www. worldsnowboardguide.com

Advertising: McMillan Scott Plc :
London - tel 020 7878 2300

Distribution:
UK - **Vine House Ltd**
tel 01825 723 398
USA & Canada - **SGB Distribution**
tel 001 - 800 729 6423

Printed By:
Stephens & George - *tel 01685 388 888*

Main cover picture
Florent Duasse - Tignes - A-Snowboards

4th cover picture
David Brownell / Sugarloaf USA

This book is dedicated to the Middleton team for all they did. Special thanks to Gary, Brian and the whole team.

MAMBO®
WHITEGOODS 2001
mambo® WHITEGOODS
MAMBO® DRYGOODS
MAMBO® SMALLGOODS

Introduction

pic - Stevie Trollands

We would like start by saying that WSG doesn't aim to win any prizes for its writing skills, so if you notice any spelling or grammar errors in this book don't fret, its the message that counts and although we do fell a bit stupid when we make the odd cock-up, we don't lose any sleep over it. However, if you spot any details that should be changed or would like to add someting new, then by all means please contact us with your information and we will feature it in WSG 2003.

WSG is the world's only snowboard guide and unlike ski guides which play lip service to snowboarding, WSG sticks solely to snowboarding with no holding back and no clap trap. We tell it as it is.

Where you stay in a resort will depend on your budget. **WSG** lists the options close to the slopes whether you're looking for hotels, chalets, apartments, bunk houses or youth hostels. We tell you what you can expect to pay for a room or a bed and when the best deals are available. We also list tour operators with package deals, where they offer their deals and web addresses to help you check out the last minute offerings.

No two mountains are the same and so **WSG** details all the relevant data with mountain heights, number of runs, rider ability levels and what style of riding the resort's terrain favours. If a resort has a halfpipe or fun park we list it and give its location on the mountain. We also give a guide to lift prices, but please note, the lift prices that we list may well have changed by the time you arrive at a chosen resort, so use the tarrifs as a guide only.

Off the slopes, **WSG** lists restaurants from expensive to budget food outlets. We try and give you an idea where the best places to hang out at night are, listing where to get a drink, shoot some pool, or chat up a local for a bit of holiday romance. We provide details on other resort attractions as well as telling you how costly or cheap a place might be and finally give it an overall rating to indicate whether a place is worth a visit or not.

When considering where to go, you will need to decide what you actually want out of a resort. Instruction, hire facilities, terrain, accommodation, location to the slopes, restaurants and night time action are the important things to consider.

In general, winter resorts open from November to the end of April. Resorts that offer summer snowboarding usually have their lifts running until mid-July and, in a few cases, mid-August. Early and late season times provide the lowest lift tariffs and accommodation rates. Some resorts even have special early season ride packages. Note that resorts which open prior to Christmas may still not have all their local services in operation, and accommodation options could be limited. Christmas, New Year, February school holidays and Easter breaks are the busiest times at any resort, with the dearest liftpass rates.

A resort's altitude is an important point to consider. Low level areas can often suffer from insufficient snow and may have to rely on artificial snowmaking. They usually have a shorter season and those that struggle beyond March, will have very little snow on the lower runs, ruling out riding back to the resort.
High altitude resorts usually guarantee snow throughout the season and often form part of a glacial area. These resorts are generally more expensive than the lower ones, but the extra cost may mean the difference between excellent or poor snow.

In Europe there are a number of regions that join up with others to form vast acreages of rideable terrain. One such example is Les Trois Vallees in France, which boasts over 600 kilometres of linked slope. However, while it may seem great to have that amount of terrain on offer, in reality, you are unlikely to cover a quarter of it in a dozen visits. Most people tend to stick to a few favourite runs.

Resorts have varying terrain features that will appeal to different styles of riders. Freestylers generally look for places that have lots of jumps, carvers prefer wide, groomed runs, whilst freeriders look for trees, bowls, backcountry slopes and cliffs. But please note, whatever type of rider you are, never ride on terrain above your ability.
Some resorts provide snowboard-only areas that can be ridden with a discounted liftpass. Details should be available at ticket offices. Snowboard-only areas don't just contain fun-parks and half-pipes; many have runs for carvers, mini-parks for kids and boardercross circuits for freeriders.

Many resorts build fun-parks and pipes, but they don't all maintain them. You could ask for a shovel at the lift hut and do some pipe-shaping yourself, but only wield a shovel with permission. If you don't know what you're doing and destroy a hit, the locals riders will have some sharp words with you.

After your travel and accommodation costs, your next main expense will be a liftpass. Resorts offer a variety of discounted tickets for kids, old age pensioners, students, and of course, locals. You can also get deals if you ride on certain days, (normally off-peak times such as week days). Tickets can usually be bought on a daily or multiple-day basis. Weekly tickets will normally require an attached picture, so take a passport-sized photo with you. Riders staying for a few months can buy season passes, and although expensive, you will make a massive saving in the long run.

Rules on snowboard leashes and the position of the back foot whilst on the lifts vary around the globe. To avoid any crap from lifties, have a leash attached to your front binding. If there are no signs at the lift stations explaining rules on leashes or back foot placement, seek advice at the ticket office or ask a local. Beginners are advised to travel on lifts with their rear foot released from the binding, as it allows for a quick getaway should you fall off the lift. Rules in the US are more established than in Europe, with most resorts insisting on leashes regardless of how well you can ride.

Should you be planning a snowboard trip with a loved one, note an important rule - don't act as their instructor! It will end in tears, and you will soon become bored and miss out on some riding. Send all novices to the snowboard school and be done with it! Most resorts offer snowboard tuition focusing mainly on beginners. However some resorts have specialist snowboard-only schools, who will often have freestyle and race training programmes, as well as facilities for kids.

If you are serious about snowboarding and really want to improve your technique, a good idea is to go on a snowboard camp. Camps offer top instruction from professional riders and are tailored to all levels and styles. Winter camps exist but the best time to attend is during the summer.

If you plan to rent snowboard equipment, it may be better to hire in-resort. Not only do you just pay for the days that you actually use the kit, but you can change the boards to suit your needs. If you have your own snowboard then obviously take it with you, but have the board pre-serviced before you leave.

Facilities for junior riders are slowly improving. Being palmed off with adult rental kit is no longer acceptable, so a mark of a good rental centre is the availability of genuine kids' equipment for hire. Look for kids' boards and boots and the option of hiring safety helmets.

Some resorts provide snowboard clothing for hire. However, it is highly unlikely you will find anywhere to rent gloves, so don't leave home without a pair. Always check on screws and other parts of your kit; if bits do come loose on the mountain, look out for tools located at most lift stations. It's a good idea to carry your own mini-binding tool.

Mountain restaurants are expensive and so if you are strapped for cash, take up a packed lunch. Having a beer on the slopes is all part of the scene, but be warned, if you're caught riding out of control because you are drunk, not only will you be a danger, but you could be arrested and stripped of your liftpass. Some resorts have police as well as ski-patrolers on the slopes.

Snowboarding is a leisure activity, not a military campaign, but do remember that mountains can be hostile places, and should be treated with respect. The higher you are, the thinner the air, which means you need to work harder. Unfit people wearing the wrong clothing and going balls-out are candidates for altitude sickness.
To avoid getting snow-blindness, wear correct goggles or glasses. Not all trendy overpriced eyewear will prevent problems, so take advice. Your skin will definitely

catch the sun even in complete cloud cover so use sun-block to avoid cooking yourself. However, always remember that snowboarders do **not,** under any circumstances, wear the silly coloured stuff that skiers love to prance around in.

When booking accommodation, the more people you squeeze into your rented accommodation, the cheaper the shared costs will be. If you are looking for accommodation that offers all the creature comforts plus easy access to the slopes, then expect to pay for it. Budget apartments are generally

those located furthest from the slopes. Chalets and apartments are good options for chilling out with ease. Some are surprisingly affordable, but note, booking will usually require a hefty deposit.

Insurance should speak for itself. In some countries you are not allowed on the slopes without personal injury cover (the US is extremely strict). You should also take out adequate cover for belongings, and if you are on a package deal, make sure you are covered for cancellation and other mishaps. Tour operators offer a number of insurance schemes but be sure you check the small print. SNOWBOARDING must be mentioned and covered in all policies. Some places have insurance cover built into a liftpass, like the French 'Carte Neige'. Ask at ticket offices for confirmation of this.

High on the need-to-know agenda is where to eat and drink after a day's riding. To save money, live off fast food. Don't bother with fancy restaurants - it's better to save your cash for boozing. Some bars thrive on a snowboard culture with music likely to be indie and hip-hop, rather than the Euro-pop played in aprés-ski bars. As far as snowboard night-life goes, remember, boarders don't 'do' aprés-ski, nor wear stupid coloured face paints and dance around at sick tea-time bar sessions whilst playing stupid party games.

One last point, if you are with your parents, ditch them as soon as you arrive at the resort. You will soon meet up with local riders who will show you the best areas. No rider should have to hang out on the slopes or at night with those dressed in '70s style clobber.

Finally, thanks to the following for their assistance with this edition of WSG.

Ruth Robinson *for US articles.*

Simon Numan-Carter *for Fernie article.*

Wess *for a couple of pictures.*

Rob Laisney *for Swiss articles.*

Parisa Urquehart *for Iran article.*

Ian & Peter Cornfoot *for bits and bobs.*

Dave Flowerdew *for his assistance.*

Eddy Spearing *for, er, er, er, god knows.*

Tammy *for US articles.*

Christie *for US articles.*

Aviemore's Rajs *for being just that!*

Kaya *for being Kaya.*

Daffy Duck *for his sound advice.*

Tennents Larger *for keeping the main. engine oiled.*

Canada

GENERAL INFO AND FACTS

Capital - Ottawa
Language - English & French
Currency - Canadian Dollar
Alcohol drinking age - 18 to 19
Drugs - Cannabis is illegal
Death Penalty - Doesn't Exist
Age of consent for Sex - 16
Military Service - Not compulsory
Electricity Supply - 110 Volts AC
International phone Code - 001
Highest Peak - Mt Logan 6,050m

DUTY FREE
1 Litre of Spirits or wine
24 x 355 ml cans of beer
200 Cigarettes
50 Cigars
200g of tobacco

CANADIAN DRIVE GUIDE
All vehicles drive on the right hand side of the road
Speed Limits -
Motorways 100kph (62mph)
Highways 90kph (55mph)
Towns 50kph (30mph)

SNOWBOARD CONTACTS
Snowboard Canada Magazine
2255BB Queen St, E.
Suite 3266. Toronto. ON. M4E
tel - 001 (416) 406 2400
info@snowboardcanada.com

Canadian Snowboard Federation
4th Floor East 235 Queen Street
Ottawa, Ontario. K1 0H6
tel - 001 (613) 954 3851

TIME ZONES
Canada has 6 time Zones

Pacific
GMT -8 hours

Mountain
GMT -7 hours

Central
GMT -6 hours

Eastern
GMT -5 hours

Atlantic
GMT -4 hours

Newfoundland
GMT -3.5hours

INTERNATIONAL AIRPORTS

1- Calgary
2 - Montreal
3 - Ottawa
4 - Quebec
5 - Toronto
6 - Vancouver

Canada has around 270 resorts, located on either the west or east coast of the country with a few resorts in the central provinces. There is even a snowboard only resort known as *'The Snowboard Ranch'* which is located 18 miles from the town of **Peterborough** in the province of **Ontario**.

The western provinces boast Canada's best mountainous areas, **Alberta** and **British Columbia (BC)**. Both regions have resorts that are a match for any in Europe. The gateway cities for flights to the west coast areas are **Calgary** in **Alberta**, and **Vancouver** in **BC**.

On the east coast there are a number of areas to ride, the majority being in the French speaking province of **Quebec**. The 100+ resorts on the east coast of Canada resemble much of what is found on the east coast of America - low level, wooded, and often windswept terrain.
Canadians treat their visitors with respect and provide a very high level of resort services to meet customer requirements. There are good slope facilities in most places, along with an abundance of places to eat and sleep close to the slopes. Prices are generally higher than those in the US but lower than in Europe. Canadians also like a beer and a good night out, so expect to party hard.

Accommodation facilities in Canada include condos and high quality hotels, as well as B&B's, lodges, hostels or dorms. Prices vary from place to place and are generally quite high wherever you go, (unless you can bunk on a floor and overload with people).

Getting around Canada by train is easy on **VIA Rail**, the Canadian national rail network, or Amtrak which runs across the Canadian/US border. **Greyhound** buses are another cheap option. Entry into Canada is liberal but you will need a passport and be advised, you can't work in Canada without a work permit as rules are strict. If you get caught scrubbing dishes in a hotel without the correct paper work, you'll soon be on your way home.

If you wish to teach snowboarding in Canada, you will need the **Canadian Association of Snowboard Instructors** (C.A.S.I.) Level 1 certificate. For details on the course, which costs from C$224, contact C.A.S.I. on 001-514 748 2648.

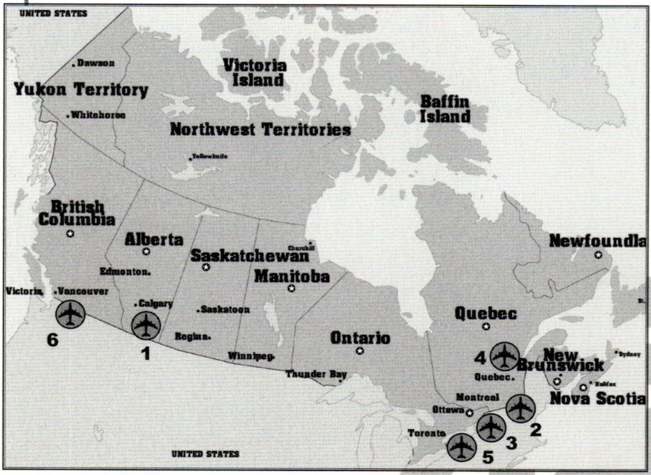

pic - Craig Farish - Kimberley Resort

PROVINCE	PAGE
Alberta	14
British Columbia	22
Quebec	42
Saskatchewan	46
Round UP	48

Alberta - AB

Resort	Page
Fortress Mountain	15
Lake Louise	16
Mt Norquay	18
Sunshine Village	19
Marmott Basin	20

GENERAL INFO AND FACTS

Capital - Edmonton
Language - English & French
Currency - Canadian Dollar
Alcohol drinking age - 18
Drugs - Cannabis is illegal
Death Penalty - Doesn't Exist
Age of consent for Sex - 16
Electricity Supply - 110 Volts AC
Area phone Code - 403
Provincial sales tax - 7% general 5% in Hotels but 0% in restaurants

ALBERTA DRIVE GUIDE

All vehicles drive on the right side of the road.

Speed Limits -

Highways	100kph (62mph)
Rural routes	80kph (50mph)
Towns	50kph (30mph)

Road Watch 001 (403) 246 5853
Fuel is sold in Litres

TRAVEL CONTACTS

International Airports
Edmonton & Calgary
Air Canada 001 (403) 298 9200
Canadian Airlines 800 426 700

Via Rail
Edmonton
001 422 890 4350
Calgary tel: 001 800 561 8630

Greyhound Buses
Edmonton 001 420 2412
Calgary 001 800 561 8630

Mountain
GMT -7 hours

AREA INFORMATION

Alberta Tourism
17811 116th Ave.
Edmonton. AB T5S 2J2
001 780 427 4321

pic - S. Metcalf - Lake Louise Resort

Fortress Mountain Alberta

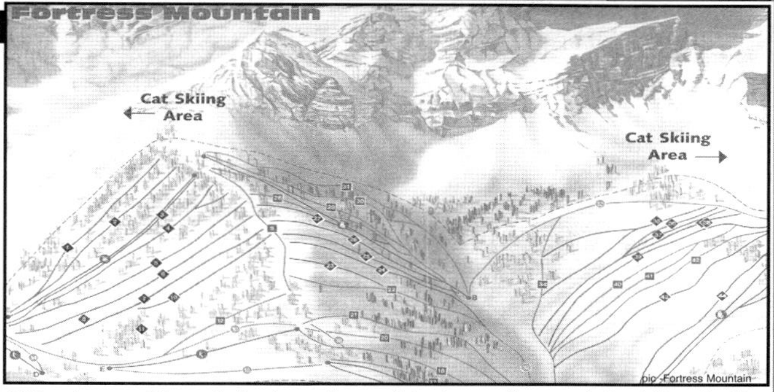

MOUNTAIN DATA

Top Lift at - 2369m
Ride Area 328 acres
Bottom Lift at - 2040m
Vertical Drop - 329m
Number of Runs - 47
Longest - 1.2 miles (2km)

TERRAIN LEVELS

Easy	20%
Intermediate	55%
Advanced	25%
Expert =	

TERRAIN TO SUITE

Freeride	20%
Trees	Yes
Backcountry	Yes
Freestyle	55%
Halfpipe	Yes 1
Terrain Park	Yes 1
Carving	25%

SNOW DATA

Average Snowfall
630cm a season
Snowmaking
40% cover of the slopes
Winter Periods
Nov to April
Summer Riding
None

SLOPE ACCESS

Total Lifts = **6**
Uplift Rate - 8,400 people an hour.
3 Chair lifts
3 Drag lifts
**Leashes Required*

Lift Times
9.00am to 4.00pm

Lift Pass Rates

1 Day pass	C$29.75
3 Day pass	C$83.55
5 Day pass	C$130.95

Travel Guide

Fly to **Calgary** with a 1¼ hour transfer to Fortress Mountain.

Bus services direct from Calgary & Edmonton.

Route Planner:
From Calgary, via Highways 1 & 40 towards Kananaskis. Fortress is 50 miles south of Banff.
The drive time to the resort is **2** hours.

Fortress Mountain is a decent but small resort that lies in the shadow of some very impressive rock faces. Located only 50 miles from Calgary, Fortress attracts a fair amount of weekend city dwellers, but don't be put off as it's a cool place to ride. There are great off-piste areas and full on tree-riding, with marked trails covering three sides of the mountain. Even though it's rated as more of an intermediate's resort, beginners and advanced riders should not feel left out. Those who can handle themselves at speed have plenty of hard-core riding to go for, especially on **Backside**, where you can find a nice double black diamond trail to test you. The mountain's layout helps to maintain a good snow covering, as well as providing some excellent powder terrain that can be ridden into May.

Freeriders should come away from Fortress as professional tree-riders as the glades are awesome. **Backside** has some of the best freeride terrain, offering a great time shredding through the spruce and hitting off some sweet banks. The off-piste opportunities are very impressive, provided you seek the knowledge of a local rider who can show you where to go. The boundary lines are not strictly adhered to, which makes a trip to the Fortress area all the more fun, though be careful.

Freestylers have a halfpipe located between the **2nd** and **3rd Chute** slopes, but at the moment there is no fun-park. The pipe is shaped with the aid of a Pipe Dragon.

Carvers are not spoilt for choice since there are a few long flats, but there is still some reasonable carving terrain. **The Jolly Jester** is a cool longhaul on the **Backside**, whilst on the front, **Friars** is the place to carve at speed.

Beginners may not find Fortress the most convenient mountain to learn on, but it's certainly not the worst. There are a number of easy trails to tackle, aided by the boys at *Fortress Snowboard School*, who offer programmes for novice and beyond

Off the slopes, basic accommodation is available around the mountain, but is limited to a few chalets or a bed at the ski dorm. A greater selection of local services are provided in the village of **Kananaskis**, which is 25 minutes away. Kananaskis has a number of hotels and a good choice of places to eat or drink in. It's not very cheap or that hot for night-life, but is still worth a visit.
For accommodation listings visit - www.worldsnowboardguide.com

Fortress Mountain Resort
111-11 Avenue, S.W Kananskis Vilage. Alberta.
***001* (403) 591 7108** **www.skifortress.com**
www.virgin.com/holidays

Overall rating out of 10 **7** **Not bad for a weekend visit.**

Lake Louise

Alberta

MOUNTAIN DATA

Top Lift at - 2637m

Ride Area 4200 acres

Bottom Lift at - 1646m

Vertical Drop - 991m

Number of Runs - 113

Longest - 5 miles (8km)

TERRAIN LEVELS

Easy	**20%**
Intermediate	**45%**
Advanced	**30%**
Expert = **12 runs**	

TERRAIN TO SUITE

Freeride	**50%**
Trees	Yes
Backcountry	Yes
Freestyle	**30%**
Halfpipe	Yes 2
Terrain Park	Yes 1
Carving	**20%**

SNOW DATA

Average Snowfall
409cm a season

Snowmaking
40% cover of the slopes

Winter Periods
Nov to May

Summer Riding
None

SLOPE ACCESS

Total Lifts = **12**

Uplift Rate -15,499 people an hour.

8 Chair lifts

4 Drag lifts

**Leashes Required*

Lift Times
9.00am to 4.00pm

Lift Pass Rates

1 Day pass	C$54
3 Day pass	C$150
5 Day pass	C$250

SLOPE ACTION

Snowboard Hire
Daily rates from C$37
Kids from C$27

Snowboard Tuition
Lesson, lift & hire
from C$39 per day

Night Riding
No

Heli Boarding
3 runs from $445

Snowmobiles
Hire & tours

Mountain Cafes
3

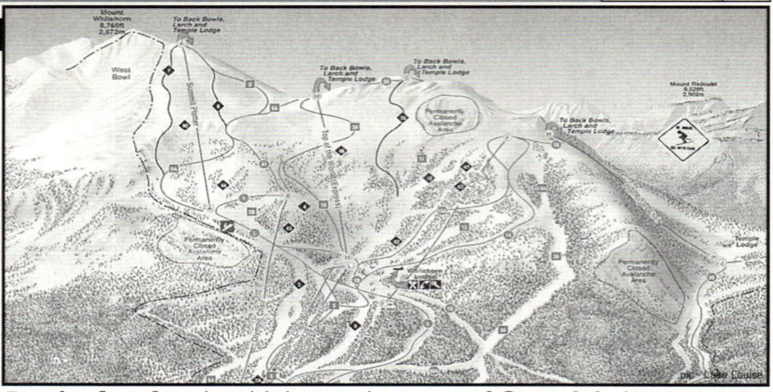

Lake Louise is widely rated as one of **Canada's** best resorts, and by far the biggest and most popular resort in **Alberta**. Being a popular place has, however, led to an area that is often unbearably busy, both on the slopes and around town. Recently the resort has undergone a few million dollar changes that include the new **Glacier Triple Chair** which starts out at the base area. The resort has also done much to improve the slopes with the edition of six new piste groomers and a brand new **Super Pipe** Grinder. **Lake Louise** is located close to the smaller resorts of **Sunshine** and **Mt Norquay** and all three share a joint lift pass.

Lake Louise is spread out over four mountain faces and collectively they offer terrain to suit all levels and styles of rider while being serviced by a well-connected lift system. A high speed quad can whisk you to **The Top of the World** in under ten minutes, from where you can access the **Back Bowls**. Unlimited and unbelievably long tree-lined powder runs lie in wait at every turn. And with new runs and lifts planned for the **Wolvern** and **Richardsons Ridge** areas, there's always new ground to explore.

Freeriders should note that it is illegal to ride in the marked out avalanche danger areas. If you're caught expect to be ejected from the hill with your pass confiscated, and even prosecuted. However, if you have the balls and fancy some out of bounds, the **Purple Bowl** in the **Larch Area** is a mega place to check out, offering a mixture of extreme and easy terrain. If you don't mind a knee-deep hike, trek up to the double black at Elevator Shaft where you'll find a host of black runs, cornice drops and rock jumps to try out. The steep blacks on the **Summit Platter** will test the best, but be warned: don't go outside the marked boundary into the **West Bowl** unless you know what you are doing.

Freestylers now have a reconstructed fun park known as the **'The Jungle'** reached off the **Olympic** chair. At 650 metres long and loaded with hits, The Jungle boast about being the largest terrain park in North America. The new pipe grinder now gives Louise a 'Super Pipe' which allows big transitions and massive air.

Carvers wanting a fast easy run should try the **Wiwaxy Trail** on the front side of the **South** facing slopes, which, at 8 kms, is the longest run in the area. Alternatively, for less crowded riding, check out a run known as **Larch.** This is a cool trail, as is the green run known as **Lookout** (which you will need to do, to avoid a sudden left hand drop into a steep black called **Ski Out**).

Beginners will find Louise a particularly good place to start out, with a host of easy to reach runs starting at the base area. The runs off **Eagle** chair are the best and allow you to have a long cruise home down trails such as **14** and **1**, which are also in a speed restricted area. The Lake Louise Snowboard School is excellent and offers loads of beginner to advanced programmes.

Lake Louise is a rather drab village that caters perfectly well for dot.com millionaires but not for budget conscious snowboarders. The truth is, Lake Louise has become far too overcrowded with holiday punters and charges excessive prices for everything. Many visitors prefer to stay in **Banff** which is only 30 miles from **Louise**. **Banff** is loaded with accommodation, shops, bars and places to hang out. Hotels can be expensive but there are cheap alternatives, including the youth hostel that costs from C$17/night for members and C$22 for non-members. The hostel also offers bed and ticket packages; for C$295 you get 5 nights accommodation with breakfast, lift pass, and return travel to the mountain included.

In **Louise** the options for eating out are okay, but very pricey. *The Chateau* is at the top end of the market and criminally expensive. However, in Banff the Hard Rock Cafe offers good food, while *Bumper's* has the biggest steaks you've ever seen. The licensed cafe at the youth hostel has the best value food.

Evenings in **Louise** are simply lame although *Charlie's* or *The Grill* are good for a beer and a game of pool. Banff offers more street-wise entertainment and goes on well into the early hours. *The Rose and Crown* is a popular pub that gets very crowded on occasions.

Accommodation in **Lake Louise** is very expensive. However, what is on offer is of a very high standard, with a number of top class hotels and lodges. Self catering is also well catered for with some very reasonable deals available for groups. If you have the cash, the *Post Hotel* is okay. However, **Banff** offers the best selection of affordable places. *The Blue Mountain* has nightly rates from $50 for B&B. *The High Country Inn* has rooms from $70 a night while the Youth Hostel has bunks from $20 per night per person.

For accommodation listings visit - www.worldsnowboardguide.com

Summary: Excellent freeriding on four mountain faces although slopes can get very busy. Facilities in Louise are a bit on the dull side, but Banff rocks.
Money wise: Expensive lodging and eating out but overall good value.

Overall rating out of 10 **7**

Lake Louise Resort
P.O. Box 5 Lake Louise
Alberta. T01 0C0
General info ***001*** **(403) 522 3555**
Reservations ***001*** **(800) 258 7669**
Snowphone ***001*** **(403) 244 6665**
www.skilouise.com
www.virgin.com/holidays

pic - Scott Rowed

pic - S.Metcalf

Travel Guide

Fly to **Calgary** International
Transfer time to resort = **2 1/4** hours.
Local airport = n/a.

Approximate global air travel times to **Calgary**:

from: London	**9**	hours
New York	**4 1/2**	hours
Frankfurt	**9 1/2**	hours

A bus from Calgary takes 2 1/4 hours. Info: (403) 762 6700
A local shuttle bus runs daily to Lake Louise from Banff.

Trains: None

Route Planner
Calgary *via Canmore/Banff*

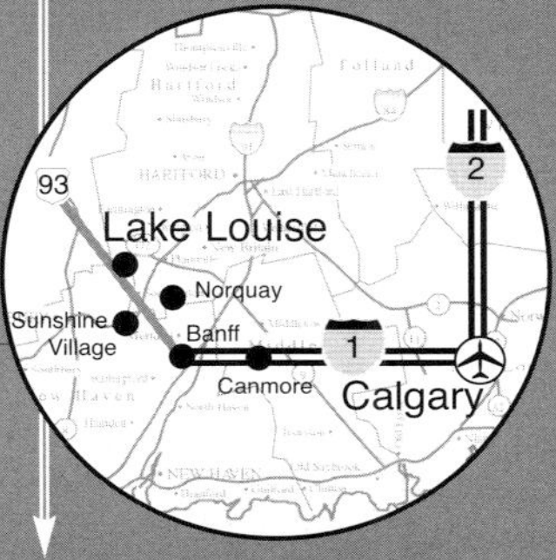

Lake Louise = 115 miles (185km)
Drive time is about **2 1/4** hours

Mt Norquay Alberta

MOUNTAIN DATA

Top Lift at - 2133m

Ride Area 162 acres

Bottom Lift at - 1636m

Vertical Drop - 2133m

Number of Runs - 27

Longest - 6 miles (10km)

TERRAIN LEVELS

Easy	11%
Intermediate	45%
Advanced	28%
Expert =	16%= 2 runs

TERRAIN TO SUITE

Freeride	50%
Trees	Yes
Backcountry	Yes
Freestyle	30%
Halfpipe	Yes 1
Terrain Park	Yes 1
Carving	20%

SNOW DATA

Average Snowfall
300cm a season

Snowmaking
90% cover of the slopes

Winter Periods
Dec to April

Summer Riding
None

SLOPE ACCESS

Total Lifts = **5**

Uplift Rate - 5000 people an hour.

3 Chair lifts

2 Drag lifts

**Leashes Required*

Lift Times
9.00am to 4.00pm

Lift Pass Rates

1/2 Day pass	C$32
1 Day pass	C$42
Night Pass	C$21

Travel Guide

Fly to **Calgary** 1 1/2 hours transfer to Mount Norquay.

Bus services from Calgary & Edmonton via Banff.

Route Planner:
From Calgary, via Highway 1 to Banff via Canmore. Mt Norquay lies north of Banff along the Norquay road. **Calgary** to Norquay is **68** miles and will take **2** hours.

pic - Dwarf

Mount Norquay is the nearest boarding area to **Banff** via a ten minute bus ride (costing C$9 leaving regularly from the main hotels). With just 6 lifts, it is the smallest resort in the area, but not without a lot of varied terrain to ride. Since 90% of the runs have snow-making machines, you shouldn't have any problem with the white stuff, even late in the season. Some of the steepest terrain in the Banff area can be found at Norquay on either side of the **North American** chair, which the locals claim can be superb after a heavy dump. Norquay has night riding from 4pm to 9pm. A night ride ticket costs C$21.

Freeriders should take the high speed **Mystic Ridge** lift to ride the best boarding area on the mountain. It gives you access to six long blue runs through the trees, with **Imp** and **Knight Flight** being favourites. There are some steeper options from this lift, like **Black Magic**, and the interestingly named **Ka-Poof**, which can either be great after a heavy fall of snow, or awful with icy hardpack late in the season.

Freestylers have a good halfpipe and fun-park, both of which are shaped by the Rockies first turbo *Pipe Grinder*. Below the pipe is a full on fun-park with all types of hits, including a massive quarter-pipe, gap jumps and table-tops. The great thing is that it's nearly always deserted and there's even a new tow rope that runs adjacent to the beginner pipe. A discounted lift pass is available for riders using the park via the **Cascade** lift at just C$27.

.

Carvers will warm to Norquay even though none of the runs are particularly long. The easy flats off the **Spirit Quad** chair are the place to head first before cranking it down **Excalibur**, a decent black run off the **Mystic Quad**.

Beginners have very easy access to tame pistes from the base station. The green runs next to the slow **Double Cascade** chair are a great place to learn some linked turns although there is otherwise a lack of easy graded terrain.

There are no local facilities at Norquay apart from *Timberline Inn* at the bottom of the ride-out (tel: (403) 762 2281). The Timberline Inn has a bar and restaurant with nightly rates from around $90 for a single. **Banff** is the better option, here you'll find all the local services that you could possibly want. Banff is only ten minutes away and is served by a regular bus to and from the slopes.

For accommodation listings visit - www.worldsnowboardguide.com

Mount Norquay
Po Box 219 Suite 7000, Banff, Alberta.
001 (403) 762 4421
www.banffnorquay.com
www.virgin.com/holidays

Overall rating out of 10 **5** **Not bad for a days hangout**

Sunshine Village Alberta

CANADA
Alberta

MOUNTAIN DATA

Top Lift at - 2730m

Ride Area 3168 acres

Bottom Lift at - 2160m

Vertical Drop - 1070m

Number of Runs - 91

Longest - 3 miles (5km)

TERRAIN LEVELS

Easy	22%
Intermediate	31%
Advanced	42%
Expert =	5%= 6 runs

TERRAIN TO SUITE

Freeride	60%
Trees	Yes
Backcountry	Yes
Freestyle	25%
Halfpipe	Yes 1
Terrain Park	Yes 1
Carving	15%

SNOW DATA

Average Snowfall
300cm a season

Snowmaking
none

Winter Periods
Dec to April

Summer Riding
None

SLOPE ACCESS

Total Lifts = **12**

Uplift Rate - 21,000 people an hour.

1 Gondola, **7** Chair lifts

4 Drag lifts

**Leashes Required*

Lift Times
8.00am to 5.00pm

Lift Pass Rates

1 Day pass	C$53
3 Day pass	C$150
Night Pass	C$21

Travel Guide

Fly to **Calgary,** with a two hour transfer to Sunshine.

Bus services from Calgary & Edmonton via Banff.

Route Planner:
From Calgary, via Highway 1 to Banff via Canmore. Sunshine is north of Banff. **Calgary** to Sunshine is **100** miles and will take **2** hours.

Sunshine and **Goat's Eye Mountain** are amongst the oldest resorts in Alberta as well as being one of the best places in the Banff area for deep snow. The area receives serious amounts of snowfall every year and is a good alternative to its neighbour, **Lake Louise**. Sunshine's high speed quad on Goat's Eye Mountain gives you the chance to ride 34 runs including some severely steep, double black diamond runs such as **The Wild Side**, **Hell's Kitchen** and **Freefall.**

Freeriders will find Sunshine very pleasing with excellent terrain, loads of trees and plenty of virgin powder to be had. The best and most challenging areas can be found on Goat's Eye Mountain. Steeper runs through the trees include **Little Angel, Ecstasy** and **Slim Pickin's** where you may find powder. From the **Standish** chair lift you can ride down a frozen waterfall on the aptly named **Waterfall** run. If you head out to **Trail 87**, you'll find some excellent freeriding. However, be careful not to enter the avalanche-prone, closed area, which is well marked.

Freestylers here have it good, with a cool halfpipe under the **Strawberry** chair and a sizeable terrain park reached off the **Standish** chair. You can also pull some big air and spin until you're dizzy, on the lots natural hits dotted all over the place. Sunshine also has a Boardercross trail down the **Birdcage** run.

Carvers will find lots of groomed runs to tackle. From the top of **Lookout Mountain** you can ride a long, lazy green down to the day lodge, whilst under the **Angel Quad** you can test your skills on some steep blacks. You can also find some okay cruising trails on **Sunshine Coast** and **Wild Fire**, but make sure you have plenty of speed for the long traverse back to the lift station.

Beginners and intermediate riders are well catered for on runs that include **The Red 90, South Divide** and **Green Run**. If you can handle riding the T-bar, the Wawa drag lift gives access to some excellent novice freeriding.

You can stay in **Sunshine Village**, at the *Sunshine Inn* which offers the only ride-in, ride-out accommodation in the **Banff** area. However, it's not particularly cheap plus there's very little to do in the evening making it unsuitable if you want to party. Banff is only 15 minutes away along Route 93 and a regular local bus services operates between Banff and Sunshine.

For accommodation listings visit - www.worldsnowboardguide.com

Sunshine Village
Suite 400,550, 11th Ave SW. Alberta.
***001* (403) 762 6500**
www.skibanff.com
www.virgin.com/holidays

Overall rating out of 10 **8** **Excellent all round riding**

Marmot Basin

Alberta

MOUNTAIN DATA

Top Lift at - 2601m

Ride Area 1000 acres

Bottom Lift at - 1704m

Vertical Drop - 897m

Number of Runs - 53

Longest - 3 miles (5km)

TERRAIN LEVELS

Easy	**35%**
Intermediate	**35%**
Advanced	**30%**
Expert =	**12 runs**

TERRAIN TO SUITE

Freeride	**60%**
Trees	Yes
Backcountry	Yes
Freestyle	**20%**
Halfpipe	Yes 1
Terrain Park	Yes 1
Carving	**20%**

SNOW DATA

Average Snowfall
418cm a season

Snowmaking
None

Winter Periods
Nov to April

Summer Riding
None

SLOPE ACCESS

Total Lifts = **8**

Uplift Rate -10,000 people an hour.

5 Chair lifts

3 Drag lifts

**Leashes Required*

Lift Times
9.00am to 4.30pm

Lift Pass Rates

1 Day pass	C$44
3 Day pass	C$128
5 Day pass	C$212

SLOPE ACTION

Snowboard Hire
Daily rates from C$35
Kids from C$28

Snowboard Tuition
Lesson, lift & hire
from C$50 per day

Night Riding
Yes

Heli Boarding
Hourly or daily trips.

Snowmobiles
Hire & tours

Mountain Cafes
3

Marmot Basin is a bit of a Canadian gem and a resort that is highly rated. Just driving to the resort is a pleasure with out of this world scenery. Located in the **Rocky Mountains, Marmot** attracts snowboarders and skiers who like their slopes hassle-free, without hordes of visitors cluttering up the runs and lifts. Despite being a popular haunt, no one spends more than a few minutes queuing in lift lines here. The lifts can shift over 10,000 people an hour uphill. The terrain is evenly split between all levels and all styles of riding, with some favourable backcountry. Bowls, trees, flats, it's all here with the most demanding areas to be found higher up. Marmot is also a place where they regularly hold snowboard events including the **New Ground Snowboard Cup** and the **Easy Rider Cup**.

Freeriders looking for powder should check out **Eagle East** where the bowls are full on. If you take the **Triple** chair lift and the **Kiefer** drag, you will eventually arrive at **Caribou Ridge** which offers an abundance of testing terrain with bumps and hits for both the freerider and freestyler. Intermediates who know what they are doing will also like this area and can ride most of the mountain one way or another. If you have the energy, advanced freeriders can hike up to **Marmot Peak** which yields an amazing ride down through powder bowls. The trees in the lower sections are pretty cool, but if you have the balls, check out **Knob Bowl** off **Knob Chair** for a taste of heaven.

Freestylers have plenty of good natural terrain for catching air, but check out **Rock Garden** for some of the best hits. There are lots of trees here and if you look out, you will find the odd log to slide. Alternatively, the fun-park decked out with a number of hits and a halfpipe is the place to head for, although it's not the most testing. Here, grommets can catch air all day long without bothering anyone else.

Carvers have some good opportunities to lay out nice, big arcs on the kind of prepared piste that carvers delight in. For some demanding riding, **Exhibition** is the place to visit, while the more sedate carver will like **Dromedary** trail.

Beginners will note one clear thing about Marmot Basin and that is how good it is for cutting their first tracks. The slopes are accessible with the easy stuff at the bottom and some good progression runs found higher up, which allows for long and gentle riding back to base. What's more, novices can get around the slopes without having to use any T-bars thanks to the way the chair lifts have been set out. Snowboard instruction services are good with a number of tuition packages available for all levels and styles of riding. There are even lessons available with video analysis to quicken your progression. A two hour group lesson costs from C$50 with lift pass and full equipment hire.

Marmot Basin doesn't offer any slopeside accommodation or full local services other than the new *Caribou Chalet* at the base of the slopes. However, the town of **Jasper** is only 10 miles away and although it isn't as big as its more famous cousin **Banff**, Jasper is less crowded and you shouldn't have any problem finding good quality lodging at prices to suit all. Marmot Basin's slopes are easy to get to and as with many resorts, there is a regular ski bus that runs all day stopping at many of the hotels en-route from Jasper to the slopes. Snowboard hire is available at the resort or in Jasper. Rates vary, costing for 6 days hire from C$90.

Eating options in **Jasper** are much the same as in any of **Alberta's** towns. If you want a slap up feast, then dine at the expensive *Edith Cavell*, or the *Tonquin Rib Village* where you can get a damn fine steak. If you like pizza, then visit *Papa George's* or *Jasper Pizza Place*.

Night-life in Jasper is best described as very low key and somewhat boring. *Pete's Bar* seems to be the in place to check out, where you can mix with a lively crowd boozing and playing pool. The *Whistle Stop* is also a cool hang out with pool and on screen sports action. *O'Shea's* is a typical Irish pub, while the Atha-Bar is the place for live music and a dance.

Accommodation in **Jasper** ranges from the usual selection of lodge-style hotels to B&B's or hostels which are widely spread out. Places like *The Amethyst Lodge* offer a selection of well equipped rooms with rates from C$70/night per person, while *The Astora*, located in central **Jasper,** has winter rates from C$40/night per person. The *Marmot Lodge,* also centrally located, offers self catering style accommodation for groups or couples as well as having an indoor swimming pool and fitness centre.

For accommodation listings visit - www.worldsnowboardguide.com

Summary: Great freeriding at this scenic crowd-free resort. However, the area is let down by the lack of slopeside facilities, although what's offered in Jasper is okay.
Money wise: Expensive lodging and eating out but overall great value.

Overall rating out of 10 **7**

Ski Marmot Basin
P.O. Box 1300, Jasper
Alberta, T0E 1E0
General info **001 (403) 852 3816**
Reservations **001 (800) 473 8135**
Snowphone **001 (403) 488 5909**
www.skimarmot.com
www.virgin.com/holidays

pics - Soft Snapper

Travel Guide

Fly to **Edmonton International**
Transfer time to resort = **4½** *hours.*
Local airport = **Hinton 38** miles.

Approximate global air travel times to **Edmonton**:

from:		
	London	**9½** hours
	New York	**4½** hours
	Frankfurt	**10** hours

A daily bus service run by **Greyhound,** operates 4 times a day from Edmonton to Jasper and takes around 5 hours.

Trains run direct into **Jasper**

Route Planner
Edmonton *via Jasper*

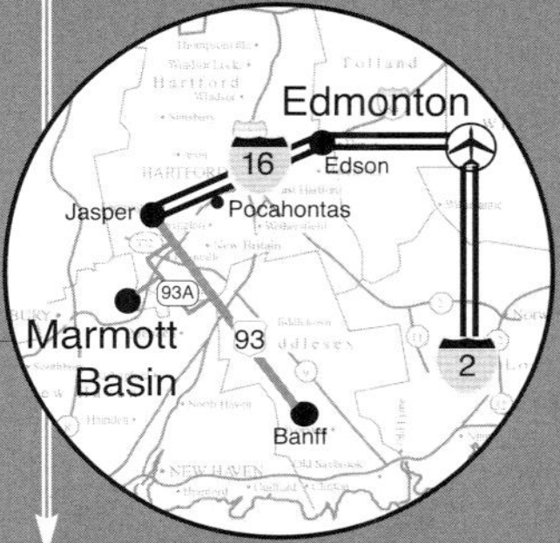

Marmot Basin = 270 miles
Drive time is about **4½** hours

British Columbia - BC

GENERAL INFO AND FACTS

Capital - Vancouver
Language - English & French
Currency - Canadian Dollar
Alcohol drinking age - 19
Drugs - Cannabis is illegal
Death Penalty - Doesn't Exist
Age of consent for Sex - 16
Electricity Supply - 110 Volts AC
Area phone Code - 403
Provincial sales tax - 7% general 8%to 10% on accommodation

BC DRIVE GUIDE

All vehicles drive on the right side of the road.
Speed Limits -
Highways 80kph (50mph)
Rural routes
Towns 50kph (30mph)
Road Watch 001 (604) 299 9000
Fuel is sold in Litres

TRAVEL CONTACTS

International Airports
Vancouver tel: [illegible]
Air Canada 001 (403) [illegible]
Canadian Airlines 800 426 7000

Via Rail
tel: 001 1-800 561 8630
BC Rail
tel: 001 (604) 631 3500

Greyhound Buses
Vancouver
tel: 001 (604) 482 8747

Mountain & West
GMT -8 hours

AREA INFORMATION
Tourism British Columbia
1117 Wharf St. Victoria
BC V8W 2Z2
tel: 001 (604) 387 1642

pic - Dan Hudson - Kimberley Resort

Apex Mountain British Columbia

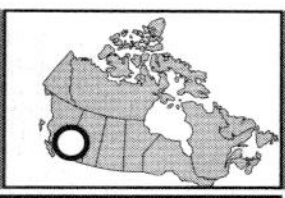

CANADA

BC

MOUNTAIN DATA

Top Lift at - 2187m

Ride Area 550 acres

Bottom Lift at - 1575m

Vertical Drop - 605m

Number of Runs - 61

Longest - 3 miles (5km)

TERRAIN LEVELS

Easy	**16%**
Intermediate	**47%**
Advanced	**18%**
Expert =	**18% 5 runs**

TERRAIN TO SUITE

Freeride	**50%**
Trees	Yes
Backcountry	Yes
Freestyle	**20%**
Halfpipe	No
Terrain Park	No
Carving	**30%**

SNOW DATA

Average Snowfall
570cm a season

Snowmaking
40% cover of the slopes

Winter Periods
Nov to April

Summer Riding
None

SLOPE ACCESS

Total Lifts = **5**

Uplift Rate - 8,700 people an hour.

3 Chair lifts

2 Drag lifts

**Leashes Required*

Lift Times
9.00am to 3.30pm

Lift Pass Rates

1 Day pass	C$38
3 Day pass	C$
5 Day pass	C$185

Travel Guide

Fly to **Vancouver,** with domestic transfers possible to Penticton.

Buses from Vancouver take around 5 hours.

Route Planner: From Vancouver, use higway 1 via Hope and Manning Park.

pic - Apex Resort

Apex Mountain may be a small resort, but with it's down-to-earth atmosphere and great riding opportunities, it's no wonder that Apex is a popular place. Located in the sunny **Okanagan Valley**, Apex is known for its great natural terrain: bowls, gullies, glades and groomed cruising runs radiate from the rounded top of the resort's main peak, **Mt Beaconsfield.** If you're a novice or intermediate, head for the wide boulevards off the **Stocks Triple** chair, where you'll find half a dozen nicely graded, rolling descents. Notice how the trail names evoke the area's mining history - **Motherlode, Gambi**t and **Sluice Box**.

Freeriders looking for some decidedly 'darker blue' cruising should head on up to **Mt Beaconsfield** and try **Ridge Run** and **Juniper** where a search for more challenging terrain won't take long. Alternatively, check out the whole series of wicked runs plunging down Apex's **North Side**. Wind your way through the woods and, if you dare, peer down **Gunbarrel**, a chute that's just 'one turn wide', and drops straight down the fall-line for 366 double black diamond vertical metres (1,200 ft).

Freestylers who expect facilities to be laid on should forget Apex, as there is no park or pipe. However, a bit of hunting will reveal some good natural gullies and hits on **Mt Beaconsfield.**

Carvers will fair well on Apex's short, but challenging trails. There are enough steep blacks for the advanced alpine rider to carve, while the novice can practice on some nice, flat blues.

Beginners should find that **Apex** allows for an easy time, as in general, this is a good mountain to learn on and allows for quick progression. **Grandfather's Trail** is a nice green that allows you to ride from the summit to the base with ease. The local snowboard school offers various *learn to ride* packages with a one day lesson, lift and full hire costing form C$42 per person.

The *New Inn* at Apex offers ride-in accommodation and some good value bed and lift ticket deals, from C$49/night mid-week. If you're planning on staying a while there are apartments available to rent, otherwise there are plenty of beds in the town of **Penticton**, forty minutes away. When the sun goes down on Apex Mountain, The Gunbarrel Saloon is the main place to eat and enjoy all sorts of entertainment. Other good food haunts are *The Rusty Spur* and *Longshot Bar.*

For accommodation listings visit - www.worldsnowboardguide.com

Apex Mountain Resort
Po Box 1060 Penticton, BC V2A 7N7
***001* (250) 292 8444**
www.apexresort.com
www.virgin.com/holidays

Overall rating out of 10 **7** **Great place to ride.**

Big White

British Columbia

MOUNTAIN DATA

Top Lift at - 2286m

Ride Area
2075 acres

Bottom Lift at - 1508m
Vertical Drop - 777m
Number of Runs - 103
Longest - 4.5 miles (7km)

TERRAIN LEVELS

Easy	**18%**
Intermediate	**56%**
Advanced	**26%**
Expert =	**17 runs**

TERRAIN TO SUITE

Freeride	**45%**
Trees	Yes
Backcountry	Yes
Freestyle	**45%**
Halfpipe	Yes 2
Terrain Park	Yes 2
Carving	**10%**

SNOW DATA

Average Snowfall
750cm a season
Snowmaking
None
Winter Periods
Nov to April
Summer Riding
None

SLOPE ACCESS

Total Lifts = **10**
Uplift Rate - 19,000 people an hour.
7 Chair lifts
3 Drag lifts
**Leashes Required*

Lift Times
9.00am to 3.30pm

Lift Pass Rates

1 Day pass	C$48
3 Day pass	C$138
5 Day pass	C$217

SLOPE ACTION

Snowboard Hire
Daily rates from C$36
Kids from C$26

Snowboard Tuition
Lesson, lift & hire
from C$55 per day

Night Riding
Yes, from 5 to 8pm

Heli Boarding
None

Snowmobiles
Hire & tours

Mountain Cafes
7

pic - Big White

Big White is a genuine snowboarder's mountain that has it all. Snowboarders and skiers in search of good mountains have been cruelly misled by the world's slack ski press for years, since **Big White** has been hardly mentioned at all in the numerous ski guides and magazines. Knowledgeable Canadians have had a freeride paradise with an annual 24 feet of champagne powder largely to themselves, at one of the country's best resorts. Big White is located in the **Okanagan Valley**, an hour from the town of **Kelowna**. The mountain is best described as a winter skate-park, with over 2,000 acres of natural terrain features spread over two mountain faces that will leave you breathless. Over recent years, large amounts of money have been spent on the resort and the results include a modern, super efficient lift system plus extremely good local services. The terrain at Big White is split evenly between freeride and freestyle, suiting beginner and intermediate riders, as well as providing some very good expert trails. The initial access to the slopes begins from the village area, with lifts taking you up the **South** face slopes, home to an array of green and blue runs that criss-cross each other.

Freeriders get the chance to ride down some impressively large powder bowls. Riders with balls (or equivalent) should take the **Alpine** T-bar and test their extreme riding on one of the double black diamond runs that are found on the **Cliff**, but only if you can ride and ride well. Likewise, the black runs off the **Powder** chair are not for the squeamish. For those not quite up to the same standard, the blue runs off the **Ride Rocket** chair are worth a blast, as is the **Blue Ribbon** over in the **West Ridge** area.

Freestylers are provided with a 450 foot quality halfpipe, located off the **Speculation** run, which regularly attracts top riders to its near perfect walls offering great transitions to catch the big one. The pipe is often used for national snowboard events. Big White also provides a small pipe for novice riders so that learners can gain their first airs and can learn the basics of pipe-riding with ease. The 8 plus acre terrain park, which is housed on the **Freeway** area, is designed for all levels of freerider and comes loaded with spines, gaps, and a monster quarter pipe.

Carvers will love Big White as the terrain is perfect for laying big turns. By taking any of the main lifts, such as **Ridge Rocket** or Bullet, you gain access to great carving slopes. **Cougar Alley** is full on and for a long carve you should crank it from the summit of the **Alpine** T-Bar, down to the base.

Beginners won't be disappointed with **Big White** as it is totally accessible and has a good selection of easy trails. First timers can ride from the summit to the base, but study your lift map first. Instruction is good and well priced, with a one day lesson, equipment hire and lift pass costing from C$55.

Off the slopes, **Big White** is a friendly and affordable place that is well set out and has the image of a laid back, sleepy mountain town with an Alpine feel. Weekends usually see an influx of extra punters from surrounding towns and cities, but the place is never so busy as to be annoying - there is room for all. Local amenities are basic but offer everything you may need during your stay, with shops and other services being well located and within walking distance of each other. Riders with too much money can throw it away at the casino, whilst families can prance around on the 7500 sq.ft, ice rink. And if that's not enough, then perhaps a snowmobile tour will suit, with over 70 miles of tracks to explore.

Eating choices are numerous and of an extremely good standard. For a hearty breakfast, check out the *Ridge Day Lodge* which opens from 8.30am daily. *Snowshoe Sam's* has a great reputation and food to match. *Dom's* serves up tender chicken while *Loose Moose* is the joint for a burger.

Night-life: By no means mad cap or hard-core drinking, but you can make it lively. *The Loose Moose* is the place to get on the dance floor, while *Raakels* is the place to chill and listen to some live music. For a bigger selection of night-life, check out the action in **Kelowna**. It is only 45 minutes away but you will need your own transport at night.

Accommodation in **Big White** is very good with much of it on, or close to the base slope areas, which allows you to ride to your door. There are a couple of classy hotels to choose from and a few chalets. For groups, there is a choice of condominiums with prices to suit even budget riders. The *White Crystal Inn* is a quality hotel located close to the slopes with a bar, a restaurant and a fitness room, but note, although the joint is loaded with facilities, this is not a cheap hotel.

For accommodation listings visit -
www.worldsnowboardguide.com

Summary: Excellent freeriding on crowd free slopes, with great terrain for all levels. Local facilities are very basic but good. Night life is tame but okay.
Money wise: Expensive lodging and eating out but overall good value.

Overall rating out of 10 — **8**

Big White Resort
P.O. Box 2039 Station Road
Kelowna. V1 4K5. BC
General info **001 (250) 765 3101**
Reservations **001 (800) 663 2772**
Snowphone **001 (250) 765 7669**
www.bigwhite.com
www.virgin.com/holidays

pic - Sang Tan

pic - Big White Resort

Travel Guide

Fly to **Vancouver** International,
Transfer time to resort = **5** hours
Local airport = **Kelowna** 45 mins

Approximate global air travel times to **Vancouver**

from:	London	9½ hours
	New York	5 hours
	Frankfurt	10½ hours

A bus from Vancouver takes around 5 hours. Local buses run daily from Kelowna to Big White and take just 45 minutes.

Trains: None

Route Planner
Vancouver *via Merritt & Kelowna*

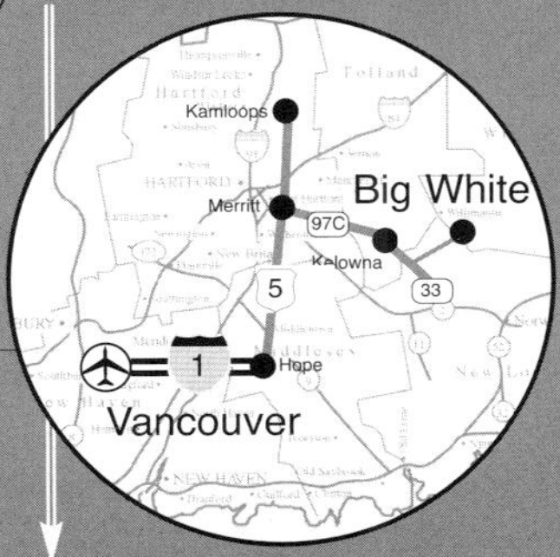

Big White = **278** miles (447km)
Drive time is about **5** hours

Cypress Bowl British Columbia

MOUNTAIN DATA

Top Lift at - 1448m

Ride Area 128 acres

Bottom Lift at - 980m

Vertical Drop - 520m

Number of Runs - 23

Longest - 1.3 miles (2km)

TERRAIN LEVELS

Easy	23%
Intermediate	37%
Advanced	40%
Expert =	

TERRAIN TO SUITE

Freeride	50%
Trees	Yes
Backcountry	Yes
Freestyle	20%
Halfpipe	Yes 1
Terrain Park	Yes 1
Carving	30%

SNOW DATA

Average Snowfall
500cm a season

Snowmaking
85% cover of the slopes

Winter Periods
Dec to April

Summer Riding
None

SLOPE ACCESS

Total Lifts = **5**

Uplift Rate - 21,00 people an hour.

4 Chair lifts

1 Drag lifts

**Leashes Required*

Lift Times
8.30am to 11.00pm

Lift Pass Rates

1 Day pass	C$35
Night pass	C$27
5 Day Pass	C$

Travel Guide

Fly to **Vancouver,** with a 30 minute transfer time to Cypress Bowl.

Bus services direct from Vancouver take 30 minutes.

Route Planner:
From Vancouver, use highway 1 westbound, direction Horseshoe Bay. Leave at exit 8 for Cypress Bowl .

pic - Mark Gunter

Cypress Bowl is one of three local mountains in the **Vancouver** area (the other two being **Grouse Mountain** and **Mt Seymour**). Situated 30 minutes drive from west Vancouver, Cypress Bowl caters largely for people living in the city. It's a relatively small resort with only four chair lifts and one drag lift, all of which are a bit outdated. The terrain on offer is very much beginner to intermediate level, but that doesn't deter the large number of 'Vancouverites' who flock here. Night-boarding is one of the biggest draws at Cypress Bowl, offering uncrowded riding for the true enthusiasts until 11pm every night.

Freeriders may find the best riding to be had on **Mt Strachan** in the east, which has two chair lifts, **Sunrise** and **Sky**, that take you to the top of the best black runs. On a clear day the view is absolutely stunning, with the enormous **Mt Baker** dominating the horizon down to Washington, USA. Snowboarding on this side of Cypress Bowl is better than anywhere else in the resort due to the steep and variable terrain. The altitude means that there is also more snow. There are some truly top class off-piste tree runs to contend with and some challenging black runs too.

Freestylers have a snowboard park called the **BoardZone** that is well maintained by the owners and a few local riders who are constantly changing the set-up. There is also a big halfpipe and if that's not enough, there are two awesome 12 foot quarter-pipes.

Carvers in search of loads of fast and extreme slopes will be a little disappointed but the runs are nicely groomed.

Beginners have it best at Cypress Bowl. The **Eagle** chair on **Black Mountain** gives access to some easy/intermediate winding runs. Alternatively, the flats on **Mt Strachan** and the **Sunrise** chair are ideal for learning the basics. Cypress Bowl Snowboard School offers courses to suit all, with a one week course that includes full equipment hire costing from C$290.

There is no accommodation or any real slope side facilities, however, a massive selection of hotels, restaurants, shops and other amenities can be found in the nearby city of **Vancouver,** BC's. capital city. In downtown **Vancouver**, there is an excellent hostel which has good facilities and runs day trips to the mountain. In terms of nightlife, Vancouver rocks with dozens of bars and clubs.
Vancouver Tourist Office *tel:* **001 (604) 683 2000.**

For accommodation listings visit - www.worldsnowboardguide.com

Cypress Bowl
PO box 91252, West Vancouver. V7V 3NR. B.C
***001* (604) 926 5612**
www.cypressbowl.com
www.virgin.com/holidays

Overall rating out of 10 — **5** — **Okay for a few days riding**

Grouse Mountain British Columbia

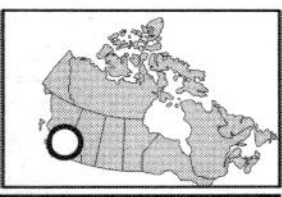

MOUNTAIN DATA

Top Lift at - 1281m

Ride Area
800 acres

Bottom Lift at - 781m
Vertical Drop - 500m
Number of Runs - 22
Longest - 1 mile (1.6km)

TERRAIN LEVELS

Easy	**30%**
Intermediate	**50%**
Advanced	**20%**
Expert =	

TERRAIN TO SUITE

Freeride	**50%**
Trees	Yes
Backcountry	Yes
Freestyle	**25%**
Halfpipe	Yes 1
Terrain Park	Yes 1
Carving	**25%**

SNOW DATA

Average Snowfall
250cm a season
Snowmaking
75% cover of the slopes
Winter Periods
Nov to April
Summer Riding
None

SLOPE ACCESS

Total Lifts = **9**
Uplift Rate - 5,500 people an hour.
1 Gondola, **4** Chair lifts
6 Drag lifts
**Leashes Required*

Lift Times
8.00am to 10.00pm

Lift Pass Rates
1 Day pass C$25
Night pass C$19
Season pass C$

Travel Guide

Fly to **Vancouver,** only 20 minutes from Grouse Mtn.

Bus services from Vancouver to Grouse daily.

Route Planner:
From Vancouver head north along Hwy 1 and turn off at the signs for the Cleveland Dam and then follow the signs for Grouse Mtn.

pic - Nidecker Snowboards

Grouse Mountain is a small resort that is located on the very northern outskirts of **BC's** capital **Vancouver**. Along with a mountain top multi-media theatre, **Grouse Mountain** has a good selection of trails that will keep the average grade snowboarder content for a day or two, satisfy an expert rider for an afternoon and totally please a beginner for a 5 day period. Regular night riding on Grouse's flood lit slopes is very popular with townies from Vancouver, who take to the slopes in the evenings after a day in the office. However, Grouse doesn't attract mass crowds due largely to the poor and unreliable snow conditions. Still, when the 22 well marked trails are covered in snow then this is a mountain that provides some good fun riding with a little for everyone. Apart from a couple of double black diamond extreme runs, however, much of the terrain is rated intermediate and overall is tame.

Freeriders will find that much of what is on offer here at will suit them so long as they are not looking for major long steeps covered in knee deep powder. There are however, some areas where the average rider can show off on runs such as the **Devil's Advocate.** This is a short but fast steep trail that winds its way down through some tress before linking up with a nice long intermediate run known as the **Inferno**. With all or most of the runs carved out of trees, there are ample opportunities to slice some wood and grind the odd fallen log.

Freestylers will soon realise that **Grouse** is not what one would call a freestyle's destination. Neither the halfpipe or the fun park are up to much or that extensive, and to be honest, the natural terrain features here will provide for a more pleasing time than any man-made hit.

Carvers have a reasonable selection of trails to choose from with some excellent wide carving to found off the **Peak Patio** and **Peak** chair lifts. Both lifts give access to some nice basic runs.

Beginners may not have dozens of novice trails to choose from, but nevertheless, the easy runs are well appointed and most first timers should have no bother negotiating the nursery areas before progressing on up to more challenging terrain. The local ski school offers a number of basic snowboard programmes.

Off the slopes, see page 37 the report on Vancouver.
Vancouver Tourist Office *tel:* **001 (604) 683 2000.**
For accommodation listings visit - www.worldsnowboardguide.com.

Grouse mountain
6400 Nancy Greene Way, North Vancouver. BC
***001* (604) 984 0661 www.virgin.com/holidays**

Overall rating out of 10 **4** **Basic small resort but okay**

Fernie Alpine

British Columbia

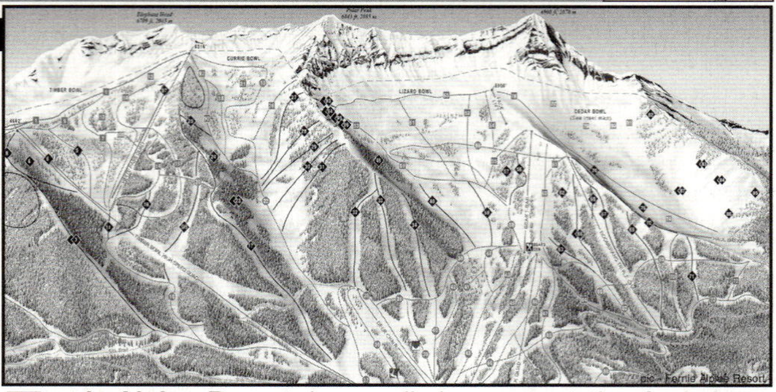

pic - Fernie Alpine Resort

MOUNTAIN DATA

Top Lift at - 1925m

Ride Area 2500 acres

Bottom Lift at - 1068m

Vertical Drop - 857m

Number of Runs - 106

Longest - 3 miles (5.1km)

TERRAIN LEVELS

Easy	**30%**
Intermediate	**40%**
Advanced	**30%**
Expert =	**12 runs**

TERRAIN TO SUITE

Freeride	**50%**
Trees	Yes
Backcountry	Yes
Freestyle	**25%**
Halfpipe	Yes 1
Terrain Park	Yes 1
Carving	**25%**

SNOW DATA

Average Snowfall
875cm a season

Snowmaking
None

Winter Periods
Dec to April

Summer Riding
None

SLOPE ACCESS

Total Lifts = **10**

Uplift Rate - 13,716 people an hour.

6 Chair lifts

4 Drag lifts

**Leashes Required*

Lift Times
8.30am to 3.30pm

Lift Pass Rates

1 Day pass	C$54
3 Day pass	C$150
5 Day pass	C$250

SLOPE ACTION

Snowboard Hire
Daily rates from C$25
Kids from C$20

Snowboard Tuition
Lesson, lift & hire
from C$42 per day

Night Riding
Yes, from 5 to 8pm

Heli Boarding
Sightseeing Tours

Snowmobiles
Hire & tours

Mountain Cafes
7

Fernie Alpine Resort deservedly has a reputation for being a powder paradise. With an average annual snowfall of 875cm and enough steep gladed terrain to keep you entertained for the longest of stays, it is not surprising that it has become so popular, especially with the *Antipodean* snowboarding contingent. Since the take over by **Banff** and **Lake Louise** owner *Charlie Locke* a few years ago the ski area has doubled in size. The two new chairs have opened the doors to three bowls, **Timber, Currie** and **Siberia** that offer some of the mountains most challenging terrain. Beginners, intermediate and advanced riders will feel equally at home on the slopes and if for some reason you decide to leave your board at home for the day, there are a number of activities from dog sledding to snowmobiling that will entertain you.

Freeriders, this is what **Fernie** is all about. Advanced Riders looking for steep tree runs could do worse than heading up to **White Pass**, then traversing around **Currie Bowl** to **Stags Leap** and the surrounding area. Or, at the top of the **Timber** quad, a quick two-minute walk will take you to the top of **Siberia Ridge**, where you can pick your line and charge through the well spaced trees. Unfortunately due to its increasing popularity you may have to fight for your fresh lines. Once the ski area is tracked out, there are a number of 30-40 minute hikes that are worth every lung-bursting step. Make sure that you are not the one to put the boot pack in. Head to **Mongolia Ridge** for more trees, **Polar Peak** for stunning panoramic views, clear powder fields or chutes back into **Currie Bowl** or **Fish Bowl** for a more cruisy ride.

Freestylers, Fernie does have a terrain park and halfpipe, but both are of poor quality and the **Deer** chair that accesses them both is frustratingly slow. Pipe etiquette is unheard of, so it can be a hazardous place with skiers and boarders dropping in left right and centre and ski schools regularly snowploughing their way down the middle, toddlers snaking behind. Instead, why not head to **Lost Boy**s in **Siberia Bowl** or the area below the **Face** lift traverse, both being ideal places to build your own kickers to huck yourself off into deep, soft powder.

Carvers, for those of you who like to wear hard boots and stay on piste, **Fernie** has plenty of wide open runs that are groomed regularly. After a fresh dump of snow, what is better than laying out some big carves on that packed powder corduroy. Try the **Bear, North Ridge** or **Falling Star**.

Beginners will enjoy learning to ride at **Fernie**. Instructors are of high standard and will have you up and going in no time. Once you have enough confidence to leave the confines of the **Mighty Moose** beginner area you will find plenty of empty, tame runs off the **Deer chair**, before trying the **Bear** and **Elk** runs which link together to give a long ride down to the **Day Lodge.**

Fernie is situated on the banks of the **Elk River** and beneath the impressive **Lizard** mountain range on which the ski area lies. Lodging, shops, and all other main local amenities can be found a few minutes down the valley in the old city of Fernie. Here plenty of affordable places to eat, sleep and drink are offered with a flavour of the wild west in a friendly small town atmosphere. There is a local shuttle bus service that operates to and from the mountain on a daily basis costing around C$4 for a return trip. Fernie offers a high level of services with a host of attractions which include ice skating, a cinema, swimming pools and other sporting facilities that are not just winter orientated Fernie is also a top summer destination.

The choices for eating out are extensive and cater for every pallet and every price range. If you wish to dine out in style then you should check the *Lizard Creek Lodge* dining room. Gabriella's is the place for Italian dishes while *Rip & Richard's* is noted for its local cuisine. *Smitty's Restaurant* is noted for its pancakes, breakfasts and light lunches.

Night-life in **Fernie** is rather tame but still enjoyable. There are a number of bars but they all seem much the same. Check out *Eldorados* for live music, *The Central* or the imaginatively named *The Pub* which has pool tables and table football.

There is plenty of budget accommodation to choose from. *The Raging Elk* is one of two conveniently located hostels downtown and there is any number of hotels and motels. *Canadian Powder Tours* is a beautiful log cabin 15 minutes walk from the centre of town. Here you'll find gourmet food, transport to and from the mountain and optional guided tours of the ski area or the backcountry. On the mountain hotels and self catering apartments include *The Wolf's Den* and *Lizard Creek Lodge* are more expensive but offer ride to your doorstep convenience.

For accommodation listings visit - www.worldsnowboardguide.com.

Summary: Excellent open bowl freeriding on crowd free slopes and a mountain with a good annual snow record. Good for beginners and ideal for freestlye riding.
Money wise: Somewhat expensive resort but damn good value.

Overall rating out of 10 **8**

Fernie Alpine Resort
Ski Area Road, Fernie.
VOB 1M1. BC
General info **001 (250) 423 4655**
Reservations **001 - 800 258 7669**
Snowphone **001 (250) 423 3555**
www.skifernie.com
www.virgin.com/holidays

pics - Wes - Riders - Simon

Travel Guide

Fly to **Calgary** International,
Transfer time to resort = **3** hours
Local airport = **Cranbrook.**

Approximate global air travel times to **Calgary**:

from:		
	London	9 hours
	New York	4 1/2 hours
	Frankfurt	9 1/2 hours

A bus service from Calgary runs twice daily and is operated by Greyhound Bus Lines .

Trains: None.

Route Planner
Calgary *via Okotoks & Sparwood*

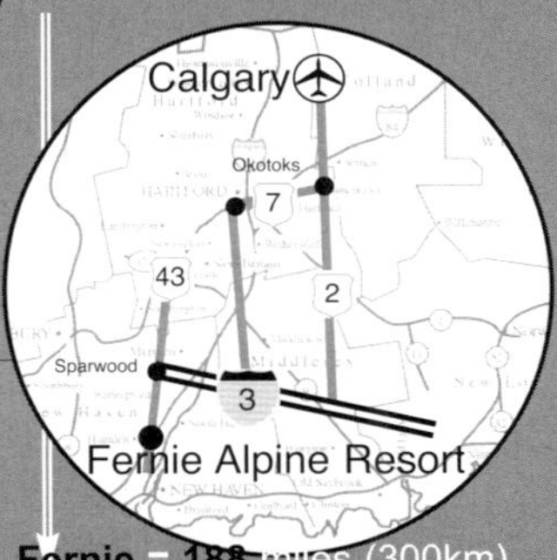

Fernie = 188 miles (300km)
Drive time is about **3** hours

Kimberley British Columbia

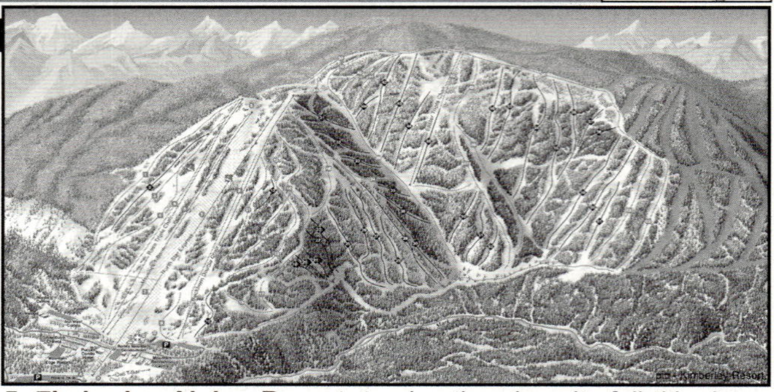

MOUNTAIN DATA

Top Lift at - 1982m
Ride Area 2500 acres
Bottom Lift at - 1280m
Vertical Drop - 702m
Number of Runs - 63
Longest - 4 miles (6.4km)

TERRAIN LEVELS

Easy	20%
Intermediate	45%
Advanced	35%
Expert =	20 runs

TERRAIN TO SUITE

Freeride	40%
Trees	Yes
Backcountry	Yes
Freestyle	20%
Halfpipe	Yes 1
Terrain Park	Yes 1
Carving	40%

SNOW DATA

Average Snowfall
400 cm a season
Snowmaking
65% cover of the slopes
Winter Periods
Dec to April
Summer Riding
None

SLOPE ACCESS

Total Lifts = **9**
Uplift Rate - 5,500 people an hour.
5 Chair lifts
4 Drag lifts
**Leashes Required*

Lift Times
9.00am to 9.30pm

Lift Pass Rates

1 Day pass	C$45
5 Day pass	C$210
Night pass	C$15

SLOPE ACTION

Snowboard Hire
Daily rates from $30
Kids from $20

Snowboard Tuition
Lesson, lift & hire
from $39 per day

Night Riding
Yes, from 5 to 9.30pm

Heli Boarding
Yes

Snowmobiles
Hire & tours

Mountain Cafes
6

Kimberley Alpine Resort, to give the place its full title, is on the up and up and is currently in the middle of a multi million dollar expansion plan that has incorporated new mountain facilities as well as a new slope side village. Kimberley's history, like many old Canadian towns, stems from the days of mining. However, you would be forgiven for not knowing this when you arrive as the area has been developed into an all year round quality outdoor recreation centre. First impressions of the place are not one of a sleepy old mining town, instead you are left feeling like you've just landed in a sausage-munching Bavarian town. Still, this strange fusion of Canada and Germany seems to work well as Kimberley is growing rapidly and is presently the fourth largest resort in **British Columbia.** Kimberley is owned by the same company that owns **Lake Louise** in **Alberta**, but that's about the only connection between two. Located 3 hours from Lake Louise, Kimberley is a resort that will appeal to everybody with a good selection of all level trails. The large percentage of easy and intermediate runs may be one reason that the slopes here attract a lot of skiers out for a simple time, however, snowboaders in the know are not left short changed with a good choice of fast black runs.

The runs are spread out over two faces and cut through a lot of thick spruce trees providing some great tree-riding. Although advanced riders are not going to be pushed much here, there are a are a couple of notable double black diamond runs that deserve full attention in order to avoid a broken collar bone.

Freeriders will find that Kimberley offers them some really cool tree-riding and some fairly good powder days. The runs off **Buckhorn** chair take you to some nice terrain, while the **Easter** triple chair lends access to the double black **Flush** run, which descends through trees that will either make or break you.

Freestylers are presented with a fairly ordinary halfpipe and funpark which are located on the **Rosa** and **Main** trails just up from the base area. There are also a few good natural hits located off the **Rosa** chair, which also gives access to some gentle terrain interspersed with wooded sections where you can practice some grinding skills on downed logs.

Carvers get the best look-in on Kimberley's slopes with some decent wide open runs allowing for big arcs. The run marked **Main** is a fast long burner which brings you out at the main base area, while **Flapper** is a shorter but faster pleaser.

Beginners who plan to spend a week here should leave far more competent than when they arrived. This is a particularly good resort for beginners with some excellent novice trails that cover the whole mountain and some nice long green runs that allow easy riding from the top to bottom.

In recent years **Kimberley** has undergone a huge amount of redevelopment that culminated in the building of new slope side facilities including a new hotel come condo unit. Downtown Kimberley is only five minutes from the slopes and offers a very good selection of facilities as well as what is said to be **Canada's** biggest cuckoo clock. Overall Kimberley is not a cheap resort in terms of accommodation and general local services. However, what is not in question is the way you are looked after; the locals are very friendly and will help you in every aspect. Kimberley is also an all year round holiday destination offering a host of sporting attractions form golf to white-water rafting and water skiing.

Around Kimberley you will find a good mix of eateries with something for everyone to sample whether on the mountain or in the village. *The Day Lodge Cafeteria* serves up a good breakfast, as does *Mingles' Grill* specialise in killer grills. *Kelsey's Restaurant* and the *Steamwinder Pub* both offer a good selection of pub food with varied menus, although both are a bit cheesy and go in for apres ski.

Night wise, **Kimberley** is a bit dull and definitely not a hot action town. Nothing really stands out or captures your attention. The place has a number of bland bars but they all go in for far too much stupid apres ski rubbish. Still, you can get very messy and drink on until the early morning hours, although partying hard and pulling a local chick is out.

Accommodation in **Kimberley** is very good with easy access slope side lodging in condo units or chalets. *The Rocky Mountain Condo* and Hotel centre is located at the very base of the slopes just a short walk from the North Star Express chair lit. The hotel offers everything you could want during your stay with units sleeping up to 14 people. Downtown Kimberley has the biggest selection of lodging with cheap B&B's and motels.

For accommodation listings visit - www.worldsnowboardguide.com.

Summary: Kimberley is an up and coming resort that will suit all levels of riders especially beginners with lots of easy to handle green runs. Excellent friendly local services.
Money wise: Generally an expensive place but good value for money.

Overall rating out of 10 **7**

Kimberley Alpine Resort
Box 40, Kimberley.
V1A 2Y5. BC

General info	***001*** **(250) 427 4881**
Reservations	***001*** **800 258 7669**
Snowphone	***001*** **(250) 427 7332**

www.skikimberley.com
www.virgin.com/holidays

CANADA
BC

pic - Gerry George pic - Craig Farish

Travel Guide

Fly to **Calgary** International,
Transfer time to resort = **4** hours
Local airport = **Cranbrook.**

Approximate global air travel times to **Calgary**:

from:		
	London	9 hours
	New York	4½ hours
	Frankfurt	9½ hours

A bus service from Calgary runs twice daily and is operated by Greyhound Bus Lines .

Trains run by Amtrax only go as far as Whitefish, Montana USA.

Route Planner
Calgary *via Invermere*

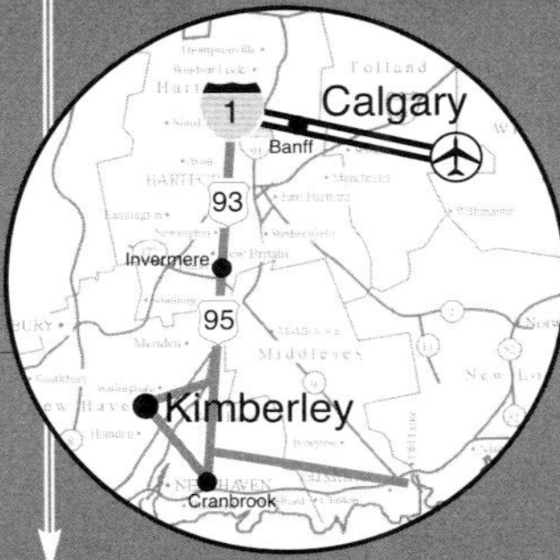

Kimberley = 188 miles (300km)
Drive time is about **4** hours

Mt Washington BC

MOUNTAIN DATA

Top Lift at - 1588m

Ride Area 1000 acres

Bottom Lift at - 1210m

Vertical Drop - 505m

Number of Runs - 42

Longest - 4 miles (6.4km)

TERRAIN LEVELS

Easy	**20%**
Intermediate	**45%**
Advanced	**35%**
Expert =	

TERRAIN TO SUITE

Freeride	**60%**
Trees	Yes
Backcountry	Yes
Freestyle	**30%**
Halfpipe	Yes 1
Terrain Park	Yes 1
Carving	**10%**

SNOW DATA

Average Snowfall
800cm a season

Snowmaking
0% cover of the slopes

Winter Periods
Dec to June

Summer Riding
Only early June

SLOPE ACCESS

Total Lifts = **7**

Uplift Rate - 9200 people an hour.

5 Chair lifts

2 Drag lifts

**Leashes Required*

Lift Times
8.30am to 4.00pm

Lift Pass Rates

1 Day pass	C$40
3 Day pass	C$
6 Day pass	C$

Travel Guide

Fly to **Vancouver**

Bus services from Vancouver to the resort.

Route Planner:
From Vancouver, drive to Horseshoe Bay and take a ferry over to Nanimo or Comox. From Nanimo, travel north on Hwys 1 &19. Mt Washington is 15 miles west of Strathcona Parkway.

Just off the west coast of Canada and floating in the Pacific Ocean is **Vancouver Island**, home to a number of resorts. The most notable and indeed the biggest is **Mt Washington**, which is located in the middle of the island. Over recent years large amounts of money has been spent on upgrading the whole area to make it modern and more fashionable. The amount of terrain available here is pretty cool offering a good mixture of off-piste, powder, trees and well groomed runs. As Mt Washington grows, so do the crowds, therefore be warned that the slopes can get busy at peak times.

Freeriders have a good selection of steep blacks reachable off the top of the **Eagle Express** chair. Here you can head down trails like **Hawk,** a fast run that starts out wide before dropping down through trees. Less adventurous but still as good is the cluster of runs off **The Gully**, such as **Scum's Delight.**

Freestylers head here en-masse to ride some great natural terrain and take advantage of the clean hits in the park. Located by the **Coaster** run off the **Whiskey Jack** chair, the park is loaded with table-tops, gaps, hits and a good halfpipe.

Carvers who only want a series of straight fast slopes to cut up will not be disappointed. If you're up to the grade, check out **Chimney** - it will prove whether you are a man or a mouse. Alternatively, **Whisky Jack** is a gentle but excellent carver's run, especially if you are still mastering the art.

Beginners will have to do introductory courses on how to cope with bruises on the lower slopes, before heading up higher. Based at the lower sections, the **Green** chair and **Discovery** lift give rise to some easy novice terrain.

In resorts that are constantly growing and developing, one is bound to find differences each time you visit. Accommodation options are fairly extensive with 4,000 tourist beds available in a variety of condos and chalets, many of which are on, or very close to, the slopes. Lodging is not overpriced here - you can get a decent condo for C$70/night or a chalet from C$100. Local facilities are a bit sparse but what is on offer is good. If you can't find what you're after, then check out the offerings in **Courtney**, 25 minutes away. This is where you will also get the best night-life.

For accommodation listings visit - www.worldsnowboardguide.com.

Mt Washington Resort
P.o Box 3069, Courtenay Comox Vallet B.C
001 (250) 338 1386 www.virgin.com/holidays

Overall rating out of 10 **5** **Basic but still an okay place**

Panorama BC

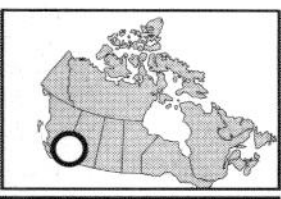

CANADA

BC

MOUNTAIN DATA

Top Lift at - 2380m

Ride Area 2400 acres

Bottom Lift at - 1160m

Vertical Drop - 1220m

Number of Runs - 1000

Longest - 3 miles (5km)

TERRAIN LEVELS

Easy	**15%**
Intermediate	**55%**
Advanced	**30%**
Expert =	**20 runs**

TERRAIN TO SUITE

Freeride	**60%**
Trees	Yes
Backcountry	Yes
Freestyle	**20%**
Halfpipe	Yes 1
Terrain Park	Yes 1
Carving	**20%**

SNOW DATA

Average Snowfall
474cm a season

Snowmaking
40% cover of the slopes

Winter Periods
Dec to May

Summer Riding
None

SLOPE ACCESS

Total Lifts = **10**

Uplift Rate - 7000 people an hour.

1 Gondola, **5** Chair lifts

4 Drag lifts

**Leashes Required*

Lift Times
9.00am to 10.00pm

Lift Pass Rates

1 Day pass	C$49
3 Day pass	C$129
3 Day pass	C$209

Travel Guide

Fly to **Calgary** with a 3 hour transfer to Panorama.

Bus services from Calgary take around 3 hours.

Route Planner:
From Calgary, use highway 1 and P93 to Radium Hot Springs, then Hwy 95 to Invermere, which is 11 miles from Panorama. **Calgary** to resort = **184** miles.3 hours drive time.

pic - San Tang

Located 3 hours from **Calgary, Panorama** is an absolute gem of a resort that is growing in popularity every year. The resort is constantly improving every aspect of the place. 2000/2001 saw the opening up of an extra 700 acres of backcountry terrain while down in the village a number of new lodging properties were added. Panorama is a retreat style resort: very quiet and uncrowded with virtually no day-trip skiers unlike many other resorts. The big news about Panorama is that it offers some of the most convenient heli-boarding around. *R.K. Heli-ski* offers hourly, daily or weekly trips that include excursions into the **Purcell Mountains**. Heli-boarding is not restricted to expert freeriders but no matter what your standard is, it's not cheap. *R.K. Heli-ski* offers various daily or weekly trips which cover 6 major mountain areas where you can ride over 700 square miles of terrain taking in massive snow bowls. Three heli-trips with a guide, breakfast and lunch cost from C$520 and is well worth the cost. Five days heli-boarding with accommodation will sting you some C$4000, but you will never forget the experience.

Freeriders will soon notice how well this resort lends itself to powder-hunting, tree-riding and natural hits. Overall, much of the terrain suits intermediate and advanced freeriders, but there is plenty for novices to get their teeth into. For a freeride rush you should check out the **Extreme Dream Zone**, located off the **Summit** T-bar, where you will find a series of black and double black steeps, trees and cliff jumps.

Freestylers have a good fun-park which is well designed and there are also loads of natural hits all over the slopes.

Carvers will find this a very good resort for laying out big turns, particularly for intermediate carvers. A couple of blue runs to the right of the **Horizon** chair are excellent.

Beginners will find Panorama perfect. The easiest runs are located on the lower sections and provide some good novice riding.

Off the slopes, accommodation is offered in a number of well-located lodges, although they are not that cheap. There are a number of eating haunts ranging from expensive restaurants to pub fare and fast food. The *T-Bar* is worth mentioning as is the *Black Forest* if you like Schnitzel. Night times are very tame with *The Glaciers* and the *Jackpine* being the "in" places

For accommodation listings visit - www.worldsnowboardguide.com.

Panorama Resort
Panorama. V0A 1KO. B.C
***001* (250) 342 6941**

www.panoramaresort.com
www.virgin.com/holidays

Overall rating out of 10 **8** **Excellent freeriding resort**

Red Mountain British Columbia

MOUNTAIN DATA

Top Lift at - 2266m

Ride Area
1200 acres

Bottom Lift at - 1187m
Vertical Drop - 880m
Number of Runs - 83
Longest - 4.5 miles (7km)

TERRAIN LEVELS

Easy	**10%**
Intermediate	**45%**
Advanced	**45%**
Expert =	**11 runs**

TERRAIN TO SUITE

Freeride	**55%**
Trees	Yes
Backcountry	Yes
Freestyle	**25%**
Halfpipe	Yes 1
Terrain Park	Yes 1
Carving	**20%**

SNOW DATA

Average Snowfall
750 cm a season
Snowmaking
0% cover of the slopes
Winter Periods
Dec to April
Summer Riding
None

SLOPE ACCESS

Total Lifts = **6**
Uplift Rate - 6,700 people an hour.
5 Chair lifts
1 Drag lifts
**Leashes Required*

Lift Times
8.45am to 3.30pm

Lift Pass Rates

1 Day pass	C$42
3 Day pass	C$108
5 Day pass	C$175

SLOPE ACTION

Snowboard Hire
Daily rates from C$34
Kids from C$22

Snowboard Tuition
Lesson, lift & hire from C$55 per day

Night Riding
None

Heli Boarding
Yes

Snowmobiles
Hire & tours

Mountain Cafes
2

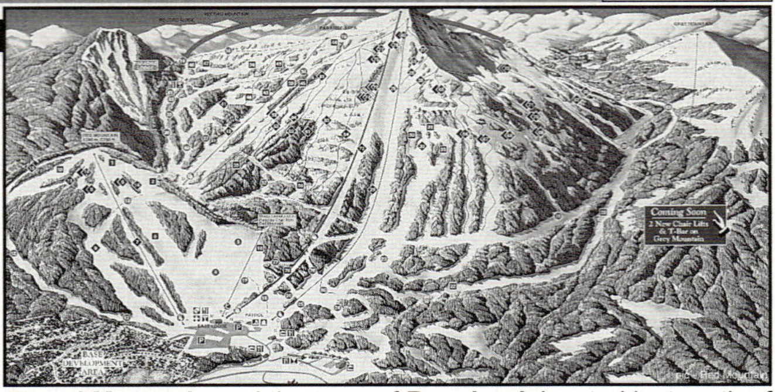

Red Mountain and the town of **Rossland,** located just north of the US/Canadian border, go back in history to the days of the Canadian gold-rush of 1896. One of the oldest resorts in Canada, Red Mountain has been operating as a ski resort since 1947 when its first chair lift was installed. Red was seen by many for a long time as a bit of a dark horse. However, as time has progressed, so has Red's reputation. As a powder heaven and home to some of the best extreme riding in Canada, Red Mountain has freeriders wetting themselves when they see what awaits them. Although this may not be in the super league of resorts, it nevertheless has a lot going for it with excellent, crowd-free runs and early powder unspoilt by morning masses. Old school riders will remember the Burton video 'Board with the World' where riders are seen at Red Mountain shredding everything in sight, coverways, table tops, downed skiers etc.

Grante Mountain and **Red Mountain** make up 1,100 acres of terrain. Both offer a variety of runs that mainly suit snowboarders who ride well. First timers are going to have their work cut out. The trail map lists many of its runs with a star to mean extreme, and that's exactly what the runs live up to. Grante is the bigger of the two areas and is easily accessed from the base lodge. Once at the top you can head off in a variety of directions, but note that most of the runs at the top are for advanced riders, although **Ridge Road** will take novices off to easier slopes.

Freeriders should check out **Buffalo Ridge** which takes you down one side of Grante into bowls, natural hits and lots of trees. **Sara's Chute**, a double black, takes you down steeps and through tight trees and eventually brings you out onto **Long Squaw**, a simple green that leads back to the base area.

Freestylers will find Red's **Rhythm Method** halfpipe located under **Red's Face**, while the well maintained fun-park is reachable from **Boardwalk**. Alternatively, there are plenty of natural hits, especially on **Grante Mountain**, to gain air from.

Carvers will find loads of good pisted runs although not all are regularly groomed. On the **Paradise** side of the mountain, the terrain will suit those wanting tamer stuff and carvers can lay out big lines on runs such as **Southern Comfort**. Other notable trails to check out are **Doug's Run** and **Maggie's Farm**.

Beginners may be a bit put off when they first see the terrain level ratings and although the slopes are rated intermediate/advanced, it doesn't mean novices can't ride here. There is ample terrain to play on at the **Upper** and **Lower Back** trails, before riding the **Long Squaw** trail that runs back to the base lodge. The staff at the local snowboard school cater well for all your first time needs, by offering a number of tuition programmes that will soon have you shredding **Red Mountain** with ease.

Red Mountain has a good but basic selection of lodging properties and facilities at the base of the slopes. Prices vary but staying close to the slopes is generally more expensive than staying down the road in the town of Rossland. **Rossland** is an old town that offers a variety of good local services from cheap eating haunts to boozy late night hangouts. Another plus is that Rossland isn't overloaded with visiting weekend skiers. You can mix with the locals who know how to party hard, and also know how to make visitors welcome. Board and boot hire is available at the slopes or in **Rossland**, check out *Powder Hounds.*
Job Seekers should call (250) 362 7384 or email: jobs@ski-red, to get the latest details.

Rossland is not noted for its restaurants, but what you'll find around the town or at **Red Mountain** is very good, and at prices to suit all pockets. *Sunshine Cafe* has a good menu while *Elmer's* serves excellent veggie food. *The Flying Shovel* dishes up good pub grub, while *Mountain Gypsy* serves pizzas.

Night-life in Rossland is not exactly the most happening, but it's still cool. It offers a number of good night-time hangouts where you can drink to jazz music or boogie to pop. Most bars play decent tunes and have pool tables. The *Flying Steamshovel* is good for a beer, as are *The Powder Keg* and *Rafter's*. (Local talent is also good)

Accommodation is as you'd expect from any resort. At the slopes there is a selection of Lodges, Chalets and Condo's. Places such as the *Red Mountain Cabins*, a short walk from the slopes, is pricey but very good. However, the best option is to stay in the town of **Rossland** which is only 2 miles from the slopes. The options include cheap B&B's and a hostel which are all close to the night-time action. Check the web site for accommodation and the latest prices.

For accommodation listings visit - www.worldsnowboardguide.com.

Summary: A fantastic resort that offers great riding on crowd free slopes, especially just after a fresh dump of snow. Low key but great local services
Money wise: Affordable lodging and eating out and overall great value.

Overall rating out of 10 — **9**

Red Mountain
P.O. Box 670,
Rossland. VOG 1Y0. BC
General info **001 (250) 362 7384**
Reservations **001 (800) 663 0105**
Snowphone **001 (250) 362 550**
www.ski-red.com
www.virgin.com/holidays

pic - San Tang

pic - Rossland

Travel Guide

Fly to **Vancouver** International
Transfer time to resort = **7** hours
Local airport = **Castlegar** 20 mins.

Approximate global air travel times to **Vancouver**:

from:		
	London	$9^{1/2}$ hours
	New York	5 hours
	Frankfurt	$10^{1/2}$ hours

A bus from Vancouver takes about 7 hours. A Local bus runs daily from Rossland to Red Mountain.

Trains go to Spokane in the US

Route Planner
Vancouver *via Osooyos & Rossland*

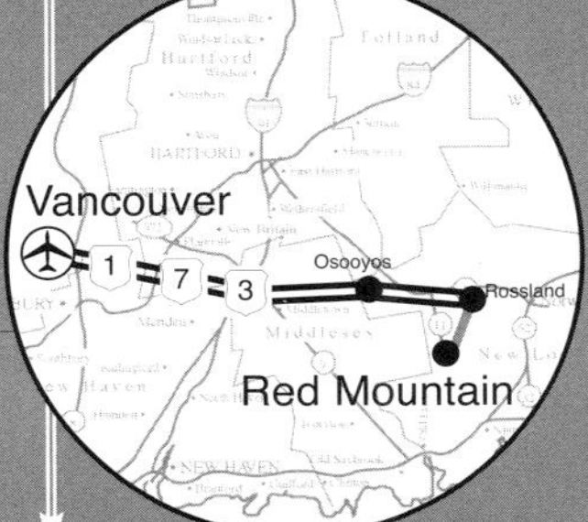

Red Mountain = 371 miles
Drive time is about **10** hours

Silver Star British Columbia

MOUNTAIN DATA

Top Lift at - 1915m

Ride Area 1440 acres

Bottom Lift at - 115m

Vertical Drop - 760m

Number of Runs - 84

Longest - 4 miles (6km)

TERRAIN LEVELS

Easy	20%
Intermediate	50%
Advanced	30%
Expert =	11 runs

TERRAIN TO SUITE

Freeride	60%
Trees	Yes
Backcountry	Yes
Freestyle	20%
Halfpipe	Yes 1
Terrain Park	Yes 1
Carving	20%

SNOW DATA

Average Snowfall
875cm a season

Snowmaking
0% cover of the slopes

Winter Periods
Dec to April

Summer Riding
None

SLOPE ACCESS

Total Lifts = **9**

Uplift Rate - 11,000 people an hour.

5 Chair lifts

4 Drag lifts

**Leashes Required*

Lift Times
8.30am to 4.00pm

Lift Pass Rates

1 Day pass	C$45
2 Day pass	C$90
5 Day pass	C$206

Travel Guide

Fly to **Vancouver** and then on to Kelowna.

Bus services from Kelowna can be arranged.

Route Planner:
From Vancouver, use as a map reference the town of Vernon, which is 12 miles from Silver Star along Hwy 97.

pic -Sam Tang

Silver Star is pure Canada and damn good at that. Any place that can boast an average snowfall of 600cm should be given a platform, and Silver Star has earned its title as a rider's paradise with stupidly large amounts of powder on an annual basis. There is plenty of good off-piste terrain, with big bowls and heaps of trees to shred. The 1,200 acres of marked runs are spread out over two faces - the **South Face** on **Vanace Creek** and the **North Face** on **Putman**, collectively suiting advanced freeriders.

Freeriders who know the score have a number of double black diamond runs to check out. The first port of call should be the **South Face** runs before heading over to the North. **Vanace Creek Express** lift takes you up to the summit where you'll find open terrain and the option of dropping down to some wide open blacks. The more gentle stuff is reached via **Sundance**. **Christmas Bowl** is really cool and if you have the bottle, try the **Attridge Face** run. **Putnam Creek** tests everybody - steeps through trees with pure freeriding territory.

Freestylers looking for air will be pleasantly surprised with the natural hits. However, with a two acre fun-park, you don't need to look far to find places to hit. The park is located below **Big Dipper** trail, off **Yellow** chair lift.

Carvers who can ride will find this a challenging resort. The **Milky Way** is an excellent open area where big arcs can be accomplished with ease. The steepest carving is on the **North Face** slopes where you'll be put to the test.

Beginners will appreciate **Silver Star** with its well connected green and blue runs. The local snowboard school runs daily programmes as well as weekly camps offering video analysis.

Off the slopes, **Silver Star's** old-fashioned Victorian theme offers accommodation for all budgets, with comfortable lodges available at the base of the slopes. Eating options are not only good, but also cheap and as with the evening hangouts, they are all within walking distance of the slopes. Silver Star's night-life may not be major, but it's still cool with a couple of drinking holes to check out. The town of **Vernon** is located only a short distance from Silver Star and offers a greater selection of facilities. Vernon is the place to go for a lively Saturday night out and to eye up some local skirt.

For accommodation listings visit - www.worldsnowboardguide.com.

Silver Star
Po Box 2, Silver Star. V1B 3M1.B.C
***001* (250) 542 0224**
www.silverstarmtn.com
www.virgin.com/holidays

Overall rating out of 10 **7** **Good all round resort**

Sun Peaks British Columbia

pic - San Tang

MOUNTAIN DATA

Top Lift at - 2080m

Ride Area 2150 acres

Bottom Lift at - 1255m

Vertical Drop - 881m

Number of Runs - 67

Longest - 5 miles (8km)

TERRAIN LEVELS

Easy	**24%**
Intermediate	**54%**
Advanced	**22%**
Expert =	**7 runs**

TERRAIN TO SUITE

Freeride	**45%**
Trees	Yes
Backcountry	Yes
Freestyle	**30%**
Halfpipe	Yes 1
Terrain Park	Yes 1
Carving	**25%**

SNOW DATA

Average Snowfall
527cm a season

Snowmaking
65% cover of the slopes

Winter Periods
Nov to April

Summer Riding
None

SLOPE ACCESS

Total Lifts = **8**

Uplift Rate - 7300 people an hour.

5 Chair lifts

3 Drag lifts

**Leashes Required*

Lift Times
8.30am to 3.30pm

Lift Pass Rates

1 Day pass	C$46
3 Day pass	C$129
5 Day pass	C$

Travel Guide

Fly to **Vancouver** with domestic flights to Kamloops.

Bus services from Vancouver takes 5½ hours.

Route Planner:
From Vancouver, take Hwy 1 east via Kamloops, then via Hwy 5 exit to Jasper for Sun Peaks.

Sun Peaks is a resort that hopes to knock Whistler off the top spot. Situated about 40 miles from **Kamloops** in the interior of the Rockies, this is a resort that has come of age. Over the past few years, huge expansion plans have been put into operation with fast modern lifts and massive changes to the layout and structure of the village. The overall results mean a damn fine mountain to ride that is not overpopulated with holiday masses. Sun Peaks is a large resort with a large vertical descent. The marked-out terrain isn't super-varied, but what is on offer is still good and well prepared with riding to suit all levels and styles.

Freeriders looking for long, wide straights with trees galore will find this mountain ideal, keeping you well occupied for a week or more. Take the long **Burfield Quad** to the top and you can gain access to some great terrain. If you plan to go outside the marked boundary, you are required to register with the ski-patrol. For some cool in-boundary riding, **Head Wall** is the place to bust a gut, with a series of short but demanding double diamond blacks. For something a little less daunting, try out the long and sweeping 5 mile trail off the Ridge, which can be tackled by intermediate riders.

Freestylers have a massive 30 acre fun park area located off the **Sunrise** chair, which is loaded with hits and a pipe. Around the slopes you also find numerous natural hits to launch off.

Carvers, Sun Peaks should appeal to you in a big way. Some of the runs here are superb and just right for laying the board over an edge at speed. If you have the balls, try the steep **Expo**; if not, try your luck down **Spillway**.

Beginners who don't appreciate the novice slopes here or manage to progress with style should give up snowboarding and take up train spotting. This is an excellent beginner's resort with some perfect novice tracks off **Sundance**.

Accommodation and all other amenities can be found in **Sun Peaks** or in the small hamlet of **Burfield**. Whichever you choose, both offer good facilities that compliment those on the slopes. Mind you, it should be pointed out that this is not a budget rider's destination as it can get expensive. There's a good choice of restaurants, bars and shops to choose from, but night-life is very tame with **Masa's** the favoured evening hangout for booze.

For accommodation listings visit - www.worldsnowboardguide.com.

Sun Peaks Mountain Resort
P.o Box 1280 Alpine Road. Sun Peaks V0E 1Z1 B.C
***001* (250) 578 7222** **www.sunpeaksresort.com**
www.virgin.com/holidays

Overall rating out of 10 **7** **A really good resort**

Whistler/Blackcomb BC

MOUNTAIN DATA

Top Lift at - 2284m

Ride Area
7071 acres

Bottom Lift at - 675m

Vertical Drop - 1609m

Number of Runs - 230

Longest - 7 miles (11km)

TERRAIN LEVELS

Easy	**25%**
Intermediate	**55%**
Advanced	**20%**
Expert =	**14 runs**

TERRAIN TO SUITE

Freeride	**50%**
Trees	Yes
Backcountry	Yes
Freestyle	**30%**
Halfpipe	Yes 3
Terrain Park	Yes 2
Carving	**20%**

SNOW DATA

Average Snowfall
914 cm a season

Snowmaking
35% cover of the slopes

Winter Riding
Dec to May

Summer Riding
June to October

SLOPE ACCESS

Total Lifts = **33**

Uplift Rate - 59,000 people an hour.

2 Gondolas, **21** Chair lifts

10 Drag lifts

**Leashes Required*

Lift Times
7.00am to 3.30pm

Lift Pass Rates

1 Day pass	C$61
3 Day pass	C$180
5 Day pass	C$294

SLOPE ACTION

Snowboard Hire
Daily rates from C$40
Kids from C$30

Snowboard Tuition
Lesson, lift & hire
from C$60 per day

Night Riding
None

Heli Boarding
Yes - 6 hours from C$400

Snowmobiles
Hire & tours

Mountain Cafes
17

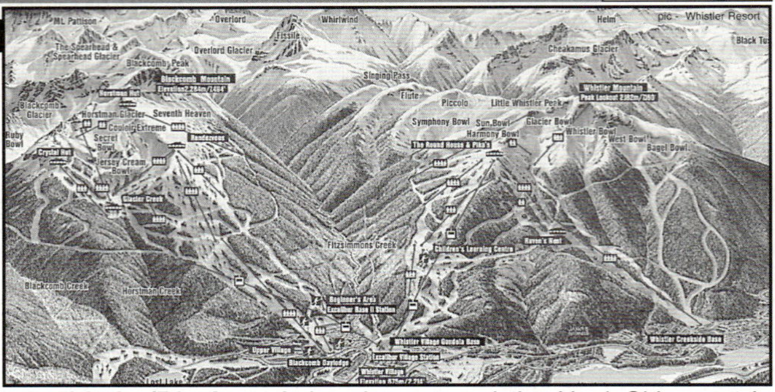

pic - Whistler Resort

Whistler/Blackcomb has been voted the No.1 Ski resort in North America 8 years running by various American magazines. And after you spend a day on the mountain it is pretty easy to see why. The reason people come here is simple: the riding on offer here is unbelievable. There is so much in terms of different terrain that if you get bored here, you must be a loser. You can choose from great bowls, terrain parks or tree runs. The two mountain areas offer over 230 marked runs with seven alpine bowls on Whistler and five bowls on Blackcomb. There are three halfpipes, 2 terrain parks, a bordercross track and some seventeen mountain restaurants. Lifts normally open at 8.30am, but early birds can take to the slopes at even earlier. Fresh Trax queues start at 7am with lifts to the top of Whistler and with as much breakfast as you can eat, you can ride the virgin trails before the rest of the public for an extra C$16 on your lift pass. If you can't make it here during the winter, don't fret as Blackcomb is the only real summer snowboard area in North America. Snowboard legend Craig Kelly holds his camps here as does Ken Achenbach, another notable snowboarder who runs the *Camp of Champions* camps. Both camps are highly rated and are open to anyone wishing to pay the camp fee.

Freeriders in search of powder have twelve bowls to pick from. **Symphony** and **Bagel** bowls on Whistler are a couple of favourites. While on Blackcomb, the **Couloir Extreme**, a double black diamond trail, will test the best. **Ridge Runner** and **Slingshot** are two more of Blackcomb's pleasers, but they are seriously extreme. For a real fix, speak to a local and ask them to direct you to '**Kyber Pass**', which is an off piste two hour trail.

Freestylers looking for air will have endless days of fun, with a major fun park on Blackcomb and a lesser one on Whistler **Blackcomb** is the main hangout, where you will find a massive halfpipe pipe with 14ft walls and a resident DJ blasting out tunes (mind you it's mostly crap techno stuff). Whichever mountain you choose, you will find plenty of great natural terrain to air off.

Carvers (those without big beards) wanting to lay out some big arcs should check out the **Dave Murray** run on Whistler**.** Novice carvers who are just finding out what it's like to hold an edge, can practice with ease down the wide open **Springboard** or **Grundy** runs, which are on the Blackcomb mountain.

Beginners are spoilt when it comes to snowboard instruction programmes. On **Blackcomb** mountain you can get lessons for any age, including classes for **Junior Jibbers** (aged 7-12) and **Kiddie Rippers** (aged 5-6). Both mountains offer plenty of good novice trails, with some of the best being at the base of Blackcomb, aided by beginner lifts. Budding young *Terjes* can also get freestyle instruction and find out just how to ride a pipe and hit a big jump with style and in safety.

Whistler is an all year round fashionable and buzzing place that attracts the rich and famous. This place can be hellishly expensive, even for a burger. In its favour, services are of a high standard, locals are very friendly and do their best to help you. All the main amenities are located in **Whistler's** smart village, which is loaded with high profile expensive retail shops and restaurants. The village has a host of attractions from swimming to ice skating in the Meadow Park sports centre. There is a number of good snowboard shops here such as 'West Beach', 'The Circle' and 'Showcase', where you can buy or hire quality snowboard gear, or get some sound advice on where or where not to ride.

Food is served from an array of restaurants, some of which attract sad Hollywood stars and disposed royals, while others cater for the more normal amongst us. For a cheap meal try *Subway* or *Tex-Mex*. For those without morals there's a *McDonald's* and a *KFC* in the market place. If steaks are your thing then check out *The Keg*. The *Longhorn* right at the base of the slopes offers reasonably priced food.

Nightlife here is possibly the one thing that lets the resort down slightly. Not that it's bad, but most places are geared towards the over 30's. That said you can have a laugh in the likes of *Garfinkel's* bar. The *Longhorn* is also a good place to get tanked up in and the staff are real cool. For clubbing check out *Tommy Africas* or *Maxx Fish.*

Accommodation in the main is expensive. There are budget options such as one of the ski dorms or hostels, but you will need to book in advance in order to get a bed. Condos are a good option for groups of riders. Lodges and hotels are of a super high standard but then so are the costs. Check out the *Blackcomb Lodge*, *Chateau Whistler* or *Pan Pacific*, all come highly recommended.

For accommodation listings visit - www.worldsnowboardguide.com.

Summary: Major riding for all styles and all levels, especially backcountry. But take note of the fact that lift queues can be very long. Great summer riding.
Money wise: Stupidly expensive with prices for everything way over the top.

Overall rating out of 10 **10**

Whistler Resort Association
4010 Whistler Way, Whistler
VON 1BA4

General info	***001*** **(604) 932 3141**
Reservations	***001*** **(888) 284 9999**
Snowphone	***001*** **(604) 932 4221**

www.whistler-resort.com
www.virgin.com/holidays

CANADA
BC

pic - Sean Littlejohn

pic - Whistler Resort

Travel Guide

Fly to **Vancouver International**
Transfer time to resort = **2** hours
Local airport = .

Approximate global air travel times to **Vancouver**:

from:	
London	**9½** hours
New York	**5** hours
Frankfurt	**10½** hours

A bus from Vancouver takes around 2 hours. A local bus runs daily around Whistler and Blackcomb.

Trains go direct to Whistler

Route Planner
Vancouver *via Squamish*

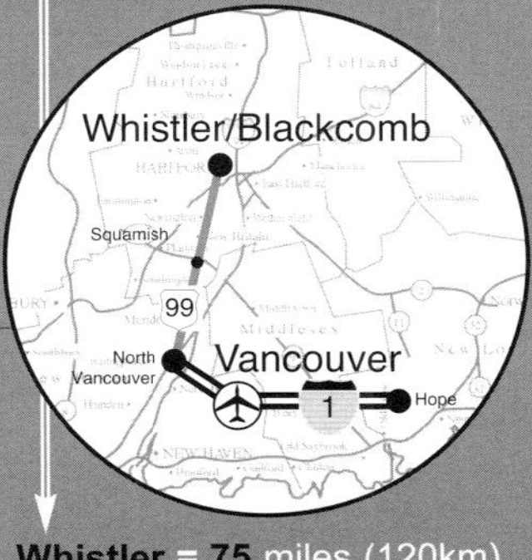

Whistler = 75 miles (120km)
Drive time is about **2¼** hours

Whitetooth

KICKING HORSE MOUNTAIN

British Columbia

MOUNTAIN DATA

Top Lift at - 1814m

Ride Area 20 miles

Bottom Lift at - 1314m

Vertical Drop - 531m

Number of Runs - 22

Longest - 3.5 miles (5km)

TERRAIN LEVELS

Easy	**20%**
Intermediate	**30%**
Advanced	**50%**
Expert =	

TERRAIN TO SUITE

Freeride	**40%**
Trees	Yes
Backcountry	Yes
Freestyle	**20%**
Halfpipe	
Terrain Park	
Carving	**40%**

SNOW DATA

Average Snowfall

Snowmaking
0% cover of the slopes

Winter Periods
Dec to April

Summer Riding
None

SLOPE ACCESS

Total Lifts = **2**

Uplift Rate -1400 people an hour.

1 Chair lift

1 Drag liff

**Leashes Required*

Lift Times
8.30am to 3.30pm

Lift Pass Rates
1/2 Day pass C$20
1 Day pass C$30
Season pass C$415

Travel Guide

Fly to **Calgary,** with a transfer time of 3 hours.

Bus services to Golden from Calgary take 3 hours.

Route Planner:
From Calgary, use the Trans-Canada Highway 1 & route P95 west to Golden, which is 2 miles from Whitetooth.
Calgary to resort = **164** miles. **3** hour drive time.

pic - Nidecker Snowboards

Three hours west of **Calgary** and close to the town of **Golden**, lies the relatively small resort of **Whitetooth,** which for some reason has changed its name to **Kicking Horse Mountain.** With large sums of dollars being spent on development, the resort is staking its claim as one of the best small areas around. It will never be a match for the likes of Fernie or Lake Louise, but to be fair, it does offer some good terrain that will help pass away a weekend or an afternoon. These are actually the only times you'll find the place open, which is probably just as well, as one week here would bore the tits off you if you know how to ride. The terrain map lets you see just how easy it is to negotiate runs and plan your routes off just two lifts. All the trails are hacked out between thick lines of ferns. The majority of runs would suit novices, although there are a couple of notable advanced runs such as **Pioneer** and **Grizzly**.

Freeriders can either take advantage of a few good pisted runs or if cash is no problem, take a heli-board trip to some more challenging areas. The trail marked out as **Porcupine** is a cool run that can be done at speed, but only if you know what you are doing. For the intermediate freerider, check out **Kicking Horse**, which starts out fairly mellow before dropping away more steeply mid-way down.

Freestylers may be forgiven for thinking that Whitetooth is not for them. Like many small areas, the splattering of natural hits and the occasional log won't keep your attention for long.

Carvers are best served here. The tree-lined trails run in a straight line down to the base area. **Pioneer** and **Grizzly** are notable carvers' trails where you can lay out some fast lines at speed, but this is an advanced rated run so be warned.

Beginners might look at the piste map and think that the place is made up of runs not suited to their ability, but on the ground it's a different story. Some of the runs are a little over-rated and could be tackled by a novice within a few days. Trails marked out as **A, C, D** and **F** offer easy flats at the lower areas, with the Waitabit run higher up being a nice progression trail.

Off the slopes, there is little to offer. At the base there is a small hire shop and a place to get a bite to eat, but that's about it. Lodging and other local facilities can be found 2 miles away in the town of **Golden**. Although not the most happening place, it's free of marauding crowds, very affordable and is still okay.
For accommodation listings visit - www.worldsnowboardguide.com.

Whitetooth
Po Box 1925, Golden, V0A 1H0. B.C
***001* (250) 344 6114**
www.rockies.net/~whitetooth
www.virgin.com/holidays

Overall rating out of 10 — **4** — **Very basic resort**

Whitewater British Columbia

CANADA
BC

MOUNTAIN DATA

Top Lift at - 2040m
Ride Area
Bottom Lift at - 1640m
Vertical Drop - 396m
Number of Runs - 24
Longest -

TERRAIN LEVELS

Easy	20%
Intermediate	40%
Advanced	40%
Expert	=

TERRAIN TO SUITE

Freeride	50%
Trees	Yes
Backcountry	Yes
Freestyle	20%
Halfpipe	No
Terrain Park	No
Carving	30%

SNOW DATA

Average Snowfall
1200cm a season
Snowmaking
0% cover of the slopes
Winter Periods
Dec to April
Summer Riding
None

SLOPE ACCESS

Total Lifts = 3
Uplift Rate - 7300 people an hour.
2 Chair lifts
1 Drag lift
**Leashes Required*

Lift Times
9.00am to 3.30pm

Lift Pass Rates

1 Day pass	C$36
3 Day pass	C$94
3 Day pass	C$525

Travel Guide

Fly to **Vancouver,** with a transfer time of 12 hours.

Bus services from Vancouver go to Nelson.

Route Planner: From Vancouver, useas a map reference the town of Nelson along Hwy3 of Hwy 6.
Calgary to resort = **478** miles.**12** hours drive time.

Whitewater is located close to the town of **Nelson** and is a very good bet for riding, even when other resorts are begging for snow. The mountain receives 1,200cm of snow each winter and due to the area's stable winter temperatures, the snow lasts and lasts. Whitewater is a huge bowl, contained by two ridges that join at the apex to form the 2,440m (800 ft) **Ymir Peak**. **Ymir** (pronounced 'why-mur') is named after a **Norse** legend and traps any westerly storm. Water vapour sucked off nearby **Kootenay Lake** is turned into consistently dry champagne powder that fills the bowl. Admittedly a 'high end' resort, with a majority of expert and intermediate terrain, Whitewater still has a lot of room for those lovers of groomed run cruising with long, easy beginner runs off the **Silver Ling** lift.

Freeriders should take the **Summit** chair to access the opposite ridge which offers steeper, groomed, intermediate runs and the most challenging off-piste through bowls and trees. Try **Dynamite**, **Catch Basin** and **Glory Basin** to lay down one powder track next to another. Get up early to challenge **Blast**, a steep fall-line under the chair lift.

Freestylers need to roam over the whole area to find places to get air as there is no permanent pipe or park. However, there is plenty of great natural freestyle terrain.

Carvers wanting fast groomed terrain will enjoy Whitewater's trails which offer every level of hard booter something to tackle.

Beginners will find that Whitewater is the kind of area that doesn't really have beginners - just learners who progress in powder by riding steeper and deeper lines. A new beginner park called The **Hunter** has been created near the day lodge. However, most people who have mastered the basics choose to head for the hills and carve up snow where groomers never reach.

There is no in-resort accommodation available at present, but there is a wide range of places to sleep in the town of **Nelson**. Nelson has good local facilities and is very affordable, if only a bit dull and basic. *The Dancing Bear Inn* has beds from C$19/person and *Stay and Ride* specials from C$45. During the day there is great food in *Shucky's Eatery* (even the soups are made with wine), and offers everything from fries to a full course lunch. *Coal Oil Jonny's* offers **Nelson** brewed beer on tap.

For accommodation listings visit - www.worldsnowboardguide.com.

Whitewater Resort
Po Box 60. Nelson. V1L 5P7.B.C
***001* (250) 354 4944**
www.skiwhitewater.com
www.virgin.com/holidays

Overall rating out of 10 **5** **Okay fun for a few days**

Resort	Page
Mont Tremblant	43
Mont sainte Ann	44

GENERAL INFO AND FACTS

Capital - QUEBEC CITY
Language - English & French
Currency - Canadian Dollar
Alcohol drinking age - 18
Drugs - Cannabis is illegal
Death Penalty - Doesn't Exist
Age of consent for Sex - 16
Electricity Supply - 110 Volts AC
Area phone Code - 514
Provincial sales tax - 7.5% on all goods and services

BC DRIVE GUIDE

All vehicles drive on the right side of the road.
Speed Limits -
Highways 100kph (60mph)
Rural routes
Towns 50kph (30mph)
Breakdown 001 (514) 861 7111
Fuel is sold in Litres

TRAVEL CONTACTS

International Airports
Montreal tel: 001 (514) 633 3105
Air Canada 001 (514) 393 3333
Canadian Airlines 800 426 7000

Via Rail
tel: 001 (514) 989 2626

Greyhound Buses
Autocars Orleans Express
tel: 001 (514) 395 4000

Eastern
GMT -5 hours

AREA INFORMATION
Tourism Quebec
CP 979, Montreal, PQ, H3C 2W3
tel: 001 (514) 873 2015

pic - Nidecker Snowboards

Mont Tremblant QUEBEC

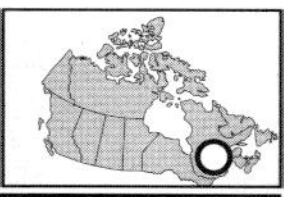

CANADA

Quebec

MOUNTAIN DATA

Top Lift at - 915m

Ride Area 500 acres

Bottom Lift at - 1575m

Vertical Drop - 694m

Number of Runs - 75

Longest - 3.5 miles (6km)

TERRAIN LEVELS

Easy	20%
Intermediate	35%
Advanced	45%
Expert =	

TERRAIN TO SUITE

Freeride	40%
Trees	Yes
Backcountry	Yes
Freestyle	20%
Halfpipe	Yes 1
Terrain Park	Yes 1
Carving	40%

SNOW DATA

Average Snowfall
370cm a season

Snowmaking
70% cover of the slopes

Winter Periods
Nov to May

Summer Riding
None

SLOPE ACCESS

Total Lifts = **12**

Uplift Rate 8,700 people an hour.

7 Chair lifts

5 Drag lifts

**Leashes Required*

Lift Times
8.30am to 4.00pm

Lift Pass Rates

1 Day pass	C$55
3 Day pass	C$161
5 Day pass	C$265

Travel Guide

Fly to **Montreal**, with a transfer time of **2** hours.

Bus services from Montreal to Tremblant.

Route Planner: From Montreal, travel north along Hwy's 15 &117, direction Ste Jovite, turning of at signs for Mont Tremblant **Montreal** to resort = **91** miles. **2** hours drive time.

pic - Mt Tremblant

Tremblant is one of the largest boarding areas in Canada and forms part of what is believed to be one of the oldest mountain ranges on the planet. Tremblant's organisational connections with **Blackcomb, Panorama** and also mighty **Stratton** in the US, helps them lay on a good time. The mountain's layout is excellent and extremely well planned, covering two sides, the **South** and the **North** which also has a new beginner slope running from the top to the bottom. The South side gives initial access to the runs which are all carved out of thick forest. The North side is a little smaller, but offers the same degree of cool riding. Both sides make up an area suited to carvers and freeriders, especially intermediate and advanced riders.

Freeriders have a really good mountain to explore, with plenty of white knuckle trails with drop offs, trees and powder. For some excellent tree-riding, go to **Emotion**. This area is graded a double black diamond trail, so it's not for the weak-kneed.

Freestylers have a decent size halfpipe and park, located under the **Express Flying Mile** chair on the South side, and only takes a few minutes to reach. The park is well looked after and you also get to listen to some decent tunes blasting out of the P.A.

Carvers buckle up tight as you'll be able to show off in style on well-pisted trails with 'carve me up' written all over them. **Geant**, a long wide black run on the **North** side, is really fun, while **Zag-Zag** on the South side is a killer double black that tames out lower down.

Beginners Tremblant offers more than enough for first timers, with easy green and blue runs on the **South** side. Take the **Express Tremblant** chair and novices can ride from top to bottom, via **La Crette** and **Nansen** green trails. If you're a late (in the day) starter then you may wish to have a late lesson; for around C$10 you can have an evening instruction session.

The village of Tremblant is only a few minutes from the slopes, although there are also some slopeside facilities with a good selection of condos and hotels to choose from. Getting around is easy on foot, alternatively there is a daily local bus service. Food and drinking options are okay and night-time can be pretty rowdy, rocking 'til the late hours. But note this is not the cheapest of places, so expect to notch up some credits on your card.

For accommodation listings visit - www.worldsnowboardguide.com.

Mont Tremblant Resort
3005 Chemin, Principal. Mont Tremblant, Quebec
1-800 567 6760 **www.tremblant.com**
www.virgin.com/holidays

Overall rating out of 10 **6** **A few good white knuckle runs**

Mont Sainte Anne QUEBEC

MOUNTAIN DATA

Top Lift at - 800m

Ride Area 428 acres

Bottom Lift at - 175m

Vertical Drop - 625m

Number of Runs - 75

Longest - 3.5 miles (6km)

TERRAIN LEVELS

Easy	23%
Intermediate	46%
Advanced	18%
Expert =	13%

TERRAIN TO SUITE

Freeride	50%
Trees	Yes
Backcountry	Yes
Freestyle	25%
Halfpipe	Yes 1
Terrain Park	Yes 1
Carving	25%

SNOW DATA

Average Snowfall
400 cm a season

Snowmaking
80% cover of the slopes

Winter Periods
Dec to April

Summer Riding
None

SLOPE ACCESS

Total Lifts = 13

Uplift Rate - 18,560 people an hour.

1 Gondolas, **6** Chair lifts

6 Drag lifts

**Leashes Required*

Lift Times
8.30am to 10.00pm

Lift Pass Rates

3 Day pass	C$117.40
4 Day pass	C$156.50
7 Day pass	C$259.95

SLOPE ACTION

Snowboard Hire
Daily rates from C$35
Kids from C$22

Snowboard Tuition
Lesson, lift & hire
from C$60 per day

Night Riding
None

Heli Boarding
No

Snowmobiles
Hire & tours

Mountain Cafes
5

pic - Mt Sainte Anne

Mont Sainte-Anne, a low level eastern ski resort makes a number of claims. It boasts for instance as being the most diverse all year round eastern sports distination, it also claims to have the best cross-country ski network in **Canada**. However, one claim it can't make, is that it's the best snowboard resort around, because it's not. That said, although a snowboarder who knows how to ride could have this place done in a day, **Mont Sainte-Anne** is still a decent resort and will certainly keep an intermediate rider content for a few days and a beginner satisified for a week with ease. With its proximity to Quebec City, the tree lined slopes here attract hoards of city dwellers at weekends, making this a busy place to ride and while the resort can boast lots of rideable terrain, this is not the highest of resorts. Still, over the years they have regularly managed to stage lots of international snowboard events so the place must have something going for it. Any resort close to a large city is often busy and suffers long lift queues, but thanks to the fast, high-tech lift system, these are greatly eliminated. Spread out on three facing slopes, **South, North** and **West**, the trails cut through thick trees that stretch to the summit. The **South Face** offers the most challenging terrain, with a number of decent black and extreme runs, which will test both freeriders and carvers alike. The intermediate terrain is quite extensive and covers all three slopes, with the **North** and **West Face**s having the best selection.

Freeriders of all levels will find something to take on at **Mont Saint-Anne,** however, should you know how to ride hard and fast, you could get round this place in a day or two. All the slopes are carved out of closely knitted trees providing for some bumpy fast trails back down to the base, but lacking on wide, open powder bowls. The south side slopes offer the most challenging runs with a cluster of fast double black diamond runs down the middle, one of which runs from the top all the way to the base and will burn up your thighs or make your eyes water if you bail.

Freestylers are free to roam the whole mountain, but they may wish to stay in the approximately 300,000 square foot fun-park which is located up on **La Grande Allee** trail. Here there is a good series of man made hits and a well shaped 75 metre halfpipe with walls cut by Quebec's first *Pipe Dragon*. The fun park, which is a good one, is unfortunately fully opened to skiers, who often wreck the top of the hits with their four edges.

Carvers may feel most at ease here. The pisted runs are well-suited to cranking over at speed. The most testing trails, including double black diamond runs, can be found on **South Face**.

Beginners are provided with gentle green runs that allow riding from top to bottom on some very tame descents. If you stay here for a week, you should be very competent by the time you leave (a two-week trip might be a bit much, even for a novice).

Mont Sainte Anne offers a very good selection of local services both at the base of the slopes or 25 miles away in down town Quebec City. Local lodging options are extensive with some 3000 visitor beds within a 3 mile stretch of the slopes. The main village is well set out and pleseant place to stay. There are a number of shops to serve your needs from boutiques to basic snowboard shops all mainly geared towards the casual visitor. The area also offers loads of other sporting attractions from snow tubing to skating on the outdoor ice rink. For those who find what's on offer close to the slopes a bit limited and too expensive, then by far the best thing thing to do is base yourself in Quebec City which is loaded with services.

Eating at the resort is pretty good but pricey. In the main base area you have a number of restaurants to choose from. The *Zig-Zag Bar* serves affordable food for those on a tight budget. *La Biscotte* and deli makes up really nice sandwiches while *La Camarine* is noted for its French food. Out of the village there is a large selection of restaurants and fast food outlets, with by the biggest selection of eateries at all price ranges in **Quebec City**.

Night-life in and around **Mont Sainte-Anne** is rather laid back and not aimed at hard core party animals. This is more of a quiet family style entertainment area with the livelyest places to be found in Quebec City. The *Zig-Zag Bar* or *The Pub* are okay night time hangouts or if you fancy a boogie, then the *Chquette Bar* is the place to go.

You can sleep close to the slopes and in varying styles of lodging. Condominiums are a popular choice with units sleeping individuals to large groups available. Costs vary but you could stay for two nights in a studio with a lift ticket thrown in from C$175. For those who like to stay in a hotel then the *Chateau Mont Sainte-Anne* is a fine place to visit with rates from C$230 for 2 nights.

For accommodation listings visit - www.worldsnowboardguide.com.

Summary: Not the worlds most interesting resort, but still okay with a few good challenging runs. Extensive local services
Money wise: Generally expensive unless you base in Quebec City which has the cheapest offerings.

Overall rating out of 10 **6**

Mont Sainte Anne
2000, Bowl Pre Cp, 400,
Beaupe, Quebec.

General info	***001*** **(418) 827 4561**
Reservations	***001*** **(418) 827 5281**
Snowphone	***001*** **(418) 827 4579**

www.mont-sainte-anne.com
www.virgin.com/holidays

pics -Mt Sainte Ann Resort

Travel Guide

Fly to **Montreal International**
Transfer time to resort = **3** hours
Local airport = Quebec City 25 miles away (40km).

Approximate global air travel times to **Montreal**:

from:		
	London	**7** hours
	New York	**2** hours
	Frankfurt	**8½** hours

A bus from **Montreal** takes around 3 hours to Quebec City with onward buses to the resort.

Trains go direct to Quebec City

Route Planner
Montreal *via Quebec City*

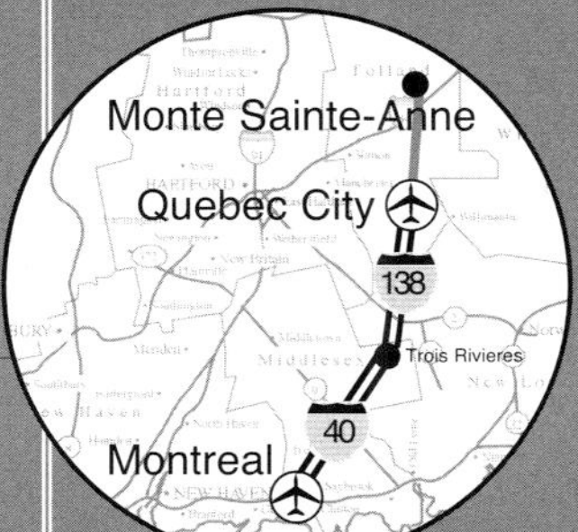

Mt Sainte Anne = 180 miles (253km)
Drive time is about **3** hours

GENERAL INFO AND FACTS

Capital - Regina
Language - English & French
Currency - Canadian Dollar
Alcohol drinking age - 19
Drugs - Cannabis is illegal
Death Penalty - Doesn't Exist
Age of consent for Sex - 16
Electricity Supply - 110 Volts AC
Area phone Code - 514
Provincial sales tax - 7.% on all goods and services

BC DRIVE GUIDE

All vehicles drive on the right side of the road.
Speed Limits -
Highways 100kph (60mph)
Rural routes
Towns 50kph (30mph)
Breakdown 001 (514) 861 7111
Fuel is sold in Litres

TRAVEL CONTACTS

International Airports
Saskatoon tel: 001 (403) 298 9200
Air Canada 001 (514) 393 3333
Canadian Airlines 800 426 7000

Via Rail
tel: 001 (561) 3949

Greyhound Buses

East
GMT -6 hours

AREA INFORMATION

Tourism Saskatchewan
500-1900 Albert St. Regina SK, S4P 4L9
tel: 001 (306) 787 2300

Blackstrap Winter Park

Po Box 612. Dundurn SK.

Located 32km south of Saskatoon via Hwy 11 and Hwy 211. Blackstrap has just 8 runs with only 88 metres of vert with the longest run just making 450m.
This small mountain is best for novices and slow intermediates. The resort also provides a cool fun park with a few table tops and a halfpipe.
No slope side lodgings exists, the nearest accommodation and services can be found at Dundurn, Hanly and Saskatoon.
ⓘ **tel-** (306) 492 2401

Blue Mountain Outdoor Cnt

RR1 North Battleford SK.

Located 32km south of Battleford, Blue Mountain is a very small retreat that offers a host of sporting activities including some limited snowboarding. There is some basic accommodation on site as well as other basic amenities.
ⓘ **tel-** (306) 445 4941

Cudworth Ski Area

Cudworth. SK

Located south on 6th Ave, Cudworth consists of just one 230 metre trail with just 24 metres of vertical with one tow.
Accommodation and other facilities are available in Cudworth.
ⓘ **tel-** (306) 256 3281

Little Red River Park

1084 Central Ave, Prince Albert SK

Located 3km east of Prince Albert via Hwy 5, Little Red River Park consists of just two runs and two lifts. One slope is of beginner level while the other is an intermediate trail. The are alos ski patrol, snowboard instruction and a halfpipe.
Accommodation and other facilities are available in Prince Albert.
ⓘ **tel-** (306) 953 4879

Mission Ridge Ski Area

Po Box 848, Fort Qu'Appelle, SK

Located 2km south east of downtown Fort Qu'Appelle. Mission Ridge, is a mountain with 8 runs, 92 metres of vert and 4 lifts. This small resort is a popular destination and can get busy. The area bosts a fun park and halfpipe and also provides night riding with special rates.
Accommodation and other facilities are available close by in Fort Qu'Appelle.
ⓘ **tel-** (306) 332 5479

Ochapowace

Po Box 190 Broadview. SK

Located 3km east of Broadview on Hwy1 and off Hwy 201. Ochapowace has a decent selection of runs with a good choice of beginner trails, okay intermediate runs and a choice of 5 fast expert trails. The longest runs measures just over a 1000 metres with maximum vert at 151 metres. There are 5 lifts, a small halfpipe and terrain park as well as piped music across the slopes during the day. Instruction and full snowboard hire is available with daily rates from C$25 a day.
Lots of accommodation and other local facilities are available in Broadview, Whitewood and in Birds point.
ⓘ **tel-** (306) 696 2522

Pasquia Ski Slope

RR 1 Tisdale, SK

Located 12km south east of Zenon. Pasquia is a tiny hangout with 4 slopes, 1 tow and only opens for afternoon riding with private bookings.
Accommodation and other facilities are available in Zenon.
ⓘ **tel-** (306) 767 2682

Ski Timber Ridge

Box 741, Big River, SK

Located 5km south of Big River on Hwy 55, Ski Timber Ridge provides 5 trails, with the longest run at 800 metres and the max vert at 90 metres. You can also get snowboard hire and instruction at the slope with daily lessons and privates. Main accommodation and other local facilities are available in Big River which is only 2 km away and has a number of okay lodging options, good places to eat as well as a host of sporting activities.
ⓘ **tel-** (306) 469 4545

Sturgis Assiniboine Ski Area

Box 520, Sturgis SK.

Located 1km south of Sturgis off Hwy 49, Tiny area offers five trails with a maximun vert of 36 metres and one drag lift.
Very basic and limited local facilities are available in Sturgis 1 km away.
ⓘ **tel-** (306) 548 2108

Table Mountain Park

Box 343, North Battleford, SK

Located 29km west of Battleford off Hwy 40. Eight trails, 107 metres of vert and 4 lifts make up this small hangout that also has night riding and a fun park.
Local services and lodging available in North Battleford and Cut Knife.
ⓘ **tel-** (306) 937 2920

Twin Towers Ski Area

Box 93, Plenty SK.

Only 3km south of Stranraer off Hwy 31, Twin Towers has six slopes, the longest being 853 metres, 91 metres of vertical and 2 lifts with a snowboard area and rentals on site.
All local services availible in Herschel, Rosetown (58km), Kindersley and Plenty.
ⓘ **tel-** (306) 377 4551

Wapiti Valley Park

Box 181, Gronlid SK.

Only 25km south of Choiceland via Hwy 6 north of Gronlid, Wapiti has eleven trails with a maximum vert of 85 metres and the longest run at 870 metres. 3 drag lifts and snowmaking equipment make up this simple resort. Local services available in Melfort, Nipawin, Gronlid and Choiceland.
ⓘ **tel-** (306) 862 5621

White Track Ski Area

Box 702, Moose Jaw, SK

Located 27km from Moose Jaw in Buffalo. Its nine slopes are evenly split between beginner, intermediate and expert levels. 3 drag lifts and a maximum vert of 70 m. All local services available in Moose Jaw, Chamberlain and Regina.
ⓘ **tel-** (306) 691 0100

Duck Mountain Saskatchewan

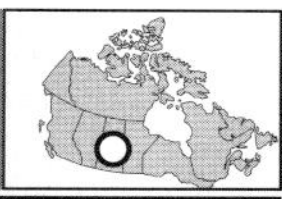

CANADA

Saskatchewan

MOUNTAIN DATA

Top Lift at - Not available

Ride Area

Bottom Lift at -

Vertical Drop - 120m
Number of Runs - 20
Longest - 1600m

TERRAIN LEVELS

Easy	**30%**
Intermediate	**45%**
Advanced	**25%**
Expert =	

TERRAIN TO SUITE

Freeride	**40%**
Trees	Yes
Backcountry	Yes
Freestyle	**20%**
Halfpipe	Yes 1
Terrain Park	Yes 1
Carving	**40%**

SNOW DATA

Average Snowfall

Snowmaking

Winter Periods
Dec to April

Summer Riding
None

SLOPE ACCESS

Total Lifts = **3**
Uplift Rate - people an hour.
1 Handle Tow
2 Drag lifts
**Leashes Required*

Lift Times
10.00am to 4.30pm

Lift Pass Rates
1/2 Day pass C$13
1 Day pass C$16
Child pass C$10

Travel Guide

Fly to **Saskatoon** International airport.

Bus services from Saskatoon are not direct.

Route Planner: From Saskatoon head east along hwy 16 to Yorkton. Then head west and north on Hwys 10 & 8 to Kamsack.
Saskatoon to resort = 241 miles. **3** hours drive time.

pic - Nidecker Snowboards

If you travel east from **Saskatoon** and drive along highway 16 towards **Yorkton** and then head north via **Kamsack,** you will eventually come to the **Duck Mountain Provincial Park** where tucked away in **Little Boggy Creek Valley** is the small but cool ski resort of **Duck Mountain.** As one of **Saskatchewain's** biggest resorts, this place is still no match for the resorts found in the neighbouring western provinces of **British Columbia** and **Alberta.** However, by no means is this place boring or not worth a visit because for beginners living close by and on a low budget, **Duck Mountain** is a fine place to try out. Intermediates will also find that this place will keep them amused for a couple of days, though, expert riders may well tire of the place after a day. There is only half a dozen black trails and none of which are that long. The 20 well marked trails are serviced by just three drag lifts. All with all the slopes link up easily and base out at the *Day lodge* which boasts a cafe-bar and snowboard rental centre. The resort operates a number of lift pass options and unlike Alberta's resorts, lift rates here are very affordable with an adult day pass costing just C$16 or a child's pass at C$13. Oldies can shred the slopes for C$10 an afternoon, provided their hearts can take it.

Freeriders shouldn't come here expecting to find an amazing amount of hardcore freeriding terrain, however, what is on offer is cool, with a few nice banks and some okay rollers. Advanced riders should take the **New T-Bar** in order to rider back down the **Timber Wolf Pass** or the **Black Bear Bowl**, both of which are fun black trails to pass away some time. The **Haywire** is another okay trail to make some tracks on and also reached off the **New T-Bar.**

Freestylers have the choice of getting air in the halfpipe which is located along side the lower section of the **New T-Bar.** The pipe is not major but it has its moments and beats having to build hits you'reself. As for natural hits, well there are a few spots to go off from, but nothing much to over excite a good freestyler.

Carvers may find that the **Hangover** or **Morning Glory** trails are the ideal places to lay out some big turns on.

Beginners have a resort that is well suited to them with some nice easy areas, although the choice of beginner runs is limited.

Some accommodation and other local services can be found a few minutes from the slopes in **Duck Mountain Lodge.** However, **Kamsack** (36km away) has the best choice of all local facilities.

Duck Mountain
Box 1673, Kamsack, SK
001 (306) 542 4111 **www.virgin.com/holidays**

Overall rating out of 10 **4** **Some nice banks and rollers**

Canadian Round up

Adanac Ski Centre *Ontario*
Near - **Sudbury** - 3 Lifts & 1 run
tel- (705) 566 9911

Agassiz Ski Resort *Manitoba*
Near - **McCreary** - 4 Lifts & 10 runs
tel- (204) 835 2246

Atitokan *Ontario*
Near - **Atitokan** - 2 Lifts & 6 runs
tel- (807) 597 6624

Beaver Valley *Ontario*
Near - **Markdale** - 3 Lifts & 21 runs
tel- (519) 986 2520

Bear Mtn Hill *British Columbia*
Near - **Dawson Creek** - 1 Lift & 10 runs
tel- (519) 986 2520

Belle Neige *Quebec*
Near - **Val Morin** - 3 Lifts & 14 runs
3 Lifts **tel-** (514) 229 2921

Big Ben *Ontario*
Near - **Cornwall** - 1 Lift & 1 run
tel- (613) 932 4422

Big Friendly *Manitoba*
Near - **Markdale** - 3 Lifts & 21 runs
tel- (204) 845 2445

Big Thunder *Ontario*
Near - **Thunder Bay** - 5 Lifts & 7 runs
tel- (807) 475 1673

Blue Mountain *Ontario*
Near - **Collingwood** - 15 Lifts & 33 runs
tel- (705) 445 0231

Bromont *Quebec*
Near - **Bromont** - 6 Lifts & 22 runs
6 Lifts **tel-** (514) 534 2200

Camp Fortune *Quebec*
Near - **Old Chelsea** - 5 Lifts &16 runs
tel- (819) 827 1717

Canada Olympic Park *Alberta*
1220m 80 Acres 5 Lifts
If you're hanging out in Calgary and fancy an afternoon's play, then try the Canada Olympic Park. But don't expect too much. This is a blip of a hill which doesn't offer much in the way of snowboard terrain other than having some flat, easy areas for novices and a funpark for freestylers.
Fly to: **Calgary** - 20 minutes away
tel- (403) 247 5452.

Canyon Ski Area *Nova Scotia*
Near - **Red Deer** - 5 Lifts & 12 runs
tel- (403) 346 5588

Cape Smokey *Ontario*
Near - **Ingonish Ferry** - 2 Lifts & 15 runs
tel- (902) 285 2778

Chedoke Park *Ontario*
Near - **Hamilton** - 4 Lifts & 7 runs
tel- (905) 528 1613

Castle Mountain *Alberta*
1981m 250 Acres 4 Lifts
Castle Mountain is a small resort located in the southern part of the province. The 36 trails are carved out through trees with a mixture of simple freeriding, nice powder bowls, and fast carving runs. It is also good for freestylers and novices. Main local services can be found in the town of Pincher Creek, a 40 minute drive away.
Fly to: **Calgary** - 2-1/2 hours away
tel- (403) 672 5101

Caribou Mountain *Ontario*
Near - **Temagami** - 1 Lifts & 3 runs
tel- (705) 569 3421

Caswell Mountain *Ontario*
Near - **Temagami** - 1 Lifts & 3 runs
tel- (705) 384 5371

Clearwater *Ontario*
Near - **Westbank** - 4 Lifts & 20 runs
tel- (604) 674 3848

Club De Ski Plessis *Quebec*
Near - **Plessisville** - 2 Lifts & 10 runs
tel- (418) 453 2357

Club Tobo Ski *Quebec*
Near - **Feliicien** - 2 Lifts & 6 runs
tel- (418) 679 5243

Cotes 40-80 *Quebec*
Near - **St. Pacome** - 2 Lifts & 4 runs
tel- (514) 229 2921

Crabbe Park *New Brunswick*
Near - **Millville** - 4 Lifts & 14 runs
tel- (506) 463 8311

Crystal Mountain *British Columbia*
Near - **Westbank** - 3 Lifts & 20 runs
tel- (604) 768 5189

Devils Elbow *Ontario*
Near - **Bethany** - 10 Lifts & 6 runs
tel- (705) 277 2012

Divine Lake *Ontario*
Near - **Port Sydney** - 1 Lift & 2 runs
tel- (705) 385 1212

Eagle Ridge *Ontario*
Near - **Ear Falls** - 1 Lift & 3 runs
tel- (807) 222 3716

Edelweiss Valley *Quebec*
Near - **Wakefield** - 3 Lifts & 19 runs
tel- (819) 459 2328

Edmonton Ski Club *Alberta*
Near - **Edmonton** - 4 Lifts & 6 runs
tel- (403) 465 0852

Fairmont Springs *British Columbia*
Near - **Fairmont** - 2 Lifts & 14 runs
tel- (604) 345 6311

Falcon Lake *Manitoba*
Near - **Falcon Beach** - 4 Lifts & 14 runs
tel- (204) 349 2201

Forbidden Mountain *British Columbia*
Near - **Courtenay** - 4 Lifts & 21 runs
tel- (604) 334 4744

Fairmont Springs *British Columbia*
Near - **Fairmont** - 2 Lifts & 14 runs
tel- (604) 345 6311

Glen Eden *Ontario*
Near - **Milton** - 5 Lifts & 10 runs
tel- (905) 878 5011

Gray Rocks *Quebec*
Near - **Saint-Jovite** - 4 Lifts & 20 runs
tel- (819) 425 2771

Harper Mountain *British Columbia*
Near - **Kamloops** - 3 Lifts & 15 runs
tel- (604) 573 5115

Hemlock Valley *British Columbia*
Near - **Agassiz** - 4 Lifts & 34 runs
tel- (604) 797 4111

Hidden Valley *Ontario*
Near - **Huntsville** - 4 Lifts & 8 runs
tel- (705) 789 1773

Holiday Mountain *Manitoba*
Near - **Riviere** - 5 Lifts & 10 runs
tel- (204) 242 2172

Horseshoe *Ontario*
Near - **Orangeville** - 4 Lifts & 10 runs
tel- (519) 942 0754

Kamiskotia *Ontario*
Near - **Timmins** - 4 Lifts & 12 runs
tel- (705) 268 9057

Kingston Hills *Ontario*
Near - **Kingston** - 5 Lifts & 7 runs
tel- (613) 378 6203

L'Avalanche *Quebec*
Near - **St-Adolphe** - 9 Lifts & 2 runs
tel- (819) 327 3232

La Crapaudiere *Quebec*
Near - **St Malachie** - 2 Lifts & 11 runs
tel- (418) 642 5171

Lakeridge Resort *Ontario*
Near - **Uxbridge** - 3 Lifts & 12 runs
tel- (905) 649 2058

Landslide *Ontario*
Near - **Marie** - 3 Lifts & 1 run
tel- (705) 946 0190

Larder Ski Club *Ontario*
Near - **Larder Lake** - 1 Lift & 4 runs
tel- (705) 643 2596

Loch Lomond *Ontario*
Near - **Thunder Bay** - 3 Lifts & 15 runs
tel- (807) 475 7787

London Ski Club *Ontario*
Near - **London** - 4 Lifts & 8 runs
tel- (519) 657 8822

Loretto Resort *Ontario*
Near - **Loretto** - 4 Lifts & 5 runs
tel- (905) 729 2385

Le Massif *Quebec*
838m 175 Acres 4 Lifts
The thick tree-covered slopes will appeal to good intermediates and carvers who ride fast. Novices and freestylers should stay away. Slopeside accommodation is available but the best and cheaper option is to stay in Quebec.
Fly to: **Quebec** - 1 hour away
tel- (418) 632 5876

Le Relais *Quebec*
Near - **Lac Beauport** - 6 Lifts & 25 runs
tel- (418) 849 1851

Le Valinouet *Quebec*
Near - **Falardeau** - 4 Lifts & 25 runs
tel- (418) 673 3455

Manning Park *British Columbia*
Near - **Manning Park** - 4 Lifts & 24 runs
tel- (604) 840 8822

Mansfield Ski Club *Ontario*
Near - **Mansfield** - 6 Lifts & 14 runs
tel- (705) 435 3838

Martock *Nova Scotia*
Near - **Wentworth** - 6 Lifts & 21 runs
tel- (902) 798 9501

Marble Mountain *Newfoundland*
Near - **Corner Brook** - 5 Lifts & 26 runs
tel- (709) 639 8531

Mission Ridge *Saskatchewan*
Near - **Fort Qu'appaelle** - 4 Lifts
tel- (306) 332 5479

Mont Alta *Quebec*
Near - **Val-David** - 2 Lifts & 22 runs
tel- (819) 322 3206

Mont Antoine *Ontario*
Near - **North Bay** - 3 Lifts & 11 runs
tel- (705) 744 2844

Mont Blanc *Quebec*
8 Lifts & 35 runs
Mont Blanc is stretched across two mountains with 35 trails cut between tree-lined terrain. A novice carver will enjoy a few days here, while a good freerider would will not. Beginners will manage a week but freestylers won't, even with the pipe. You can lodge slopeside at the hotel.
Fly to: **Montreal** - 1 hour away
tel- (514) 476 1862

Mt Baldy *British Columbia*
Near - **Oliver** - 2 Lifts & 15 runs
tel- (604) 498 2262

Mt Cain *British Columbia*
Near - **Port McNeill** - 3 Lifts & 18 runs
tel- (604) 949 9496

Mt Castor *Quebec*
Near - **Matane** - 3 Lifts & 12 runs
tel- (418) 562 1513

Mont Christie *Quebec*
Near - **Christieville** - 3 Lifts & 12 runs
tel- (514) 226 2412

Mont Daniel *Quebec*
Near - **Lac des Iles** - 2 Lifts & 16 runs
tel- (819) 597 2388

Mont Edouard *Quebec*
Near - **Anse-St. Jean** - 3 Lifts & 20 runs
tel- (418) 272 2112

Mont Farlagne *New Brunswick*
Near - **Edmundston** - 4 Lifts & 17 runs
tel- (506) 735 8401

Mont Fortin *Quebec*
Near - **Jonquiere** - 4 Lifts & 11 runs
tel- (418) 695 7707

Mont Gabriel *Quebec*
433m 11 runs 10 Lifts
Mont Gabriel is one of the haunts that serves Montreal's city dwellers offering something for everyone. Some good carving areas, wide open trails for freeriding piste lovers, and a halfpipe for freestylers that was once voted the second best in Quebec.
Local services offer a few tourist beds. Better to stay in Montreal.
Fly to: **Montreal** - 40 minutes away
tel- (514) 227 1100

Mont Garceau *Quebec*
Near - **Saint Donat** - 6 Lifts & 17 runs
tel- (819) 424 2784

Mont Grand Fonds *Quebec*
Near - **La Malbaie** - 4 Lifts & 14 runs
tel- (418) 665 4405

Mont Habitant *Quebec*
3 Lifts & 14 runs 300 Acres
Mt Habitant is a small mountain north of Montreal that appeals largely to 'happy family' types, with parents in one-piece ski-suits, and kids in ugly hats. Although it is snowboard-friendly, it doesn't offer much except to those at novice level. Local facilities are basic and boring .
Fly to: **Montreal** - 45 minutes away
tel- (514) 227 2637

Mont Joye *Quebec*
Near - **North Hatley** - 3 Lifts & 18 runs
tel- (819) 842 2447

Mont Labelle *Quebec*
Near - **Labelle** - 2 Lifts & 11 runs
tel- (819) 686 2626

Mont Orford *Quebec*
Near - **Orford** - 6 Lifts & 39 runs
tel- (819) 843 6548

Mont Orignal *Quebec*
Near - **Lac Etchemin** - 4 Lifts & 15 runs
tel- (418) 625 1551

Mont Pontbriand *Quebec*
Near - **Rawdon** - 5 Lifts & 10 runs
tel- (514) 834 6660

Mont Rigaud *Quebec*
Near - **Rigaud** - 2 Lifts & 8 runs
tel- (514) 415 5316

Mont St Bruno *Quebec*
Near - **St Bruno** - 7 Lifts & 14 runs
tel- (514) 653 3441

Mont St Castin *Quebec*
Near - **Lac Beauport** - 5 Lifts & 14 runs
tel- (418) 849 1893

Mont Saint-Sauveur *Quebec*
416m 175 Acres 9 Lifts
Saint-Sauver is yet another small resort just outside Montreal with around 30 trails that will appeal to carvers. Weekends can be very busy with novices, but those riders who like to give it some, can try a few blacks and a double diamond expert trail. Basic slopeside lodging, but better in Montreal.
Fly to: **Montreal** - 40 minutes away
tel- (514) 227 4671

Mont Saint -Maire *Quebec*
Near - **Lac Sainte-Marie** - 3 Lifts & 17 runs
tel- (819) 467 5200

Mont Sauvage *Quebec*
Near - **Val-Morin** - 3 Lifts & 9 runs
tel- (819) 322 2337

Mont Sutton *Quebec*
Near - **Sutton** - 9 Lifts & 53 runs
tel- (514) 538 2545

Mount Arrowsmith *British Columbia*
Near - **Port Alberni** - 3 Lifts & 12 runs
tel- (604) 723 7899

Mount Mackenzie *British Columbia*
Near - **Revelstoke** - 4 Lifts & 26 runs
tel- (604) 837 5268

Mount St Louis *Ontario*
Near - **Coldwater** - 13 Lifts & 33 runs
tel- (705) 835 2112

Murray Ridge *British Columbia*
Near - **St James** - 2 Lifts & 20 runs
tel- (604) 996 8513

Mystery Mountain *Manitoba*
Near - **Thompson** - 4 Lifts & 17 runs
tel- (204) 677 4729

Nakiska *Alberta*
2260m 734 Acres 5 Lifts
Built to host the 1988 winter Olympics, Nakiska, which has a well equipped modern lift system, straddles the slopes of Mount Allan and offers basic snowboarding that will suit intermediates. Freeriders will find the double black trails off the Eagle chair the place to get a fix, while freestylers are presented with a halfpipe off the Silver chair. Beginners have a good selection of novice areas. Accommodation can be found slopeside or in nearby Kananaskis.
Fly to: **Calgary** - 1 hour away
tel- (403) 591 7777

Onaping *Ontario*
Near - **Onaping** - 3 Lifts & 10 runs
tel- (705) 966 3939

Owl's Head *Quebec*
Near - **Mansonville** - 7 Lifts & 27 runs
tel- (514) 292 3342

Phoenix Mountain *British Columbia*
Near - **Grand Forks** - 2 Lifts & 9 runs
tel- (604) 442 2813

Powder King *British Columbia*
Near - **Mackenzie** - 3 Lifts & 18 runs
tel- (604) 561 1776

Purden Village *British Columbia*
Near - **Prince George** - 2 Lifts & 13 runs
tel- (604) 565 9038

Mt Seymour *British Columbia*
2260m 300 Acres 5 Lifts
The terrain here consists of huge rollers, steep powder lines, perfect cliff-drops, and masses of trees to please freeriders of all levels in areas such as **City Booter, McGuire Hip, Whisky Hip**, and **Dave Lee Gap**. But beware! There is considerable avalanche danger. Freestylers have a number of park and pipe areas, but with so much natural terrain, they're not needed. The **Lodge** chair offers access to some easy runs making this a good place for novices. There are no local services at the slopes, but **Vancouver** is only 30 minutes away. Here you'll find all you need including, alleyways and pavements to kip on.
Fly to: **Vancouver** - 30 minutes away
tel- (403) 591 7777

Stoneham *Quebec*
630m 300 Acres 4 Lifts
300 acres of well-linked terrain is spread over four mountains that are tree-lined to the summit. Mixed ability runs snake down through trees towards the base area. There's a good offering of double diamond black trails for advanced riders and a number of simple greens for novices. Local services are okay but not cheap.
Fly to: **Quebec** - 20 minutes away
tel- (418) 848 2411

Tabor Mountain *British Columbia*
Near - **Prince George** - 3 Lifts & 10 runs
tel- (604) 963 7542

The Snowboard Ranch *Ontario*
Near - **Peterborough** - 4 Lifts & 10 runs
tel- (705) 277 9211

Wintergreen *Alberta*
190 Acres 4 Lifts
Wintergreen is okay for a small resort, with just 10 runs that are evenly shared out between beginner and expert levels. However, riders who like to ride hard will have the resort licked in an hour, while beginners will need a day to conquer this place. There is a good halfpipe here which is floodlit, enabling night-riding. Lodging and services are best found in Calgary 30 mins away.
Fly to: **Calgary** - 30 minutes away
tel- (403) 949 5100

GENERAL INFO AND FACTS

Capital - Washington D.C
Language - English (just)
Currency - US Dollar
Alcohol drinking age - 21
Drugs - Cannabis is illegal
Death Penalty - Exists in 32 states
Age of consent for Sex - 16
Military Service - Not compulsory
Electricity Supply - 110 Volts AC
International phone Code - 001
Highest Peak - Mt Mckinley 6194m

DUTY FREE
1 Litre of Alcohol
200 Cigarettes
100 Cigars
Up to $100 for gifts and goods.

AMERICAN DRIVE GUIDE
All vehicles drive on the right hand side of the road
Speed Limits -
Motorways 100kph (62mph)
Highways 90kph (55mph)
Towns 50kph (50mph)

SNOWBOARD CONTACTS
Transworld Snowboard Mag
353 Airport Rd, Oceanside. CA
tel - 001 (760) 722 7777

Snowboarder Magazine
PO Box 1028, Dana Point.CA
92629. tel - 001 (949) 496 5922

US Snowboard Association
PO Box 44oo Frisco, Colorado
80443. tel - 001 (303)668 3350

www.virgin.com/holidays

TIME ZONES
Canada has 6 time Zones

Pacific
GMT -8 hours

Mountain
GMT -7 hours

Central
GMT -6 hours

Eastern
GMT -5 hours

Atlantic
GMT -4 hours

Newfoundland
GMT -3.5hours

INTERNATIONAL AIRPORTS
1 - **Seattle** - WA
2 - **Portland** - OR
3 - **San Francisco** - CA
4 - **Los Angles** - LA
5 - **Reno** - NE
6 - **Salt Lake City** - UT
7 - **Denver** - CO
8 - **Portland** - MA
9 - **Boston** - MA
10 - **New York** - NY

There are hundreads of resorts in the US spread out over the northern eastern states, the central Rockie states and the north western states, however, many are no more than a backyard affair operated by a dollar-hungry hillbilly.

The usual season lasts from November until mid-April, with a few northern areas staying open until mid-May. US resorts are generally much smaller than ones in Europe. However, the Rockies do have peaks that rise up to 3,000 metres.

Flights to US cities are frequent, with many having transfer flights to resorts. From various airports you can reach the resorts by bus (sometimes a free shuttle service), or by hire car. If you're touring around the US, you can fly very cheaply using an Air Pass costing from $375.

Travel to a resort by train is limited in terms of direct routes. In most cases you will need to take a train to the nearest city and then transfer by bus. East coast resorts are the easiest to reach by train from international airports. A 30 day rail pass for unlimited travel costs from $400.

Greyhound Buses operate the largest cross-country network of routes, with dozens of options. Like trains, it may be necessary to take a Greyhound bus to a city and then transfer by a local bus. A 30-day adult *Ameripass* costs from $450.

Visa requirements vary, but generally, Europeans can enter without a visa and stay for 90 days. All foreigners need a valid passport. If you want to work in the US, you will need to obtain a work visa, which is difficult. If you are caught working without a visa, you will be deported.

Accommodation comes in the form of hotels, motels, guest houses and condominiums (apartments), which are reasonably priced and usually of a very high standards. A low cost option would be to stay in a youth hostel or a ski dorm.

Restaurants vary considerably in price from cheap to ridiculous, and remember that you are expected to tip in restaurants. Proof of age is constantly required when buying alcohol, so keep some form of ID on you wherever you go. Baby-faced snowboarders forget it.

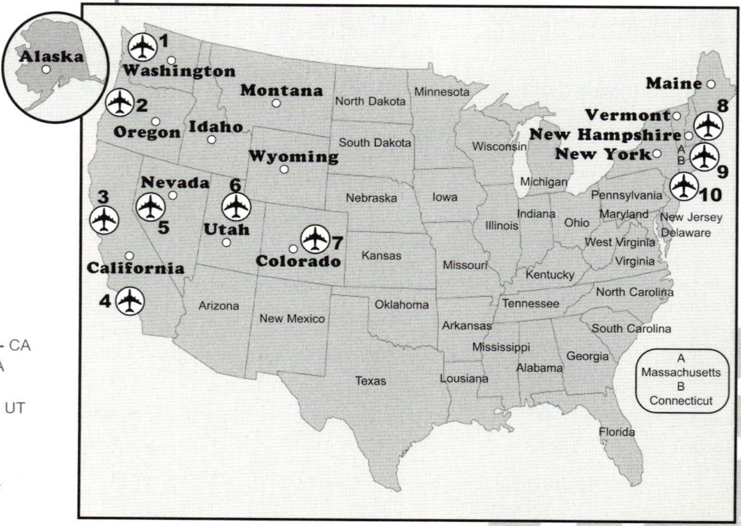

pic - Hank deVr / Rider - Shaun Palmer at Big Bear California

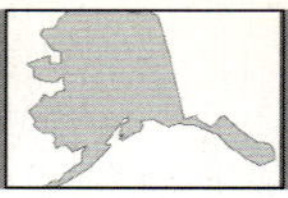

GENERAL INFO AND FACTS

Capital - Juneau
Language - English
Currency - US Dollar
Alcohol drinking age - 21
Drugs - Cannabis is illegal
Death Penalty - Doesn't Exist
Age of consent for Sex - 16
Electricity Supply - 110 Volts AC
Area phone Code - 907
Provincial sales tax - 0% on all goods and services

ALASKA DRIVE GUIDE

All vehicles drive on the right side of the road.

Speed Limits -
Motorways 62mph (100kph)
Highways 55mph (90kph)
Towns 30mph (50kph)
Road Info 001 (907) 273 6037
Fuel is sold in Gallons

TRAVEL CONTACTS

Gateway Airports
Anchorage
tel: 001 (907) 266 2525
Juneau

Alaska Railroad
tel: 001 (907) 265 2494

Alaskon Express

Alaskan
GMT -9 hours
(1 hour earler than Pacific)

AREA INFORMATION

Anchorage Convention & Visitors
524 W. 4th Ave. Anchorage, Alaska
tel: 001 (907) 276 4118

Alaska State Tourism
P.O Box 110801, Juneau AK 99811
tel: 001 (907) 465 2010

If you mention the name **Alaska** to most people, they will shiver with the thought of huge ice bergs, wild snow cape mountain ranges and dridiculously cold tempreatures.

In terms of terrain for snowboarding, most believe that the only people who can snowboard in Alaska are expert riders who know how to ride high altitude, steep, extreme back-country areas. While much of this is ture with some 90% of the ridable terrain only accessable via a helicopter or by long hikes form barron and remote out post, Alaska is infact not just for a select few of big headed sponsored riders doing a video shot, its a place that welcomes all riders no matter what you're ability and although this is a very cold state with recorded low tempreatures of -70°C, don't be put of. Alaska has all the modern resort facilites found in any other US snowboard/ski resort. The only difference is that what Alasks offering are a lot more limited with infact only one majorly developed resort, **Alyeska** which is a fully developed resort with some 62 runs and many purpose bulit facilities at the base of the slopes. (see page 54. As well Alyesa, there are a number of smaller ridable areas, but the remainder are very basic and are not resorts as we know them. They are more or less for locals and run by clubs and private companies.

Where you won't get any of the standard resort set up style of services is in **Valdez**, which lies some 300 miles east of Anchorage. Valdez, which is actually a busy oil port, is the snowboaders heaven and for the place for purist only. This is where backcountry, means '*Backcountry*'. There are no lifts with lines of skiers in sad clothing and headbands moaning about snowboarders, no groups of ski classes getting in the way all over the place, no ski patrols, no marked runs, no pisted runs. Nothing other than pure virgin terrain that sholud only be ridden if one, you can ride, and two, you only ride in a group and with a local guide and are propley equiped with backcountry clothing and safety equipment.

A number of establised and professional companies are based here and operate proper backcountry tours with local guides who know the mountains and are fully trained in mountain safety and rescue. Organised trips in areas such as the **Chugach Mountains** and the **Thompson Pass** can be arranged with travel options that range from flying in by helicopter, snow-plane, snow-cat or on foot by hiking. Its even said that if you can show that you are the first to ride a particular slope, you get the honour of naming the slope or face, after your self or what ever name you choose.

Fully inclusive trips that include travel, accommodation, food and guiding are available all yera round and all though a weeks all in tour will cost you dearly, it will be a trip of a life time.

As for local aminites, accommodation and restaurants, Valdez is a hard town that is home to oil workers who can drink stupid amounts of alchol and who don't give a shit what snowboard you ride. The town has a number lodges and bed and breakfast homes with affordable rates. The **Totem Inn** is one of the main places to hang out in the evenings, where you can get a decent meal, shot some pool or drink you self stupid well in to the night trying to keep up with the locals.

pic - Ride Snowboards

Alyeska Alaska

MOUNTAIN DATA

Top Lift at - 838m

Ride Area
790 acres

Bottom Lift at - 175m
Vertical Drop - 762m
Number of Runs - 62
Longest -1.5 miles (2.4km)

TERRAIN LEVELS

Easy	**11%**
Intermediate	**52%**
Advanced	**37%**
Expert =	**6 runs**

TERRAIN TO SUITE

Freeride	**60%**
Trees	Yes
Backcountry	Yes
Freestyle	**20%**
Halfpipe	Yes 1
Terrain Park	Yes 1
Carving	**10%**

SNOW DATA

Average Snowfall
1422 cm a season
Snowmaking
37% cover of the slopes
Winter Periods
Nov to April
Summer Riding
None

SLOPE ACCESS

Total Lifts = **9**
Uplift Rate -10,355 people an hour.
1 Tram, **6** Chair lifts
2 Drag lifts
**Leashes Required*

Lift Times
10.30am to 9.30pm

Lift Pass Rates
1 Day pass $45
3 Day pass $101
Season pass $1000

SLOPE ACTION

Snowboard Hire
Daily rates from $38
Kids from $22

Snowboard Tuition
Lesson, lift & hire
from $45 per day

Night Riding
Over 27 trails

Heli Boarding
Yes

Snowmobiles
Hire & tours

Mountain Cafes
2

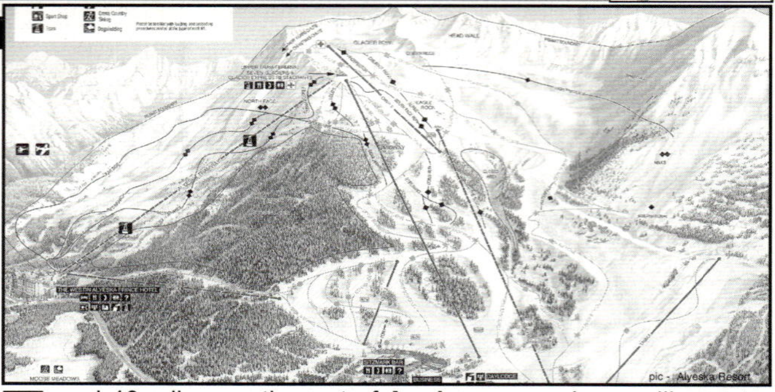

pic - Alyeska Resort

Travel 40 miles south west of **Anchorage** and you will eventually arrive at the somewhat unusual, but interesting resort of **Alyeska.** It happens to be Alaska's only traditional purpose-built resort which, now celebrating its 40th year and has a lot going for it. Forget the impression of severe weather conditions and ice slabs that one normally associates with Alaska. What you find here is a great mountain, with excellent terrain serviced by a modern lift system and is spread out over a series of slopes that begin at almost sea-level. Over the years, places like Alyeska have been largely left alone by the mass holiday crowds. Hardly any ski guides or magazines feature this resort, which is a shame because despite its location in the far northern reaches of the US and Canada, Alyeska has as much to offer, if not more, than many Rocky Mountain-based resorts. A huge plus for this resort is not only its excellent snow record, with average yearly dumps of 600 plus inches, but also the fact that you can ride deep powder in early and late spring. The 790+ acres are excellent and offer something for every style and ability, especially advanced riders. The double black diamond runs on the **North Face** are a match for anything found anywhere else in the US. There's plenty of diverse terrain with a number of damn good bowls and gullies. Across the lower slopes are glades, while higher up you will find nice open slopes and well groomed trails.

Freeriders who know the score, have a damn fine mountain to check out with some very challenging terrain on offer. The double blacks on **North Face** will give you the chance to go wild at speed, as will the double black listed as **Max's**. There is also plenty of intermediate freeride terrain with lots of okay red and blue trails both on and off-piste. If you hike to the summit, you can gain access to the **Glacier Bowl** which has a superb descent down a wide, open expanse of deep snow. For those not content with the easy access slopes there is heli-boarding and snowcats tours in the Chugach mountain range, where you will get to see Alaska as it should be, wild, un-tamed, spectacular, orgasmic.

Freestylers are well catered for here with an abundance of natural hits to get air, such as the nice banks on the **Mambo**. The resort also has a good terrain park which is furnished with a good set of obstacles. Alyeska 300 foot halfpipe is located on the Don's Gully area off lift 4, and is groomed to perfection with Alaskas only pipe grooming machine providing 10 foot high walls.

Carvers would be the ones to feel a little left out here, as this place couldn't really be described as a good carvers resort.

Beginners don't have a vast area of novice slopes but what is on offer is not bad especially on the lower areas off **Lift 3**. Avoid this area at the end of the day as it becomes the busy homebound route for everyone coming down off the mountain. A beginners programme of instruction cost from $45 for lesson lift and hire.

Off the slopes you will find all the creature comforts required to make your stay a pleasant one and although not extensive, local services are very good. There is a good choice of lodging and eating joints conveniently located either at the base of the slopes or in the small town of **Gridwood**, a few minutes away by shuttle bus. The area also boasts an array of local activities ranging from river rafting, to para -gliding on skis or a board. You can even do a cruise around some of the glaciers or try your hand at salmon fishing.

Job Seekers: If you fancy doing a season here and need to work, then call the Jobs Hot Line to find out what employment vacancies exists.
tel 001 (907) 754 2250

Alaska my not be world renowned for its culinary skills, however, the choice and quality of restaurants along with fast-food outlets is particularly good in and around the resort. You can pig out on fine cajun food at *Double Musky's Inn*, or sample some well-prepared sea food at *Simon's Saloon*. *The Bake Shop* is a local's favourite for quick snacks, whilst the *Teppanyaki Katsura* offers traditional Japanese nosh, but at a price.

Night-life around Gridwood is somewhat tame, but nevertheless not bad. There is a decent selection of laid back hangouts. The *Sitzmark* and *Aurora* bars are well visited and lively spots. But if you want some real late night action, check out what's going down 40 miles away in **Anchorage**, where you are able to party hard.

You can lodge at the base of the slopes, most notably in the *Westin Alyeska Prince* Hotel which is located just yards from the cable car's base station. Around *Gridwood* there's a good selection of condos and B&B's, but it's not the cheapest place to stay. The cheaper option is to stay in *Anchorage*, which has a far bigger selection of accommodation, but you will have to commute to the slopes.
For accommodation listings visit -
www.worldsnowboardguide.com

Summary: An excellent resort with great freeriding that will please freeriders of all levels. There is a high level of good local facilities within easy reach of the slopes.
Money wise: A bit on the expensive side, but well worth the money.

Overall rating out of 10 — **8**

Alyeska Resort
P.O Box 249 Gridwood
Alaska 99587
General info **001 (907) 754 1111**
Reservations **001 (907) 754 1111**
Snowphone **001 (907) 754 7669**
www.alyeskaresort.com
www.virgin.com/holidays

pic - Alyeska Resort

pic - Ride Snowboards

Travel Guide

Fly to **Anchorage International**
Transfer time to resort = **50** mins
Local airport = **n/a**

Flight times to **Anchorage** via **Vancouver** and Seattle are approximate:
from: London **18** hours
New York **7** hours (direct)

There is a daily bus service between Alyeska and Anchorage run by Gray Line Buses. A return ticket cost from $12 or $8 single.

Trains go direct to Gridwood

Route Planner
Anchorage *via Highway 1*

Alyeska = 45 miles (72km)
Drive time is about **50** minutes

pic - Diamond Peak Resort

GENERAL INFO AND FACTS

Capital - Sacaamento
Language - English
Currency - US Dollar
Alcohol drinking age - 21
Drugs - Cannabis is illegal
Death Penalty - Exists
Age of consent for Sex - 16
Electricity Supply - 110 Volts AC
Area phone Code - 916
Provincial sales tax - 7% to 8% on all goods and services

CALIFORNIAN DRIVE GUIDE

All vehicles drive on the right side of the road.
Speed Limits -
Motorways 70mph (112kph)
Highways 55mph (90kph)
Towns 30mph (50kph)
Road Info 001 (916) 445 7623
Fuel is sold in Gallons

TRAVEL CONTACTS

Gateway Airports
Los Angeles - Reno - San Francisco

Amtrax Railroad
tel: 001 1-800 872 7245

Western
GMT -8 hours

AREA INFORMATION

California Division of Tourism
800 TO-CALIF
tel: 001 (916) 322 2881

Lee Canyon Nevada

USA Nevada

MOUNTAIN DATA

Top Lift at - 2846m

Ride Area

Bottom Lift at -

Vertical Drop - 304.8m

Number of Runs - 10

Longest - 1500m

TERRAIN LEVELS

Easy	20%
Intermediate	60%
Advanced	20%
Expert =	4 runs

TERRAIN TO SUITE

Freeride	40%
Trees	Yes
Backcountry	Limited
Freestyle	20%
Halfpipe	Yes 1
Terrain Park	Yes 1
Carving	40%

SNOW DATA

Average Snowfall
254 cm a season
Snowmaking
50% cover of the slopes
Winter Periods
Dec to April
Summer Riding
None

SLOPE ACCESS

Total Lifts = 3
Uplift Rate - 3500 people an hour.
3 Chair lifts

**Leashes Required*

Lift Times
Call the resort

Lift Pass Rates
1 Day pass $28
1 Day kit hire $27
1 Day package $55

Travel Guide

Fly to **Reno or Las Vegas** International airport.

Bus services from Las Vegas take around 1 hour.

Route Planner: Route **95** out of **Las Vegas** towards **Reno.** After 30 miles turn left onto Route 156, then15 miles or so to **Lee Canyon.**

Not many people will know this or indeed will believe it, but yes it's true, it's a fact, it exists: a snow-capped mountain to ski and ride on just outside the world's gambling heaven **Las Vegas. Lee Canyon** is a small resort only 45 miles from the Las Vegas Strip. It is weird to drive up from the heat of the desert to arrive in just 20 minutes at altitude with snowdrifts all around. The mountains get regular snow throughout the winter with an average of 254 centimetres a yearl. The resort can also cover 50% of the slopes with artificial snow should the real stuff be lacking.
Set at 8500ft in the **Spring Mountains** to the north west of Las Vegas, what you actually get is a slope area offering a respectable 1000ft of vertical drop. There are three slow chairlifts, one on the nursery slopes accessing a total of 11 trails, one of them dotted with ramps and kickers (plus a sign that says "No aerial flips allowed" (most people seemed to ignore it!). All standards from beginner to snowgod would find something here to keep them amused for a while - if only an afternoon or two. What's more, this place never gets too crowded. The car park often seems full yet the slopes never seem to number more than 50 people at a time. At the slopes you can get full snowboard hire but like most hire kit the quality varies - getting there early gets you better equipment. There is also a shop, bar and cafe for your standard burger hit.

Freeriders should find the 4 black runs, which are not groomed and are basically mogul fields, a cool place to ride offering a fun challenge. Two of the blacks descend through some trees which only adds to the fun. There are a few bits where you can get off piste but the powder soon gets shredded out so don't expect any hardcore backcountry terrain.

Freestylers are best looking out for natural hits as the man made offerings are a bit lame. The snowboard park, which is designed as a long trail, has a pretty mundane halfpipe which looked more like a long depression in the snow (March 2001).

Carvers may find that this is not a place for them due to the lack of pisted trails. The terrain is often to bumpy to hold a good edge.

Beginners only have a few rather dull areas to slide around on.

To find out what's going on off the slopes, get your self a guide book on **Las Vegas** as there is no way that we can even begin to tell you all that is on offer in this massive gambling city.

Lee Canyon
State Route 156. Nevada
001 (702) 593 9500

www.skilasvegas.com
www.virgin.com/holidays

Overall rating out of 10 — **3** — **Very very basic indeed**

Alpine Meadows California

MOUNTAIN DATA

Top Lift at - 2632m

Ride Area 2100 acres

Bottom Lift at - 2083m

Vertical Drop - 549m

Number of Runs - 100

Longest -2.5 miles (4km)

TERRAIN LEVELS

Easy	**25%**
Intermediate	**40%**
Advanced	**35%**
Expert =	**9 runs**

TERRAIN TO SUITE

Freeride	**60%**
Trees	Yes
Backcountry	Yes
Freestyle	**20%**
Halfpipe	Yes 1
Terrain Park	Yes 1
Carving	**20%**

SNOW DATA

Average Snowfall
1800 cm a season

Snowmaking
20% cover of the slopes

Winter Periods
Nov to April

Summer Riding
None

SLOPE ACCESS

Total Lifts = **12**

Uplift Rate - 16,000 people an hour.

10 Chair lifts

2 Drag lifts

**Leashes Required*

Lift Times
9.30am to 4.00pm

Lift Pass Rates

1 Day pass	$50
3 Day pass	$141
5 Day pass	$233

SLOPE ACTION

Snowboard Hire
Daily rates from $25
Kids from $20

Snowboard Tuition
Lesson, lift & hire from $56 per day

Night Riding
None

Heli Boarding
None

Snowmobiles
Hire & tours

Mountain Cafes
3

pic - Alpine Meadows

Trrgasmic.**Alpine Meadows** only opened its doors to snowboarders in 1996, but within that short space of time, Alpine has now become one of the most popular boarding mountains in the Tahoe region. For years, Alpine was the number one ski resort in the US for skiers - and now we know why they kept it to themselves for so long! Alpine Meadows has all sorts of natural terrain that lends itself to the specific needs of snowboarders. There is a wide variety of trails from beginner to expert, lots of tree runs, great off-piste with amazing views of Lake Tahoe, if you care to stand and stare. On a week-day, you will hardly ever stand in line for the lifts, giving maximum riding time and ample reason to rest and chill at one of the mountain restaurants. Combine all this with a very snowboard-friendly and generally mellow attitude, Alpine Meadows is simply magic place for all snowboarders.

Freeriders of an advanced level should take the high speed, 6-person **Summit Six** chair for access to endless off-piste, via short traverses and hikes. On powder days check out some awesome off-piste available from **Scott** chair and **Lake View**. Unlike other nearby resorts, Alpine has an 'open boundary' policy, meaning that providing the area boundary is marked 'OPEN', you can ride wherever you desire. However, you must observe all 'CLOSED' signs, or risk riding in dangerous areas and losing both your lift pass and your life. If you are prepared to explore at Alpine you will find some excellent powder, long after a storm - it's worth hiring a guide for the day. Intermediates can enjoy long cruises from the **Roundhouse** detachable quad, and also over the back of **Alpine** on **Sherwood**, where the best early sun can be found.

Freestylers have a great halfpipe known as the **'Gravity Cavity'** which is now shaped by a new device called the 'Scorpion'. The pipe is located on **Sympathy Face** off the Roundhouse chair, while the 'Roos Ride' terrain park, which is open to skiers and snowboarders, can be found off the **Kangaroo** chair. For those who like their hits spread naturally across the mountain, you may need to ask a local where the best ones are located as they are not always obvious but are in abundance. Be sure to use a spotter for reasons of safety.

Carvers are presented with great corduroy slopes, with the best advanced and intermediate stuff off the **Summit** chair lift, where you will find some nice blacks that mellow out into blue trails.

Beginners may only have a few marked green runs, but they are more than adequate. First timers should ride the chair lifts at the bunny slopes on the base of the mountain, before graduating to the **Weasel** chair for smooth, wide, open runs. The local ski-school offers a high level of tuition, with a full day's package costing from $56 which includes, lesson, lift and snowboard hire for the day. Budding freestylers can also sign up for halfpipe and basic freestyle lessons.

Alpine Meadows, doesn't have any real slope side services. However, just about anything you need can be found in nearby **Tahoe City.** Tahoe City has a surplus of accommodation, eating out and sporting facilities. There are loads of shops, including loads of souvenir outlets so beloved by tourists and skiers. With the **Tahoe** area being so popular, it is quite possible that you could be hanging out here with some of the biggest names in snowboarding as a number of pros live in the area.

For **Job Seekers,** the whole area offers dozens of job opportunities ranging from work in the catering trade to lift operators. To find out more and see what jobs exist, call 001(530) 581 8212

If you can't find anywhere in this area to suit your taste buds, then you have a serious medical problem. There are loads of eating outlets in every price range - the choice and range are excellent. For a decent breakfast before hitting the slopes, check out *The Alpine Riverside Cafe*. For good food at reasonable prices, check out *Bridgetender* or the *Mandrian Villa* in **Tahoe City**. *Jasons Saloon* also serves up some decent nosh.

Night-life here is pretty cool with lots of night spots in the area. Partying options are great, with excessive drinking and chatting up of local birds made easy. Some of the best talent can be found in places such as *Naughty Dog, Pierce St Annex, or Humpty's*. The *River Ranch,* which is en-route to Alpine, is also noted for being a lively place.

Alpine dosen't offer any convenient slopeside lodgings, but with over 10,000 visitor beds spread throughout the Tahoe area, you can't fail to find suitable and affordable accommodation. The nearest lodging for Alpine is at **Tahoe City** which is 6 miles away. Here you can find a good selection of hotels, condos, apartments or cabins.

For accommodation listings visit - www.worldsnowboardguide.com

Summary: Great freeriding and natural freestyle resort with a good annual snow record. No slopeside facilities, but excellent services within easy reach.
Money wise: Very expensive resort for just about everything.

Overall rating out of 10 — 9

Alpine Meadows Resort
P.O Box 5279, Tahoe City
CA 96145

General info	***001*** **(530) 583 4232**
Reservations	***001*** **(800) 949 3296**
Snowphone	***001*** **(530) 581 8374**

www.skialpine.com
www.virgin.com/holidays

pic - Martin Robinson

pic - Alpine Meadows

Travel Guide

Fly to **Reno** International
Transfer time to resort = **1** hour
Local airport = .

Approximate global air travel times to **Reno**:

from:		
	London	**9** hours
	New York	**4** hours
	Frankfurt	**10** hours

A bus from Reno takes around 1 hour. A Grey Hound bus from San Francisco takes 5 hours via Tahoe City, 6 miles away.

Trains to Truckee, 6 miles away

Route Planner
Reno *via Truckee*

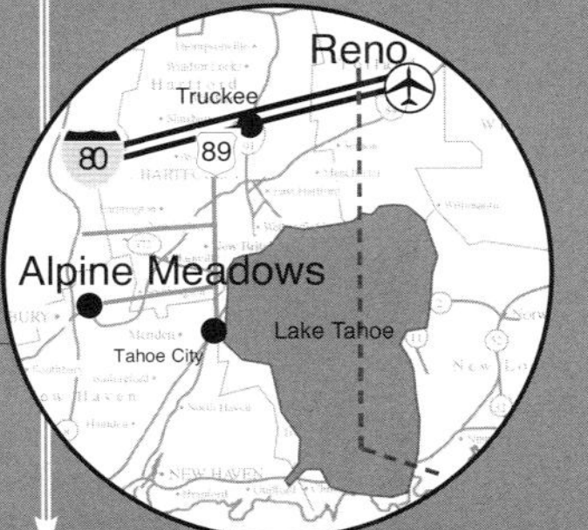

Alpine Meadows = **45** miles
Drive time is about **1** hour

Bear Mountain

California & Nevada

MOUNTAIN DATA

Top Lift at - 2685m

Ride Area 195 acres

Bottom Lift at - 2177m

Vertical Drop - 507m

Number of Runs - 22

Longest - 3.5 miles (5km)

TERRAIN LEVELS

Easy	**25%**
Intermediate	**50%**
Advanced	**25%**
Expert =	

TERRAIN TO SUITE

Freeride	**40%**
Trees	Yes
Backcountry	Yes
Freestyle	**40%**
Halfpipe	Yes 2
Terrain Park	Yes 4
Carving	**20%**

SNOW DATA

Average Snowfall
254cm a season

Snowmaking
100% cover of the slopes

Winter Periods
Dec to April

Summer Riding
None

SLOPE ACCESS

Total Lifts = **12**

Uplift Rate not available an hour.

9 Chair lift

3 Drag liff

**Leashes Required*

Lift Times
8.30am to 4.00pm

Lift Pass Rates
1/2 Day pass $29
1 Day pass $35
2 Day pass $65

Travel Guide

Fly to **Los Angeles**, transfer time is 2 hours.

Bus services from Los Angeles are available.

Route Planner:
From Los Angeles use Interstates 10 & 215 east to Hwy's 30, 330 & Hwy travelling via Redlands. **Los Angeles** to resort = **100** miles. **2** hour drive time.

pic - Hank deVr / Palmer Board X Team @ Bear Mountain

Bear Mountain Valley is home to two mountain resorts, **Big Bear** and **Snow Summit**. Both play host to numerous top snowboarding events including the *Annual Board Aid Festival* at Snow Summit. As a rule, resorts' marketing slogans are trite and meaningless, but Bear Mountain's billing as a 'Good Time' place is quite accurate. Anyone who has ridden the parks or pipes, and afterwards sat in the sun on the outdoor *deck* for lunch, would be hard-pressed to dispute this claim. Part of the *deck's* inherent allure is the fact that riders need a place to kick back after spending time on Bear's slopes, where vertical is the name of the game. The high speed quad, **Big Bear Express**, reaches the top of **Goldmine Mountain** in about seven minutes, where you can ride the **Claim Jumper** trail to notch up over 500 vertical metres. Bear Mountain offers riding for all abilities, from carving to freestyle and all species in-between. Big Bear is also a black diamond bliss.

Freeriders have a good choice of areas to ride.The double black diamond **Geronimo** run is a real tester, however the **Gambler**, off the top of **Showdown Mountain**, is also super cool ride area.

Freestylers now have four big terrain parks and halfpipes. **The Zone** is located immediately above the deck. There is a snack shack at the top of the pipes called **The Yurt** with a judging stand and a DJ station. The **Outlaw Snowboard Park** features enormous table tops, and the famous **Serpentine.**

Carvers have a number of good trails to cruise, although in fairness this is not a Euro-carver's place. For a quick burst plus a show-off, check out **Grizzly**, a short but steep trail.

Beginners, Bear is an excellent place to learn. The local snowboard school offers an introduction to Snowboarding scheme, and a *Vertical Improvement Program* for riders who want to enhance their carving and jumping skills. Kids under 9 can also sign up for the magic Minors Snowboard Camp.

There is a huge range of accommodation available at **Big Bear Lake** with apartments to rent at the base of the slopes. Local services are varied, with hundreds of places to eat and drink. The *Grizzly Manor Cafe* is the place for breakfast or lunch, whilst *Village Pizza* is the place for a take-away. *Pine Knot* is a wicked bakery where you can get a good cup of coffee. As for night-life, with a choice of over 50 bars, no-one should miss out.

For accommodation listings visit - www.worldsnowboardguide.com

Bear Mountain Resort
P.o Box 6812, 43101 Goldmine Drv, Big Bear Lake, CA
***001* (909) 585 2519**
www.bearmtn.com
www.virgin.com/holidays

Overall rating out of 10 **7** **Excellent snowboarders resort**

Diamond Peak Nevada

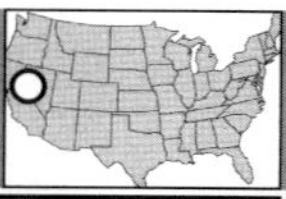

MOUNTAIN DATA

Top Lift at - 2602m
Ride Area 655 acres
Bottom Lift at - 2042m
Vertical Drop - 561m
Number of Runs - 30
Longest - 2.5 miles (3km)

TERRAIN LEVELS

Easy	18%
Intermediate	46%
Advanced	36%
Expert =	0

TERRAIN TO SUITE

Freeride	45%
Trees	Yes
Backcountry	Yes
Freestyle	30%
Halfpipe	Yes 1
Terrain Park	Yes 1
Carving	25%

SNOW DATA

Average Snowfall
762cm a season
Snowmaking
75% cover of the slopes
Winter Periods
Dec to April
Summer Riding
None

SLOPE ACCESS

Total Lifts = 6
Uplift Rate - not available an hour.
6 Chair lifts

**Leashes Required*

Lift Times
8.30am to 4.00pm

Lift Pass Rates

1 Day pass	$41
2 Day pass	$73
3 Day pass	$105

Travel Guide

Fly to **Reno,** transfer time to the resort is 30 minutes.

Bus services from Reno are available to the resort.

Route Planner:
From Reno take either the route 28 or 431 south to the Country Club Drive and then Ski Way.
Reno to resort = **35** miles.
30 minutes drive time.

pic - Diamond Peak

Diamond Peak is one of **Lake Tahoe's** lesser talked of resorts, yet it's one of the most enjoyable for a number of reasons. The main reason being that it is less stuck up and far more friendly than some of its neighbours. There's no fancy pretence here just a simple mountain that despite being fairly small can offer everybody a cool time. Diamond Peak is a resort that places a strong emphasis on fun, families and snow, and they succeed in many ways as this is a cool hang-out that attracts all ages with the slopes getting a good annual snow covering. Located on the shores of **Lake Tahoe** in **Nevada**, Diamond Peak is only 30 minutes south of **Reno** making this an easy place to get to. The slopes are set out in a simple manner with a good mixture of runs spread out over the whole mountain. Being a quiet resort, the trails don't get busy and there aren't long lift lines.

Freeriders who can cut the mustard, will find the longest and most challenging terrain up in the area known as the **Solitude Canyon**, which is reached off the **Crystal Quad** chair. But note you are not allowed to go past the marked boundary and if you do you will be prosecuted, so study your lift map. Solituide offers some fast uneven terrain with some trees to weave in and out of. For those who like to take it a bit easier then the **Crystal Ridge** is a long intermediate trail with a number of black trails that drop off to one side, should you feel up to it.

Freestylers should find **Diamond Peak** ideal for getting high in more ways than one. The cool terrain park is located off the **Ridge** chair with the back drop of **Lake Tahoe** to take in as you catch some big air, while around the slopes hits are always being built.

Carvers should give the **Crystal Ridge** a go first, and then the **Great Flume**, both of which are nice intermediate trails. However, for a faster blast then check out the series of blacks off the **Lakeview** chair, where you will find a number of slalom runs.

Beginners have only a few green trails at the base area but don't fret, some of the blue intermediate trails are a bit overrated.

Base facilities are provided in **Incline Village** and at **Crystal Bay**. Both have a good selection of condo's, hotels and lodges. The *Crystal Bay Motel* is a good budget option with nightly rates from around $35. Nightlife is basically non-existence, but so what.
For accommodation listings visit - www.worldsnowboardguide.com

Diamond Peak
1210 Ski Way, Incline Village, NV 89451
***001* (775) 832 1177**
www.diamondpeak.com
www.virgin.com/holidays

Overall rating out of 10 **7** **Good all round fun resort**

Heavenly California/Nevada

MOUNTAIN DATA

Top Lift at - 3060m

Ride Area 1994 acres

Bottom Lift at - 1994m

Vertical Drop - 1607m

Number of Runs - 84

Longest - 5.5 miles (9km)

TERRAIN LEVELS

Easy	**20%**
Intermediate	**45%**
Advanced	**35%**
Expert =	**8 runs**

TERRAIN TO SUITE

Freeride	**45%**
Trees	Yes
Backcountry	Yes
Freestyle	**25%**
Halfpipe	Yes 4
Terrain Park	Yes 4
Carving	**30%**

SNOW DATA

Average Snowfall
864 cm a season

Snowmaking
69% cover of the slopes

Winter Periods
Nov to May

Summer Riding
None

SLOPE ACCESS

Total Lifts = **29**

Uplift Rate - 30,000 people an hour.

1 Tram, **1** Gondola,
19 Chair lifts, **7** Drag lifts

**Leashes Required*

Lift Times
8.30am to 4.00pm

Lift Pass Rates

1 Day pass	$57
3 Day pass	$162
5 Day pass	$260

SLOPE ACTION

Snowboard Hire
Daily rates from $28
Kids from $25

Snowboard Tuition
Lesson, lift & hire
from $80 per day

Night Riding
None

Heli Boarding
None

Snowmobiles
Hire & tours

Mountain Cafes
7

pic - Heavenly Ski Resort

This is an over hyped resort. The new gondola that runs from downtown **South Lake Tahoe** makes access to the mountain easier but you can't make use of this facility if you are still a beginner as it does not access any beginner slopes. This is something that the resort are looking into.You can, however, ride up to look at the beautiful views of the Lake for a steep price**. Heavenly** is a large resort that stretches across the two states of **California** and **Nevada**. Heavenly has over 40 years of operation under its belt, as well as some of the largest snowboard/ski acreage in the US, and by far the biggest vertical out of the Lake Tahoe resorts. Snowboarders are drawn from afar, especially at weekends and during holidays. In the past, the International Snowboard Federation has held world cup events that have attracted riders from around the world, who came for the challenge of a big mountain with hardcore terrain. However, Heavenly is not just for the pro's - there is something here for everyone - but the slopes do favour riders of intermediate and advanced levels, with steeps and big air possibilities on double black diamond runs, like those of **Mott** & **Killebrew Canyons** and the **Gunbarrel**.

Freeriders will find the most challenging terrain is located on the Nevada side of the resort in the **Milky Way bowl**. However, it does become tracked out very quickly and would be best left until just after a fresh dump. Still, the **Milky Way Bowl** is major and offers some great powder. Advanced riders who like their slopes steep and covered with trees should check out the **North Bowl**. But for those who really want to fill their pants should make for the white-knuckle rides on the **Mott & Killebrew Canyon** area. Here you will find a series of expert double black diamond runs through a series of chutes. For something a little less intimidating try the blues off **Tamarack** and **Sky** chairs on the **California** side.

Freestylers are provided with four terrain parks and a boarder cross trail that may alter depending on the snow depths. They are spread out across both sides of the mountain. One of the terrain parks, which is designed by top riders, is built to accommodate all riders whatever your ability. However, for those who prefer natural hits, Heavenly has an abundance of them all over the place.

Carvers are not to be outdone since Heavenly is a highly rated carvers' resort. There are plenty of well prepared pistes for laying out big tracks on, such as **Liz's** and **Big Dipper**. The **Olympic** on **Milky Way** entails a bit of skating on a flat section but is worth it.

Beginners may at first feel a little left out with the lack of green runs. However, there are plenty of excellent blue trails to check out. Be aware that in various areas there are a number of blacks that turn off and drop away from some of the easier trails, so check your piste map. The cluster of greens off the **Waterfall** lift, on runs like **Mombo Meadows,** are good for whetting the appetite before trying out the blues off **Ridge** and **Canyon lifts**.

Off the mountain, local action is lively and plentiful. The choice of accommodation, eating and booze joints is massive and many within easy reach of the slopes. However, local services are a bit spread out and having a car here is a must. Locals make you feel at home and services are of a very high standard. However, the popularity of the area does mean that the place can be excessively busy, especially at weekends. **South Lake Tahoe** has heaps of shops, loads of sporting facilities as well as a number of casinos.
Jobseekers: For those wanting to work, this is an area that employs thousands of seasonal staff to work in hotels, shops or as lifties.
Call Human Resources 001 702 586 7000

Eating options are good, plentiful and at prices to please everyone. There is also the chance to pig out in various fast-food joints. Every type of food is available here from Chinese, Italian, Mexican to standard American fair. It's all on offer. The list of good eating places is too long to mention in this short journal, but loacls will point you in the right direction if you ask for some recommendations. In the meantime *Red Hutt* or *Chris's* are both good.

Nightlife in Heavenly is dull. However in **South Lake Tahoe** there is plenty of gambling if that is your thing and many of the casinos have nightclubs. Some of the better ones are *Club Z* and *Nero's. Hoss Hogs* host some great band nights and *Mulligans* Irish bar is always a favourite for late night drinking.

Accommodation: Although there is lodging within walking distance of the slopes, it is very expensive. **South Lake Tahoe** is heaving with hotels and motels from very cheap to very expensive. If you are on a budget try '*Doug's Mellow Mountain Retreat*' (916) 544 8065 at $13-$15 per night for a small dormitory. *The Blu Zu Hostel* 4140 Pine Park (916) 541 9502 $15 per night for a bed in the dormitory. It's a bit hippyish but okay.

For accommodation listings visit - www.worldsnowboardguide.com

Summary: Great all-round freeriding and carving with some excellent steeps. Very busy most of the time especially holidays. Good local services.
Money wise: Overall this is a very expensive resort, but good value.

Overall rating out of 10 **8**

Heavenly Resort
295 Highway 50, Suite 8.
State Line Nevada 89449
General info **001 (775) 586 7000**
Reservations **001 (800) 243 2836**
Snowphone **001 (775) 586 7000**
www.skiheavenly.com
www.virgin.com/holidays

pic - Steve Barker

pic - Scott Markewitz

Travel Guide

Fly to **Reno** International
Transfer time to resort = **1** hour
Local airport = **South Lake Tahoe** 6 miles away.
Approximate global air travel times to **Reno**

from:	London	**9** hours
	New York	**4** hours
	Frankfurt	**10** hours

A bus from Reno takes 1½ hours. A Grey Hound bus from San Francisco takes 6 hours via South Lake Tahoe, 6 miles away.

Trains: Nearest station at Reno.

Route Planner
Reno *via Carson City*

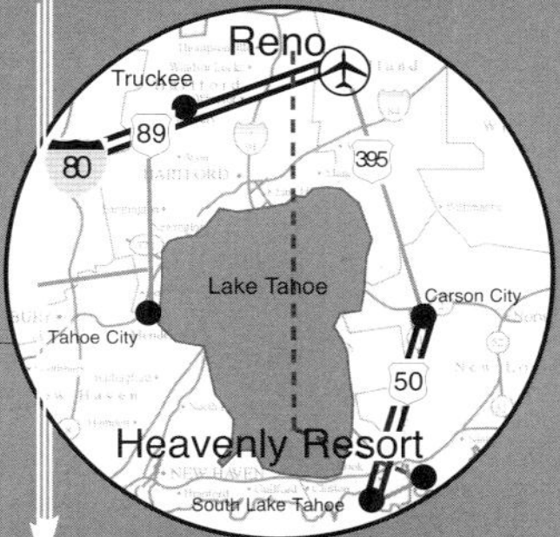

Heavenly = **58** miles (93)
Drive time is about **1** hour

Dodge Ridge California

MOUNTAIN DATA

Top Lift at - 2499m

Ride Area 815 acres

Bottom Lift at - 2011

Vertical Drop - 488m

Number of Runs - 60

Longest - 2.5 miles (4km)

TERRAIN LEVELS

Easy	20%
Intermediate	50%
Advanced	30%
Expert =	7 runs

TERRAIN TO SUITE

Freeride	40%
Trees	Yes
Backcountry	Yes
Freestyle	30%
Halfpipe	Yes 2
Terrain Park	Yes 1
Carving	30%

SNOW DATA

Average Snowfall
1016cm a season

Snowmaking
10% cover of the slopes

Winter Periods
Nov to April

Summer Riding
None

SLOPE ACCESS

Total Lifts = **12**

Uplift Rate not available an hour.

8 Chair lift

4 Drag liff

**Leashes Required*

Lift Times
9.00am to 4.00pm

Lift Pass Rates

1 Day pass	$30
1 Day pass	$39 weekends
Child pass	Free

Travel Guide

Fly to **San Francisco**, transfer time is $2^{1/2}$hours.

Bus services from **San Francisco** are available.

Route Planner:
From **San Francisco**, take the 580 & 205 east to Manteca and then the 120 and 108 via Oakdale and Sonora, turning of first at signs for Pinecrest and then left to Dodge Ridge.

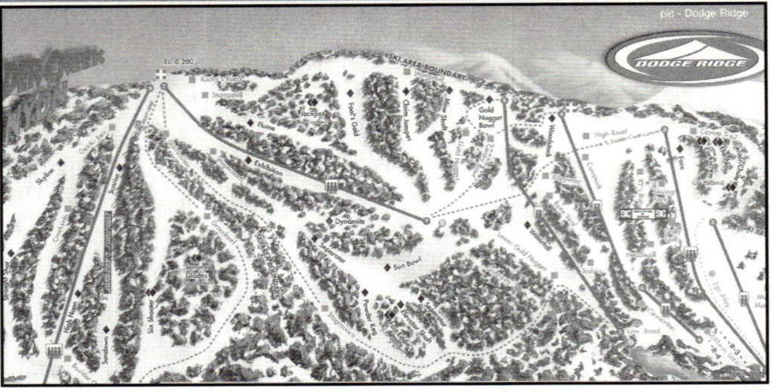

Dodge Ridge is not one of those resorts that springs to mind when one is thinking about where to go for a few days riding. Come to think about it, Dodge Ridge is almost unknown outside of those who live in the area or by a few hardcore riders who travel around in a van searching out the small haunts. Anyway, why would this relatively new resort be of much interest? After all, it's only been going for 15 years. Well Dodge Ridge has some 60 trails with 12 lifts which take you over a mountain that has a lot to offer, especially advanced riders, with a good series of double black diamond runs such as the trails that can be found off of lift **3**. The slopes are well maintained and well set out offering something for all levels with a good mixture of trails.

Freeriders who like to experience rough, hard core and fast terrain will like what they find here. There is a good selection of expert runs to take on with the most interesting being the **Six Shooter** and the **Sonora Glades**, which is a tricky steep section with heaps of trees. A little more sedate trails to try out are the **Sunrise** or the **Exhibition** while the **Gentle Ben** is even easier.

Freestylers have had a halfpipe and terrain park here for years. The **Santa Cruz Snowpark** and **DC Rythm Zone** are loaded with hits and are located off the number **8** down the Sunrise trail, but note, this is a steep trail and not for **novices**. A new **Santa Cruz** sponsored pipe is located on a more gentle area at the top of lift **8** while lower down there is an area called the **Mountain Dew Fun Zone** designed for younger riders just learning to get air.

Carvers have a couple of cracking trails to let loose on, namely the **Sunrise** if you have the balls or the **Quicksilver** which is a nice long blue trail off lift **8. Fools Gold** is another cool fast trail.

Beginners will find the best areas to take on are located at the lower sections of lifts 2 and 1. Please note that these are novice areas and although tame, should not be ridden over at speed.

Off the slopes things suddenly change and become a little different as well as very basic indeed. Local services, provided in nearby town of **Pinecrest** are very good with good rates for accommodation and other services. There are a number of good eating joints but don't expect a lot of night life. There is none of note really, which is not to say that you can't have a good time out.

For accommodation listings visit - www.worldsnowboardguide.com

Dodge Ridge
P.o Box 1188 Pinecrest, CA 95364
***001* (209) 965 3474**
www.dodgeridge.com
www.virgin.com/holidays

Overall rating out of 10 **6** **Some excellent fast riding**

Kirkwood California

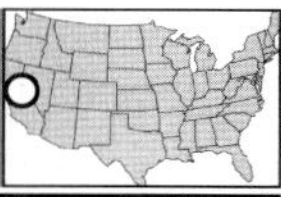

MOUNTAIN DATA

Top Lift at - 2987m
Ride Area 2300 acres
Bottom Lift at - 2377m
Vertical Drop - 609m
Number of Runs - 30
Longest - 2.5 miles (3km)

TERRAIN LEVELS

Easy	15%
Intermediate	50%
Advanced	20%
Expert =	15%

TERRAIN TO SUITE

Freeride	50%
Trees	Yes
Backcountry	Yes
Freestyle	25%
Halfpipe	Yes 1
Terrain Park	Yes 1
Carving	25%

SNOW DATA

Average Snowfall
1270cm a season
Snowmaking
10% cover of the slopes
Winter Periods
Nov to May
Summer Riding
None

SLOPE ACCESS

Total Lifts = **12**
Uplift Rate - 15,300 people an hour.
10 Chair lifts
2 Drag lifts
**Leashes Required*

Lift Times
9.00am to 3.30pm

Lift Pass Rates

1 Day pass	$49
3 Day pass	$147
5 Day pass	$245

Travel Guide

Fly to **Reno,** transfer time to is 90 minutes.

Bus services from Reno are available to the resort.

Route Planner:
From Reno take US route 395 south and then take the state route 88 west to Kirkwood.
Reno to resort = **70** miles.
90 minutes drive time.

pic - Kirkwood Ski Resort

Kirkwood has the reputation of being an advanced rider's mountain, and in many ways it is, as proved by their hosting of a leg of the US Extremes Pro-snowboard Tour. With a number of steep, double black diamond trails and the highest base elevation in the area, Kirkwood has great freeriding, on and off-piste, excellent carving and full-on freestyle terrain. The resort is located south of **South Lake Tahoe**, along Highways 88 and 89. Although it's not far from the resort of **Heavenly**, it is far less crowded, leaving the slopes free for riders who know what they are doing.

Freeriders in particular will like the natural terrain here, like open tree-riding in areas like **Larry's Lip**, and fast steeps on the double black diamond trails below an area known as **The Sisters**, which is reachable off **Wagon Wheel** chair lift. Don't venture into these trails if you're not up to the mark as they are steep runs which mellow out only at the lower sections. If it's powder you're after, look no further as Kirkwood receives lots of it annually.

Freestylers get an excellent mountain to discover lots of natural hits. **Snowsnake Gully** offers all sorts of excitement, but the fun-park, located off **Caple's Crest** chair lift, is loaded with so many toys that freestylers hardly need go in search of anything else.

Carvers are presented with some first class carving terrain that is a match for anywhere else in the Tahoe region. For a long, fast descent, you should give **Thunder Saddle** or **Larry's Lip** a try, but be warned - this is not for knuckle heads. For something a little less daunting, **Buckboard** is fun.

Beginners need to get their act together fast if they want to appreciate Kirkwood's offerings to the full, and with the fact that this resort has some great novice trails, it shouldn't be too long. Although the piste map shows a low percentage of easy trails, there are plenty of rideable areas to be found at the lower section, like **Graduation**, which has its own easy-to-use lift. Make it to **Timber Creek** and you can practice with ease, before having a killer hot-dog at the cafe.

If your name is Mr Dull then you will love what is on offer at the base of Kirkwood. What you get is not up to much with expensive accommodation, dull eateries and dull night-life. For the best local happenings and night-action, head to **South Lake Tahoe**, which is only 15 miles away.

Kirkwood Mountain Resort
P.O Box 1, Kirkwood, CA 95646
***001* (209) 258 6000**
www.skikirkwood.com
www.virgin.com/holidays

Overall rating out of 10 — **5** — **Okay on the slopes but dull off.**

Mammoth Mountain California

pic - Mammoth Mountain

MOUNTAIN DATA

Top Lift at - 3369m

Ride Area 3500 acres

Bottom Lift at - 2424m
Vertical Drop - 944m
Number of Runs - 150
Longest -3 miles (5km)

TERRAIN LEVELS

Easy	**30%**
Intermediate	**40%**
Advanced	**40%**
Expert =	**20 runs**

TERRAIN TO SUITE

Freeride	**55%**
Trees	Yes
Backcountry	Yes
Freestyle	**25%**
Halfpipe	Yes 2
Terrain Park	Yes 3
Carving	**20%**

SNOW DATA

Average Snowfall
945 cm a season
Snowmaking
25% cover of the slopes
Winter Periods
Nov to May
Summer Riding
Early June

SLOPE ACCESS

Total Lifts = **28**
Uplift Rate - 56,000 people an hour.
2 Gondolas,
25 Chair lifts, **1** Drag lift
**Leashes Required*

Lift Times
8.30am to 4.00pm

Lift Pass Rates

1 Day pass	$54
3 Day pass	$146
5 Day pass	$235

SLOPE ACTION

Snowboard Hire
Daily rates from $28
Kids from $25

Snowboard Tuition
Lesson, lift & hire from $79 per day

Night Riding
From 4pm to 9pm

Heli Boarding
None

Snowmobiles
Hire & tours

Mountain Cafes
6

California has given us Hollywood, *Daffy Duck* and thankfully, **Mammoth Mountain.** Located in the Eastern Sierra region, Mammoth has welcomed snowboarders onto its slopes for many years, and with a good snow record, riding is often possible into June. A point to note is that Mammoth's slopes can often get busy at weekends when the place fills up with California's city dwellers. Don't let that put you off though as by normal American standards, Mammoth is a pretty big place. In fact, it's one of the biggest resorts in America, with over 150 trails set out on a long-since dead volcano. The well planned runs and connecting lifts are backed up by an excellent piste map that will give every rider, no matter what their style or ability, plenty to do.

Freeriders have a great mountain to ride with trees, big bowls and loads of natural hits to catch air, especially in areas such as **Huevos Grande** and **Hangman's Hollow**. Experienced riders normally head up to the ridge reached by **Gondola 2** Here there is a host of chutes that lead into a wide bowl, perfect for freeriders to show what they're made of. The **Cornice** run is the one to go for - it's awesome and will give you a major buzz. If you really have the balls, check out **Wipe Out**, a double black run off **Chair 23**. If you emulate the name of this run, not only will it make your eyes water, but everyone on the chair lift above will be able to watch and laugh as you wipe out in style (give them two fingers and then get on your way).

Freestylers have a resort that is well in tune with their needs, whether you're after natural hits or purpose built jumps. A good spot to check out is the area known as **Lower Dry Creek** which is a natural halfpipe. Alternatively, the **Dragon's Back** gives the advanced freestyler plenty of air time. If you aren't content with either of these runs, check out the **Unbound Snowboard Arena**, off **Chair 6** on the **Bowling Alley** trail, which has a very good half-pipe and a terrain park that is loaded with a series of hits both big and small. There is a second pipe on the area marked as Roller Coaster. Alternatively **June Mountain** is only 20 minutes away where you can try out its well established park and pipe.

Carvers who like to sign the snow with their tracks will love Mammoth. The runs are super-well pisted and make for good carving terrain, both for those wanting to go at speed or for the more sedate carver. Check out the trail off **Chair 3** known as the **Saddle Bowl**, where you will find a nice, tame, long blue run.

Beginners, if you can't learn or improve at Mammoth, then you're into the wrong sport. The area is perfect for novices, with plenty of green and easy progression blue runs at the lower sections and excellent snowboard tuition available. Lesson, lift and rental packages start from $59 and are well worth the money. The local snowboard school has a good reputation and caters for all levels with a number of teaching programmes available.

At the base area you will find some accommodation and basic facilities. However, it's best to stay down in the town of **Mammoth Lakes** which is 4 miles from the mountain. Mammoth Lakes has a huge selection of good local services and although the area is not noted for being affordable, riders on a budget will still be able to swing it with a number of cheap supermarkets and low priced dorms to lodge at. For all your snowboard needs, Mammoth has a number of snowboard shops, such as *Stormriders* tel (760) 934 2471 and *Mountain Riders,* tel (760) 934 0679.
For **Jobseekers,** there are dozens of positions available in catering and on the slopes.
Call the Job Line, (800) 472 3168

You can get almost any type of food here, ranging from expensive to mega bucks. There are a number of cheaper food-stops such as *Berger's*, where you can dine on chicken or burgers. *The Breakfast Club* is the place for early starters, while *Roberto's* serves hot Mexican nosh. If pizzas is your thing, then try a slice at *Nik-N-Willie's* which is noted for its food. *Grumpy's* is noted for chicken served up in a sporting setting.

Night-life hits off in Mammoth Lakes and while not fantastic, it is still pretty good with bars playing up-to-date sounds. Amongst the more popular hangouts are *Whiskey Creek* and the *Stonehouse Brewery. Grumpy's* is a cool place that serves booze and burgers, set to a back drop of TV screens showing the latest slope action.

Mammoth Lakes has over 3,000 visitor bed spaces, but note, on the whole, most are very expensive. You will find condo-overload plus a few B&B joints and a bunk house. Good packages can be had at Mammoth Mountain Inn or the Alpine Lodge. The *Ullr Lodge* is a reasonable priced bunk house with beds from $18 a night.

For accommodation listings visit -
www.worldsnowboardguide.com

Summary: Great freeriding on open slopes, but very busy at weekends and over holiday periods. Good local facilities but limited, affordable slopeside beds
Money wise; Very expensive overall resort, but very good value for money

Overall rating out of 10 **9**

Mammoth Mountain
P.o Box 24. 1 Minaret Road.
Mammoth Mountain Lakes CA 93546
General info **001 (760) 934 2571**
Reservations **001 (800) Mammoth**
Snowphone **001 (760) 934 2571**
www.mammoth-mtn.com
www.virgin.com/holidays

pic - Roger Witney   pic - Mammoth Mountain Resort

Travel Guide

Fly to Reno International
Transfer time to resort = **4** hours
Local airport= **Mammoth Lakes**, 20 away
Approximate global air travel times to **Reno**

from:		
	London	9 hours
	New York	4 hours
	Frankfurt	10 hours

A bus from Reno takes $3^{1/2}$ hours. **Grey Hound** buses operate daily services from Reno and Los Angeles, which is a 6 hours away.

Trains: None

Route Planner
Reno *via Mammoth Lakes*

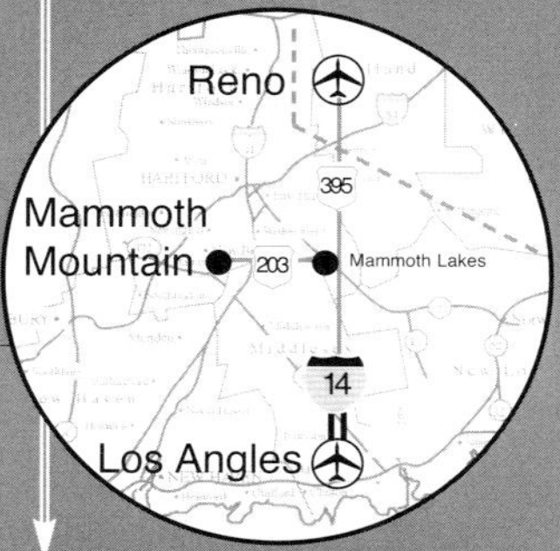

Mammoth Mtn = 163 miles
Drive time approx **4** hours

Mountain High California

MOUNTAIN DATA

Top Lift at - 2499m

Ride Area 220 acres

Bottom Lift at - 1829m

Vertical Drop - 488m

Number of Runs - 150

Longest -1.6 miles (2.5km)

TERRAIN LEVELS

Easy	25%
Intermediate	35%
Advanced	40%
Expert =	6 runs

TERRAIN TO SUITE

Freeride	55%
Trees	Yes
Backcountry	Yes
Freestyle	25%
Halfpipe	Yes 2
Terrain Park	Yes 5
Carving	30%

SNOW DATA

Average Snowfall
457 cm a season

Snowmaking
95% cover of the slopes

Winter Periods
Nov to May

Summer Riding
None

SLOPE ACCESS

Total Lifts = **12**

Uplift Rate - people an hour.

10 Chair lifts,

2 Drag lifts

**Leashes Required*

Lift Times
8.30am to 10.00pm

Lift Pass Rates

8 Hour pass	$35
200 Points	$39
All Day pass	$39

SLOPE ACTION

Snowboard Hire
Daily rates from $27
Kids from $20

Snowboard Tuition
Lesson, lift & hire
from $49per day

Night Riding
From 4pm to 9pm

Heli Boarding
None

Snowmobiles
-

Mountain Cafes
-

pic - Mountain High Resort

Have you heard about the resort that although located in the southern reaches of **California** and only ninety minutes from **Los Angeles**, boasts at having five terrain parks, two half pipes, forty-seven named trails, twelve lifts and night riding seven days a week over seventeen flood lit slopes? No ? Well let me introduce to you **Mountain High**, a no nonsense resort with riding over two mountain areas with a summit of over 2499 metres. By no means is this a big resort, indeed Mountain High is relatively small when compared to the likes of its more northern neighbour **Mammoth Mountain**. However, unlike Mammoth Mountain this place is far less over-hyped, far less crowded and a lot more affordable. There may only be just over 200 acres of ridable terrain, but as the saying goes, 'size doesn't always matter, it's what you do with the size that counts. And to be fair, Mountain High does very nicely with what it has with tow mountain areas covered in tight trees and offering a good selection of well laid out trails. The **East Resort** mountain has the highest summit elevation of 2499 metres but the smallest selection of trails, while the **West Resort** has the largest selection of trails. Both mountain areas have terrain parks and halfpipes however, the two areas are not connected by mountain lifts and you can't ride between the two, instead you will need to take the resort shuttle bus to reach either. They have been doing things here on the mountains since 1937 so in that time the management have learnt a thing or two. It's noticeable today with innovative lift ticket schemes such as the *Flexi* ticket system where you buy a pass for a certain number of hours or the *Point* system which is a system where you buy points that let you ride whenever you want throughout the season. You can even share the points by transferring them to a buddy.

Freeriders will no doubt find the slopes on the **East Resort** to there liking, especially the **Olympic Bowl** which is a double black diamond stretch. On the **West Resort** there are a number of nice trails to check out with lots of trees and some fine steeps. The runs off the **Inferno Ridge** are particularly good as is the **Vertigo** which is also a night time run. For those who like to take it easy then the **Upper** and **Lower Chisolm** trails are first class trails.

Freestylers are extremely well looked after here with choice of five terrain parks and two halfpipes as well as loads of natural hits from which to get air from. The terrain parks, which are sponsored by *Vans* are spread across both mountains and known as the Faultline. Two of the parks are for beginners while both half pipes have their own drags lifts.

Carvers will find that the **East Resort** offers some of the best cruising with a good selection of runs from the top to the base.

Beginners should also like **Mountain High** with a nice selection of gentle slopes laid out at the base areas with the best runs on the **West Mountain** off the **Coyote** and **Roadrunner** lifts.

Off the slopes things are somewhat different and not what you would totally expect. The resort itself, doesn't own or provide any slope linking accommodation or provide a multi complex resort with all the normal holiday attractions. Around the base areas are a few sport shops and snowboard hire outlets and cafeterias, but that's about it. However, **Mountain High** is located next to the town of **Wrightwood** which provides a host of local facilities from lodges to bed and breakfast joints. **Los Angeles** is only 90 minutes away so you could even base yourself there or at any one of the many towns en route. If you were to choose to stay in Los Angeles, provided you don't mind the travelling to and from, you would be spoilt for facilities. Wrightwood is a simple and laid back place and the best way to find about what is on offer is to contact the *Wrightwood Chamber of Commerce* on 001 (760) 249 432.

Where you eat depends basically on where you decided to stay. Most lodges and hotels in the area have restaurants or are close to one. There are also loads of fast food joints to seek out all the way back to **Los Angeles** or in **Wrightwood**.

Nightlife and other evening entertainments vary from place to place, but basically things in **Wrightwood** are laid back and not very exciting while **Los Angeles** rocks big style and offers millions of things to do.

Accommodation

Golden Acorn Bed & Breakfast
001 (760) 249 6252
Corcoran's Corner - 001 (760) 249 6365
Finch House - 001 (760) 249 6897
Pine View House - 001 (760) 249 4348
Wrightwood Mountain realty
001 (760) 249 3257
Wrightwood Sales and Rentals
001 (760) 249 3339
Don Oster Realty - 001 (760) 249 3000

Summary: What you get here is a fun resort which offers something for everyone although this is not an extensive mountain and can be ridden with ease in a few days.
Money wise: Very affordable resort offering great value for money.

Overall rating out of 10 **7**

Mountain High
Po Box 3010, 24510 Highway 2.
Wrightwood, CA 92397
General info **001 (760) 249 5808**
Reservations **001 (760) 249 5808**
Snowphone **001 (888) 754 7878**
www.mthigh.com
www.virgin.com/holidays

pic - Shawn Frederick - Mountain High Resort/Rider Todd Melinn

pic - Mountain High Resort

Travel Guide

Fly to Ontario International
Transfer time to resort = **45** mins
Local airport=

Approximate global air travel times to **Reno**

from:	London	**9** hours
	New York	**4** hours
	Frankfurt	**10** hours

A bus from Ontario airport takes 45 minutes, Los Angeles takes 90 minutes, while from Orange County the time is 75 minutes.

Trains: None

Route Planner
Reno *via Wrightwood*

Mammoth Mtn = 163 miles
Drive time approx **4** hours

Squaw Valley California

MOUNTAIN DATA

Top Lift at - 2758m

Ride Area 4000 acres

Bottom Lift at - 1890m

Vertical Drop - 869m

Number of Runs - 100

Longest - 3 miles (5km)

TERRAIN LEVELS

Easy	25%
Intermediate	45%
Advanced	30%
Expert =	

TERRAIN TO SUITE

Freeride	50%
Trees	Yes
Backcountry	Yes
Freestyle	25%
Halfpipe	Yes 2
Terrain Park	Yes 2
Carving	25%

SNOW DATA

Average Snowfall
1142 cm a season

Snowmaking
20% cover of the slopes

Winter Periods
Nov to May

Summer Riding
None

SLOPE ACCESS

Total Lifts = **30**

Uplift Rate - 49,500 people an hour.

2 Gondolas & Cables cars, **25** Chair lifts, **3** Drag lifts

**Leashes Required*

Lift Times
8.30am to 4.00pm

Lift Pass Rates

1 Day pass	$52
3 Day pass	$138
5 Day pass	$220

SLOPE ACTION

Snowboard Hire
Daily rates from $30
Kids from $25

Snowboard Tuition
Lesson, lift & hire from $65 per day

Night Riding
From 4pm to 9pm

Heli Boarding
None

Snowmobiles
Hire & tours

Mountain Cafes
3

Squaw Valley is full-on and has been snowboard-friendly for many years. Squaw is a total snowboarder's resort in every sense and is one of the best known in the Tahoe area. With its European-alpine feel, and its history in hosting the 1960 Winter Olympics, Squaw is well used to looking after its visitors, with a substantial mountain on which to do so.

4000 acres of open bowl riding, 6 peaks, 30 lifts, a total capacity of 49,500 people per hour, 2 fun-parks and a halfpipe, combined with an average of 450 inches of snow a year (with massive amounts of snowmaking too), makes Squaw a great riders' hang-out. Countless snowboard action videos feature the slopes of Squaw and it's easy to see why. Located a stone's throw from its neighbour **Alpine Meadows**, Squaw has heaps of terrain for all styles of rider to conquer - steeps, trees, long chutes, as well as easy flats for novices. Like many of the resorts in the Tahoe region, Squaw serves the weekend city dweller. Don't despair though as the slopes can still be fairly quiet during the week-days leaving plenty of powder and open runs to shred.

Freeriders wanting an adrenalin rush will be able to get it in an area known as the **KT22.** This particular area is rated double expert, and it's for no mean reason. Lose it up here and its all over - your own dear mother wouldn't even recognise your body, so be warned. Powder-seekers will find some nice offerings around **Headwall**, or over at **Granite Chief** which is a black graded area (not for wimps) with well spread out trees.

Freestylers have been able to ride Squaw's excellent halfpipe and park for a good number of years. The **Central Park** fun-park features many obstacles to catch air and is one the best kept terrain parks in the US. The halfpipe is shaped with a *Pipe Dragon* and has perfectly cut walls that most resorts only dream about. You can also ride the park and pipe at night until 9 pm. Squaw also has a fast *Boarder Cross* circuit

Carvers in hard boots and piste-loving freeriders in softs, will not want to leave the amazingly well groomed slopes at **Squaw**. The runs off **Squaw** and **Siberia Express** are superb for laying big carves and can be tackled by all levels. **Gold Coast** is a long trail that will leave you breathless if you manage to do it in one.

Beginners have a great resort to start mastering the art of staying upright. Much of the novice terrain is to be found at the base area, while the bulk of easy trails are located further up the slopes and reached off **Super Gondola** or the cable car. Once up, the smattering of greens and blues are serviced by a number of chair lifts, so you can avoid the T-bars during the early stages of snowboarding. The local ski-school can handle all rider levels and styles, with daily ride packages to suit everone starting from around $65 for hire, lift pass and lesson.

Away from the slopes, **Squaw** has gained a reputation of being both expensive and a bit snobbish, and in both cases, it's true. But don't be put off as the place has a good buzz about it, and the locals are really friendly. Lodging, feeding, partying and all other local services are convenient for the slopes. The village packs in a raft of activities with ice skating, climbing walls and a games hall. Getting around is easy, although having a car would allow you to travel around at your own leisure, especially if you want to head down to Tahoe City. The area is serviced by a local shuttle bus.
Jobseekers, will find plenty of vacancies at Squaw or in nearby towns. Call Squaw's Job Hotline for details on, (530) 581 7117

Like any dollar-hungry mountain resort, expect to notch up some mileage on the credit card. Even a burger can set you back a small fortune. But as there are so many eating options, even the tightest of tight riders will be able to grab some affordable scram. For a good choice of eats, pay *Dave's Deli* a visit for take away sandwiches. While *Mother Barclays* serves up a hearty breakfast, designed to get your day going in style.

Night-life is aimed at the rich, so if you find that Squaw's local offerings are not your style, then try out the far more extensive facilities on offer in nearby **Truckee** or **Tahoe City** where you'll find the best night spots and local talent. You can either drive down, or catch a bus or taxi. Check out *Red Dog* or *Naughty bar.*

Accommodation is offered with a number of places close to the slopes. But it will cost you. Condo's are plentiful and well equipped, but not all affordable. For a cheap and comfortable place to stay, check out the *Youth Hostel* - it has bunks at happy prices but bring your own sleeping bag.
Check Squaws web site for the latest deals.

For accommodation listings visit - www.worldsnowboardguide.com

Summary: Great all-round resort with snowboarding to suit all levels and styles. Excellent halfpipe and good novice slopes. Very good local services.
Money wise: Very expensive, on and off the slopes, but worth it.

Overall rating out of 10 — 9

Squaw Valley Resort
P.O Box 2007 Squaw Valley
CA 96146

General info	***001*** **(530) 583 6985**
Reservations	***001*** **(800) 545 4350**
Snowphone	***001*** **(530) 583 6955**

www.squaw.com
www.virgin.com/holidays

pics - Squaw Valley Resort

Travel Guide

Fly to **Reno** International
Transfer time to resort = **1** hour.
Local airport = n/a

Approximate global air travel times to **Reno**

from:		
	London	9 hours
	New York	4 hours
	Frankfurt	10 hours

A bus from Reno takes around 1 hour. A Grey Hound bus from San Francisco takes 5 hours via Tahoe City, 6 miles away.

Trains to Truckee, 6 miles away

Route Planner
Reno *via Truckee*

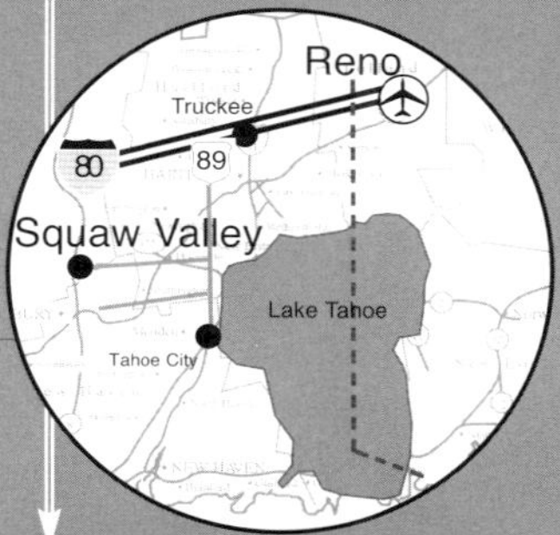

Squaw Valley = 45 miles (72km)
Drive time approx **1 hour**

Sierra-At-Tahoe California

MOUNTAIN DATA

Top Lift at - 2698m

Ride Area 2000 acres

Bottom Lift at - 2024m

Vertical Drop - 674m

Number of Runs - 46

Longest - 2.5 miles (4km)

TERRAIN LEVELS

Easy	**25%**
Intermediate	**50%**
Advanced	**25%**
Expert =	

TERRAIN TO SUITE

Freeride	**40%**
Trees	Yes
Backcountry	Yes
Freestyle	**50%**
Halfpipe	Yes 1
Terrain Park	Yes 2
Carving	**10%**

SNOW DATA

Average Snowfall
1219cm a season

Snowmaking
20% cover of the slopes

Winter Periods
Nov to April

Summer Riding
None

SLOPE ACCESS

Total Lifts = **9**

Uplift Rate - 14,920 people an hour.

7 Chair lift

2 Drag liff

**Leashes Required*

Lift Times
8.30am to 4.00pm

Lift Pass Rates

1 Day pass	$48
3 Day pass	$119
5 Day pass	$195

Travel Guide

Fly to **Reno,** transfer time is around 35 minutes.

Bus services from **Reno** are available to the resort.

Route Planner:
From Reno, use I-395 south via Carson City & Hwy 50 to Echo Summit & then to Sierra-at-Tahoe.
Reno to resort = **31** miles.
35 mins drive time.

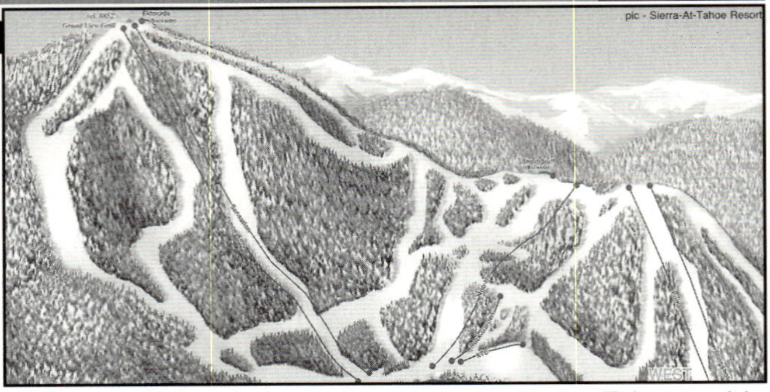

Sierra-at-Tahoe is located south-west of **Lake Tahoe** and is one of the lesser known or visited resorts in the Lake Tahoe Region. This means that the 2,000 acres of freeriding and freestyle terrain is left relatively crowd-free. 46 trails cut through thick trees that spread out over three areas, offering excellent snowboarding for all abilities, but mainly favouring intermediates. Advanced riders are provided with some very challenging riding on a number of good black trails, especially those found under the **Grand View Express**.

Freeriders who get their fix by shredding trees will love this resort. Sierra is covered with tight trees that will rip you apart if you drop down the wrong line. However, much of the area is rated as intermediate standard.

Freestylers will find this mountain a bit of a gem, apart from the shameful fact that fun-parks are open to skiers. However, **Pipeline** is a long, well looked after pipe, that is snowboard-only. There are four parks here called **Fun Zones** which are dotted around the slopes and marked out on the piste map in pink. For those who like their hits to come naturally, you will find plenty of banks and big walls to ride, especially where snow banks up alongside the trees.

Carvers who look only for perfectly flat, bumpless slopes may not be too impressed. This is not a resort that can lay claim to having lots of great piste on which to lay some fast turns. In general the terrain is a little unforgiving. However, there is some quite good riding to be had on the **West Bowl Slopes** where carvers can show off in style and at speed.

Beginners will find plenty of easy slopes, with the chance of riding from the summit down the green **Sugar 'n' Spice** trail. Other cool novice trails are off **Rock Garden** and **Nob Hill** lifts. **Broadway**, located at the base area, is good for the total beginner and it even has its own beginner chair so you won't have to suffer the embarrassment of continually falling off a drag lift.

There is some basic slopeside accommodation, but for the best local happenings and night-life, head back down to the **South Lake Tahoe** area, only 12 miles away. Get the free shuttle bus if you don't have car. Around town you will find every thing you could possibly want to make your stay a worth while one.

For accommodation listings visit - **www.worldsnowboardguide.com**

Sierra-at-Tahoe Resort
1111 Sierra-atTahoe Road, Twin Bridges, CA 95735
***001* (530) 659 7453** **www.sierratahoe.com**
www.virgin.com/holidays

Overall rating out of 10 — 6 **Excellent freestylers resort**

Sugar Bowl California

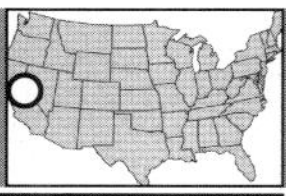

USA California

MOUNTAIN DATA

Top Lift at - 2555m

Ride Area
2083 acres

Bottom Lift at - 2083m
Vertical Drop - 457m
Number of Runs - 80
Longest - 3 miles (5km)

TERRAIN LEVELS

Easy	**17%**
Intermediate	**43%**
Advanced	**40%**
Expert =	

TERRAIN TO SUITE

Freeride	**50%**
Trees	Yes
Backcountry	Yes
Freestyle	**25%**
Halfpipe	Yes 1
Terrain Park	Yes 1
Carving	**25%**

SNOW DATA

Average Snowfall
1270cm a season
Snowmaking
13% cover of the slopes
Winter Periods
Nov to April
Summer Riding
None

SLOPE ACCESS

Total Lifts = **13**
Uplift Rate - 12,622 people an hour.
1 Gondola, **10** Chair lifts
2 Drag lifts
**Leashes Required*

Lift Times
9.00am to 4.00pm

Lift Pass Rates

1 Day pass	$50
3 Day pass	$132
5 Day pass	$220

Travel Guide

Fly to **Reno,** transfer time is 40 minutes.

Bus services from Reno are available to the resort.

Route Planner:
From Reno take I-80 south west past Truckee and via Donner Lake along the Donner Pass road to Reach Sugar Bowl.

Sugar Bowl has numerous points that it likes to draw to people's attention, such as the fact that it is one of the oldest resorts in **California** and was fathered by no less than **Walt Disney** many years ago. However, don't be alarmed, **Donald Duck** and **Mickey Mouse** are nowhere to be seen, although many of the skiers here do resemble a bunch of **Plutos.** Sugar Bowl is a nice little gem of a place that should keep you amused for a few days, but it should be pointed out that this place can become a little crowded over holiday periods etc. The terrain is evenly split over three main areas that are connected, **Lincoln, Mt Judah,** and **Mt Disney.** Lincoln and Mt Disney offer some of the most testing runs with a cool selection of black trails and a couple of double black diamonds. Mt Judah has the most sedate terrain and best for beginners and intermediates. The resort offers base facilities where you can get snowboard hire.

Freeriders will be pleased with **Sugar's** nice offering of trees, back bowls and morning powder trails. The black runs on **Mt Disney** will sort out the wimps from the men, with some very challenging trails especially the area off the **Silver Belt** chair lift where you will find a steep cliff section.

Freestylers are more than welcome here and have full access to all three areas. On **Mt Judah** there is an extremely well constructed terrain park which was originaly designed by the one time pro-rider **Noah Salasnek**. The park is easily accessed via the **Mt Judah** lift and is loaded with a cool series of hits. The resort also boasts a well carved out halfpipe known as the '**Scorpion Halfpipe'**, where air heads can get some big air.

Carvers are not noted for loving this place as either the trails are a little uneven or not particulary long, but that said **Sugar Bowl** is still okay with a few good cruising trails.

Beginners will find that the best laid out easy terrain is available on **Mt Judah**, which has a particulary good easy section for novices to shine on. The section of the **Christmas Tree** chair is also noted for being a good easy area.

Off the slopes there is some very limited accommodation in the base lodge, which houses a hotel and can be reached via the gondola. However, the best option and biggest choice of local services can be found in the nearby town of **Truckee** which is only 10 miles away.

Sugar Bowl Resort
Norden, CA 95724
***001* (530) 426 9000**

www.sugarbowl.com
www.virgin.com/holidays

Overall rating out of 10 — **6** — **A good fun resort**

Resort	Page
Berthoud Pass	75
Beaver Creek	76
Breckenridge	78
Crested Butte	80
Copper Mountain	82
Durango	84
Keystone	85
Lovelands	86
Snowmass	87
Steamboat	88
Vail	90
Telluride	92
Winterpark	93

GENERAL INFO AND FACTS

Capital - Denver
Language - English
Currency - US Dollar
Alcohol drinking age - 21
Drugs - Cannabis is illegal
Death Penalty - Exists
Age of consent for Sex - 16
Electricity Supply - 110 Volts AC
Area phone Code - 303 & 720
Provincial sales tax - 4% on all goods and services

COLARIDO DRIVE GUIDE

All vehicles drive on the right side of the road.
Speed Limits -
Motorways 70mph (112kph)
Highways 55mph (90kph)
Towns 30mph (50kph)
Road Info 001 (303) 639 1111
Fuel is sold in Gallons

TRAVEL CONTACTS

Gateway Airports
Denver
Flights from London take around 9 hours 50 mins.

Amtrax Railroad
tel: 001 (303) 534 2812

Greyhound Buses
tel: 001 (303) 293 6550

Mountain
GMT -7 hours

AREA INFORMATION

Denver Convention
Visitor Centre
1668 Larimer St
Denver, Colorado 80202
tel: 001 (303) 892 1112

pic - Bob Winsett

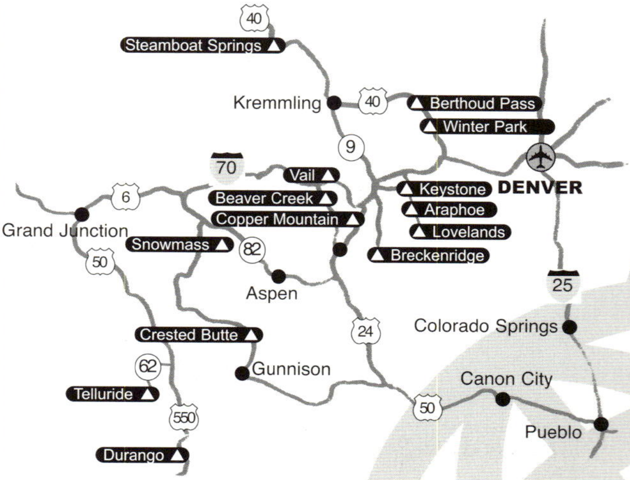

Berthoud Pass Colorado

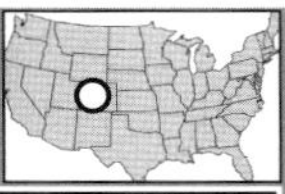

MOUNTAIN DATA
Top Lift at - 3672m
Ride Area 1220 acres
Bottom Lift at - 3447m
Vertical Drop - 365m
Number of Runs - 65
Longest -

TERRAIN LEVELS

Easy	20%
Intermediate	30%
Advanced	50%
Expert =	11 runs

TERRAIN TO SUITE

Freeride	45%
Trees	Yes
Backcountry	Yes
Freestyle	30%
Halfpipe	Yes 1
Terrain Park	Yes 1
Carving	25%

SNOW DATA
Average Snowfall
1270 cm a season
Snowmaking
0% cover of the slopes
Winter Periods
Dec to April
Summer Riding
None

SLOPE ACCESS
Total Lifts = 2
Uplift Rate - 3500 people an hour.
2 Chair lifts

**Leashes Required*

Lift Times
9.00 to 3.30pm

Lift Pass Rates
1/2 Day pass $22
3 Day pass $34
Season pass $325

Travel Guide

Fly to **Denver** International airport, 1 1/4 hours away.

Bus services are available from Reno via Winter Park.

Route Planner: From Denver head west along the I-70 and exit at gate 232 on to Hwy 40 and drive north via Winter Park to reach Berthoud Pass.

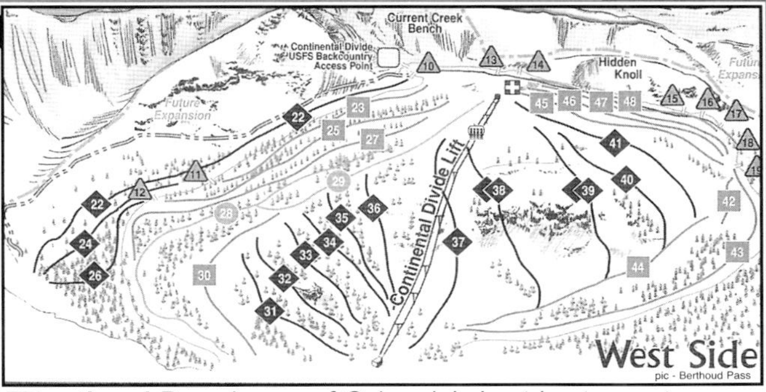

pic - Berthoud Pass

Berthoud Pass is one of Colorado's best kept secrets - anyone taking a holiday to nearby **Winter Park** will drive straight through it. Most people don't realise just what they're missing here, with exciting, varied terrain and an average snowfall of 1,270 centimetres on offer. **Berthoud Pass** has long been a favourite of locals seeking good backcountry powder. Berthoud Pass has around 2,000 acres of terrain, served by two chair lifts and a fleet of shuttle buses running from two pick-up stops on either side of the Pass. The two mountain peaks, **Russell** and **Colorado**, are split into five areas providing a riding experience to suit good/expert and intermediate riders.

Freeriders are in for a treat - there's an abundance of great terrain to ride. The **Continental Divide** chair gives access to a mixture of steep blacks and double diamond chutes, cliffs and drop offs - not for the faint hearted, or the beginner. There is also a backcountry access point here for those powder lovers and steep freaks. Tree lovers should check out the half-a-dozen gladed runs in the **Pumphouse Basin** area where there is usually a fresh layer of thick powder. **Floral Park**, reached off **Mines Peak** chair, also gives access to some steep gladed runs. However, it's the **Current Creek** slopes that offer the best cluster of steep blacks.

Freestylers are also in for a good time at Berthoud. The slopes are peppered with amazing drop offs and big hits. **The Hell's Half Acre/East Side** slopes are full-on. Make sure you have balls or firm tits, because the **High Trail Cliffs** are super-scary - attempt these at your peril. However, the fun-park, also on Hell's Half Acre, is not so daunting and easily reached from the **Lodge.**

Carvers who can ride fast, hard and hold an edge, welcome, as this place is for you. The **West Side** slopes off the **Continental Divide** chair offer a number of good cruisey blues and blacks, with a couple of double diamond blacks thrown in for good measure, such as **Rush Chute** and **Nitro Chute**.

Beginners, since Berthoud is not for you, go to **Winter Park** which is only a few minutes away. Saying that, if you're a competent first timer and can learn quickly, there are a few easy trails to check out before taking on the harder stuff.

For local services, see *Winter Park*, as there are no facilities on offer at **Berthoud Pass**. However, *The Pub,* located at the base of the slopes serves a damn fine selection of burgers and booze.

Berthoud Pass Ski Area
P.O Box 3314, 93475 US Hwy 40. CO 80482
***001* (800) 7754 2378.**
www.berthoudpass.com
www.virgin.com/holidays

Overall rating out of 10 **6** **A nice all round resort**

Beaver Creek Colorado

MOUNTAIN DATA

Top Lift at - 3488m

Ride Area 1625 acres

Bottom Lift at - 2255m

Vertical Drop - 1018m

Number of Runs - 146

Longest -3.5 miles (5.6km)

TERRAIN LEVELS

Easy	34%
Intermediate	39%
Advanced	27%
Expert =	

TERRAIN TO SUITE

Freeride	55%
Trees	Yes
Backcountry	Yes
Freestyle	25%
Halfpipe	Yes 2
Terrain Park	Yes 4
Carving	20%

SNOW DATA

Average Snowfall
838 cm a season

Snowmaking
50% cover of the slopes

Winter Periods
Nov to May

Summer Riding
None

SLOPE ACCESS

Total Lifts = **14**

Uplift Rate - 24,700 people an hour.

13 Chair lifts

1 Drag lifts

**Leashes Required*

Lift Times
8.30am to 4.00pm

Lift Pass Rates

1 Day pass	$63
3 Day pass	$189
5 Day pass	$285

SLOPE ACTION

Snowboard Hire
Daily rates from $30
Kids from $25

Snowboard Tuition
Lesson, lift & hire
from $95 per day

Night Riding
None

Heli Boarding
Yes

Snowmobiles
Hire & tours

Mountain Cafes
2

pic - Beaver Creek

Beaver Creek, a short distance from its more famous cousin **Vail**, has a classy and expensive reputation - an ex-US President even has a house here. But don't let that put you off as this is a resort that has come of age with a really healthy attitude towards snowboarding, as seen by the provision of so many snowboard services. Even some of the local riders give up their time to form what they call the *Snowboard Courtesy Patrol*, which is a group of snowboarders that patrol the area's slopes to offer assistance and keep everyone in check. **Beaver Creek** is a relatively new resort, but unlike some old timers, it has managed to get things right. The well set out lift system is located on four areas, with runs that favour intermediate riders for the most part. The trails, which are cut through thick wooded areas, are shaped in a way that allows you to get around with ease, making riding here an ideal experience.

Freeriders are presented with a series of slopes, covered in trees from top to bottom. Recently the resort has added over 100 acres of extra tree cover terrain, to please riders even more. If you like to ride hard and fast, then the double black diamonds on **Grouse Mountain** off the **Grouse** chair will satisfy you. Here you can drop down a line of four steep trails, where the longest, **Royal Elk**, sweeps in an arc through trees, whilst **Osprey** is the shorter of the four. Alternatively, the **Half Hitch** and single black trails found off the **Centennial** chair are less daunting, but just as much fun. To ride the best spots, hook up with a local snowboard guide.

Freestylers will find plenty of big natural hits to float air. If you're a park rider, then head for the **Stick Line** snowboard park (located off the **Centennial** lift). It's loaded with a well-shaped halfpipe, rails and other obstacles to catch air. However, the park is located on a steep section of terrain so novice freestylers take note. Riders can even get freestyle tuition should you not be too clever on take off and landing techniques.

Carvers are much in evidence here, and with so many good carving trails, it's no wonder. Edge-to-edge stylers are attracted by the extremely well groomed trails that descend from all areas of the resort, which twist and wind their way through the tree-lined trails. The **Centennial** trail is an extremely popular run that starts off at the top of the **Centennial** lift. Starting as a black run and descending into a more sedate blue down to the base area, it can be done in a short space of time if you can hang on at the start.

Beginners will find the best easy trails are to be found at the top. This means that unless you can learn fast and ride back home, you may have to chair it back down - which is always a pain. Still, a nice touch at **Beaver Creek** is the kid's fun-park, *Chaos Canyon Adventure Zone,* which has a series of small hits. Riders who have never been on a snowboard will learn quickly if they visit the local snowboard school, which has a high reputation.

Beaver Creek is a major in terms of dullness. However, the village is a laid back place and locals are very friendly. Beaver is a much quieter hangout than nearby Vail, which may be why the place attracts nice family groups that walk around holding hands and smiling as they go. The resort offers all the normal Colorado tourist attractions from hot air baloon rides to sleigh rides and an attraction called the Adventure Ridge. You can hire full snowboard equipment at Beaver or in Vail with prices much the same wherever you go, from around $35 a day. Check out the *Edgewise* snowboard shop tel (970) 845 5420.
Jobseekers will find loads of vacancies - call Human Resources Dept. tel (970) 845 2460

If your sole reason for visiting Beaver is the food, you will find a variety of mostly costly, but good restaurants to choose from. Vegetarians, vegans, or monster meat lovers will find their every desire well catered for from one end of the village to the other. The *Coyote Cafe*, which is near the lift ticket office, is noted for good food at okay prices. Other good eateries to try, are *The Saddleridge*, the *Mirabelle* or *On The Fly* for great sandwiches.

Nightlife: put simply, is dull and basically non-existent. The bars cater in the main for rich ski-types in expensive cowboy boots, who prefer to sit around log fires talking bull. However, the *Coyote Cafe* is good and worth a visit for a few beers. The best thing to do is head for Vail - but remember to have plenty of dollars on you.

Accommodation: There are no real cheap options for lodging in **Beaver** - in short, prices start at silly and go up to downright criminal. There are plenty of condo's offering beds close to the slopes, or within a short distance, but for budget riders, you are better looking for somewhere to kip in the small, nearby town of **Avon** which has quite a few cheap bed and breakfast homes.
For accommodation listings visit - www.worldsnowboardguide.com

Summary: Generally a good riders resort with good carving and freestyling. Also noted for excellent tuition programmes. However, night-life is crap.
Money wise: Super expensive, with prices that are not always justified.

Overall rating out of 10 **8**

Beaver Creek Resort
P.O Box 915 Avon
CO 81620

General info	**001 (970) 476 5601**
Reservations	**001 (800) 404 3535**
Snowphone	**001 (970) 476 4888**

www.beavercreek.com
www.virgin.com/holidays

pic - Beaver Creek pic - Bob Winsett

Travel Guide

Fly to **Denver** International
Transfer time to resort = $2^{1/4}$ hours.
Local airport = **Eagle County,** 10 miles away
Approximate global air travel times to **Denver**

from:		
	London	9 hours
	New York	$3^{1/2}$ hours
	Frankfurt	10 hours

There are daily bus services from both Denver and Vail/Eagle County airports direct to Beaver Creek

Trains: None

Route Planner
Denver *via Interstate 70*

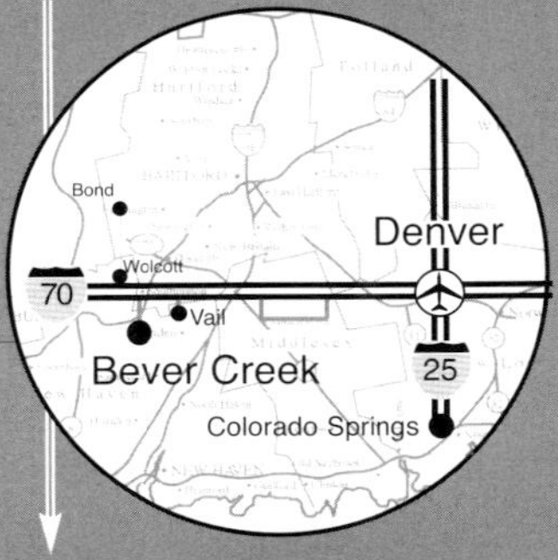

Beaver Creek = 110 miles
Drive time is about $2^{1/4}$ hours

Breckenridge Colorado

MOUNTAIN DATA

Top Lift at - 3962m

Ride Area 2043 acres

Bottom Lift at - 2962m
Vertical Drop - 1036m
Number of Runs - 139
Longest - 3.5 miles (5.6km)

TERRAIN LEVELS

Easy	13%
Intermediate	36%
Advanced	51%
Expert =	10 runs

TERRAIN TO SUITE

Freeride	60%
Trees	Yes
Backcountry	Yes
Freestyle	30%
Halfpipe	Yes 2
Terrain Park	Yes 2
Carving	10%

SNOW DATA

Average Snowfall
761 cm a season
Snowmaking
26% cover of the slopes
Winter Periods
Oct to April
Summer Riding
None

SLOPE ACCESS

Total Lifts = **25**
Uplift Rate - 30,600 people an hour.
14 Chair lifts
11 Drag lifts
**Leashes Required*

Lift Times
8.30am to 4.00pm

Lift Pass Rates

1 Day pass	$57
3 Day pass	$171
5 Day pass	$245

SLOPE ACTION

Snowboard Hire
Daily rates from $29
Kids from $26

Snowboard Tuition
Lesson, lift & hire from $70 per day

Night Riding
None

Heli Boarding
Yes

Snowmobiles
Hire & tours

Mountain Cafes
9

Breckenridge is a true snowboard classic, and has been for many years, having played a leading role in the development of snowboarding in the US. The resort is constantly improving by adding new features to the mountain and around town. Located off Interstate 70, to the west of **Denver** and part of the **Ten Mile Range**, Breckenridge is a big and impressive area with terrain that spreads over four excellent snowboarding peaks, all offering something different for everyone. Some say that the 'new school' style of snowboarding started here, but whether you're from the new or the old, you should have no problems cutting big turns on the mainly wide, open flats.

Freeriders with their powder-searching heads, will not have to hunt for long when they see what's available in the **Back Bowls** off **Peak 8** and off **Peak 9's North Face**. Here you'll find plenty of terrain for riders who know how to snowboard. At the top of **Chair 6**, you'll find loads of good hits and drop offs, while lower down there are some wicked tree runs. You'll find good powder here, even after everywhere else has been tracked out. The **Imperial Bowl** on **Peak 8** has over 1,000 metres of vert to tackle, but there's no lift, so you will need to hike up.

Freestylers should have no reason to complain as apart from having some fantastic natural freestyle terrain, there are also two terrain parks and two pipes of competition standard. The latest addition to Breckenridge is what they call a 'Super Pipe Dragon', the only one in the US which can cut perfectly smooth deep walls. The **Lechman** trail is known for being one of the best natural freestyle runs on the mountain, with loads of hits formed from big wind-lips running down the sides of certain sections. Head for **Peak 9** and you'll find the **Gold King** fun-park which is pretty awesome and well-maintained: there are some big, big jumps to go for and thankfully it's groomed at least twice a week, although it does get icy. There is also a halfpipe, located just above the park, which is shaped with the Pipe Dragon every Thursday and is therefore closed on that day. However, when it's re-opened on Friday mornings, it's perfect - but get up early, because everyone wants to get there first. **Peak 8** is home to the other park and pipe on the **Fairway** area.

Carvers have a mountain here that will allow for some very fast and challenging riding on well groomed alpine trails. Speed-freaks should try out the **Centennial** trail, which is a long flat and perfect for cranking big turns on. Intermediates will find the runs off **Peak 10** the place to be, in particular the **Crystal**.

Beginners have plenty of easy runs, many of which can be found on **Peaks 8** and **9**. The fact that novice trails like **Silverthorne** are wide enough for all newcomers helps to make this a great beginners' resort, especially around the **Quicksilver** lift. Beginner programmes start from around $70 for a day's session.

As with many of **Colorado's** resorts, **Breckenridge** can be uncomfortably expensive. However, for riders on a tight budget, providing you shop around for accommodation and other local services, you will be able to stay here. The town is spread out, and has a rustic wild west feel about it. You can spend until you drop here with a staggering 225 plus shops, including a number of good outlets for snowboard hire with the option to rent demo boards and step-in set. Other attractions include a new 5 million dollar ice rink and a cool area for skateboarders to do their thing.

Jobseekers will find sacks of vacancies existing all season for waiters and even lifties. Contact for details 001 (970) 453 6018

Around town you will find a massive selection of good restaurants and fast food joints ranging from cheap to steep with over 100 places to choose from. Breakfast is dished up in numerous places. The *Prospect* does a nice sunny side up as does the *Mountain Lodge Cafe*. Veggies should head to *Noodle & Bean* for the very same, while meat lovers may want to try a grill at '*Breckenridge Cattle Co*' which is also noted for its fish food.

Nightlife is pretty good and rocks until late. There's plenty of beer, dancing and fine local talent to check out, including four main nightclubs and some 80 odd bars. Head to the *Underworld Club*, or *Jake T Pounders* which is young, trendy, fun and one of the main hangouts that has darts, football and pool tables. *Eric's* is another cool hangout.

Accommodation options are vast with some 23,000 visitor beds up for grabs. Those on a tight budget will manage to find a cheap B&B, while those wanting some luxury will be able to chill out in a classy hotel. *Breckenridge Mountain* Lodge is an okay and affordable place to spend a few nights in while the Great *Divide Lodge* is an expensive alternative that offers lots of services.

For accommodation listings visit - www.worldsnowboardguide.com

Summary: Despite being an expensive location, this is a super resort with great snowboard terrain, and excellent local services.

Money wise: Very expensive, both on and off the slopes, but worth the costs.

Overall rating out of 10 — **8**

Breckenridge Resort
P.O Box 1058. Breckenridge.
CO 80424

General info	***001*** **(970) 453 5000**
Reservations	***001*** **(800) 221 1091**
Snowphone	***001*** **(970) 453 6118**

www.breckenridge.com
www.virgin.com/holidays

pics - Bob Winsett

Travel Guide

Fly to **Denver** International
Transfer time to resort = **1 1/2** hours.
Local airport = **Eagle County**

Approximate global air travel times to **Denver**

from:		
	London	9 hours
	New York	3 1/2 hours
	Frankfurt	10 hours

There are daily bus services from both Denver and Vail/Eagle County airports direct to Breckenridge

Trains: None

Route Planner
Denver *via Interstate 70 & Hwy 9*

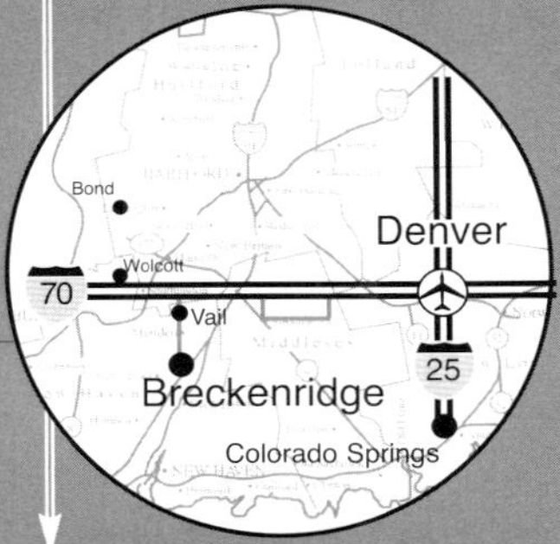

Breckenridge = 81 miles
Drive time is about **1 1/2** hours

Crested Butte Colorado

MOUNTAIN DATA

Top Lift at - 3707m

Ride Area 1160 acres

Bottom Lift at - 2857m
Vertical Drop - 850m
Number of Runs - 85
Longest - 2.5 miles (4km)

TERRAIN LEVELS

Easy	13%
Intermediate	30%
Advanced	57%
Expert =	10 runs

TERRAIN TO SUITE

Freeride	60%
Trees	Yes
Backcountry	Yes
Freestyle	25%
Halfpipe	Yes 1
Terrain Park	Yes 1
Carving	15%

SNOW DATA

Average Snowfall
582 cm a season
Snowmaking
25% cover of the slopes
Winter Periods
NOv to April
Summer Riding
None

SLOPE ACCESS

Total Lifts = **14**
Uplift Rate - 17,400 people an hour.
9 Chair lifts
5 Drag lifts
**Leashes Required*

Lift Times
8.30am to 4.00pm

Lift Pass Rates
1 Day pass $53
3 Day pass $159
5 Day pass $245

SLOPE ACTION

Snowboard Hire
Daily rates from $27
Kids from $22

Snowboard Tuition
Lesson, lift & hire from $80 per day

Night Riding
None

Heli Boarding
Yes

Snowmobiles
Hire & tours

Mountain Cafes
8

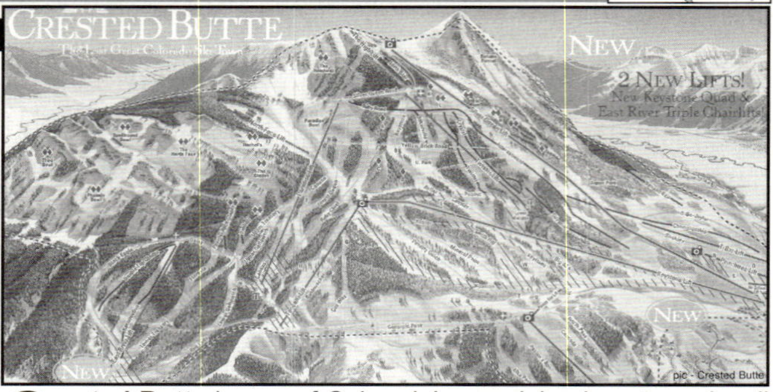

pic - Crested Butte

Crested Butte is one of Colorado's ex-mining haunts and well worth a visit. It has gained a good reputation as a snowboard-friendly resort, but is best known for is its extreme and hard core terrain. Indeed, you could call this place the extreme freerider's heaven in the USA, as it has successfully staged several *US Extreme Snowboarding Championships*. Crested Butte easily offers some of the most challenging snowboarding in America.

What you get is a serious mountain for serious riders, and not your typical dollar-hungry Colorado destination. If you like your mountain high with steeps, couloirs, trees, major off-piste in big bowls, then Crested Butte is for you. With 85 runs, spread over 1,160 acres, no-one needs to feel left out, on crowd-free slopes, with a good average snow record. What's more, if you fancy riding during November, pre-Christmas, as well as the latter part of April, you can ride for nothing, or put another way, free of charge!

Freeriders are in command here, with much of the terrain best suited to riders who know how to handle a board and prefer off-piste. **Extreme Limits** which has recently had an exta 280 acres added via the **Teocalli Bowl**, is a gnarly, un-pisted heaven for extreme lovers wanting big hits and steeps. Check out **Headwall** and **North Face** for some serious double black diamond trails, offering cliffs, couloirs and trees. In order to stay safe and appreciate Crested Butte's extreme terrain, you are strongly advised to get a copy of the Extreme Limits Guide, which is a separate lift and trail guide, pinpointing how and where to ride. Ignore its advice, and you may not live to regret it. However, don't simply read the guide and head off, you MUST also seek the services of a local snowboard or ski guide as well.

Freestylers will find that a two week stay would still not be enough time to check out all the natural options for going airborn. Check out Crested Butte's gnarly fun-park, which has rails, logs, table-tops, quarter-pipes and is also skier-free. To get to the park, take the **Silver Queen** or **Keystone** lift.

Carvers who choose a resort because of its motorway-wide, perfectly groomed slopes without a bump in sight, may feel a bit left out, but not too disappointed. You can still carve hard on a number of selected trails. For a fast trail, give **Ruby** a try, or check out the flats on the **Paradise Bowl**.

Beginners cutting their first runs would do best to ride on the lower slopes near the village, before trying out **Poverty** or **Mineral Point** off the **Keystone** lift. There are a number of green runs to tackle before trying some of the easy connecting blues. The runs off **Gold Link** lift are pretty cool and worth a go. The local ski/snowboard school offers a host of teaching sessions with a beginners learn to snowboard programme that includes lift, lessons and hire, costing from around $80.

Visitors coming here expecting to find the all too often horrible Colorado-style, glitzy ski-tourist trap, will be pleased to note that **Crested Butte** is none of that. This is a friendly and welcoming place with services located at the base area or in the the old town, a short bus journey away. Wherever you stay, there is plenty to keep you entertained at prices that don't always hurt. Local facilities include basic sporting outlets, a swimming pool, a gym, and an ice ring. There is also a cinema with the latest movies on show. But note, this is not a place loaded with attractions, but more of a place where you can sit back and relax without being over pampered. *Colorado Boarders Shop* is the place to go for board hire and snowboard sales.

Fatties on a mission to eat fast, hard and cheaply, welcome - you have arrived in heaven. This place is littered with eateries in every price range. For a hearty breakfast, there are a number of good places to visit such as *Forest Queen*, *The Woodstone Grill* or the *Timberline Cafe*, all three open early. Later on in the day, check out *Idle Spur* where they serve damn fine steaks cooked exactly to the way you like it.

Night-life comes with a cowboy theme without the flashness or bright lights. You can drink in a relaxed atmosphere at a number of joints that go on until the early hours. *Talk of the Town* has a punkish reputation and worth a visit. The *Idle Spur* is another cool hang which offers a good selection of beers and often has live music.

Accommodation is available at the slopes or in the old town, and together they can sleep 5,000 visitors in a choice of condos, hotels and B&B's. Prices vary, with rates as low as $25 a night in a B&B, or as high as $300 in a fancy hotel. The nearer you stay to the slopes, the more costly things are, making the old town the cheapest option.

For accommodation listings visit - www.worldsnowboardguide.com

Summary: The dog's balls for backcountry riding, but also a piste-loving carver's destination and good for beginners. Good and friendly local services.
Money wise: Moderately expensive resort, both on and off the slopes.

Overall rating out of 10 **8**

Crested Butte Resort
500 Gothic Rd, Mt Crested Butte. CO 81245
General info **001 (970) 349 2333**
Reservations **001 (800) 544 8448**
Snowphone **001 (970) 349 2323**
www.butte.com
www.virgin.com/holidays

pics - Crested Butte

Travel Guide

Fly to **Denver** International
Transfer time to resort = **6½** hours.
Local airport = **Gunnison,** 30 miles south.

Approximate global air travel times to **Denver**

from:		
	London	**9** hours
	New York	**3½** hours
	Frankfurt	**10** hours

There are daily bus services from both Denver and Gunnison airports direct to Crested Butte.

Trains: None

Route Planner
Denver *via Gunnison*

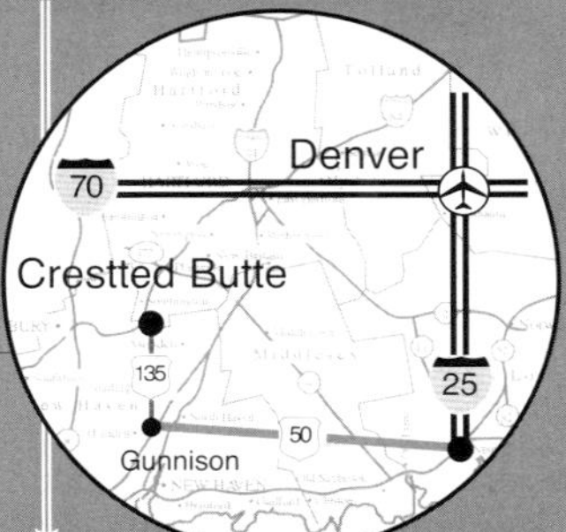

Crested Butte = 233 miles
Drive time is about **6½** hours

Copper Mountain
Colorado

MOUNTAIN DATA

Top Lift at - 3767m
Ride Area 2433 acres
Bottom Lift at - 2926m
Vertical Drop - 793m
Number of Runs - 125
Longest - 3 miles (5km)

TERRAIN LEVELS

Easy	**21%**
Intermediate	**25%**
Advanced	**36%**
Expert =	**4 runs**

TERRAIN TO SUITE

Freeride	**45%**
Trees	Yes
Backcountry	Yes
Freestyle	**25%**
Halfpipe	Yes 2
Terrain Park	Yes 1
Carving	**30%**

SNOW DATA

Average Snowfall
710cm a season
Snowmaking
15% cover of the slopes
Winter Periods
Nov to April
Summer Riding
None

SLOPE ACCESS

Total Lifts = **23**
Uplift Rate - 30,630 people an hour.
15 Chair lifts
8 Drag lifts
**Leashes Required*

Lift Times
8.30am to 3.30pm

Lift Pass Rates

2 Day pass	$104
3 Day pass	$147
5 Day pass	$215

SLOPE ACTION

Snowboard Hire
Daily rates from $31
Kids from $26

Snowboard Tuition
Lesson, lift & hire from $80 per day

Night Riding
None

Heli Boarding
Yes

Snowmobiles
Hire & tours

Mountain Cafes
2

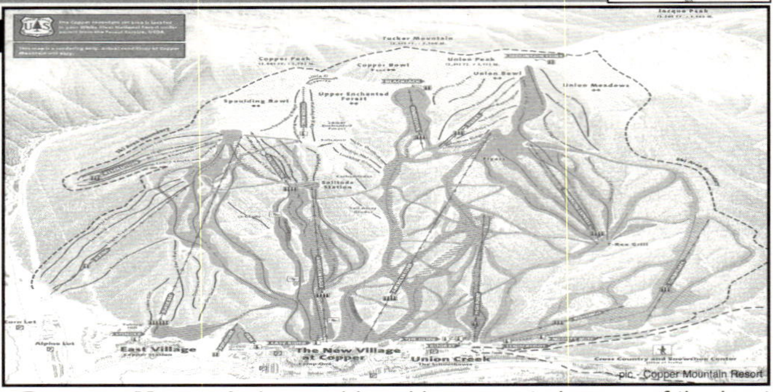

pic - Copper Mountain Resort

Copper Mountain is considered by many to be one of the best mountains in the USA and since being bought by *Intrawest Resorts*, the whole place has seen heavy investment to greatly improve a place that was good before. They have not only been improving what is available on the slopes but a lot of work has taken place around the town with the centre part now becoming a car free area. Copper's crowd free slopes with long trails and few traverses appeal to tree-riding fans and those looking for something interesting to tackle. Powder is in abundance here with four big bowls holding massive amounts of it. Most of the main chairs take around ten minutes to reach their drop off points, although it seems double that time when you're dangling hundreds of feet in the air, with wind driving snow up your nose and down your neck. Still, the lifts are modern and connect well with the runs. Once you get to the top of each run, you will not regret the chair ride as you are presented with a mountain that is lovingly pisted, well marked out and will make for a great time.

Freeriders, welcome to sex on snow! Copper has it all for you. Powder, deep bowls and trees all on offer from expert double blacks to tame piste trails. Take the **Flyer** chair to reach the Flyer area where you will find a series of blue runs that cut through trees. Alternatively ride the **Sierra** lift to get a powder fix. More advanced riders should take **Lift E** to take on a cluster of short blacks. These are perfect for freeriders, especially the **Union Bowl**. If you keep right off the E-lift, you hit some decent trees. Intermediate freeriders will find plenty to interest them on the run known as **Andy's Encore**, reached off the **B-1** chair.

Freestylers have a great mountain to explore with great natural terrain and numerous man made hits in the shape of two halfpipes and a cool terrain park. The **Tsunami** halfpipe is a massive pipe that's regularly used for competitions. To get to it, simply take the **American Flyer** lift via the **Carefree** trail. Coppers terrain park is noted for having a great series of hits and furthermore all the hits are colour-graded for different rider standards, just like the runs. Natural terrain seekers should find **Union** and **Spaulding Bowls** the areas to check out for wind-lips, rock jumps and hits galore. Copper has a programme called the **'Team'**. If you volunteer to help look after the park and pipe, you will get a free season pass. tel 001 970 968 2318 for details.

Carvers will find that this is definitely a place for them, with plenty of advanced and intermediate wide open well pisted trails to choose from. Runs like **Bittersweet** are a carver's dream

Beginners who come here won't be disappointed. Copper has more than sufficient areas for learning the basics and progressing onwards. There are plenty of easy green trails. The tree-lined runs off the **American Flyer Quad** are a real joy. The flats off **K** and **L** lifts are also perfect for first timers.

Copper Mountain is very much a snowboard-friendly place and the locals will make your stay a good one. However, Copper has the usual pitfalls of many Colorado resorts - it can be painfully expensive. But if you're a good scammer, you can stay here on a low budget if you put yourself about and get to know the locals. The resort facilities are very good and unlike many resorts, Copper isn't overloaded with dozens of soppy tourist shops, but rather a need to have selection. There is also a sports centre, a swimming pool and gym.
Jobseekers: Copper has several work programmes of interest to the foreign travellers, which enable you to work legally and earn lift passes instead of cash. Call (970) 968 2882.

The menus on offer here are perfect for the holiday crowds, but nothing comes cheap - a burger and a coke at *Copper Commons* is about $6. Still, *Farley's* does do an affordable steak, while *O'Shea's* serves up killer breakfasts at very reasonable prices. *Pesce Fresco's* is another noted eatrie with a big menu to chose from. However, for a burger and other light snacks, check out the *B-Lift Pub*, a favourite with locals and visitors alike.

Nightlife around Copper is somewhat tame. The main hang outs being *B-Lift Pub*, *O'Shea's and Farleys.* However, the better option for a night out drinking or pulling a local bit of skirt, is in nearby Breckenridge or Vail. The choice of bars is much better, but unless you're 21+, and have ID to prove it, you're going to be seriously bored.

Accommodation in Copper offers slopeside beds, but prices range enormously from $20 up to $800 a night. Staying in nearby **Dillon** or **Frisco** would be a good alternative if you're on a tight budget, both have a good selection of cheaper accommodation. For all your lodging needs, contact Copper Mountain Lodging Services.

For accommodation listings visit - www.worldsnowboardguide.com

Summary: One of Colorado's best resorts, with some great natural freestyle terrain. Excellent for beginners. Limited but very good local services.
Money wise: High prices for most things but good value for your money.

Overall rating out of 10 — **9**

Copper Mountain Resort
P.O Box A 3001. Copper Mountain. CO 08443

General info	***001*** **(970) 968 2882**
Reservations	***001*** **(800) 458 8386**
Snowphone	***001*** **(800) 789 7609**

www.ski-copper.com
www.virgin.com/holidays

pics - Copper Mountain

Travel Guide

Fly to **Denver** International
Transfer time to resort = **1½** hours.
Local airport = **Eagle County,** 20 miles away.
Approximate global air travel times to **Denver**

from:		
	London	**9** hours
	New York	**3½** hours
	Frankfurt	**10** hours

There are daily bus services from both Denver and Vail/Eagle County airports direct to Copper Mountain

Trains: None

Route Planner
Denver *via Interstate 70*

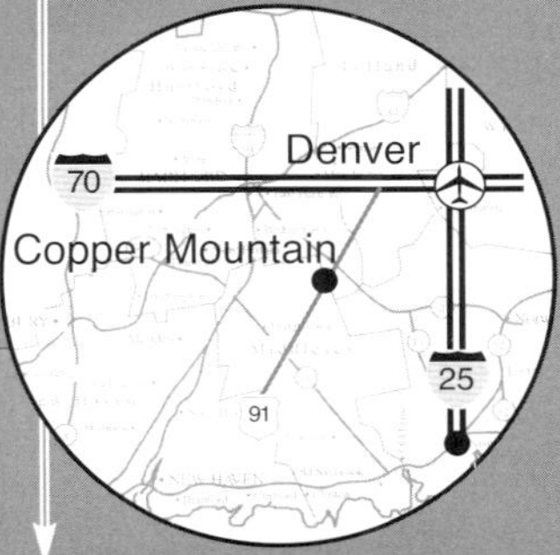

Copper Mountain = 78 miles
Drive time is about **1½** hour

Durango Colorado

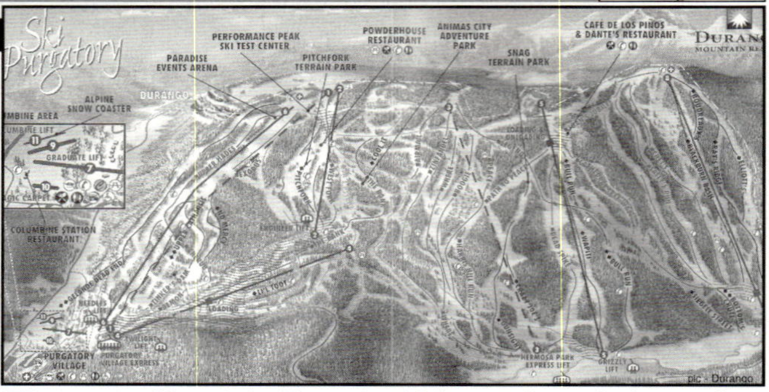

MOUNTAIN DATA

Top Lift at - 3298m

Ride Area 1200 acres

Bottom Lift at - 2680m

Vertical Drop - 618m

Number of Runs - 75

Longest -

TERRAIN LEVELS

Easy	**23%**
Intermediate	**51%**
Advanced	**26%**
Expert =	**5 runs**

TERRAIN TO SUITE

Freeride	**40%**
Trees	Yes
Backcountry	Yes
Freestyle	**30%**
Halfpipe	Yes 1
Terrain Park	Yes 2
Carving	**30%**

SNOW DATA

Average Snowfall
660cm a season

Snowmaking
34% cover of the slopes

Winter Periods
Nov to April

Summer Riding
None

SLOPE ACCESS

Total Lifts = **9**

Uplift Rate -15,600 people an hour.

9 Chair lifts

2 Drag lifts

**Leashes Required*

Lift Times
8.30am to 4.00pm

Lift Pass Rates

1 Day pass	$45
3 Day pass	$135
5 Day pass	$215

Travel Guide

Fly to **Denver**, transfer time is around 6 hours.

Bus services from **Denver** are available but not direct.

Route Planner:
From Denver, head west on I-70 to Grand Junction and then head south on Hwy's 50 & 50 down to Durango.

Durango Mountain Resort, which was formerly known has **Purgatory,** and only changed recently when the resort was taken over, is a fantastic place and one that doesn't come with all the razzamatazz and ponciness that many of **Colorado's** other resorts have. What's more, this place is not an over priced hunt designed for Dot.Com millionaires, this is a place where riders who like to ride hard and then relax with ease, can do so at resort that is friendly and extremely well set out. This can be said for both on and off the mountain and down town in **Durango**, which is 25 miles away. Although Durango is under new management, there has been a ski centre here for the past 36 years, and the future looks good for this place with a number of major developments taking place up on the slopes and down in the base village of Purgatory. On the slopes you have a surprisingly well laid out selection of runs that provide something for everyone with a good choice of advanced and excellent intermediate slopes.

Freeriders have a wonderful mountain to play on. A weeks visit won't be wasted here with a good selection of runs to choose from with some very fast descents through trees and some fine powder stashes to seek out. The runs located under and around the **Grizzly** chair lift are cool and will offer the advanced rider a good time. The **Bull Run** is especially good but be warned, the lower section is not for the faint hearted. For some less daunting descents try the runs off the **Hermosa Quad.**

Freestylers have plenty to do here with a choice of terrain parks and halfpipes. The main park, which is known as the **Pitchfork** and covers some 10 acres, is located next to the **Engineer** chair lift and has a series of hits that include table tops. The **Snag** terrain park is located near the **Path of Peace** trail.

Carvers have a series of cool cruising trails but in truth this place is more of a freerider's resort. Still, runs like the **Path of Peace** is a good intermediate cruising trail.

Beginners can almost ride from the top to the bottom on a nice cluster of easy green trails reached off the Hermosda lift.

If you wish to lodge close to the slopes, then you can but the choice is very limited with only a couple of options. The best thing to do is base yourself down in **Durango** which has a good choice of places to stay in as well as okay restaurants and bars.

For accommodation listings visit - www.worldsnowboardguide.com

Durango Mountain Resort
One Skier Place, Durango, CO 81301
***001* (970) 247 9000** **www.durangomountainresort.com**
www.virgin.com/holidays

Overall rating out of 10 **8** **Really good resort for all**

Keystone Colorado

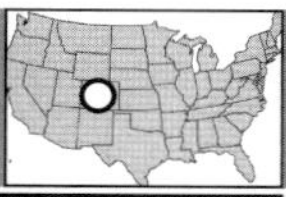

MOUNTAIN DATA

Top Lift at - 3719m

Ride Area 1861 acres

Bottom Lift at - 2835m

Vertical Drop - 713m

Number of Runs - 116

Longest - 3 miles (5km)

TERRAIN LEVELS

Easy	12%
Intermediate	29%
Advanced	55%
Expert =	54%

TERRAIN TO SUITE

Freeride	60%
Trees	Yes
Backcountry	Yes
Freestyle	20%
Halfpipe	Yes 1
Terrain Park	Yes 1
Carving	20%

SNOW DATA

Average Snowfall
584cm a season

Snowmaking
50% cover of the slopes

Winter Periods
Nov to April

Summer Riding
None

SLOPE ACCESS

Total Lifts = **20**

Uplift Rate - 27,273 people an hour.

2 Gondolas, **13** Chair lifts

5 Drag lifts

**Leashes Required*

Lift Times
9.00am to 4.00pm

Lift Pass Rates

1 Day pass	$57
3 Day pass	$171
5 Day pass	$245

Travel Guide

Fly to **Denver,** transfer time is 1¾ hours.

Bus services from Denver are available to the resort.

Route Planner:
From Denver head west along I-70 via the Eisenhower Tunnel to Dillion. Exit at junction 205 to Hwy 6 to reach Keystone.

pic - Susie

Keystone has been a ski resort since 1970, but it was only in 1997 that the management finally broke down and allowed snowboarders to use their mountain. The new found tolerance of 'knuckle draggers' has not impressed all parties, (ie skiers) especially since Keystone seems to have embraced snowboarding whole-heartedly. A snowboard-specific section combines a halpipe with a snowboard park. There's also a snowboard school and the largest board rental shop in North America. Keystone is owned by *Vail Associates*, who also own **Vail, Beaver Creek, Breckenridge** and **Arapahoe Basin** - all these resorts offer a multi-area pass. Boarders were excited at the opening of Keystone for many reasons: they have the only gondola in **Summit County** and it also offers the county's only night-boarding area, where you can ride 14 lit trails until 9pm.

Freeriders can roam freely over **Keystone's** three connected mountains: **Keystone Mountain**, **North Peak** and **The Outback.** Keystone is the front mountain and is laden with jib runs like **Paymaster** and **Spring Dipper**. It's a good idea to have someone to spot your blind landings off the big rollers as it gets real busy. North Peak and Outback offer steeps and open tree runs.

Freestylers now have a 20 acre fun-park and two halfpipes located in the **Packside Bowl**. The main pipe is widely hailed as excellent, with walls reaching 3m in high season. The park's hits and layout have received less praise, but it's hoped that the new season will see changes. One major problem with the park is that it is next to the slalom course and the main ski-school area: more than one day-glow, spandex-clad racer has nearly been decapitated as they stupidly take a short cut across the park.

Carvers will be delighted to know that **Keystone** grooms some of their runs twice a day, leaving lots of terrain to lay out big turns.

Beginners may find that overall the area is not a great novice resort as there are too many flats and too much traversing.

Over the past few years **Keystone** has been engaged in a multi-dollar redevelopment plan. This has lead to the building of the *River Run* area which is a collection of condos within walking distance of the slopes. Keystone overall offers a lot of condos and a handfull of hotels with nothing coming in that cheaply. However, eating and drinking options are plentiful, although night time action is lame to say the least.

Keystone Resort
P.o Box 38 Keystone, CO 80435.
***001* (800) 222 0188**
www.keystone.com
www.virgin.com/holidays

Overall rating out of 10 **4** **This place is not up to much**

Lovelands Colorado

MOUNTAIN DATA

Top Lift at - 3871m

Ride Area 1365 acres

Bottom Lift at - 3231m

Vertical Drop - 735m

Number of Runs - 70

Longest -

TERRAIN LEVELS

Easy	**17%**
Intermediate	**42%**
Advanced	**41%**
Expert =	**6 runs**

TERRAIN TO SUITE

Freeride	**60%**
Trees	Yes
Backcountry	Yes
Freestyle	**20%**
Halfpipe	Yes 1
Terrain Park	Yes 1
Carving	**30%**

SNOW DATA

Average Snowfall
1097cm a season

Snowmaking
12% cover of the slopes

Winter Periods
Oct to May

Summer Riding
None

SLOPE ACCESS

Total Lifts = **11**

Uplift Rate 12,500 people an hour.

9 Chair lifts

2 Drag lifts

**Leashes Required*

Lift Times
8.30am to 4.00pm

Lift Pass Rates

1 Day pass	$41	Adult
1 Day pass	$17	Child
5 Day pass	$	

Travel Guide

Fly to **Denver,** transfer time is around 1 hour.

Bus services from **Denver** available by arrangement.

Route Planner:
From Denver, head west on I-70 via Idaho Springs and turning left onto the route 6 past Georgetown, to reach Loveland. The distance from Denver is 56 miles.

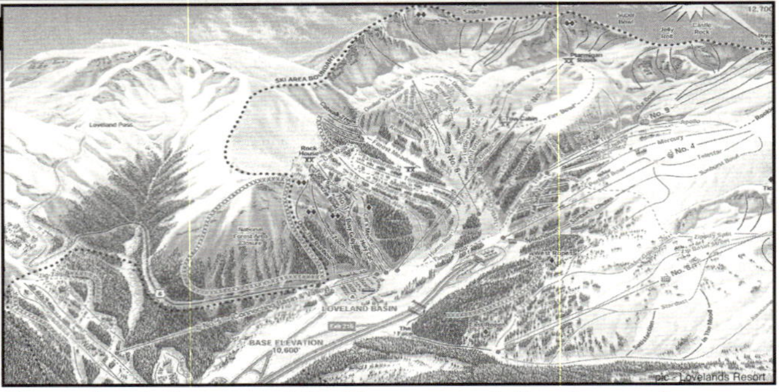

pic - Lovelands Resort

Lovelands is a resort that has a reputation for good snow, a long season, and a claim to have the world's highest quad chair lift which lets you off at an elevation of 3871 metres. Located close to **Denver**, is definitely a place that is worth a visit and a great one for day trippers, especially for the city slickers from Denver. Despite being close to Denver, however, overcrowding is not a problem and both the lift lines and pistes are often deserted. The resort has recently been investing a lot of dollars in expanding the terrain with the addition of another 400 acres of extreme slopes at the area known as the **Ridge**. A lot of money has also been spent on upgrading the snowmaking facilities to help boost the snowcover. Loveland is not the biggest hill in **Colorado**, but what you get is more than adequate and there are certainly smaller places than this one. What you have is a ridable area that stretches up from two points, **Loveland Valley** and **Loveland Basin** that are linked by chairlift and road. Loveland Valley is the smaller of the two areas with a cluster of runs that rise up through some thick wooded glade's that eventually thin out the further up you go. Loveland Basin, who's slopes stretched out around a high bowl above the entrance to the **Eisenhower Tunnel**, is the main area to ride with a good choice of runs from basic intermediate trails to some hardcore extreme runs with a few double black diamond extreme slopes.

Freeriders should grab the number **2** lift and head up to the **Ptarmigan** area where you will find lots of cool freeriding terrain. However, some of the best freeride terrain can be found off lift **8** in the **Zip Basin**. Here you will find some nice backcountry type terrain with a few gullies and bowls.

Freestylers have a decent terrain park along with an okay pipe, but in truth some of the natural features are better for air.

Carvers have a good resort with well maintained trails that are nicely laid out. Some of the best carving is off the number **6** lift.

Beginners can take a lesson here to help then tackle what is largely not a beginner's resort. That's not to say novices should stay away, it's just that the resort is more of an intermediate level.

While there area boasts a few shops and places to eat, this is not a resort as such. One okay option would be to stay down in **Denver** where you can't fail to find good local facilities.

For accommodation listings visit - www.worldsnowboardguide.com

Loveland Ski Area
P.O Box 899 Georgetown, CO 80444
***001* (303) 569 3203**
www.skiloveland.com.
www.virgin.com/holidays

Overall rating out of 10 **6** **Very good resort.**

Snowmass Colorado

MOUNTAIN DATA

Top Lift at - 3752m
Ride Area 3010 acres
Bottom Lift at - 2506m
Vertical Drop - 1246m
Number of Runs - 83
Longest - 4 miles (6.2km)

TERRAIN LEVELS

Easy	7%
Intermediate	55%
Advanced	18%
Expert =	20%

TERRAIN TO SUITE

Freeride	60%
Trees	Yes
Backcountry	Yes
Freestyle	25%
Halfpipe	Yes 2
Terrain Park	Yes 2
Carving	25%

SNOW DATA

Average Snowfall
762cm a season
Snowmaking
5% cover of the slopes
Winter Periods
Nov to April
Summer Riding
None

SLOPE ACCESS

Total Lifts = 20
Uplift Rate - 50,000 people an hour.
17 Chair lifts
3 Drag lifts
**Leashes Required*

Lift Times
8.30am to 4.00pm

Lift Pass Rates

1 Day pass	$63
3 Day pass	$177
5 Day pass	$285

Travel Guide

Fly to **Denver,** transfer time is 3½ hours.

Bus services from Denver are available to the resort.

Route Planner:
From Denver head west along I-70 via the Eisenhower Tunnel until you come to the junction for Hwy 82 with directions for Aspen. Head southwards to reach Snowmass.

pic - Snowmass Resort

Snowmass is the biggest of the resorts that make up the **Aspen** area, and the second largest resort in Colorado. With its four seperate peaks, Snowmass is an impressive resort with a lot going for it and warmly welcomes snowboarders. This has not always been the case within the Aspen group, where snobbish areas such as Aspen Mountain, still ban snowboarders. However, the 1,246 metres of vertical available here, means you don't have to go anywhere else. Snowmass is mainly an advanced/intermediate rider's retreat, with a good choice of double black diamond runs and trails through trees, steeps and awesome powder making this a place where everyone can get a fix.

Freeriders will go crazy here. **Snowmass** is a real pleasure and offers fantastic riding. Those wanting to cut some serious terrain should check out **Hanging Valley** and **Cirque** for double black steeps and powder bowls. The run known as **Baby Ruth** is also where advanced riders will get a real buzz. Snowmass offers lots of backcountry riding with organised tours: A*spen Powder Tours* runs trips for riders wanting the ultimate thrill, from $230 a day.

Freestylers have three halfpipes and a good terrain park, as well as a mountain riddled with natural hits. The main pipe is some 500ft long, with big walls and perfect transitions for getting massive amounts of air. The pipe was originally designed by pro *Jimi Scott*, and is easily reached off the **Funnel lift**. There is also a very good fun-park reached off the **Coney Glade** chair lift.

Carvers have a good selection of wide, open motorway flats for putting in some big carves, with an array of all-level, well groomed trails set out across the area. **Big Burn** reached off Lift **Number 4** is a good intermediate trail.

Beginners cutting their first snow should start at the base area from the **Fanny Hill** chair lift, before trying out the steeper stuff on the **Big Burn**. The local ski-school has a 3 day beginner's programme, that guarantees you will learn to ride: if you don't, you get an extra day's tuition free.

The base village has dozens of lodging options, with beds within easy reach of the bottom runs. Evenings are not up to much, but there is a lot more going on in nearby **Aspen**. For a drink, check out the *Copper Street Pier*, or *Eric's* for a game of pool. Be aware that Aspen is super $$$ dollar-hungry.

For accommodation listings visit - www.worldsnowboardguide.com

Snowmass Village at Aspen
P.O Box 1248 Aspen. CO 81611
***001* (970) 925 1220**
www.skiaspen.com
www.virgin.com/holidays

Overall rating out of 10 **5** **Okay resort but expensive**

Steamboat Colorado

MOUNTAIN DATA

Top Lift at - 3221m

Ride Area
2939 acres

Bottom Lift at - 2103m
Vertical Drop - 1118m
Number of Runs - 141
Longest - 3 miles (5km)

TERRAIN LEVELS

Easy	**13%**
Intermediate	**56%**
Advanced	**31%**
Expert =	**6 runs**

TERRAIN TO SUITE

Freeride	**60%**
Trees	Yes
Backcountry	Very good
Freestyle	**20%**
Halfpipe	Yes 2
Terrain Park	Yes 2
Carving	**20%**

SNOW DATA

Average Snowfall
744cm a season
Snowmaking
15% cover of the slopes
Winter Periods
Nov to April
Summer Riding
None

SLOPE ACCESS

Total Lifts = **22**
Uplift Rate - 34,658 people an hour.
20 Chair lifts
2 Drag lifts
**Leashes Required*

Lift Times
8.30am to 4.30pm

Lift Pass Rates

1 Day pass	$59
3 Day pass	$174
5 Day pass	$265

SLOPE ACTION

Snowboard Hire
Daily rates from $32
Kids from $27

Snowboard Tuition
Lesson, lift & hire
from $86 per day

Night Riding
None

Heli Boarding
Yes

Snowmobiles
Hire & tours

Mountain Cafes
9

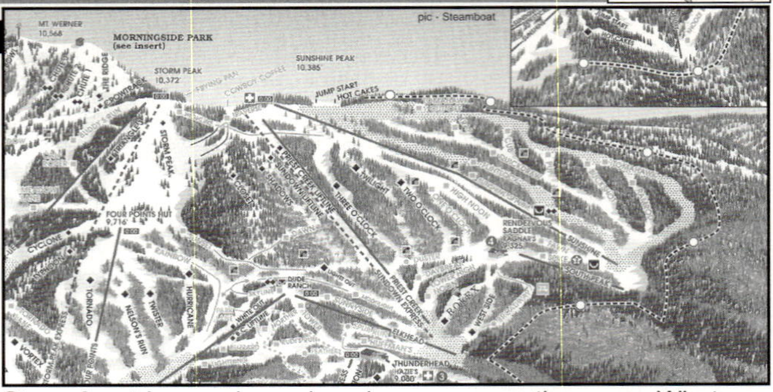

Steamboat is a curious place in more ways than one. What you get is an old mining town with a seemingly laid back approach coupled with a mountain that offers some great riding with over 2939 acres of terrain that is spread out over four tree-lined mountain peaks. Unfortunately, many will find Steamboat is certainly not the best place to spend a weeks vacation. Although this is not a bad place to visit in terms of the riding opportunities and the good annual snow record, its tacky dollar hungry, fur-clad ski-cowboy image will make most normal snowboarders want to throw up. However, Steamboat has a growing snowboard population and has made a real effort to drag itself into the 21st century (although having live bands playing on the lower slopes on a Friday afternoon is hardly ground breaking stuff). Still, the resort has several things in its favour. The resort offers some fantastic tree-riding, there's ample deep powder and some great carving slopes. There is also a couple of double black diamond trails offering extreme slopes for advanced riders to tackle along with some over-rated blacks for intermediate riders to try out. What is most notable here, are the trees and the options for backcountry snowboarding, which can be explored by taking a snowcat trip organised locally.

Freeriders can have a good time at Steamboat. If you're up to the grade, try riding the steeps on the **Meadows** of **Storm Peak**, where **Christmas Tree Bowl** and the neighbouring chutes will give you a good challenge. Alternatively, try cutting some deep powder tracks in areas like **Toutes**.

Freestylers can catch some decent natural air or sample the man-made hits in the **Maverick** terrain park on **Big Meadow.** There is also a good pipe called **'Dude Ranch'** ('Dude' - what a seriously lame name) which is located on the **Bashor** area and is of competition standard cut by a Pipe Dragon. Less poorly named is the **Beehive**, a small fun-park with a series of mini-hits for kids only, located on the **Spike** trail reachable off the **South Peak** lift.

Carvers have a number of very good descents on which to perfect their technique. **Steamboat** is also noted for its **Olympic** race runs, which can be used by snowboarders. Further more, this is also a place where speed skiers, and indeed extreme down hill mountain bikers, often come to practice their thing. Which means the mountain certainly has a number of very gnarly slopes where you can cut it at great speed, but don't go racing down fast runs in an out of control or dangerous manner, because not only will someone get seriously hurt, but the ski patrol will take a very dim view of your actions and throw you off the mountain.

Beginners and total novices will feel most left out here, for apart from some green runs snaking in and out of the higher grade trails, the easy stuff at the base area is often very tiresome. However, on a more positive note, **Steamboat** has an excellent ski and snowboard school and offers a number of teaching programmes with clinics aimed at all levels and ages.

Steamboat is a welcoming town even if it has a poncy feel about it. The town is loaded with all manner of attractions and is well equipped for making your stay a good one. You can choose to stay on or close to the slopes and the main resort facilities are well located to each other and for the slopes. However, being a dollar-hungry place, those of you on a tight budget may not be able to survive beyond a couple of days here. The cost of most things is unjustifiably high. Which is a shame (perhaps its a deliberate resort policy so they can attract dot.com millionaire's and keep low-lifes away). Around town you will find a host of things to do, from a climbing gym to an indoor ice rink. The town also has a number of shops, with most now catering for snowboarders, some even offer reasonable deals on board sales.

If you are rider intending to do a season here and will be looking for a job, then call the Human Resources department on (970) 871 5132, as there are always vacancies going.

Steamboat has a good selection of restaurants from fancy dining out joints to a number of fast food places, whether you have a steak or a burger, one thing is for sure, you can guarantee it will be top notch (mind you so will the price). You can eat out in style on the mountain at places like the *Bear River Bar & Grill* or the *Rendezvous Saddle* cafeteria.

Night-life in this over hyped town leaves a lot to be desired and can be best described as crap and aimed at middle-aged skiers with sad dress sense. They have way too much apres-ski nonsense here. However, the *Cellar bar* has a good deal going. For around $12 you get to drink as much as you can for two hours.

Steamboat has a very good selection of accommodation with loads of lodges, chalets and condo's to choose from, but nothing comes cheaply.
For accommodation listings visit - www.worldsnowboardguide.com

Summary: On the mountain this a great place to ride with some excellent treeriding to try out and some cool carving runs. But off the slopes the place is way too stuck up.
Money wise: Everything is way over priced and not always good value.

Overall rating out of 10 **8**

Steamboat Resort
2305 Mount Werner Circle, Steamboat Springs. CO 80487
General info **001 (970) 879 6111**
Reservations **001 (800) 922 2722**
Snowphone **001 (970) 879 7300**
www.steamboat-ski.com
www.virgin.com/holidays

pic - Cynthia Hunter/ Steamboat

pic - Cynthia Hunter

Travel Guide

Fly to **Denver** International
Transfer time to resort = **3** hours.
Local airport = **Yampa Valley,** 22 miles away.
Approximate global air travel times to **Denver**

from:		
	London	9 hours
	New York	$3^{1/2}$ hours
	Frankfurt	10 hours

There are daily bus services from both Denver and Yampa Valley airports direct to Steamboat.

Trains: None

Route Planner
Denver *via Kremmling 70*

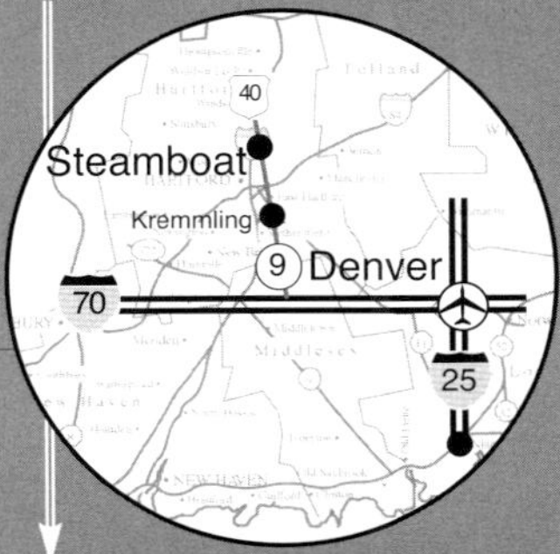

Steamboat = 157 miles
Drive time is about **3** hours

Vail Colorado

MOUNTAIN DATA

Top Lift at - 3500m

Ride Area 2091 acres

Bottom Lift at - 2475m

Vertical Drop - 1024m

Number of Runs - 174

Longest -4.5 miles (7.2km)

TERRAIN LEVELS

Easy	**28%**
Intermediate	**32%**
Advanced	**40%**
Expert =	

TERRAIN TO SUITE

Freeride	**60%**
Trees	Yes
Backcountry	Yes
Freestyle	**20%**
Halfpipe	Yes 2
Terrain Park	Yes 2
Carving	**20%**

SNOW DATA

Average Snowfall
850cm a season

Snowmaking
3% cover of the slopes

Winter Periods
Nov to April

Summer Riding
None

SLOPE ACCESS

Total Lifts = **32**

Uplift Rate -51,781 people an hour.

1 Gondola, **22** Chair lifts

9 Drag lifts

**Leashes Required*

Lift Times
8.30am to 4.00pm

Lift Pass Rates

1 Day pass	$63
3 Day pass	$189
5 Day pass	$285

SLOPE ACTION

Snowboard Hire
Daily rates from $35
Kids from $28

Snowboard Tuition
Lesson, lift & hire
from $105 per day

Night Riding
Yes

Heli Boarding
Yes

Snowmobiles
Hire & tours

Mountain Cafes
20

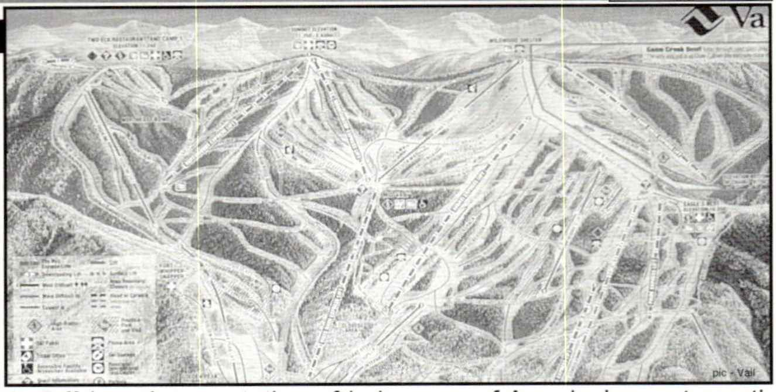

pic - Vail

Vail has the reputation of being one of America's most prestigious (ie snobbish) ski resorts, and in some respects it's true. The town of Vail, a bizarre imitation of a 'typical' Swiss alpine village, is centred around the base of the resort and is hellishly expensive. However, there are loads of good reasons to visit Vail, which include the large amount of terrain on offer (over 4,000 acres) and Vail's extremely healthy and positive attitude towards snowboarding. The terrain park has 3 halfpipes and 12 runs, and is also open to skiers although thankfully, it's frequented almost exclusively by snowboarders. One major point regarding Vail, is that it is a very popular resort resulting in some long lift queues throughout the season. But in terms of climate and cost, a good time to visit is late season when the snow is soft and the price of lift tickets drop dramatically.

Freeriders will find this place heaven. Vail's **Back Bowls** will stoke you beyond belief when you see what is on offer. In order to find out where the best places are, you should pick up a copy of the free pocket-sized snowboard mountain map which will point you in the direction of the best boarding trails and hits. The most popular backcountry includes **Ptarmigan Ridge**, a 25ft cornice jump and **Kengis Khan**, another cornice not suitable for sufferers of vertigo. The cliffs under **Chair 4** are easier to access, as long as you don't mind your slams being applauded by everyone on the lift. The tree run **Cheeta Gully** is marked as one of the special snowboard trails and will test the most proficient rider.

Freestylers are extremely well catered for on **Vail's** slopes. *Burton Snowboards* have an area called the **Burton Super Centre** located off lift **4**, where you can try out Burtons latest kit or ride their small park which has a few hits. Vail also provides a major half pipe and terrain park known as the Golden Peak. Both park and pipe are groomed to perfection. The pipe has huge walls offering great transitions while the park is loaded with not only a major series of gaps, spines etc, but also a chill out area that has video screens, pumping music and drink vending services.

Carvers have some excellent blue trails and some challenging fast blacks. Many of the runs start out as one grade and then suddenly become another, so study a lift map in order to negotiate the best spots with ease. The **Avanti** lift gives access to some really nice carving trails. The Mountain Top lift also allows you to ride in style on a number of extremely good trails.

Beginners have a mountain with so many easy trails and excellent progression possibilities, that if you fail here, you must be a complete loser. The areas of **Golden Peak** are perfect for learning the basics, although it can become a little clustered around midday, especially at weekends and holidays. Vail's snowboard school is excellent and has a number of instruction programmes with prices from $105 high peak for a full days session.

If you reckon that **Vail** is just about the slopes, think again as there are heaps of things going on with an amazing amount of great local services. The area is huge, so use of the free shuttle bus may be necessary depending on where you base yourself. But, and it's a big but, the people who set the charges should all be locked up. Vail is super dollar-hungry - nothing comes cheap, not even bubble-gum. The place also has an overdose of visiting punters. Still locals know exactly what to do to make your stay a good one. They offer a high level of service whether you're buying a burger or booking in to a hotel.

Jobseekers: Stacks and stacks of vacancies exist all season, tel for details (970) 349 2333

Eating in the resort or around the main area will destroy your bank balance or father's credit card. Prices are silly, but there are plenty of semi-affordable, fast-food joints to check out. To tickle your taste buds, why not check out *Pazzo's,* which serves a good helping of cheap pasta or where you can have a 'do it yourself pizza'. *Ti Amo* is another noted restaurant, where you can get a large and reasonably priced steak .

Night-life, as you'd hope, is extremely good. The offerings are excellent, with good bars and okay places to boogie well into the early hours. But if you want to pull a local chick for the night, you better have the money to impress her because nothing comes cheap, not even the talent. Check out *Nick's* or *Skieka's* which are very popular.

Accommodation consists of a selection of some 30,000 visitor beds and providing you don't mind not being slopeside, you will find affordable lodging. Many opt to stay out in one of the nearby villages with cheaper housing and on average, only a 20 minute 'commute' to the slope. Check Vails web site for a full listing of accommodation.

For accommodation listings visit - www.worldsnowboardguide.com

Summary: Absolutely fantastic mountain offering great riding for ever style and level of rider. Great local services in and around the resort with lots going on.
Money wise: Criminally insane prices for everything, but worth it.

Overall rating out of 10 **10**

Vail Associates
P.O Box 7 Vail
CO 81658
General info **001 (970) 476 5601**
Reservations **001 (970) 476 5601**
Snowphone **001 (970) 476 5601**
www.vail.com
www.virgin.com/holidays

pics - Vail Associates

Travel Guide

Fly to **Denver** International
Transfer time to resort = **2** hours.
Local airport = **Eagle County,** 30 miles away.
Approximate global air travel times to **Denver**

from:		
	London	**9** hours
	New York	**3**$^{1/2}$ hours
	Frankfurt	**10** hours

There are daily bus services from both Denver and Vail/Eagle County airports direct to Vail.

Trains: None

Route Planner
Denver *via Interstate 70*

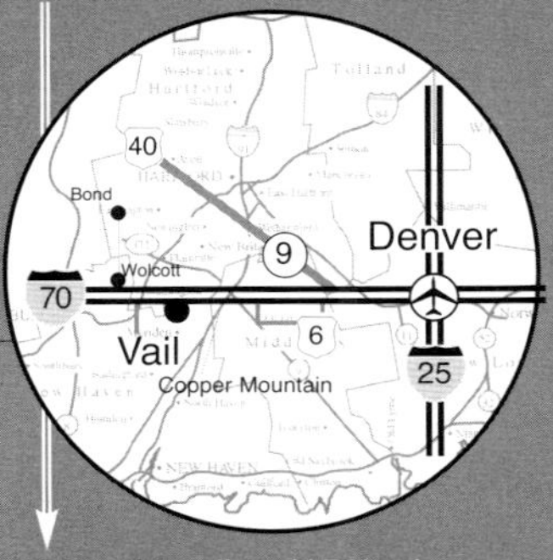

Vail = 97 miles (156km)
Drive time is about **1**$^{3/4}$ hours

Telluride Colorado

MOUNTAIN DATA

Top Lift at - 2660m

Ride Area
1050 acres

Bottom Lift at - 3735m

Vertical Drop - 1074m

Number of Runs - 64

Longest - 3 miles (5km)

TERRAIN LEVELS

Easy	21%
Intermediate	47%
Advanced	32%
Expert =	18 runs

TERRAIN TO SUITE

Freeride	60%
Trees	Yes
Backcountry	Yes
Freestyle	20%
Halfpipe	Yes 2
Terrain Park	Yes 4
Carving	30%

SNOW DATA

Average Snowfall
762cm a season

Snowmaking
15% cover of the slopes

Winter Periods
Nov to April

Summer Riding
None

SLOPE ACCESS

Total Lifts = **12**

Uplift Rate - 12,500 people an hour.

2 Gondolas, **8** Chair lift

2 Drag lifts

**Leashes Required*

Lift Times
8.30am to 4.00pm

Lift Pass Rates

1 Day pass	$57
3 Day pass	$165
5 Day pass	$245

Travel Guide

Fly to **Denver,** with flights to Telluride Domestic Airport, 6 miles away.

Buses from airports are available by arrangement.

Route Planner: From Denver, go west on I-70 to Grand Junction and then south on Hwy's 50 & 550 unit you pick up signs for route 62 for Placerville and to Telluride along the 145.

Telluride sticks two fingers up to convention when it comes to the norm in **Colorado**! Why? Well it's simple, no tackiness, no bull, no hype, no snotty nose yuppies, none of it, what you have here is easily summed up as '*superb*'. Telluride, which is said to have been robbed over a hundred years ago by **Butch Cassady**, is full on, but unlike other resorts in Colorado, this wild west town won't rob you blind. Telluride, which is an old mining town, is set in the **San Juan Mountains** and is a skiers and snowboarders heaven that offers every style and ability of rider something to saviour, especially beginners as this place has to be one of the best novices resort in the whole state.

Freeriders who like fast hard steeps will love it here as Telluride offers some fantastic riding. The **Kant-Mak-M**, the **Spiral** and the **Plunge** runs are a series of really challenging steeps that will either leave you seriously bruised if you bail, or make you feel like a god if you complete them in style. These are serious double black diamond trails and not for wimps.

Freestylers who are happy to roam around riding off natural hits are in for a pleasant surprise. The mountain has a number of natural pipes and banks. The **West Drain** slope offers some cool riding due in part to it being a natural half pipe. The mountain also boasts a big 8 metre plus terrain park which is loaded with toys for gaining air, such as logs, rails, spines etc. Along with a number of smaller terrain parks dotted around the mountain, there is also a massive man made halfpipe.

Carvers have a mountain that lends itself perfectly well to cruising at speed, although it should be said that many of the trails are a bit short. Note also that some runs are only pisted on oneside, which means one side being smooth and the other bumpy.

Beginners are probably the one group who will feel most pleased here and most at ease because **Telluride** not only has a good percentage of easy trails, they are also extremely well set out and very easy to negotiate. Instruction services are also very good.

Off the slopes things are just as good as on the them. There are two options to choose from for lodging and local facilities in either **Telluride's** main town or up in the **Mountain Village**. Which every you choose you wont be disappointed as both offer good accommodation, great places to dine and a number of cool bars.

For accommodation listings visit - www.worldsnowboardguide.com

Telluride
565 Mountain Village Boulevard, Telluride CO 81435
***001* (970) 728 6900**
www.skiloveland.com.com
www.virgin.com/holidays

Overall rating out of 10 **8** **Excellent place to ride**

Winterpark Colorado

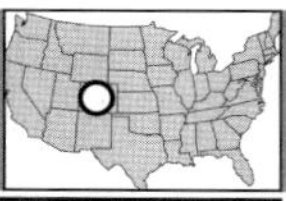

MOUNTAIN DATA

Top Lift at - 3676m
Ride Area 2886 acres
Bottom Lift at - 2743m
Vertical Drop - 933m
Number of Runs - 134
Longest - 5 miles (8km)

TERRAIN LEVELS

Easy	22%
Intermediate	41%
Advanced	20%
Expert =	9%

TERRAIN TO SUITE

Freeride	50%
Trees	Yes
Backcountry	Yes
Freestyle	25%
Halfpipe	Yes 1
Terrain Park	Yes 2
Carving	25%

SNOW DATA

Average Snowfall
950cm a season
Snowmaking
11% cover of the slopes
Winter Periods
Nov to April
Summer Riding
None

SLOPE ACCESS

Total Lifts = **22**
Uplift Rate - 35,000 people an hour.
19 Chair lifts
3 Drag lifts
**Leashes Required*

Lift Times
8.30am to 4.00pm

Lift Pass Rates

1 Day pass	$50
3 Day pass	$129
5 Day pass	$210

Travel Guide

Fly to **Denver Int**, with a transfer time of 1½ hour.

Bus services from **Denver** available by arrangement. **Trains** services go to Fraser a few miles away.

Route Planner:
From Denver, head west on I-70 via Eisenhower tunnel to exit 232 on Hwy 40 direction Granby.
Denverto resort = **67** miles.

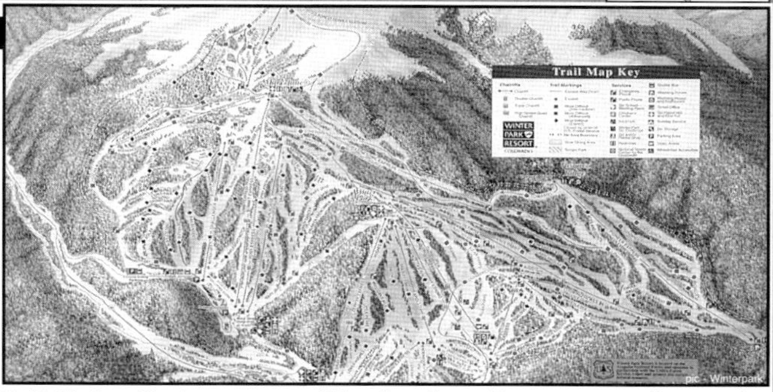

pic - Winterpark

Winter Park - a mere 67 miles from **Denver**, nestling at the base of **Berthoud Pass** at an altitude of 2,743 feet, is said to be the fifth largest resort in the USA, with over 2886 acres of terrain. The old saying that 'size always matters' doesn't ring true at Winter, since although this place is vast, it is not as great as the hype dictates. However, **Colorado** is famous for its powder snow and in fairness, Winter Park snags more than its fair share, with an average annual snowfall of 350 inches and plenty of blue sky days. The high tree line of Winter Park means that even when there is low cloud, visibility is still good. Winter Park is actually two mountains, **Winter Park** and **Mary Jane**. Winter Park has trails for all standards of rider and is well groomed. What makes this place somewhat dull is that it is really tame, with hardly any fast, challenging terrain. The best runs (if such exist) are on the **Mary Jane** slopes and are mostly black trails.

Freeriders will find plenty of okay tree runs around both mountains with near perfect spaced trees. However, don't expect to ride all the ferns at any great speed. There is some good riding to be had in **Parsenn Bowl** on **June Mountain**, and on the runs of the **Challenger**.

Freestylers are presented with two fun-parks. One runs through a wooded glade and is an interesting idea, but you need to be wary of going too fast since the trees can painfully stop you dead in your tracks. The other snowboard park is quite compact in size, but instead of having the standard jump following jump, there is a far more 'line' orientated layout.

Carvers content with wide pistes where they can pose doing big arcs, will find Winter Park right up their street. Much of what you find on Winter Park mountain will suit carvers.

Beginners also fair well here. The easy trails, and indeed some of those classed as intermediate, can be ridden within a few days if you put your mind to it.

Winter Park's lodging is 6 miles down the valley, where you can find a good selection of places to stay at affordable prices. The evenings are not too hectic, but you can party. Check out *Lord Gore Arms* which shows videos every night with DJ's and bands, or *The Pub* for Sunday night disco mayhem.

For accommodation listings visit - www.worldsnowboardguide.com

Winter Park Resort
677 Winter Park Drive, Po Box 36 W/Park. CO 80482
001 (970) 726 5514 **www.skiwinterpark.com**
www.virgin.com/holidays

Overall rating out of 10 **4** **Ideal place for old age pensioners**

GENERAL INFO AND FACTS

Capital - Boise
Language - English
Currency - US Dollar
Alcohol drinking age - 21
Drugs - Cannabis is illegal
Death Penalty - Exists
Age of consent for Sex - 16
Electricity Supply - 110 Volts AC
Area phone Code - 208
Provincial sales tax - 4% on all goods and services

IDAHO DRIVE GUIDE

All vehicles drive on the right side of the road.
Speed Limits -
Motorways 70mph (112kph)
Highways 55mph (90kph)
Towns 30mph (50kph)
Road Info 001 (208) 336 6600
Fuel is sold in Gallons

TRAVEL CONTACTS

Gateway Airports
Boise (Gowen Field)
Flights from London take around 9 hours 50 mins (not direct).

Mountain
GMT -7 hours

AREA INFORMATION

Denver Convention
Idaho Department of Commerce
Po Box 83720
700 West State. ID
tel: 001 (208) 334 2470

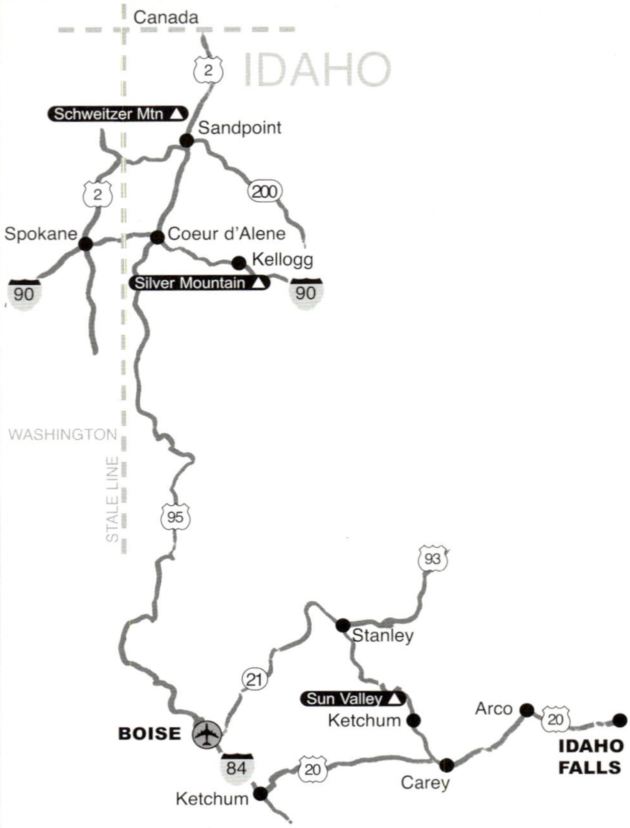

pic - Burton Snowboards

Schweitzer Mountain

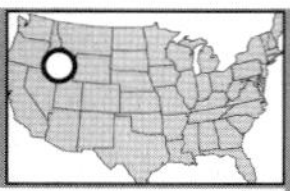

U S A

Idaho

MOUNTAIN DATA

Top Lift at - 1951m

Ride Area 2350 acres

Bottom Lift at - 1217m

Vertical Drop - 732m

Number of Runs - 58

Longest - 2.7 miles (4km)

TERRAIN LEVELS

Easy	**20%**
Intermediate	**40%**
Advanced	**35%**
Expert =	

TERRAIN TO SUITE

Freeride	**50%**
Trees	Yes
Backcountry	Yes
Freestyle	**25%**
Halfpipe	Yes 1
Terrain Park	Yes 1
Carving	**25%**

SNOW DATA

Average Snowfall
762 cm a season

Snowmaking
10% cover of the slopes

Winter Periods
Nov to April

Summer Riding
None

SLOPE ACCESS

Total Lifts = **6**

Uplift Rate - 7092 people an hour

6 Chair lifts

**Leashes Required*

Lift Times
9.00 to 4.00pm

Lift Pass Rates
1 Day pass $35
Night pass $20
Season pass $249

Travel Guide

Fly to **Spokane Int,** which is 86 miles south west.

Bus services from Spokane take 90 mins to the resort.

Route Planner:
From Spokane, take I-90 east and then Hwy 95 north via the town of Sandpoint. Schweitzer is another 2 miles on.

Lying about an hour's drive north of **Couer D'Alene, Idaho,** (and about an hour and a half south of the **Canadian** border) is the town of **Sandpoint**. Sandpoint is in the lucky position of having one of the coolest snowboarding spots in the North-western United States. A mere 10 minutes drive up a beautiful wooded ascent takes you to the **Schweitzer** basin. Probably unheard of by anyone that hasn't spent time in the area. On top of the amazingly laid back atmosphere of the Northwest in general, Schweitzer enjoys a very low "I snowboard so I'm great" bullshit factor, a problem that needs addressing both in the **UK** and central states like **Utah** and **Colorad**o. The resort has a good lift system with reasonably priced lift tickets at $35 a day for the whole mountain - this may also include some excellent night riding on one of the many well lit runs. If you haggle, you might get some bargains for multi-day tickets, or if you are with a group.

Freeriders are assured plenty of powder days and an enormously varied selection of terrain from the super steep chutes on the west side of the front half of the mountain, to an amazingly long (and tiring) blue run that starts from one of several high speed, no-queue lifts about 100 feet from the day-lodge. The ridge that links the runs together along the top of the mountain also provides a breathtaking view of **Lake Pend O'Reille.**

Freestylers have a magical mountain do to their tricks on. A favourite with local students, this overlooked mountain provides some great natural kicks, a fantastic half pipe, a boardercross course and an altogether impressive fun park called **Ground Zero** where competitions are held throughout the season period.

Carvers have plenty of groomed stuff on offer and speed perverts can make good on runs such as Cathedral and Zip

Beginners have no need to worry here as all the novice runs (recently expanded), are well away from the main runs so helping to prevent mass collisions, and serviced by a separate chair lift.

All your local needs are mainly provided down in Sandpoint 2 miles away. There is some accommodation available at the base area close to the slopes such as *The Green Gables Lodge*. Far cheaper lodging can be found in **Sandpoint** where you will find a basic but okay selection of shops, restaurants and bars. For a burger try the *Powder House* and for a beer give *Roxy's* a try.

For accommodation listings visit - www.worldsnowboardguide.com

Schweitzer Mountain
10000 Schweitzer Basin Mtn, Sandpoint, ID 83864
***001* (208) 263 9555**
www.schweitzer.com
www.virgin.com/holidays

Overall rating out of 10 **6** **Really cool resort**

Silver Star Idaho

MOUNTAIN DATA

Top Lift at - 1920m

Ride Area 1500 acres

Bottom Lift at - 1250m

Vertical Drop - 671m

Number of Runs - 50

Longest - 3 miles (5km)

TERRAIN LEVELS

Easy	**15%**
Intermediate	**45%**
Advanced	**40%**
Expert =	

TERRAIN TO SUITE

Freeride	**30%**
Trees	Yes
Backcountry	Yes
Freestyle	**20%**
Halfpipe	Yes 1
Terrain Park	Yes 1
Carving	**50%**

SNOW DATA

Average Snowfall
635cm a season

Snowmaking
15% cover of the slopes

Winter Periods
Nov to April

Summer Riding
None

SLOPE ACCESS

Total Lifts = **7**

Uplift Rate - 8,200 people an hour.

1 Gondolas, **5** Chair lifts

1 Drag lift

**Leashes Required*

Lift Times
9.30am to 3.30pm

Lift Pass Rates

1 Day pass	$34 week
1 Day pass	$34 week end
Season pass	$199

Travel Guide

Fly to **Spokane Int,** which is 70 miles west of the resort.

Buses from Spokane take 80 mins to Kellogg.

Route Planner:
From Spokane, take I-90 west past Coeur d'Alene and then a further 40 miles on to Kellogg. Silver Mountain is only 1/4 of a mile form Kellogg.

A **smaller** resort than Schweitzer, and much closer to civilisation, is Kellogg, Idaho. A small mining town in north central Idaho, about 40 minutes from Couer D'Alene, Kellogg has the honour of running the longest gondola ride in the world, which culminates at the day lodge of **Silver Mountain**. Essentially composed of two resorts, the new Silver Mountain lift system and the incorporated "**Jackass Ski Bowl**" provide a superb set of runs, although the intermediate rider is better catered for than freestylers or super euro-carvers. In fact, the only real downside to this hidden gem of a mountain is the fact that it is infested with cat tracks linking one run to the next. Easy on skis, a real drag on a board. However, to be fair to the resort management, they are dealing with the problem by getting rid of a lot of the cat tracks. Overall, the mountain offers a fair selection of long steeps with generally great snow and weather conditions. The seven lifts are quick and easy to negotiate and mercifully lift lines are tiny. Slope facilities are a bit suspect, the day lodge is far less impressive than that at Schweitzer, and the food is both mediocre and extortionate. But a major plus is the very low lift prices, with a day pass from only $24 bucks during the week.

Freeriders will find that the backcountry stuff is thin on the ground - unlike tree stumps, grit, and large rocks, which seem to litter a good deal of the area outside the fences. However, some very nice, but challenging, freeriding can be had on areas like the **Rendezvous** or down the **Warner Peak.**

Freestylers note that this is not a place loaded with natural freestyle terrain. However, to counter this there is a good terrain park and halfpipe called the **Trench** which is built and shaped to conform with competition standards located up on Noah's.

Carvers can ride with some degree of style here, with a number of long cruising trails that are groomed to perfection. The **Tamarack** is a fantastic two and a half mile long trail to try out.

Beginners have a mountain that is well suited to their needs, with a host of novice trails offering easy sedate descents.

You can lodge close to the slopes, but in general the main thing to do is base yourself down **Kellogg**, which is 2 minutes away. The town offers a good choice of local facilities with very reasonable prices for lodging and general living. The *Silver Ridge Mountain Lodge* offers some good packages.

Silver Mountain Ski Area
610 Bunker Avenue, Kellogg ID 83837
***001* (208) 783 1111**
www.silvermt.com
www.virgin.com/holidays

Overall rating out of 10 **5** **Okay resort but very basic**

Sun Valley Idaho

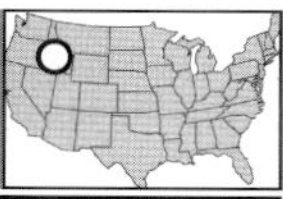

MOUNTAIN DATA

Top Lift at - 2789m
Ride Area 2054 acres
Bottom Lift at - 1753m
Vertical Drop - 1036m
Number of Runs - 78
Longest - 3 miles (5km)

TERRAIN LEVELS

Easy	36%
Intermediate	42%
Advanced	22%
Expert =	

TERRAIN TO SUITE

Freeride	50%
Trees	Yes
Backcountry	Yes
Freestyle	20%
Halfpipe	Yes 1
Terrain Park	Yes 1
Carving	20%

SNOW DATA

Average Snowfall
589cm a season
Snowmaking
78% cover of the slopes
Winter Periods
Nov to April
Summer Riding
None

SLOPE ACCESS

Total Lifts = **18**
Uplift Rate - 28,180 people an hour.
17 Chair lifts
1 Drag lift
**Leashes Required*

Lift Times
8.30am to 4.00pm

Lift Pass Rates
1 Day pass $59
3 Day pass $171
5 Day pass $284

Travel Guide

Fly to **Boise Int**, with a transfer time of **2 1/2** hours.

Bus services from **Boise** available by arrangement.

Route Planner:
From Boise, head south on I-84 and then via hwy 20 at Mountain Home to hwy 75 heading north following signs for Ketchum and then onto Sun Valley.

pic - Sun Valley

Sun Valley dates back decades and comes with a fair share of its own history. Said to be the **USA's** oldest ski resorts, Sun Valley has managed stay up with the times and today is a resort that is a match for any other destination in the country. Located in the southen part of **Idaho** and east of the capital **Bosie**, what you have here is a resort for every one from advanced air heads to total first timers, although it's fair to say that the beginner terrain is a bit limited. On and off the slopes the whole area has a rather strange feel to it with a mixture of the *Old Wild West* and a hint of **Europe** thrown in. It isset to a back drop of a large ridable area which covers over 2000 acres and split over two main areas known as **Dollar/Elkhorn** and **Bald Mountain**. Dollar/Elkhorn area the smaller and best for beginners while Bald Mountain is the place to head for to ride some advanced steeps. Whichever area you try out, you will be met with excellent slope facilities which incorporates a high tech snowmaking system that covers over 78% of the slopes.

Freeriders who know what life is about and can handle a board at speed will be able to prove it on the slopes up on **Bald Mountain** which has a good selection of advanced and intermediate trails. The bowls below the **Seattle Ridge** are superb and will keep you amused for days with some nice powder stashes.

Freestylers are well catered for here with a halfpipe that measures 350 foot long by 80 foot wide and is located on the **Dollar** area. Riders can also purchase a budget priced lift ticket that covers Dollar and the pipe area. Around the whole area freestylers will find loads of awesome natural hits to get air off.

Carvers who consider themselves to be of the advanced grade, should look no further than the slopes off **Bald Mountain** where you'll find a first class selection of long, well pitched cruising runs.

Beginners should be aware of the difference between the main areas. If you are a total first timer to snowboarding then stay away from **Bald Mountain** and check out the offerings on **Dollar**. The local ski school offers clinics from $40 a session for all grades.

Off the slopes, **Sun Valley** is a resort that is fully geared up to handle visitors needs. There is a good selection of slope-side accommodation and excellent resort services with some nice restaurants and good bars, but note this is not a cheap resort.

For accommodation listings visit - www.worldsnowboardguide.com

Sun Valley Resort
1 Sun Valley Road, Box 10, Sun Valley, ID 83353
001 (208) 622 2231
www.sunvalley.com
www.virgin.com/holidays

Overall rating out of 10 **8** **Very good all round resort**

Resort	Page
Sugarloaf/USA	99
Sunday River	100

GENERAL INFO AND FACTS

Capital - Augusta
Language - English
Currency - US Dollar
Alcohol drinking age - 21
Drugs - Cannabis is illegal
Death Penalty - Dosen't Exist
Age of consent for Sex - 16
Electricity Supply - 110 Volts AC
Area phone Code - 207
Provincial sales tax -

MAINE DRIVE GUIDE

All vehicles drive on the right side of the road.
Speed Limits -
Motorways 70mph (112kph)
Highways 55mph (90kph)
Towns 30mph (50kph)
Road Info 001 (207) 287 3427
Fuel is sold in Gallons

TRAVEL CONTACTS

Gateway Airports
Portland
Flights from London take around 5 hours 30 mins (direct).

Amtrax Railroad
tel: 001-800 872 7245

Greyhound Buses
tel: 001 (207) 772 6587

Mountain
GMT -5 hours

AREA INFORMATION

Visitor Information
Maine Publicity Bureau
Po Box 2300, Hallowell 04347
tel: 001 (207) 772 0690

pic - K2 Snowboards - Brian Savard

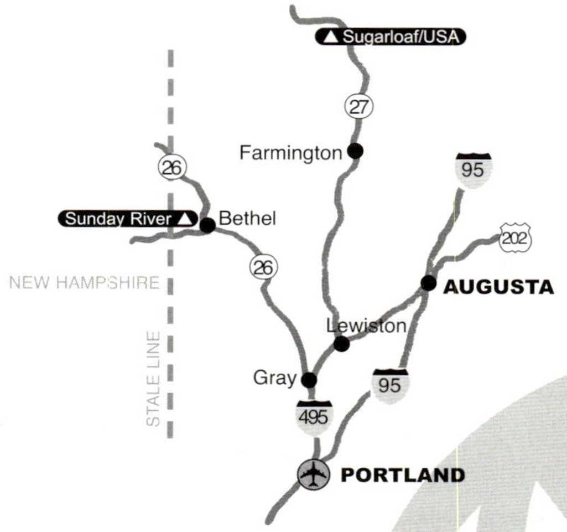

Sugarloaf/USA

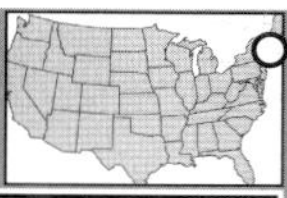

pic - David Brownell/Sugarloaf/USA

MOUNTAIN DATA

Top Lift at - 1291m

Ride Area 1400 acres

Bottom Lift at - 427m
Vertical Drop - 865m
Number of Runs - 126
Longest - 3 miles (5km)

TERRAIN LEVELS

Easy	24%
Intermediate	28%
Advanced	48%
Expert =	

TERRAIN TO SUITE

Freeride	35%
Trees	Yes
Backcountry	Yes
Freestyle	20%
Halfpipe	Yes 1
Terrain Park	Yes 1
Carving	45%

SNOW DATA

Average Snowfall
609 cm a season
Snowmaking
92% cover of the slopes
Winter Periods
Oct to May
Summer Riding
None

SLOPE ACCESS

Total Lifts = **14**
Uplift Rate - 20,000 people an hour.
13 Chair lifts
1 Drag lift
**Leashes Required*

Lift Times
8.30 to 3.30pm

Lift Pass Rates

1 Day pass	$51
2 Day pass	$147
5 Day pass	$245

Travel Guide

Fly to **Portland** which is 110 miles away.

Bus services from Portland can take a good 3 hours.

Route Planner:
From Portland travel north on the I-95 to Augusta, then take the 27 via Farmington to reach the resort. The journey by car will take about $2^{1/2}$ hours.

By east coast standards, **Sugarloaf/USA** is a big resort and a highly rated one that is well worth taking the time to visit. Located around two and a half hours drive time from Portland, this is a relatively easy place to get to and one could quite easily spend a week riding here on a mountain that has the only tree-less summit with lift access in the east. Another notable point is that unlike many other east coast resorts, Sugarloaf/USA manages a longer season than many other east coast destinations as the resort is able to keep hold of its snow very well. What's more, they back up their real snow with snowmaking facilities that cover almost 92% of the mountain. In truth this is a mountain that will mainly appeal to freeriders and carvers. The 126 well groomed and well set out runs offer some very very challenging runs with the option to ride down some extreme steeps and fast double diamond black trails.

Freeriders are going to feel very much at home here, with a good choice of descents that include acres of summit bowl riding and over 500 acres of treeriding terrain. Some of the most challenging terrain to check out can be found off the **Spillway** chair lift, while for a less stressing descent, the **Gauge** is okay.

Freestylers can be seen kicking off natural hits all over this mountain as the place lends itself very nicely to natural freestyling. If you can't find a decent hit to please your desires, than Sugarloaf/USA has a massive terrain park and large halfpipe with huge walls and nice transitions. The terrain park comes loaded with hits galore with rails, spines and big gaps, there is also a boarder cross circuit with a number of hits and banks.

Carvers of all levels will find an abundance of runs to choose from which are laid out all over the mountain starting out at the summit and allowing for long cruising runs all the way back home.

Beginners are presented with numerous trails that are mainly laid out across the lower section of the mountain and although the resort has a lot of good novice areas, the main section is often clogged up with skiers and others using the routes as access to the base, and base lifts.

Local facilities are well placed for the slopes with lots of condo's available for letting at reasonable rates. Around the resort you will find a good selection of restaurants and a number of nightspots.
For accommodation listings visit - www.worldsnowboardguide.com

Sugarloaf/USA
RR 1 Box 500, Carrabassett Valley, ME 04947
***001* (207) 237 2000**
www.sugarloaf.com
www.virgin.com/holidays

Overall rating out of 10 **7** **Good east coast resort**

Sunday River Maine

MOUNTAIN DATA

Top Lift at - 975m

Ride Area 640 acres

Bottom Lift at - 244m

Vertical Drop - 713m
Number of Runs - 126
Longest - 3 miles (5km)

TERRAIN LEVELS

Easy	**26%**
Intermediate	**36%**
Advanced	**38%**
Expert =	**6 runs**

TERRAIN TO SUITE

Freeride	**60%**
Trees	Yes
Backcountry	Poor
Freestyle	**20%**
Halfpipe	Yes 3
Terrain Park	Yes 5
Carving	**20%**

SNOW DATA

Average Snowfall
635cm a season
Snowmaking
92% cover of the slopes
Winter Periods
Oct to May
Summer Riding
None

SLOPE ACCESS

Total Lifts = **18**
Uplift Rate - 32,000 people an hour.
15 Chair lifts
3 Drag lifts
**Leashes Required*

Lift Times
8.30am to 4.00pm

Lift Pass Rates

1 Day pass	$49
3 Day pass	$138
5 Day pass	$230

SLOPE ACTION

Snowboard Hire
Daily rates from $28
Kids from $22

Snowboard Tuition
Lesson, lift & hire from $60 per day

Night Riding
No

Heli Boarding
No

Snowmobiles
Hire & tours

Mountain Cafes
6

Sunday River, which happens to be one of the major resorts in the **American Skiing Co's** portfolio, has rapidly grown from a local snowboarder's haunt to a fairly happening place in a very short space of time. Located a stone's throw away from the state border with **New Hampshire**, Sunday River attracts a lot of city dwellers from **Portland** and other nearby towns, to its simple but extremely well laid out slopes that cover eight linked mountains with three resort base areas. Once you arrive, it's not long before you appreciate just why this place is a popular destination with many of **Maine's** snowboarders and skiers alike as this is an excellent east coast resort which is thick with trees from the top to bottom on all the mountains. All the runs are hacked out from the dense pine to form a cluster of trails suitable for all styles and level of rider, in particular freeriders who know how to go for it. The eight mountain peaks are all open to snowboarders, with over 120 well looked after runs that get a good annual covering of real snow and are backed up by major snowmaking facilities that covers nearly all of the trails. The one off putting point is the crowds, particularly at weekends when the whole mountain can become a bit busy. However, to be fair, with such a good lift system linking all the spread out trails, time spent in lift lines is kept to a minimum.

Freeriders will find that a week's stay here will not be wasted provided you get out and explore all eight mountains. Each one offers something a little different to the last, although in the main they don't vary too much. Still, the resort management have planned the runs and offer different slope pitches and terrain features that will catch you out if you are not concentrating on what you are doing. For those riders who can handle fast steeps, the double blacks on **Oz Peak** and **Jordan Bowl** (especially the double black Caramba) are the places to head for. However, beware of **Kansas**, a long, flat muscle-pumping traverse used to get you back to the main area, the trick here is to keep you speed up. Some good tree-riding can be found on the **Baker Mountain**.

Freestylers will find lots of natural hits to catch air, and plenty of places for jibbing off logs and other obstacles. However, for those who like things laid on, **Sunday** offers a lot more than many other resorts by providing five terrain parks loaded with all sorts of hits, a boardercross circuit and three halfpipes.

Carvers who like speed and steeps mixed in together can crank some fast turns on the **White Heat** trails, which is one of the steepest runs on the east coast. The trails on the North Peak are ideal for intermediate riders who like to take it easy.

Beginners here have a resort that is superb for learning at with a large choice of easy runs to try out. The local ski-school offers a great teaching programme called the *'Perfect Turn Snowboard 'Clinic'*, where they guarantee to teach you to ride in a day, with a maximum of six people in a class.

Off the slopes, local services are initially provided in the base areas where you will find a good selection of slope side lodging with condo's being the main choice. However, you may find it better to take the four mile drive back down to **Bethel** which plays host to all your needs. This is an easy-going and laid back kind of place that offers far more options for lodging, eating out or going for a beer. Bethel also offers cheaper facilities because as with most resorts, if you stay on or near the slopes, prices go up, and this place is no exception. Bethel is not the most happening of places, it tends to cater for families with attractions. This is not a young persons town. But don't be put off it's still okay.

Sunday River hasn't always had a good reputation for it's eating out. But things are changing and with a good selection of restaurants on the slopes or close by in many of the lodges or hotel-condo's one is able to fine something that will please. You can get a decent steak in places like the *Hill Trading* restaurant, or a good Italian meal at *Rosett's.* In **Bethel** you could try out the *Sud's Pub* for bar food or the *Matterhorn* for a really tasty pizza.

Nightlife is probably **Sunday River's** main let down. This is basically a place for lame heads into apres and all the horrible stuff that comes with it. There are a number of okay bars such as *Bumps* and the *Foggy Goggle* (what a lame name) or *Suds Pub* and the *Sunday River Brewery,* but they all seem to think that sad music and silly games are cool.

Good accommodation exists at the base of **Sunday's** slopes with a big choice of condo's slope side. For riders on a budget then *The Snow Cap Lodge Dorm* is a good place to stay and is close to the slopes. On the other hand, if you have the cash then the *Jordan Grand Hotel,* which is on the slopes, is the place. Here they have all the facilities of a hotel which include a swimming and health club, bar lounge and dining room.

For accommodation listings visit - www.worldsnowboardguide.com

Summary: This is a place that offers some great all round freeriding to suit all levels. There is some excellent treeriding to be had and good beginner areas.

Money wise: Not a cheap place, but at the same time not over expensive.

Overall rating out of 10 — **7**

Sunday River
P.O Box 450, Bethel,
ME 04217
General info **001 (207) 824 3000**
Reservations **001 (800) 543 2754**
Snowphone **001 (207) 824 5200**
www.sundayriver.com
www.virgin.com/holidays

pic - John Quigley

pic - Norm Hersom

Travel Guide

Fly to **Portland** International
Transfer time to resort = **1½** hours.
Local airport = **Bethel,** 6 miles away.

Approximate global air travel times to **Portland**

from: London 7 hours
New York 5 hours
Frankfurt 8 hours

There are daily bus services from both Portland airport by arrangement.

Trains to **Bethel** 6 miles away.

Route Planner
Denver *via Bethel*

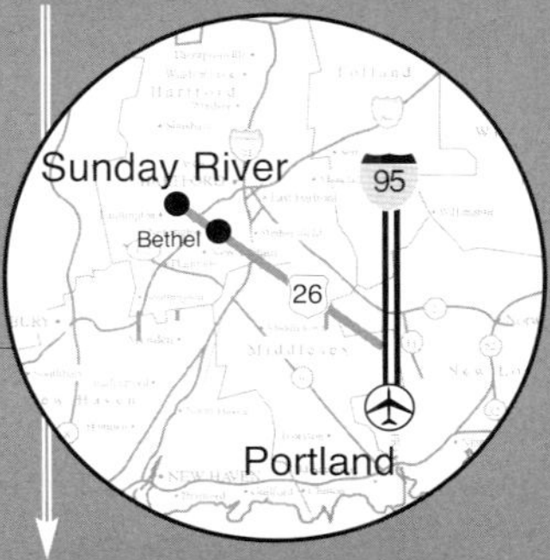

Sunday River = 75 miles
Drive time is about **1½** hours

Montana

GENERAL INFO AND FACTS

Capital - **Helena**
Language - English
Currency - US Dollar
Alcohol drinking age - 21
Drugs - Cannabis is illegal
Death Penalty - Exists
Age of consent for Sex - 16
Electricity Supply - 110 Volts AC
Area phone Code - 406
Provincial sales tax - 0%

pic - Ride Snowboards - Brushie

MONTANA DRIVE GUIDE

All vehicles drive on the right side of the road.
Speed Limits -
Motorways 70mph (112kph)
Highways 55mph (90kph)
Towns 30mph (50kph)
Road Info 001 (406) 444 6339
Fuel is sold in Gallons

TRAVEL CONTACTS

Gateway Airports
Bozeman
Flights from London take around 10 hours 30 mins (not direct).

Amtrax Railroad
tel: 001-800 872 7245

Greyhound Buses
tel: 001 (406) 245 5116

Mountain - West
GMT -6 hours

AREA INFORMATION
Montana Travel
Po Box 200533, 1424 9th Avenue
Helena, MT 59620-0533
tel: 001 (406) 444 2654

Big Sky Montana

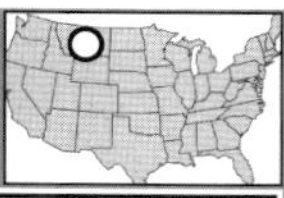

MOUNTAIN DATA

Top Lift at - 3404m

Ride Area 3500 acres

Bottom Lift at - 2124m

Vertical Drop - 1247m

Number of Runs - 100

Longest - 6 miles (9.6km)

TERRAIN LEVELS

Easy	**10%**
Intermediate	**47%**
Advanced	**43%**
Expert =	

TERRAIN TO SUITE

Freeride	**45%**
Trees	Yes
Backcountry	Yes
Freestyle	**35%**
Halfpipe	Yes 1
Terrain Park	Yes 1
Carving	**20%**

SNOW DATA

Average Snowfall
1015 cm a season

Snowmaking
75% cover of the slopes

Winter Periods
Nov to April

Summer Riding
None

SLOPE ACCESS

Total Lifts = **15**

Uplift Rate - 20,000 people an hour.

12 Chair lifts

3 Drag lift

**Leashes Required*

Lift Times
8.30 to 4.00pm

Lift Pass Rates

1 Day pass	$54
3 Day pass	$156
5 Day pass	$250
$27	

Travel Guide

Fly to **Bozeman Int,** with a transfer time of 1 hour.

Bus services from Bozeman take 1 hour.

Route Planner:
From Bozeman, head south on Hwy 191 direct to Big Sky.

Bozeman
to resort = **45** miles
1 hour drive time

pic - Big Sky

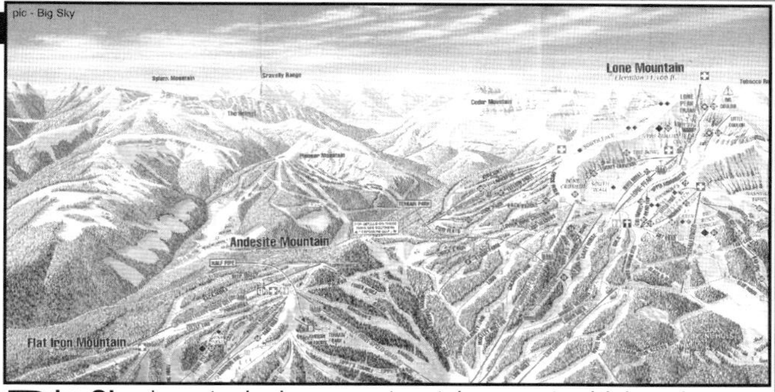

Big Sky is a typical corporate style resort which only goes back to around 1973, when the place was first built aided by millions of corporate dollars. Located just south of **Bozeman** in the northern *Rockies*, Big Sky is an impressive place, where you can do some serious riding on crowd-free slopes that rise above the tree lines. The rideable area is reached by Big Sky's tram and is spread over **Andesite Mountain** and **Lone Mountain**, which rise up to 3,400 meters. This has led to the claim that Big Sky has the largest vertical in the US. The two mountains, with a total of 75 trails, are connected by just fifteen lifts, consisting of some very fast chair lifts that can move 17,000 people uphill per hour.

Freeriders will find this is a great place to get a fix. A good trail is the Big Horn which begins as an unchallenging trail that passes through woods, before dropping sharply into a bowl with banks and some good hits. Some of the most challenging terrain can be found if you first take the Lone Peak chair, and then hike up to reach the ridge off the south-facing summit. For those who know what they're doing, you get the option to go for it down loads of chutes.

Freestylers looking for some natural hits, would do well to check out the gully formed down the side of **Lower Morning Star**, which is pretty cool. And if this is not enough, then Big Sky has a wheel-carved halfpipe and a good series of hits in the terrain park, which will keep grommets happy for days on end.

Carvers should get a good buzz out of these slopes, with plenty of wide open flats that allow for some serious carving. Check out the stuff off the **Ram Charger** quad, where you can lay out with style. Carvers will also prefer the wide terrain on **Elk Park Ridge**, where you can crank some wide turns.

Beginners will find plenty of easy terrain to practice their first moves, with the best novice stuff on the south side of Andesite, off **Southern Comfort** chair lift. The local ski-school handles all levels of tuition with full beginner programmes.

Big Sky is not a place for the budget conscious. The modern town is a friendly place which looks after its visitors well and offers all the things you would expect of a tourist trap. Lodging is a mix-ture of condos and hotels along with a number of expensive restaurants and a few okay bars. .

For accommodation listings visit - www.worldsnowboardguide.com

Big Sky Resort
P.O Box 160001, 1 Lone Mountain Trail. Big Sky MT
***001* (406) 995 5000** **www.bigskyresort.com**
www.virgin.com/holidays

Overall rating out of 10 **6** **Good freeriding resort**

Big Mountain Montana

MOUNTAIN DATA

Top Lift at - 2100m

Ride Area 3020 acres

Bottom Lift at - 1350m

Vertical Drop - 750m

Number of Runs - 81

Longest - 3 miles (5km)

TERRAIN LEVELS

Easy	25%
Intermediate	50%
Advanced	25%
Expert =	4 runs

TERRAIN TO SUITE

Freeride	55%
Trees	Yes
Backcountry	Yes
Freestyle	25%
Halfpipe	Yes 1
Terrain Park	Yes 1
Carving	20%

SNOW DATA

Average Snowfall
838cm a season

Snowmaking
0% cover of the slopes

Winter Periods
Nov to April

Summer Riding
None

SLOPE ACCESS

Total Lifts = **11**

Uplift Rate - 13,800 people an hour.

8 Chair lifts

3 Drag lifts

**Leashes Required*

Lift Times
9.00am to 9.00pm

Lift Pass Rates

1 Day pass	$44
3 Day pass	$129
4 Day pass	$168

SLOPE ACTION

Snowboard Hire
Daily rates from $28
Kids from $22

Snowboard Tuition
Lesson, lift & hire
from $46 per day

Night Riding
4pm to 9pm Wed to Sat

Heli Boarding
Yes

Snowmobiles
Hire & tours from $140

Mountain Cafes
2

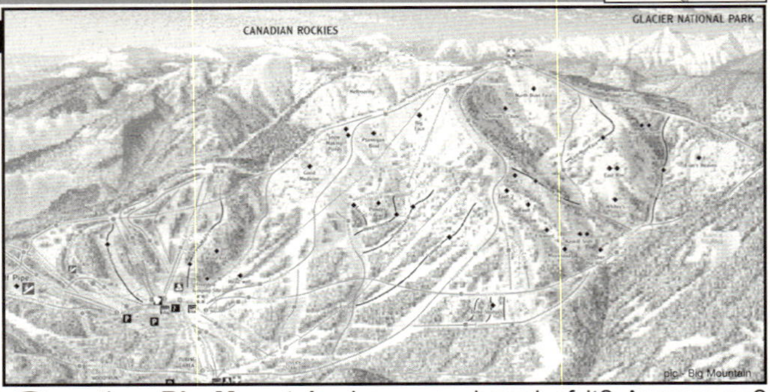

pic - Big Mountain

Question, **Big Mountain,** have you heard of it? Answer no? Well other than those in the area and those from surrounding states, not many people have, and those in the know who have discovered this gem, may want to keep this place a secret. But it could be said that to not tell others about this rider's heaven could be criminal. Located in the far north of **Montana**, **Big Mountain** has attracted a lot of attention recently and is steadily growing in popularity due to it not only having great riding available, but also because of the resort's super laid back attitude and no nonsense approach. This place isn't one of those horrible glitzy haunts visited by fur clad skiers out to pose as is so often the case in many of **Colorado's** resorts. No, this is a purist's resort, a place where you come to ride and take it easy without gimmicks. Big Mountain, which is closely linked to the nearby town of **Whitefish**, attracts visitors from places such as **Seattle** and up in neighbouring **Canada.** However, it doesn't attract too many of them so it never becomes overpopulated here. Excellent transport links exist making this an easy place to get to either by plane or by train. **Amtrax** runs a daily service to Whitefish, called the *Empire Builder Passenger* service to and from major cities like **Seattle** and even **Chicago**. Overall this is a place that keeps things simple and affordable, both on the mountain and around town. The slopes operate a good lift system and provide heaps of annual snow. They don't bother with snowmaking here as they simply don't need it. The real stuff covers a mountain that offers a mixture of wide open bowls, wooded glades and great cruising runs.

Freeriders are in for a major treat at this place with a fantastic offering of deep powder, big bowls, lots of trees and great natural terrain features. Recently the resort has installed a new T-bar which has not only opened up more terrain but also provided better access to some existing runs. Basically, the mountain splits into three marked out areas. There's the **Main Mountain**, which has the most trails and something for every level, the **North Side**, which has a splattering of tree line black and blue runs and the **Hellroaring Basin,** which is an area mainly suited to advanced freeriders with some open riding on black and double black trails.

Freestylers can have lots of fun here and any rider that doesn't appreciate this mountain should give up boarding and become a girl guide. This place is ideal for freestylers. Apart from lots of good natural features, there is a massive terrain park and a cool halfpipe off the **Tenderfoot** chair **3.**

Carvers will appreciate the long and wide corduroy trails that can be found all over the mountain making this a carver's paradise.

Beginners also have a great mountain with lots of easy trails especially at the lower sections. A number of the blues are also suitable for quick learners and allow novices to ride from the top to bottom on the runs off the **Glacier Chaser** chair lift **1.**

Close to and even on the slopes there is a good choice of local services to choose from with a wide range of options for lodging, eating and having a good night out. The facilities at the base of the slopes are very good and will provide you with most of your basic needs with condo's that have restaurants and bars. Around the base village you will also find a few shops, but in truth the biggest choice of shops and all other local services can be found back down in the sprawling and old fashioned town of Whitefish. Here you will find a place where locals treat you with respect, look after you and get on with their lives. They don't over pamper you, they won't bug you, they simply provide a laid back town that is both affordable and good.

Big Mountain and **Whitefish** provide good and simple choices for going out and filling your stomach at a price to please everyone. You can pig out at *The Stube & Chuckwagon Grill* which serves excellent food all day long. The *Moguls Bar and Grill* is an ideal place to get breakfast before hitting the slopes and is located near the base of *Swift Creek chair lift*. In **Whitefish** the *Buffalo Cafe* is a good place to get a simple affordable meal.

Nightlife attractions here are some what tame and on the whole very laid back, but that's not to say that you can't have a stomping time. Highly rated by the visiting ski groups is the *Stube & Chuckwagon Grill* which goes in for too much apre ski stuff, is still a cool bar. The **Great Northern** in **Whitefish** is not a bad joint which has a good selection of beers.

Good accommodation is provided at the slopes or in **Whitefish.** If you stay near the slopes you will be able to find a condo or a bed in one of the lodges at reasonable prices. Rates start from $56 per person a night, but if you base yourself down in Whitefish, you will be able to get better deals. There is a hostel called the *Non Hostile Hostel* that offers cheap bunks 001 (406) 862 7383.
For accommodation listings visit - www.worldsnowboardguide.com

Summary: Top resort that is a riders dream and very welcoming. The riding is excellent especially for freeriders and novices.
Money wise: This is an excellent value for money resort and definitely not and over-priced place.

Overall rating out of 10 — **10**

Big Mountain
P.O Box 1400, Whitefish
Montana 59937
General info **001 (406) 862 1900**
Reservations **001 (800) 858 4157**
Snowphone **001 (406) 862 19007669**
www.virgin.com/holidays

pics - Big Mountain

Travel Guide

Fly to **Calgary** International CDA
Transfer time to resort = **20** mins.
Local airport = **Glacier,** 19 miles away.

Approximate global air travel times to **Seattle**

from:		
	London	12 hours
	New York	5 hours
	Frankfurt	13 hours

There are daily bus services from both airports by arrangement.

Trains to **Whitefish,** 8 miles on.

Route Planner
Calgary (in Canada) *via Browning*

Big Mountain = **298** miles
Drive time is about **6** hours

New Hampshire

Resort	Page
Bretton Woods	107
Loon Mountain	108
Waterville Valley	109

GENERAL INFO AND FACTS

Capital - **Concord**
Language - English
Currency - US Dollar
Alcohol drinking age - 21
Drugs - Cannabis is illegal
Death Penalty - Exists on paper
Age of consent for Sex - 16
Electricity Supply - 110 Volts AC
Area phone Code - 603
Provincial sales tax - 0%

NEW HAMPSHIRE DRIVE GUIDE
All vehicles drive on the right side of the road.
Speed Limits -
Motorways 70mph (112kph)
Highways 55mph (90kph)
Towns 30mph (50kph)
Road Info 001 (603) 271 6900
Fuel is sold in Gallons

TRAVEL CONTACTS

Gateway Airports
Manchester & Boston (in Maine)
Flights from London take around 5 hours 30 mins (direct).

Amtrax Railroad
tel: 001-800 872 7245

Greyhound Buses
tel:

Eastern
GMT -5 hours

AREA INFORMATION
Montana Travel
Office of Travel & Tourism
Po Box 856, Concord
03303. USA
tel: 001 (406) 444 2654

pic - Ride Snowboards

Bretton Woods New Hampshire

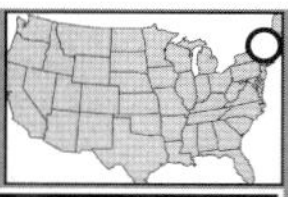

USA New Hampshire

MOUNTAIN DATA
Top Lift at - 945m
Ride Area 345 acres
Bottom Lift at - 488m
Vertical Drop - 457m
Number of Runs - 66
Longest - 2 miles (3km)

TERRAIN LEVELS
Easy **31%**
Intermediate **41%**
Advanced **28%**
Expert =

TERRAIN TO SUITE
Freeride **40%**
Trees Yes
Backcountry Yes
Freestyle **15%**
Halfpipe Yes 1
Terrain Park Yes 1
Carving **45%**

SNOW DATA
Average Snowfall
430 cm a season
Snowmaking
95% cover of the slopes
Winter Periods
Nov to April
Summer Riding
None

SLOPE ACCESS
Total Lifts = **8**
Uplift Rate - 8,000 people an hour.
6 Chair lifts
2 Drag lift
**Leashes Required*

Lift Times
8.30 to 4.00pm

Lift Pass Rates
1 Day pass $42
3 Day pass $90
5 Day pass $142

Travel Guide

Fly to **Boston,** in Maine, transfer time of 2 1/2 hour.

Bus services from Boston will take 3 hours.

Route Planner:
From Boston, head north on I-93 via Manchester and Concord turning left at signs for Twin mountain along route 302.
Boston to the resort = **165** miles

pic - Soft Snapper

Bretton Woods lies 165 miles north of **Boston** and 100 miles north of **Manchester** and claims to be the largest resort in **New Hampshire.** However, claiming to be the biggest at something is not always an indicator of how good you are. What you have here is a respectable mountain that by east coast standards is fairly decent. Some 66 runs are hacked out of dense trees that cover the whole mountain from the summit to base. The slopes, which are in view of **Mt Washington**, are currently spread out over two peaks, **Mt Rosebrook** and **West Mountain** with the trails all working their way back down into one main base area. Soon to open will be another ridable area, that of **Mt Stickney.** What **Bretton** seems to be about to the casual observer, is a place that likes to keep things simple and one that attracts a lot of family ski groups. Constantly expanding, this is a resort that is best suited to beginners and intermediate carvers although freeriders who like easy slopes with trees will also fair well here. In recent years major expansion plans have lead to the area almost doubling in size with the opening of the **West Mountain** which is a nice area for advanced riders who like to shred tight trees. All the trails and lifts connect up well and getting around the three slope faces can be done with ease. But that said, riders who prefer steep trails that last more than a few turns, may find that anything more than a couple of days on these slopes may become a bit tedious. On the other hand, a 10 year old kid taking their first snowboard trip with their parents will enjoy a weeks stay.

Freeriders do have a mountain that allows for easy going riding which also means taking in some treeriding. But this place is by no means a good freerider's resort, there's nothing that adventurous to take on and the few advanced runs that there are, don't take long to conquer.

Freestylers are presented a mountain that is basically dull when it comes to finding good natural hits. They do exist but not many. However, there is an okay halfpipe to check out.

Carvers who like to take it easy will enjoy **Brettons Woods**. In the main, this is a good simple cruising resort, with a number of decent trails especially those on **Mt Rosebrook.**

Local attractions and services are provided at the base of the slopes. What you are offered is of a very high standard, the only problem being that the place is very boring and not much fun.
For accommodation listings visit - www.worldsnowboardguide.com

Bretton Woods
Route 302, Bretton Woods. NH 03575
***001* (603) 278 3320**
www.brettonwoods.com
www.virgin.com/holidays

Overall rating out of 10 **4**

Overall a bit of a dull place

Loon Mountain New Hampshire

MOUNTAIN DATA

Top Lift at - 930m

Bottom Lift at - 289m
Vertical Drop - 640m
Number of Runs - 46
Longest - 2.5 miles (4km)

TERRAIN LEVELS

Easy	**20%**
Intermediate	**64%**
Advanced	**16%**
Expert =	

TERRAIN TO SUITE

Freeride	**50%**
Trees	Yes
Backcountry	Poor
Freestyle	**20%**
Halfpipe	Yes 1
Terrain Park	Yes 1
Carving	**30%**

SNOW DATA

Average Snowfall
300cm a season
Snowmaking
97% cover of the slopes
Winter Periods
Oct to April
Summer Riding
None

SLOPE ACCESS

Total Lifts = **8**
Uplift Rate - 10,550 people an hour.
1 Gondolas, **6** Chair lifts
1 Drag lift
**Leashes Required*

Lift Times
8.30am to 4.00pm

Lift Pass Rates

1 Day pass	$47
3 Day pass	$116
5 Day pass	$149

Travel Guide

Fly to **Boston,** with a transfer time of 2 1/4 hours.

Bus services from Boston can take 3 hours to Loon.

Route Planner:
From Boston, head north on I-93 to exit 32 at Lincoln. Then go east along R-122 to Loon Mountain

Boston to resort = **132** miles.

pic - Loon Mountain

New Hampshire breeds a lot of resorts, most of which are frankly crap. However, **Loon Mountain** is one of the state's better offerings with a good friendly snowboard attitude. Located in **White Mountain National Forest**, Loon is the highest mountain in New Hampshire and a very popular resort that attracts a lot of punters. The resort has been going through a multi-million dollar expansion programme and has recently expanded the ride area with new lifts and services. The 275 acres of terrain is nearly all covered by snow cannons, so when the real stuff is lacking, they can still ensure good coverage. Despite Loon's small size and the odd lift line, it's a good place to ride, with a mixture of varied terrain to appeal to most recreational boarders.

Freeriders have a tree-covered mountain that allows for some good riding experiences. **The Kissin' Cousin** is a popular warm-up area, before trying out the likes of **Speakeasy**, reached by the **Kancamagus** chair. The **East Basin** is also a popular freeride area, where you'll find some decent wind-lips to track up.

Freestylers have a full-on fun-park called **Skid Road,** which snowboarders travel a long way to ride. Located on **Lower Flying Fox** and approximately 1,500m long, the park has plenty of very big hits including a 100 metre halfpipe.

Carvers will soon realise that Loon is the mountain for them. It offers a great chance to perform to watching onlookers, as you carve big turns on long, well prepared trails. Some of the best runs are the **Flume** and the **Upper** and **Lower Walking Boss**, an area that offers some cool carving on either blue or black trails. There is also plenty for novice and intermediate alpine riders.

Beginners will find plenty here. The best and easiest stuff is found on the **West Basin**, while the mid-section of the **Seven Brothers** chair offers something a little more testing. Loon Ski School offers a very good learning snowboard clinic.

Local services are plentiful in either **Loon**, **Lincoln** or down in the famous hippy hangout of **Woodstock**. All three towns are friendly and look after their visitors well. Food around the area caters well for all tastes and pockets. The *Old Mill* is good for seafood, while *Elvios* is the pizza place, and *The Woodstock Inn* is good for bar food. There are also a few good late-night hangouts in either Loon, Lincoln or Woodstock.

For accommodation listings visit - www.worldsnowboardguide.com

Loon Mountain Resort
RR1, P.O Box 41 Kancampagus, Lincoln. NH 03251
***001* (603) 745 8111** **www.loonmtn.com**
www.virgin.com/holidays

Overall rating out of 10 **5** **A bit dull and basic but okay.**

Waterville Valley New Hampshire

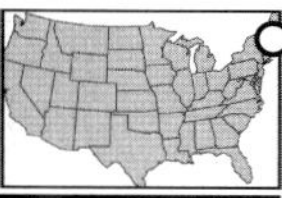

MOUNTAIN DATA

Top Lift at - 1220m

Ride Area 255 acres

Bottom Lift at - 604m

Vertical Drop - 616m

Number of Runs - 52

Longest - 3 miles (5km)

TERRAIN LEVELS

Easy	20%
Intermediate	60%
Advanced	20%
Expert =	2 runs

TERRAIN TO SUITE

Freeride	40%
Trees	Yes
Backcountry	Yes
Freestyle	20%
Halfpipe	Yes 1
Terrain Park	No
Carving	20%

SNOW DATA

Average Snowfall
355cm a season

Snowmaking
100% cover of the slopes

Winter Periods
Nov to April

Summer Riding
None

SLOPE ACCESS

Total Lifts = **11**

Uplift Rate - 14,867 people an hour.

7 Chair lifts

4 Drag lift

**Leashes Required*

Lift Times
9.00am to 4.00pm

Lift Pass Rates

1 Day pass	$47
3 Day pass	$115
5 Day pass	$168

Travel Guide

Fly to **Boston Int,** with a transfer time of **2** hours.

Bus services from **Boston** available by arrangement.

Route Planner:
From Boston, head north on the I-93 to exit 28 at Campton. Then head easy along the route 49 to Waterville Valley.

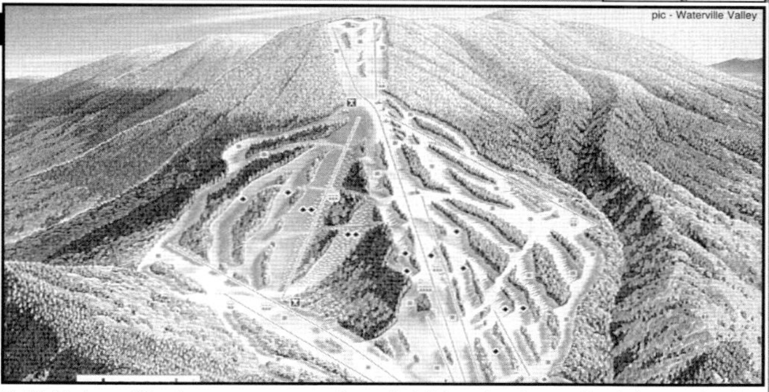

Waterville is an easy-going, laid back place that is part of a programme called the Peaks of Excitement, a group of resorts working together. This means that your lift pass can be used at over 20 other places, giving a combined area of around 2,000 acres. The resort is only two hours from **Boston** and can be easily reached by bus or car. The slopes are a two minute drive from the village and serviced by a regular shuttle bus to the lifts. Waterville really tries hard to please snowboarders, with four fun-parks. However, the resort is a busy place at weekends, and being quite small, it can feel a bit cluttered at times. Advanced riders don't have a host of challenging trails, in the main this is an intermediate's and fast learning novice's resort.

Freeriders may not have the biggest or most happening playground at Waterville, but you still have areas to cut, with plenty of trees to shred like **Lower Bobby's.**

Freestylers and trick merchants have four fun-parks and a massive halfpipe to play in. The parks (shamefully open to skiers), are spread out around the slopes and offer something for all levels. The **Boneyard** (located on **Periphery**) is a pro-level park and features quarter-pipes, rail slides, table-tops and gaps. **Park Place** at **Lower Sel's Choice** is less intimidating, while **Broad Walk** is the biggest park area containing the most hits. **Snow Wonder** is a mini-park for novice air catchers.

Carvers who can handle a board on its side have just one steep double black to go for - **True Grit**. Alternatively, the cluster of blues that descend from the summit make for nice easy carving on pleasant and well groomed trails.

Beginners only have a couple of dull green trails at the base, with a number of over-rated blues higher up that can be tackled quite easily by those with a few days under their belt.

Local facilities, a few minutes from the slopes, are without frills. Accommodation covers condos, hotels and an array of B&B's. Prices are affordable and a number of weekly packages are available at reduced rates. Dining out offers no great surprises, with a simple choice of restaurants providing local dishes, fast-food and deli stuff. For some decent food check out *Chile Peppers* or *Alpine Pizza*. Night action is dull, but the *Zoo Station* and *Legends 1291* are okay for a beer.

For accommodation listings visit - www.worldsnowboardguide.com

Waterville Valley
Ski Area Rd., Waterville Valley. NH 03215
***001* (603) 236 8311**
www.waterville.com
www.virgin.com/holidays

Overall rating out of 10 **6** **Not hot but then its not bad.**

Oregon

GENERAL INFO AND FACTS

Capital - Salem
Language - English
Currency - US Dollar
Alcohol drinking age - 21
Drugs - Cannabis is illegal
Death Penalty - Exists
Age of consent for Sex - 16
Electricity Supply - 110 Volts AC
Area phone Code - 503
Provincial sales tax - 0%

OREGON DRIVE GUIDE

All vehicles drive on the right side of the road.
Speed Limits -
Motorways 70mph (112kph)
Highways 55mph (90kph)
Towns 30mph (50kph)
Road Info 001 (503) 588 2941
Fuel is sold in Gallons

TRAVEL CONTACTS

Gateway Airports
Portland
Flights from London take around 12 hours 30 mins (not direct).

Amtrax Railroad
tel: 001 (503) 335 1234

Greyhound Buses
tel: 001 (503) 243 2357

Mountain
GMT -8 hours

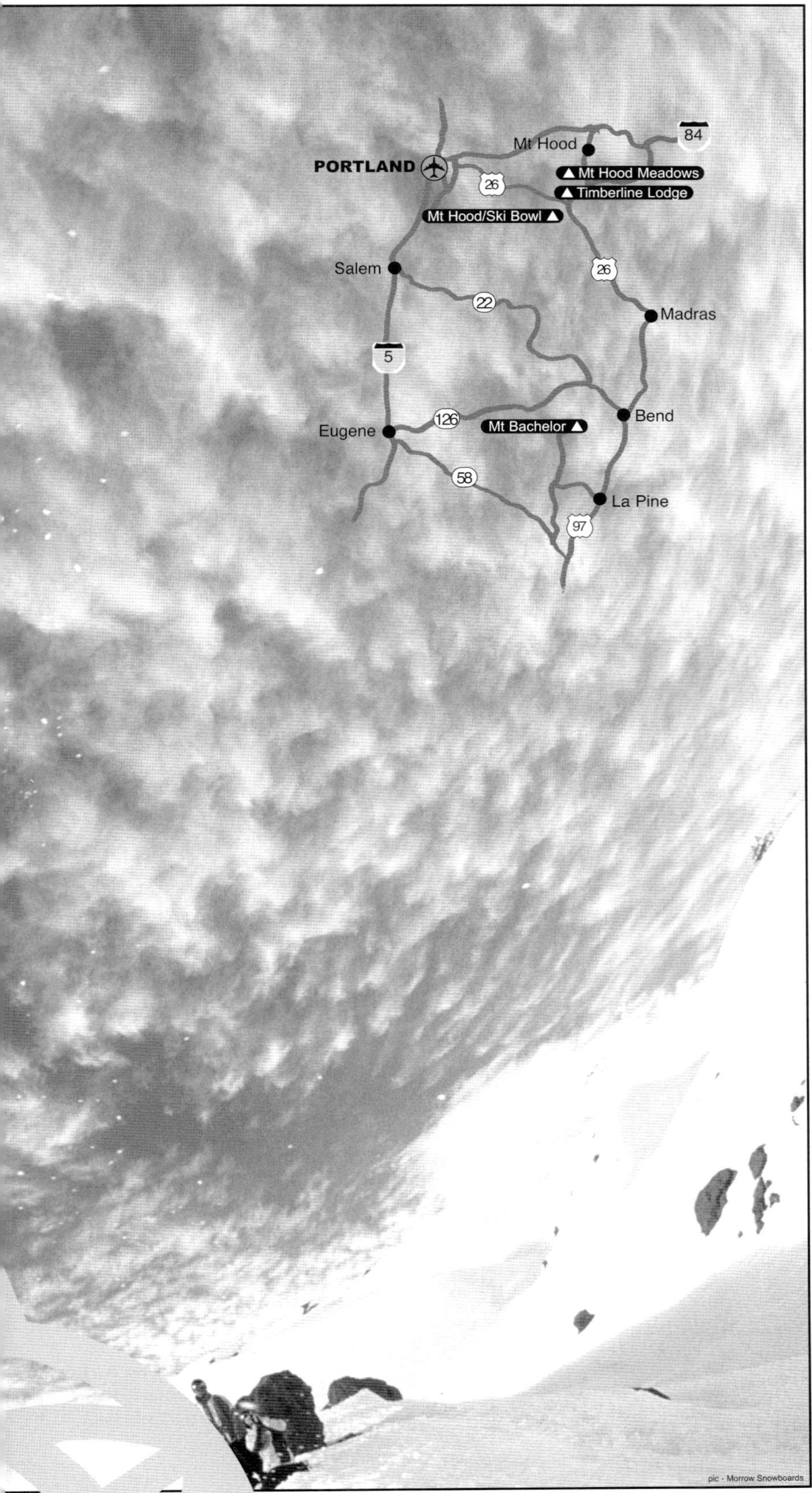

pic - Morrow Snowboards

Mt Bachelor Oregon

MOUNTAIN DATA

Top Lift at - 2763m
Ride Area 3683 acres
Bottom Lift at - 1818m
Vertical Drop - 946m
Number of Runs - 70
Longest - 2 miles (3km)

TERRAIN LEVELS

Easy	15%
Intermediate	25%
Advanced	35%
Expert =	4 runs

TERRAIN TO SUITE

Freeride	70%
Trees	Yes
Backcountry	Yes
Freestyle	20%
Halfpipe	Yes 2
Terrain Park	Yes 4
Carving	10%

SNOW DATA

Average Snowfall
826cm a season
Snowmaking
0% cover of the slopes
Winter Periods
Nov to June
Summer Riding
None

SLOPE ACCESS

Total Lifts = **12**
Uplift Rate - 21,000 people an hour.
10 Chair lifts
2 Drag lifts
**Leashes Required*

Lift Times
8.30am to 4.00pm

Lift Pass Rates

1 Day pass	$45
3 Day pass	$126
4 Day pass	$200

SLOPE ACTION

Snowboard Hire
Daily rates from $26
Kids from $20

Snowboard Tuition
Lesson, lift & hire from $45 per day

Night Riding
Yes

Heli Boarding
No

Snowmobiles
Hire & tours

Mountain Cafes
20

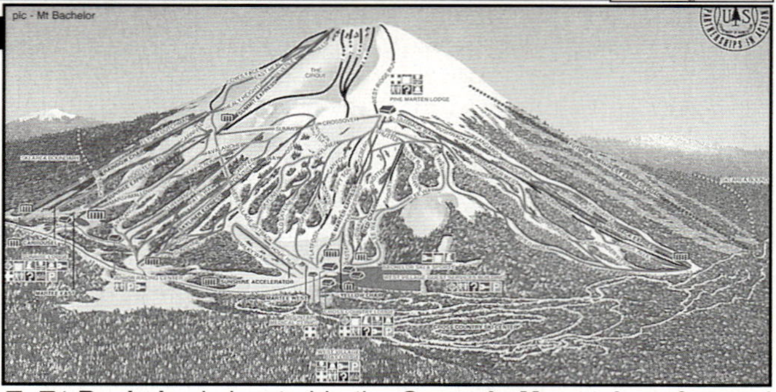
pic - Mt Bachelor

Mt Bachelor is located in the **Cascade Mountains** of central **Oregon**, 16 miles from the booming city of **Bend.** The snow-capped, extinct volcano is unique in that it is conical-shaped with six high-speed quads, offering 360° access to the whole area. Chutes and gullies created long ago by lava flows, gives the terrain a shape and contour found in few other places. Combine 200 inches of annual snowfall, howling winds that create fairy-tale wind-lips, and you're left with acres of terrain that rival the best of any man-made park. Weekly storms rock the mountains, forcing you to frequently use force to steer through the dense weather systems. But even before the clouds clear and the sky is blue again, Mt Bachelor is damn fun!

Freeriders-if the summit is open, be sure to make the 15 minute hike to the top of the **Cirque Bowl**. You will find here an extra large cornice (that grows to 45 feet) and the infamous **Jamo Jump**, where you can fling yourself silly. Also accessible from the summit chair is Mt Bachelor's **Backside**, where you are sure to find fresh snow and solitude. You can use the new 2 mile long **Northwest Express** chair to access a vast amount of steep bowls and perfect tree runs. There are minimal man-made runs here, and the ones that are cut are narrow and winding.

Freestylers-the Outback has many BMX and skate park-like runs that are easy to find by following the tracks. On crowded days, head over to **Rainbow** chair, which unfortunately is as slow as shit, but there are many natural quarter-pipes and rollers untouched by the weekend crowd. If you're man enough, ask some local jackass about the **Compression** jump, which on good days allows you to travel an unlimited distance before shooting up the side of the **Cindercone**. If natural terrain is not for you, Mt Bachelor maintains a decent park, and **High Cascade Snowboard Camp** lends its Pipe Dragon to keep the 60 metre halfpipe (off the **Skyliner** chair) in top condition.

Carvers will find that Bachelor has them in mind and grooms its trails to perfection. The runs off **Skyliner** and **Marten** chairs are great intermediate and novice trails, but if you have the bottle then head to the summit and ride the unpisted open steeps of the **Cirque** - but don't bail!

Beginners-this is a mountain that you'll appreciate, with its selection of good, easy green runs that can be ridden from the mid-section of the **Pine Marten** chair. The runs descend in a manner that allow you to steer onto a more interesting and challenging blue as you gain confidence. The local snowboard school is really good, and the staff know how to turn you into a fast freeriding god within a day or two. A day's all-in programme will set you back just $45, and for those who want to make it big, should sign up for one of High Cascade's winter camps where you will receive top instruction by pros.

Mt Bachelor doesn't offer any substantial slopeside facilities. However, excellent laid back local services with a warm welcome are available 16 miles away in **Bend.** A free, daily and regular shuttle bus service runs to and from the slopes. Hitching to the mountain is also a good bet and cars do stop to pick you up. Bend and the surrounding area has everything you need for your stay, shops, banks, postal services and a huge array of in and out-door sporting attractions. Good snowboard hire services are at the *Bachelor Snowboard Shop* and *Smoked Monkey*.

Jobseekers: Some employment options on the slopes, but most casual work is available in Bend. Call for details (541) 382 2442

There are no big surprises when it comes to restaurants. What you are offered is a good, but somewhat basic selection of eateries where you can wine and dine down in **Bend,** or have a snack attack up on **Bachelor.** The *Taco Stand* is the place to fill yourself with a burrito bomber: this beauty will clog up any 15 gallon pressure-locked toilet. *Stuft Pizza* is the place for pasta dishes. Pasta and pizza lovers should make for the *Stuft Pizza* restaurant

Night-life at Bachelor is not exactly the most happening. However, things liven up in Bend where there are enough joints to drink and dance in until you drop. Try *Evil Sister Saloon* if you're inclined to the 'alternative' end of the spectrum. *Legends* is also a cool hang-out with large screens showing sports and music videos, they also serve decent beer.

Accommodation: The area can accommodate over 7,500 visitors, but nothing directly on the slopes. The nearest lodging is only a few miles from the slopes at the *Inn of The Seventh Mountain*, but the best choice of condos, B&B's and lodges can be found in the town of **Bend**, 16 miles away from Bachelor.

For accommodation listings visit - www.worldsnowboardguide.com

Summary: Full-on freeriders resort offering great open and tree-lined riding on crowd free slopes ideal for all levels. Excellent local facitities of a high quality.
Money wise: Prices vary for lodgings, but overall this an affordable resort.

Overall rating out of 10 — **10**

Mt Bachelor Resort
P.O Box 1031 Bend
Oregon 97709
General info **001 (541) 382 2442**
Reservations **001 (541) 382 7888**
Snowphone **001 (541) 382 2442**
www.mtbachelor.com
www.virgin.com/holidays

pics - Mt Bachelor

Travel Guide

Fly to **Portland** International
Transfer time to resort = **4¼** hours.
Local airport = **Redmond,** 15 miles away.

Approximate global air travel times to **Portland**

from: London	**12** hours	
New York	**5** hours	
Frankfurt	**13** hours	

There are daily bus services from both Portland airport and Redmond domestic airport.

Trains to Chemult 60 miles on.

Route Planner
Portland *via Madras & Bend*

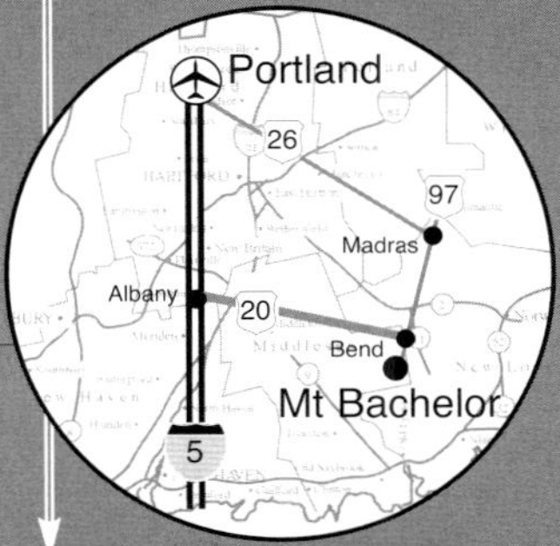

Mt Bachelor = 203 miles
Drive time is about **4¼** hours

Mt Hood Meadows Oregon

MOUNTAIN DATA

Top Lift at - 2225m

Ride Area 2150 acres

Bottom Lift at - 1379m

Vertical Drop - 846m

Number of Runs - 87

Longest - 3 miles (5km)

TERRAIN LEVELS

Easy	**15%**
Intermediate	**50%**
Advanced	**20%**
Expert =	**15%**

TERRAIN TO SUITE

Freeride	**60%**
Trees	A few
Backcountry	Yes
Freestyle	**30%**
Halfpipe	Yes 1
Terrain Park	Yes 3
Carving	**10%**

SNOW DATA

Average Snowfall
915cm a season

Snowmaking
0% cover of the slopes

Winter Periods
Nov to June

Summer Riding
July to August

SLOPE ACCESS

Total Lifts = **12**

Uplift Rate - 16,145 people an hour.

10 Chair lifts

2 Drag lifts

**Leashes Required*

Lift Times
8.00am to 4.00pm

Lift Pass Rates
1 Day pass $42
5 Day pass $150
Season pass $1000

SLOPE ACTION

Snowboard Hire
Daily rates from $25
Kids from $20

Snowboard Tuition
Lesson, lift & hire
from $45 per day

Night Riding
Yes on 22 runs

Heli Boarding
No

Snowmobiles
N/A

Mountain Cafes
2

pic - San Tang

There are three main resorts on **Mt Hood**, a dormant (not extinct!) volcano: **Mt Hood Meadows**, **Ski Bowl** and **Timberline**. Although small, Meadows is the most popular and has a huge range of interesting riding crammed into its space and, joy of joys, virtually no traversing anywhere. It maybe tempting fate, but it is hard to get lost on Hood. You can spend a whole day taking different lines, but know that you are not too far from where you started. This is a very mixed ability mountain, with some nice basic novice terrain to pockets of testing trails for the more advanced rider, but in truth this not the most testing place, Steep descents will only be found in very short doses, like on **Waterfall** or around the back of **Nightmare Knoll** (a 40+ft cliff).

The locals have their own names for most of the stuff they ride and are more than happy to show you their favourite little stash(!). The lifties are cool too, and a large proportion ride. If you can't afford the daily rates, the mountain is open for night-riding until March, although not extensively: take advantage of the special offers at *Safeway's Supermarkets* ($8.50 for Sunday 4pm-10pm) and you can't complain. Meadows is a popular destination for summer riding, with *Tim Windell's High Cascade* and *Mt Hood Snowboard Camp,* but you have to be enrolled on a camp to use their facilities.

Freeriders-this mountain is very much for you: the terrain, which may not offer a super amount of challenging stuff or be the most extensive in the world, is still perfect wherever you go. The **Super Bowl** is a black graded area, with a series of descents on open terrain. The notable thing about the Super Bowl, is that it's not serviced by a lift line; instead you get up on a snowcat for around $12 a go or $50 for 5 runs.

Freestylers-there are natural hits everywhere and also a good fun-park off the Hood River chair. However, the fact that skiers are allowed in the park with so much good natural terrain on offer, make it hardly worth using. You can have a great time riding the hits around **Chunky Swirl** and the **Texas** run. If you're a pipe hound, then you'll usually find it well maintained but often very busy with local air heads.

Carvers-the runs from **Cascade** are the best in terms of wide, open carving trails, with a couple of decent blue trails down to choose from. There isn't an abundance of steeps for long fast carving, but what is there is is excellent.

Beginners are treated to a good number of trails that are easy to reach and easy to negotiate. **Mt Hood Express** gives access to some interesting green runs and some tame blues. The local snowboard school which is staffed by a number of good snowboarders, has a host of teaching programmes for all levels, including a *Mountain Master Programme*.

If you're the sort of person that doesn't want the normal, tacky, overpriced tourist facilities found in many resorts, then this place will please you. What you have is a laid back and very basic place where the locals are cool. Timberline Lodge (the location for the film 'The Shining') has recently had an overhaul and is the only real slopeside accommodation which is open all year, but prices can be a bit steep. A good option would be to stay down in **Government Camp** opposite **Ski Bowl** which is only a few miles away. Alternatively you could base yourself in the town of **Hood River**, 36 miles away, which has loads of facilities.
For your hire needs visit *Hood River Outfitter* or the *Demo Board Centre* tel (503) 337 2222.

If you're the sort of person that wants to dine out night after night eating fine haute cuisine dressed in a tuxedo, then firstly see a shrink, and secondly visit another resort. This place is for those who like their food served man style, big portions no frills and cheap. Wherever you stay, there are plenty of budget food-stops. *Huckleberry's* does a damn fine breakfast and is open 24 hours. While down in **Hood River**, *Big City Chicks* is good.

Night-life: Hood may seem to be quiet and tame from the outside, but in fact things can get very lively and in a snowboard way, kick off nightly with a lot of hardcore boozing, especially in the no frills **Goverment Camp** or in **Mt Hood** at the likes of the *Alpenstube*. The biggest selection of night action takes place in **Hood River.**

Accommodation is provided in various locations, with the more expensive near the slopes at **Mt Hood.** *Mt Hood Hamlet B&B* has rates from $95 tel (800) 407 0570. While down on **Hood River** you can get a bed at *Prater's* Motel for around $40 a night. The *Bingen School Hostel* has nightly rates from $15 and is a good budget hangout.

For accommodation listings visit - www.worldsnowboardguide.com

Summary: Full-on freerider's resort offering great, open and tree-lined terrain with crowd-free slopes suited to novices. Good but very basic local services.
Money wise: Prices vary, but overall this is a very affordable place.

Overall rating out of 10 **10**

Mt Hood Meadows
P.O Box 470, Mt Hood
Oregon 97041

General info	***001*** **(503) 246 1810**
Reservations	***001*** **(800) 754 4663**
Snowphone	***001*** **(503) 246 1810**

www.skihood.com
www.virgin.com/holidays

pics - Mt Hood Meadows

Travel Guide

Fly to **Portland** International
Transfer time to resort = **1½** hours.
Local airport = n/a

Approximate global air travel times to **Portland**

from:	London	**12** hours
	New York	**5** hours
	Frankfurt	**13** hours

There are daily bus services from Portland airport as well as good car hire services.

Trains to Portland 69 miles on.

Route Planner
Portland *via Hwy's 26 & 35*

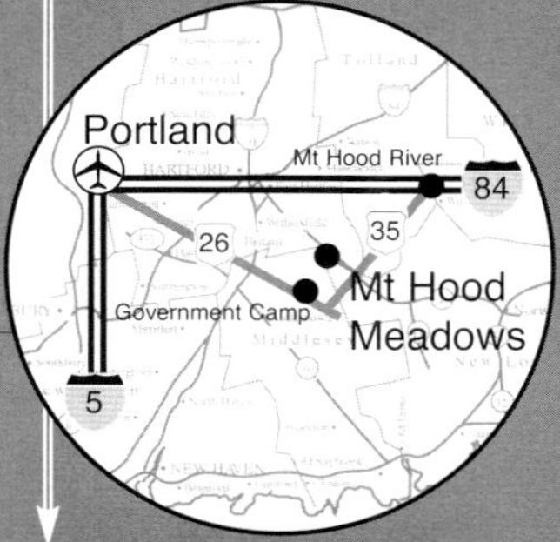

Mt Hood Meadows = 75 miles
Drive time is about **1½** hours

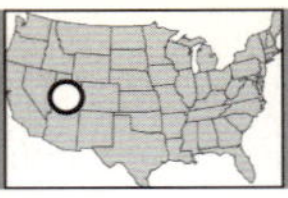

Resort	Page

pic - Snowbird

GENERAL INFO AND FACTS

Capital - **Salt Lake City**
Language - English
Currency - US Dollar
Alcohol drinking age - 21
Drugs - Cannabis is illegal
Death Penalty - Exists
Age of consent for Sex - 16
Electricity Supply - 110 Volts AC
Area phone Code - 801
Provincial sales tax - 0%

UTAH DRIVE GUIDE

All vehicles drive on the right side of the road.
Speed Limits -
Motorways 70mph (112kph)
Highways 55mph (90kph)
Towns 30mph (50kph)
Road Info 001 (801) 964 6000
Fuel is sold in Gallons

TRAVEL CONTACTS

Gateway Airports
Salt Lake City
Flights from London take around 12 hours 30 mins (not direct).

Greyhound Buses
tel: 001 (800) 231 2222

Mountain
GMT -7 hours

AREA INFORMATION

Salt Lake Visitors Bureau
90 South West Temple
Salt Lake City.
Utah 84101
USA
tel: 001 (801) 521 2822

Utah Ski & Snowboard Ass
150 West 500 South Salt Lake City
Utah 84101
USA
tel: 001 (801) 534 1779

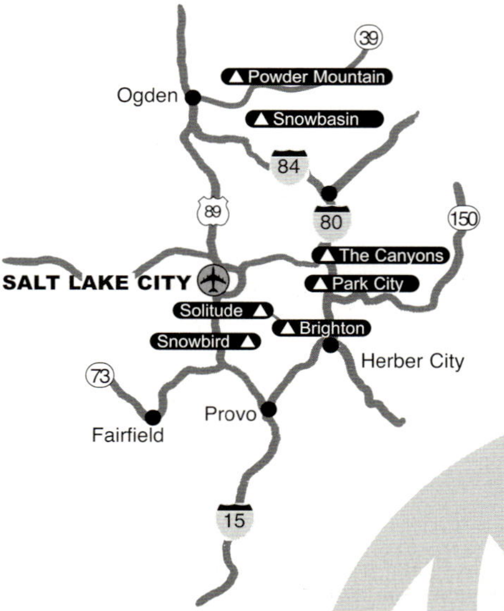

Brighton Utah

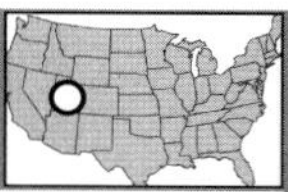

U S A

Utah

MOUNTAIN DATA

Top Lift at - 3200m

Ride Area 850 acres

Bottom Lift at - 2668m

Vertical Drop - 532m

Number of Runs - 66

Longest - 3 miles (5km)

TERRAIN LEVELS

Easy	21%
Intermediate	40%
Advanced	39%
Expert =	

TERRAIN TO SUITE

Freeride	**60%**
Trees	Yes
Backcountry	Yes
Freestyle	**20%**
Halfpipe	Yes 2
Terrain Park	Yes 1
Carving	**20%**

SNOW DATA

Average Snowfall
1269 cm a season

Snowmaking
24% cover of the slopes

Winter Periods
Nov to April

Summer Riding
None

SLOPE ACCESS

Total Lifts = **7**

Uplift Rate - 10,100 people an hour.

7 Chair lifts

**Leashes Required*

Lift Times
9.00 to 9.00pm

Lift Pass Rates
1 Day pass $37
Night pass $20
Season pass $895

Travel Guide

Fly to **Salt Lake City**, with transfer time of 35 minutes.

Bus services from Salt Lake City takes 45 mins

Route Planner:
From Salt Lake City head east along highway 190 Canyon Road all the way up to Brighton
Salt Lake City to the resort = **35** miles.

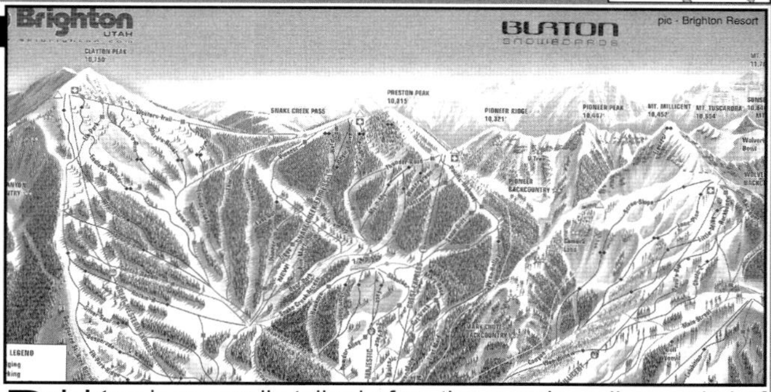

pic - Brighton Resort

Brighton is generally talked of as the snowboarding capital of **Utah**, but that is over-rated. Brighton is located at the top of **Big Cottonwood Canyon** and most of the mountain is lacking in vertical and challenging terrain. The pipe sucks and the regulars here are not a friendly crowd. There are some really good riders but they don't appreciate visitors crowding the snowboard parks and they will always be the first to let you know it. However, **Brighton** has been welcoming pleasure seekers to its slopes since 1936 and is fully open to snowboarders, which is not the case in all of Utahs resorts such as nearby **Alta** or **Dear Valley** who still ban snowboaders because of their stuck up attitude (don't worry, both are crap anyway). Brighton is also close to the snowboard friendly resort of **Solitude**.

Freeriders will want to head straight for the **Millicent** lift. The **Wolverine Cirque** backcountry is out of this world. This area may require a hike out, but it is well worth the effort. **Scree-Slope** rocks too. It accesses a sweet cliff/shoot area, which goes all the way over to **Camera Land** and **Mary Chutes** backcountry. An easy hike to the top of **Preston Peak** from the **Snake Creek Express** leads to some super tree runs in **Snake Bowl. Hidden Country** backcountry also has a limitless possibility of tree runs and powder shoots after a good storm, but it tends to get tracked out pretty fast.

Freestylers will be disappointed with the pipe but the park is very well maintained. It has a bunch of decent table tops and spine jumps and is not usually crowded during the week.

Carvers will find that **Brighton** doesn't have a lot to offer. There are only a few fast groomers off of **Millicent** and **Evergreen**. The rest of the mountain just does not maintain enough vertical.

Beginners would really enjoy learning on this mountain. A large portion of the terrain is not too steep or technical. The **Explorer** lift is a great place to start and there are numerous runs off of the Majestic lift that beginners would be comfortable with. Sunshine off the **Snake Creek Express** is a long run, but mellow.

Off the slopes things are remarkably different to on the slopes because in truth there is nothing here other than a couple of basic lodges and a few bed and breakfasts haunts. You should stay in a neighbouring resort or down in **Salt Lake City**

For accommodation listings visit - www.worldsnowboardguide.com

Brighton
Star Route, Brighton. UT 84121
***001* (801) 532 4731**
www.skibrighton.com
www.virgin.com/holidays

Overall rating out of 10 **5** **Basic, and too much attitude**

Park City Utah

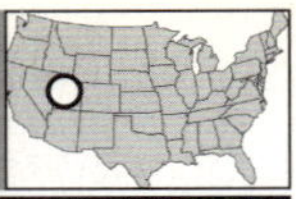

MOUNTAIN DATA

Top Lift at - 3056m

Ride Area 3300 acres

Bottom Lift at - 2014m

Vertical Drop - 944m

Number of Runs - 97

Longest - 3.5 miles (5km)

TERRAIN LEVELS

Easy	18%
Intermediate	43%
Advanced	39%
Expert =	

TERRAIN TO SUITE

Freeride	50%
Trees	Yes
Backcountry	Poor
Freestyle	20%
Halfpipe	Yes 1
Terrain Park	Yes various
Carving	30%

SNOW DATA

Average Snowfall
889cm a season

Snowmaking
47% cover of the slopes

Winter Periods
Nov to April

Summer Riding
None

SLOPE ACCESS

Total Lifts = **14**

Uplift Rate - 27,200 people an hour.

14 Chair lifts

**Leashes Required*

Lift Times
9.00am to 9.00pm

Lift Pass Rates

1 Day pass	no set price
3 Day pass	$165
5 Day pass	$245

Travel Guide

Fly to **Salt Lake City**, with transfer time of 45 minutes.

Bus services from Salt Lake City takes 45 mins

Route Planner:
From Salt Lake City head east along I-80 and exit at the junction for route 224 for Park City.
Salt Lake City to the resort = **32** miles

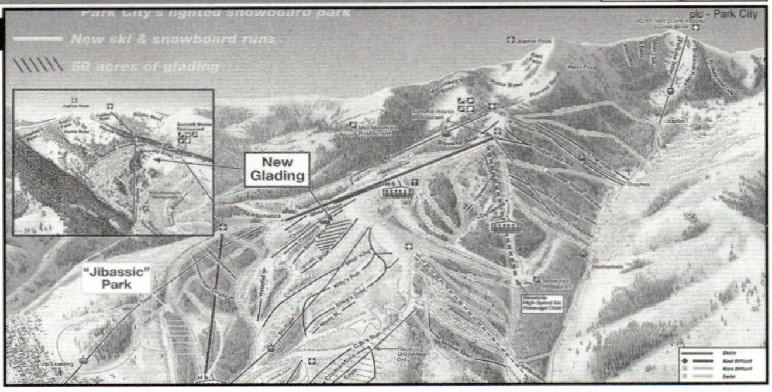

Park City, which is to play host to the **2002 Olympic Winter Games**, is by far the most famous resort in **Utah** and also one of the most expensive. However, don't let the fact that this is a costly place with a bit of an attitude put you off. In terms of what there is to ride and the way the place is laid out, **Park City** is truly awesome. With some 97 named trails and over 3300 acres of linked terrain, no-one is going to feel left out here. For the 2002 Olympic Winter Games, Park City will be hosting skiing's giant slalom and as well as the snowboard races and when you see this place, it's easy to see why. This is a place that knows how to put on a show.

Freeriders will be wetting themselves once they see what awaits them on these slopes, which stretch out over a number of peaks. If you like backcountry riding then check out **McConkey's** bowl where there are some great double diamond runs that weave through the trees. If riding deep powder in bowls is your thing then this place has some fantastic bowls that involve some hiking and then dropping in, notably the trails on **Jupiter**. Here you will find some orgasmic black diamond rated trails that can be ridden down to a chair lift, but be warned, this area is for experts.

Freestylers who want to catch big air off natural hits are going to love this place. The mountain is littered with hits galore whether it be up in the bowls or down on the lower pisted areas. The resort also builds numerous terrain parks with man-made hits of every shape, and to cap it all, there is a serious halfpipe located at the top of the **Payday** trail. The pipe is also flood lit for night riding.

Carvers are also in for a good time here. There is a fine choice of good cruising trails such as the runs off the **King Con** chair lift.

Beginners who have never ridden will soon be able to get to grips with things here, as this is a very good first timers resort.

No other resort in **Utah** packs in as many facilities as this one. There is every imaginable type of accommodation available although not many are aimed at budget riders. However, a good cheap option is the *Park City Youth Hostel* (www.parkcity.com tel 435 655 7255). Around town there are lots of things to do as well has offering fantastic nightlife. Don't listen to the stories about the Mormon drinking laws, they do exist but they just make things more amusing. Ask a local bartender what the score is on this.

For accommodation listings visit - www.worldsnowboardguide.com

Park City Mountain Resort
P.O. Box 39, Park City, UT 84060
***001* (435) 649 8111**
www.parkcitymountain.com
www.virgin.com/holidays

Overall rating out of 10 **7** **Top resort but damn expensive**

Powder Mountain Utah

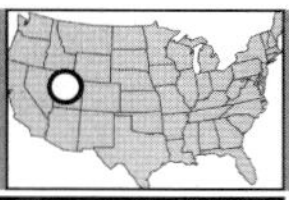

MOUNTAIN DATA

Top Lift at - 2713m
Ride Area 5500 acres
Bottom Lift at - 2316m
Vertical Drop - 395m
Number of Runs - 72
Longest - 3 miles (5km)

TERRAIN LEVELS

Easy	**10%**
Intermediate	**50%**
Advanced	**40%**
Expert =	

TERRAIN TO SUITE

Freeride	**70%**
Trees	Yes
Backcountry	Yes
Freestyle	**10%**
Halfpipe	Not yet
Terrain Park	Not yet
Carving	**30%**

SNOW DATA

Average Snowfall
1270cm a season
Snowmaking
0% cover of the slopes
Winter Periods
Nov to April
Summer Riding
None

SLOPE ACCESS

Total Lifts = **6**
Uplift Rate - not available an hour.
3 Chair lifts
3 Drag lifts
**Leashes Required*

Lift Times
9.30am to 10.00pm

Lift Pass Rates

1 Day pass	$37
3 Day pass	$100
5 Day pass	$166

Travel Guide

Fly to **Salt Lake City**, with transfer time of 1 hour.

Bus services from Salt Lake City takes 1 hour.

Route Planner:
From Salt Lake City head north on the I-15 north to Ogden 12th Street exit
Salt Lake City to the resort = **55 miles**

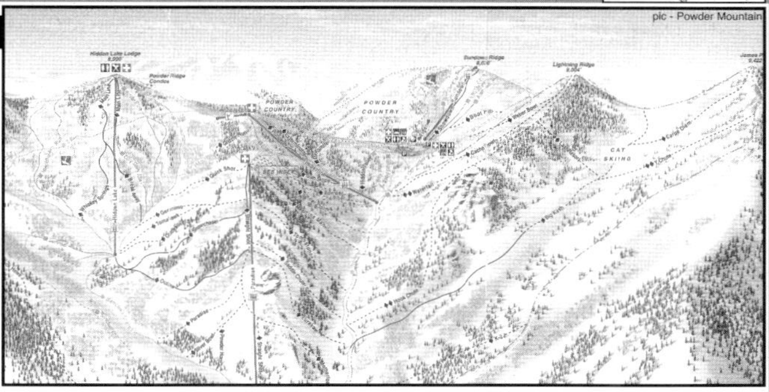

pic - Powder Mountain

Powder Mountain: the name of this resort doesn't lie as this place gets a lot of **Utah's** fine snow. Powder Mountain can be considered as Utah's best kept secret. It is just outside of the small mountain town of **Eden,** north of **Salt Lake City**, and does not attract the crowds like many of the larger destination resorts near **Salt Lake City** and **Park City**. The snowboard attitude around this resort is relaxed and friendly with many of the riders being regular locals from **Ogden** and other surrounding towns.

Freeriders will be stoked to find that **Powder Mountain** is one giant playground. Most of the terrain is a variety of tree shots, rock drops, and open powder fields. There are great lines off either side of **Straight Shot** and from the top of **Cobabe Canyon**. Powder has super cat skiing to the top of **Lightning Ridge**. Riders will also fall in love with the backcountry area known as **Powder Country** which is well known throughout the region. These impressive steeps are easily accessible from the **Sundown** lift and drop to the highway where a shuttle service runs for another ride up. For heli-boarding around the **Ogden** area call *Diamond Peaks Heli-Ski Adventures* (801) 745-4631.

Freestylers will find a decent well maintained halfpipe off the **Hidden Lake Run** and a smaller pipe off of **Sundown** lift near **Confidence**. Unfortunately, there is not a designated park area. If you search a little, you can find plenty of natural hits to play on. The boulder field on lower **Straight Shot** and the trees off of **East 40** have some nice kickers.

Carvers have a smaller selection of ccruising runs but most of the trails are not groomed. There are a few quality pistes off each lift, like **Whiskey Springs, Runaway**, and **Dr. C** all being pretty nice.

Beginners should all learn to ride at this resort with ease. **Sunrise, Sundown**, or **Hidden Lake** lift would be good places to start while the **Picnic** and **Mushroom** runs are nice mellow runs to follow up on. Instruction is offered at $25 for a group lesson.

Resort lodge restaurants are the only places to eat nearby and the only accommodation at the mountain is the **Columbine Inn**, where rooms and condos are available. The best bet for inexpensive food and accommodations is 19 miles away in the city of **Ogden**. Here you will find a large selection of everything, birds, booze and music, to mention but a few.

For accommodation listings visit - www.worldsnowboardguide.com

Powder Mountain
P.O. Box 450, Eden, UT 84310
***001* (801) 745 3772**
www.powdermountain.com
www.virgin.com/holidays

Overall rating out of 10 **6** **Great mountain - boring town**

Snowbird Utah

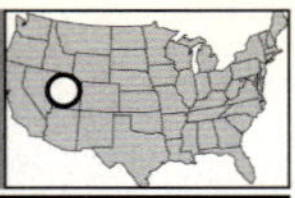

MOUNTAIN DATA

Top Lift at - 3352m

Ride Area 2500 acres

Bottom Lift at - 2365m

Vertical Drop - 988m

Number of Runs - 82

Longest -3.5 miles (5.2km)

TERRAIN LEVELS

Easy	**25%**
Intermediate	**35%**
Advanced	**40%**
Expert =	

TERRAIN TO SUITE

Freeride	**50%**
Trees	Yes
Backcountry	Yes
Freestyle	**20%**
Halfpipe	Yes 1
Terrain Park	Yes 1
Carving	**20%**

SNOW DATA

Average Snowfall
1270cm a season

Snowmaking
1% cover of the slopes

Winter Periods
Nov to May

Summer Riding
None

SLOPE ACCESS

Total Lifts = **12**

Uplift Rate - 15,000 people an hour.

1 Tram - **9** Chair lifts

2 Drag lifts

**Leashes Required*

Lift Times
9.00am to 8.30pm

Lift Pass Rates

1 Day pass	$54
3 Day pass	$141
5 Day pass	$215

Travel Guide

Fly to **Salt Lake City**, with transfer time of 45 minutes.

Bus services from Salt Lake City takes 45 mins

Route Planner:
From Salt Lake City head east along I-80 and I-215 south and leave at exit 6 following the route for ittle Cottonwood Canyon.
Salt Lake City to the resort = **25** miles

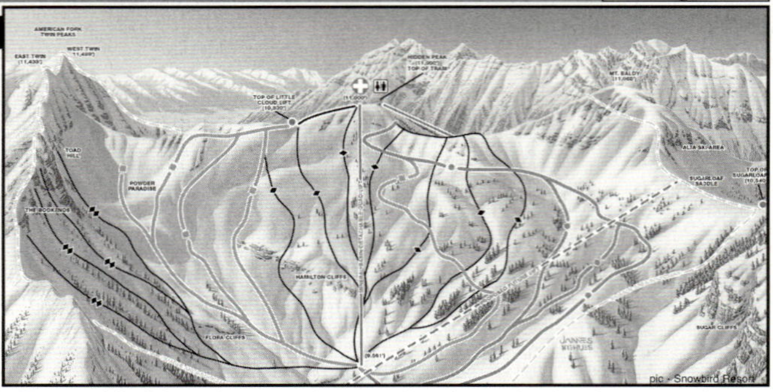

pic - Snowbird Resort

Snowbird is a favoured resort by those in the know and certainly one of **Utah's** most treasured snowboard destinations. Snowbird is unquestionably the choice mountain for intermediate and expert snowboarders. It has the most vertical terrain of any **Utah** resort and a pretty decent halfpipe. Skiers tend to out-number riders on this mountain, but the attitude is not competitive. The locals who ride here are definitely serious about what they do, but the atmosphere is still carefree and the regular crowd is always out to have a good time. During the ski season there is usually always some celebration or activity going on. Over the years, this is a resort that has become well known for its steep terrain and fantastic powder, trees, bowls and gullies along with some okay novice terrain. In all honesty, this place is for riders who can ride, because nearly half of the mountain is rated as advanced. If you like going balls out down serious steeps then **Snowbird** is your heaven, but be warned, if you fail to respect any of the slopes, you may go home in a body bag.

Freeriders should take the **Mineral Basin** lift off the backside of **Hidden Peak** which accesses some of the most epic snow and terrain imaginable. It is easy to spend an entire day there after a good storm and never get bored. On the other hand, once you take the tram to the top of **Hidden Mountain**, you can't really go wrong no matter what face you drop in off. There are plenty of cool runs like **Silver Fox, Great Scott**, and **Upper Cirque**, and **Gad Valley**. It is also not a bad idea to save some quality time for **Thunder Bowl**, accessible by the **Gad 2** lift.

Freestylers have a decent pipe accessed by the **Mid-Gad** lift. Besides that, you will have to use some creativity to find hits.

Carvers have a fairly limited selection of good runs. Groomed trails are generally traverses, cat tracks, or the easy way down.

Beginners will quickly find that **Snowbird** is really an intermediate to expert mountain and might get bored on the limited availability of easy runs. However, the opening of the easy area known as the **Baby Thunder,** which although may be a bit tricky to first get to, is the spot of first timers.

Local services are sparse to say the least. There are a couple of lodges close to the base lifts along with a few restaurants and a couple of bars. But don't expect much, or anything cheap.

For accommodation listings visit - www.worldsnowboardguide.com

Snowbird Ski Resort
P.O. Box 929000, Snowbird UT 84092-9000
***001* (801) 742 2222**
www.snowbird.com
www.virgin.com/holidays

Overall rating out of 10 **7** **Epic mountain for good riders**

Solitude Utah

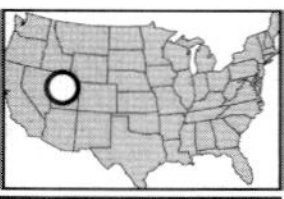

MOUNTAIN DATA

Top Lift at - 3059m

Ride Area 1200 acres

Bottom Lift at - 2435m

Vertical Drop - 624m

Number of Runs - 63

Longest -3.5 miles (5.2km)

TERRAIN LEVELS

Easy	20%
Intermediate	50%
Advanced	30%
Expert =	

TERRAIN TO SUITE

Freeride	70%
Trees	Yes
Backcountry	Yes
Freestyle	0%
Halfpipe	No
Terrain Park	No
Carving	30%

SNOW DATA

Average Snowfall
1143cm a season

Snowmaking
9% cover of the slopes

Winter Periods
Nov to April

Summer Riding
None

SLOPE ACCESS

Total Lifts = 7

Uplift Rate - 10,750 people an hour.

7 Chair lifts

**Leashes Required*

Lift Times
9.00am to 4.00pm

Lift Pass Rates

1 Day pass	$39
3 Day pass	$111
5 Day pass	$185

Travel Guide

Fly to **Salt Lake City**, with transfer time of 50 minutes.

Bus services from Salt Lake City takes 50 mins

Route Planner:
From Salt Lake City head east along I-80 and south on I-215 and exit at the junction 6 to Wasatch **Salt Lake City** to the resort = 33 miles.

pic - Solitude

Solitude is a nice change of pace because it does not seem to attract hoards of people like the other **Salt Lake** resorts, plus the mountain kicks ass! There is also a great variety of terrain and a way of spreading out the crowds so that the lines in any one area do not get too long. The attitude is low key and the regulars are super friendly. The down side is the weird *no air policy* at this resort. That's right, no parks, kickers, or halfpipes. No jumping allowed. Another major complaint is the electronic pass card and gate system used at every lift which is a real pain in the ass.

Freeriders will have no problem having the time of their lives at this resort. The summit lift is sure access to some of the sweetest powder country in **Utah**. **Honeycomb Canyon** is long and extreme and offers freeriding at its best. The **Evergreen** area is a must and the **Headwall Forest** rarely gets tracked out. The best freeriding on this mountain is the **Solitude** backcountry area, only accessible by hiking. These impressive steeps and powder fields drop down onto **Brighton Ski Resort**, but by staying far left, you will find trails that wrap back around to **Solitude**.

Freestylers will probably hate it here. No air? Enough said.

Carvers will want to concentrate on the area accessed by the **Eagle Express** where there are plenty of fast cruiser runs like the **Challenger, Gary's Glade** and **Inspiration**. Carvers will also be happy with a handful of smooth runs off of the Summit chair such as **Dynamite** and **Liberty**. The **Apex** chair will get you to a few short groomers as well.

Beginners will find that this mountain is a great place to first try snowboarding at. There is a good area for learning right off of the **Moonbeam II** chair, where you will find plenty of good easy runs to keep you happy for a while. **North Star** and **South Star,** off the **Sunrise** lift, are also great beginner runs. First timers can also warm up on **Easy Street** off the Link chair.

You can stay close to the slopes in one of the lodges or condo units offering a choice rooms at generally high rates. The *Powderhorn* is **Solitude's** newest place for lodging offering visitors somewhere to stay that is both good and convenient, but it's not cheap. Eating out options are basic, however, the *Creekside* makes fantastic pizza's.

For accommodation listings visit - www.worldsnowboardguide.com

Solitude Ski Resort
12000 Big Cottonwood Canyon, Solitude, UT 84121
***001* (801) 534 1400** **www.skisolitude.com**
www.virgin.com/holidays

Overall rating out of 10 - **7** **Super terrain but no air**

Snowbasin Utah

MOUNTAIN DATA

Top Lift at - 2850m

Ride Area 3200 acres

Bottom Lift at - 1951m

Vertical Drop - 899m

Number of Runs - 55

Longest - 3 miles (5km)

TERRAIN LEVELS

Easy	20%
Intermediate	50%
Advanced	30%
Expert =	

TERRAIN TO SUITE

Freeride	60%
Trees	Yes
Backcountry	Yes
Freestyle	0%
Halfpipe	Not yet
Terrain Park	Not yet
Carving	40%

SNOW DATA

Average Snowfall
1016cm a season

Snowmaking
over 579 acres

Winter Periods
Nov to April

Summer Riding
None

SLOPE ACCESS

Total Lifts = 9

Uplift Rate - 14,650 people an hour.

9 Chair lifts

**Leashes Required*

Lift Times
9.00am to 4.00pm

Lift Pass Rates
1 Day pass $43
1/2 Day pass $37
5 Day pass $

Travel Guide

Fly to **Salt Lake City**, with transfer time of 45 minutes.

Bus services from Salt Lake City takes, 45 mins

Route Planner:
From Salt Lake City head north on the I-15 north and exit to the I-89 & I-84 east for Mt reen/Huntsville to Hwy 167.

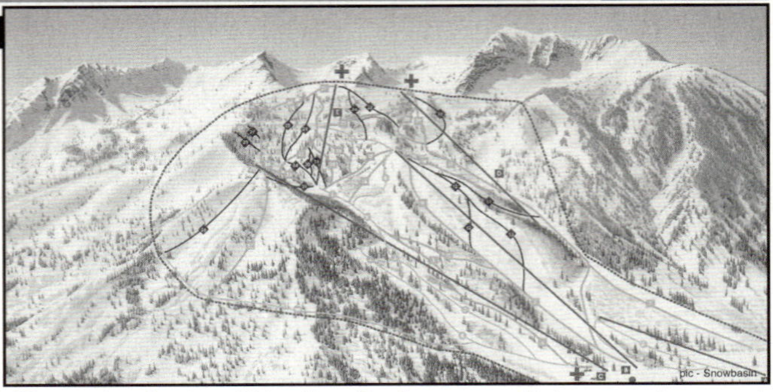

Snowbasin is within the **Ogden** area. It is a pretty sweet mountain but unfortunately everyone else has figured that out too. Located north of the city of **Ogden,** they regularly hold a bunch of ski races here, like the *Men's and Women's NorAm Superseries*, The *Men's World Cup Downhill and Super G*. **Snowbasin** will hold the *Men and Women's Downhill, Super G*, and *Combined Downhill* races for the **2002 Olympic** games. Unfortunately, they hold so many races here that the **John Paul Express,** which takes you to the men and women's downhill courses and which accesses a large kick ass part of the mountain, is usually closed of for competitions. Still, there are a lot of other runs to check out with a good supply of black ones at the upper area and a number of intermediate trails leading from the top to the bottom, taking in a few trees en-route. The whole mountain is open to boarders, but only if you have a safety strap on your board. If you arrive without one, you won't be allowed up.

Freeriders will like this mountain more than anyone else. In general the mountain is not extensive and a week's stay would be overdoing it. However, there is a good selection of black marked slopes to keep most riders interested for a day or two. The **Strawberry Express** is good for access to backcountry gates. It is not a long hike to some shoots to the south called the **Seven Sisters**. The north face of **De Moisy** is super nice too.

Freestylers will note that the **Snowbasin** doesn't have a whole lot to offer them. No parks or pipes are built yet, hopefully this will change in the near future. However, until such time that the resort sees fit to sculpture some hits, you can either build your own kickers or seek out the odd natural spot.

Carvers have some nice options like the men's and women's downhill courses when races are not going on. Most of the mountain is intermediate groomers with some nice long trails.

Beginners have a good resort for learning the basics at and although there are not loads of green easy trails, what is on offer is okay, especially the beginner terrain off of **Becker Chair**.

Forget about any slope side facilities, however, **Ogden** has everything you could possibly want. The **Alaskan Inn** 001 (801)-621-8600 is pricey and the rooms fill up fast, but it is fun and is right in **Ogden Canyon**, closer to the resorts.

Accommodation: Visit www.worldsnowboardgiuide.

Snowbasin
P.O. Box 460 Huntsville, UT 84317
***001* (801) 620 1000**
www.snowbasin.com
www.virgin.com/holidays

Overall rating out of 10 **5** **Decent terrain, but too commercial.**

The Canyons Utah

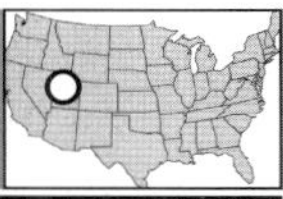

MOUNTAIN DATA

Top Lift at - 3045m

Ride Area 3625 acres

Bottom Lift at - 2073m

Vertical Drop - 853m

Number of Runs - 134

Longest - 2.5 miles (4km)

TERRAIN LEVELS

Easy	**14%**
Intermediate	**44%**
Advanced	**42%**
Expert =	

TERRAIN TO SUITE

Freeride	**60%**
Trees	Yes
Backcountry	Yes
Freestyle	**30%**
Halfpipe	No
Terrain Park	No
Carving	**10%**

SNOW DATA

Average Snowfall
826cm a season

Snowmaking
4% cover of the slopes

Winter Periods
Nov to April

Summer Riding
None

SLOPE ACCESS

Total Lifts = **14**

Uplift Rate - 24,000 people an hour

12 Chair lifts

2 Drag lifts

**Leashes Required*

Lift Times
9.00am to 4.00pm

Lift Pass Rates

1 Day pass	$58
3 Day pass	$150
5 Day pass	$240

Travel Guide

Fly to **Salt Lake City**, with transfer time of 45 minutes.

Bus services from Salt Lake City takes 45 mins

Route Planner:
From Salt Lake City head east along I-80
Salt Lake City to the resort = **32** miles.

pic - The Canyons

The **Canyons** is **Utah's** newest resort and one of the largest with over 3625 acres of fantastic terrain to check out that makes this part of the **Rockies** a pure dream. Newest Canyons may be, but in fact this place has been around for quite some time but under another name, that of **Park West**. However, that's neither here nor there, what this place is about is the future. This massive mountain, which is covered in trees from top to bottom, is constantly expanding by opening new areas all the time and upgrading base facilities year on year off. Indeed Canyons has big ambitions and plans to one day be the biggest resort in the US. And when you see what they have achieved so far, perhaps it could happen. But for now this is a mountain that has everything to turn the aspiring freestyle junkie into a pro air head, or a freeride grommet into a mountain guru. You have deep gullies, massive powder bowls and natural hits galore wherever you go.

Freeriders have landed in paradise when they get here. You simply won't believe not only the amount of terrain, but also the diversity of it all. The **Tombstone Express** will take you to some super terrain, but make sure you study your lift map, it would be easy to head off down a steep trail above your ability. However, one of the best areas to visit is the **South Side Chutes** off the **Condor** chair lift, where you will find a series of steep chutes.

Freestylers who have been wondering which place to check out in **Utah**, should look no further than this resort. **The Canyons** is a mega freestylers hangout having loads of natural halfpipes with excellent banked walls. And as if having perfectly formed natural pipes wasn't enough, the resort also has a first class man-made pipe called the **Painted Horse** (or **CIA** by locals) and is off the **Saddleback Express** chair lift.

Carvers of any level will find that this is a fine resort to practice carving at. There are loads of carefully prepared pistes that will keep you happy for days on end.

Beginners must study a lift map or seek advice from a local in order to get to the best of the easy terrain, which in truth, is rather limited. However, if you're a quick learner then it's fine.

The Canyons has some base area accommodation and other local services. However, the best option in terms of choice and prices is either down in **Park City** or back along in **Salt Lake City**.

For accommodation listings visit - www.worldsnowboardguide.com

The Canyons
4000 The Canyons Resort Drive, Park City, UT 84060
001 **(435) 649 5400** **www.thecanyons.com**
www.virgin.com/holidays

Overall rating out of 10 **8** **Big mountain, great riding**

Vertmont

Resort	Page
Jay Peak	125
Killington	126
Mt Snow-Haystack	128
Okemo	129
Stratton	130
Stowe	132
Sugar Bush	133

GENERAL INFO AND FACTS

Capital - Montpelier
Language - English
Currency - US Dollar
Alcohol drinking age - 21
Drugs - Cannabis is illegal
Death Penalty - Dosen't Exist
Age of consent for Sex - 16
Electricity Supply - 110 Volts AC
Area phone Code - 802
Provincial sales tax - 5%

VERMONT DRIVE GUIDE

All vehicles drive on the right side of the road.

Speed Limits -
Motorways 70mph (112kph)
Highways 55mph (90kph)
Towns 30mph (50kph)
Road Info 001 (801) 964 6000
Fuel is sold in Gallons

TRAVEL CONTACTS

Gateway Airports
Burlington for internal and **Boston** in **Massachusetts** for international
Flights from London take around 6 hours 30 mins (not direct).

Amtrax Railroad
tel: 001 (802) 879 7298

Greyhound Buses
tel: 001 (802) 864 6811

Eastern
GMT -5 hours

AREA INFORMATION

Vermont Travel Bureau
134 State St, Montpelier.
VT 05602
USA
tel: 001 (802) 828 3237

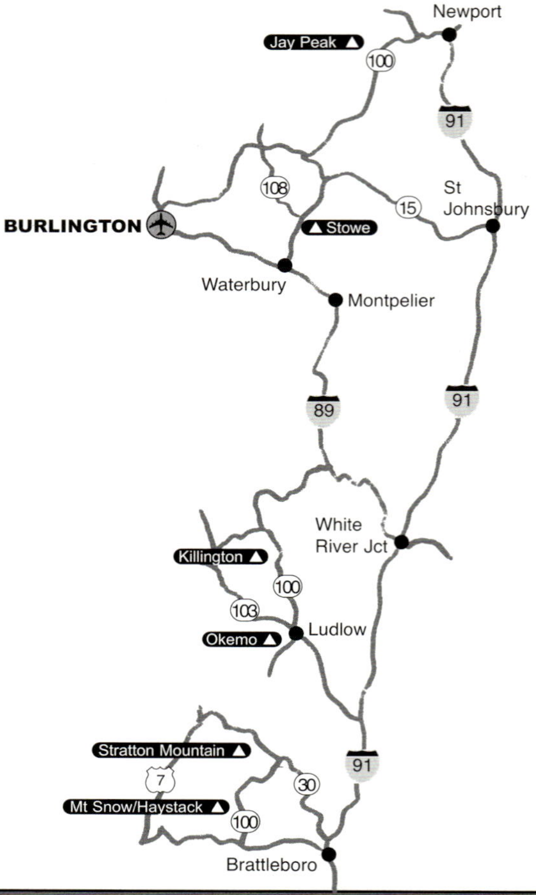

pic - Killington Resort

Jay Peak Vermont

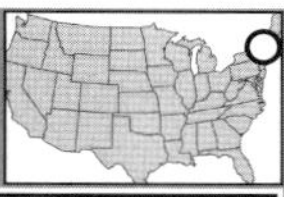

MOUNTAIN DATA

Top Lift at - 1209m

Ride Area 385 acres

Bottom Lift at - 553m

Vertical Drop - 656m

Number of Runs - 65

Longest - 3 miles (5km)

TERRAIN LEVELS

Easy	**20%**
Intermediate	**40%**
Advanced	**40%**
Expert =	

TERRAIN TO SUITE

Freeride	60%
Trees	Yes
Backcountry	Yes
Freestyle	20%
Halfpipe	Yes 1
Terrain Park	Yes 1
Carving	20%

SNOW DATA

Average Snowfall
117 cm a season

Snowmaking
75% cover of the slopes

Winter Periods
Nov to April

Summer Riding
None

SLOPE ACCESS

Total Lifts = **7**

Uplift Rate - 11,500 people an hour.

1 Tram 5 Chair lifts

1 Drag lift

**Leashes Required*

Lift Times
8.30 to 4.00pm

Lift Pass Rates

1 Day pass	$49
Night pass	$
5 Day pass	$

Travel Guide

Fly to **Monteal** in Canada, transfer time of 1 1/2 hours.

Bus services from Montreal takes 1 1/2 hours.

Route Planner:
From Montreal head south on I-10, 35 & 91 & Hwy 100 via Newport.
Montreal to the resort = **70** miles.
Boston is 3 1/2 hours
New York City is 6 1/2 hours.

pic - Burton Snowboards

Jay Peak, located in the far northern part of **Vermont** and close to the **Canadian** border, is not a bad place and one that attracts a fair few riders from within the state and across the border in **Canada**. Indeed the resort is actually owned by a Canadian resort company and you can even use Canadian dollars to pay for your lift ticket. For an east coast resort, **Jay** has a fairly good annual snow record, and although the amount of snow that falls here is no match for the resorts in the **Rocky Mountains**, is still good for the east and you can usually be guaranteed some fine powder each year. It is also notable that although it may not be a very big place, the amount of good hardcore and tree riding stands out's. Much of the mountain is fully open to snowboarders and is rated for advanced and intermediate riders, novice terrain is very limited. The resort has a modern lift system which includes a 60 person tramway and a series of chair lifts and T-bars. The location of **Jay Peak** may be the chief reason for this place for not becoming overcrowded while lift lines are either nonexistent or very small, except over holiday periods and the odd weekend.

Freeriders will find that the offerings on **Jay Peak** are pretty good and will allow advanced and intermediate riders the chance to ride hard and fast with some excellent powder spots, some very fast chutes and lots of tight trees. Note, the resort has a strict policy when it comes to riding in the woods. Basically you must take responsibility for your own actions if you ride out of bounds, you must be a competent rider and you must not go alone. Areas such as **Buckaroo**, the **Everglade** or the **Beaver Ponds Glades** are pure nectar and will excite all riders.

Freestylers have a terrain park, halfpipe and boardercross trail. But with so much natural freestyle terrain on offer, the man made hits are almost not needed. The **Canyonland** is home to an amazing natural halfpipe that should keep you amused for hours.

Carvers have a nice number of cruising trails set out everywhere.

Beginners are the one group who may find this place not for them. There are novice areas but they are very limited.

Jay Peak is a small town and has a limited amount of accommodation on offer. However, prices are not too bad and around town you will be able to go out and get a good meal with a reasonable choice of restaurants. Night life, however, is very tame.

For accommodation listings visit - www.worldsnowboardguide.com

Jay Peak
Route 242, Jay, VT o5859
***001* (802) 988 2611**

www.jaypeakresort.com
www.virgin.com/holidays

Overall rating out of 10 **5** **Okay east cost freeriding**

Killington Vermont

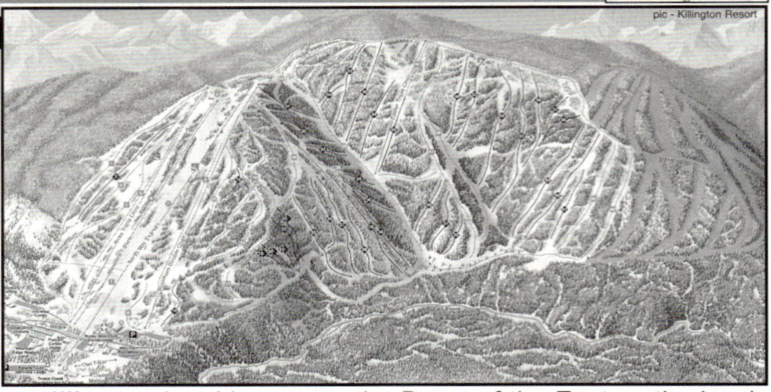

MOUNTAIN DATA

Top Lift at - 1292m

Ride Area 1160 acres

Bottom Lift at - 332m

Vertical Drop - 960m

Number of Runs - 205

Longest - 10 miles (16km)

TERRAIN LEVELS

Easy	**15%**
Intermediate	**60%**
Advanced	**26%**
Expert =	**10** runs

TERRAIN TO SUITE

Freeride	**45%**
Trees	Yes
Backcountry	Yes
Freestyle	**30%**
Halfpipe	Yes 2
Terrain Park	Yes 2
Carving	**25%**

SNOW DATA

Average Snowfall
640cm a season

Snowmaking
72% cover of the slopes

Winter Periods
Oct to May

Summer Riding
None

SLOPE ACCESS

Total Lifts = **31**

Uplift Rate - 53,973 people an hour.

2 Gondolas **24** Chair lifts

7 Drag lifts

**Leashes Required*

Lift Times
8.30am to 4.00pm

Lift Pass Rates

1 Day pass	$56
3 Day pass	$156
5 Day pass	$230

SLOPE ACTION

Snowboard Hire
Daily rates from $27
Kids from $22

Snowboard Tuition
Lesson, lift & hire from $65 per day

Night Riding
No

Heli Boarding
No

Snowmobiles
N/A

Mountain Cafes
9

Killington is a big resort - the Beast of the East as the locals like to call it. If you thought the east coast of **America** was lame and no match for the central or western resorts, then think again. Killington has seven mountains of steeps, bumps, mega carving terrain, loads of fun-parks and halfpipes, all serviced by a modern and well equipped lift system that includes an artistically painted and heated gondola. Visitors arriving here thinking that they will have the place licked in a day or two will be surely tested. You will need at least a couple weeks to ride all the runs and then a further month just to get to know what you have just been down. Killington reportedly has the largest snow-making facilities in the east, and like a number of other US resorts, it's a particularly snowboard-friendly place having hosted many snowboard events. The *United States Amateur Snowboard Association* once chose Killington as its training ground, and it's easy to see why: the terrain is perfect for all levels and all styles. One thing that boarders should be aware of is traversing, as it's very easy to end up spending a lot of time travelling across the mountain, trying to get around. An excellent tool here is the free *Ride Guide* which tells you everything worth knowing, from a snowboarder's perspective, about the mountain and surrounding town - you can pick up a copy at the ticket office.

Freeriders have a mountain that often seems to vary at every turn: you get to ride lots of bumps - **Superstar** on **Skye Peak** and **Outer Limits** on **Bear Mountain** for instance; plus there are lots of trees to ride in, with numerous 'secret' trails to search out. If you're after a heart tester, check out the steeps at **Killington Peak** off the **Cascade** chair, where you have a choice of tree-lined steep blacks.

Freestylers have two terrain parks and two halfpipes. The main pipe with its 12ft walls is superb and located close to the base lodge. And as well as the pipe having great transitions and sounds blasting out, you can also get a burrito pipe side. As well as featuring two terrain parks, one of which is now on the Timberline, there is now a boardercross course on the Dream Maker area. Killington offers a pipe-only pass for $20.

Carvers will love Killington's steep terrain, which ranges from ultra-wide, straight down trails like **Double Dipper** (which is good for big carves), to narrower, more traditional runs such as **East Fall** or **Royal Flush**. Other notable carving spots are on **Ram's Head, Snowdon** or **Skye Peak**.

Beginner's areas are excellent. However, like a lot of **New England** resorts, they can get busy at weekends. Stick to mid-week if possible as there are no crowds and empty runs. The *Killington Snowboard School* has a very good reputation and offers every level of tuition at prices worth paying. A day's ride package costs $65.

Local facilities are extensive and varied, with a purpose-built village at the base of the slopes. However, by far the bulk of local hospitality is stretched along the access road. If you're prepared to pay for the convenience, then try to stay at the base; the cheaper thing to do is move away from Killington and hang out in one of the smaller hamlets. This way you get a better feel of the place and the locals are easier to get to know. Wherever you stay, it's always good to have a car, although there are shuttle bus services. For snowboard services check the *Ride On* or *Darkside* shops.

Jobseekers: Lots of vacancies exist all season on or off the slopes, working in bars and cafes. Call Human Resources (802) 422 6100.

Food is standard grade, east coast, with big portions, lots of variety with over 60 restaurants throughout the area and in every price bracket. *Churchills* is noted for its steaks but isn't cheap and may entail a drive to get to it along route 4. Also highly rated is *Hemingways,* a super dollar hungry restaurant. For a decent and filling breakfast, why not check out the *Kodiak Cafe.* Or for a reasonably priced burger visit Peppers bar.

Night-life in and around Killington is noted for being well suited to snowboarders. There is a host of evening spots where beer and local birds are available to all ,and which can be very lively most evenings while rocking 'til late. The *Pickle Barrel* is known for having a good vibe as is the *Wobbly Barn* with live bands and rowdy crowds.

Accommodation here is a bit hit and miss, in the sense that there is no real town to speak of. There are some slopeside condos, but they don't come cheap. A full range of lodging options can be found stretched along the five mile access road, and offers dozens of cheap B&B joints to motels.

For accommodation listings visit - www.worldsnowboardguide.com

Summary: Very good snowboarder's resort with ample, diverse terrain to suit all styles and levels. Lots of good local services but not a convenient layout.

Money wise: Main very pricey but with options for budget riders.

Overall rating out of 10 **8**

Killington Resort
Killington Raod
Killington. VT 05751

General info	**001 (802) 422 3333**
Reservations	**001 (800) 621 6867**
Snowphone	**001 (802) 422 3261**

www.killington.com
www.virgin.com/holidays

pic - Killington Resort   pic - Nathan Bilow

Travel Guide

Fly to **Boston** International
Transfer time to resort = **3** hours.
Local airport = **Rutland** 12 miles.

Approximate global air travel times to **Boston**

from:	
London	**7** hours
Los Angeles	**5** hours
Frankfurt	**8** hours

There are daily bus services from Boston airport as well as good car hire services.

Trains to Rutland 12 miles on.

Route Planner
Boston *via Manchester & Woodstock*

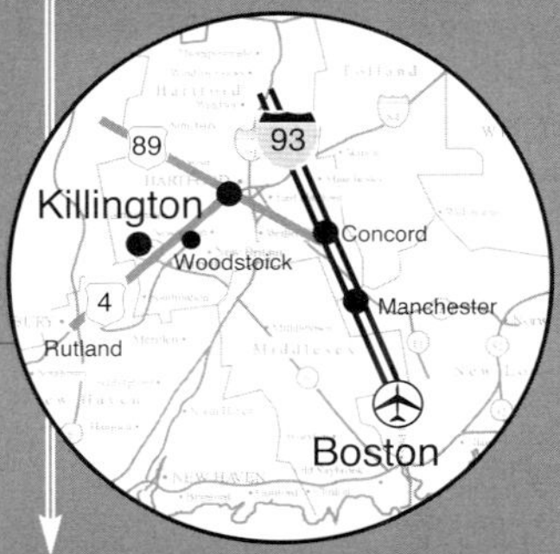

Killington = 162 miles
Drive time is about **3** hours

Mt Snow–Haystack vermont

MOUNTAIN DATA

Top Lift at - 1097m

Ride Area 767 acres

Bottom Lift at - 579m

Vertical Drop - 365m

Number of Runs - 130

Longest - 2.5 miles (4km)

TERRAIN LEVELS

Easy	**20%**
Intermediate	**60%**
Advanced	**20%**
Expert =	

TERRAIN TO SUITE

Freeride	**40%**
Trees	Yes
Backcountry	Poor
Freestyle	**25%**
Halfpipe	Yes 2
Terrain Park	Yes 5
Carving	**40%**

SNOW DATA

Average Snowfall
350cm a season

Snowmaking
86% cover of the slopes

Winter Periods
Nov to April

Summer Riding
None

SLOPE ACCESS

Total Lifts = **26**

Uplift Rate - 38,525 people an hour.

20 Chair lifts

6 Drag lifts

**Leashes Required*

Lift Times
8.30am to 4.00pm

Lift Pass Rates

1 Day pass	$55
3 Day pass	$148
5 Day pass	$239

Travel Guide

Fly to **Boston** Int, transfer time of around 2¾ hours .

Bus services from Boston and Bradley.

Route Planner:
From Boston, head west along Hwy 2, then north on I-91, west along Rte 9 and then finally north on Rt 100 to Mt Snow.
Boston = to resort = **134** miles.

pic - John Quigley

Mount Snow and **Haystack** are located in the **Green Mountain National Forest,** and like many of the east coast resorts within easy reach of major towns and cities, the area sees plenty of weekend ski-dwellers. Mount Snow and Haystack are, in fact, two separate resorts that are not, unfortunately, linked by lifts or snow trails. However, they are only a few minutes apart via the regular shuttle bus operating between the two areas. Collectively, the two areas have some 130 trails that are sold as one when you buy a lift pass. In the main, the whole place forms a cruisy mountain, best suited to intermediates and novices, with some decent-sized runs and interesting terrain features with hits, rollers, flats and trees. Be warned that at weekends and holiday periods, long lift queues do appear.

Freeriders coming here for the first time will find that the slopes on Mount Snow will offer challenging and difficult terrain. Advanced freeriders should head up to **North Face** with its series of blacks and double blacks which will test you with a mixture of bumps and groomed terrain. On Haystack, **The Witches** double blacks offer some interesting riding, but they're quite short.

Freestylers are best checking out the slopes on Mount Snow, where you'll find a good series of well constructed man-made hits in **Un Blanco Gulch** fun-park, which is over 1,000 metres long. Close by, is the 120 metre professional standard halfpipe, which has flood lights and is shaped to competition level.

Carvers wanting to lay down arcs can do so with ease on **Snowdance**, one of the blues from the **Summit Cafe**. The **North Face** area on **Mount Snow** is good for fast carving on steeps.

Beginners tend to stay on Mount Snow, where there is a good layout of easy trails. Haystack has a complete beginner-only area. *Ride On Snowboard School* offers a *Guaranteed Learn to Ride session*, at $50 all-in.

There is accommodation at the base of the slopes. *Mount Snow Condominiums* offer very good facilities which include a pool, but it's not a cheap option. A far greater selection of services can be found at **West Dover** or **Wilmington**, both inside a 10 mile radius. The lifestyle here is nothing amazing: a few bars and a number of places to eat give a laid back feel to the place, without any ego.

For accommodation listings visit - **www.worldsnowboardguide.com**

Snowbasin
P.O. Box 460 Huntsville, UT 84317
001 (801) 399 1135
www.snowbasin.com
www.virgin.com/holidays

Overall rating out of 10 **5** **Basic mountain but good riding**

Okemo Vermont

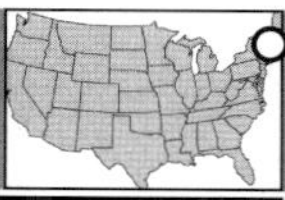

U S A

Vermont

MOUNTAIN DATA

Top Lift at - 1029m

Ride Area 500 acres

Bottom Lift at - 367m

Vertical Drop - 662m

Number of Runs - 98

Longest - 4 miles (7km)

TERRAIN LEVELS

Easy	25%
Intermediate	50%
Advanced	25%
Expert	=

TERRAIN TO SUITE

Freeride	40%
Trees	Yes
Backcountry	Poor
Freestyle	20%
Halfpipe	Yes 2
Terrain Park	Yes 3
Carving	40%

SNOW DATA

Average Snowfall
635cm a season

Snowmaking
95% ccver of the slopes

Winter Periods
Nov to April

Summer Riding
None

SLOPE ACCESS

Total Lifts = **13**

Uplift Rate 23,200 people an hour

10 Chair lifts

3 Chair lifts

**Leashes Required*

Lift Times
8.030am to 4.00pm

Lift Pass Rates

1 Day pass	$56
3 Day pass	$156
5 Day pass	$230

Travel Guide

Fly to **Boston**, with a transfer time 3 hours.

Bus services from Boston can be arranged.

Route Planner:
From Boston, head north on I-93 to Hwy 89, turning off at junction 9 for route 103 via Ascutney and Ludlow.
Boston to resort = **150** miles.

pic - Okemo Resort

After spending a couple of days on **Okemo**, you will notice the incredible core of talented riders who call Okemo home. There is tons of diverse terrain to ride, with nearly 90 trails, so you can find plenty of room, no matter what type of rider you happen to be. The lift system at Okemo is rarely busy, but if you don't have a leash you won't be welcome, so come equipped.

Freeriders who like bumps must check out **Ledges, Chief** and **The Plunge**. Recommended gladed runs are **Double Diamond** and **Outrage**. Both are long, steep and covered by snowmaking machines, which means that they open early and stay open late into the season. Okemo has expanded and now has new glades in the **South Face** area known as **Forest Bump** offering even more tree riding! Once you're clear of the trees and bumps, you won't believe the huge, ultra-long, rolling trails that are Okemo's trademark. **Sapphire**, **World Cup**, **Coleman Brook**, and **Tomahawk** are just a few trails that are perfect for going fast and boosting huge airs. For safety's sake, always use a spotter.

Freestylers won't want to miss **Okemo's** snowboard park, located at the bottom of **Sel's Choice**. Aside from the 420ft halfpipe, there is an array of jumps, rails, spines and boxes for every ability. Every season there is at least one jump (usually a table-top) that is so big, it takes a week for locals to clear.

Carvers have 90 trails to choose from, so every arc merchant should find something to please them, with the best terrain to lay out fast turns on being located on the upper sections.

Beginners are extremely well catered for at **Okemo** and for those who need to brush up or learn something new,there is an award-winning snowboard school catering for all levels and style of rider, with the beginner terrain being easy to handle. A *First Tracks* programme costs from $45 a day.

Off the slopes there are plenty of places to stay, with the usual array of hotels, motels and even a youth hostel. Prices will suit every budget, whether it be a slopeside condo or a giant B&B. To dine in style, *Nikki's* or *DJ's* is the place, whilst *Savannah's* is the joint for burgers. If you want a good drink with your food, then head for the *Black River Brew Pub*. Okemo in a nutshell: big mountain riding, small mountain atmosphere.

For accommodation listings visit - www.worldsnowboardguide.com

Okemo Mountain Resort
77 Okemo Ridge Road, Ludlow, VT 05149
***001* (802) 228 4041**
www.okemo.com
www.virgin.com/holidays

Overall rating out of 10 **6**

Stacks of diverse terrain to ride

Stratton Vermont

MOUNTAIN DATA

Top Lift at - 1181m

Ride Area 583 acres

Bottom Lift at - 571m

Vertical Drop - 610m

Number of Runs - 90

Longest - 3 miles (5km)

TERRAIN LEVELS

Easy	**35%**
Intermediate	**37%**
Advanced	**28%**
Expert =	**6** runs

TERRAIN TO SUITE

Freeride	**45%**
Trees	Yes
Backcountry	Okay
Freestyle	**25%**
Halfpipe	Yes 1
Terrain Park	Yes 1
Carving	**30%**

SNOW DATA

Average Snowfall
432cm a season

Snowmaking
82% cover of the slopes

Winter Periods
Nov to May

Summer Riding
None

SLOPE ACCESS

Total Lifts = **13**

Uplift Rate - 36,000 people an hour.

1 Gondola **10** Chair lifts

2 Drag lifts

**Leashes Required*

Lift Times
8.30am to 4.00pm

Lift Pass Rates

1 Day pass	$59
5 Day pass	$165
5 Day pass	$251

SLOPE ACTION

Snowboard Hire
Daily rates from $27
Kids from $22

Snowboard Tuition
Lesson, lift & hire
from $79 per day

Night Riding
Yes on Friday & Saturdays

Heli Boarding
No

Snowmobiles
N/A

Mountain Cafes
8

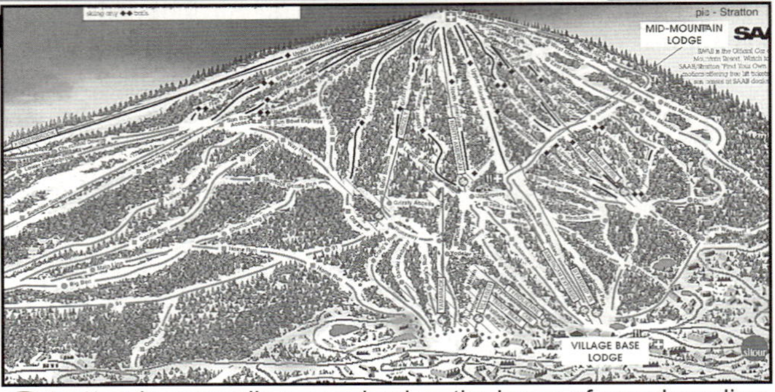

pic - Stratton

Stratton is generally recognised as the home of snowboarding, well at least on the east coast. A decent-sized resort, Stratton was one of the first areas in the US to give snowboarders access to its mountain. It is also noted for not only being the original home and test area for Jake Burton and his Burton Snowboards, but also as the place where America's first pro-snowboard school was set up and the home to the world's longest running snowboard competition, *The US Open*, which uses what is reputed to be the best halfpipe on the planet. *The Green Mountain Race Series* also comes to Stratton for a couple of events. Midweek you are up and down the mountain in a flash, but at the weekend, lift queues appear as everybody from **New York** and **Boston** arrive en-mass. However, with 40 years history as a ski resort, the management know how to keep things moving along to everyone's satisfaction. The future for Stratton also looks good, with a multi million dollar expansion plan. Riding here will suite everyone although riders who look for extreme or big cliff jumps may be a little disappointed. Still this is a resort that has a good annual snow record, and one which offers snowmaking facilities covering over 82% of the terrain on offer.

Freeriders who like their terrain carved out of tight trees, won't be disappointed as all the trails are hacked out of thick wood from top to bottom. For a good ride fix, the rollers and banks on the intermediate/novice terrain of **Black Bear** and the **Meadows** should do the trick. Riders with some know-how should check out the **Upper Tamarack** and if you are looking for some open trees, **Freefall** is the place.

Freestylers hanging around the lower mountain can use the high-speed, six-person chair to access one of three fun-parks and the 300ft long halfpipe. All the parks have a series of table-tops, gaps and ramps and to keep you interested they regularly build new hits. The pipe also has a loud sound-system, and floodlights for hitting the walls at night. On the lower mountain is the **Daniel Webster** terrain park, a novice park set out with a series of small hits for catching your first air without too much landing pain. The fun-park even has its own ranger, whose job it is to preen and rebuild the hits.

Carvers will notice that **North American**, **Upper Standard** and **Lifeline** will grab the alpine rider for big turns. The runs are well pisted and wide enough to allow you to put in some long, continuous turns, without too much fear of a collision.

Beginners and novice riders will have the whole of the lower mountain to explore, plus easy routes from the summit. The runs are particularly well suited for first timers, but at weekends the flat pitches become crowded, so expect a few collisions. Snowboard tuition is first class at **Stratton** with loads of teeching programmes to choose from.

Whether you're planning a week's trip or a two week stay, you won't be disappointed with what you find both on the slopes and off them. At the base of the mountain is a compact alpine style village with more or less everything you need. The scene can't be described as wild and in your face, but it is out there and with plenty going on. The place has a warm and welcoming atmosphere, and although you pay for it, services are very good. Shopaholics will love it here as there are dozens of stores and malls to help while away your time. There's also a very good sports centre in Stratton, where you can tone up, have a massage, or simply perve at the women doing their exercises. **Jobseekers:** Call for vacancies (802) 297 2200

Eating out options are a little disappointing, with the choice of expensive, bland food in a pompous restaurant, or cheap, bland nosh at a fast-food outlet. However, if you search around, you will find something to please your pallet. The *Sirloin Saloon* fries up some damn fine steaks and the *Base Lodge Cafeteria* dishes up a decent breakfast. Pizza lovers should check out the offerings from *La Pizzeria* while *Red Fox* is the Italian place.

Night-life in Stratton is okay but not spectacular. The *Base Lodge* is the first port of call in the early evening hours, where you can play pool, pinball and a juke box pumping out up-to-date sounds. Later on, check out the *Green Door Pub* for a few lively beers, or *North Grill* to sample some blues in a laid back atmosphere.

Accommodation: With nigh on 20,000 visitor beds around the area, lodging options are really good, with the usual offerings of condos, lodges, fancy, over-priced hotels or basic B&B haunts. The *Lift Line Lodge* has rates from $70, while *the Stratton Mountain Inn* has rates from $90 and offers good services in the centre of the village.

For accommodation listings visit - www.worldsnowboardguide.com

Summary: Good snowboarder's resort with ample, diverse terrain to suit all styles and levels. Lots of good local services, but a bit hit and miss!
Money wise: Good value for a weeks stay, but not a cheap resort.

Overall rating out of 10 **8**

Stratton Mountain Resort
P.O Box 145 Stratton
VT 05155

General info	***001*** **(802) 297 2200**
Reservations	***001*** **(800) 782 8866**
Snowphone	***001*** **(802) 297 2200**

www.stratton.com
www.virgin.com/holidays

pics - Stratton Mountain

Travel Guide

Fly to **Boston** International
Transfer time to resort = **3¼** hours.
Local airport = **Albany** 90 miles.

Approximate global air travel times to **Boston**

from:	London	**7** hours
	Los Angeles	**5** hours
	Frankfurt	**8** hours

There are daily bus services from Boston airport and from Albany airport.

Trains to Brattleboro (40 miles).

Route Planner
Boston *via Brattleboro & I-91*

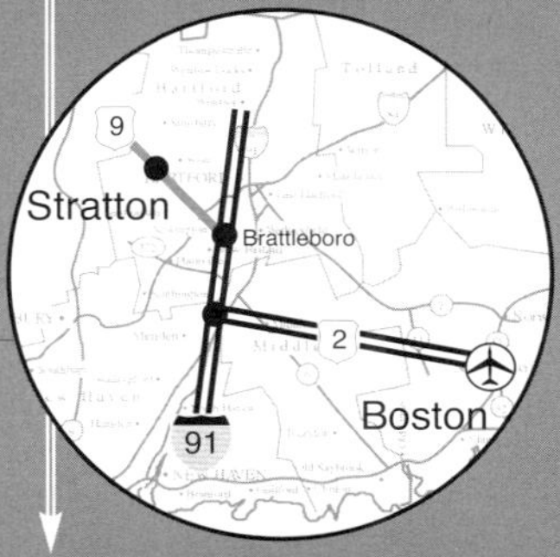

Stratton = 146 miles
Drive time is about **3¼** hours

Stowe vermont

MOUNTAIN DATA

Top Lift at - 1109m

Ride Area 480 acres

Bottom Lift at - 290m

Vertical Drop - 720m

Number of Runs - 46

Longest - 2.5 miles (4km)

TERRAIN LEVELS

Easy	16%
Intermediate	59%
Advanced	25%
Expert =	

TERRAIN TO SUITE

Freeride	40%
Trees	Yes
Backcountry	Yes
Freestyle	25%
Halfpipe	Yes 1
Terrain Park	Yes 2
Carving	35%

SNOW DATA

Average Snowfall
635cm a season

Snowmaking
75% cover of the slopes

Winter Periods
Nov to April

Summer Riding
None

SLOPE ACCESS

Total Lifts = **11**

Uplift Rate - 16,600 people an hour.

1 Gondola **8** Chair lifts

2 Drag lifts

**Leashes Required*

Lift Times
8.30am to 4.00pm

Lift Pass Rates

1 Day pass	$54
3 Day pass	$135
5 Day pass	$207

Travel Guide

Fly to **Boston Int**, with a transfer time of $2^{1/2}$hours.

Bus services from Boston take $3^{3/4}$ hours.

Route Planner:
From Boston, head north on 89 and turn off at junction 10 on to route 100 to Stowe

Boston
to resort = **198** miles.
$2^{1/2}$ hours drive time.

pic - Stowe

If you're after some serious east coast riding, then the popular resort of **Stowe** is your place. It's a proper mountain spread over three distinct areas, each one lending itself to a different level of ability: **Spruce Peaks** is the beginner/intermediate area (a little isolated from the main ride area); **Mt Mansfield** is accessed by the fastest 8-person gondola in the world, and is an intermediate's paradise with great cruising terrain, perfect for those who like to carve. The final area is the largest, and a perfect mix for each style in the advanced stages. Because **Stowe** is a popular hangout with city slickers and weekend tourists, the lifts can get clogged on weekend mornings, but don't be put off - a short wait will be awarded with a good long run.

Freeriders may find the area under the gondola fun with heaps of tracks through trees, and plenty of places within the main area to disappear into. **Liftline** and **National** are rather tame trails having been widened over the years, and are only cool if you are into bumps. **Nosedive** is good for freeride and carving, with the rest of the **Mansfield** area consisting of intermediate terrain, including a few good natural hits and jumps on the trail's edge.

Freestylers are going to kick arse on any mountain after a session in one of four fun-parks at Stowe. The top choice park is the specially designed **Jungle**, located on the **Lower Lord** area which is easily reached from **Lift 4**. Stowe also has a pipe, and the resort even provides a park for beginners and novices, alongside 20 minute lessons called *Quick Trick* at $15.

Carvers are much in evidence at Stowe, with the runs on Mt Mansfield having some nice, tame carving trails.

Beginners will surprise themselves when they see how quickly they can progress on the abundance of easy slopes, especially if they are aided by the teaching staff at the local snowboard school who have more teaching programmes available than you could poke a stick at, ranging from novice to freestyle camps.

The village is about six miles from the main slopes and is reached by a free shuttle bus. There are plenty of places to lay your head along the road to the lifts, with the usual choice of condos and B&B's. Stowe doesn't have the most radical night-life, although you can eat and drink well in a number of restaurants and bars, with the cool, friendly locals. *The Rusty Nail* is a hot spot for beer.

For accommodation listings visit - www.worldsnowboardguide.com

Stowe Mountain Resort
5781 Mountain Road, Stowe. VT 05672
***001* (802) 253 3000**
www.stowe.com
www.virgin.com/holidays

Overall rating out of 10 **6** **Okay fun all round resort**

Sugar Bush Vermont

USA Vermont

MOUNTAIN DATA

Top Lift at - 1260m

Ride Area 432 acres

Bottom Lift at - 453m
Vertical Drop - 804m
Number of Runs - 112
Longest - 3 miles (5km)

TERRAIN LEVELS

Easy	22%
Intermediate	46%
Advanced	32%
Expert =	

TERRAIN TO SUITE

Freeride	40%
Trees	Yes
Backcountry	Poor
Freestyle	20%
Halfpipe	Yes 1
Terrain Park	Yes 1
Carving	40%

SNOW DATA

Average Snowfall
716cm a season
Snowmaking
68% cover of the slopes
Winter Periods
Nov to April
Summer Riding
None

SLOPE ACCESS

Total Lifts = **18**
Uplift Rate - 24,363 people an hour.
16 Chair lifts
4 Chair lifts
**Leashes Required*

Lift Times
8.030am to 4.00pm

Lift Pass Rates

1 Day pass	$55
3 Day pass	$125
5 Day pass	$195

Travel Guide

Fly to **Boston,** with a transfer time 3¾ hours.

Bus services from Boston can be arranged.

Route Planner:
From Boston, head north on I-93 to Hwy 89, turning off at the junction for Bethel taking Hwy 107 and on up to Hwy 100. Boston to Sugarbush is 195 miles.

pic - John Quigley

Located along the **Mad River Valley** is the very snowboard friendly resort of **Sugarbush,** a mountain resort that is not bad and well worth a visit if you are in the area. Sugarbush is split over six connected mountain areas, all of which offer different features for different abilities. A short distance from Sugarbush is a resort called **Mad River Glen**, however, don't bother with this arse hole of a place because seven years ago they banned snowboarders due to a dispute with the management. Still, today there's no such problem here at Sugarbush, which has been operating as a resort since 1958. Today Sugarbush is a modern and well equipped resort with state of the art snowmaking facilities that reach almost 70% of the slopes. Mind you the resort has a respectable real annual snow fall of some 716 cm per season, making artifical snow not always so important. The six ridable areas are split up as, **Castlerock Peak,** which is home to some major expert terrain, **Cadd Peak,** which is the location for the *Mountain Range Snow Park* and good intermediate runs, **Lincoln Peak,** which has a splattering of good carving trails and some trees, **Mount Ellen,** which is the highest in the resort, **North Lynx Peak** home to a lot of novice terrain and finally **Slide Brook Basin.** You can ride all the areas on one lift pass and all are connected by the array of chair and drag lifts.

Freeriders should first make for the **Lincoln Peak** where you will be able to sample some major runs via the **Castlerock** chair. This area is mainly for riders who know the score, if you are easily frightened, forget it. However, if you are up to it then you won't be disappointed.

Freestylers are presented with the massive terrain park and pipe **Godzilla,** located on **Mount Ellen.** Around the resort there is also an abundance of natural hits for catching air off.

Carvers can pick and choose really. The area has a cool choice of groomers. Some of the runs on **Lincoln** are ideal for carving.

Beginners can take a lesson at the local ski school before trying out the easy slopes on **Lincoln Peak** or the **North Lynx Peak**

Off the slopes **Sugarbush** offers a large number of accommodation options, from quality hotels to basic bed and breakfast homes. Dining out is also rather good around here, however, the same can't be said for the nightlife, it's very lame indeed.

For accommodation listings visit - www.worldsnowboardguide.com

Sugarbush
2405 Sugarbush Access Road, Warren, VT 05674-9572
001 (802) 583 6300
www.sugarbush.com
www.virgin.com/holidays

Overall rating out of 10 **6** **Not a bad series of mountains.**

GENERAL INFO AND FACTS

Capital - Olympia
Language - English
Currency - US Dollar
Alcohol drinking age - 21
Drugs - Cannabis is illegal
Death Penalty - Exists
Age of consent for Sex - 16
Electricity Supply - 110 Volts AC
Area phone Code - 360
Provincial sales tax - 8.1%

WASHINGTON DRIVE GUIDE

All vehicles drive on the right side of the road.
Speed Limits -
Motorways 70mph (112kph)
Highways 55mph (90kph)
Towns 30mph (50kph)
Road Info 001 888 766 4636
Fuel is sold in Gallons

TRAVEL CONTACTS

Gateway Airports
Seattle -Tacoma International
Flights from London take around 12 hours (direct).

Amtrax Railroad
tel: 001 (206) 872 7245

Greyhound Buses
tel: 001 (206) 628 5526

Western
GMT -8 hours

AREA INFORMATION

Washington State Tourrism
Po Box 42500, Olympia
98504-2500
tel: 001 (360) 586 2088

pic - Soft Snapper

Crystal Mountain Washington

USA Washington

MOUNTAIN DATA

Top Lift at - 2134m

Ride Area 2300 acres

Bottom Lift at - 1341m
Vertical Drop - 945m
Number of Runs - 50
Longest - 3 miles (5km)

TERRAIN LEVELS

Easy	13%
Intermediate	57%
Advanced	30%
Expert =	

TERRAIN TO SUITE

Freeride	50%
Trees	Yes
Backcountry	Yes
Freestyle	25%
Halfpipe	Yes 1
Terrain Park	Yes 1
Carving	25%

SNOW DATA

Average Snowfall
812 cm a season
Snowmaking
1% cover of the slopes
Winter Periods
Nov to April
Summer Riding
None

SLOPE ACCESS

Total Lifts = **9**
Uplift Rate - 20,000 people an hour.
9 Chair lifts

**Leashes Required*

Lift Times
8.30 to 4.00pm

Lift Pass Rates

1 Day pass	$40
3 Day pass	$111
5 Day pass	$185

Travel Guide

Fly to **Seattle,** which is 76 miles north of Crystal.

Bus services from Seattle take around 1 3/4 hours.

Route Planner:
From Seattle head south on I-5 and exit onto Hwy 164 and then Hwy 410 east to Crystal Mountain.

Seattle to resort = **76** miles. **1 1/2** hours drive time.

pic - Ride Snowboards

Located mid-way into **Washington State**, an hour and twenty minutes from **Seattle**, **Crystal** is yet another yankee freeride classic, unspoilt by skiers, for riders in the know. The terrain is spread out over four peaks, with an awesome amount of back-country riding. Over the next few years, the planned investment programme will deliver new lift facilities and improve existing services. It will also raise Crystal's profile which may have the adverse effect of bringing in more skiers - presently there is a balanced mix, leaving the slopes crowd-free and lift queues short.

Freeriders, miss this place and you're missing out on life; the terrain is pure freeriding and **South Back** is the place to check out if you're willing to do some hiking. From the summit of **Throne**, you get to ride what can best be described as heaven - unfortunately it is not for wimps being a steep with a double black diamond rating. Less daunting but still a big buzz are the runs off **Summit House**, while the trails in the **North Back** area on the likes of **Paradise Bowl** are total joy.

Freestylers won't need man-made facilities at Crystal Mountain, as there is plenty of natural freeride terrain to catch big air. However, there is a pipe off the **Rendezvous** chair, but it's not up to much. **The Boarder Zone** fun-park, located off the **Quicksilver** chair, has a number of hits, but like the halfpipe, it doesn't live up to what nature can offer.

Carvers can have as good a time as freeriders, with a choice of excellent slopes that will please advanced and intermediate riders, even if some of the trails are not too long.

Beginners can't do much worse than at Crystal. Only 13 of its trails are fine for novices, but what is on offer is excellent and easily reached from the base. And like many US resorts, a number of the higher rated runs are not that tricky, so many of the red trails can be licked by a competent, fast-learning novice.

No big surprise here, the village at the base of the slopes is simple, basic, but good enough, with affordable places to sleep and eat in to suit all tastes and pockets. For a bed check out *The Alpine Inn*, which is close to the slopes and good value. And for a feed try the *The Cascade Grill* which serves a good breakfast. The main hangout for booze is the **Snorting Elk Cellar,** but unfortunately it's not a place for babes.

For accommodation listings visit - www.worldsnowboardguide.com

Crystal Mountain Resort
1 Crystal Mtn Blvd. Crystal Mt. WA 98022
001 (360) 663 2265
www.skicrystal.com
www.virgin.com/holidays

Overall rating out of 10 **6** **Good fun resort**

Mt Baker

Washington

MOUNTAIN DATA

Top Lift at - 1535m

Ride Area 1000 acres

Bottom Lift at - 455m

Vertical Drop - 457m

Number of Runs - 38

Longest -1.75 miles (3km)

TERRAIN LEVELS

Easy	**24%**
Intermediate	**45%**
Advanced	**31%**
Expert =	**2** runs

TERRAIN TO SUITE

Freeride	**60%**
Trees	Yes
Backcountry	Lots of it
Freestyle	**20%**
Halfpipe	Yes 1
Terrain Park	Yes 1
Carving	**20%**

SNOW DATA

Average Snowfall
1638cm a season

Snowmaking
0% cover of the slopes

Winter Periods
Nov to May

Summer Riding
None

SLOPE ACCESS

Total Lifts = **9**
Uplift Rate - 6,000 people an hour.
8 Chair lifts
1 Drag lift
**Leashes Required*

Lift Times
8.30am to 4.00pm

Lift Pass Rates

1 Day pass	$22 weekday
1 Day pass	$32 weekend
5 Day pass	$

SLOPE ACTION

Snowboard Hire
Daily rates from $25
Kids from $20

Snowboard Tuition
Lesson, lift & hire
from $43 per day

Night Riding
No

Heli Boarding
No

Snowmobiles
N/A

Mountain Cafes
3

pic - Mtn Baker

If sex was a mountain, **Mt Baker** would be the orgasm, because this treasure is pure snowboarding heaven, with a snowboard history that is written in big letters. In the early days when other ski resorts had their heads up their arses and were banning snowboarders, this amazing place took a far different view. That foresight has crowned Baker as one of the best unspoilt snowboard resorts in the world, with a snow record to be envious of. Mt Baker is also the home to the legendary *Banked Slalom* race, which is held every year. Located in the far north of **Washington** state, Mt Baker is home to all-time legend Craig Kelly, who liked riding Baker's terrain so much, he moved there. Due to Baker's isolation it has the added advantage that it doesn't attract hoards of day-tripping skiers, leaving the slopes bare and the lift queues at a big fat 'zero'. The slopes span two mountains - **Mount Shuskan** rising to 2,963m (9,720ft), and **Panorama Dome** with its more modest summit of 1,524m (5,000ft). Both mountains offer the opportunity to ride steeps and deep powder, with the majority of advanced piste set out on the Panorama side. Runs like the **Chute** are set to test anyone, but be warned, parts of it are really steep and carry avalanche warnings. Overall, Baker is a mountain where you need be fully aware of your surroundings and not take any chances. One wrong turn could easily see you returning home to mum in a black body bag!.

Freeriders wanting to explore the amazing off-piste should seek the advice of a local rider; it's the only way to locate the best stuff, of which there are heaps. The amazing amount of unrestricted freeriding terrain is truly awesome and will keep you riding happily forever and a day. For the less adventurous, the blue off Number **8** chair in the **Shuskan** area is well worth a ride, offering piste-loving freeriders the opportunity to shine at speed.

Freestylers will love the whole area, particularly the natural half-pipe that runs from the top of the two Shuskan chair lifts. This is where the Banked Slalom is held and, apart from beginners, is a must for all freestylers and freeriders. The run drops down a long winding gully and is totally magic.

Carvers who only want to pose whilst laying fast tracks on perfectly prepared piste should stay away. Mt Baker is not a hard-booter's resort, although there are some runs to blast down. Instead, buckle in with soft boots and go freeriding which this places is meant for, (lame heads who want to pose in hard boots stay away).

Beginners won't be disappointed with Mt Baker, with the option of learning on plenty of easy runs that are spread out around the area, the best being located on Shuskan. The local snowboard school is well established and offers a number of teaching programmes for all levels, with an emphasis on general freeriding. A days learn to ride package cost from $43.

Riders who like everything on their doorstep will not be happy as the only facility at the base is a car park. **Mt Baker** is not a gimmick, so you do have to put yourself out which is another reason why it's so good. The slopes of Mt Baker are located 17 miles from the main local services which can be found in the low-key town of **Glacier**, a simple and unspoilt place. Local services may be a bit thin on the ground, but don't let that put you off. What is offered is cheap and damn good value, making a week or even two, well worth the trip up. The town of Bellingham, just over an hour away has an even greater selection of lodgings, sporting facilities and other visitor attractions.
Jobseekers: Call for details: (360) 734 6771.

The options for getting a meal on the slopes or down in Glacier may be a bit limited in terms of choices of restaurants, but what is available will do nicerly. During the day you can pig out on the slopes at the *White Salmon Day Lodge* which has very reasonable rates. The new *Raven Hot* cafe has fast become a major day time hangout whilst also serving up some wicked food. Down in Glacier, *Milano's Cafe* is the place to check out, where they do great pasta dishes.

One of the beautys of this place is it's laid back atmosphere, which applies equally to the night life in **Glacier,** the perfect snowboard scene-laid back and cool. There is no hype, no apres-ski crap and no gits in silly hats playing party games. What you get is basic, offering a good laugh and messy late night drinking sessions, resulting in some killer hangovers.

Accommodation is only possible down in Glacier which has a number of options at very reasonable prices. Cool places to contact for a bed, are *Glacier Creek Lodge*, *Mt Baker B&B*, *Diamond Ridge B&B* or a condo at the *Mt Baker Chalets & Condos.*

For accommodation listings visit - www.worldsnowboardguide.com

Summary: Fantastic snowboarder's resort with ample diverse terrain to suit all styles and levels. Lots of good local services but not convenient for the slopes.
Money wise: Extremely affordable resort both on and off the slopes.

Overall rating out of 10 — **10**

Mt Baker Resort Office
1017 Iowa Street.
Bellingham. WA 98226
General info **001 (360) 734 6771**
Reservations **001 (360) 734 6771**
Snowphone **001 (360) 671 0211**
www.mtbakerskiarea.com
www.virgin.com/holidays

pics - Mt Baker

Travel Guide

Fly to **Seattle** International
Transfer time to resort = **2** hours.
Local airport = **Bellingham** 52 miles away
Approximate global air travel times to **Seattle**

from: London	**12** hours
New York	**5** hours
Frankfurt	**13** hours

Buses from **Seattle** take 3 hours and 1 1/4 hours from **Bellingham** airport.

Trains to Bellingham (5 miles).

Route Planner
Seattle *via Bellingham*

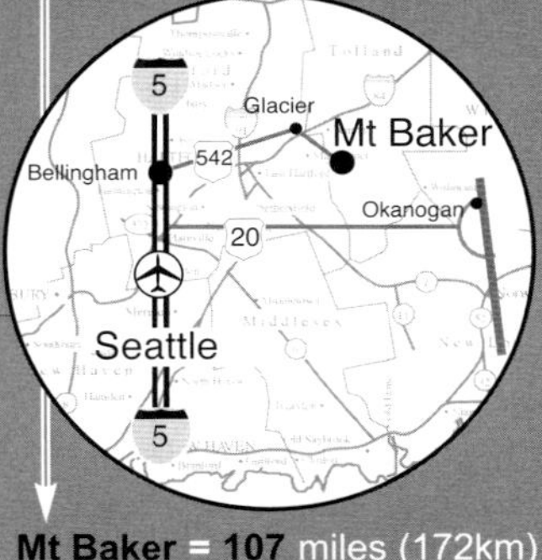

Mt Baker = **107** miles (172km)
Drive time is about **2** hours

Wyoming

Resort	Page
Grand Targhee	140
Jackson Hole	142

GENERAL INFO AND FACTS

Capital - **Cheyenne**
Language - English
Currency - US Dollar
Alcohol drinking age - 21
Drugs - Cannabis is illegal
Death Penalty - Exists
Age of consent for Sex - 16
Electricity Supply - 110 Volts AC
Area phone Code - 307
Provincial sales tax - 6%

WYOMING DRIVE GUIDE

All vehicles drive on the right side of the road.

Speed Limits -

Motorways 70mph (112kph)
Highways 55mph (90kph)
Towns 30mph (50kph)
Road Info 001 (307) 772 0824
Fuel is sold in Gallons

TRAVEL CONTACTS

Gateway Airports
Jackson Hole Airport
Cheyenne Airport
Flights from London take around 12 hours (not direct).

Amtrax Railroad
tel: 001

Greyhound Buses
tel: 001 800 231 2222

Mountain & West
GMT -7 hours

AREA INFORMATION

Wyoming Division of Tourism
125 & College Dr, Cheyenne
82002 WY
tel: 001 (307) 777 7777

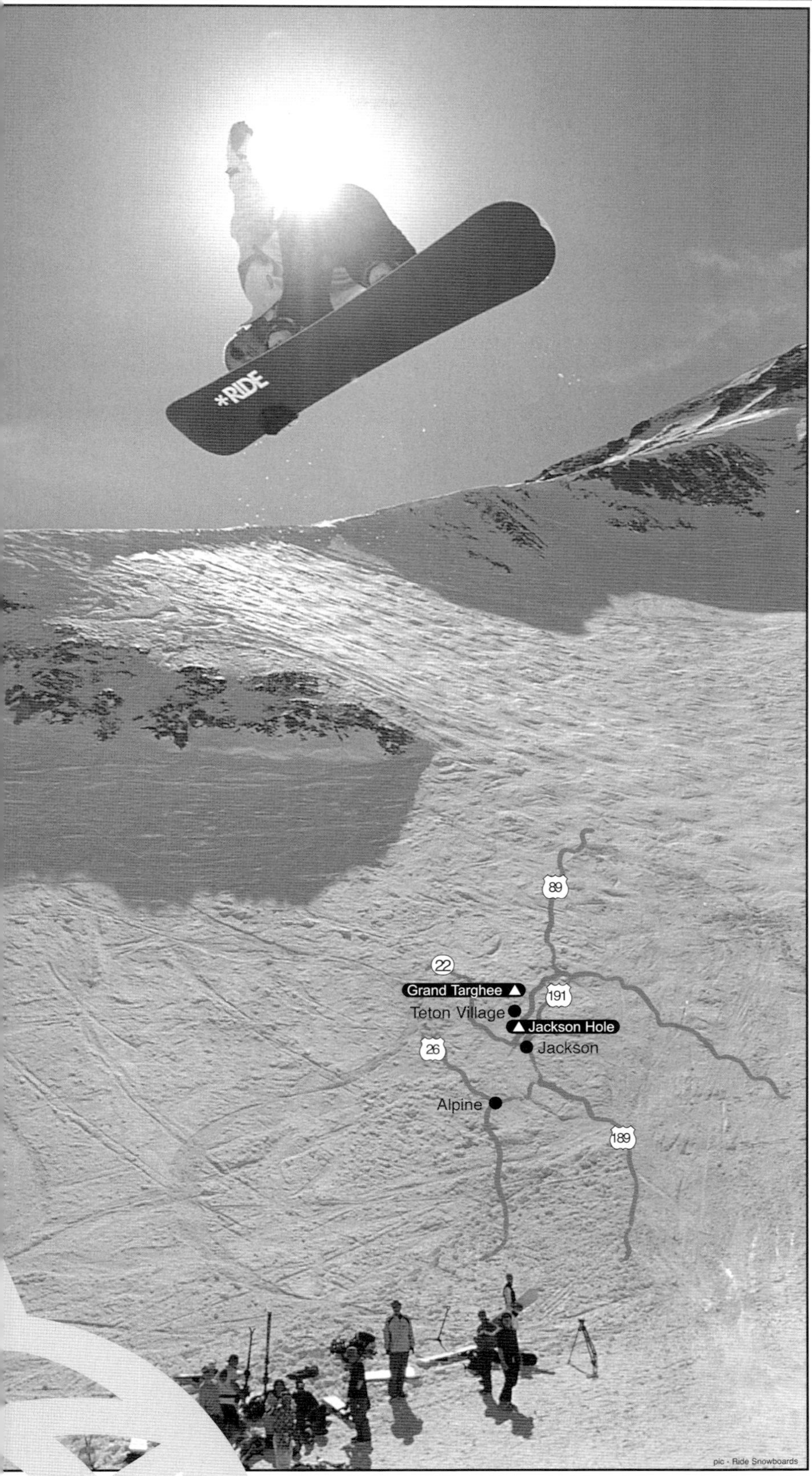

pic - Ride Snowboards

Grand Targhee Wyoming

MOUNTAIN DATA

Top Lift at - 3110m

Ride Area 1500 acres

Bottom Lift at - 2438m

Vertical Drop - 672m

Number of Runs - 62

Longest - 2.5 miles (3km)

TERRAIN LEVELS

Easy	**10%**
Intermediate	**35%**
Advanced	**35%**
Expert =	**20%**

TERRAIN TO SUITE

Freeride	**70%**
Trees	Yes
Backcountry	Lots of it
Freestyle	**20%**
Halfpipe	Yes 1
Terrain Park	No
Carving	**10%**

SNOW DATA

Average Snowfall
1280 cm a season

Snowmaking
0% cover of the slopes

Winter Periods
Nov to April

Summer Riding
None

SLOPE ACCESS

Total Lifts = **4**
Uplift Rate not available

3 Chair lifts
1 Drag lift
**Leashes Required*

Lift Times
9.30am to 4.00pm

Lift Pass Rates

1 Day pass	$44
3 Day pass	$123
5 Day pass	$205

SLOPE ACTION

Snowboard Hire
Daily rates from $26
Kids from $20

Snowboard Tuition
Lesson, lift & hire
from $59 per day

Night Riding
No

Heli Boarding
No

Snowmobiles
Hire and tours

Mountain Cafes
5

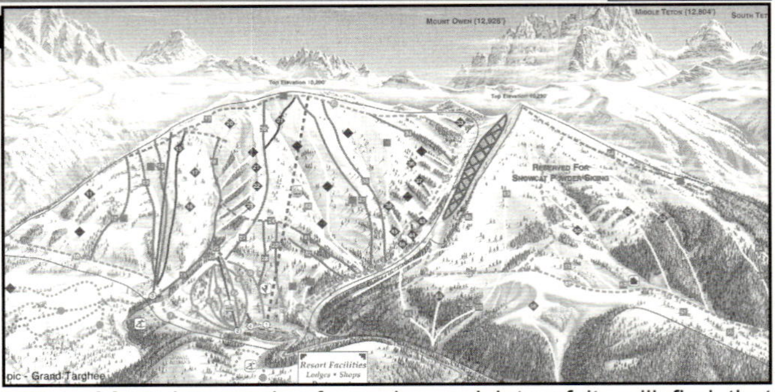

pic - Grand Targhee

Freeriders in search of powder and lots of it, will find that **Grand Targhee** is the perfect place to find it. This fantastic resort is a US powder heaven, with an average snowfall of over 1,280cm a year making riding powder a buy word here, even the piste map shows the powder terrain levels so novices can even try out powder stashes. What you have here in this low key resort are two mountains - **Fred's Mountain** which can be reached via three chair lifts and a drag lift, and **Peaked Mountain** accessible only by snowcats. Both mountains offer the chance to do some full-on freeriding on crowdfree slopes that will suit advanced and intermediate riders in the main. The trails on Fred's Mountain are a collection of short blacks that snake through a smattering of trees with a couple of nice, wide open blue runs. If you're the adventurous sort, then **Peaked Mountain** should be the place to get your fix. This is where you get to ride perfect freeride territory with the help of snowcats - a local company offers snowcat tours for around $210 a day. Tours are accompanied by guides and limited to 10 people per cat; prices include a lunch. Peaked Mountain is not exclusively for advanced riders; in fact most of what is on offer is graded green and blue, with a couple of black descents that take in some thick trees.

Freeriders will soon work out that this is a resort for them. The terrain on both mountains lends itself perfectly for both piste and backcountry riding. You'll find a number of steep black trails on **Fred's Mountain**, but most of them are quite short. However, for a real buzz, there is the option to take a snowcat tour on **Peaked Mountain** where you can freeride thousands of metres of untracked terrain. A one day cat board tip may set you back as much as $250, but it won't be wasted money. You can even sign up for a lesson in riding powder.

Freestylers have a naturally formed halfpipe that provides air heads with some interesting walls to ride up. There is also a killer boardercross circuit that needs to be treated with full respect. However, man-made obstacles aren't really necessary in **Targhee**; the place is riddled with natural hits, many of which are known only to the locals. However, the riders here are cool and will happily take you to the best launch pads and show you how much diverse, natural freestyle terrain there actually is.

Carvers forget it, especially Euro-faggots who only own a pair of hard boots. The terrain here is not really suited to big arcs and posey turns for lift-line riders. What's more, as there's not too much smooth grooming here, the generally uneven slopes will take you out if you edge over without good speed control.

Beginners are the one group who may feel left out here. Although there is some novice areas around the base, there's not much of it. Still, if you're a fast learner then don't be put off. Lesson programmes are available with a days packakge rate from $59.

Off the slopes what you get is both basic and very limited. There is only a handful of buildings at the base area offering a number of high quality lodges, hotels and a few local shops all close to the slopes. The village has a very relaxed and laid back appeal to it, but if you're the sort that wants a resort loaded with the usual tourist gizmo's, forget it. There is an outdoor swimming pool and a few spa baths. Snowmobiling is another past time on offer, as is dog sledding. But overall your leasure time will mainly be taken up with either, eating, drinking or sleeping. Still, the locals are a cool bunch. Furthermore this place is reasonably priced and can be done on a tight budget making a weeks trip well worth it.

Foodies on a serious quest to eat nightly at dozens of eatries are in for a massive shock. **Grand Targhee** only has half a dozen restaurants although the main lodges have their own restaurants. What is available, is very good. *Wild Bills,* centrally located in the *Rendezvous Lodge,* serves a variety of dishes all day long, with mexican dishes available alongside hot grills etc. *Snorkels* is noted for being able to offer a good breakfast while the *Trap* fries a good burger and at a decent price.

Night owls who normally ride hard during the day, and then party all night long won't be doing that here. **Grand Targhee** is a sedate family style hang out that doesn''t go in for serious hardcore night-life action. There is almost zero here in terms of bars or discos, but you can have a beer and while the night away in the *Trap Bar, or Snorkels* which is the laid back but dull night time hang out.

The resort only has 430 tourist beds available in a couple of hotel/lodges and in a condo unit. Various weekly packages are on offer from throughout the season. A two person condo at the Sioux Lodge will set you back some $500 for five nights. Call reservations for full details.
See www.worldsnowboardguide.com.

Summary: A very good resort for powder hounds and freeriders. But this is not a place for the total novice nor for those individuals looking for a big loaded resort.
Money wise: A great value for money resort in all aspects.

Overall rating out of 10 — **8**

Grand Targhee
Ski Hill Road, Box Ski, Alta
Wyoming 83422
General info **001 (307) 353 2300**
Reservations **001 (800) 827 4433**
Snowphone **001 (307) 353 2300**
www.grandtarghee.com
www.virgin.com/holidays

pic - Zip

pic - Grand Targhee

Travel Guide

Fly to **Salt Lake City** International
Transfer time to resort = **5$^{3/4}$** hours.
Local airport = **Teton Peaks** 13 miles away

Approximate global air travel times to **Salt Lake City**

from:		
	London	**9** hours
	New York	**3$^{1/2}$** hours
	Frankfurt	**10** hours

Buses from **Idaho Falls** take 1$^{1/2}$ hours and 5$^{3/4}$ hours from **Salt Lake City** airport (289 miles).

Trains: None

Route Planner
Idaho Falls *via Driggs*

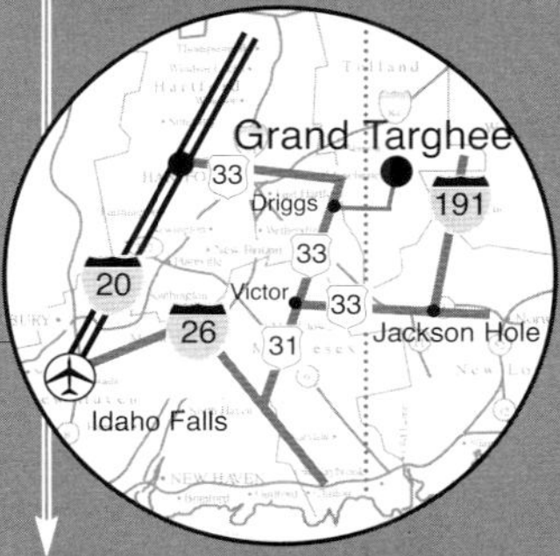

Grand Targhee = 87 miles
Drive time is about **1$^{3/4}$** hours
***Salt Lake City** is **289** miles which will take about **5$^{3/4}$ hours**

Jackson Hole Wyoming

MOUNTAIN DATA

Top Lift at - 3185m

Ride Area 2500 acres

Bottom Lift at - 1924m

Vertical Drop - 1216m

Number of Runs - 80

Longest -4.5 miles (7.2km)

TERRAIN LEVELS

Easy	10%
Intermediate	40%
Advanced	50%
Expert =	

TERRAIN TO SUITE

Freeride	**55%**
Trees	Yes
Backcountry	Lots of it
Freestyle	**25%**
Halfpipe	Yes 1
Terrain Park	Yes 1
Carving	**20%**

SNOW DATA

Average Snowfall
765cm a season

Snowmaking
20% cover of the slopes

Winter Periods
Dec to April

Summer Riding
None

SLOPE ACCESS

Total Lifts = **10**

Uplift Rate - 12,000 people an hour.

1 Tram

9 Chair lifts

**Leashes Required*

Lift Times
8.30am to 4.00pm

Lift Pass Rates

1 Day pass	$56
3 Day pass	$162
5 Day pass	$250

SLOPE ACTION

Snowboard Hire
Daily rates from $30
Kids from $25

Snowboard Tuition
Lesson, lift & hire
from $60 per day

Night Riding
Yes

Heli Boarding
No

Snowmobiles
Hire and tours

Mountain Cafes
3

pic - Jackson Hole

Jackson Hole is a truly all American resort and comes with cowboys, saloon bars and high peaks. Not the typical tree-lined rolling mountains found in a lot of US resorts, Jackson is a high peaked mountain resort that is located in a large valley some 10-40 miles wide and 50 miles long. At the base of the slopes is a small village called **Teton**, 10miles away from the main town of Jackson Hole, which has the much smaller resort of **Snow King** rising out of it. Jackson Hole is a resort that will appeal to snowboarders that like a challenge. Much of the terrain is rated black, offering some steep sections with trees and long chutes. Back country riding is also a major option as there are vast amounts of terrain to check out. To get the best of it, there are a number of specialist backcountry tour operators, offering daily tours with prices starting at around $300.

Freeriders should love it on Jackson's slopes, with a host of marked out trails and acres of backcountry terrain to explore in areas such as the **Green River Bowl** or **Cody Bowl.** Backcountry guides are on hand to help you, and you can sign up for half day, full, or two day guiding sessions for around $325. But note that you are strongly advised to always check with the areas Bridger-Teton Backcountry avalanche hazard and weather forecast before going anywhere. Some of the best riding can be found on **Rendezvous** mountain which was once noted for having the biggest vertical descent in the US, some 1261 metres. Once you get off Rendezvous' old tram, you drop down into a cool play-ground, offering a great selection of chutes, jumps and big drop-ins, Jackson also features **Corbett's Couloir**, a famous vertical drop into a marked run that will leave you breathless.

Freestylers will certainly appreciate Jackson. From the **Thunder Chair** you will be able to reach a natural pipe. The **Paintbrush** and **Toilet Bowl** also offer loads of hits, where you can ride for hours off and over loads of good natural stuff. If this isn't enough, then check out the man-made pipe of the **Teewinot** chair lift.

Carvers who can and like to do so at speed, should check out **Gros Venture** as this is the place for experienced speed mer-chants. The run is over 3 km long and drops away, forming an excellent testing trail Intermediates (and those not so sure of themselves) should try out **Casper Bowl** or **Moran Face** on **Apres Vous Mountain**.

Beginners will find Jackson's mostly steep and testing terrain a bit daunting, but don't fret, most novices should manage to get around after a few days, although they should probably avoid the **Rendezvous** area. First timers have the chance to progress quickly, especially on the runs found at the bottom of **Apres Vous** mountain, reached off the **Teewinot** chair. A high level of instruc-tion is available including halfpipe training run camps for women.

Immediately at the base area of the slopes lies the resort of **Teton Village** which is more or less your typical horrid ski resort all in set up. That's not to say it's not welcoming, it is, and locals will make your stay a good one. However, the town of Jackson which is a 20 minute bus ride away operating on an-all day basis, offers a more sedate time with a heavy dose of pure outback Americana. Around town there is a lot of activities and not all costing the earth, which makes the place cool and worth it. There is a number of good snowboard shops to check out: such as the *Hole in the Wall,* or the *Bomb Shelter.*

Jobseekers: Big area attracting lots of visitors thus offering lots of jobs. Details-(307)733 2292

If you don't leave here over weight, then see a shrink. The place has dozens of places to get food from, whether it be a super-market, fast food joint or an up-market restaurant frequented by fur clad clueless city slickers. Prices to suite all are possible but on the whole, dining out is not a cheap experience here. However, *Bubba's* is comes highly recommrnded and serves some great chicken dishes. The *Snake River* and *Otto Brothers* brew pub are also noted for their good food.

Night life here is just how it should be, with something for all with a snowboard flavour. Options for some night action exist in either **Teton Village** or Jackson itself. Tretton is a lot quieter than Jackson, with *Mangy Moose,* the *Stagecoach* or the *Rancher* all being popular hangouts. As for local talent, the place seems a bit of a guy place but there is some skirt to be had.

Accommodation; The area has a vast array of lodging. There isplenty near the slopes in **Teton Village** where you can kip close to the slopes at the Hostel for around $5 a night. For a bigger selection and cheaper prices check out the offerings in **Jackson,** 10 miles from the slopes.

For accommodation listings visit - www.worldsnowboardguide.com

Summary: Great resort with lots of challenging terrain offering some excellent backcountry freeriding. Good and friendly local services, although a bit spread out.

Money wise: This is an expensive resort but it can be done on the cheap.

Overall rating out of 10 — 8

Jackson Hole
P.O Box 290, Teton Village
WY 83025
General info ***001*** **(307) 733 2291**
Reservations ***001*** **(800) 443 6931**
Snowphone ***001*** **(307) 733 2291**
www.jacksonhole.com
www.virgin.com/holidays

pic - Team Rajs - Cornfoot and Drumond

pic - Jackson Hole

Travel Guide

Fly to **Salt Lake City** International
Transfer time to resort = **5 3/4** hours.
Local airport = **Jackson** 10 miles away

Approximate global air travel times to **Salt Lake City**

from:	London	**9** hours
	New York	**3 1/2** hours
	Frankfurt	**10** hours

Buses from **Idaho Falls** take 1 1/2 hours and 5 3/4 hours from **Salt Lake City** airport (299 miles).

Trains: None

Route Planner
Idaho Falls *via Victor*

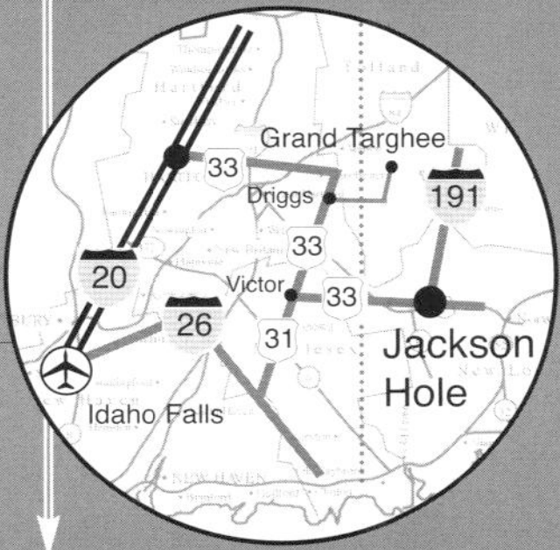

Jackson Holw = 111 miles
Drive time is about **1 3/4** hours
***Salt Lake City** is **299** miles which will take about **5 3/4 hours**

49 Degrees North *Washington*
Near - **Chewelah** - 4 Lifts & 23 runs
tel- (509) 935 6649

Afton Alps *Minnesota*
Near - **Hastings** - 20 Lifts & 36 runs
tel- (612) 436 5245

Alpenglow *Alaska*
Near - **Anchorage** - 4 Lifts & 20 runs
tel- (907) 248 0367

Al Quaal *Michigan*
Near - **Ishpeming** - 3 Lifts & 3 runs
tel- (906) 486 6181

Alpental Snoqualmie *Washington*
Near - **Snoqualmie** - 0 Lifts & 33 runs
tel- (206) 232 8182

Alpine Mtn *Pennsylvania*
Near - **Analomink** - 3 Lifts & 18 runs
tel- (717) 595 2150

Alpine Valley *Michigan*
Near - **White Lake**- 22 Lifts & 23 runs
tel- (313) 887 2180

Andes Tower Hill *Minnesota*
Near -**Kensington** - 5 Lifts & 14 runs
tel- (612) 965 2455

Angel Fire *New Mexico*
▲3255m 400 Acres 6 Lifts
This is an all year holiday destination, that offers its winter visitors a mountain suited to beginners looking for a simple resort. The slopes offer a mixture of easy freeride, to basic flat terrain. Excellent off-slope local services.
Fly to: **Albuquerque -**
tel- (505) 377 6401

Anthony Lakes *Oregon*
Near - **Island City** - 2 Lifts & 23 runs
tel- (503) 963 4599

Arapahoe Basin *Colorado*
▲3978m 490 Acres 5 Lifts
Arapahoe Basin is said to be the highest altitude lift serviced area in the US. Although this is a very small resort, with rather slow lifts (but no lift lines), it's still worth a visit. The terrain is very much of intermediate to advanced level. Freeriders have some great bowls and long chutes to check out. Freestylers also have a good terrain park.
All local services can be found at Keystone, just 5 miles away.
Fly to: **Denver** - 2 hours away
tel- (970) 468 4242

Arizona Snowbowl *Arizona*
Near - **Flagstaff** - 4 Lifts & 32 runs
tel- (602) 779 1951

Antelope Butte *Wyoming*
Near - **Dayton** - 3 Lifts & 5 runs
tel- (307) 655 9530

Aspen Highlands *Colorado*
▲3559m 650 Acres 8 Lifts
This is a resort with a big vertical and a good attitude towards snowboarders. Freeriders who like trees will be pleased to find that there are plenty. Freestylers have a good fun-park and lots of natural hits which can be checked out with the aid of the Ride Guide. Full local services are available in Aspen a few miles away. Beware, Aspen is super dollar-hungry.
Fly to: **Denver** - 3 hours away
tel- (800) 262 7736.

Attitash Bear *New Hampshire*
▲701m 273 Acres 12 Lifts
Attitash is the largest resort in **Mt Washington Valley**. The runs are well maintained and provide a good surface for carvers to ride. The fun-park is not the most happening, but it still offers a number of good hits. Beginners have a fine area to learn on. Plenty of slopeside beds but dull facilities.
Fly to: **Boston**
tel- (603) 374 2368

Bald Mountain *Idaho*
Near - **Orofino** - 2 Lifts & 15 runs
tel- (208) 464 2311

Beech Mtn *North Carolina*
Near - **Banner Elk** - 9 Lifts & 13 runs
tel- (704) 387 2011

Berkshire East *Massachusetts*
Near - **Charlemont** - 4 Lifts & 31 runs
tel- (413) 339 6617

Big Powderhorn *Michigan*
Near - **Bessemer** - 9 Lifts & 24 runs
tel- (906) 932 4838

Big Rock *Maine*
Near - **Mars Hill** - 4 Lifts & 9 runs
tel- (207) 425 6711

Big Tupper *New York*
Near - **Tupper Lake**- 5 Lifts & 24 runs
tel- (518) 359 3651

Bittersweet Resort *Michigan*
Near - **Otsego** - 13 Lifts & 14 runs
tel- (616) 694 2820

Blackjack *Michigan*
Near - **Bessemer** - 6 Lifts & 17 runs
tel- (906) 229 5115

Black Mountain *Maine*
Near - **Rumford** - 2 Lifts & 9 runs
tel- (207) 364 8977

Blandford Ski *Massachusetts*
Near - **Blandford** - 4 Lifts & 24 runs
tel- (413) 848 2860

Blue Hills *Massachusetts*
Near - **Canton** - 7 Lifts & 4 runs
tel- (617) 828 5090

Blue Knob *Pennsylvania*
Near - **Claysburg** - 7 Lifts & 21 runs
tel- (814) 239 5111

Bogus Basin *Idaho*
Near - **Boise** - 10 Lifts & 46 runs
tel- (208) 332 5100

Boston Mills *Ohio*
Near - **Peninsula** - 16 Lifts & 17 runs
tel- (216) 467 2242

Bousquet Ski *Massachusetts*
Near - **Pittsfield** - 5 Lifts & 21 runs
tel- (413) 442 8316

Boyne Highlands *Michigan*
Near - **Harbour Springs** - 9 Lifts & 32 runs
tel- (616) 549 2441

Boyne Mountain *Michigan*
Near - **Boyne Falls** - 10 Lifts & 17 runs
tel- (616) 549 2441

Bradford *Massachusetts*
Near - **Haverhill** - 6 Lifts & 10 runs
tel- (508) 373 0071

Bridger Bowl *Montana*
▲2469m 1200 Acres 6 Lifts
Not your usual tourist trap, **Bridger Bowl** is a fantastic freerider's place with a nice selection of steep terrain, lots of trees, great backcountry options and deep powder stashes. However, carvers who only want long and well-pisted slopes, forget it. They only piste a few trails leaving most of the surface untouched and a bit bouncy. Not hot for novices but okay. Good local services.
Fly to: **Bozeman** - 50 minutes away
tel- (406) 586 2389

Brodie Mtn *Massachusetts*
Near - **Ashford** - 6 Lifts & 28 runs
tel- (413) 443 4752

Brundage Mountain *Idaho*
Near - **McCall** - 4 Lifts & 36 runs
tel- (208) 634 7462

Bryce Resort *Virginia*
Near - **Basye** - 4 Lifts & 6 runs
tel- (703) 856 2121

Buckhorn Ski Area *California*
Near - **La Canada** - 2 Lifts & 2 runs
tel- (714) 775 7513

Burke Mountain *Vermont*
Near - **East Burke** - 5 Lifts & 30 runs
tel- (802) 626 3305

Buttermilk *Colorado*
▲3017m n/a Acres 7 Lifts
Buttermilk should keep basic intermediate riders occupied for a week's stay. Advanced riders may prefer nearby Aspen or Snowmass. Freestylers have a well equipped fun-park and a good halfpipe. Carvers will find some fast trails of the Tiehack lift. Full local services are available in Aspen a few miles away. Beware, Aspen is super dollar-hungry.
Fly to: **Denver** - 3 hours away
tel- (800) 262 7736.

Butternut Basin *Massachusetts*
Near - **G/Barrington** - 8 Lifts & 20 runs
tel- (413) 528 2000

Caberfae Peaks *Michigan*
Near - **Cadillac** - 9 Lifts & 20 runs
tel- (616) 862 3300

Camden Snow Bowl *Maine*
Near - **Camden** - 3 Lifts & 11runs
tel- (207) 236 3438

Canonsburg *Michigan*
Near - **Cannonsburg** - 12 Lifts & 18 runs
tel- (616) 874 6711

Cannon Mtn *New Hampshire*
▲1274m 164 Acres 6 Lifts
Cannon Mountain is a tin pot east coast resort and as big as they get in New Hampshire. Still, Cannon is an unspoilt place with the biggest vertical in the state. All the runs are hacked out of tightly knitted trees from top to bottom.
Full services, are available at nearby **Franconia**.
Fly to: **Boston** - 1 1/2 hours away
tel- (603) 823 5563

Catamount *Massachusetts*
Near - **South Egremont** - 6 Lifts & 23 runs
tel- (413) 528 1262

Chestnut Mountain *Illinois*
Near - **Galena** - 8 Lifts & 17 runs
tel- (815) 777 1320

Cleary Summit *Alaska*
Near - **Anchorage** - 3 Lifts & 20 runs
tel- (907) 456 5520

Cloudmont Ski Resort *Alabama*
Near - **Mentone** - 2 Lifts & 2 runs
tel- (205) 634 4344

Copper Spur *Oregon*
▲1524m ◊100 Acres ☒ 2 Lifts
Copper Spur is a tiny resort located an hour from **Portland**. The resort is a favourite with family ski groups as the terrain is mainly suited to total beginners. There's nothing much for advanced riders, however freeriders may wish to take a snowcat tour to sample more interesting terrain at **Cloud Cap District**. Basic local facilities exist nearby.
Fly to: **Portland** - 1 hour away
ⓘ **tel-** (503) 352 7803

Cottonwood Butte *Idaho*
Near - **Cottonwood** - ☒ 2 Lifts & 4 runs
ⓘ **tel-** (208) 962 3631

Cranmore *New Hampshire*
▲518m ◊185 Acres ☒ 6 Lifts
Cranmore is a bit of a nothing place. The area is more or less a family ski haunt, and will appeal to first time snowboarders with no adventure in them. The park and pipe are also pretty poor. Lots of slopeside beds but dull facilities.
Fly to: **Boston**
ⓘ **tel-** (603) 356 5544

Crystal Mtn *Michigan*
Near - **Lindy Rd** - ☒ 7 Lifts & 23 runs
ⓘ **tel-** (616) 378 2000

Cuchara Valley *Colorado*
Near - **Cuchara** - ☒ 4 Lifts & 24 runs
ⓘ **tel-** (719) 742 3163

Deer Valley Resort *Utah*
Near - **Park City** - ☒ 12 Lifts & 66 runs
ⓘ **tel-** (801) 649 1000

Discovery Basin *Montana*
Near - **Anaconda** - ☒ 5 Lifts & 30 runs
ⓘ **tel-** (406) 563 2184

Donner Ski Ranch *California*
Near - **Norden** - ☒ 6 Lifts & 40 runs
ⓘ **tel-** (916) 426 3635

Eagle Crest Ski Area *Alaska*
Near - **Juneau** - ☒ 3 Lifts & 30 runs
ⓘ **tel-** (907) 790 2000

Eaton Mountain *Maine*
Near - **Skowhegan** - ☒ 2 Lifts & 14 runs
ⓘ **tel-** (207) 474 2666

Eldora Resort *Colorado*
Near - **Nederland** - ☒ 8 Lifts & 44 runs
ⓘ **tel-** (303) 440 8800

Four Lakes Village *Illinois*
Near - **Lisle** - ☒ 6 Lifts & 6 runs
ⓘ **tel-** (708) 964 2551

Fun Valley *Iowa*
Near - **Montezuma** - ☒ 5 Lifts & 10 runs
ⓘ **tel-** (515) 623 3456

Granlibakken *California*
Near - **Tahoe City** - ☒ 2 Lifts & 2 runs
ⓘ **tel-** (916) 583 9896

Hesperus Ski Area *Colorado*
Near - **Durango** - ☒ 2 Lifts & 18 runs
ⓘ **tel-** (303) 259 3711

Hidden Valley *New Jersey*
Near - **Breakneck** - ☒ 3 Lifts & 12 runs
ⓘ **tel-** (201) 764 6161

Holiday Valley *New York*
Near - **Ellicottville** - ☒ 11 Lifts & 52 runs
ⓘ **tel-** (716) 699 2345

Hood/Ski Bowl *Oregon*
▲1544m ◊960 Acres ☒ 9 Lifts
Ski Bowl boasts the largest night-ride area in America, yet has a reputation for being either really wide and flat or scarily steep with no intermediate terrain. Only the faithful few ride here. There is a fun-park with a killer halfpipe. Lodging, is available in nearby Government Camp.
Fly to: **Portland** - 1 1/2 hours away
ⓘ **tel-** (503) 272 3206

Indianhead Mtn *Michigan*
Near - **Gaylord** - ☒ 5 Lifts & 9 runs
ⓘ **tel-** (517) 939 8919

June Mountain *California*
Near - **June Lake** - ☒ 32 Lifts & 8 runs
ⓘ **tel-** (619) 648 7733

Kelly Canyon *Idaho*
Near - **Idaho Falls** - ☒ 5 Lifts & 20 runs
ⓘ **tel-** (208) 538 6261

Kratka Ridge *California*
Near - **La Canada** - ☒ 3 Lifts & 14 runs
ⓘ **tel-** (818) 578 1079

Lassen Park *California*
Near - **Red Bluff** - ☒ 2 Lifts & 2 runs
ⓘ **tel-** (916) 595 3376

Little Ski Hill *Idaho*
Near - **McCall** - ☒ 1 Lifts & 5 runs
ⓘ **tel-** (208) 634 5691

Lookout Pass *Idaho*
Near - **Wallace** - ☒ 2 Lifts & 12 runs
ⓘ **tel-** (208) 744 1301

Lost Valley *Maine*
Near - **Auburn** - ☒ 3 Lifts & 15 runs
ⓘ **tel-** (207) 784 1561

Magic Mountain *Idaho*
Near - **Kimberley** - ☒ 3 Lifts & 20 runs
ⓘ **tel-** (208) 423 6221

Massanutten Resort *Virginia*
Near - **Harrisonburg** - ☒ 5 Lifts & 14 runs
ⓘ **tel-** (703) 289 9441

Maverick Mountain *Montana*
▲2810m ◊500 Acres ☒ 9 Lifts
This is one of those resorts that you either love or hate. The terrain rates equally for beginners and intermediates, with a number of steep sections including double diamond blacks for advanced riders. Good, cheap selection of local facilities.
Fly to: **Bozeman** - 2 hours away
ⓘ **tel-** (406) 834 3454

Mission Ridge *Washington*
Near - **Wenatchee** - ☒ 6 Lifts & 33 runs
ⓘ **tel-** (509) 663 7631

Mohawk Mtn *Connecticut*
Near - **Cornwall** - ☒ 5 Lifts & 23 runs
ⓘ **tel-** (203) 672 6100

Monarch Ski Resort *Colorado*
Near - **Monarch** - ☒ 4 Lifts & 55 runs
ⓘ **tel-** (719) 539 3578

Moose Mountain *Alaska*
Near - **Fairbanks** - ☒ 1 Lifts & 10 runs
ⓘ **tel-** (907) 479 8362

Mt Ashwabay *Wisconsin*
Near - **Bayfield** - ☒ 5 Lifts & 13 runs
ⓘ **tel-** (715) 779 3227

Mt Ashlamd *Oregon*
▲2286m ◊120 Acres ☒ 4 Lifts
Mt Ashland is located close to the town of **Ashland**. The mountain itself offers some good snowboard terrain with a high percentage of advanced trails. Carvers can shine on runs such as the **Romeo**. Local services are very pricey and a bit stuck up.
Fly to: **Portland** - 1 1/2 hours away
ⓘ **tel-** (503) 822 3799

Mt Baldy *California*
Near - **Mt Baldy** - ☒ 4 Lifts & 28 runs
ⓘ **tel-** (909) 982 0800

Mt Crescent Ski Area *Iowa*
Near - **Cresent** - ☒ 3 Lifts & 10 runs
ⓘ **tel-** (712) 545 3850

New Hermon Mtn *Maine*
Near - **Searsport** - ☒ 2 Lifts & 18 runs
ⓘ **tel-** (207) 848 5192

Mt Jefferson *Maine*
Near - **Lee** - ☒ 2 Lifts & 10 runs
ⓘ **tel-** (207) 738 2377

Mt Lemmon *Arizona*
Near - **Tucson** - ☒ 3 Lifts & 30 runs
ⓘ **tel-** (602) 885 1181

Mt Rose Ski Area *Nevada*
Near - **Reno** - ☒ 5 Lifts & 22 runs
ⓘ **tel-** (916) 926 8610

Mt Shasta Ski Park *California*
Near - **Mt Shasta** - ☒ 3 Lifts & 41 runs
ⓘ **tel-** (800) Ski Rose

Mt Southington *Connecticut*
Near - **Souhington** - ☒ 6 Lifts & 14 runs
ⓘ **tel-** (203) 628 0954

Mt Sunapee *New Hampshire*
Near - **Sunapee** - ☒ 7 Lifts & 36 runs
ⓘ **tel-** (603) 763 2356

Mt Waterman *California*
Near - **La Canada** - ☒ 3 Lifts & 23 runs
ⓘ **tel-** (818) 440 1041

Nor-Ski Runs *Iowa*
Near - **Decorah** - ☒ 3 Lifts & 5 runs
ⓘ **tel-** (319) 382 8373

North Star *California*
▲2625m ◊2400 Acres ☒ 12 Lifts
Snowboarders were banned here until 1997, but the whole place is now open to riders, with good freeriding terrain and powder. Freeriders should find the back bowls pretty cool, with a series of black trails that will appeal to advanced riders. Freestylers have a very well equipped fun-park and pipe on Sundance and Pinball trails. Carvers have a good mountain to roam with some nice trails to rush down. Advanced carvers may not love it though. Beginners have plenty of easy trails. General lodging and local services at the base. **Truckee**, only 6 miles away.
Fly to: **Reno** - 40 minutes away
ⓘ **tel-** (530) 562 1010.

North South Bowl *Idaho*
Near - **Maries** - ☒ 2 Lifts & 15 runs
ⓘ **tel-** (208) 245 4222

Norwich University *Vermont*
Near - **Northfield** - ☒ 2 Lifts & 4 runs
ⓘ **tel-** (802) 485 2145

Nub's Nob *Michigan*
Near - **Harbour Springs** - ☒ 8 Lifts & 23 runs
ⓘ **tel-** (616) 526 2131

Olympia Village *Wisconsin*
Near - **Oconomowoc** - ☒ 3 Lifts & 5 runs
ⓘ **tel-** (414) 567 2577

Perfect North Slopes *Indiana*
Near - **Lawrenceburg** - ☒ 9 Lifts & 14 runs
ⓘ **tel-** (812) 537 3754

Pebble Creek *Idaho*
Near - **Pocatello** - ☒ 3 Lifts & 25 runs
ⓘ **tel-** (208) 775 4451

Pico Ski Area *Vermont*
Near - **Rutland** - ☒ 9 Lifts & 40 runs
ⓘ **tel-** (802) 775 4346

Pine Creek *Wyoming*
Near - **Cokeville** - ☒ 2 Lifts & 13 runs
ⓘ **tel-** (307) 279 3201

Plumas-Eureka *California*
Near -**Quincy** - ☒ 3 Lifts & 6 runs
ⓘ **tel-** (916) 836 2317

Plumtree Ski Area *Illinois*
Near - **Lake Carroll** - 2 Lifts & 10 runs
ⓘ **tel-** (815) 493 2881

Pomerelle Ski Resort *Idaho*
Near - **Albion** - 3 Lifts & 17 runs
ⓘ **tel-** (208) 638 5599

Powderhorn Ski *Colorado*
Near - **Mesa** - 4 Lifts & 27 runs
ⓘ **tel-** (303) 242 5637

Powder Ridge *Connecticut*
Near - **Middlefield** - 5 Lifts & 14 runs
ⓘ **tel-** (203) 349 3454

Potawatomi Park *Wisconsin*
Near - **Sturgeon Bay** - 3 Lifts & 3 runs
ⓘ **tel-** (414) 743 7033

Ragged Mtn *New Hampshire*
Near - **Danbury** - 4 Lifts & 23 runs
ⓘ **tel-** (603) 768 3475

Ragged Mtn *New York*
Near - **Highmount** - 8 Lifts & 33 runs
ⓘ **tel-** (914) 254 5600

Red River *New Mexico*
▲3155m 200 Acres 7 Lifts
Red River is located 35 miles north of **Taos**, and is an evenly mixed-ability mountain offering the chance to ride some south state trees. Freeriders have a number of good slopes to try out whilst beginners are well catered for on the lower sections. There are good local services at the base.
Fly to: **Albuquerque -**
ⓘ **tel-** (505) 754 2223

Riverside Hills *Iowa*
Near - **Estherville** - 3 Lifts & 6 runs
ⓘ **tel-** (712) 362 5376

Rocking Horse *New York*
Near - **Highland** - 2 Lifts & 3 runs
ⓘ **tel-** (406) 278 5308

Rocky Mountain *Montana*
Near - **Choteau** - 3 Lifts & 25 runs
ⓘ **tel-** (406) 278 5308

Saddleback *Maine*
▲1256m 120 Acres 5 Lifts
As one of Maine's lesser known resorts, **Saddleback** is a simple place offering equal ability riding on a mountain that provides some nice freeriding, with trees and powder spots to search. Carvers have a number of black trails while novices have the long **Lazy River** to learn the basics on.
Low key, affordable local services are available near the slopes.
Fly to: **Portland**
ⓘ **tel-** (403) 591 7777

Santa Fe Ski Area *New Mexico*
▲3155m 200 Acres 7 Lifts
One of **New Mexico's** main resorts, **Ski Santa Fe** is a resort that should please advanced freeriders. Freestylers can find man-made hits in a temporary fun-park, while beginners are provided with good easy trails. Local services are 15 miles away.
Fly to: **Albuquerque -**
ⓘ **tel-** (505) 754 2223

Shawnee Peak *Maine*
▲594m 210 Acres 5 Lifts
Shawnee Peak may be a small resort, but it has long been big on snowboarding, allowing riders on the slopes long before many other areas. A favourite with local riders, the slopes are crowd-free and offer intermediate carvers well-pisted trails for big turns. Beginners should also like it here.
Fly to: **Portland**
ⓘ **tel-** (207) 647 8444

Silvercreek *Colorado*
Near - **Silvercreek** - 4 Lifts & 25 runs
ⓘ **tel-** (303) 887 3384

Silver Creek *Iowa*
Near - **Humboldt** - 6 Lifts & 11 runs
ⓘ **tel-** (515) 332 3329

Ski Apache *New Mexico*
Near - **Ruidosp** - 10 Lifts & 52 runs
ⓘ **tel-** (505) 336 4356

Ski Copper *Colorado*
Near - **Leadville** - 4 Lifts & 26 runs
ⓘ **tel-** (719) 486 3684

Ski Denton *Pennsylvania*
Near - **Coudersport** - 4 Lifts & 20 runs
ⓘ **tel-** (814) 435 2115

Ski Land *Alaska*
Near - **Fairbanks** - 3 Lifts & 25 runs
ⓘ **tel-** (907) 381 2314

Ski Mt. Abram *Maine*
Near - **Locke Mills** - 5 Lifts & 25 runs
ⓘ **tel-** (207) 875 5003

Ski Paoli Peaks *Indiana*
Near - **Paoli** - 8 Lifts & 14 runs
ⓘ **tel-** (812) 723 4696

Ski Squaw Mountain *Maine*
Near - **Greenville** - 4 Lifts & 18 runs
ⓘ **tel-** (207) 695 2272

Ski Sundown *Connecticut*
Near - **New Hartford** - 4 Lifts & 16 runs
ⓘ **tel-** (203) 379 9851

Ski Sunrise *California*
Near - **Wrightwood** - 4 Lifts & 22 runs
ⓘ **tel-** (619) 249 6150

Ski Valley *Indiana*
Near - **La Porte** - 6 Lifts & 5 runs
ⓘ **tel-** (219) 326 0123

Ski Valley *Iowa*
Near - **Boone** - 4 Lifts & 10 runs
ⓘ **tel-** (515) 432 2423

Ski Windham *New York*
Near - **Windham** - 8 Lifts & 33 runs
ⓘ **tel-** (518) 734 4300

Ski World *Indiana*
Near - **Nashville** - 5 Lifts & 12 runs
ⓘ **tel-** (812) 988 6638

Snowhaven *Idaho*
Near - **Grangeville** - 2 Lifts & 3 runs
ⓘ **tel-** (208) 983 2581

Snow King Resort *Wyoming*
Near - **Jackson** - 0 Lifts & 3 runs
ⓘ **tel-** (307) 733 5200

Snowy Range *Wyoming*
Near - **Laramie** - 4 Lifts & 24 runs
ⓘ **tel-** (307) 745 5750

Snowstar Ski Area *Illinois*
Near - **Taylor Ridge** - 4 Lifts & 9 runs
ⓘ **tel-** (309) 798 2666

Soda Springs *California*
Near - **Truckee** - 2 Lifts & 16 runs
ⓘ **tel-** (916) 427 3666

Soldier Mounatin *Idaho*
Near - **Fairfield** - 3 Lifts & 36 runs
ⓘ **tel-** (208) 764 2300

Spirit Mountain *Minnesota*
Near - **Duluth** - 8 Lifts & 20 runs
ⓘ **tel-** (218) 628 2891

Sundown Mountain *Iowa*
Near - **Duduque** - 6 Lifts & 26 runs
ⓘ **tel-** (319) 556 6676

Sunrise Park *Arizona*
Near - **McNary** - 11 Lifts & 65 runs
ⓘ **tel-** (602) 735 7676

The Homestead *Michigan*
Near - **Glen Arbor** - 4 Lifts & 14 runs
ⓘ **tel-** (616) 334 5000

Tiehack *Colorado*
Near - **Aspen** - 7 Lifts & 45 runs
ⓘ **tel-** (303) 925 1221

Timberline *Oregon*
▲2591m 1430 Acres 6 Lifts
Timberline is a small area, and the second of only two places in the USA that offers summer riding. The terrain is flat and a bit dull, apart from the area off **Palmer Express** lift. In summer, the Palmer area plays host to summer fun, with pipes and parks spread out from May to October. Slopeside beds and services are available at the base in the **Timberline Lodge**.
Fly to: **Portland** - 1 1/2 hours away
ⓘ **tel-** (503) 272 3311

Titcomb Mountain *Maine*
Near - **Farmington** - 2 Lifts & 10 runs
ⓘ **tel-** (207) 778 9031

Tyrol Basin *Wisconsin*
Near - **Mt Horeb** - 5 Lifts & 12 runs
ⓘ **tel-** (608) 437 4135

Villa Olivia *Illinois*
Near -Bartlett - 8 Lifts & 7 runs
ⓘ **tel-** (708) 289 5200

Vernon Valley *New Jersey*
Near - **Vernon** - 17 Lifts & 52 runs
ⓘ **tel-** (201) 827 2000

Whitecap Mountains *Wisconsin*
Near - **Montreal** - 8 Lifts & 33 runs
ⓘ **tel-** (715) 561 2227

Wildcat *New Hampshire*
▲1234m 225 Acres 6 Lifts
Wildcat hasn't always been a great favourite with those who like perfectly groomed trails. However, freeriders may like what's on offer, if only to see out a day's riding. Freeriders will find lots of hits and uneven terrain for catching air. Lodging is only five mins away.
Fly to: **Boston**
ⓘ **tel-** (603) 466 3326

Willamette Pass *Oregon*
▲2037m 210 Acres 5 Lifts
Located just off Route 58, an hour or so from the city of **Eugene,** lies this well-known US speed-skiing resort. However, you don't have to be a speed-freak to enjoy **Willamette**, although it will help since you have a high level of fast expert freeriding slopes. Novices need not be put off, there are good flats; freestylers have a park and pipe. Lodging nearby is okay.
Fly to: **Portland** - 1 1/2 hours away
ⓘ **tel-** (503) 2484 5030

Williams Ski Area *Arizona*
Near - **Williams** - 2 Lifts & 5 runs
ⓘ **tel-** (602) 635 9330

Wisp Ski Area *Maryland*
Near - **McHenry** - 7 Lifts & 23 runs
ⓘ **tel-** (301) 387 4911

Woodbury *Connecticut*
Near - **Woodbury** - 4 Lifts & 12 runs
ⓘ **tel-** (203) 263 2203

pic - John Quigley - Rider - Seth Miller at Sugar Bush

ANDORRA

GENERAL INFO AND FACTS

Capital - Andorra La Vella
Language - Spanish - French
Currency - Spanish Pesetas
Alcohol drinking age - 18
Drugs - Cannabis is illegal
Death Penalty - Doesn't exist
Age of consent for Sex - 16
Military Service - Not compulsory
Electricity Supply - 240 Volts AC
International phone Code ++376
Highest Peak -

DUTY FREE
Andorra is a duty free country on with no tax duty on most goods sold in shops throught the whole country.

ANDORRA DRIVE GUIDE
All vehicles drive on the right hand side of the road
Speed Limits -
Motorways
Highways 70kph (44mph)
Towns 40kph (25mph)

Ministeri de Turisme
Carrer Prat de La Casa
62-64 Andorra La Vella
tel - ++376 829 345

TIME ZONES
Central European
GMT +1 Hour
Between March and October
GMT+2 Hours

INTERNATIONAL GATEWAY AIRPORTS
Barcelona *in Spain = 4 hours away.*
Toulouse *in France = 4 hours away.*

Apart from **Andorra** being the self-governing principality under the joint sovereignty of France and Spain, Andorra has also become known as the cheap package tour centre of Europe - a reputation richly deserved. Nestled high in the Pyrenees, Andorra is a very friendly, laid back place where locals try hard to make your visit a good one. Over the past few years a lot of effort has gone into improving the on-slope facilities, especially in terms of snowmaking. This area has not always had a great snow record.

No amount of artificial snow can make up for the fact that Andorra is more or less a country with a number of very small resorts, that are ideal for total beginners, and just okay for intermediates on a three day visit. In general, Andorra does-n't have any challenging terrain for expert riders, or at least nothing that can't be ridden within a day at the most. A week here will bore the tits off any rider who likes to ride steep, fast and challenging terrain, so forget it.

All the areas are located within a short distance of each other and can be reached via France or Spain. The nearest inter-national airport is in **Barcelona**, 140 miles away, but transfer is not easy if you don't have a car. All the resorts offer basic cheap local services. Apartments are abundant, but because this is a tour operator's place, bookings are often a must.

Andorra is well known for its very boozy night action. Plenty of lager louts and skiers getting drunk on shandy, all help to make this a very party-style hangout. This isn't a bad place to snowboard, as long as it's for no more than a week.

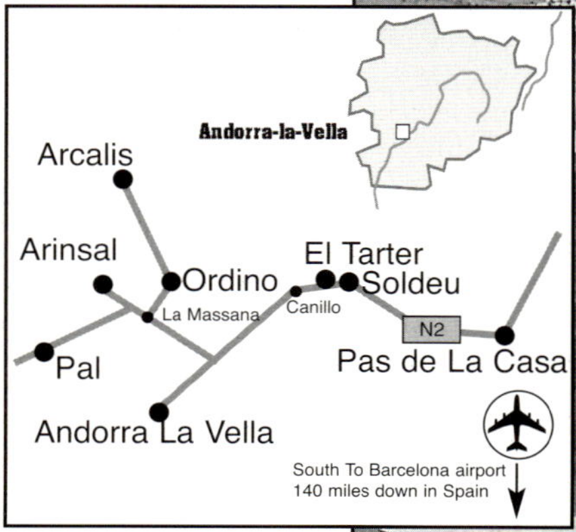

ARCALIS - ORDINO

Arcalis is the least known, least visited, and most remote of all Andorra's resorts. An undeveloped area, Arcalis doesn't come with the immediate resort facilities demanded by tour operators and skiers. The 18 miles of snow-sure terrain is perched much above the tree line, and offers some of the best terrain in the whole principality, with a small number of modest but quite difficult trails. All styles will find that a day or two here is not a waste of money. There are some nice spots for intermediate freeriders to check out, but hardcore freestylers forget it. There's nothing in the way of big jumps, although you will always find plenty of small kickers to trip off. One thing the slopes do offer, is excellent areas for beginners, with easy to reach trails, that make up some 55% of the snowboard area.

Local facilities can be found in down **Ordino** which is about 10 miles or 16 km away What you get is very dull.

Top Lift at
2600m
Ride Area
15.6 miles (25km)
Halfpipe Yes 1
Fun Park No
Slope Access
Total Lifts = **12**

Overall rating out of 10 — 2 — **This dump sucks= Super dull**

++376 836 963

ARINSAL

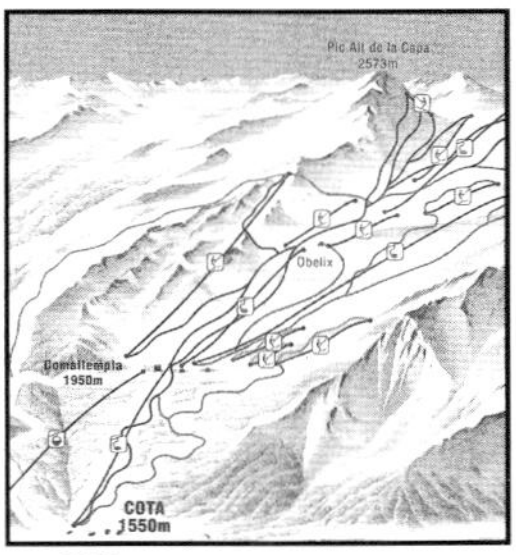

Arinsal is basically a very boring resort with miserable features and super dull terrain. This place really isn't worth bothering with unless you're into very flat and dull trails which allow for an average maximum speed of 2 miles per hour. However, saving grace is at hand, while on its own this is a small place, being located close to a couple of **Andorra's** other resorts, **Ordino** and **Pal,** you are able to escape the tedium of Arinsal with ease. In Arinsal's defence, a group of beginners on their first snowboard holiday will find the place absolutely perfect and well worth the money - just don't expect any progression once you pass the novice rating. Intermediate carvers may also find a few trails to while away an hour or two but for advanced freestylers forget it.

Cheap lodging is available in the village of Arinsal which is a few minutes from the slopes and has the reputation of having very lively night-life. Local services are basic but cheap.

Top Lift at
2560m
Ride Area
17 miles (28km)
Halfpipe Yes 1
Fun Park No
Slope Access
Total Lifts = **14**

Overall rating out of 10 — 1 — **Miserable and very dull - Rubbish**

++376 838 438

PAL

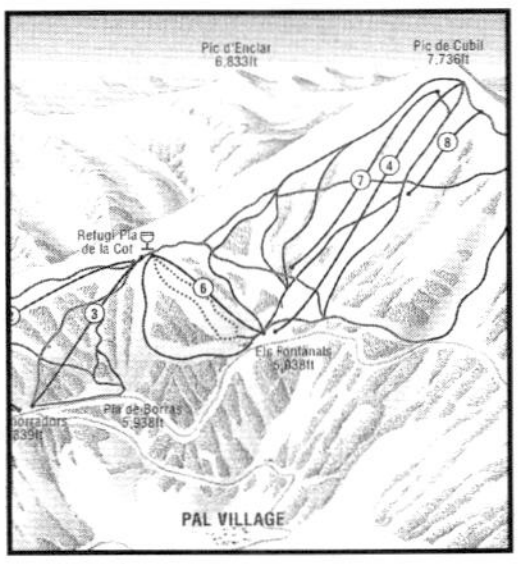

Pal is a slightly bigger and better resort than that of its near neighbour Arinsal, with which it shares a lift pass. It also has more interesting terrain than Arinsal and is not quite as rowdy both on and off the slopes. The area is, however, a place for total novices and slow learning intermediates with 95% of the terrain graded blue and red. There's absolutely nothing of note for advanced riders, no matter your style of riding. Only 5% of marked-out trails are black, and even some of these are over-rated, especially if you can ride at a competent level. Most riders will have the whole joint licked in the time it takes to smoke a good joint. Easy-going freeriders will find some wooded areas that on a good day allow for some off-piste through the trees; beginners have nearly the whole place to roam around with a degree of total ease. Freestylers may find the odd log to grind, but that's about all.

Pal has very basic local services a few miles away.

Top Lift at
2358m
Ride Area
20 miles (32km)
Halfpipe Yes 1
Fun Park No
Slope Access
Total Lifts = **12**

Overall rating out of 10 — 3 — **Okay for beginners**

+376 838 438

Pas De La Casa

MOUNTAIN DATA

Top Lift at - 2600m

Ride Area 100km of piste

Bottom Lift at - 2030m

Vertical Drop - 550m

Number of Runs - 52

Longest - 2.5 miles (4km)

TERRAIN LEVELS

Easy	**25%**
Intermediate	**55%**
Advanced	**20%**
Expert =	

TERRAIN TO SUITE

Freeride	**40%**
Trees	A few
Backcountry	A bit
Freestyle	**10%**
Halfpipe	Yes 1
Terrain Park	Yes 1
Carving	**50%**

SNOW DATA

Average Snowfall

Snowmaking
15% cover of the slopes

Winter Periods
Dec to April

Summer Riding
None

SLOPE ACCESS

Total Lifts = **33**

Uplift Rate - 44,600 people an hour.

18 Chair lifts

15 Drag lifts

**Leashes Required*

Lift Times
8.30am to 4.00pm

Lift Pass Rates

1 Day pass	5000 Pts
5 Day pass	18000 Pts
7 Day pass	

Travel Guide

Fly to **Toulouse**, or **Barcelona**, both 3 hours away.

Bus services from airports take 4 hours.

Route Planner: From Barcelona, head north on the A17 and N152 roads.

pic - Pas De La Casa

Pas de La Casa is the second largest snowboard resort in Andorra, lying in the eastern section of the country along Route N2, close to the French border. Each year, the resort attracts more and more riders in groups of lively revellers at novice stage, looking for an easy resort to sample a few beginner bruises. Pas de La Casa shares its slopes with an area known as **Grau Roig** (pronounced 'grau rosh'). Both are lift-linked, offering a collective area of easy-to-master intermediate terrain, with an excellent walk to beginner slopes and a few advanced black runs which can be ridden over a day or two. Three days or more will bore adventurous riders, but a week for beginners is ideal. The mountain is well serviced by some 33 lifts, although quite a few are drag lifts and not beginner friendly.

Freeriders should be advised that this is not a freeriding metropolis. However, the area can offer some good powder stashes after a recent dump. The best riding is on the Grau Roig, up on the main slope and down the other side. Once in the Grau Roig, you can take a chair up the mountain to gain access to a whole new area, and if you take the main run down the hill and across the top of the black run, you will find some okay powder fields.

Freestylers will find a number of natural hits on the **Grau Roig** area. However, you will need to plan your route using the piste map if you want to avoid a long walk back to the lift station. Overall, this is not a hot freestyle resort even though there is a well looked after fun-park and pipe off the **Coma 111** trail, which is reached by taking the **Number 1** chair.

Carvers have a respectable 25 mile trail which can be done at speed. Avoid trail **37** or **Isards**, which are pure crap.

Beginners can take most advantage here, with good novice areas reached by foot from the village. The flats are perfect for novices and it won't be too long before you can tackle the rest.

Local services at the foot of the slopes are cheap and cheerful, offering a host of duty-free shops, supermarkets, restaurants and bars that stay open very late, and see a fair share of hardcore partying. Shops and night-life are within walking distance, doing away with the need for a car or public transport in the evenings. Cool hangouts are *Pub Milwaukee* for happy hour with a lively atmosphere and *Billboard* for a late beer and holiday talent.

For accommodation listings visit - www.worldsnowboardguide.com

Pas de La Casa
AV. Carlemany 46, Escaldes. Andorra.
++376 80 10 60 **www.pasdelacasa.ad**

Overall rating out of 10 **5** **Okay but a bit limited**

Soldeu

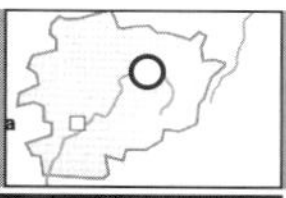

MOUNTAIN DATA

Top Lift at - 2560m

Ride Area
49km of piste

Bottom Lift at - 1800m
Vertical Drop - 850m
Number of Runs - 62
Longest - 5 miles (8km)

TERRAIN LEVELS

Easy	37%
Intermediate	41%
Advanced	20%
Expert =	

TERRAIN TO SUITE

Freeride	40%
Trees	A few
Backcountry	A bit
Freestyle	20%
Halfpipe	Yes 1
Terrain Park	Yes 1
Carving	40%

SNOW DATA
Average Snowfall

Snowmaking
25% cover of the slopes
Winter Periods
Dec to April
Summer Riding
None

SLOPE ACCESS
Total Lifts = **21**
Uplift Rate - 21,000 people an hour.
1 Cable Car, **6** Chair lifts
14 Drag lifts
**Leashes Required*

Lift Times
8.30am to 4.00pm

Lift Pass Rates

1 Day pass	5000 Pts
5 Day pass	18000 Pts
7 Day pass	

Travel Guide

Fly to **Toulouse**, or **Barcelona**, both 3 hours away.

Bus services from airports take 4 hours.

Route Planner:
From Barcelona, head north on the A17 and N152 roads.

pic - Soft Snapper

Soldeu - El Tarter makes up the biggest rideable area in Andorra, with some 52 miles of linked terrain. This is also the country's most popular resort which makes the place hellishly busy, with clogged up lifts and slopes. Budget-conscious skiers have been flocking here for years, and it is now also becoming a popular snowboard destination. Cheap and tacky, maybe, but it is still okay for your first snowboard holiday. Although this is the largest area in Andorra, there is still not much to brag about. The terrain is not adventurous, and basically poor for riders with ability. There is only a couple of black runs to choose from. However, Soldeu has a good snowboard scene and plays host to a number of locally organised snowboard events.

Freeriders will find that Soldeau has the best terrain in Andorra, especially for off-piste. The unpisted runs graded black and red, running down from the summit area of **Pic D'enc Ampadana**, are good freeriding areas. The trail starts off in a fast open section before dropping through a thick tree-lined area. For something to suit a novice rider, the red run that descends from the main summit, through the open expanse of the **Riba Escorxada,** is cool.

Freestylers are offered park and pipe, neither of which are well maintained. There are also plenty of cool natural hits to catch air, but nothing is really big so there's no need to call air traffic control. Look out for locals spotting hits to know where to ride.

Carvers have plenty of flats, with the option to ride hard and fast down a number of blacks, or the more sedate, pisted red and blue trails off the **Tosa Espiolets** chair.

Beginners have a great little mountain to explore with lots of easy, green nursery slopes to learn on, even if they do get clogged. Unfortunately, the easy runs are serviced by T-bars. Novices can ride down a series of open green trails, which will take you through trees and back to **Soldeau**.

An overload of apartments are available at the base of the slopes, with some very cheap lodging options. Like the rest of **Andorra**, local facilities are basic, somewhat dull, but perfectly adequate for a week's stay. Night-life is fast, raunchy, with booze, booze and more booze - the streets are pebble-dashed with diced carrots on a nightly basis. Lively bars to check out are the *Piccadilly*, *Pub Iceberg* or *Fat Alberts*.
For accommodation listings visit - www.worldsnowboardguide.com

Soldeau/ El Tarter
Ensasa El Tarter-Canillo
++376 851 144 **www.soldeu.ad**

Overall rating out of 10 **5** **Will suit beginners for a week**

AUSTRIA

GENERAL INFO AND FACTS

Capital - Vienna
Language - German
Currency - Schillings & Euros
Alcohol drinking age - 18
Drugs - Cannabis is illegal
Death Penalty - Doesn't exist
Age of consent for Sex - 16
Military Service - Compulsory
Electricity Supply - 240 Volts AC
International phone Code ++43
Highest Peak - Grossglockner 3797m

DUTY FREE
10 Litres of Alcohol
90 Litres of Wine - 110 of beer
800 Cigarettes
200 Cigars

AUSTRIAN DRIVE GUIDE
All vehicles drive on the right hand side of the road
Speed Limits -
Motorways 130kph (81mph)
Highways 100kph (62mph)
Towns 50kph (31mph)

Contacts and general info

Austrian Snowboard Association
Leopoldstrasse 4, Innsbruck
tel - ++43 (0) 512 565 675

International Snowboard Federation
Pradlerstrasse 21, A-6020, Innsbruck
tel - ++43 (0) 512 342 834

Snowboard Revue Magazine
Lohnsteinstrasse. 17, 2380 Pechtoldsdorf, **Austria**
+43 (0) 222 865 04 04

Hotel Sursilva - Lech
Situated 80m from the slopes. Bar, Restaurant,Gym, Lech
+43 (0) 558 32 97 02 2

Hotel Montana Garni - St Anton
Situated 200m from the slopes. 13 beds, Lounge, Rates from £35.
+43 (0) 544 632 53

Pension Paula - Innsbruck
Situated 5 minutes walk from city centre. Rates from £15 a night bed and breakfast.
+43 (0) 5357 2949

Chalet Stein - St Anton
Ride in/ride out, 4 twin rooms. Rates from £35 a night B&B .
+43 (0) 5446 2342

TIME ZONES
Central European
GMT +1 Hour
Between March and October
GMT+2 Hours

Austria is seen by many as the snowboard capital of Europe. With great resorts, a cool attitude, and a willingness to adopt new ideas. Austrian resorts aren't stretched out like the mega-sized places found in the French Alps. Apart from being far more affordable than France, the slopes are better laid out with excellent mountain facilities, modern lift systems, easy access to the slopes, and great traditional local slopeside services.

Many resorts are mid-range in height which can make them a little sketchy, as far as guaranteed snow goes. The best options are the glacial areas above 1,300 metres, like **Kaprun** or **Solden.**

Austrian's don't go in for the purpose-built style resorts so common in France and Italy. You will find traditional villages adapted to accommodate tourists. Standards are extremely high and affordable, with hotels and pensions the main form of lodging. Apartment blocks and cheap bunk-houses are almost non-existent, and despite the postcards, chalets are not a common form of letting property.
However, Austria does lose out in its reputation for food, and its lack of fast-food outlets. Yes, the Austrian's do make a wicked Goulash soup, but on the whole, nosh is very bland, consisting of dishes like Tafelspitz (boiled beef), or various cured hams and German-style sausages. If you're a veggie (vegetarier), you're in for a hard time - the Austrian's don't go in for rabbit-food.

An important and useful thing to note about Austria, is that credit cards are not that widely accepted: cash, travellers cheques or Euro-cheques are the norm.

Flying to the resorts is easy via the international airports in Austria, Switzerland or Germany, then taking onward travel via the excellent rail or road services. Only 25% of resorts have their own train station, although connections from the nearest towns are easy by post-bus. Bus travel is inexpensive with many daily services from major towns and cities .

Driving in Austria is convenient and easy, with the roads and resorts being well sign-posted. In some parts, snow-chains are required. Austria has an autobahn tax called the Vignette which costs ATS 70/week (ATS 560/year), and can be purchased at petrol stations or border crossings. If you are caught without the tax, you'll be liable to a costly on-the-spot fine.

EU nationals won't need either a visa or working permit, and can stay for as long as they want. But if you want to teach snowboarding, you may need to have the relevant Austrian snowboard instructors teaching qualifications.

pic - Wilder Kaiser Brixental - Soll Tourism

Main international Gateway Airports

Innsbruck
Salzburg
Munich *in Germany*
Zurich *in Switzerland*

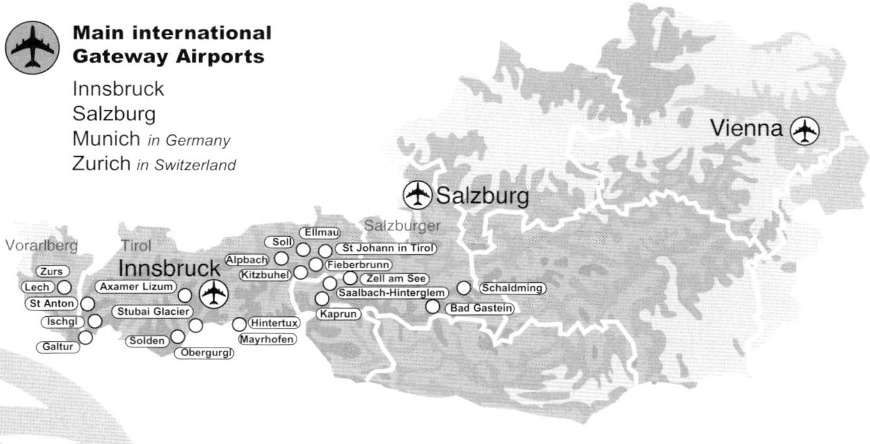

Axamer Lizum

MOUNTAIN DATA

Top Lift at - 2340m

Ride Area

100km of piste

Bottom Lift at - 878m

Vertical Drop - 1420m

Number of Runs -

Longest - 7 miles (4.3km)

TERRAIN LEVELS

Easy	**50%**
Intermediate	**40%**
Advanced	**10%**
Expert =	

TERRAIN TO SUITE

Freeride	**50%**
Trees	Yes
Backcountry	A bit
Freestyle	**30%**
Halfpipe	Yes 1
Terrain Park	Yes 1
Carving	**20%**

SNOW DATA

Average Snowfall
n/a cm a season

Snowmaking
0% cover of the slopes

Winter Periods
Dec to April

Summer Riding
None

SLOPE ACCESS

Total Lifts = **10**

Uplift Rate -12,400 people an hour.

1 Funicular Train, **5** Chairs

4 Drag lifts

**Leashes Required*

Lift Times
8.30am to 4.00pm

Lift Pass Rates

1 Day pass	250 Sch
4 Day pass	1,710 Sch
5 Day pass	2,290 Sch

SLOPE ACTION

Snowboard Hire
Daily rates from 350 Sch
Kids from 250 Sch

Snowboard Tuition
Group lessons, from
from 580 Sch

Night Riding
Yes in the pipe

Heli Boarding
No

Snowmobiles
No

Mountain Cafes
6

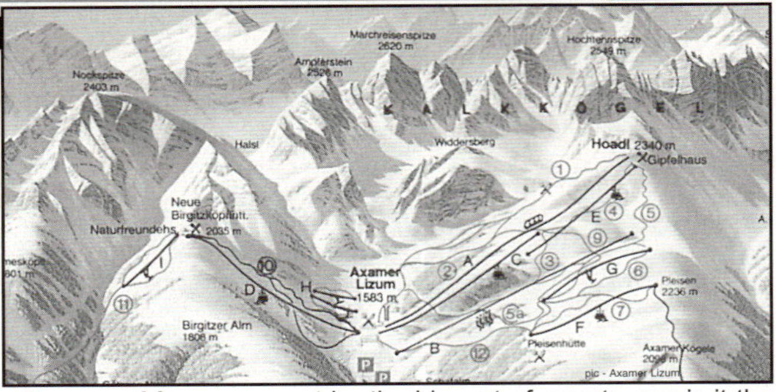

Axamer Lizum may not be the biggest of resorts, nor is it the chosen resort for holiday package tour operators, and yes the ski press may slag the place, but then what would that clueless lot know. Built in 1964 for the winter Olympics, Axams is a full-on no nonsense great natural freeride-freestyle snowboarder's paradise. The resort has everything you could possible ask for and although not extensive, the terrain in places is as natural as it gets. Don't be fooled by its small size as **Axamer Lizum** (and Axams), is the playground for the Innsbruck crowd that includes Max Plotzeneder and top racer Christine Rauter - and it's easy to see why. Axams is a quiet place, free of holiday ski crowds (although weekends are very busy), big on air and short on lift queues. Having twice hosted Olympic disciplines, the runs are obviously of a decent standard, with something to suit all. Freeriders and freestylers are going to get the best out of the slopes, with loads of great hits, big banks, and gullies that form natural pipes to drop in and out of and tight trees to weave through. The atmosphere on the slopes is really cool, and on certain days snowboarders actually out-number skiers, especially when the ISF are running one of their international competitions.

Freeriders wanting off-piste and trees won't be disappointed, although it should be pointed out that the resort management frowns upon shredding through the spruce since it kills off the trees. Off-piste terrain is limited, but if you get the conditions, great powder can be ridden without a trek. There's a great area if you go right at the exit point off the funicular train, and follow the line of reds, Trail **4** and **3**. Riders already past the novice stage and with a few bruises under their belts, will be able to collect a few more down Trails **5** and **5a.** Experienced riders can go for it down the blacks on Piste **10** where the trail is on a bumpy, steep run, and is not the greatest descent in the world.

Freestylers looking for the best hits should take the funicular train to the top, then follow the Number **1** blue run off to the left, which will bring you out onto a really cool mixture of red runs, with the best hits on Run **2**. The fun-park and halfpipe are located at the base area and reached from the beginner's T-bars or by hiking up. The fun-park is basic, and the pipe is not up to much, but with such good natural terrain, you don't need man-made hits.

Carvers will look and feel a little out of place here, as this is not long, wide autobahn territory. Saying that, there is room to crank some big carves, especially on piste Numbers **1** and **2**.

Beginners having their first go at snowboarding can loosen up and get to grips with the basics, on easy trails located at the base area just up from the ticket booths. The only drawback is that the easy slope is serviced by two T-bars, which may cause shy ones a few problems at first, but not for long.

Off the slopes, this is one of those places where you will have to put yourself out, and having a car may also be a preferred option. There is some accommodation at the base of the slopes consisting of a couple of B&B pensions and hotels, but that's it. Staying slopeside is not recommended, unless you're a hermit. The village of **Axams** is only a few miles away and has a decent selection of local services, which include a few shops and a sports centre. However, the best option is to stay down in Innsbruck, (the biggest and best snowboard resort-city in Europe). There are regular transfer buses to get you there, and once there you are bombarded with services, shops galore, an Olympic ice ring, swimming pools, concert halls, the list is endless. What's more, Innsbruck is an inexpensive and friendly place.

Innsbruck is the place for food with loads of restaurants, although fast food joints are limited to basically *McDonalds* (the eco warriors favourite). There are a number of first class pizza restaurants, along with a few Chinese and Indian restaurants and loads of Austrian restaurants serving dishes such as Tafelspitz (boiled beef).

Night-life in Axams is dull, without much happening. *Off Limits* is Axam's main hangout. Innsbruck, on the other hand, is a different story with simply loads going on and a large choice of cafe bars. There's an Irish bar called *Limerick Bills* and a club under *Jimmy's Bar* that rocks until very late.

Accommodation at the base of the slopes is very limited, while down in **Axams** the choice is greater. However, the best thing to do is to stay in **Innsbruck**, which offers everything you could want and more. There are lots of B&B's and loads of hotels, along with a couple of hostels and backpackers style lodging. *Pension Paul* is the most popular with nightly rates from 300sch, tel ++43 (0) 512 29 22 62 to book.

For accommodation listings visit - www.worldsnowboardguide.com

Summary: A great resort that will appeal to freestylers and intermediate freeriders spoilt only by the weekends queues. Some might find a full weeks stay a bit to long.

Money wise: Great value with low price lift tickets and accommodation.

Overall rating out of 10 — **10**

Axamer Lizum Tourism
Sylvester-Jordan Str 12
A6094 Axams, Tirol

General info	**++43 (0) 5234 681 780**
Reservations	**++43 (0) 5234 681 780**
Avalanche info	**++43 (0) 512 1588**

www.tiscover.com/innsbruck

pic - Axamer Lizum

Travel Guide

Fly to **Innsbruck** International
Transfer time to resort = **25** mins
Local airport = **Innsbruck**.

Approximate global air travel times to **Innsbruck**

from:		
London	2	hours
Los Angeles	13	hours
New York	9	hours

Buses from Innsbruck, leave the train station hourly for Axams and back again. Bus services also from Munich to Innsbruck.

Trains go only to Innsbruck.

Route Planner
Innsbruck *via motorway A12*

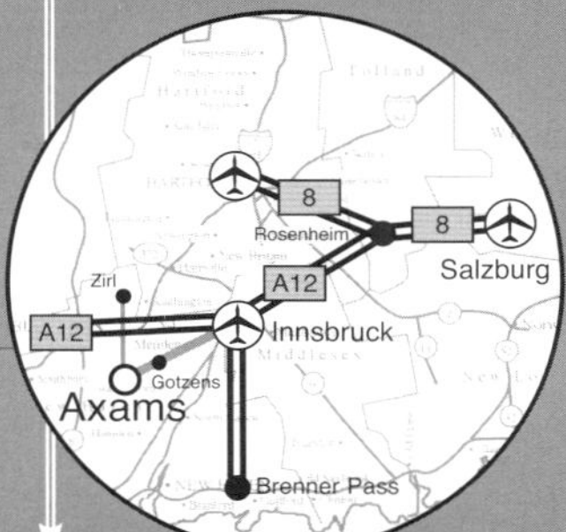

Axamer Lizum = **15** miles (24Km)
Drive time is about 20 minutes

*From **Calais** 646 miles (1039 Km)
Drive time is around **11½** hours.

Alpbach

MOUNTAIN DATA

Top Lift at - 2928m

Ride Area
42km of piste

Bottom Lift at - 816m

Vertical Drop - 1212m

Number of Runs -

Longest - 5 miles (8km)

TERRAIN LEVELS

Easy	**30%**
Intermediate	**60%**
Advanced	**10%**
Expert =	

TERRAIN TO SUITE

Freeride	**40%**
Trees	A few
Backcountry	A bit
Freestyle	**20%**
Halfpipe	Yes 1
Terrain Park	Yes 1
Carving	**40%**

SNOW DATA

Average Snowfall
600cm a season

Snowmaking
50% cover of the slopes

Winter Periods
Dec to April

Summer Riding
None

SLOPE ACCESS

Total Lifts = **20**

Uplift Rate - 19,000 people an hour.

1 Gondola - **5** Chair lifts

14 Drag lifts

**Leashes Required*

Lift Times
8.30am to 4.00pm

Lift Pass Rates

1 Day pass	325 Sch
6 Day pass	1350 Sch
Season Pass	-

Travel Guide

Fly to **Innsbruck,** airport 50 minutes transfer time.

Bus services direct from Innsbruck airport.

Route Planner:
From Innsbruck head east along the A12 and exit at junction 32 via Brixlegg and on to Alpbach.

* Drive time from **Calais** is $11^{1/2}$ hours. 676 miles (1088 km)

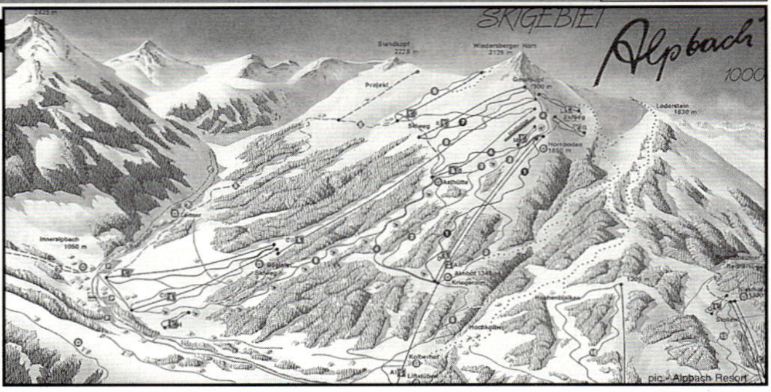

Alpbach is a cool, all-Austrian alternative to some of its more famous nearby cousins. This perfect picture postcard resort, decked out with traditional chalets dotted in and around a gently rising mountain, is one of those places beloved by skiers in one-piece ski-suits who seem to spend more time sunning themselves outside mountain restaurants than checking out the slopes. However, this small and easy-going resort is host to part of the *ISF World Pro Tour*, so it's not all bad news. Alpbach is without doubt, an intermediate's resort and one that won't take too long to conquer; you wouldn't spend more than a week here, and certainly not a whole season, unless you're easily pleased and like an unadventurous mountain.

Freeriders have a small area to explore, with some interesting terrain to ride. On the upper sections, you can check out some wide, open powder fields, that eventually descend through trees en route to the base area. Advanced riders will find that the few black runs are not to be treated with arrogance. Unpisted routes from **Loderstein** back to the gondola station, give freeriders in soft boots a great time, as do the runs around the **Wiedersbergerhorn**, which often have excellent powder.

Freestylers fed up with looking for natural hits, should make their way to the halfpipe and fun-park, located on **Gahmkopf**, where grommets can take their frustrations out in this average play area.

Carvers with a good pair of boots will love **Alpbach.** It's a full-on carver's resort, with wide pistes devoid of any trouble spots. Although there isn't an abundance of pisted runs, what is available is well looked after, and easily negotiated.

Beginners have a great learner's mountain. There are some perfect flats around the base areas to start out on, with excellent wide, open novice trails up in the **Skiweg** area.

Alpbach offers some slopeside accommodation with the bulk of beds available within easy reach of the village a two minute bus ride from the base lifts. Being a resort used by package tour operators means that on the one hand, the place can become very busy, but on the other, some cheap package deals are available. The village is a relaxed affair offering a number of restaurants, swimming and skating. But as for night-life, apart from a few bars, you won't find much to shout about. But overall Alpbach is a nice place, just a bit bland.

Alpbach Tourism
311- 6236 Alpbach. Tirol
++43 (0) 5336 5233 www.alpbach.com

Overall rating out of 10 — **5** — **Okay but a bit limited**

Bad Gastein

AUSTRIA

MOUNTAIN DATA

Top Lift at - 2230m

Ride Area 200km of piste

Bottom Lift at - 1080m
Vertical Drop - 1150m
Number of Runs - 25
Longest - 5 miles (8km)

TERRAIN LEVELS

Easy	**24%**
Intermediate	**66%**
Advanced	**10%**
Expert =	

TERRAIN TO SUITE

Freeride	**40%**
Trees	A few
Backcountry	A bit
Freestyle	**20%**
Halfpipe	Yes 1
Terrain Park	Yes 1
Carving	**40%**

SNOW DATA

Average Snowfall
600cm a season
Snowmaking
30% cover of the slopes
Winter Periods
Dec to April
Summer Riding
None

SLOPE ACCESS

Total Lifts = **53**
Uplift Rate - 23,400 people an hour.
9 Cable Cars, **29** Chair lifts
15 Drag lifts
**Leashes Required*

Lift Times
8.30am to 4.00pm

Lift Pass Rates

1 Day pass	430 Sch
6 Day pass	2050 Sch
Season Pass	

Travel Guide

Fly to **Salzburg** airport 2 hours away.

Bus services on a daily basis from the airport.

Route Planner:
From Salzburg head south along the A10 to junction 46 and then take the 168 route until signs for Badgastein along the 167.

pic - Bad Gastein

Bad Gastein is an old **Austrian** spa town that is located in the Tirol region along the **Gastein Valley** and perched up at a height of some 1080 metres, it is only a short distance from the village of **Bad Hofgastein**. What you have here is a relatively unknown but large ridable area which is basically split into four resorts that although are simlar, nevertheless offer something different. Collectively you have over 200km of marked out piste to ride, though it should be pointed out that not all the areas or pistes are linked up by lifts. So study the local piste maps to ensure that you don't have any problems finding slopes and lifts. Overall, this is an area that predominantly favours intermediate riders with an excellent choice of cruising runs to enjoy. **Bad Gastein** gives direct access to the slopes on the **Stubnerkogel, Sportgastein** and higher up to the summit of **Kreuzkogel**. You can also gain access via Bad Gastein to the half dozen or so runs on the **Gravkoe**l where you will find some decent trees to shred. Bad Hofgastein and the area known as **Dorfgastein** are two other locations where you can do some cool riding.

Freeriders can basically pick and choose from any one of the areas in order to have a good time. The collection of slopes on the **Dorfgastein** are okay for freeriding.

Freestylers might not embrace this place with its rather dull freestyle appeal. However, you will still be able to find some good hits and be able to catch some big air. There is also a pipe and terrain park up on the **Dorfgastein** slopes.

Carvers will possibly like this place the most no matter which area you select. The whole area is littered with good pisted cruising runs, especially the runs up on the **Stubnerkogel** area.

Beginners should think about choosing another resort as this is not really a hot place for learning snowboarding at.

Off the slopes, hotels, chalets and other local facilities are in abundance but not very convenient to reach all the slopes and other areas. Having a car around **Bad Gastein** may be a good idea as local transport is not hot. Accommodation options within the area are not overpriced and cheap budget priced lodgings are easy to find. Eating out options are not mega in terms of selection. What you have is a lot of hotel restaurants selling much the same style of food. As for a good lively night out, forget it.

For accommodation listings visit - www.worldsnowboardguide.com

Badgastein
Kaiser Franz Josef Strasse 1, Bad Gastein A5640
++43 6434 25310 www.gastein.com

Overall rating out of 10 **6** **Not a bad group of mountains.**

Ellmau

MOUNTAIN DATA

Top Lift at - 1829m

Ride Area
35km of piste

Bottom Lift at - 820m
Vertical Drop - 1009m
Number of Runs -
Longest - 4.5 miles (7km)

TERRAIN LEVELS

Easy	**43%**
Intermediate	**48%**
Advanced	**9%**
Expert =	

TERRAIN TO SUITE

Freeride	**40%**
Trees	A few
Backcountry	A bit
Freestyle	**10%**
Halfpipe	Not local
Terrain Park	Not local
Carving	**50%**

SNOW DATA

Average Snowfall

Snowmaking
15% cover of the slopes
Winter Periods
Dec to April
Summer Riding
None

SLOPE ACCESS

Total Lifts = **92**
Uplift Rate -19,000 people an hour.
9 Gondolas - **30** Chair lifts
55 Drag lifts
**Leashes Required*

Lift Times
8.30am to 4.00pm

Lift Pass Rates

1 Day pass	380 Sch
6 Day pass	1890 Sch
Season Pass	

Travel Guide

Fly toSalzburg airport 90 minutes transfer time.

Bus services direct from Salzburg airport.

Route Planner:
From Salzburg head south along routes 21 and 312 to Ellmau. A 45 mile (70km) journey.

* Drive time from **Calais** is $11^{1/2}$ hours. 692 miles (115 km)

pic - Ellmau Resort

Ellmau forms part of the massive **Ski Welt,** which is said to be **Austria's** largest linked ridable area located in the Tirol and is only 90 minutes from **Salzburg**. 250km of linked piste covered by 92 lifts should mean utopia, but unfortunately this place is not that hot. The resort's low altitude means that good annual snow is not a feature of this place although to be fair, the place has a good snowmaking set up to help when the real stuff is lacking. As for the slopes, this is mountain that tends to suffer from a lack of a good selection of advanced freeriding areas, come to that, it lacks good natural freestyle terrain as well. The biggest let down here are the hordes of novice ski groups clogging up the place and littering the slopes with skis and poles as they fall over all over the place. This is a very popular ski resort which on the one hand means long lift queues, but on the other hand, and in the resorts defence, this is also an affordable destination.

Freeriders who know their stuff, won't find the offerings here to their general liking. You can have a good time but nothing is that testing or too prolonged in terms of long runs and although the **Ski Welt** offers a lot of riding opportunities, a week's trip would be better spent at a more adventurous resort. However, an okay run to check out is the trail down from **Brandstadl** to **Scheffau**.

Freestylers should make the trip back down to the resort of **Soll** to check out their halfpipe and terrain park because it's about the best place to get any big air from. This is not a freestylers resort whether you want natural hits of man mad offerings. But like any resort, if you look hard enough, you will find something to leap off.

Carvers of limited experience can have a great time at **Ellmau** or at any of the nearby linked resorts. The area boasts a lot of wide and well groomed runs that will let you cruise with ease for hours on end. Check out the Hohe Salve for some fun.

Beginners are the one group who should have no problems with this resort even if the place is a bit fragmented. There are plenty of easy to reach nursery slopes to seek out.

Ellmau may be a quaint **Austrian** village, but it is also a bit of a miss-mash of a place. Getting around can be a real pain in the arse and local transport services are poor. Still, accommodation is affordable and there are lots of hotel restaurants to get a meal in. Night life is super dull, unless you're into aprés ski games.

For accommodation listings visit - www.worldsnowboardguide.com

Ellmau Tourist Office
Ellmau A 6352. Tirol
++43 (0) 5358 2301 www.ellmau.com

Overall rating out of 10 **4** **Poor freestylers resort**

Fieberbrunn

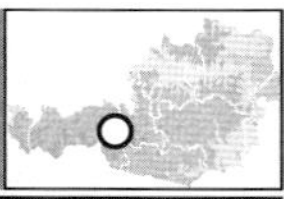

MOUNTAIN DATA

Top Lift at - 2020m

Ride Area
50km of piste

Bottom Lift at - 878m
Vertical Drop - 1220m
Number of Runs -
Longest - 5 miles (8km)

TERRAIN LEVELS

Easy	**34%**
Intermediate	**50%**
Advanced	**16%**
Expert =	

TERRAIN TO SUITE

Freeride	**45%**
Trees	A few
Backcountry	A fair bit
Freestyle	**15%**
Halfpipe	Yes 1
Terrain Park	Yes 1
Carving	**40%**

SNOW DATA

Average Snowfall

Snowmaking
40% cover of the slopes
Winter Periods
Dec to April
Summer Riding
None

SLOPE ACCESS

Total Lifts = **14**
Uplift Rate ---- people an hour.
2 Gondolas, **5** Chair lifts

**Leashes Required*

Lift Times
8.30am to 4.00pm

Lift Pass Rates
1 Day pass 350 Sch
6 Day pass 1600 Sch
Season Pass 1600 Sch

Travel Guide

Fly to **Salzburg,** airport 1 1/4 hours transfer time.

Bus services with links from Salzburg .

Route Planner:
From Salzburg head west along route 312 St Johann, then turn right on the 164 to Fieberbrunn. (44 miles)
* Drive time from **Calais** is **11 1/2** hours
696 miles (1119 km)

pic - Fieberbrunn Resort

Fieberbrunn is a rather strange tale in terms of its popularity with snowboarding. It's not a high resort, nor is Fieberbrunn an adventurous place, and most good riders will have had enough after three or four days. Its snowboard status must be something to do with either the fantastic halfpipe, or else someone at the *International Snowboard Federation* has got a thing going with a local chick. The area lies in a natural snow pocket receving 50% more snow than nearby **Kitzbuhel** over a course of a season. Two years ago saw another new hi-speed quad replacing a t-bar in the middle of the resort and new for this season will be the **Sky-Liner** gondola from the car park to the top of the **Doischberg** replacing the last t-bar on the mountain. Fieberbrunn has never really attracted tour operators, the result being that the slopes are mainly inhabited by either locals or their cousins from Germany. **Like** most resorts, the well-prepared slopes do have busy periods (mainly at weekends and holidays), but don't be put off as this is a cool snowboard-friendly place.

Freeriders will find that the terrain is not the most testing, with only a couple of black runs that offer nothing much for advanced riders. The main runs on **Streuboden** are reached via a short journey on an unusual gondola system that arrives at two levels: the first of which will bring you out on easy terrain around trees, whilst the second takes you to open reds and a black run.

Freestylers looking for an endless supply of natural hits will be disappointed with Fieberbrunn. This is not the place to seek big air, but the extremely well-shaped halfpipe is superb and is open until 10 o'clock each night!

Carvers will find that the slopes appeal very much to intermediate hard booters, especially if you like well pisted and easy flats.

Beginners have a very good choice of beginner-friendly areas for learning the basics. As a decent novice's resort, you can avoid the drag lifts by riding the runs down off the first gondola station.

Fieberbrunn is a small village. Hotels, pensions and rooms in private houses are the main form of accommodation. Some of which are very close to the slopes. Prices vary, but in general the place is affordable. Night-life is definitely not one of Fieberbrunn's strong points. The *Londoner* and the *River House* are both popular bars. The *Biwak* is a new bar which looks out on to the halfpipe while *Tenne* night club is the late night hangout.

Fieberbrunn Tourism
Dorfplatz 1, Fieberbrunn, Austria
++43 (0) 5354 56304
www.fieberbrunn.com
www.snowscape.co.uk

Overall rating out of 10 **6** **Rapidly up and coming resort**

Hintertux

MOUNTAIN DATA

Top Lift at - 3250m

Ride Area
120km of piste

Bottom Lift at - 1500m

Vertical Drop - 1750m

Number of Runs - 18

Longest - 5 miles (8km)

TERRAIN LEVELS

Easy	**25%**
Intermediate	**65%**
Advanced	**10%**
Expert =	

TERRAIN TO SUITE

Freeride	**40%**
Trees	None
Backcountry	A bit
Freestyle	**20%**
Halfpipe	Yes 1
Terrain Park	Yes 1
Carving	**40%**

SNOW DATA

Average Snowfall

Snowmaking
20% cover of the slopes

Winter Periods
Dec to April

Summer Riding
May to Nov

SLOPE ACCESS

Total Lifts = **33**

Uplift Rate -30,000 people an hour.

6 Gondolas - **17** Chair lifts

10 Drag lifts

**Leashes Required*

Lift Times
8.30am to 4.00pm

Lift Pass Rates

1 Day pass	430 Sch
3 Day pass	1130 Sch
6 Day pass	2050 Sch

Travel Guide

Fly to **Innsbruck,** 1 1/2 hours away.

The nearest train stop is at Mayrhofen 20 min away.

Route Planner: From Innsbruck go west on the A12. Exit at B169 along the Zillertal Valley past Mayrhofen onto Hintertux.
* Drive time from **Calais** is 12 hours
700 miles (1126 km)

The base of **Hintertux** sits at a height of 1,500m at the far end of the **Zillertal** valley, which is also home to the resorts of **Mayrhofen** and **Eggalm**. Hintertux has a number of advantages and disadvantages: on the plus side, it's a glacial resort, and apart from being one of the best summer snowboard resorts in Europe, it also has an enviable snow record in winter. However, in winter the same pluses mean that when the lower altitude resorts of the valley are suffering from a lack of snow, Hintertux can become very busy. Still, the open expanse of freeride terrain provides some excellent powder fields that are seldom tracked out by the morning ski masses. In summer the extent of snow cover over the length of the runs is often more than many resorts get during the winter season. Slopes are always crowd-free and riding in a t-shirt is the norm.

Freeriders have the pick of the slopes with various terrain on and off-piste. There are huge open expanses and loads of gullies and natural walls to ride. There's no tree riding as the altitude deters their growth, but it's no big loss as the terrain is more than sufficient, especially if you take a look at what's available to ride off Number **3** chair.

Freestylers have loads of hits to check out, which include a few cliff drops and a number of wide, natural gap jumps. If you're still not content, there's a fun-park and two halfpipes which they maintain all year, although it's not always possible in July and August.

Carvers can feel as much at home here as anyone else. The pistes are really good for laying out big turns, and tend to be long with a few sharp turns here and there.

Beginners may find **Hintertux** a bit too daunting, especially if you're a total novice. There are some easy runs, but in truth you may be better off at another resort.

Hintertux has a lot going for it on the slopes, but off the mountain, the place is totally crap with little or no real local services. It's not that cheap either, with only a few restaurants and no decent drinking holes whatsoever. The best thing is to stay down the valley at **Mayrhofen**, which is about a forty minute bus ride away. Mayrhofen is a cool place with loads of places to stay, lots of restaurants and heaps of other things going on. Mayrhofen also has a very good and lively night life.

For accommodation listings visit - www.worldsnowboardguide.com

Hintertux - Tourism TUX
Lanersbach 472. A6293 Tux. Tirol
++43 (0) 5287 8506 www.tux.at.

Overall rating out of 10 - **7** **Fantastic summer destination**

Galtur

AUSTRIA

MOUNTAIN DATA

Top Lift at - 2292m

Ride Area

47km of piste

Bottom Lift at - 1584m

Vertical Drop - 700m

Number of Runs -

Longest - 2 miles (3km)

TERRAIN LEVELS

Easy	10%
Intermediate	60%
Advanced	30%
Expert =	

TERRAIN TO SUITE

Freeride	35%
Trees	A few
Backcountry	Okay
Freestyle	5%
Halfpipe	Yes 1
Terrain Park	Yes 1
Carving	60%

SNOW DATA

Average Snowfall
528 cm a season

Snowmaking
10% cover of the slopes

Winter Periods
Dec to April

Summer Riding
None

SLOPE ACCESS

Total Lifts = **12**

Uplift Rate not available an hour.

2 Chair lifts

10 Drag lifts

**Leashes Required*

Lift Times
8.30am to 4.00pm

Lift Pass Rates

1 Day pass	375 Sch
3 Day pass	950 Sch
6 Day pass	1710 Sch

Travel Guide

Fly to **Innsbruck** airport **2** hours transfer time.

Trains stop at Landeck which is 30 minutes away.

Route Planner:
From Innsbruck head west along the A12 to Landeck and then take the 316 to Ischgl and then the A188 to Galtur.

Calais is 11½ hours
620 miles (998 km)

plc - Galtur Resort

Galtur, the less famous cousin of **Ischgl** (20 minutes away at the head of the Paznaun Valley), was made famous for all the wrong reasons during the winter of '98/'99. The resort suffered an avalanche that wiped out much of the village and left many people dead. Although a small resort, Galtur proves that size doesn't always matter. Whilst Ischgl gets all the attention, Galtur is left relatively alone, making it a far quieter place to ride. Galtur is a very Austrian resort, with all the usual trappings. The terrain doesn't measure to mega status and piste are fairly ordinary. However, it is possible to buy a lift ticket for the **Silvretta** area (of which Galtur is a part), that includes **Ischgl**, opening up some 155 miles of terrain. You can also do night riding here, which is not a common thing in **Austria.**

Freeriders in softs looking for interesting terrain should check out the **Innere Kopsalpe** area. It won't test advanced riders too much, but should keep intermediates happy for a few days.

Freestylers won't love Galtur as it doesn't offer any real big air opportunities - though like any resort there are hits to be found if you look. The best thing to do is either take the 20 minute bus journey to Ischgl to ride their amazing fun-park, or check out the halfpipe at **Samnaun**, a small neighbouring Swiss resort.

Carvers will find this a good place, but not exhausting. The well-pisted runs allow carvers to progress with ease, and the red and black runs on the **Saggrat** should give you a rush.

Beginners are the one group of riders who will really like Galtur. The flats are easy to reach from the village and riders should have no real problems, unless they are scared of using the drag lifts that serve many of the runs (including the easy ones). Still, as the lift lines are non-existent and quiet, you'll be able to keep trying without too much hassle from irate skiers. The local ski-school, which caters mainly for beginners, will help you out.

Off the slopes, **Galtur** is a typical Austrian village with normal accommodation offerings, from pricey hotels to well priced pensions. Everything is within easy access of the slopes and for such a small resort, there are plenty of things to do. Eating out is all Austrian, which is average but bland. There is, however, way too much aprés-ski which will appeal to some sad types, but not the hardcore rider who likes to party hard.

For accommodation listings visit - www.worldsnowboardguide.com

Galtur Tourism
Postfach 10, A-6563, Galtur.
++43 (0) 5443 521 **www.galtuer.com**

Overall rating out of 10 **7** **Good freeriding resort**

Innsbruck

MOUNTAIN DATA

Top Lift at - 3200m

Ride Area
323km of piste

Bottom Lift at - 850m

Vertical Drop - 1460m

Number of Runs -

Longest - 6 miles (9.6km)

TERRAIN LEVELS

Easy	**54%**
Intermediate	**40%**
Advanced	**6%**
Expert =	

TERRAIN TO SUITE

Freeride	**35%**
Trees	Yes
Backcountry	Yes
Freestyle	**35%**
Halfpipe	Yes 6
Terrain Park	Yes 6
Carving	**30%**

SNOW DATA

Average Snowfall

Snowmaking
40% cover of the slopes

Winter Periods
Dec to April

Summer Riding
May to Nov

SLOPE ACCESS

Total Lifts = **210**

Uplift Rate not available an hour.

**Leashes Required*

Lift Times
8.30am to 4.00pm

Lift Pass Rates

1 Day pass	510 Sch
5 Day pass	1400 Sch
6 Day pass	

Travel Guide

Fly to **Innsbruck** direct.

The nearest train station is in the centre of the city

Route Planner:
From Munich, head south on the A8 and A12 Autobahn routes direct to Innsbruck.
* Drive time from **Calais** is 11 1/2 hours
649 miles (1044 km)

pic - Innsbruck Tourism

Innsbruck is not actually a resort but a gate way city to dozens of resorts. Five of the resorts on the city's doorstep are, **Axams, Igls, Seegrübe, Mütters** and **Stubai Glacier**. The close areas around Innsbruck (apart from Stubai Glacier), are low altitude, and not always snowsure. None of them are very big or adventurous. You can buy a special pass that covers you for all five resorts and the bus to each place. However, although local bus services are excellent, it may be an advantage to have your own car so you can travel around the resorts or further afield. All the road links are superb so you won't have any problems, but remember to take some snow-chains.
Burton Snowboards set up their first non-American headquarters in Innsbruck in 1992. *Snowboard Klinik* is also based in the city as are the offices of the *International Snowboard Federation (ISF)*.

Innsbruck, may not be New York or London, but it still has a good scene and is home to a big snowboard culture. There are loads of things to do: you could visit the Olympic ice-rink, hang out and skate at loads of good spots, or simply party.

Innsbruck also holds the annual 'Air 'N' Style snowboard event up on the **Bergisel**, which is an Olympic ski jump stadium located on the outskirts of the city. The event is a big attraction and apart from snowboarding, loads of pop bands perform for the crowds (mind you only to boost their record sales - *scumbags*).

Innsbruck has simply loads of restaurants. There's a *McDonald's* which pumps out its cardboard crap, and a *Wiener Wald*, a version of *Kentucky Fried Chicken*.

Night-life in Innsbruck is particularly good, simply because there are no stupid aprés-ski crowds. There are plenty of late night bars - check out *Limerick Bills,* a cool Irish pub or *Jimmy's* Bar a very popular hangout and the club.

Accommodation is well located: you can bed down cheaply within walking distance of the city centre. Prices are extremely reasonable. *Pension Paula* the local backpacker's place, is only five minutes from the town centre and is without doubt the best place to stay in the city, with rates from 300sch a night. There is also a hostel and numerous hotels. *Hotel Central* is a budget place that also has a bar, and is only two minutes from the city centre with nightly rates from 280sch.
For accommodation listings visit - www.worldsnowboardguide.com

Innsbruck Tourist Bureau
Burggraben 3, A-6020 Innsbruck
++43 (0) 512 5356 **www.tiscover.com/innsbruck.**

Overall rating out of 10 **10** **Great gate-way city**

Stubai Glacier

AUSTRIA

MOUNTAIN DATA

Top Lift at - 3200m

Ride Area
30km of piste

Bottom Lift at - 1721m
Vertical Drop - 1500m
Number of Runs - 20
Longest - 6 miles (9.6km)

TERRAIN LEVELS

Easy	**64%**
Intermediate	**29%**
Advanced	**7%**
Expert =	

TERRAIN TO SUITE

Freeride	**35%**
Trees	No
Backcountry	No
Freestyle	**15%**
Halfpipe	Yes 1
Terrain Park	Yes 1
Carving	**50%**

SNOW DATA

Average Snowfall
n/a cm a season
Snowmaking
10% cover of the slopes
Winter Periods
Nov to April
Summer Riding
May to Sept

SLOPE ACCESS

Total Lifts = **19**
Uplift Rate - 22,000 people an hour.
4 Gondolas/Cable cars
3 Chair lifts - **12** Drag lifts
**Leashes Required*

Lift Times
8.30am to 4.00pm

Lift Pass Rates

1 Day pass	430 Sch
3 Day pass	1150 Sch
6 Day pass	1890 Sch

Travel Guide

Fly to **Innsbruck** airport 40 mins away.

Bus services run almost hourly from Innsbruck .

Route Planner:
Via Innsbruck, head south on the A13 toll road until the Staubi turn. Then head up the B183 to Staubi.
* Drive time from **Calais** is 12 hours 676 miles (1088 km)

pic - Doppelmayr/Bohler

Stubai Glacier is the biggest resort under the **Innsbruck** area. It's also the only Innsbruck resort that has summer snow-boarding. A common factor in the summer months are the hoards of day-tripping US students, with no idea what they are doing or where they are. Stubai is a great mountain to try out with open runs that are well groomed and serviced by a set of efficient lifts. The only drawbacks are that, being a high glacier resort, it can be stupidly cold in the winter where the temperature can make it almost impossible to ride. The other problem is that because Stubai nearly always guarantees snow when lower areas are short on the stuff, the masses head here, making the place very busy, especially at weekends. Munich is only two and a half hours away and so the place also gets a regular German overload. Access to the slopes involves a twenty minute cable car ride, but once up, you're presented with a great selection of runs.

Freeriders will find an abundance of trails to ride, without having to go over the same ones every twenty minutes. Although this may not be the most demanding resort, with only a couple of steep trails, there's plenty to keep you content. Trail **8** is a short black that will keep you on your toes. But more interesting is the **4a** black trail off the **Schlepplift Fernau** drag lift. It offers a fast, uneven descent that's not for wimps. The Number **14** red trail is the longest run, and winds its way down over 6 miles; don't try it unless you're a competent rider and have first studied a lift map.

Freestylers have a fun-park with a halfpipe, but neither are up to much and are hardly ever used by the locals. The natural hits that are all over the place give much better air time.

Carvers will enjoy the runs here the most. The management take great care in preparing the slopes: they don't just piste once at night, but keep the runs pisted all day, so carvers can enjoy some of the finest carving trails in the whole Tirol area.

Beginners are well taken care of with a number of perfectly well-appointed, easy, flat blue runs. But watch out for the drag lifts.

En route to **Stubai,** there are a number of villages to stay in with full local services. However, you're better off staying down in Innsbruck which has the best options. Staying in **Neustiff**, which is only 20 minutes away, is not a bad idea and has a number of accommodation options, restaurants and bars.

For accommodation listings visit - www.worldsnowboardguide.com

Staubi Gletsvherbahn
A-6167 Neustiff im Stubaital
++43 (0) 52 26 81 41 **www.tiscover.com/innsbruck.**

Overall rating out of 10 **7** **Good open flat runs for carving**

Ischgl

MOUNTAIN DATA

Top Lift at - 2864m

Ride Area 200km of piste

Bottom Lift at - 1400m

Vertical Drop - 1472m

Number of Runs - 62

Longest - 4.3 miles (7km)

TERRAIN LEVELS

Easy	**27%**
Intermediate	**63%**
Advanced	**10%**
Expert =	

TERRAIN TO SUITE

Freeride	**40%**
Trees	Yes
Backcountry	Some
Freestyle	**20%**
Halfpipe	Yes 2
Terrain Park	Yes 2
Carving	**20%**

SNOW DATA

Average Snowfall

Snowmaking
20% cover of the slopes

Winter Periods
Dec to April

Summer Riding
None

SLOPE ACCESS

Total Lifts = **41**

Uplift Rate - 58,000 people an hour.

3 Gondolas & Cable cars

11 Chair lifts **25** Drag lifts

**Leashes Required*

Lift Times
8.30am to 4.00pm

Lift Pass Rates

1 Day pass	415 Sch
6 Day pass	2060 Sch
12 Day pass	3260 Sch

SLOPE ACTION

Snowboard Hire
Daily rates from 450 Sch
Kids from 350 Sch

Snowboard Tuition
Group lessons, from from 600 Sch

Night Riding
Yes in the pipe

Heli Boarding
No

Snowmobiles
No

Mountain Cafes
11

Ischgl has gained a reputation as being one of Austria's best resorts - and it's a worthy reputation at that. Mind you, it's also one of Austria's more snobbish areas and can be very expensive. Ischgl may not be the most testing place, but it offers something for everyone, with well groomed slopes serviced by fast modern lifts. Snowboarders have been coming here for years to sample the excellent selection of wide, open, long runs which suit all standards and styles of rider. The *International Snowboard Federation* regularly stage slalom and halfpipe events here, so it must have something to offer. If what you find at Ischgl is not enough, then you can ride into the neighbouring Swiss duty-free resort of **Samnaun**. It can be reached by connecting lifts and is covered by the **Silvretta** lift pass, which can be used at three other nearby resorts (**Galtur, Kappl** and **See**).

Freeriders have a high altitude mountain that ensures a good annual snow record, providing excellent wide open powder fields. For some easy freeriding, check out the stuff in the **Idjoch** area, which has a good mixture of blues and reds to play around on. Advanced riders will find plenty of stuff to keep them busy, although you won't be tested too often. **Pardatschgrat**, a black run leading back into the village (with the lower section cutting through some trees), is well worth a go, and you'll also find good off-piste opportunities and fine freeriding down the runs off **Palinkopf.**

Freestylers are probably going to be the most pleased with Ischgl for one reason, and one reason only - the **Boarder's Paradise** fun-park is the dog's bollocks. It is without doubt, one of the best parks in Europe and is equipped with all sorts of interesting obstacles with marked areas such as Freeride, New School, and Mogul, which starts at the top. At the bottom there is a well-shaped halfpipe. The whole area is designed with the intention of satisfying air heads of all levels (there's also a halfpipe at **Samnaun**). However, freestylers who are still not content will find plenty of natural hits to get that extra air fix, with big drop ins, banks and gullies all over the mountain.

Carvers, especially hard boot riders, will love this resort, with its wide, motorway pistes where you can put down big arcs and easily make those 360° snow turns. Ischgl often hosts top slalom and giant slalom events so there must be good quality, fast carving terrain. The runs are so well-marked and pisted, that carving up Ischgl is a total pleasure, no matter what is on your feet.

Beginners will soon see the benefits of learning here. The novice-marked runs are just that, being well located and offering some long, easy-to-negotiate trails. The only drawback is the amount of drag lifts that beginners need to use, but you've got to learn some time. The local ski school has a lot of snowboard instruction and lesson programmes are very resonable.

The village of Ischgl is a modern affair, rather than the oldie world style more prevalent in **Austria**. However, this is a resort popular with the ski tour groups who come here by the coachload, so it can get very busy both on and off the slopes. Ischgl is also not the cheapest of places, so skint or budget-conscious riders will need to do some serious scamming to see a seven day trip through. Around the village there are a number of attractions from the adventure swimming pool, squash courts and a number of shops (selling tack mostly). There is a few snowboard hire outlets, with prices much the same from 350sch a day for set-up, check out *Sport Mahoy.* **Jobseekers:** As a resort visited by lots of Brits, English-speaking snowboard instructors and reps are always required.

Depending on what you're into may have a lot do with how you eat here. There are quite a lot of restaurants in Ischgl, mostly hotel restaurants. However, they are nearly all Austrian style, offering a lot of bland menus. Fast food around here is a shop-lifter running out of the supermarket with a packet of biscuits. The Pizzeria is good, so it's not all bad news.

Night-life in Ischgl is dire and really lets the place down. There is a number of okay bars and late night hangouts. But the big problem is that most places are full of those sickly aprés-ski bores, wearing silly coloured lipsticks and face paints. They also go in for lots of tacky tea-time bar games.

Accommodation is of a very high standard but with high rates to match. There are plenty of typical Austrian hotels, pensions and a number of Austrian-style apartment suites, with self-catering sleeping 6 or more. Nothing is more than a few minutes from the base lifts, with many of the places located in areas where cars are banned. Many tour operators come here offering lots of package deals for weekly and two week stays.

For accommodation listings visit - www.worldsnowboardguide.com

Summary: Ischgl has one of the greatest fun-parks in Europe and offers some excellent all-round terrain for all levels. However, off the slopes things are a bit poncy.
Money wise: Very expensive resort, with over priced accommodation.

Overall rating out of 10: 9

Ischgl Tourism
Po Box 24,
A-6561 Ischgl.
General info ++43 (0) 5444 52660
Reservations ++43 (0) 5444 52660
Avalanche info ++43 (0) 5522 1588
www.ischgl.com

pics - Ischgl Tourist Office

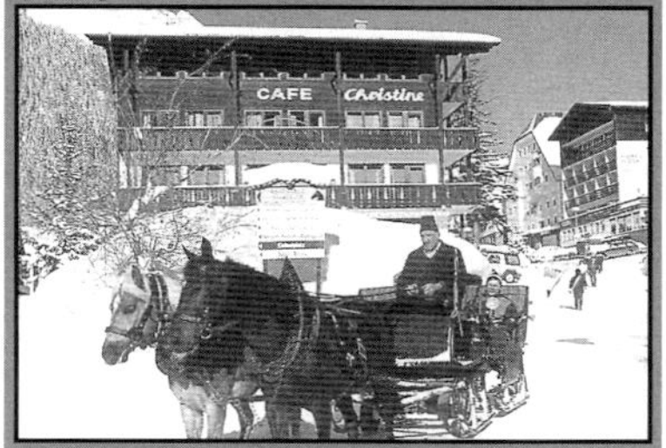

Travel Guide

Fly to **Innsbruck** International
Transfer time to resort = **3½** hours.
Local airport = **Innsbruck**.

Approximate global air travel times to **Innsbruck**

from:	London	2 hours
	Los Angles	13 hours
	New York	9 hours

Buses from Innsbruck, can be taken via Landeck to Ischgl on a daily basis. Landeck is 55 mins.

Trains go to Landeck - 55 mins

Route Planner
Innsbruck *via motorway A12*

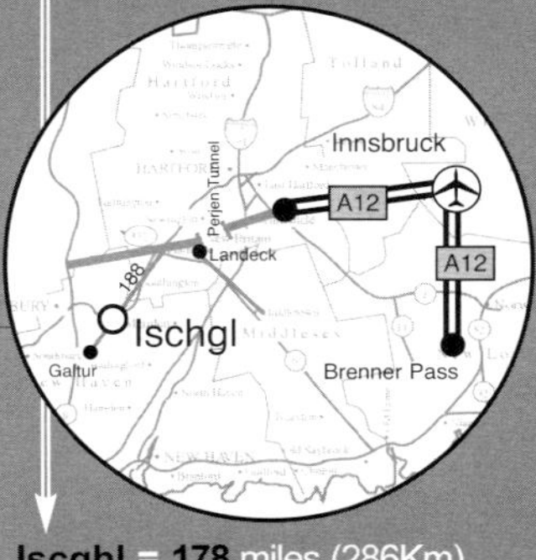

Iscghl = **178** miles (286Km)
Drive time is about **3½** hours

*From **Calais** 639 miles (1028Km)
Drive time is around **11½** hours.

Kaprun

MOUNTAIN DATA

Top Lift at - 3029m

Ride Area

129km of piste

Bottom Lift at - 800m

Vertical Drop - 1132m

Number of Runs -

Longest - 5 miles (8km)

TERRAIN LEVELS

Easy	53%
Intermediate	20%
Advanced	30%
Expert =	

TERRAIN TO SUITE

Freeride	50%
Trees	No
Backcountry	A bit
Freestyle	20%
Halfpipe	Yes 2
Terrain Park	Yes 1
Carving	30%

SNOW DATA

Average Snowfall
1030 cm a season

Snowmaking
30% cover of the slopes

Winter Periods
Nov to April

Summer Riding
May to Sept

SLOPE ACCESS

Total Lifts = **27**

Uplift Rate - 30,000 people an hour.

8 Trains-Gondolas-Cables

3 Chair lifts - **19** Drag lifts

**Leashes Required*

Lift Times
8.30am to 4.00pm

Lift Pass Rates

1 Day pass	435 Sch
6 Day pass	2050 Sch
Season pass	

Travel Guide

Fly to **Salzburg,** 1 1/2 hours transfer.

The nearest train stop is at Zell an See 10 mins away

Route Planner: From Salzburg head south on the A10. Then south west on the 168 via Taxenbach to Kaprun (56 miles)

* Drive time from **Calais** is 12 1/4 hours 714 miles (1159 km)

pic - San Tang

Winter or summer, Kaprun cuts it big style. The ride area is located on one of Austria's best glaciers, the **Kitzsteinhorn Glacier**, which reaches an altitude of 3,203 metres, making it a perfect place to ride. Being a glacier resort, you can ride here all year and no matter what month you visit, riders of all levels will find something to shred. It has to be said however, that much of what is here (or at nearby **Zell am See**), is best suited to intermediate freeriders and carvers.

Freeriders wanting to gain access to **Kaprun's** best terrain and main runs, should head for the **Kitzsteinhorn** via the cable car or funicular train to the **Alpencentre**. Further up, you can reach good off-piste powder stashes, which can often still be found in the summer months of June and July.

Freestylers are provided with a halfpipe at Kaprun all year round, and there's another one down in **Zell am See** during the winter. Kaprun's pipe is not the world's best but it still allows for some okay riding. The fun-park has an array of hits, but really freestylers should search out Kaprun's natural hits.

Carvers will be at ease whether they ride here or Zell am See, as both resorts have some great, open carving runs. At Kaprun you can access some excellent spots via the **Alpencentre**.

Beginners can get going on a number of easy runs on the Maiskogel mountain, which is reached by a drag lift from the centre of the village. If you can't handle a drag lift, take the cable car at the north end of the village to reach the east slopes. Beginners are spoilt when it comes to snowboard instruction; Kaprun was the first Austrian resort to have an independent snowboard school. If you get bored with Kaprun, Zell am See is only a ten minute bus ride away, which gives you access to an extra 50 miles of piste covered by the same pass.

Kaprun is a fairly large and stretched out affair. Having a car may save a lot of walking but there is also a good and regular local bus service. Around town, you get a mixture of the old and new with a typical **Austrian** flavour. Accommodation options are excellent and Kaprun will satisfy both rich and skint snowboarders alike. Evenings in Kaprun are laid back - check out the *Austrian Pub*, *Bauber's*, or the *Fountain* bar. Nothing great about any of them, but there are worse places.

For accommodation listings visit - **www.worldsnowboardguide.com**

Kaprun Tourism
Salzburger Platz 601. A-5710 Kaprun
++43 (0) 6547 86430

Overall rating out of 10 — **6** — **Good winter and summer resort**

Kitzbuhel

AUSTRIA

MOUNTAIN DATA

Top Lift at - 2000m

Ride Area
160km of piste

Bottom Lift at - 800m
Vertical Drop - 1200m
Number of Runs - 54
Longest - 6 miles (9.6km)

TERRAIN LEVELS

Easy	**50%**
Intermediate	**42%**
Advanced	**8%**
Expert =	

TERRAIN TO SUITE

Freeride	**45%**
Trees	A few
Backcountry	A bit
Freestyle	**10%**
Halfpipe	Yes 1
Terrain Park	Yes 1
Carving	**45%**

SNOW DATA

Average Snowfall
180 cm a season
Snowmaking
25% cover of the slopes
Winter Periods
Dec to April
Summer Riding
None

SLOPE ACCESS

Total Lifts = **61**
Uplift Rate - 65,000 people an hour.
6 Gondolas/Cable cars
27 Chair lifts - **28** Drag lifts
**Leashes Required*

Lift Times
8.30am to 4.00pm

Lift Pass Rates

1 Day pass	430 Sch
6 Day pass	2080 Sch
Season pass	7500

Travel Guide

Fly to **Salzburg** airport 1 3/4 hours transfer time

The nearest train station is in Kitzbuhel

Route Planner:
Via Salzburg, head south via the route 312 and 161 all the way to Kitzbuhel 50 miles (82km).
* Drive time from **Calais** is 11 3/4 hours 700 miles (1126 km)

pic - Kitzbuhel Tourism

The chances are that if you know Austria, you'll know about **Kitzbühel**, famed for the **Hahnenkamm** (a World Cup ski downhill course), and noted for the billions of ski-package tour groups. Yep, Kitzbühel is Austria's Benidorm, due to the hoards of skiers cluttering up the slopes and making fools of themselves around town. A shame really, for apart from the long lift queues and the fact that it is a low-level resort, which doesn't guarantee snow cover on the bottom runs, it is a cool place to ride. Still, when the snow has dumped, no rider should get bored as there is enough room to ride without constantly bumping into skiers.

Freeriders should look under **Bichlam** in order to ride some cool powder, while advanced riders will find the more testing runs on **Ehrenbach** (a part of the Hahnenkamm), and down the steeps of **Ehrenbachgraben**. The best way to cut the off-piste is to seek out the assistance of a local guide at the off-piste school.

Freestylers are attracted to **Kitzbühel** for its extensive amounts of natural hits, like the stuff found on **Pegelstein**, or those hits dotted around **Safari**, which starts at Pegelstein. The park and pipe also provide plenty of air time, even if they're not that well looked after.

Carvers are primarily drawn to **Kitzbühel** by the thought of tackling the **Hahnenkamm**. The rest of the area has plenty of good advanced and intermediate terrain that also allows for some fast carving descents.

Beginners in particular are well suited to these slopes, as there's the chance of riding some long, easy runs serviced by chair lifts, and not just drags, offering the nervous T-bar virgin good, alternative options for getting around. The long **Hagstein** run is ideal for first timers; the only problem with this area is that it is often littered with fallen down skiers.

Lodging in a town like Kitzbühel is no problem, with heaps of beds at average prices in pensions and apartments. Mercifully, **Kitzbühel** has loads of cheap eating joints, including take-away outlets. Boozing goes off in a number of places, allowing drinking into the early hours of the morning. But beware, skiers aprés all over the place, although most are in bed by 9pm having had their two glasses of gluhwein. Popular hangouts are *Take 5* (er) and the *Londoner* bar (points for names Zero).

For accommodation listings visit - www.worldsnowboardguide.com

Kitzbuhel Tourisn
Hinterstadt 18, Postfact 42, A-6370 Kitzbuhel. Tyrol
++43 (0) 5356 621 550-0 www.kitzbuehel.com

Overall rating out of 10 — **6** — **Overated, stuck up & cheesy**

Mayrhofen

MOUNTAIN DATA

Top Lift at - 2250m

Ride Area
160km of piste

Bottom Lift at - 630m
Vertical Drop - 1648m
Number of Runs - 133
Longest - 4.2 miles (7km)

TERRAIN LEVELS

Easy	**50%**
Intermediate	**42%**
Advanced	**8%**
Expert =	

TERRAIN TO SUITE

Freeride	**50%**
Trees	No
Backcountry	Poor
Freestyle	**10%**
Halfpipe	Yes 1
Terrain Park	Yes 1
Carving	**40%**

SNOW DATA

Average Snowfall
100 cm a season
Snowmaking
35% cover of the slopes
Winter Periods
Dec to April
Summer Riding
None

SLOPE ACCESS

Total Lifts = **64**
Uplift Rate - 35,000 people an hour.
4 Gondolas -1 Cable car
27 Chair lifts - **32** Drag lifts
**Leashes Required*

Lift Times
8.30am to 4.00pm

Lift Pass Rates
1 Day pass 370 Sch
6 Day pass 2130 Sch
Season pass

Travel Guide

Fly to **Innsbruck,** 1 1/4 hours transfer.

The nearest train stop is at Mayrhofen- Jenbach.

Route Planner:
From Innsbruck go west on the A12. Exit at B169 along the Zillertal Valley to Mayrhofen .
* Drive time from **Calais** is 12 hours 692 miles (1113 km)

pic - Krissy

Mayrhofen is situated in the **Ziller Valley,** and although it's a fairly unassuming resort, it offers some of the best riding in the area. Mayrhofen is linked with **Finkenberg** and **Hippach** which have a healthy snowboard presence, as well as stupidly large amounts of package tour ski groups. The resort is favoured by hoards of British and German two-plankers who clog up the lift system almost to bursting point. Lift queues are among the worst in the country, but at least the resort is working on solutions: ever since a gondola was installed in the centre of town, access to the mountain is much quicker. In the early days, Mayrhofen had the reputation of being a bit of a hard boot carver's place; this has changed and today there's a good influx of freeriders.

Freeriders willing to make the short hike past the **Gspeilkopf** lift, will find a side of the mountain that is only tracked by locals. It offers some rocky steeps and trees to slice through that eventually allow you to ride right back to the lift.

Freestylers have a halfpipe and a park that's loaded with various style jumps and a sound system, situated next to the **Hintertrett** chair. They try to keep the park for snowboarders only, but skiers are often allowed in (shameful).

Carvers have a mountain that seems to be made for them, with a number of super-wide and open cruising trails, that will give the edge-cranking lovers multiple orgasms.

Beginners have plenty of wide and well-prepared corduroy tracks to play on, and although many are serviced by drag lifts, you can also get around on chair lifts. The only bugs are the queues and hordes of ski-school classes hogging the easy slopes most of whom are total beginners leaving the base runs littered with fallen bi-plankers.

Although **Mayrhofen** isn't actually that big, there's plenty to keep you busy, with a good selection of accommodation and local services. Every winter there's an *Air and Style* competition, which involves a lot of partying. Down by the river there's also a skate ramp. Cheap eating options are plentiful and evenings are pretty cool. You can party hard well into the early hours in a couple of okay bars and late discos, but be warned, skiers do a lot of their stupid aprés-ski nonsense here, giving the whole place a cheap (which it's not) and cheesy feel about it.

For accommodation listings visit - **www.worldsnowboardguide.com**

Mayrhofen Tourism
Postfach 21. A-6290 Mayrhofen, Zillertal. Tirol
++43 (0) 5285 6760 www.mayrhofen.com

Overall rating out of 10 **4** **Limited and over all a bit dull**

Obergurgl

AUSTRIA

MOUNTAIN DATA

Top Lift at - 3035m

Ride Area: 110km of piste

Bottom Lift at - 1930m

Vertical Drop - 1105m

Number of Runs - 35

Longest - 5 miles (8km)

TERRAIN LEVELS

Easy	**32%**
Intermediate	**50%**
Advanced	**18%**
Expert =	

TERRAIN TO SUITE

Freeride	**30%**
Trees	None
Backcountry	No
Freestyle	**10%**
Halfpipe	Yes 1
Terrain Park	Yes 1
Carving	**60%**

SNOW DATA

Average Snowfall

Snowmaking
45% cover of the slopes

Winter Periods
Dec to April

Summer Riding
At Solden

SLOPE ACCESS

Total Lifts = **23**

Uplift Rate - 65,000 people an hour.

1 Cable car **11** Chair lifts **11** Drag lifts

**Leashes Required*

Lift Times
8.30am to 4.00pm

Lift Pass Rates

1 Day pass	460 Sch
6 Day pass	2230 Sch
Season pass	

Travel Guide

Fly to **Innsbruck** airport
$1^{3/4}$ hours transfer time

Bus services run almost hourly from Innsbruck .

Route Planner:
Via Innsbruck head along the A12 and turn off on to the B186 down the Otztal Valley to Obergurgl
* Drive time from **Calais** is $12^{3/4}$ hours
672 miles (1082km)

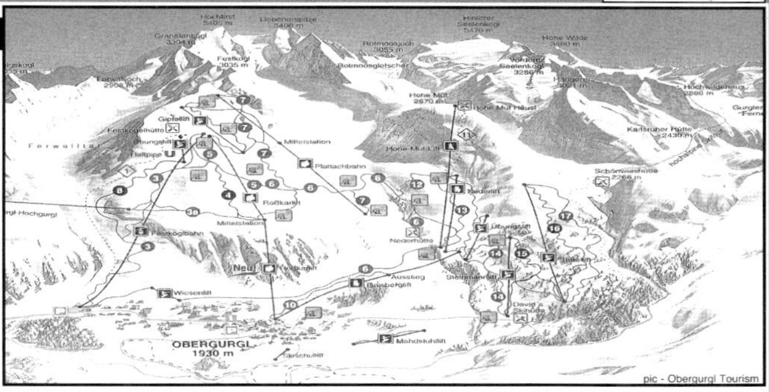

pic - Obergurgl Tourism

Obergurgl sits at the head of the **Otzal Valley,** a mere 90 minutes form **Innsbruck** and only 20 minutes from the more popular resort of **Solden**. Although Obergurgl and Solden are located along the same valley and both are base locations for summer snowboarding up on the **Tiefenbach** glacier, the similarity esnd there. Obergurgl, with its linked neighbouring resort **Hochgrugl**, is far smaller and far less diverse than Solden especially when it comes to freeriding. Where Obergurgl shines and gets top marks is as a carver's resorts. The resort's high altitude also scores highly in its favour, this place has a very good annual snow record with heaps of the stuff falling every year. Mind you, being a high altitude resort means that prices are also high. Another distinction is that it is a bit stuck up and visited by a lot of snotty nosed skiers with bad attitudes. On the slopes what you have is a wide open plateau that is completely void of any trees and is in general a tame mountain to ride. However, don't be put off, Obergurgl is still worth a visit. You could stay in Solden and visit this place for a day's riding by taking the local bus up or driving yourself. What ever, the runs are set out neatly and conveniently serviced by a series of lifts that go to a staggering summit elevation of some 3035 metres. Most of the runs are of an intermediate level with a series of reds, a few easy blues and only a couple of advanced black trails to check out.

Freeriders don't bother making the trek up to **Obergurgl** as the freeriding on offer down in **Solden** is far superior. You can still have a good time here but the slopes are not too adventurous.

Freestylers will largely be wasting their time up here, this is not an air head's retreat. There are of course a few natural hits as with most mountains covered in snow, but they are few and far between. Still, the resort does have a pipe and terrain park.

Carvers are the ones in for a treat. Obergurgl is dream for those who want to arc over in style on well groomed runs that are wide and free of obstacles (apart form the odd skier in drag).

Beginner should have no real problems with this place. The mountain is nicely laid out and novices can ride from the mid point all the way to the base via the number 5 and 6 trails.

Obergurgl off the slopes is boring and lacking in most things. You are far better off staying down in **Solden** which is excellent.

For accommodation listings visit - www.worldsnowboardguide.com

Obergurgl Tourisn
Obergurgl, A 6456
++43 (0) 5256 6466 www.obergurgl.com

Overall rating out of 10 — 6 — **Very good carver's resort**

Saalbach-Hinterglemm

MOUNTAIN DATA

Top Lift at - 2864m

Ride Area 200km of piste

Bottom Lift at - 1003m

Vertical Drop - 1095m

Number of Runs - 61

Longest - 4.3 miles (7km)

TERRAIN LEVELS

Easy	**50%**
Intermediate	**42%**
Advanced	**8%**
Expert =	

TERRAIN TO SUITE

Freeride	**50%**
Trees	Yes
Backcountry	Yes
Freestyle	**20%**
Halfpipe	Yes 2
Terrain Park	Yes 2
Carving	**30%**

SNOW DATA

Average Snowfall

Snowmaking
20% cover of the slopes

Winter Periods
Dec to April

Summer Riding
None

SLOPE ACCESS

Total Lifts = **63**

Uplift Rate - 64,000 people an hour.

10 Gondolas & Cable cars

14 Chair lifts **39** Drag lifts

**Leashes Required*

Lift Times
8.30am to 4.00pm

Lift Pass Rates

1 Day pass	430 Sch
6 Day pass	2070 Sch
12 Day pass	

SLOPE ACTION

Snowboard Hire
Daily rates from 480 Sch
Kids from 370 Sch

Snowboard Tuition
Lesson, lift & hire
from 610 Scg per day

Night Riding
Yes

Heli Boarding
No

Snowmobiles
No

Mountain Cafes
7

pic - Saalbach-Hinterglemm

Saalbach-Hinterglem are two closely linked villages. They lie along a valley floor where the mountain slopes rise up on both sides of each village. The first village you arrive at is Saalbach with Hinterglem a few minutes up the road. Together they become one large snowboard area, that covers 124 miles of piste, and forms a massive and good rideable area. Over the years, this has become a very popular place for visiting snowboarders, but it's not so favoured by many Austrian riders. This has nothing to do with the terrain since the area boasts some of the best in the country, with excellent advanced freeriding and fantastic beginner areas. It has more to do with the fact that this is a very busy tourist retreat, which can often see stupidly long lift lines and way overcrowded slopes, especially at weekends and holiday periods. Mornings can be stupidly busy, especially the first lifts up via the **Schattberg** cable car, but mercifully, once up, things get a lot better.

For a resort to host world ski events, you would expect some great terrain - and that is exactly what you get at Saalbach-Hinterglemm. There are trees, steeps, powder and natural hits, not to mention eight miles of snowboard-only runs for freeriders and carvers, as well as two halfpipes and a fun-park to suit all levels and styles of freestyler. If you get bored here or can't handle it, take up brass rubbing as it will suit you better.

Freeriders wanting off-piste powder will find some good stuff on the slopes of the north side of the valley, where you can gain access to some great runs which are not messed up by skiers. There's also a boardercross circuit for freeriders to shred.

Freestylers will find a large amount of natural hits dotted all over the place, many of which are favourite spots of the locals. The eight mile snowboard-only area, which has a good fun-park loaded with a series of hits and gaps, is well maintained and a pleaser. **Saalbach** and **Hinterglem** also have separate halfpipes; the one at Saalbach on the **Bernkogel** area is the better of the two; the pipe at Hinterglem is more tame and will suit mainly novice air heads, having a less scary vert, and lower walls.

Carvers of all grades will do well here - the place is a carver's dream. Those at advanced level who want a testing black run, should take the **Schattberg** cable car, from where you'll find what you're looking for. Those less adventurous carvers will find the red run named **Limberg-Jausern**, a nice long treat.

Beginners will quickly see improvements in their riding as **Saalbach-Hinterglem** is an ideal place for first to visit. The mountain have ample slopes that are easy to reach and negotiate; but note this place is littered with drag lifts, so expect a bit of T-bar tackling. The numerous ski/snowboard schools here all offer snowboard tuition for all level and will soon help you sort out any T-bar problems.

Being a popular tourist place, the area can sometimes feel tacky and overpopulated - but don't let that put you off. Whichever village you choose to stay in, you'll find a high level of service and plenty of off-slope things to do, from shopping for tourist toys, pigging out, drinking or body fitness. It should be mentioned though, that nothing comes cheap as this is an expensive place. Spread out between the two villages you'll be able to find an indoor swimming pool, a bowling alley, numerous saunas and fitness gyms. Ice skaters also have an ice ring to perform on. Snowboard hire is available in both villages, with prices the same wherever you go. You need a passport as security when hiring.
Jobseekers: English-speaking qualified snowboard instructors have no problems, as do tour reps, but that's about it.

There are many eating holes, with all the hotels serving typical Austrian dishes. There's also a number of pizza joints so getting a meal around here should pose no real problems, however, you sould remember that this is not a cheap place. Riders on low funds may have to resort to supermarket offerings.

Night-life is very lively, spoilt by the fact that most places go in for aprés-ski for some very sad groups, who don't know how to party on their own. The Ice Bar is a popular hangout and stays open late. The stupidly named *Londoner* bar is also popular; both are aprés haunts, so be warned.

Accommodation ranges from cosy chalets to schilling-hungry hotels. Prices are mainly on the high side, but you can find pensions with rates from 300 schillings a night. *Pension Montan* or *Pension Scharnagl* are both good, while *Bergers Sporthotel* is a good choice. *Thomson* offer a good choice of package rates with hotels in both villages. To book call ++44 0870 606 1470.

For accommodation listings visit - www.worldsnowboardguide.com

Summary: Together these two resorts make any snowboard trip worthwhile, with a good selection of all-round and all-level terrain. Good off-slope services.
Money wise: Very expensive resort, with over priced accommodation.

Overall rating out of 10 **9**

Saalbach-Hinterglem
Fremden Vertkehrs Verband
A-5753 Saalbach 550. Tirol

General info	**++43 (0) 6541 6800 68**
Reservations	**++43 (0) 6541 6800 68**
Avalanche info	**++43 (0) 512 1588**

www.saalbach.com

pics - Saalbach-Hinterglem

Travel Guide

Fly to **Salzburg** International
Transfer time to resort = **1½** hours.
Local airport = **Salzburg**.

Approximate global air travel times to **Salzburg**

from:	
London	**2** hours
Los Angles	**13** hours
New York	**9** hours

Buses from Salzburg, can be taken to Zell am See, then transfer by local bus to Saalbach.

Trains to Zell am See (12 miles)

Route Planner
Salzburg *via motorway A10 & 311*

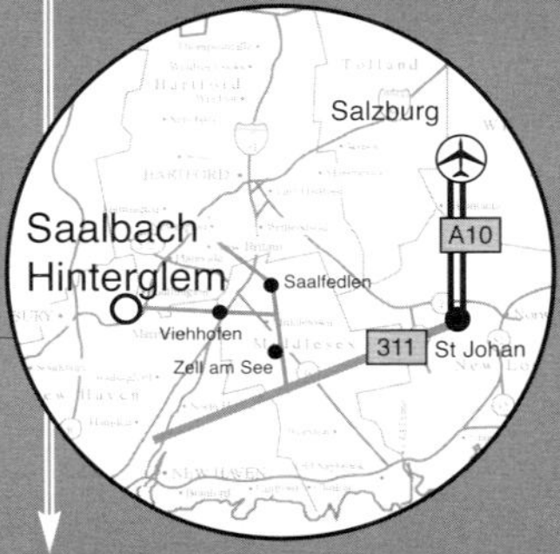

Saalbach = 59 miles (94Km)
Drive time is about 1½ hours

*From **Calais 723** miles (xx Km)
Drive time is around **12½** hours.

Schaldming

MOUNTAIN DATA

Top Lift at - 1850m

Ride Area
152km of piste

Bottom Lift at - 745m
Vertical Drop - 1105m
Number of Runs - 74
Longest - 4.2 miles (7km)

TERRAIN LEVELS

Easy	25%
Intermediate	71%
Advanced	4%
Expert =	

TERRAIN TO SUITE

Freeride	**40%**
Trees	A few
Backcountry	Okay
Freestyle	**20%**
Halfpipe	Yes 3
Terrain Park	Yes 1
Carving	**40%**

SNOW DATA

Average Snowfall
500 cm a season
Snowmaking
30% cover of the slopes
Winter Periods
Dec to April
Summer Riding
None

SLOPE ACCESS

Total Lifts = **88**
Uplift Rate - 88,000 people an hour.
7 Gondolas
14 Chair lifts - **65** Drag lifts
**Leashes Required*

Lift Times
8.30am to 4.00pm

Lift Pass Rates
1 Day pass 420 Sch
6 Day pass 2035 Sch
Season pass

Travel Guide

Fly to **Salzburg** 1 hour away.

The nearest train station is in Schladming.

Route Planner:
Via Salzburg, head south on the A10 and exit at junction 63 on to 146 to Schaldming turn off
* Drive time from Calais is 12½ hours
741 miles (1192 km)

pic - Burton Snowboards

Schladming is an all year-round resort, with summer riding on the **Dachstein Glacier,** and is a popular snowboard haunt. The riding is spread out over a number of areas which offer basic intermediate terrain, and perfect beginner stuff. Schladming is not a hardcore or advanced rider's destination, but that's not to say there aren't any testing runs. There are actually seven different mountains, but not all of them are connected by lifts. The **Hauser Kaibling** mountain has lots of intermediate terrain, with a series of long reds that are ideal for carvers. There are excellent novice trails, with the option to ride a long blue all the way down to the base at the village of **Haus,** just up the road from Schladming. **Hochwurzen**, which rises up to 1,850m, has lots of trees for freeriders to drop through, and a number of reds at the top that base out into simple blues, with easy runs back to Schladming. The Planai mountain holds the main trails and is reached from the edge of Schladming by gondola. Planai's runs offer something for everyone, with some interesting intermediate freeriding terrain. The **Reiteralm** is much the same as **Hochwurzen** and although it has a bigger ride area, it's less convenient for Schladming.

Freeriders will find that any of the areas listed above can suit their needs, with some cool tree runs to be found on the **Planai**, and favourable powder to be found at **Hauser Kaibling.**

Freestylers will find natural hits in most areas, with the Planai and the **Dachstein Glacier** having the best spots. There are also now three halfpipes and a fun-park to catch air on. One of the pipes is also well maintained during the summer months.

Carvers will find all seven areas great, with some of the best pistes on the Hauser Kaibling mountain.

Beginners will find the **Rohrmoss** area at 869m is flat and boring, but should still appeal to novices. Snowboard instruction is very good, and they even have a children's snowboard school.

Accommodation is spread out around a large area, but the old town of Schladming has the biggest selection and offers the best facilities. Prices vary throughout the area, but as there is a youth hostel with cheap bunks, life is made easy for riders on a budget. The area offers a vast amount of sporting facilities as well some good restaurants like *Giovanni's*. Night-life is okay but nothing outstanding.

Accommodation: Visit www.worldsnowboardgiuide.

Schaldming Tourism
A-8970 Erzerog-johann Str 213 Schaldming
++43 (0) 3687 22268-0 www.schladming.com

Overall rating out of 10 **7** **A good all round fun resort**

St Johann in Tirol

AUSTRIA

MOUNTAIN DATA

Top Lift at - 1700m

Ride Area
60km of piste

Bottom Lift at - 670m

Vertical Drop - 1030m

Number of Runs - 19

Longest - 3 miles (5km)

TERRAIN LEVELS

Easy	41%
Intermediate	47%
Advanced	12%
Expert =	

TERRAIN TO SUITE

Freeride	30%
Trees	Yes
Backcountry	No
Freestyle	10%
Halfpipe	Yes 1
Terrain Park	Yes 1
Carving	60%

SNOW DATA

Average Snowfall
560 cm a season

Snowmaking
11% cover of the slopes

Winter Periods
Dec to April

Summer Riding
At Solden

SLOPE ACCESS

Total Lifts = **17**

Uplift Rate - 20,000 people an hour.

2 Cable cars - **6** Chair lifts

9 Drag lifts

**Leashes Required*

Lift Times
8.30am to 4.00pm

Lift Pass Rates

1 Day pass	360 Sch
6 Day pass	1730 Sch
Season pass	

Travel Guide

Fly to **Salzburg** airport 1 3/4 hours transfer time

Bus services run regulary from the airport daily.

Route Planner:
From Salzburg head south on the route 312 direction Worgl to reach the resort.

* Drive time from **Calais** is 11 3/4 hours 672 miles (1082km)

pic - K2 Snowboards / Ostler Electra

St Johann in Tirol is **Austrian** through and through, read any one of the numerous dull ski guides and see how this place is often described as 'quaint, charming, traditional, lovely and picturesque. Well forget all that sort of pointless bull, its what the place has to offer for snowboarding that is important. And frankly St Johann doesn't have a great deal to offer. Yes, there is 60km of well groomed piste (pretty poor for this area) to ride, and yes, the place is fine for first timers and slow learners (a 90 year old granny would manage to ride here) No, the problem with this place is that it is dull and tedious. There is no decent hardcore adventurous terrain, albeit one okay, but fairly ordinary black run, which is not actually that hard to master. St Johann is located close to a lot of low level resorts and none of them can provide you with a good annual snow record. What St Johann can provide you with is a mountain that can often be stupidly busy resulting in some long lift lines. This is largely due to tour operators shipping out bucket loads of wannabe skiers. An advanced rider will have this place licked within a matter of hours, intermediates may take two days. The slopes are a collection of easy reds, a handful of so called blacks and a load of easy blues. Still slope facilities are good and the mountain is serviced by a modern lift system and unusually for a place of this size, some 15 mountain cafes and bars. On the plus side for St Johann, this is a cheap resort.

Freeriders, if you can ride forget it, you will be bored stupid with this place in a stupidly quick time. If you are a basic intermediate freerider then this mountain may suit you and help to kill an afternoon. But the best thing for advanced riders to do is check out the offerings at nearby **Kitzbuhel** (although a bit over-rated) or a little further away at **Saalbach-Hinterglem.**

Freestylers, despite the resort providing a fairly decent halfpipe and park, this is not by any stretch of the imagination a freestylers place, although you will find something to hit off.

Carvers, you will hate this place if you like to ride fast down big steeps. But if you're a bit of a nerd on a slow board then fine.

Beginners who holiday with their parents and don't plan to do a lot of riding in their lives will be suited to a T.

Around the town you will find lots of hotels, Pensions (B&B's) and other local services close to the slopes. Nightlife can be okay.

For accommodation listings visit - www.worldsnowboardguide.com

St Johann in Tirol
Postfach 114, St Johann in Tirol. A-6380
++43 (0) 5352 63335 www.st.johnn.tirol.at

Overall rating out of 10 **4** **Low level boring resort**

Solden

MOUNTAIN DATA

Top Lift at - 3235m

Ride Area
180km of piste

Bottom Lift at - 1377m

Vertical Drop - 1771m

Number of Runs -

Longest -7.5 mile s(12km)

TERRAIN LEVELS

Easy	**42%**
Intermediate	**44%**
Advanced	**14%**
Expert =	

TERRAIN TO SUITE

Freeride	**40%**
Trees	Yes
Backcountry	Yes
Freestyle	**20%**
Halfpipe	Yes 2
Terrain Park	Yes 1
Carving	**40%**

SNOW DATA

Average Snowfall
250cm a season

Snowmaking
20% cover of the slopes

Winter Periods
Dec to April

Summer Riding
May to November

SLOPE ACCESS

Total Lifts = **33**

Uplift Rate - 40,000 people an hour.

3 Gondolas & Cable cars

18 Chair lifts **12** Drag lifts

**Leashes Required*

Lift Times
8.30am to 4.00pm

Lift Pass Rates
1 Day pass 380 Sch
6 Day pass 1890 Sch
Season pass

SLOPE ACTION

Snowboard Hire
Daily rates from 490 Sch
Kids from 390 Sch

Snowboard Tuition
Group lessons, from
from 610 Sch

Night Riding
No

Heli Boarding
No

Snowmobiles
No

Mountain Cafes
25

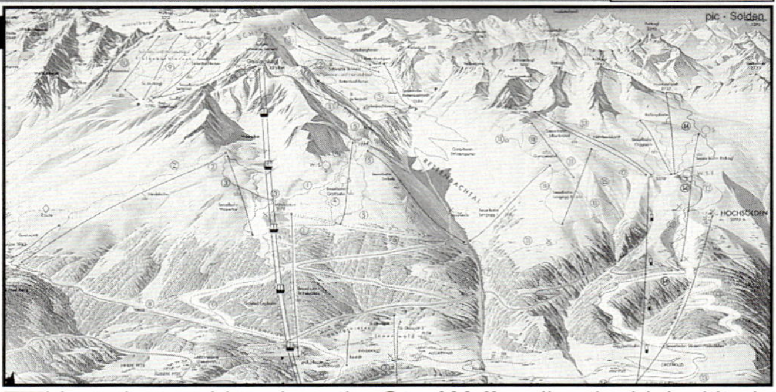

Thirty minutes drive along the **Otzal Valley**, lies the high altitude resort of Solden and the smaller village of Hochsolden, a well established haunt for snowboarders and other adventure sports enthusiasts (summer sees major canoeing events take place on the river that runs through the village). **Solden** has allowed snowboarders on its slopes for years, learning the difference between snowboarders and skiers in order to provide good snowboard services, without it being a hassle. This easy-to-reach resort has all year round snowboarding, with available slopes on two of its neighbouring glacier areas: part of which remains closed during the winter to preserve the runs for the summer months. The combined areas of both Solden and **Hochsolden** are predominantly a carver's-come-freerider's place, with a lot of good on and off-piste to shred. There is a number of long wide open runs to fly down, which thread through the tree-lined pistes of the lower areas.

Freeriders have a resort that caters extremely well for their needs, with some great tree runs that go from thick to even thicker and off-piste areas to please all. Those wanting to go for it, should try out some of the stuff on the **Hochsolden** area, where you can find some cool black pistes that run all the way back to the base gondola - so you can go straight back up the mountain to do it all again. The off-piste stuff under the top section of the **Gaislachkogl** cable car is well worth a look: the run is steep at the top (not for the weak-kneed), and mellows out onto some reds and blacks, which descend back to the village offering lots of cool hits along the way.

Freestylers may initially feel that Solden isn't a major air heads resort, but after a short while you'll think differently. There are loads of big natural hits and gullies with high walls. Solden also has a halfpipe where grommets can play, but it's only well maintained during the summer camps in July and August. If you do come in the summer months, August is the cheapest time, with a day lift pass costing about 250 schillings.

Carvers, Solden should rate very highly on your score-card, as this is one of the best carving resorts in Austria. There are loads of extremely well prepared pistes that descend the mountain slopes in varying degrees of difficulty. Marked trails don't just drop down in a straight line; the runs turn in and out of tree lines, and bank on corners at varying sections.

Beginners can cut it with ease on the lower slopes, which can be reached by foot from **Solden**. Alternatively, head up to the main runs via the gondola to avoid using the drag lifts. Once up on the main slopes, there's plenty of space to fool around on, and at the end of the day, there's a long blue run back down into Solden, perfect for novices. Solden local ski school has been offering snowboard instruction for years and they do it were well her with a group lesson costing from around 610Sch per session.

Solden is a popular tourist resort because it is so snowsure due to its height and glaciers. Unfortunately, Solden is also an expensive place, and gets stupidly busy throughout most of the season. The high street often resembles that of Oxford Street on a Saturday afternoon. However, this is a well laid out town with good local services, all in easy reach of most accommodation. There is also a free daily shuttle bus, provided you have a valid lift ticket. The village also has an excellent centrally located sports complex, that houses a swimming pool, sauna and solarium as well as a weights room for those who need a gym fix each evening before hitting the night spots.

Jobseekers: A few places exist for English-speaking qualified snowboard instructors. However, there's always places for tour reps, ski-techs and general tour operator dogs bodies.

Solden has a big choice of restaurants and cafe-bars to choose from and although the type of offerings doesn't differ too much, most none choosy people will find something to please there pallet. The *Pizzeria* is highly recommended while for 'cheap-ish' food, check out *Cafe Heiner* .

Night-life in **Solden** is okay, and can get very messy due to the number of bars and hangouts, but there are a lot skiers in green lipstick around. The *Das Stampel Bar* is a favourite hangout with locals and visitors alike. The main disco nearby is a cool place to pull a holiday chick, but it plays crap music.

With 9,500 bed spaces, all within easy distance of the slopes, there's a pillow for everyone unless you're skint. For a cheaper, out of town bed, the small neighbouring village of **Zwieselstein** has a place known as the *German Alpine Club.* This is a basic house with self catering facilities, that sleeps up to 30 people, 200sch a night. *Pension Mina* is a good option, as is *Pension Arnold* which is centrally located.

For accommodation listings visit - www.worldsnowboardguide.com

Summary: Solden is one of Austria's best all round resorts, with great terrain. The two let downs being far too many skiers, and the price of accommodation.

Money wise: Very expensive resort, but excellent services.

Overall rating out of 10 — **10**

Solden Tourism
Otztal Arean, Postfach 80
Solden A-6450. Tirol

General info	**++43 (0) 5254 22120**
Reservations	**++43 (0) 5254 22120**
Avalanche info	**++43 (0) 512 1588**

www.solden.com

pic - Phillipe

pic - Solden

Travel Guide

Fly to **Innsbruck** International
Transfer time to resort = **1 1/4** hours.
Local airport = **Innsbruck**.

Approximate global air travel times to **Innsbruck**

from:		
	London	2 hours
	Los Angles	13 hours
	New York	9 hours

Buses from **Innsbruck** go direct to **Solden** with daily return services from Innsbruck train station.

Trains to **Otztal** (20 minutes).

Route Planner
Innsbruck *via motorway A12*

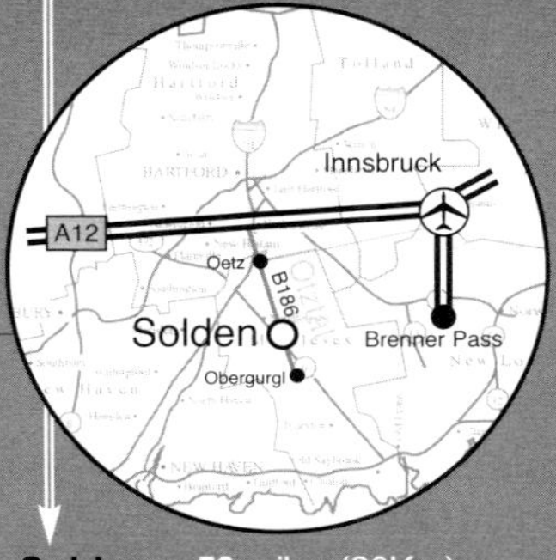

Solden = **50** miles (80Km)
Drive time is about 1 1/4 hours

*From **Calais** 654 miles (1052 Km)
Drive time is around **12** hours.

St Anton

MOUNTAIN DATA

Top Lift at - 2811m

Ride Area
260km of piste

Bottom Lift at - 1304m
Vertical Drop - 1507m
Number of Runs - 134
Longest -6.2 miles (10km)

TERRAIN LEVELS

Easy	**30%**
Intermediate	**40%**
Advanced	**30%**
Expert =	

TERRAIN TO SUITE

Freeride	**50%**
Trees	Yes
Backcountry	Yes
Freestyle	**20%**
Halfpipe	Yes 2
Terrain Park	Yes 1
Carving	**30%**

SNOW DATA

Average Snowfall
250cm a season
Snowmaking
10% cover of the slopes
Winter Periods
Dec to April
Summer Riding

SLOPE ACCESS

Total Lifts = **84**
Uplift Rate - 54,000 people an hour.
1 Train **10** Gondolas & Cables
35 Chair lifts **36** Drag lifts
**Leashes Required*

Lift Times
8.30am to 4.00pm

Lift Pass Rates

1 Day pass	485 Sch
3 Day pass	1350 Sch
6 Day pass	2410 Sch

SLOPE ACTION

Snowboard Hire
Daily rates from 485 Sch
Kids from 370 Sch

Snowboard Tuition
Group lessons, from from 620 Sch

Night Riding
No

Heli Boarding
No

Snowmobiles
No

Mountain Cafes
10

pic - St Anton Tourism

Those who about where to ride would have to agree that **St Anton** has the best terrain in **Austria,** making this place an absolute must. This is a resort that has it all and will suite all styles of riding, though favouring freeriders the most. Honestly, the place will suite whether you're a freestyle freak, a piste carving poser, a freeride speed king or simply a nappy-wearing new kid. The area does have the reputation for being expensive and attracting the fur-clad, Ferrari-owning skiers, but whilst they sip pink gins in mountain bars, snowboarders can roam freely over miles of excellent terrain. With steeps, deep powder, air, and trees on all sides of the mountain slopes, it's hard to beat. The **Arlberg** ski pass allows you to ride the linked areas of **St Christoph** and **Stuben**, which also both offer great snowboarding terrain, with amazing amounts of powder.

Freeriders are best suited to St Anton as it's the perfect playground, with a little of everything: steeps, powder, trees and big drop offs. Riders who know what they're doing should worm their way up to **Kapall** where they'll find loads of great freeriding terrain, with good natural hits. Alternatively, head to the summit of **Valluga Grat** via the **Galzig** cable car to reach some major off-piste, with long runs back down to St Anton and **St Christoph.** Intermediates just getting it together will find loads to ride, especially on **Gampen** and **Kapall**. The runs on **Galzig** are easier, but tend to get busy with skiers. Advanced riders will love Rendl, a separate mountain on the opposite side of St Anton across to the Gampen runs. Whenever there's a fresh dump, expect to find the locals and ski-bums cramming into **Rendlbahn** for first tracks. This area is absolutely amazing for full-on freeriding terrain with tight and open trees and crowd-free slopes.

Freestylers spending a month or two here will never find every natural hit - the resort is simply littered with great take off points and drop ins. It's a great freestyler's place, and if you're not content with the natural stuff, then there's a park and pipe at Rendl Beach to play on. Although the pipe is not really that good, it is improving with each new season.

Carvers are much in evidence on St Anton's slopes. Some are obviously rich Germans who have the kit because they think it's cool, whilst others have heard how good the terrain is for laying big arcs. You can perform here with no trouble on countless well groomed runs like Osthang, but in truth, any rider spending more than an hour in hard boots here should have his balls hacked off, since this is a true soft boot resort.

Beginners with a little adventure will be able to handle St Anton, but wimps may have trouble if they stray too far from the easy runs. A learner's slope at **Nasserein** provides a good starting point for a number of easy blue trails.

The one big depressing thing about **St Anton** is that it's very stuck up and attracts some of the worst of the so called rich elete. The place positively stinks with money drenched posers who haven't got the slightest interested in the slopes, they simply come to rub shoulders with their ilk. Another sorry point is the cost of things, in fact, this is one of the most expensive resorts in Austria. That said, you at least pay for quality and good local services. For those with the cash, there is a host of local attractions. At present the whole town is under renovation, so expect to see major changes over the next two years (lets hope the attitude changes as well). For all your snowboard hire needs, check *Jennewein Snowboarding* near the tourist office, or *Sno Control* in the main street, both offer great advice and good services.

Got a gold credit card? If yes, proceed to one of the many restaurants, if the answer is no, then OPPs' because eating out daily will be beyond most. However, there are some relatively cheap options in the centre of town like the *Funky Chicken*, frying the very thing or *Pizzeria Pomodora*.

Night-life is lively. *Taps* which is located on **Gampen** home run is where riders chill after a day's ride. *Amadeus* is popular with a pool table and cheapish beer. The *Funky Chicken* is also good for a beer. At the end of the night most end up in either the *Platz'l* bar or the *Postkeller* for a snog.

Accommodation: There's plenty of lodging but nothing cheap, and anyone on a low budget will find it hard going. B&B's are available in and around the small hamlets of **Bach**, **St Jakob** and **Nasserein**, and are less expensive than central St Anton. A free, regular ski-bus will save you a walk. Apartments allow you to cram in extra people, but look out as Austrian iin-keepers are strict.

For accommodation listings visit - www.worldsnowboardguide.com

Summary: The best resort in Austria, with great freeriding for advanced and intermediate riders. The biggest problem is the stuck up snobbery of the place.
Money wise: Super expensive, but worth the money just for the slopes.

Overall rating out of 10 — **10**

St Anton Tourism
A-6580
St Anton am Arlberg

General info	**++43 (0) 5254 22690**
Reservations	**++43 (0) 5254 22690**
Avalanche info	**++43 (0) 5522 1588**

www.stanton.com

pic - Peter mathis - Palmer Snowboards

pic - St Anton

Travel Guide

Fly to **Innsbruck** International
Transfer time to resort = **1 1/4** hours.
Local airport = **Innsbruck**.

Approximate global air travel times to **Innsbruck**

from:		
	London	**2** hours
	Los Angles	**13** hours
	New York	**9** hours

Buses from **Innsbruck** go direct to **St Anton** with daily return services from Innsbruck.

Trains direct to **St Anton** center

Route Planner
Innsbruck *via Landeck*

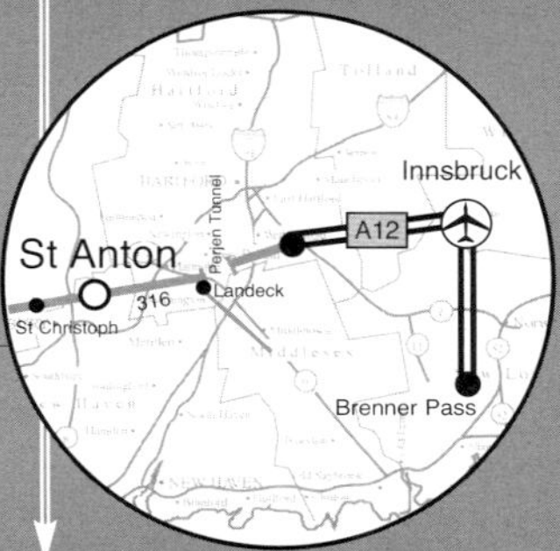

St Anton = 61 miles (98Km)
Drive time is about 1 1/4 hours

*From **Calais** 618 miles (994 km)
Drive time is around **11** hours.

Soll

MOUNTAIN DATA

Top Lift at - 1829m

Ride Area

34km of piste

Bottom Lift at - 620m

Vertical Drop - 1129m

Number of Runs - 15

Longest -4.7 miles (7.5km)

TERRAIN LEVELS

Easy	43%
Intermediate	48%
Advanced	9%
Expert =	

TERRAIN TO SUITE

Freeride	**40%**
Trees	A few
Backcountry	A bit
Freestyle	**20%**
Halfpipe	Yes 1
Terrain Park	Yes 1
Carving	**40%**

SNOW DATA

Average Snowfall
250 cm a season

Snowmaking
12% cover of the slopes

Winter Periods
Dec to April

Summer Riding
None

SLOPE ACCESS

Total Lifts = **12**

Uplift Rate - 37,000 people an hour.

3 Gondolas

5 Chair lifts - **4** Drag lifts

**Leashes Required*

Lift Times
8.30am to 4.00pm

Lift Pass Rates

1 Day pass	380 Sch
3 Day pass	1050 Sch
6 Day pass	1890 Sch

Travel Guide

Fly to Salzburg airport 90 minutes transfer time.

Bus services direct from Salzburg airport.

Route Planner:
From Salzburg head south on the routes 21 and 312 to Ellmau on the left, a 45 mile (70km) journey.
* Drive time from **Calais** is **11**½ hours. 692 miles (115km)

pic - Soll Tourism

Soll can be summed up in a few simple words: 'traditional appealing village with excellent slopes for beginners'. This is one of **Austria's** most popular resorts for package tour operators who send ski groups here en-masse. Soll is located a short distance from the resorts of **Ellmau**, **Scheffau**, **Going** and nearby **Brixen**, **Hopfgarten** and **Westendorf**, all of which form part of **Austria's** largest linked ski and snowboard area, known as the **Ski Welt**. All the resorts are similar in style and character yet still have something different to offer whether it be on the slopes or around one of the traditional styled villages. **Soll** has two distinctions, one, it's a pretty lame mountain for advanced riders and two, the so called picturesque village offers a high level of good services. The slopes here are ideal for no hopers and cross-over skiers (those with an identity crisis who don't really want to snowboard but feel they should try it just once so they can boast about there endeavours when they get home). Getting to this resort is very easy from either **Salzburg** (only 90 minutes away) or Innsbruck, however, trying to appreciate the opportunities on the slopes when you arrive is a different matter. Expert riders will soon tire of the resort while slow carvers and beginners will love it. This is also a cool place if you're on a tight budget and planning to take a cheap package holiday.

Freeriders will find this place a bit limiting. However, the black graded slope that runs down from the **Hohe Salve** is not a bad trail and not to be treated too lightly, same goes for the slope under the **Brixen Gondola.**

Freestylers have a halfpipe and terrain park to practice tricks in, but that's about all as the natural freestyle terrain is poor.

Carvers not wanting to be tested will be happy apart from the fact that the well groomed slopes can often be so busy with skiers that it's impossible to link up more than a few turns.

Beginners are the ones who will appreciate **Soll** the most.

Soll is a small village that offers high quality services, but the layout is not the most convenient for the slopes, you may find yourself staying a fair distance from the base lifts. Still, there are lots of restaurants and surprisingly nightlife around here can be very good. There is a good choice of bars and a few night spots which are not over-priced just over full with sad skiers doing aprés crap.

For accommodation listings visit - www.worldsnowboardguide.com

Soll Tourism
Soll A6306
++43 (0) 5333 5216 **www.soll.com**

Overall rating out of 10 — 6 **A very good beginners resort**

Lech

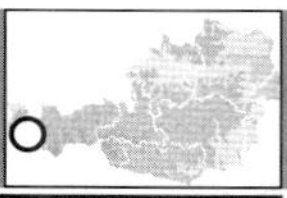

MOUNTAIN DATA

Top Lift at - 2444m

Ride Area 97km of piste

Bottom Lift at - 1450m

Vertical Drop - 994m

Number of Runs - 32

Longest - 3 miles (5km)

TERRAIN LEVELS

Easy	**40%**
Intermediate	**40%**
Advanced	**20%**
Expert =	

TERRAIN TO SUITE

Freeride	**50%**
Trees	A few
Backcountry	Good
Freestyle	**20%**
Halfpipe	Yes 1
Terrain Park	Yes 1
Carving	**30%**

SNOW DATA

Average Snowfall
260 cm a season

Snowmaking
10% cover of the slopes

Winter Periods
Dec to April

Summer Riding
None

SLOPE ACCESS

Total Lifts = **33**

Uplift Rate - 44,000 people an hour.

5 Gondolas **18** Chair lifts

10 Drag lifts

**Leashes Required*

Lift Times
8.30am to 4.00pm

Lift Pass Rates
1 Day pass 485 Sch
6 Day pass 2230 Sch
Season pass

Travel Guide

Fly to **Innsbruck,** 2 hours transfer

The nearest train stop is at St Anton 10 minutes away

Route Planner:
Via Innsbruck head west on the A12 to Landeck then take the 316 via St Anton to reach Lech.
* Drive time from Calais is 10¼ hours
615 miles (989 km)

pic - Lech Tourism

The **Arlberg**, in the far eastern section of Austria, is home to all the top classy resorts that the country has to offer. **Lech** is just one of them, along with its close neighbours **Zurs**, **Stuben**, **St Christoph** and **St Anton**. More closely linked with Zurs, Lech sits at the back of **St Anton**, and is without doubt Austria's number one poncy retreat. Year in, year out, this high altitude resort attracts numerous royals along with the finest from the film and pop world - and all the arse-lickers they can muster to join them. Skiers come here to be seen, not to ski. But Lech is a great place to ride, for all levels and styles, with some major freeride terrain and excellent off-piste powder. So although you may have to push past a fur coat or two, you can ride happily on a mountain where the management have been keen to make Lech a snow-board-friendly resort.

Freeriders will love this place, with large amounts of steeps and deep powder. The runs off **Kriegerhorn** are the total dog's 'B's', as are the powder trails down from **Zuger Hochlicht**, which can take you from top to bottom free of any piste-loving pop star.

Freestylers have a fantastic 300 metre long fun-park area, located on **Schlegelkopf**. The park is loaded with gaps, quarter-pipes and a decent halfpipe, which like all the best areas here, are free of posing image junkies.

Carvers who turn up here with hard boots should have their balls boiled while still attached. This is soft boot heaven; only the poser patrol have hards here, and their boots are just for show.

Beginners have a perfectly acceptable series of novice runs and good trails to progress on, making Lech a good first timer's resort. The only drawback is sharing the easy slopes with moaning no-hopers from the pop world, or a public school kid who thinks he's street wise (stick a finger in his eye and see what he thinks then).

The town at the base of the slopes is expensive and dripping with sad people in fur coats and gold, so expect to pay highly for everything. Even the pensions cost an arm and a leg; you may find that a stay here is beyond the reach of most. Try lodging in one of the nearby hamlets. If you do give **Lech** the one night treatment, remember that night-life is dull and super poncy. However, to spruce things up, try seeing how many animal killers in fur coats you can cover with yellow spray paint.

For accommodation listings visit - www.worldsnowboardguide.com

Lech Tourism
A-6764 Lech. Arlberg
++43 (0) 55832161-0 www.lech.at/.com

Overall rating out of 10 **8** **Great slopes stuck up village**

Zell am See

MOUNTAIN DATA

Top Lift at - 1949m

Ride Area
43km of piste

Bottom Lift at - 758m
Vertical Drop - 1191m
Number of Runs - 59
Longest - 2.5 miles (4km)

TERRAIN LEVELS

Easy	**43%**
Intermediate	**38%**
Advanced	**19%**
Expert =	

TERRAIN TO SUITE

Freeride	**40%**
Trees	Not allowed
Backcountry	A bit
Freestyle	**20%**
Halfpipe	Yes 2
Terrain Park	Yes 2
Carving	**40%**

SNOW DATA

Average Snowfall

Snowmaking
25% cover of the slopes
Winter Periods
Dec to April
Summer Riding
None

SLOPE ACCESS

Total Lifts = **31**
Uplift Rate - 20,000 people an hour.
4 Gondolas
19 Chair lifts - **8** Drag lifts
**Leashes Required*

Lift Times
8.30am to 4.00pm

Lift Pass Rates

1 Day pass	435 Sch
6 Day pass	2050 Sch
Season pass	

Travel Guide

Fly to **Salzburg**, 1½ hours transfer.

The nearest train stop is at Zell am See 10 mins away.

Route Planner: From Salzburg head south on the A10. Then south west on the 168 via Taxenbach to Kaprun (56 miles)
* Drive time from **Calais** is 12¼ hours
714 miles (1159 km)

pic - Ride Snowboards

Zell am See is located close to a large lake and not far from the glacier resort of **Kaprun. Zell** offers over 130km of marked out piste, much of which is treelined. A third of the runs are covered by snowmaking facilities, which is a good thing, as this resort doesn't have the greatest annual snow record. This resort has long been popular with snowboarders in **Austria** and has always been welcoming. The management do frown when it comes to riding in the trees, as you are not allowed to snowboard through the wooded sections. In general this is a pretty good snowboarders resort with the added advantage of a glacier at **Kaprun** just down the road should the snow here turn out to be crap or you simply fancy a change. Zell's main disadvantage is its own popularity as it's high on tour operators lists and therefore very crowded. Each Saturday the resort sees a fresh intake of thousands of two plankers in their new holiday clothes ready to make a mess of the overnight grooming of the pistes. Whatever level of a rider you are or whatever style of riding you do, this place will give you the opportunity to practice your skills, and most people will be able to make a 5 day trip well worthwhile.

Freeriders have a varying selection of runs to choose from. Advanced riders may want to take the cable car up to the **Berghotel** where you will be able to gain access to a couple of good steep sections. There are also a number of cool runs down the **Sonnkogel**. If you are looking for deep powder and open bowl riding, then head on up to the glacier at **Kaprun**

Freestylers can choose to ride the pipe and park at **Zell** or try out the same at **Kaprun**, which has a pipe all year round. Around Zell locals often build their own hits but if you can't be bothered, you will be able to find lots of stuff to fly from.

Carvers have an ordinary mountain to cut up with plenty of well groomed trails to try out, more so at **Zell** than at **Kaprun**.

Beginners have lots of nursery areas as well as spots that allow for easy progression making this a good novice resorts.

Zell am See is a busy village with a lot going on and plenty of accommodation at all price ranges. The village is a lively one and as well as having loads of restaurants, mainly hotel ones, nightlife here is also quite good with some okay bars to check out.
For accommodation listings visit - www.worldsnowboardguide.com

Zell am See Tourism
Zell am See, A5700
++43 (0) 6542 770 www.zellamsee.com

Overall rating out of 10 — **6** — **Not a bad resort but too busy**

Zurs

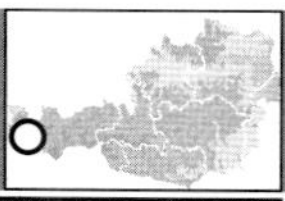

AUSTRIA

MOUNTAIN DATA

Top Lift at - 2450m

Ride Area 88km of piste

Bottom Lift at - 1725m
Vertical Drop - 728m
Number of Runs - 55
Longest - 3 miles (5km)

TERRAIN LEVELS

Easy	**40%**
Intermediate	**40%**
Advanced	**20%**
Expert =	

TERRAIN TO SUITE

Freeride	**60%**
Trees	A few
Backcountry	Good
Freestyle	**20%**
Halfpipe	Yes 1
Terrain Park	Yes 1
Carving	**20%**

SNOW DATA

Average Snowfall
280 cm a season
Snowmaking
10% cover of the slopes
Winter Periods
Dec to April
Summer Riding
None

SLOPE ACCESS

Total Lifts = **32**
Uplift Rate - 43,000 people an hour.
1 Cable car **17** Chair lifts
14 Drag lifts
**Leashes Required*

Lift Times
8.30am to 4.00pm

Lift Pass Rates
1 Day pass 445 Sch
6 Day pass 2130 Sch
Season pass

Travel Guide

Fly to **Innsbruck** 1 1/2 hours transfer.

The nearest train stop is at St Anton 10 minutes away

Route Planner:
Via Innsbruck take the A12 to Landeck then take the 316 via St Anton to reach Lech. (70 miles).
* Drive time from Calais is 11 3/4 hours
611 miles (983 km)

pic - Zurs Tourism

Who knows or cares what **Zurs** means in Austrian; what we can tell you is that in plain English, Zurs stands for super-sad, super-rich, super ponces, and the worst level of stuck-up skiers known to man. This relatively small resort is in the same locality as that other fur-dripping hangout, **Lech**. However, on a more positive side, the slopes are surprisingly free of champagne-drinking 'wa wa's', which means that riders can roam freely over some excellent slopes. Zurs is without doubt, one of Austria's most spectacular resorts and could rival any in Europe when it comes to the type of terrain it has to offer. Its diverse and interesting slopes make it a great place to snowboard, offering powder fields and miles of pistes.

Freeriders will literally be able to pick a line as they travel on a chair lift over vast areas of untracked mountain. You're never far away from marked areas and the lifts, so no hiking is involved with this side of the mountain. There are so many ways down that there aren't really any no-go areas; just be careful and pay attention to the avalanche warnings. Alternatively, the other side of the valley which makes up the resort, has plenty of long, steep pistes, gullies and chutes - take a piste map with you.

Freestylers would do well to check out the 300 metre pipe and park area on Lech's slopes. However, Zurs has a lot of good natural terrain for grabbing big air. There are loads of cliff drops of various sizes, and plenty of banked walls to pull off tricks.

Carvers will find lots of challenging terrain. The marked-out slopes are groomed to perfection, and perfect corduroy tracks are left just waiting to be sliced up at Mach 6.

Beginners-although Zurs is primarily an intermediate/advanced freeriding area, some of the lower slopes offer perfect conditions for learning. The lifts are slow, but redeemed by the generally patient and friendly lift attendants (yes, they do exist!).

Lodging, eating and drinking in **Zurs** is classicly Austrian, and will burn a big hole in your wallet. You can stay out of Zurs in neighbouring villages that are far cheaper and have a better local feel to them, offering a more relaxed atmosphere. In Zurs, the streets are littered with poodle-carrying idiots in search of posh hang-outs, but you'll be surprised at how many snowboarders you'll come across, so don't be too put off by the hideous reputation.

For accommodation listings visit - www.worldsnowboardguide.com

Zurs Tourism
Zurs Am Arlberg. A-6763
++43 (0) 5583 2245

Overall rating out of 10 **8** **Great powder freeriding**

Austrian Round up

Abtenau
Tiny resort with 7 lifts & 10 runs
Located 45 minutes from Salzburg.

Altenmarkt-Zauchense
Linked area with 135 lifts & 55 runs
Located 50 minutes from Salzburg

Auffach
▲ 1900m 12 miles 11 Lifts
Auffach is a tiny, relatively boring resort, that will please family ski groups. Auffach has a joint lift pass with neighbouring areas, which is a good thing because there's nothing here for riders with any know-how. However, Auffach is good for beginners. Okay slope-side loding available.
Fly to: **Innsbruck -** 1 1/4 hours away
ⓘ **tel-** ++43 (0) 5339 8255.

Bad Hofgastein
▲ 2295m 175miles 31 Lifts
Bad Hofgastein is located centrally in the Salzburg region, and forms part of one of Austria's largest rideable areas. Intermediate carvers are well suited to these slopes, with a nice long seven mile run to practice some wide carves. Total beginners will love it, and its not bad for freestylers with a good pipe. There is plenty of slopeside lodging and good local services.
Fly to: **Salzburg -** 1 1/2 hours away
ⓘ **tel-** ++43 (0) 6432 7110

Bad Kleinkirchheim
Novices resort 32 lifts & 30 runs
1 hour from Klagenfurt airport.

Bad Mitterndorf

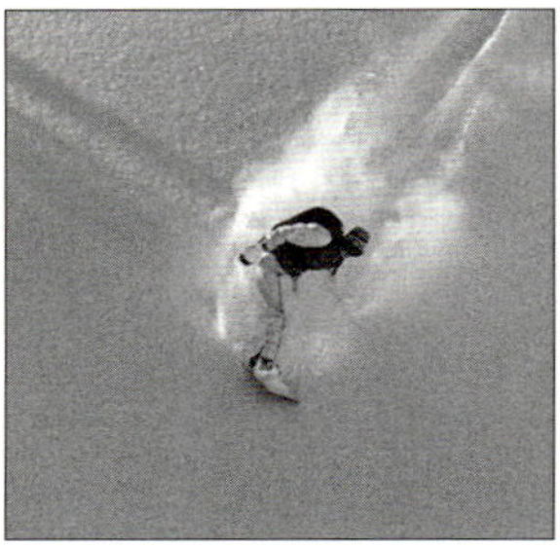

▲ 1965m 16 miles 20 Lifts
Bad Mittendorf is a spa town that likes to shroud itself in strange old tales. What isn't fiction is that this is not the greatest of snowboard destinations. The 15 miles of piste rarely allows an adrenalin rush, although there are a couple of okay black trails and the odd red that's worth a look. Crap for freestylers but perfect for beginners. Off the slopes you will find simple and affordable slopeside accommodation and services.
Fly to: **Salzburg -** 1 1/2 hours away
ⓘ **tel-** ++43 (0) 3623 2444

Bad Brixen im Thale
Large circuit area 260 lifts & 170 runs
60 minutes from Innsbruck airport.

Ehrwald
Big ride and okay 46 lifts & 22 runs
60 minutes from Innsbruck airport.

Filzmoos
Small and basic 14 lifts & 20 runs
1 1/4 hours from Salzburg airport.

Finkenberg
Very boring 30 lifts & 40 runs
1 1/4 hours from Innsbruck airport.

Flachau
Big pipe & park 51 lifts & 55 runs
50 minutes from Salzburg airport.

Fugenberg
Novices only 18 lifts & 20 runs
30 minutes from Innsbruck airport.

Fulpmes
Very basic & dull 9 lifts & 15 runs
20 minutes from Innsbruck airport.

Gargellen
Small & dull 10 lifts & 14 runs
2 hours from Innsbruck airport.

Grossarl
Fun & easy area 20 lifts & 26 runs
60 minutes from Salzburg airport.

Haus in Ennstal
Very basic runs 14 lifts & 30 runs
1 1/2 hours from Salzburg airport.

Hopfagarten in Brixental
Large ride area 260 lifts & 328 runs
1 1/2 hours from Salzburg airport.

Igls

▲ 2247m 8 miles 6 Lifts
Igls is perched high above Innsbruck, 3 miles from the city centre. There's nothing here, especially for competent riders. This is a beginner's area with half a dozen trails easily accessed by a cable car. Great local facilities in Innsbruck, 10 minutes away.
Fly to: **Innsbruck -** 10 minutes away
ⓘ **tel-** ++43 (0) 512 37 71 01

Kaunertal

▲ 3160m 12 miles 7 Lifts
Kaunertal is a glacial resort open all year round. Overall, the terrain is great for novices but a bit dull for advanced riders. What you get is a mixture of easy freeriding with powder areas and excellent carving terrain. Freestylers have one of the most perfectly shaped half-pipes on the planet. Lodging and local services can be found at **Feichten,** 16 miles down the valley, so a car is a must.
Fly to: **Innsbruck -** 90 minutes away
ⓘ **tel-** ++43 (0) 5475 292

Kirchberg in Tyrol
Okay area 61 lifts & 56 runs
1 1/2 hours from Salzburg airport.

Kirchdorf
Ok expert trails 8 lifts & 8 runs
60 minutes from Salzburg airport.

Landeck
Very basic area 8 lifts & 8 runs
55 minutes from Innsbruck airport.

Lermoos
Not hot at all 9 lifts & 15 runs
60 minutes from Innsbruck airport.

Mutters
▲ 1800m 6 miles 8 Lifts
Mutters is a small rideable area nestled between **Innsbruck** and **Axamer Lizum**. But this is no match for Axams, which can be reached with a backcountry hike. There are only a few runs, mainly suited to beginners and intermediates. Mutters attracts a lot of cross-country skiers. Great local facilities in Innsbruck, 20 mins.
Fly to: **Innsbruck -** 15 minutes away
ⓘ **tel-** ++43 (0) 512 54 67 15

Neustif
Good for carvers 30 lifts & 38 runs
25 minutes from Innsbruck airport.

Niedrau
▲ 1600m 25 miles 28 Lifts
Niederau/Oberau are two tiny hamlets with little interest for snowboarders. Freeriders have nothing of real note, although the blacks under the gondola are not for the squeamish. Carvers who can ride will have this place done by lunch. Perfect for beginners. Good slope side local services.
Fly to: **Innsbruck -** 60 minutes away
ⓘ **tel-** ++43 (0) 533 8225

Obertauren

▲ 2350m 40 miles 27 Lifts
Just when you thought that Austria was all the same, along comes **Obertauren**, noted for its excellent snow records. The terrain here is very much freeride-orientated with lots of areas to check out suited to all levels. Advanced riders have plenty of good, testing blacks where carvers can leave some nice lines. Freestylers have a pipe, and novices have good areas.

Excellent lodging and local facilities are at the base of the slopes.
Fly to: **Salzburg -** 1¼ hours away
ⓘ **tel-** ++43 (0)

Partenen
Very dull indeed 28 lifts & 26 runs
2 hours from Innsbruck airport.

Pettneu an Arlberg
Very small resort 8 lifts & 4 runs
1 hour from Innsbruck airport.

Pitztal

▲3440m 60miles 12 Lifts
Pitzal is a high altitude resort, allowing for summer riding on the **Pitztal Glacier**. The glacier is reached by an unusual funicular train that travels through the mountain, and gives access to good, intermediate carving runs and off-piste freeride areas. Set aside is a 4 mile snowboard-only area with a good pipe and fun-park. There's even a kid's park!
Local services in **St Leonard** are in a basic Austrian format.
Fly to: **Salzburg -** 20 minutes away
ⓘ **tel-** ++43 (0)

Radstadt
Lots of lift links 292 lifts & 240 runs
50 minutes from Innsbruck airport.

Ramsau am Dachstein
Okay halfpipes 20 lifts & 18 runs
11/4 hours from Salzburg airport.

Rauris
Very basic and uneventful 9 lifts
50 minutes from Salzburg airport.

Scheffau
Mixed riding 15 lifts & 25 runs
50 minutes from Salzburg airport.

Seefield

▲2100m 15 miles 14 Lifts
Seefield is a blip on the outskirts of **Innsbruck**. Freeriders will find that there's not much to do here. Freestylers have a long pipe and park, which attracts locals from Innsbruck. Carvers will manage okay. Beginners will also be okay. Good, slopeside services.
Fly to: **Innsbruck -** 20 minutes away
ⓘ **tel-** ++43 (0) 5212 2313

Schruns
▲2400m 13 miles 13 Lifts
Schruns is a tiny resort close to the Swiss boarder. The slopes make for an okay one day visit if you can ride or a week if you can't. The place only has one noted black trail but it also has a long 8 mile run which will keep an intermediate freerider happy. Great place for begiunners but crap for freestylers.
Very basic but good local facilities at the base of the slopes.
Fly to: **Innsbruck -** 2 hours away
ⓘ **tel-** ++43 (0) 556 721 660

Schwaz-Pill
Very boring terrain 7 lifts & 8 runs
25 minutes from Innsbruck airport.

Serfaus
▲1427m 50 miles 21 Lifts
Serfus is a cool place with a decent mountain. Overall, the area provides good all-round snowboarding, no matter your style or standard.
Well appointed and affordable local services
Fly to: **Zurich -** 120 minutes away
ⓘ **tel-** ++43 (0) 556 721 660

Sibratsgfall
Low level with boring slopes 4 lifts
3 hours from Zurich airport.

St Christoph

▲2811m 106 miles 86 Lifts
St Christoph is a small, glitzy outpost in the **Arlberg** close to its far more famous cousin, **St Anton**. And like its neighbour, this is a money mountain that provides great slopes with miles of backcountry freeriding, and natural freestyle terrain. Advanced riders have enough runs to keep them occupied for a week, while carvers have more than enough to last them a month. Great for beginners. Off the slopes you'll pay dearly for everything.
Fly to: **Innsbruck -** 1½ hours away
ⓘ **tel-** ++43 (0)

St Wolfgang
▲1350m 15 miles 9 Lifts
St Wolfgang put simply, is not a good snowboarding resort. There is nothing much here, not even for beginners. Granny may manage a few turns, but others will soon tire of it. In truth, this is a family-orientated, beginner's ski resort. Freestylers do have a small park and pipe, but don't blink or you'll miss it. Lots of close by accommodation.
Fly to: **Salzburg -** 45 minutes away
ⓘ **tel-** ++43 (0) 5352 6335

Wagrain
▲2190m 217 miles 120 Lifts
As a base to reach any one of a dozen other ride areas, offering over 200 miles of linked cool, freeriding terrain, with a number of good parks and pipes, then this is a great place to be. Beginners are spoilt for choice, as are piste-hugging carvers, who have dozens of well groomed trails.
Off the slopes, it's Austrian picture postcard stuff, but dull.
Fly to: **Salzburg -** 60 minutes away
ⓘ **tel-** ++43 (0)

Waidring
▲1900m 16 miles 12 Lifts
Waldring is a dull, geriatric heaven, and of interest only to those who are brain-dead. Its only saving grace is that the place is close to other resorts so you can at least escape the tedium of the place. Anyone planning more than an hour's stay here needs to see a shrink.
Local services consist of a few old people's homes and a morgue.
Fly to: **Salzburg -** 60 minutes away
ⓘ **tel-** ++43 (0) 5353 5242

Westendorf
▲1865m 25 miles 14 Lifts
Westendorf is all but the same as its nearby neighbours, **Soll** and **Ellmau**. Unlike Ellmau, however, there is at least a decent halfpipe and park for air heads to try out. Carvers also have a good choice of trails on which to practice the art of signing snow with an edge. There are a couple of black trails for advanced riders and good beginner's areas.
Local services at the base of the slopes are cheap and cheerful.
Fly to: **Salzburg -** 120 minutes away
ⓘ **tel-** ++43 (0) 5334 6230

Windischgarsten
Total crap with only 4 runs.
120 minutes from Salzburg airport.

Worgl
Forget it totally. This place is crap
50 minutes from Innsbruck airport.

Zams
▲2212m 16 miles 7 Lifts
Zams is a relatively unknown and small resort. There's a grand total of eight runs, all suited to beginners going backwards. The best thing to do is pass by and check out the Kaunertal Glacier which is far better. Off the slopes forget it, the place may be traditionally Austrian, but it is dull.
Fly to: **Innsbruck -** 90 minutes away
ⓘ **tel-** ++43 (0) 5442 6339

Zell am Ziller
Boring terrain 22 lifts & 60 runs
50 minutes from Innsbruck airport.

Zeutschach
Low level boaring resort with 4 lifts
Fly to Klagenfurt airport.

Zoblen
Low level boaring resort with 3 lifts
Fly to Innsbruck airport.

Zug
Low level boaring resort with 5 lifts
Fly to Zurich airport.

FINLAND

GENERAL INFO AND FACTS

Capital - Helsinki
Language - Finnish
Currency - Markka (Fmk)
Alcohol drinking age - 18
Drugs - Cannabis is illegal
Death Penalty - Doesn't exist
Age of consent for Sex - 16
Military Service - Not compulsory
Electricity Supply - 240 Volts AC
International phone Code ++358
Highest Peak - Haltia 1328m

DUTY FREE
10 Litres of Alcohol
90 Litres of Wine - 110 of beer
800 Cigarettes
200 Cigars

FINLAND DRIVE GUIDE
All vehicles drive on the right hand side of the road
Speed Limits -
Motorways 120kph (74mph)
Highways 100kph (80mph)
Towns 50kph (32mph)

Finnish Snowboard Federation
Radiokatu 20,00240 Helsinki.
Finland
tel- ++358 400 414 587
e-mail:ari.mentu@amen.pp.fi

TIME ZONES
Central European
GMT +1 Hour
Between March and October
GMT+2 Hours

International gateway Airports
Helsiniki
Domestic gateway airports
Kithila
Kuusamo
Pori

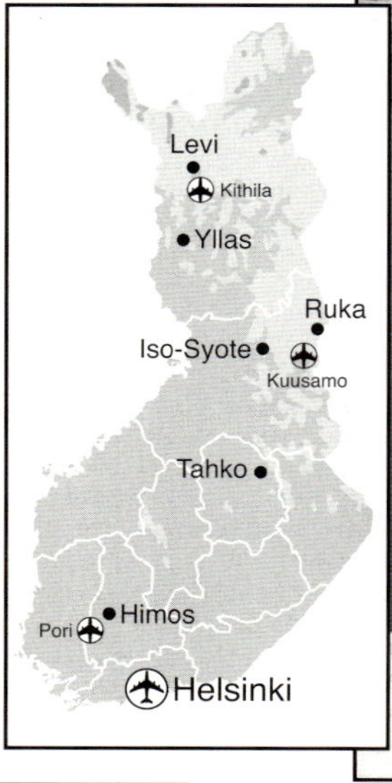

Finland produces some of the best young freestylers in the world. You may ask how such a small country, with a small population, can do this, well the answer must lie in the fact that Finnish resorts offer so little in terms of terrain that the main challenge is the halfpipes.

Being so close to the Arctic regions it can be damn cold, temperatures often plummet to below -50° C. Whats more, the resorts are small and nothing is high or adventurous. Many places mean long journey times to reach them and one thing for sure is that Finland's not cheap. Whichever resort you go to, there are no major resort facilities to choose from, although what you do find is of a high standard. The locals are really cool and despite the small hills, you could do worse in other countries.

Travelling around Finland by air is possible: you can fly international to main cities, with domestic flights to some resorts, transfering by public transport. Driving around Finland should pose no problems. Just remember that fuel is very expensive. Train travel is a good option, but will usually mean the final leg needs to be completed by bus, as most resorts are around an hour from the nearest train station.

Visas are not required for EU nationals, but US, Canadian and Australian nationals need the relevant visa's.

Accommodation ranges from hotels, apartments, cabins and chalets of which apartments shared by groups will be the cheapest option. A 6 person Chalet ranges from 350 Finnish Markka a night.

pic - San Tang - Rider Hamish Mcknight

Alhovuori
Flat ride area 4 lifts & 9 runs
Located 40 mins from **Helsinki**

Ellivuori
Boring ride area 5 lifts & 9 runs
Located 2 hours from **Helsinki**

Heinapaa
Very boring ride area 1 lifts & 2 runs
Located 14 hours from **Helsinki**

Hirvensalo
Very boring ride area 3 lifts & 3 runs
Located 2 hours from **Helsinki**

Huukajavuori
Ultra boring ride area 2 lifts & 3 runs
Located 2 hours from **Helsinki**

Iso-Syote
▲432m 80 km of piste 11 Lifts
Iso-Syote is one of Finlands biggest resorts with a total of 21 runs. What you have here are two small mountains, offering you an area of gentle snowboard terrain that allows for some okay freeriding with some fantastic novice trails from top to bottom. There is a good halfpipe and some of the trails are flood lit for late riding! Lots of very basic lodging is available near the slopes in cabins and chalets. You can also party late but not hard.
Fly to: **Helsinki-** 14 hours away by car
ⓘ **tel-** ++358 (9) 88 838 150

Jurttivaara-Bomba
Very boring ride area 3 lifts & 7 runs
Located 9 hours from **Helsinki**

Kalli
Ultra boring ride area 1 lift & 1 run
Located 14 hours from **Helsinki**

Kalpalinna
Okay ride area 18 lifts & 18 runs
Located 2 hours from **Helsinki**

Kasurila
Very boring ride area 3 lifts & 8runs
Located 9 hours from **Helsinki**

Kauniainen
Very boring ride area 2 lifts & 1 runs
Located 20 mins from **Helsinki**

Kaustinen
Small halfpipe 4 lifts & 5 runs
Located 10 hours from **Helsinki**

Kolin _ Hiihtokeskus
Flat and very dull 4 lifts & 6 runs
Located 7 hours from **Helsinki**

Koykkyri
Total crap 2 lifts & 1 runs
Located 12 hours from **Helsinki**

Lakis
Not worth the effort 3 lifts & 3 runs
Located 10 hours from **Helsinki**

Loma-Kolin Rinteet
Small halfpipe 5 lifts & 7 runs
Located 10 hours from **Helsinki**

Levi
▲530m 29 km of piste 15 Lifts
Levi is a small resort that boasts 140 miles of trails although 125 of them are for oldies on cross country skis. The terrain is set out over a stump of a hill and offers freeriders a little bit of uneven rough to ride, including some trees. Carvers have a few good trails while freestylers have a natural halfpipe and a 100 metre man made version. Levi is also ideal for beginners.
Local facilities are well located.
Fly to: **Helsinki-** 20 hours away by car
ⓘ **tel-** ++358 16 643 466

Loma - Kolin Rinteet
Small halfpipe 5 lifts & 7 runs
Located 10 hours from **Helsinki**

Luosta
Okay for beginners 4 lifts & 7 runs
Located 16 hours from **Helsinki**

Maarianvaara
Okay for beginners 4 lifts & 7 runs
Located 10 hours from **Helsinki**

Meri - Teijo Ski Cnt
Small halfpipe 3 lifts & 8 runs
Located 8 hours from **Helsinki**

Messila
Ok slopes & halfpipe 9 lifts & 9 runs
Located 7 hours from **Helsinki**

Mielakka
Very flat ride area 2 lifts & 3 runs
Located 2 hours from **Helsinki**

Mustavaara
Small halfpipe 3 lifts & 4 runs
Located 6 hours from **Helsinki**

Myllymaki
Small halfpipe 4 lifts & 5 runs
Located 7 hours from **Helsinki**

Olos
Flat area with a pipe 4 lifts & 6 runs
Located 1hour from **Rovanemi**

Ounasvaara
Tiny area with a pipe 4 lifts & 10 runs
Located 1hour from **Kittila**

Paaskyvouri
Flat dull area 2 lifts & 4 runs
Located 8 hours from **Helsinki**

Paljakka
Best for novice carvers 8 lifts & 15 runs
Located 10 hours from **Helsinki**

Palls
Very boring ride area 2 lifts & 9 runs
Located 20 hours from **Helsinki**

Parnavaara
Small halfpipe 1 lifts & 3 runs
Located 8hours from **Helsinki**

Parra
A few easy runs 3 lifts & 4 runs
Located 8 hours from **Helsinki**

Peuramaa
Good for carvers 10 lifts & 9 runs
Located 10 hours from **Helsinki**

Puijon Rinteet
Only for novices 2 lifts & 2 runs
Located 10 hours from **Helsinki**

Pukkivuori
Small halfpipe 2 lifts & 4 runs
Located 8 hours from **Helsinki**

Purnuvuori
Small halfpipe 2 lifts & 4 runs
Located 10 hours from **Helsinki**

Pyha
▲280m 13 km of piste 6 Lifts
Phya is as small as they can possible get, with just eight or so runs and nothing longer than two turns on a long carving board. However, it is a snowcovered hill that has a half-pipe and a couple of fairly steep runs. A good intermediate will manage quite easily, but an advanced rider really shouldn't bother with this place. Actually, only novices should give it a go, if you live locally because its not worth trecking up otherwise.
Fly to: **Helsinki-** 18 hours away by car
ⓘ **tel-** ++358 692 812 081

Ruosniemi
Pipe & park but dull 3 lifts & 3 runs
Located 10 hours from **Helsinki**

Saariselka
Pipe & park but dull 6 lifts & 12 runs
Located 20 mins from **Ivalo**

Salla
▲230m 14 km of piste 6 Lifts
Salla seems a rather remote resort but it's no more remote than any other Finnish outback. This place is located in the mid to northern section of the country and on the Russian border, infact you can take a snowcat trip in to the Russian side to ride back down. The 9 runs on the Finnish side are basic but an easily-pleased freerider may find it okay. At the base are there is a hotel and not much more.
Fly to: **Helsinki-** 14 hours away by car
ⓘ **tel-** ++358 (9) 692 879 712

Sappee
▲120m 10 km of piste 4Lifts
Sappee is one of the closest resorts to **Helsinki** and a place that attracts a few weekend city dwelling snowboarders. However never to the point of bursting, which is surprising because this place is small, half a dozen riders giving it shit at mach 6 six would crowd the slopes as well as clear them. Great for novices and ideal for freestyles who like man made hits, crap for any one else.
Expensive but okay lodging and local services are in easy reach
Fly to: **Helsinki-** 2 hours away by car
ⓘ **tel-** ++358 36 538 2160

Simpsio
Very boring ride area 5 lifts & 5 runs
Located 8 hours from **Helsinki**

Solvalla - Swinghill
Very boring ride area 3 lifts & 3 runs
Located 8 hours from **Helsinki**

Sotkanrinteet
Very boring ride area 2 lifts & 2 runs
Located 8 hours from **Helsinki**

Suomu
Very basic terrain 4 lifts & 10 runs
Located 16 hours from **Helsinki**

Talma
Small pipe, ok slopes 6 lifts & 7 runs
Located 120 mins from **Helsinki**

Ukko-Koli
Okay for carvers 3 lifts & 6runs
Located 8 hours from **Helsinki**

Vihti
Very boring ride area 5 lifts & 6 runs
Located 8 hours from **Helsinki**

Vuokatti
Longest run 500m 5 lifts & 12 runs
Located 30 mins from **Helsinki**

Yllas
▲530m 29 km of piste 15 Lifts
Yllas is much in keeping with what is found at most Finnish resorts and while it is bigger than many places, it's not mega. What you get is a hill rising above the tree line, which allows for some okay intermediate freeriding, as well as some powder spots and decent carving terrain. Freeriders are usually found in the halfpipe, or pulling air off one of the many natural hits. Ideal for novices.
Local facilities can be found in two small villages nearby.
Fly to: **Helsinki-** 17 hours away by car
ⓘ **tel-** ++358 695 565 511

Himos

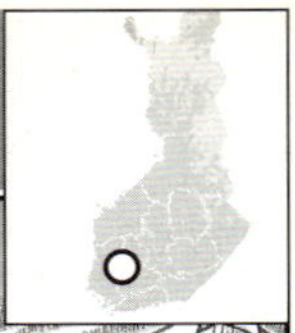

MOUNTAIN DATA

Top Lift at - 220m

Ride Area 110 acres

Bottom Lift at - 80m

Vertical Drop - 140m

Number of Runs - 15

Longest - .6 miles (1km)

TERRAIN LEVELS

Easy	**20%**
Intermediate	**55%**
Advanced	**25%**
Expert =	

TERRAIN TO SUITE

Freeride	**25%**
Trees	Poor
Backcountry	No
Freestyle	**50%**
Halfpipe	Yes 2
Terrain Park	Yes 2
Carving	**70%**

SNOW DATA

Average Snowfall
80 cm a season

Snowmaking
100% cover of the slopes

Winter Periods
Nov to May

Summer Riding
None

SLOPE ACCESS

Total Lifts = **10**

Uplift Rate - 11,200 people an hour.

9 Chair lifts

1 Drag lift

**Leashes Required*

Lift Times
10.00am to 4.00pm

Lift Pass Rates

1 Day pass	160 Fmk
6 Day pass	640 Fmk
Season pass	

Travel Guide

Fly to **Helsinki,** 3 hours transfer time.

Bus services direct from Helsinki airport.

Route Planner:
Via Helsinki, head north on motorway 4/E75 direction Lahti and then Jamsa to reach Himos which is a distance of 140 miles (225 km).

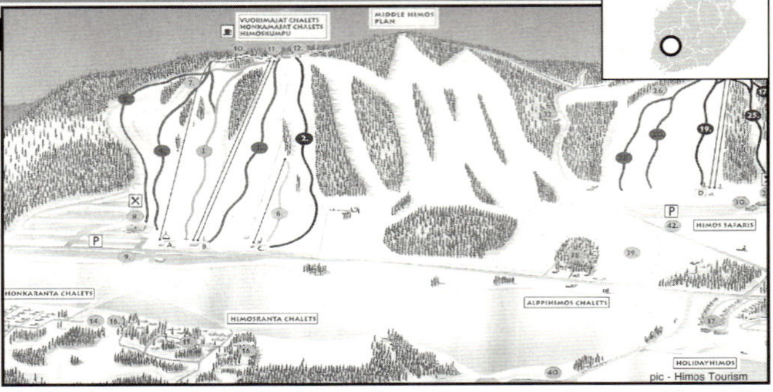

pic - Himos Tourism

Most resorts in **Finland** are tiny blips spread over rolling hills and although **Himos** is small, it is by no means the smallest resort in the country. But compared to elsewhere in central western Europe, it's almost a joke that only **Scotland** could match. Located in the southern part of the country and three hours by road from the Finnish capital of Helsinki, Himos is a very popular resort with a large number Finland's snowboarders, especially freestylers. The resort opened in 1984 and first impressions will have you wondering what the hell you are doing there. The tiny hill that rises above the shores of the frozen lake is split into two slope areas, both offering the same terrain: a mixture of flat, unadventurous trails.

Freeriders are not going to find this place up to much as there's nothing really to excite. The longest trails are on the north slopes, with one black and a couple of red runs on offer. The runs on the west slope offer a few more challenges, with some blacks that weave through the trees, but don't expect powder.

Freestylers are provided with two half-pipes and a fun park, which they call **'The Street'**, comprising of hits and rails which at least make up for the boring terrain. Locals often build the odd hit and you may even find a few logs to session in the trees.

Carvers who don't ask for much in life will probably get the best out of the slopes here, although the longest trail only just manages about 1000m, equalling at best 3 or 4 good carves. The slopes on the west hill give you the chance to shred at speed down some well prepared black trails and the short red runs are good for carvers who want progress.

Beginners have only a few, very short green trails to get started, but as the blue trails and even the reds are overrated difficulty-wise, novices have more on offer than it first seems. To help total first timers, there is a slope with a free lift. Most novices should have this place sorted in three days, if not, take up cross country skiing as you'll be more in tune with that.

Accommodation, which is spread out but within easy reach of the slopes, is offered mainly in chalet form with a number of hotels, but nothing is cheap! Don't expect any happening night life: the main place is the *Himos Hotel* which is dull to the extreme. The place isn't totally crap, it just doesn't offer very much.

For accommodation listings visit - **www.worldsnowboardguide.com**

Himos Information Cnt
Himosvuri 42100 Jamsa. Finland
++358 42 786 1051 www

Overall rating out of 10 **3** **Over all this a rather dull place**

Tahko

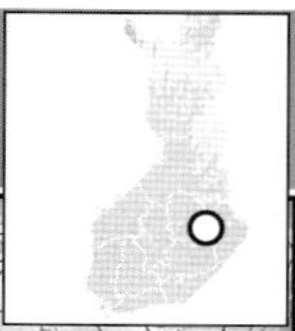

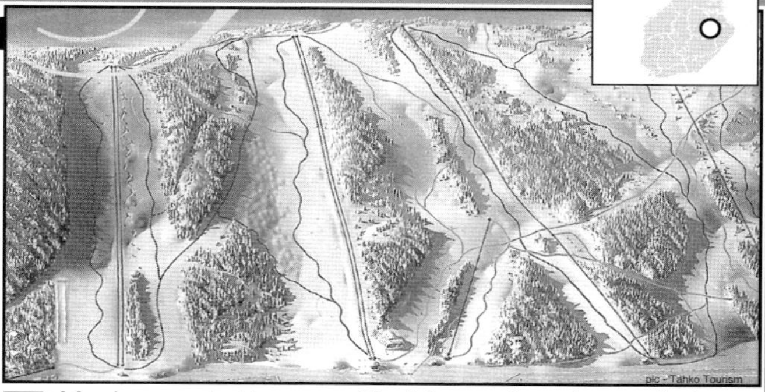

pic - Tahko Tourism

MOUNTAIN DATA

Top Lift at - 220m
Ride Area 40 acres
Bottom Lift at - 80m
Vertical Drop -
Number of Runs - 17
Longest -

TERRAIN LEVELS

Easy	50%
Intermediate	50%
Advanced	0%
Expert =	

TERRAIN TO SUITE

Freeride	30%
Trees	Poor
Backcountry	Poor
Freestyle	5%
Halfpipe	Yes 1
Terrain Park	Yes 1
Carving	65%

SNOW DATA

Average Snowfall
66 cm a season
Snowmaking
100% cover of the slopes
Winter Periods
Nov to May
Summer Riding
None

SLOPE ACCESS

Total Lifts = **8**
Uplift Rate - 9,000 people an hour.
8 Drag lifts

**Leashes Required*

Lift Times
10.00am to 4.00pm

Lift Pass Rates

1 Day pass	160 Fmk
6 Day pass	640 Fmk
Season pass	

Travel Guide

Fly to **Helsinki,** 10 hours transfer time.

Bus services with transfers will take around 10 hours

Route Planner: Via Helsinki, head north on motorway 4/E75 to Lahti and then take the M5 to Heinola and then A5 to Siilinjarvi via Kuopio before taking the B75 to Tahko.

Tahko is regarded by many Finnish snowboarders as their premier resort, which when compared with what else is on offer in the country, is easy to see why: even the **ISF** like Tahko enough to sanction snowboard events here. Tahko is a resort that attracts many cross-country skiers, but these strange creatures that dress in spray-on clothing set off into the trees and thankfully aren't seen again until the later hours of the day. Lucky, as the terrain is not very extensive and can easily become clogged up with two plankers of all types. The riding on the Tahkovuori hill is not going to excite you for very long: a few hours and you have done the lot. Still, the terrain is not bad and the pistes are well looked after, with full snowmaking facilities to help when the real stuff is in short supply. All the runs are cut through trees, offering slopes to suit intermediate and novice riders, but absolutely nothing for advanced riders to get their teeth into.

Freeriders have nothing to write home about. There are some tree areas which most of the runs are carved out of, but most are unrideable. However, on a good day there are some okay powder spots , but don't get up late thery're all gone within an hour.

Freestylers have a well shaped halfpipe located at the lower section alongside the tree line. Apart from the pipe, locals like to build their own hits, but as for big natural hits, forget it. There are a number of banks to ride up, however.

Carvers who dare to be seen in hard boots here will find some decent trails, with a couple of good red pistes to cut big wide turns on. But you won't be putting in too many before you hit the bottom and are being stared at again by everyone else in the lift queuewho will be in soft boots for certain.

Beginners have an ideal resort with half of the runs suited to novices, even if all the lifts are drags. Snow Valley is an area set aside for kids and first timers, but if you're a 300 pound, hairy arsed learner with no sense of control, stick to the main beginner runs as wiping out three year olds is not funny, and not on.

Tahko has a small, but good selection of accommodation options near the slopes. You can opt for a hotel, chalets or a bungalow. Alternatively if you're driving here, and on a tight budget, you could park up in a caravan spot, but it will be freezing in winter. Night life is quite sad and expensive, but there are worse haunts.
For accommodation listings visit - www.worldsnowboardguide.com

Tahko Information Centre
Tahko
++358 71 464 8200

Overall rating out of 10 **4** **Overall dull but okay for a day**

Ruka

MOUNTAIN DATA

Top Lift at - 1300M
Ride Area
28km of piste
Bottom Lift at - 150m
Vertical Drop - 200m
Number of Runs -
Longest -1.1 miles (1.8km)

TERRAIN LEVELS

Easy	**61%**
Intermediate	**32%**
Advanced	**7%**
Expert =	

TERRAIN TO SUITE

Freeride	**50%**
Trees	A few
Backcountry	A bit
Freestyle	**30%**
Halfpipe	Yes 2
Terrain Park	Yes 1
Carving	**20%**

SNOW DATA

Average Snowfall
300cm a season
Snowmaking
100% cover of the slopes
Winter Periods
Oct to May
Summer Riding

SLOPE ACCESS

Total Lifts = **22**
Uplift Rate - 21,000 people an hour.
4 Chair lifts
18 Drag lifts
**Leashes Required*

Lift Times
9.00am to 8.00pm

Lift Pass Rates
1 Day pass 150 Fmk
6 Day pass 360Fmk
Season pass 6000 Fm

SLOPE ACTION

Snowboard Hire
Daily rates from 135 Fmk
Kids from 120 Fmk

Snowboard Tuition
Group lessons, from from 140 Fmk

Night Riding
until 8.00pm

Heli Boarding
No

Snowmobiles
No

Mountain Cafes
5

pic - Ruka Tourism

Finland is generally a flat country with lots of lakes and the **Kusamo** region, where this typical Finnish resort is located, is no exception. The journey to **Ruka** involves no great uphill climbs or winding mountain passes, you simply arrive to see the hill popping out of the landscape like a volcano. **Ruka** is just about Finland's largest resort and during the 1996 season hosted the *International Snowboard Federation Junior World Championships,* indicating that the place has something to offer. Don't get too excited though as this is not hardcore freeriding territory and you can explore the whole area in half a day. However, the mainly intermediate slopes do offer carvers some nice flats to carve up and the slopes can be accessed with ease from any of the 5 car-parks dotted along the road that circles most of the hill. Trees cover much of the mountain, so all the trails are cut through the forest giving you the feeling you are on a different run every time, rather than just riding 100 metres across from where you were originally. All the slopes are well groomed and pisted constantly, so bumps don't get a chance to build up. Most of the area has blue and easy red runs, with only a couple of blacks down the front side.

Freeriders will find some interesting terrain to explore, although it won't take too long. There are some nice areas to ride including open and tight tree sections, especially round the side of the ski jump. **Ruka** is also known for having some good powder stashes. Although it's never super deep, it's still good fluffy stuff.

Freestylers have two fun park areas and two halfpipes, all serviced by T-bars. Both parks have a good range of gaps and table tops of all sizes and are groomed daily, so you won't need to hike up with your own shovel to shape hits. One of the parks and pipes are located up off lift number **17**, where it gets cold but you will find a shelter with a wood fire burning to warm you up between runs. Don't leave your gloves drying above the fire though, as a pair of $200 smoked *Fishpaws* are not as trendy as you may think.

Carvers are provided with flats and well spaced out trails, allowing for some interesting carving, most of which needs to be done on a series of red runs. The runs off the **7** lift are nice, long descents which allow novice carvers the option to move across from some tamer blue trails. Lift **15** also gives access to a good tree-lined carving trail that can be taken at speed.

Beginners are presented with plenty of gentle runs that allow for long descents from the summit, making **Ruka** a good place to learn the basics. Lifts stay open with the help of flood-lights until 8 pm most nights, so you can get loads of riding in if early mornings aren't your thing. Instruction facilities are very good here and you can get tuition for riding the flats or the halfpipe.

Ruka is an all year round tourist destination, so add that to the fact that Finland is an expensive country, and what you get is a super expensive but good resort. Ruka, which is only half hour bus ride from **Kuusamo** airport, has a good selection of well appointed local facilities which include a damn fine sports centre and a number of shops. If Ruka is not your thing, Kuusamo is the nearest big town with a far greater selection of everything with slightly lower prices, which will help the budget conscious rider.

Jobseekers: The chances of a job are poor for non locals. But as Ruka is a tourist haunt, skivvies are always needed.

The options for eating out are fairly good, with a choice of restaurants around town and near the slopes, but it hurts having to pay so much money even for a burger. Still *The Ampan* is well known for serving up a good pizza, while *Ali-Baba* does great grills to order, burnt or rare, it's your call.

Night life in Ruka is tame and not bright lights and disco style. However, things are very lively and the Fins know how to party hard (mind you how they manage to get drunk with the cost of booze in this place is a mystery). The only main night time hang out is *Ruka Mesta Club*, forgetting how much things costs, will initially take a while and it won't be until you're drunk that you can loosen up.

Accommodation; The choice of accommodation is extremely good, both at the slopes and back along in Ruka. Options range from very expensive hotels to very expensive shared chalets. If you find staying in Ruka or at the slopes is just too expensive then the town of **Kuusamo** is only 20 miles away and offers a greater selection of places to stay with a wider price. You will have to commute to the slopes however.

For accommodation listings visit - www.worldsnowboardguide.com

Summary: Not a bad place with terrain that allows for freeriding and some really good carving. Great for novices. Good but expensive slope side facilities.
Money wise: Nothing is cheap around this place, on or off the slopes.

Overall rating out of 10 — **6**

Ruka Information Cnt
Ruka-Rukakeskus Centre Oy
Rukatunturi, SF 93825
General info **358 89 868 1231**
Reservations **358 89 868 1395**
Snowphone **358 89 868 1231**
www.travel.fi/ruka.com

pics - San Tang

Travel Guide

Fly to **Helsinki** international
Transfer time to resort = **14** *hours.*
Local airport = Kuusamo, 20 miles

Approximate global air travel times to **Helsinki:**

from:		
	London	$4^{1/2}$ hours
	New York	**15** hours
	Frankfurt	$3^{1/2}$ hours

Buses from **Helsinki** can be taken via a change over at **Kuusamo** with a jouney time of around 14 hours

Trains to Taivalkoski (50 miles)

Route Planner
Helsinki *via Kuusamo*

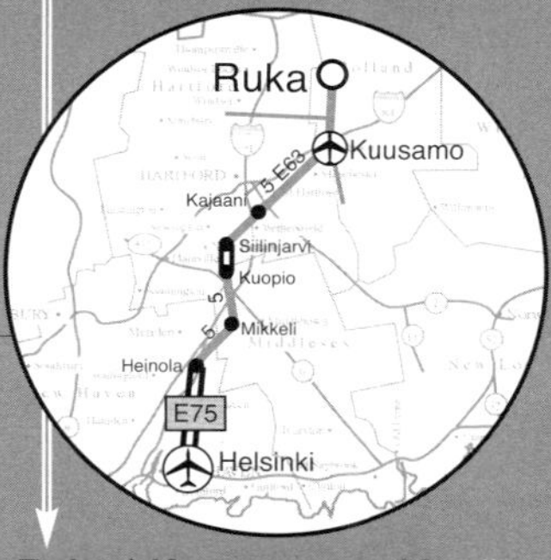

Ruka / *Kuuusamo* = **20** miles
Drive time is about **14** hours

GENERAL INFO AND FACTS

Capital - Paris
Language - French
Currency - Francs & Euros
Alcohol drinking age - 18
Drugs - Cannabis is illegal
Death Penalty - Doesn't exist
Age of consent for Sex - 16
Military Service - Voluntary
Electricity Supply - 240 Volts AC
International phone Code ++33
Highest Peak - Mont Blanc 4808

DUTY FREE
10 Litres of Alcohol
90 Litres of Wine - 110 of beer
800 Cigarettes
200 Cigars

FRENCH DRIVE GUIDE
All vehicles drive on the right hand side of the road
Speed Limits -
Motorways 120kph (74mph)
Highways 100kph (62mph)
Towns 50kph (31mph)

Contacts and general info

French Snowboard Association
Le Solaris, Z.A de Pre. France
+33 76 52 37 74

TIME ZONES
Central European
GMT +1 Hour
Between March and October
GMT+2 Hours

Main international Airports

Paris, Lyon, Grenoble, Toulouse and Geneva in *Switzerland.*

Fifty-six-and-a-half million French people are the lucky owners of some of the best snowboard resorts in the world, (Chamonix and Serre Chevalier should be on the calling card of all snowboarders) and without doubt, the most extreme and largest areas in Europe.

Resorts vary from the old to the new, but what makes them stand out is the variety of resorts themselves. Some are ugly, semi-modern dumps, whilst others are olde worlde hamlets. What is common however, are the facilities on offer. Fast-food and good bars are plentiful and all help to create a good snowboard scene.

Getting to French resorts is no problem; most are reached by road, although please note that motorways have expensive tolls. Flying to France offers a number of routes, with the principal airports to resorts being Grenoble, Lyon, Chambery and Geneva in Switzerland.
Train services in France are affordable, excellent and fast. Furthermore, during the winter months there is a direct train service from London's Waterloo station to Bourg St Maurice station, a short five minute walk to the funicular that serves the resort of Les Arcs. Most resorts can be reached indirectly by train and bus.

EU nationals won't need a visa to work in France, however, France is the worst country in the world to get a job as a snowboard instructor. The authorities are very protective of their own. If you're caught teaching on the slopes and don't hold the French ski instructor's certificate. you will be arrested and jailed. However, more mundane forms of work such as bar work are permitted. Many opportunities do exist, especially at the bigger resorts.

Accommodation in most places consists of apartment blocks sleeping any number from 1-21, which are usually quite easy to overload with floor scammers, provided they pay up with some beers.

On the money side, France is expensive, but you can get by if you eat fast-food or buy in supermarkets (where alcohol is really cheap). Avoid the over-priced discos as late night bars are just as good. n snowboard instructors teaching qualifications.

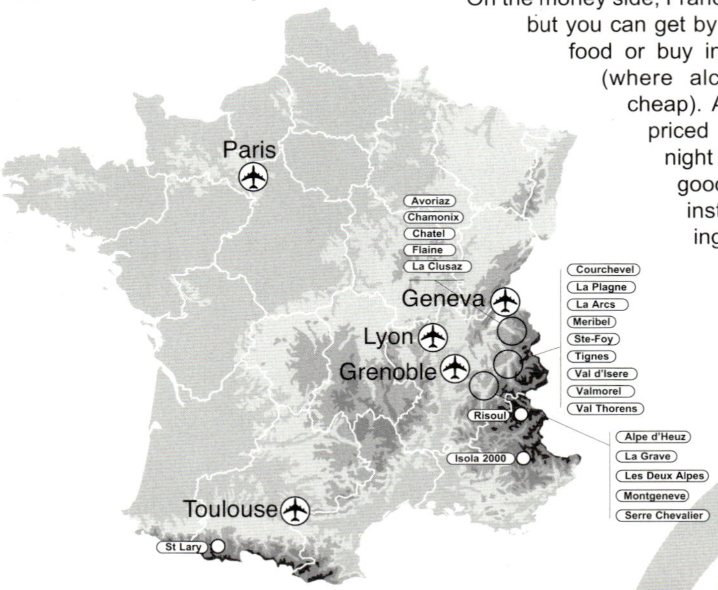

pic - A-Snowboards - Rider - Jamie Baker at Tignes

Avoriaz

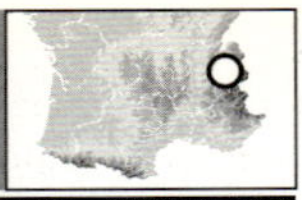

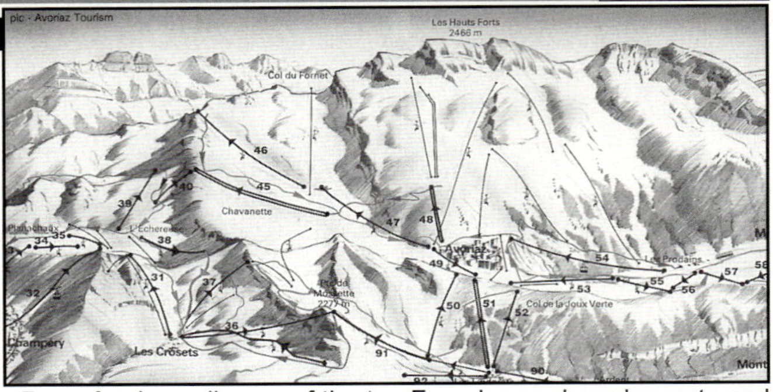

MOUNTAIN DATA

Top Lift at - 2350m

Ride Area
153km of piste

Bottom Lift at - 1000m

Vertical Drop - 1470m

Number of Runs - 50

Longest - 3 miles (5km)

TERRAIN LEVELS

Easy	**54%**
Intermediate	**33%**
Advanced	**13%**
Expert =	

TERRAIN TO SUITE

Freeride	**40%**
Trees	A few
Backcountry	Yes
Freestyle	**30%**
Halfpipe	Yes 2
Terrain Park	Yes 2
Carving	**30%**

SNOW DATA

Average Snowfall
915cm a season

Snowmaking
17 snow cannons

Winter Periods
Dec to April

Summer Riding
None

SLOPE ACCESS

Total Lifts = **42**

Uplift Rate - 47,000 people an hour.

2 Gondolas & **1** Cable car

21 Chair lifts **18** Drag lifts

**Leashes Required*

Lift Times
8.30am to 4.00pm

Lift Pass Rates
1 day area pass 207 Fr
6 day area pass 998 Fr
1 day Avoriaz pass 171 Fr

SLOPE ACTION

Snowboard Hire
Daily rates from 198 Fr
Kids from 175 Fr Sch

Snowboard Tuition
Group lessons from from 205 Fr

Night Riding
No

Heli Boarding
Flights from 300 Fr a go

Snowmobiles
No

Mountain Cafes
20

Avoriaz is easily one of the top French snowboard resorts and is seen by many as the snowboard capital of Europe. The management have been very positive in promoting snowboarding here since day one. For instance, Avoriaz was one of the first areas to have a snowboard-only section, including a pipe, a park-and-ride area and its own lift. Furthermore, the resort has been producing a snowboarder's passport, covering all aspects of Avoriaz, for a number of years.

153km of piste in **Avoriaz** links up with **Les Portes du Soleil**, a group of areas straddling the French/Swiss border, creating one of the largest circuits in Europe with some major off-piste to shred. The terrain on offer in Avoriaz is more than amazing and will suit every level and style of rider: trees, big cliff drops, powder bowls and easy, wide flats - it's all here. And as everybody gets the odd off day and fancies doing something other than riding, Avoriaz puts on a choice of services that are normally found only in US resorts: quad-bike riding, snowmobiling and climbing are all an alternative buzz.

Freeriders with bottle will find the steep blacks on **Hautes Forts** well worth the effort, where you can cut some nice unspoilt terrain at speed and in style. However, riders who really want to explore the major off-piste terrain can do so by going heli-boarding, since Avoriaz is one of the few resorts in France that allows this pursuit. Prices range from 250Fr a person for one descent with a guide.

Freestylers flock here for the natural hits and big air opportunities, of which some of the best are found around the tree-lined **Linderets** area. Avoriaz's fun-park has been established for years now and can be found near the **Arare** piste, off the **Lac du Bleu** drag lift. The park has a great selection of hits including a buried Beetle car. The halfpipe is deep and long, with sounds that blast out to accompany you on your way down. And if the pipe and park areas on Avoriaz slopes were not enough, then there is another terrain park with its half pipe located at Les Crosets, on the swiss side of the resort area.

Carvers, this resort is as much suited to you as any other rider, with plenty of wide, open slopes for Euro's to lay out big turns. The reds down **Chavanette** and **Arare** are good carving lines.

Beginners should find Avoriaz no problem. There are plenty of easy flats around the base area to try out your first falls, before progressing up to the higher blues and reds reachable by chairs (which will help those who can't get to grips with T-bars and the Poma button lifts). One note of caution is that a lot of ski classes use the easy runs, which means they can be very busy at times, so expect congestion. The resort has recently included a new mini terrain park for kids and the younger generation. But note that it's still a fun park so take care when going off the small hits.

As for the local services, what you get is a wonder of contemporary architecture - a purely purpose-built, dirty and ugly sham, perched way up the mountain with most of the buildings being made of wood - tons of it. However, whatever your opinion on the looks, the resort provides excellent access from all accommodation to the slopes, with riding to your door the norm. Overall **Avoriaz** caters well for snowboarders and is not too fancy (in fact its pretty damn cheesy and down market). There are heaps of local attractions with a number of sporting complexes and cinemas to help while away your evenings, although most people just party the night away.

Jobseekers: Lots of seasonal work is available whether you speak French or not. This is a very popular package tour-operators resort.

Avoriaz can feed everyone so long as they're not too choosy. The main menu is based around two-week old pieces of cardboard pizza costing a few francs or costly 3 course French cusine which could sting you for 300fr a throw. *Marie Brech* is a very good eateriewhile Us1 serves an okay grill.

Nightlife here resembles what you would find in a sea side resort on the south coast of England. Pure holiday camp designed for the world's dole cheats making the place pretty lively and often roudy. Booze flows freely all day and all night. *The Place* is a main hangout as is *Le Choucas* and *Les Ruches*, which all play cool sounds and have plenty of holiday talent to check out.

Accommodation: There are loads of wooden apartment blocks, with self-catering being the main choice. Prices vary but you can get great deals. *Chalet Snowboards* ++44 (0)1235 767 575 or *Snowboard Lodge* ++44 (0) 01562 743 888 offer good holiday packages and are based close to the slopes. Thomson Holidays ++44 (0)870 606 1470 also offer a number of inclusive holiday trips.

Summary: Good resort with excellent freeriding and carving areas. The main problem with Avoriaz are the crowds and long lift queues. **Money wise;** This is an affordable place if you take a package tour Prices for all main services are reasonable.

Overall rating out of 10 **8**

Tourist Office Avoriaz
Place Centrale, 74110,
Avoriaz

General info	**++33 (0) 450 74 02 11**
Reservations	**++33 (0) 450 74 02 11**
Avlanche info	**++33 (0) 836 681 020**

www.avoriaz.com

pics - Avoriaz Tourism

Travel Guide

Fly to **Geneva** international
Transfer time to resort = **2** *hours.*
Local airport = none

Approximate global air travel times to **Geneva:**

from:		
	London	2 hours
	Los Angles	13 hours
	New York	9 hours

Bus services from Geneva airport in Switzerland, are available on a daily basis to Avoriaz via Clues

Trains stop at **Clues** (20 mins)

Route Planner
Geneva

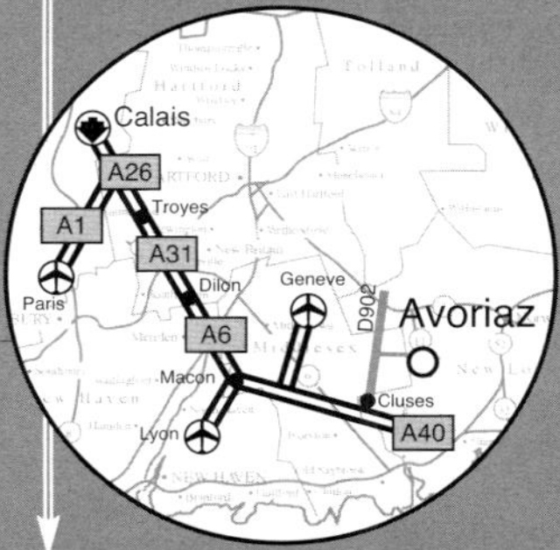

Avoriaz = 52 miles (80km)
Drive time is about **120** minutes

*From **Calais** 554 miles (891 Km)
Drive time is around 9½ hours.

Alpes D'Huez

MOUNTAIN DATA

Top Lift at - 3330m

Ride Area 225km of piste

Bottom Lift at - 1450m

Vertical Drop - 1880m

Number of Runs - 108

Longest - 10 miles (16km)

TERRAIN LEVELS

Easy	36%
Intermediate	54%
Advanced	10%
Expert =	

TERRAIN TO SUITE

Freeride	50%
Trees	No
Backcountry	A bit
Freestyle	20%
Halfpipe	Yes 2
Terrain Park	Yes 2
Carving	40%

SNOW DATA

Average Snowfall

Snowmaking
20% cover of the slopes

Winter Periods
Dec to April

Summer Riding
None

SLOPE ACCESS

Total Lifts = **86**

Uplift Rate - 90,000 people an hour.

9 Gondolas **6** Cable cars

23 Chair lifts - **48** Drag lifts

**Leashes Required*

Lift Times
8.30am to 4.00pm

Lift Pass Rates
1 Day pass 207 Fr
6 Day pass 1070 Fr
Season pass

Travel Guide

Fly to **Lyon** with a transfer time of around 2 hours.

Bus services go direct from Lyon to the resort.

Route Planner: Via Grenoble, head south on the N75 and turn off at Le Pont de-Clax on to the N91 turning off for Alp d'Heuz.
*Drive time from **Calais** is 10 hours 569 miles (915 km)

pic - Soft Snapper

Anyone planning a two-week trip to **Alpe d'Huez**, will not have enough time to ride all the amazing and varied terrain that this place has to offer. Each year, this high altitude resort offers amazing amounts of great powder days covering some fantastic backcountry and wide open plateaus. The terrain is as much for the advanced rider as it is for the novice. Due to its location and mostly south-facing slopes, the runs here get a lot of annual sunshine. This has the benefit of letting you ride in great sunny conditions and also helps to soften up certain areas early on in the day. There's heaps of snow here so don't be worrying if the odd bit thins out early. The resort has a well-equipped and fast lift system that can shunt over 90,000 punters up the mountains per hour. Unfortunately, its popularity with overseas holiday crowds means that Alpe d'Huez can get a bit clogged up, especially at weekends. Holiday periods are absolutely crazy, so avoid this time at all costs if you want to escape millions of day-glow two-plankers. However, during normal periods you can ride freely all week long from top to bottom, on and off-piste, without having to cross-track your own path or that of another skier.

Freeriders can be forgiven for thinking that they are in heaven. Alpe d'Huez is a backcountry freeride gem with miles of off-piste powder, in areas such as **Gorges de Sarenne** and **Glacier de Sarenne**. Please note that, riding without a guide is total folly. For assistance seek out the services of a local guide through one of the ski-schools, or via *Planet Surf* snowboard shop.

Freeriders are provided with a fun-park that in many ways isn't necessary. There are loads of natural air spots to make you feel spoilt for choice.

Carvers are teased with so many well groomed trails, that picking one as a favourite is just not possible.

Beginners are bombarded with a easy green runs at the lower areas, the only bug being that these areas are usually very busy.

Off the slopes, the whole place is cheesy and very tacky. On the other hand it provides great all-round affordable local services close to the slopes. You can dine very affordably with cheap pizza restaurants in abundance. Night-life ranges from a cinema to loud partying which is brash and full-on, although this place does go in for a lot of aprés crap.

For accommodation listings visit - www.worldsnowboardguide.com

Alpe d'Heuz Tourist office
Bp 28, F-38750 Alpe d'Heuz, Dauphine
++33 (0) 476 11 44 44 www.alpedhuez.com

Overall rating out of 10 **7** **Really good carvers slopes**

Chatel

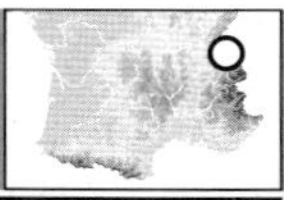

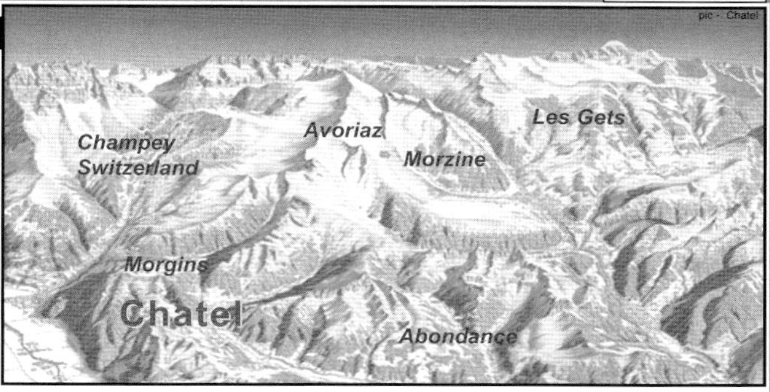

MOUNTAIN DATA

Top Lift at - 2200m

Ride Area
225km of piste

Bottom Lift at - 1200m
Vertical Drop - 1000m
Number of Runs - 42
Longest - 4 miles (6km)

TERRAIN LEVELS

Easy	49%
Intermediate	39%
Advanced	12%
Expert =	

TERRAIN TO SUITE

Freeride	40%
Trees	Yes
Backcountry	Yes
Freestyle	20%
Halfpipe	Yes 1
Terrain Park	Yes 1
Carving	30%

SNOW DATA

Average Snowfall
400 cm a season
Snowmaking
10% cover of the slopes
Winter Periods
Dec to April
Summer Riding
None

SLOPE ACCESS

Total Lifts = **40**
Uplift Rate - 41,600 people an hour.
2 Gondolas
28 Chair lifts - **12** Drag lifts
**Leashes Required*

Lift Times
8.30am to 4.00pm

Lift Pass Rates
1 Day pass 207 Fr
6 Day pass 998 Fr
Season pass

Travel Guide

Fly to **Geneve,** 1 1/2 hours away.

Train services are possible to Thonon les bains which is a 45 minute away.

Route Planner: Via Geneva, head north west on the N2 turning on to the D902 at Thonon. Chatel lies along the D22
*Drive time from
Calais is 9 1/2 hours
524 miles (843 km)

Chatel is a two-levelled, low lying resort that forms part of the massive **Portes du Soleil** area, and is linked by a local bus service to a number of nearby resorts. There are two distinctive architectural styles - the old and the new. The old comes by way of a traditional French mountain village; the new is what has sprung up since the place became stupidly busy with skiers. At the base of the wooded slopes is the village of Chatel, set 1,200m above sea-level. Initial access to the mountain is via a gondola that can be annoyingly busy in the mornings. However, once up the slopes you are set above the second area of **Super Chatel**, which sits at 1,630m. Above this mid-point lies a series of lifts that cover a wide open expanse of good snowboard terrain, with the possibility of being able to ride all the way back to Chatel. You wouldn't rate Chatel in the major league of resorts, but it is not a bad haunt, especially for carvers.

Freeriders will find that Chatel offers some excellent terrain, with uncrowded powder areas to play in. The **Pre-La-Joux** area can often have a decent powder stash, while the long black run near the **Linga** gondola can be done at speed.

Freestylers are better off going to nearby **Avoriaz**, as the so-called fun-park and pipe at **Chatel** is poxy and not worth the effort. However, some natural hits are and you can always ollie over fallen skiers for some extra fun.

Carvers may find **Chatel** best suited to their needs, especially if they're a crossover skier who is not out for much other than showing off to their two-planked cousins. A cool place for laying out big turns is around **Super Chatel,** on the intermediate trails.

Beginners will find the best terrain for their needs up at **Super Chatel**, but overall it is a poor learning area since many of the novice trails are cluttered with ski classes. However, beginners can ride a long trail from the highest point to the base when snow cover permits.

Off the slopes, **Chatel** sucks. It is too stuck up with an underlying pompous attitude. Fashion-conscious dickheads are everywhere, and the only saving factor about this place is leaving it. That said, you can find affordable accommodation and cheap food outlets, but night-life is geared around happy groups wanting aprés nonsense, so avoid like the plague.

For accommodation listings visit - www.worldsnowboardguide.com

Chatel Tourist Office
F-74390 Chatel-Haute Savoie
++33 (0) 450 73 22 44 **www.chatel.com**

Overall rating out of 10 **4** **This place is far to it's own arse**

Chamonix

MOUNTAIN DATA

Top Lift at - 3840m

Ride Area
140km of piste

Bottom Lift at - 1035m

Vertical Drop - 2850m

Number of Runs - 50

Longest - 13 miles (21km)

TERRAIN LEVELS

Easy	54%
Intermediate	33%
Advanced	13%
Expert =	

TERRAIN TO SUITE

Freeride	65%
Trees	Yes
Backcountry	Yes 'mega'
Freestyle	25%
Halfpipe	Yes 2
Terrain Park	Yes 2
Carving	10%

SNOW DATA

Average Snowfall
960cm a season

Snowmaking
47 snow cannons

Winter Periods
Dec to April

Summer Riding
None

SLOPE ACCESS

Total Lifts = **62**

Uplift Rate - 47,000 people an hour.

6 Gondolas & **7** Cable car

16 Chair lifts **33** Drag lifts

**Leashes Required*

Lift Times
8.30am to 4.00pm

Lift Pass Rates

1 Day pass	241 Fr
6 Day pass	999 Fr
Season pass	

SLOPE ACTION

Snowboard Hire
Daily rates from 210 Fr
Kids from 195 Fr Sch

Snowboard Tuition
Group lessons, from
from 210 Fr

Night Riding
No

Heli Boarding
Flights from 370 Fr a go

Snowmobiles
No

Mountain Cafes
21

pic - Chamonix Tourism

Chamonix couldn't be any more different than **France's** other well-known boarding resorts, yet many see it as a mecca. It doesn't have a huge area of well-connected lifts or groomed pistes and the crowds, slow and old lifts and queues can be a real grind. You may want to think about the time of year you visit as the lower valley runs are often closed due to a lack of snow. It does have some of the most heart pumping off-piste anywhere in the world set under Europe's highest mountain, with amazing views of **Mont Blanc**. There is plenty to do if you want to take a break from boarding in Chamonix as it is a real French town, much larger than other purpose built resorts. Take this warning though; you will most certainly need a guide to appreciate it, as this place can be really dangerous.

Freeriders will find the extreme centre of boarding in **Chamonix** has to be at **Argentiere** at the top of the valley in the **Grands Montets,** where the top cable car takes you up to 3300m. You will have to fork out some extra cash for this lift, but strangely not if you have a day pass. From the top there are two black pistes **Point de Vue** and **Pylones**, with heaps of off-piste alternatives. From the top of the **Bochard** bubble you can head into the **Combe de la Pendant** bowl for 1000m of unpisted descent. The runs down are amazing with loads of cliffs, hits and chutes, but the area can be avalanche prone. Another area that is worth a visit is the linked area of **Brevent** and **La Flegere**. **Flegere** is smaller and quieter, but there is some nice off-piste, small bowls and trees to ride, which can be okay in flat light. Make sure you get to the bottom of the cable car early though as there is only one way up and you could be queuing for more than an hour if you time it wrong. If you've got some cash for a guide you could do the **Vallee Blanche**, which is easy boarding, but there are some nasty large crevasses for the unsuspecting rider. For many riders it's going to be a once in a lifetime experience. A final area that is worth a try is **La Tour** at the head of the valley. It's one of the smallest areas, with pretty basic lifts but it can be good and there is some off-piste potential here if you link up with the train.

Carvers should note that although there are a number pisted runs here they are not very wide, making this not the resort for carvers.

Freestylers don't really need a fun-park or pipe as there's so much natural freestyle terrain. It seems that the attitude is to build a pipe for competitions and then leave it to rot. Most of the time the pipes are totally unridable, whilst the 2 or 3 jumps in the park are a joke and badly maintained. **Chamonix** is a mountain resort, so if you stay in the park you'll never get the best from it.

Beginners can ride Chamonix. If you are a novice or visiting with children, **La Plange** may be the resort for you as there are plenty of greens and blues with really good lifts nearby and you can easily get to the highest points of the resort.

This resort is very apartment dominated, but there are still plenty of choices for chalets. All the centres are self contained with bars, restaurants and shops. **La Plange** is pretty quiet and dull in the evenings and certainly isn't a party town. However you could always try out the *Olympic Bobsleigh* run of 1.5km, reaching speeds of 100kmh. There are plenty of things to do in **Chamonix** with a large sports centre, swimming pool, arcades and bowling alley. **Argentiere** at the head of the valley has a good choice of bars and restaurants and is a great place to stay.

Food of every kind is available at most prices but excludes the budget range. There are simply dozens of restaurants from cheap to steep. In Chamonix, the *Jeckyl & Hyde* does good pub grub.

As for nightlife, there are plenty of bars in **Chamonix** (usually packed with Swedish chicks). The *Jeckyl and Hyde*, (full of Brits abroad) and the *Drivers* bar, which is more French, are popular bars. **Argentiere** at the head of the valley has a good choice of bars and restaurants and is a great place to stay. The *Office* is one of the busiest spots, but there are many more traditional French bars too that have cheaper drinks.

Accommodation: There is a wide range of places to stay that will cover all budgets, with apartments, hotels, and chalets. A good cheap, basic and clean place that is close to the slopes is in **Argentier**e - the *Belvedre Bunk House*, which is a 5 minute walk to the bottom lift and has prices from 80ff a night. Another good bet in Argentiere is with the *Kommunity Camps* run by *Neil McNab*. *Kommunity Snowboard Camps* offer great full snowboard packages close to the slopes at **Grands Montets.** ++33 (0) 450 54 22 84. **www**.mcnab.co.uk.

For accommodation listings visit - www.worldsnowboardguide.com

Summary: Chamonix offers some truly excellent freeriding and great natural freestyle terrain. However, this is not the friendliest of places and is a bit run down.
Money wise: Although a shoddy place, Chamonix is super expensive.

Overall rating out of 10 **10**

Tourist Office Chamonix
85 Place du Triangle de L'Amitie
F74400 Chamonix, Mont Blanc
General info **++33 (0) 450 53 00 24**
Reservations **++33 (0) 450 53 23 33**
Avlanche info **++33 (0) 836 681 020**
www.chamonix.com

pic - Chamonix Tourism

Travel Guide

Fly to **Geneva** international
Transfer time to resort = **3** *hours.*
Local airport = none

Approximate global air travel times to **Geneva:**

from: London	**2** hours
Los Angles	**13** hours
New York	**9** hours

Bus services from Geneva airport in Switzerland, are available on a daily basis to the centre of Chamonix.

Trains stop in **Chamonix**

Route Planner
Geneva - *Calais*

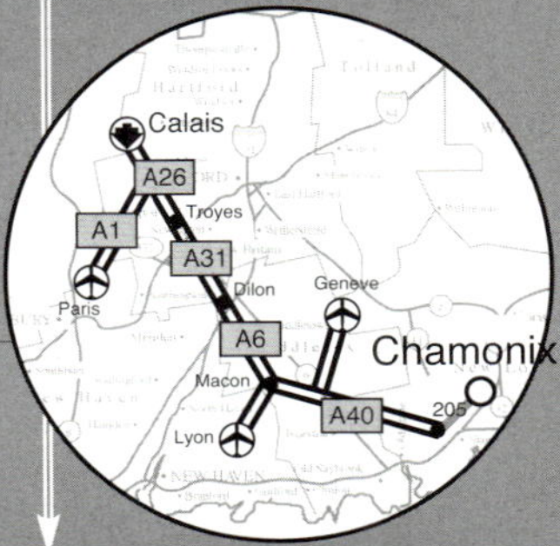

Chamonix = 50 miles (905 km)
Drive time is about **1** hour

*From **Calais 551** miles (886 Km)
Drive time is around **9** hours.

Courchevel

MOUNTAIN DATA

Top Lift at - 3500m

Ride Area
160km of piste

Bottom Lift at - 1250m

Vertical Drop - 1438m

Number of Runs - 275

Longest - 3 miles (5km)

TERRAIN LEVELS

Easy	**25%**
Intermediate	**64%**
Advanced	**11%**
Expert =	

TERRAIN TO SUITE

Freeride	**40%**
Trees	Yes
Backcountry	Yes
Freestyle	**20%**
Halfpipe	Yes 2
Terrain Park	Yes 2
Carving	**40%**

SNOW DATA

Average Snowfall
600cm a season

Snowmaking
26 snow cannons

Winter Periods
Dec to April

Summer Riding
None

SLOPE ACCESS

Total Lifts = **67**

Uplift Rate - 68,000 people an hour.

9 Gondolas & **1** Cable car

16 Chair lifts **41** Drag lifts

**Leashes Required*

Lift Times
8.30am to 4.00pm

Lift Pass Rates

1 Day pass	353 Fr
6 Day pass	1160 Fr
Season pass	

SLOPE ACTION

Snowboard Hire
Daily rates from 205 Fr
Kids from 188 Fr Sch

Snowboard Tuition
Group lessons, from
from 235 Fr

Night Riding
No

Heli Boarding
Flights from 365 Fr a go

Snowmobiles
Yes

Mountain Cafes
10

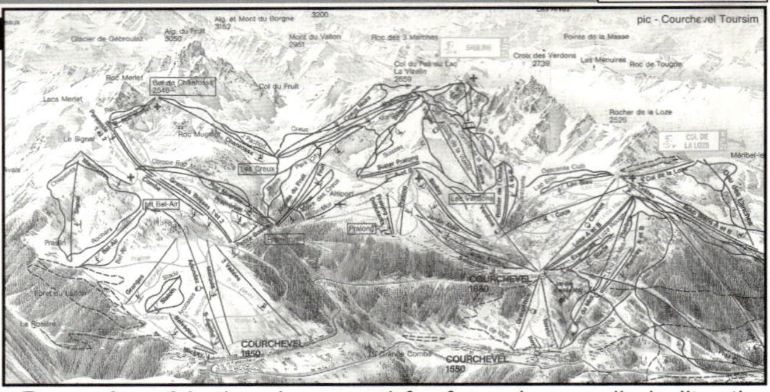

Courchevel is the playground for france's so called elite, the ridiculously rich and the just plain ridiculous. Here you'll find silk, money, Brits and bull, but despite it all, this is a pretty good place to board and party. Pop stars and their ilk are often seen posing on the slopes here along with miserable film stars. Still, you can quite easily avoid the aforementioned group of scum. This is an area that offers a lot of snow and a good uplift system, taking you away to stupid amounts of rideable slopes. Courchevel, which is one of the vast **Les Trois Vallees** ski domains, is actually consists of four purpose-built stations, towns, centres, call them what you want. At the bottom is **1300,** otherwise known as **Le Praz** and is the only real village out of the lot. Next up is **1550** followed closely by **1650** and finally (at the top) **1850,** which also stands for attitude and ugliness and is the snob's the snobs spot. All the areas have easy access onto the mountain and a good variety of terrain. However, this is a stupidly busy place that not only caters for millions of visiting foreign skiers, but also Frances own who consider this one of their best resorts. During school holidays and other public holiday periods, the whole place can get pretty busy, but even then lift queues are rarely long and there's still plenty of space to avoid the crowds due to a lot of well spread terrain.

Freeriders will be happy as there are loads of cracking intermediate pistes and some long, open blacks to keep advanced riders entertained. Even after a big dump the pistes don't get too bumped up, but there are a lot of long flat sections between the steeps where you may find yourself walking if you're not careful. Off-piste, check out either side of the **Chanrossa** chair and the hugebowl underneath the **Vizelle** bubble and **Dou des Lanche** chair. The latter is well worth the haul and powder stays in these spots for longer than elsewhere in the resort. 1650 has some superbly open and tight tree runs off the central drag lifts.

Freestylers looking for a good supply of natural hits should try the tunnel off the **Grand Boss** drag at **1650**, the rollers to the side of **Verdon** and **Biollay**, and follow some of the locals off **Creux Noir**. A good place to hang out is the big snow-park and halfpipe by the **Plantrey** chair. There's also a free drag.

Carvers will be in hard boot heaven in Courchevel. There are acres of well groomed, wide, open pistes for all standards of rider. Ear-splitting stuff! Truly one of the best carving resorts in France

Beginners have big areas to learn the basics in **1850** and **1550,** for example the motorway pistes in the **Pralong** area. Nearly all lifts at **1650** are drags, so watch out if you're venturing off the nursery slopes for the first time. Courchevel has several zillion ski-schools, but in the main, they are still exactly that - SKI-schools. Be warned, go to one of the a registered ski school, which offer good rates for tution with qualified instructors.

Why do the French build such blots on their landscapes? **1850** is like hell on a bad day and **1650** is worse. However, if you can put up with the grim buildings, the upper-class twits that inhabit them, and the tour reps, you'll find easy access to the slopes with good local facilities - ice-rink, climbing walls and a well equipped gym. If you visit in March, you must do the 45 second freefall jump - a flying orgasm! Each level has bars and shops. **Le Praz,** which still looks and feels like a village, has the fewest tour operators and is the cheapest place to stay. Wherever you stay, your francs (or euros) will start dematerialising faster than Captain Kirk as this place is with out doubt one of the most expensive resorts in France, although it dosen't warrant the super cost.

When eating out, you only have three choices in Courchevel - flashy restaurants, Savoyarde hill food or pizza. The first are five-course feed-ins, the second is melted cheese, dried meat and tatties in varying combinations, and well, pizza's pizza! And they're all expensive! If you're a veggie, expect to eat a lot of cheese. Find some overpriced rabbit nosh at *FiFi's* in **1850.**

Night-life comes with either bars full of tour operator punters playing aprés-ski games, supported by their 18-year-old debutante chalet girls, or bars full of merchant bankers and old Etonians. For an early beer, try *L'Equipe* in 1850, or *Le Signal* in **1650** then the *D'Arbeilo* in *Le Praz* or *Bang Bang*.

Accommodation: You can pick up some really cheap deals in all four villages by trying one of the many agencies for apartments. Alternatively, *Pleisure Holidays* offer affordable and great snowboard trips with well equipped chalets on the slopes from £200 a week. Stay at Chalet Martel with prices for individuals to groups or Chalet Barragiste, 1550 (on the slopes), which can accommodate up to 18 people. Hotel Olympic is a well appointed B&B with self-catering and is ideal for short breaks. Tel ++44 (0) 24 7668 6835

Summary: Good all-round resort with excellent terrain for all styles, particularly carvers and off-piste freeriders. The main drawbacks are crowds and costs.
Money wise: Hellishly expensive resort but offering good value in parts.

Overall rating out of 10 **9**

Tourist Office Courchevel
La Croisette - Bp 37
73122 Courchevel. Cedex
General info **++33 (0) 4 79 08 00 29**
Reservations **++33 (0) 4 79 08 00 29**
Avlanche info **++33 (0) 836 681 020**
www.courchevel.com
www.pleisure.co.uk

pic - Robbie Allan

Rider Stevie Trollands

Travel Guide

Fly to **Lyon** international
Transfer time to resort = **2¼** hours.
Local airport = none

Approximate global air travel times to **Lyon:**

from:		
	London	2 hours
	Los Angles	13 hours
	New York	9 hours

Bus services from Lyon or Geneva airport in Switzerland, are available on a daily basis to the centre of Courchevel.

Trains to **Moutiers,** 15 miles on.

Route Planner
Lyon

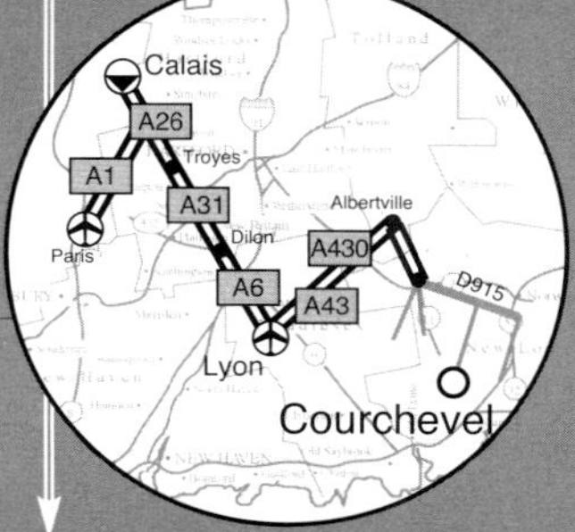

Courchevel = 118 miles (189 km)
Drive time is about **2¼** hours

*From **Calais** 586 miles (928 Km)
Drive time is around **9¾** hours.

Flaine

MOUNTAIN DATA

Top Lift at - 2500m

Ride Area 161km of piste

Bottom Lift at - 1600m

Vertical Drop - 900m

Number of Runs - 108

Longest -8.7 miles (14km)

TERRAIN LEVELS

Easy	**10%**
Intermediate	**65%**
Advanced	**25%**
Expert =	

TERRAIN TO SUITE

Freeride	**50%**
Trees	Yes
Backcountry	Yes
Freestyle	**20%**
Halfpipe	Yes 1
Terrain Park	Yes 1
Carving	**30%**

SNOW DATA

Average Snowfall
500cm a season

Snowmaking
5% cover of the slopes

Winter Periods
Dec to April

Summer Riding
None

SLOPE ACCESS

Total Lifts = **31**

Uplift Rate - 28,000 people an hour.

1 Gondola **1** Cable car

10 Chair lifts - **19** Drag lifts

**Leashes Required*

Lift Times
8.30am to 4.00pm

Lift Pass Rates

1 Day pass	193 Fr
6 Day pass	970 Fr
Season pass	

Travel Guide

Fly to **Geneva**, about 1 hours transfer to Flaine.

Train services to Cluses which is 10 minutes away.

Route Planner: Via Geneva, head south on the A40 to Cluses and then take the B road on the left up to Flaine. (44miles)
*Drive time from **Calais** is 9 1/4 hours
545 miles (877 km)

pic - Flaine Tourism

Flaine is a purpose-built, 1960's mess, whose architects must have designed the resort in the space of five minutes, then built it with five million tonnes of waste concrete. Ugly? Yep, and designed purely for hordes of skiers. However, as far as snowboarding is concerned, Flaine offers some great and varied terrain for different abilities. Flaine sits in a big bowl and forms part of **Le Grand Massif** area, which includes the linked resorts of **Samoens, Morillon**, and **Les Carroz**, offering good off-piste.

Freeriders have some great opportunities for off-piste riding, with long, interesting runs to tackle. The area above the **Samoens** lift is pretty good, but alternatively, you should check out the trees in **Les Carroz**, where you will get a good lesson on how to treat wood at speed. Advanced riders should check out **Combe de Gers**, which is a steep back bowl that drops away with 700 metres of vert (don't bail this one). To get the best off-piste riding, hire a guide, which will cost about 360FF for two hours. Heli-boarding is also possible here.

Freestylers may at first feel they are invading a Euro-carver's hangout, but air heads have a good two mile long fun-park area, loaded with big hits to get high. There's even a kid's halfpipe called the **Fantasurf**. The park is supported by a reduced lift pass, so check at the ticket office for the latest deals.

Carvers are certainly at home here: Flaine was one of the first carving capitals in France and like most of the country, there are many good areas for Alpiners to show off.

Beginners have a number of very easy flat runs which are serviced by a free lift located a short walk from the village area. However, to progress, you will need to buy a pass and head up to the more interesting runs. There are a couple of long blues leading away from the top of **Les Grandes Platieres** cable car, that will allow novices to find out what linking turns are like.

Flaine is not a massive village, nor is it the most expensive, but it's hell on earth in terms of the way it is presented as a holiday camp on a mountain. The Brits have over the years done a good job in turning Flaine it into a tacky hole. Lodging is basic, and apartments are the main accommodation with most either next to the slopes, or within a short walk. Evenings are noisy with lots of aprés-ski going on. In truth this is an utter dire place of the slopes.

For accommodation listings visit - www.worldsnowboardguide.com

Flaine Tourist office
Galerie des Marchants, 74300 Flaine
++33 (0) 450 90 80 01 www.flaine.com

Overall rating out of 10 — 6 **Okay slopes, dire village**

Isola 2000

FRANCE

MOUNTAIN DATA

Top Lift at - 2610m

Ride Area
120km of piste

Bottom Lift at - 1800m
Vertical Drop - 810m
Number of Runs - 46
Longest - 2.5 miles (4km)

TERRAIN LEVELS

Easy	**48%**
Intermediate	**39%**
Advanced	**13%**
Expert =	

TERRAIN TO SUITE

Freeride	**40%**
Trees	Yes
Backcountry	Yes
Freestyle	**20%**
Halfpipe	Yes 1
Terrain Park	Yes 1
Carving	**50%**

SNOW DATA
Average Snowfall

Snowmaking
15% cover of the slopes
Winter Periods
Dec to April
Summer Riding
None

SLOPE ACCESS
Total Lifts = **25**
Uplift Rate - 20,000 people an hour.
2 Gondolas
7 Chair lifts - **16** Drag lifts
**Leashes Required*

Lift Times
8.30am to 4.00pm

Lift Pass Rates

1 Day pass	210 Fr
6 Day pass	800 Fr
Season pass	

Travel Guide

Fly to Nice, 50 miles away.

Train services are possible all the way to Nice, which is a 50 minute transfer.

Route Planner:
Via Nice, head north on the N202 and then the D2205 to Isola turning left on to the D97 for Isola 2000

pic - Isola 2000 Tourism

Isola 2000, situated in the south of **France,** has more to offer than you'd expect. A calculated and very purpose-built resort, the French seem to have got their sums a bit wrong in the early days when they built this rather cheesy and tacky mess, whose original destiny was to pack in hordes of cheap package tour groups fresh out of jail. However, things have changed a little, and the place is losing its poor reputation and gaining a lot of respect. The resort has easy access to lifts, and all the slopes offer plenty of terrain to keep even the most adventurous rider busy for a good week or two, but a season here would be pushing it.

Freeriders scoping the land will touch the piste only to hop between tree runs, or to get back on the lift. Isola has ample tree coverage over the mid to lower areas. Natural gullies can be hit near **Melezes**, plus look out for the drop offs in the trees as you're going up the chair lift - they're all over the place. Turn to the north-facing slope when conditions are good, above Grand Tour, as it is well worth hiking the ridge for freshies. Do watch your run out though as you come to a severe drop off onto a flat piste below.

Freestylers Isola 2000 is home to the Back to Back Snowboard Club, and a dedicated and maintained snowboard park. They don't have a residential Pipe Dragon yet, but with the experienced locals, you can be sure of a park with table-tops, spined tomb-stones and gaps.

Carvers The whole area was planned to make runs long, well groomed and easy to return to base, with good cruising and carving on both sides of the mountain.

Beginners have a massive designated area near the base lift station. This keeps them out of trouble on a good area for progression, before they take on the higher grade runs, allowing quick learners the chance to ride the whole resort.

The easiest option with accommodation would be to stay in one of the apartment blocks - comfortable, unfussy and just a stone's throw away from the lift station and amenities. If you're after a bit more style and want to impress your other half, take up space in one of the chalets available. For food, why not try the *Crocodile Bar*, which serves up some decent *Tex-Mex*. It's also a good local snowboard hangout and stays open long into the early hours, with good measures and good sounds.

For accommodation listings visit - www.worldsnowboardguide.com

Isola 2000 Tourist Office
Isola F-06420.
++33 (0) 4 93 23 15 15 **www.isola-2000.com**

Overall rating out of 10 **5** **Okay slopes but cheesy town**

La Clusaz

MOUNTAIN DATA

Top Lift at - 2600m

Ride Area
129km of piste

Bottom Lift at - 1100m
Vertical Drop - 1200m
Number of Runs - 76
Longest - 2 miles (3km)

TERRAIN LEVELS

Easy	**65%**
Intermediate	**27%**
Advanced	**8%**
Expert =	

TERRAIN TO SUITE

Freeride	**50%**
Trees	Limited
Backcountry	Yes
Freestyle	**20%**
Halfpipe	Yes 1
Terrain Park	Yes 1
Carving	**30%**

SNOW DATA

Average Snowfall
500cm a season
Snowmaking
10% cover of the slopes
Winter Periods
Dec to April
Summer Riding
None

SLOPE ACCESS

Total Lifts = **56**
Uplift Rate - 28,000 people an hour.
5 Gondola **1** Cable car
13 Chair lifts - **39** Drag lifts
**Leashes Required*

Lift Times
8.30am to 4.00pm

Lift Pass Rates
1 Day pass 157 Fr
6 Day pass 820 Fr
Season pass

Travel Guide

Fly to **Geneva,** which is around a 1hour transfer.

Train services go to Annecy, 10 minutes away.

Route Planner: Via Geneva, head south on the A40 and exit at Bonneville on to the D12 via Borne to La Clusaz
*Drive time from **Calais** is 9 hours 533 miles (858 km)

pic - La Clusaz Tourism

La Clusaz is located in the distant shadow of **Mont Blanc** and is only an hour-and-a-half from **Geneva**. La Clusaz is a cluster of five low-level rideable areas, linked by a series of lifts. The two very noticeable problems with La Clusaz are a) the low altitude, which can mean poor snow levels, and b) the French disease of overpopulation by ski-tour groups. Collectively, snowboarding can be described as poor. It lacks anything of great interest, unless you're a carver who likes to pose alongside lift lines on blue runs. Advanced riders will have this place licked in a few days, with the only decent challenge being a long black on the **Massif de Balme** area. You can ride four of the five areas via a network of connecting lifts, while the fifth, the **Massif de Balme**, can be reached by road or chair lift. Here you ride down a red or black before taking the gondola back up.

Freeriders will like the less crowded area of the **Massif de Balme,** where a series of red runs and a long black that covers open slopes, allows you to ride off-piste, hitting some powder stashes. The **Combe du Fernuy** is the area that descends a red section, down a tree line onto a cool run, en route to the Massif de Balme area. There are lots of trees, but no great challenges.

Freestylers usually have a halfpipe and park on the **Massif de Balme** slopes, but neither are shit hot or particularly big. The way the area is spread out means that there is a lot of okay natural terrain for catching air, but this is not a great freestyle place.

Carvers are very well matched to all five areas. The slopes allow for some good, wide arcs on intermediate terrain; the longest run is on the **Balme** slopes, whilst on **Massif de Beauregard**, there's an interesting long run to tackle at speed.

Beginners can achieve a lot here, with slopes that are excellent for finding out what snowboarding is like at the early stages. The Beauregard and L'Etale areas have good, easy slopes; the only potential problem is that they are mostly serviced by drag lifts.

Off the slopes, the village has everything you would expect from a tourist trap. There's a good selection of beds ranging from expensive chalets to cheap, shared apartments. Accommodation shops, and restaurants are located within easy reach of the slopes, with many slope side hangouts. Evenings are dull and uneventful, unless you're a brain-dead aprés fan.

For accommodation listings visit - **www.worldsnowboardguide.com**

La Clusaz Tourist office
Place de L'Eglise BP7, La Clusaz
++33 (0) 450 326 500 www.laclusaz.com

Overall rating out of 10 **5** **Basic riding but still okay**

La Plagne

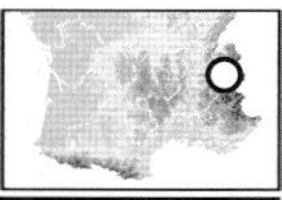

FRANCE

MOUNTAIN DATA

Top Lift at - 3250m

Ride Area 209km of piste

Bottom Lift at - 1800m

Vertical Drop - 2000m

Number of Runs - 123

Longest - 9 miles (15km)

TERRAIN LEVELS

Easy	**10%**
Intermediate	**84%**
Advanced	**6%**
Expert =	

TERRAIN TO SUITE

Freeride	**40%**
Trees	A few
Backcountry	Yes
Freestyle	**10%**
Halfpipe	Yes 1
Terrain Park	Yes 1
Carving	**50%**

SNOW DATA

Average Snowfall
520cm a season

Snowmaking
20 snow cannons

Winter Periods
Dec to April

Summer Riding
None

SLOPE ACCESS

Total Lifts = **110**

Uplift Rate - 117,000 people an hour.

8 Gondolas **1** Cable car

32 Chair lifts - **69** Drag lifts

**Leashes Required*

Lift Times
8.30am to 4.30pm

Lift Pass Rates

1 Day pass	175 Fr
6 Day pass	850 Fr
Season pass	

Travel Guide

Fly to **Lyon** which is 2 hours away.

Train services are possible to Aime, 10 minutes away.

Route Planner: Via Lyon, on A43 - A430 to Albertvile and then head south on the N90 to Moutiers , then N90 via Amie to La Plagne.
*Drive time from **Calais** is 10 hours 597 miles (960 km)

pic - La Plagne

There are 11 resorts that compose the **La Plange** boarding area, ranging from traditional villages to modern purpose high altitude resorts built resorts, some of which are horrible such as **Aime la Plange**, a single great apartment block. La Plange is mainly suited to intermediate boarders as there is not that much steep terrain and few challenging runs. There are some good wooded areas, which can be a blessing in white outs, especially around the areas of **Les Coches** and **Champagny**. This resort is ideally suited to the Euro carver with mile after mile of motorway cruising.

Freeriders, for advanced boarders there are some great runs down from the **Bellecote** glacier, which goes up to 3250m, so there shouldnt be a shortage of snow here even at the end of the season. You can also head off piste down to **Peisey- Nancroix** to link up to the Les Arcs area. In 2003 there will be a jumbo two-tiered cable car linking the 2 resorts that will only take 4 minutes, which will greatly improve the attractiveness of this resort. Another great long piste run runs from the top of **Les Verdons** down to **Champagny**, with a vertical drop of 1250m. It has some sweet trees to cruise through at the bottom, but you will have to catch it on a good day to get the best snow.

Freestylers won't find many natural hits in **La Plange**, but you can always use your shovel or go looking and you will find something to get some air off. There is a fun park at **Plange Soleil**.

Carvers are very well matched to all five areas. The slopes allow for some good, wide arcs on intermediate terrain; the longest run is on the **Balme** slopes, whilst on **Massif de Beauregard**, there's an interesting long run to tackle at speed.

Beginners can achieve a lot here, with slopes that are excellent for finding out what snowboarding is like at the early stages. The Beauregard and L'Etale areas have good, easy slopes; the only potential problem is that they are mostly serviced by drag lifts.

Off the slopes, the village has everything you would expect from a tourist trap. There's a good selection of beds ranging from expensive chalets to cheap, shared apartments. Accommodation shops, and restaurants are located within easy reach of the slopes, with many slope side hangouts. Evenings are dull and uneventful, unless you're a brain-dead aprés fan.

For accommodation listings visit - www.worldsnowboardguide.com

La Plagne
Le Chalet B.P 62, 73211 Aime, Cedex
++33 (0) 4 79 09 79 79   www.skifrance.fr/~laplagne

Overall rating out of 10 **4** **Okay slopes but cheesy town**

Les Arcs

MOUNTAIN DATA

Top Lift at - 3226m

Ride Area
241km of piste

Bottom Lift at - 1600m

Vertical Drop - 1626m
Number of Runs - 121
Longest - 4.3 miles (7km)

TERRAIN LEVELS

Easy	**50%**
Intermediate	**33%**
Advanced	**17%**
Expert =	

TERRAIN TO SUITE

Freeride	**40%**
Trees	Yes
Backcountry	Yes
Freestyle	**40%**
Halfpipe	Yes 2
Terrain Park	Yes 1
Carving	**20%**

SNOW DATA

Average Snowfall
500cm a season
Snowmaking
25% cover of the slopes
Winter Periods
Dec to April
Summer Riding
None

SLOPE ACCESS

Total Lifts = **79**
Uplift Rate - 68,000 people an hour.
5 Trains-Gondolas-Cables
29 Chair lifts - **45** Drag lifts
**Leashes Required*

Lift Times
8.30am to 4.30pm

Lift Pass Rates
1 Day pass 220 Fr
6 Day pass 1065Fr
Season pass

SLOPE ACTION

Snowboard Hire
Daily rates from 200 Fr
Kids from 189 Fr Sch

Snowboard Tuition
Group lessons, from from 220 Fr

Night Riding
Yes

Heli Boarding
No

Snowmobiles
Yes

Mountain Cafes
14

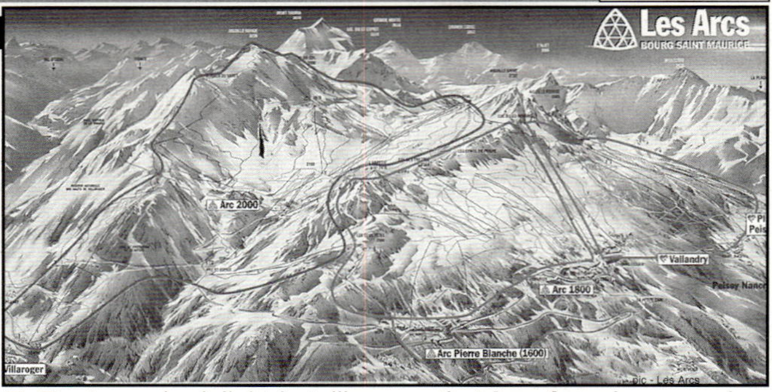

Most people delight in telling you that **Les Arcs** is a massive, concrete carbunkle on the arse of the French Alps - but these people probably haven't been here, let alone spent any sort of time in the place. Ignore such comments, come with an open mind, and ride one of the best sets of mountains in the world. Les Arcs itself is split into four distinctive resorts - **1600, 1800, 2000** and **Bourg-St-Maurice**. Each place has a different feel to it, so choose wisely. 1600, where most of the chalets are situated, is quite chilled out with loads of trees. 1800 is the party place, while 2000 is a bit hideous and isolated, but has good access to some amazing terrain. Despite having a huge riding area, Les Arcs has managed to retain a cosy feel as its dead easy to get from one area to another and you are only likely to run into heavy lift queues during the height of the French holidays. On the mountain, Les Arcs has it all, from mellow beginner slopes to some of the most challenging runs anywhere in France, with hardly any moguls. What Les Arcs does have however, is a lot of punters as this is a very popular resort, but with such a vast expanse of snow to explore, the slopes are left fairly quite.

Freeriders, it's all here and it's all good! If there is fresh snow on the ground, you can be guaranteed an amazing day through trees in **Peisey** or above **1600**, off cornices in **2000**, or just straightlining anything all day long. The area off the **Trans Arc** cable car gives access to some great off-piste riding.

Freestylers might not see a lot of jumps on first arrival, and in truth, there aren't many natural jumps waiting to be hit. However, there are plenty of kickers all over the place, especially in **Peisey, 2000** and high above **1800** - use your eyes and feel the force when you get up there. The hits on an area known as **Les Clocherets** are also worth a visit. If you're into man-made jumps, then there's a park above the Altiport restaurant, which should keep everyone happy from the grommet learning to jump, to the seasoned pro. However, it's true to say that the park is not well maintained, even though locals help out.

Carvers are in hard boot heaven here, with amazingly well groomed, wide open pistes, that are generally crowd free most of the time especially the higher grade runs. Les Arcs piste lends itself perfectly for big slashing turns. The **Mont Blanc** piste on 1600 is ideal for intermediate carvers, and the **Belette** and **Myrtille** runs are good for advanced carvers who can handle a board at speed.

Beginners are sorted here and it shouldn't be long before you're riding all over the place aided by the quality of the piste and the fact that most areas are connected by fairly easy trails and lifts. There are a lot of drag lifts, so expect a bit of embarrassment as you fall off after the first two yards.

The four areas of Les Arcs are somewhat spread out, although they link up by both lift and road. Each area has quick access to the slopes, making riding back to your accommodation the norm at the end of the day. 1800 is the most popular place to stay, where there is a good selection of apartment blocks and hotels. The best thing about all the areas is that prices for accommodation, eating out and partying are largely the same throughout, with something to appeal to everyone. The general feel to the whole area is one of a gigantic, spread-out holiday camp that rocks 'til late, looks tacky, but has heaps going on with all manner of sporting facilities and shopping.

No matter what area you base yourself in, you will be able to find somewhere that serves up food to your liking. The place is littered with restaurants with cheap and chearful offerings being the favoured selection. 1800 has the best offerings with places like *Mountain Cafe,* where they serve huge portions of everything including *Tex-Mex*. The *Red Rock Bar* is also noted for grills etc.

Night-life, you can pickle your liver during your stay with a large selection of pretty good lively bars in both **1600** or **1800.** *Cafe Sol* being the number one place to go in 1600, while up the road in **1800**, you should. check out the *Red Hot Saloon* before hitting the late spot, *Apokalypse*.

Accommodation: Many operators run package holidays using chalets, hotels and apartments throughout the resort. Prices vary however - you can rent an apartment for four people for a week from 2,500FF, loading in at least four more bodies, and then split the cost. Most lodging is next to the slopes, with nothing involving a long trek. *Thomson Holidays* ++44 (0) 0870 606 1470 offer a number of inclusive holiday trips.

For accommodation listings visit - www.worldsnowboardguide.com

Summary: A great freerider's resort with lots of off-piste and powder, plus natural hits to explore. A major busy tourist spot with a lively night-life.
Money wise: Very good value with budget options for accommodation.

Overall rating out of 10 **8**

Tourist Office Les Arcs
BP 45, 73706 Les Arcs
Bourg Saint Maurice

General info	**++33 (0) 4 79 07 12 57**
Reservations	**++33 (0) 4 79 07 12 57**
Avlanche info	**++33 (0) 836 681 020**

www.lesarcs.com

pic - A Snowboards

pic - Les Arcs

Travel Guide

Fly to **Lyon** international
Transfer time to resort = **2** hours.
Local airport = none

Approximate global air travel times to **Lyon:**

from:		
	London	**2** hours
	Los Angles	**13** hours
	New York	**9** hours

Bus services from Lyon airport, are available on a daily basis via Bourg St Maurice to Les Arcs.

Trains to **Bourg-St-Maurice**
10 min utes away

Route Planner
Lyon

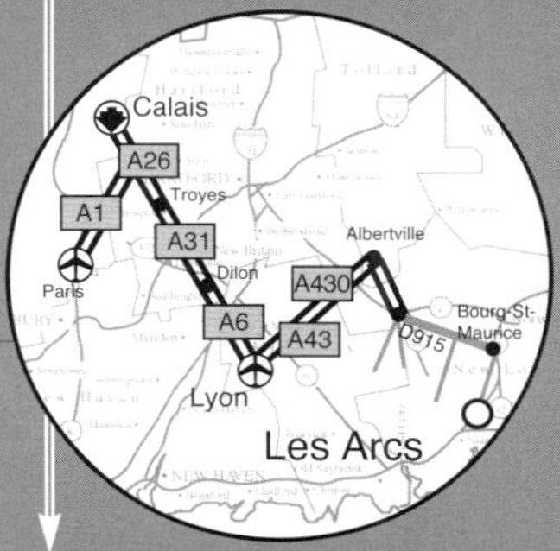

Les Arcs = 130 miles (210 km)
Drive time is about **2** hours

*From **Calais** 709 miles (1140 Km)
Drive time is around **11½** hours.

Les Deux Alpes

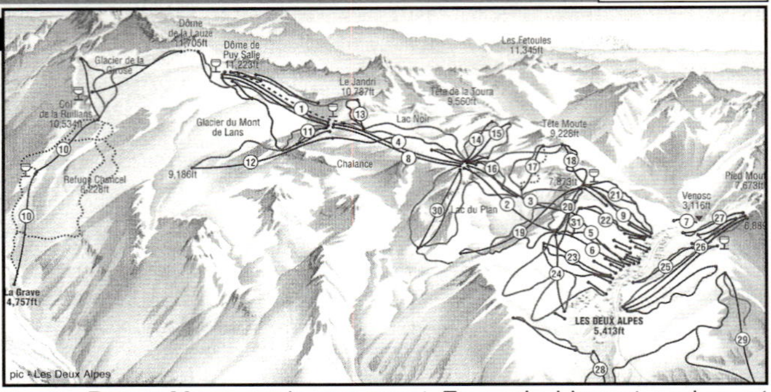

MOUNTAIN DATA

Top Lift at - 3568m

Ride Area 200km of piste

Bottom Lift at - 1270m

Vertical Drop - 2298m

Number of Runs - 70

Longest - 7.5 miles (9km)

TERRAIN LEVELS

Easy	**61%**
Intermediate	**27%**
Advanced	**12%**
Expert =	

TERRAIN TO SUITE

Freeride	**40%**
Trees	No
Backcountry	Yes
Freestyle	**10%**
Halfpipe	Yes 1
Terrain Park	Yes 1
Carving	**50%**

SNOW DATA

Average Snowfall

Snowmaking
20% cover of the slopes

Winter Periods
Nov to April

Summer Riding
May to October

SLOPE ACCESS

Total Lifts = **64**

Uplift Rate - 68,000 people an hour.

5 Trains-Gondolas-Cables

24 Chair lifts - **33** Drag lifts

**Leashes Required*

Lift Times
8.30am to 8.30pm

Lift Pass Rates
1 Day pass 195 Fr
6 Day pass 960 Fr
Season pass

SLOPE ACTION

Snowboard Hire
Daily rates from 185 Fr
Kids from 165 Fr

Snowboard Tuition
Group lessons, from from 190 Fr

Night Riding
Yes

Heli Boarding
Yes

Snowmobiles
Yes

Mountain Cafes
6

Les Deux Alpes ranks amongst France's biggest and most friendly resorts. Not just friendly, but snowboard-friendly. Home to world class performers like Alexis Parmentier, the resort has plenty of testing and rider-friendly terrain. As a glacial resort, when other areas are suffering from a lack of the white stuff, Les Deux Alpes has no such problem. The end of October sees the now legendary **Mondial**, a huge event that attracts most of the world's snowboard equipment manufacturers, holding a 'come and try it' session of next season's kit. Hand in your passport, and ride off on next year's board! Five thousand boarders, an ISF Big Air jump, a boardercross and full-on night-life, makes it a wild time. A great time to vist this place is summer, as the glacier allows for some fine summer riding in T-shirts. A lot of camps are held here in June and July, with camp programmes mainly aimed at freestylers.

Freeriders While skiers with poor imagination brand it a motorway resort, the same is not true for boarders. When there is a fresh dump, you can ride almost everywhere you can see - the off-piste is huge and challenging. The only terrain missing is that of trees, but with a free day on the lift pass in nearby **Serre Chevalier**, tree huggers should feel catered for. Check out the Dome for a powdergasm, and routes off the new 6-man chair, La Fee, for steep, deep and testing riding.

Freestylers can pipe and park ride all year round. Winter sees the park located at the mid-station with a well prepared pipe and a permanent boardercross course. In the summer, the park is on the glacier, which features in virtually every European snowboard video, such is its reputation. Summer sees the addition of two pipes serviced by a separate drag lift and the funicular train under the glacier.

Carvers This is an alpine rider's dream retreat, with nicely pisted runs like the **Roch-Mantel** and the **Signal** for a warm up. The glacier itself is great for ballistic speed. The **Sandri** run at the foot of the glacier to the mid-station is a warp factor 9, if you adhere to the essential turn only rule. So, for those of you who think turning is to admit defeat, tuck'em away and go for it.

Beginners starting out couldn't ask for a better place to make steady progress. The only problem is that the home runs down the front face are amongst the steepest in the resort, but there is a winding green run as an alternative. A real bonus is that the gentlest terrain is at the very top of the resort, where you can find the best snow. Due to the layout of the lift system, other than your first morning on the beginner's slope, you need never take a drag for the remainder of your stay. The chairlifts, gondolas and other lifts make the whole uplift problem easier to sort out than a wonderbra, which should please the wimps.

Off the slopes and at the base of the runs, Les Deux Alpes sits conveniently for most local services, but being a large town, not everything is within walking distance. The resort is a mix of old school and purpose-buildings, with accommodation ranging from quaint chalets, ritzy hotels, to apartment blocks that wouldn't look out of place in a New York suburb. There are loads of off-slope services, including a cinema, bowling alley, sports complex and an outdoor climbing wall. There are lots of the usual shopping outlets, and a mini-mall selling the usual tourist junk and pricey snowboard gear. It should also be pointed out that this is a busy package tour destination.

Food-wise, this place caters well for people on a budget, as well as those who want to splash out. There are some reasonably priced pizza and burger bars that are very good indeed. The Thai takeaway is much better than the disappointing Chinese. For a Tex-Mex, visit *Smokey Joes* or *Saxo* - also home to some of France's loveliest bar staff (top french tottie).

Night-life goes off seven nights a week, and it's common to see aprés-ski idiots throwing up all over the place early on, having had a glass of gluwein at a poxy teatime bonding session. Okay for a laugh is the *Brazilian Bar*, while *Mike's* and the *Dutch Bar* are for those who just want to get wasted.

Accommodation: Standard grade apartment blocks, and a number of traditional-style chalets and modern hotels at prices that won't always hurt. *Chalet Snowboard* ++44(0)1235 767 575 is the place to check into here - they offer full weekly packages from 3,400FF, and have a *Burton* test centre and snowboard guiding services. *Thomson Holidays* ++44 (0) 0870 606 1470 offer a number of inclusive holiday trips.

For accommodation listings visit - www.worldsnowboardguide.com

Summary: Good all-year, all-style resort, with some great carving terrain and good off-piste, but the place can be hellish busy at weekends and over holidays
Money wise: This is not a cheap resort, but with prudence you can manage

Overall rating out of 10 **7**

Tourist Office Les Deux Alpes
BP 7-38860.
Les Deux Alpes
General info **++33 (0) 4 76 79 22 00**
Reservations **++33 (0) 4 76 79 22 00**
Avlanche info **++33 (0) 836 681 020**
www.les2alpes.com

pic - Johnny Barr

Travel Guide

Fly to **Lyon** international
Transfer time to resort = **2** hours.
Local airport = Grenoble

Approximate global air travel times to **Lyon:**
from: London **2** hours
Los Angles **13** hours
New York **9** hours

Bus services from Lyon airport, are available on a daily basis via Grenoble to Les Arcs.

Trains to **Grenoble** (25 minutes)

Route Planner
Lyon

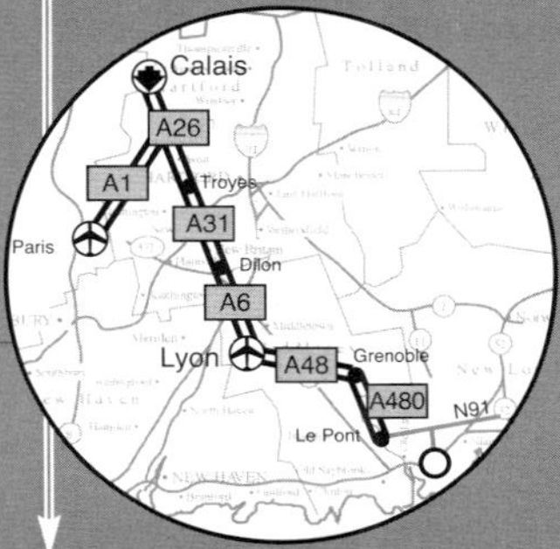

Les Deux Alpes = **106** miles (170 km)
Drive time is about **2** hours

*From **Calais** 571 miles (950 Km)
Drive time is around **9¾** hours.

Meribel

pic - San Tang

MOUNTAIN DATA

Top Lift at - 952m

Ride Area 150km of piste

Bottom Lift at - 1400m

Vertical Drop - 1200m

Number of Runs - 76

Longest - 2.5 miles (4km)

TERRAIN LEVELS

Easy	58%
Intermediate	28%
Advanced	14%
Expert =	

TERRAIN TO SUITE

Freeride	40%
Trees	Yes
Backcountry	Yes
Freestyle	20%
Halfpipe	Yes 2
Terrain Park	Yes 1
Carving	40%

SNOW DATA

Average Snowfall
500cm a season

Snowmaking
26% cover of the slopes

Winter Periods
Dec to April

Summer Riding
None

SLOPE ACCESS

Total Lifts = **60**

Uplift Rate - 50,000 people an hour.

16 Gondolas

24 Chair lifts - **20** Drag lifts

**Leashes Required*

Lift Times
8.30am to 4.30pm

Lift Pass Rates

3 Day pass 526 Fr
6 Day pass 897 Fr
Season pass

Travel Guide

Fly to **Lyon,** which has a 2¼ hour transfer time.

Train services go to Moutiers, 10 minutes away

Route Planner: Via Lyon, head south to Moutiers via A432, A43, N90 and then the D915 to Meribel
*Drive time from **Calais** is 9¾ hours
585 miles (941 km) **Calais**

Meribel is certainly the place to avoid if you don't like hordes of British skiers, due partly to the large number of British owned chalets here. However, don't be put off too easily as Meribel has loads to offer all ages and abilities. This resort has serious amounts of terrain as it's linked to the Three Valleys with 600km of piste and great snowmaking facilities. So despite its relatively low altitude, you can nearly always board to the base.

Freeriders have a massive area to explore in areas like the **Campagnol** and **Combe Vallon**, there is some off piste to be had in the **Glacier du Borgne**, although go with a guide if you want to go seriously out of bounds. Meribel provides links to some more great adventures in the Three Valleys area, with links to **Val Thorens** and **Les Menuires**. Be careful with the last lifts though as a taxi back to Meribel will heavily eat into your drinking money. If you are looking for some powder head over towards the edge of the **Reserve Naturelle de Tueda**, but be careful not to enter the national park closed zone.

Freestylers are presented with two halfpipes, a boardercross track and a fun park which allow for some serious air time. The main pipe and park are located at **Plattieres 2,** with the other at the **Arpasson** drag near to **Tougnette** mid station.

Carvers will find some really sweet runs over the mountain to **St Martin de Belleville**, like **Jerusalem**. The **Burgin-Saulire** gondla takes you up to 2738m, where you have a number of choices. You can take the reds or blacks into **Courchevel 1850**, which can get quite busy at peak times, or head back down to **Mottaret**. For some gentle cruising try **Chamois** then **Biche**.

Beginners have lots of opportunities to master those linked turns around the **Altiport** area, although some of the lifts are very old and slow. The **Rhodos** lift that services this area is one of the latest to close so you'll have plenty of time to practice.

Meribel is so tainted with the UK's so called upper class ski twits, that to stay here is almost a crime. But if you want any sort of night-life, food, or use of a toilet, then Meribel will do. However, **Mottaret** has the cheapest lodging and the easiest access to the valley's ride areas. Most of the idiots that flock here stay in the snootier scene of Meribel, where everything is expensive and night-life is ruined by the aprés-skiing Brits.

For accommodation listings visit - www.worldsnowboardguide.com

Tourist Office Meribel
BP1, F-732551 Meribel
++33 (0) 4 79 08 60 01 www.meribel.com

Overall rating out of 10 **5** **Criminally stuck up**

Montgenevre

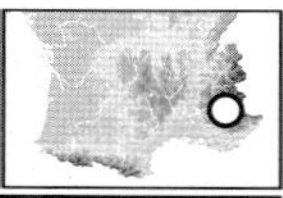

FRANCE

MOUNTAIN DATA

Top Lift at - 2680m

Ride Area
64km of piste

Bottom Lift at - 1850m
Vertical Drop - 1300m
Number of Runs - 45
Longest - 4.3 miles (7km)

TERRAIN LEVELS

Easy	**49%**
Intermediate	**32%**
Advanced	**19%**
Expert =	

TERRAIN TO SUITE

Freeride	**30%**
Trees	A few
Backcountry	Yes
Freestyle	**5%**
Halfpipe	Yes 1
Terrain Park	Yes 1
Carving	**65%**

SNOW DATA

Average Snowfall

Snowmaking
26% cover of the slopes
Winter Periods
Dec to April
Summer Riding
None

SLOPE ACCESS

Total Lifts = **24**
Uplift Rate - 6500 people an hour.
2 Gondolas
8 Chair lifts - **16** Drag lifts
**Leashes Required*

Lift Times
8.30am to 4.30pm

Lift Pass Rates
1 Day pass 150 Fr
6 Day pass 750 Fr
Season pass

Travel Guide

Fly to **Turin** in Italy which is 1 hour away.

Train services are go to to Briancon, 10 away.

Route Planner: Via Turin head west along the A21 and the E70, turning off at Oulx and precede down the B24 to Montgenevre
*Drive time from
Calais is 10½ hours
622 miles (1001 km)

pic - Montgenevre Tourism

Montgenevre forms the only French part of a circuit known as the **Milky Way**: a collection of resorts that extends along a number of valley floors and criss-crosses over into **Italy. Montgenevre** is basically at the opposite end to its more famous relation, the Italian resort of **Sauze d 'Oulx.** Collectively, the circuit offers over 250 miles of rideable terrain on slopes that have a good, reliable snow record, thanks to the average height of each area. Montgenevre's own 65km of marked out trails are an interesting mixture of mainly intermediate trails and poor, advanced terrain, rising from the village which is at an altitude of 1850m. Although this is a popular tourist resort, it is not as tainted with package tours as some other resorts in the region. Easy access to the slopes is made possible by a number of base lifts that will take you up to the main slopes of **Les Anges** and **Le Querelay** areas, or in the opposite direction to **Le Chalvet.**

Freeriders can cut decent off-piste powder and ride some nice tree lines, although you won't find much of it a great challenge. The trails on **Le Chalvet,** located in what tends to be the quietest area to ride, give access to some cool freeride terrain and has a nice big powder bowl.

Freestylers are presented with what they call a fun-park, but in truth it is a little dire with only a few man-made hits. The best options for air is to seek out the natural terrain features.

Carvers are a common sight here, with boy wonders in hards posing on **Les Anges** and **Le Querelay**, which are both popular and easy. The two blacks down the **Pian del Sole** en route to the village of **Claviere**, are a little more interesting and worth a blast.

Beginners are well catered for here, with a host of easy trails that can be reached (having first studied the piste map), without needing to ride a drag lift. Fast learners will soon be able to ride from the summit of **Les Anges** to the base, via a mixture of blue trails.

Local facilities are based conveniently for the slopes with a mixture of apartment blocks, chalets, shops, sporting facilities and restaurants, styled in a sober manner but aimed at the package tour ski groups. The village is okay, although there isn't a great deal to get excited about. Lodging is very affordable, whilst evenings can be very lively, with a number of bars that have young crowds partying every night all night.

For accommodation listings visit - www.worldsnowboardguide.com

Montgenevre Tourist Office
F-05100, Hautes Alpes. Montgenevre
++33 (0) 4 92 21 90 22 www.

Overall rating out of 10 **4** **Okay but basic**

Risoul

MOUNTAIN DATA

Top Lift at - 2750m

Ride Area
161km of piste

Bottom Lift at - 1650m
Vertical Drop - 1100m
Number of Runs - 104
Longest - 5 miles (8km)

TERRAIN LEVELS

Easy	40%
Intermediate	34%
Advanced	11%
Expert =	

TERRAIN TO SUITE

Freeride	40%
Trees	Yes
Backcountry	Yes
Freestyle	35%
Halfpipe	Yes 1
Terrain Park	Yes 1
Carving	40%

SNOW DATA

Average Snowfall

Snowmaking
10% cover of the slopes

Winter Periods
Dec to April

Summer Riding
None

SLOPE ACCESS

Total Lifts = **55**
Uplift Rate - 41,000 people an hour.
1 Gondola
13 Chair lifts - **41** Drag lifts
**Leashes Required*

Lift Times
8.30am to 4.30pm

Lift Pass Rates
1 Day pass 185 Fr
6 Day pass 880 Fr
Season pass

Travel Guide

Fly to **Grenoble,** 2 1/4 hours transfer time.

Train services go to on Dauphin which 20 minutes.

Route Planner: Via Grenoble head south east along route 91 via Briancon. 117 miles.
*Drive time from **Calais** is 9 3/4 hours 585 miles (941 km)

pic - Ride Snowboards

Risoul is located between **Gap** and **Briancon**, and combined with the neighbouring resort **Vars**, the whole area offers about 170 km of terrain. The big men of the resort are more than happy to have snowboarders here, since the image of non-conformity fits in nicely with the way the resort is run - clearly with the young in mind. **Risoul 1850** offers everything from easy slopes for beginners, to double black diamond runs for extreme freaks.

Freeriders tend to show up here around New Year in search of decent terrain, which they can find on **Pic de Razies, Melezet** and **Platte De La Nonne**, or **Pic De La Mayt**. Ride in these big powder bowl areas, and you can forget about sex being the best thing in the world. One warning - you won't decide on which is your favourite run for days or even weeks, as there are so many damn good ones.

Freestylers should take **De Cezier** chair to reach **Surfland,** where the jibbing begins. This playground (which is akin to paradise), offers a complete boardercross run, rails, several quarter-pipes, small practice kickers, a pro-jump over a bus, and one of the best halfpipes in Europe. 100m long, 20m wide and with 3m walls, this pipe will probably offer you more air-time than you actually want. Every Friday night there's a high-jump contest, with local riders jumping to World Pro Tour levels (there's also a barbecue in the evening).

Carvers All the slopes are designed and prepared for hardcore edge-to-edge activities, and there are even special slopes for race practice (poles available at the ski school).

Beginners If you take the cabin lift named **Accueil**, you'll find the area that Risoul has set aside for its snowboard kindergarten - the short and easy run is perfect for your first try on a board. There are also two small, slow drag lifts to practice on, before going up into the real snowboard world.

Risoul is a small village where the inhabitants still treat you as a guest. There is a good selection of slopeside accommodation, with seven nights in an apartment costing around 800fr per rider. Eating out is cool at places like *Snack Attack*, but for night-life, head to the *Yeti* (little Holland), where you must drink more booze than the Dutch dude, then leave him on the floor and take off with his girlfriend.

For accommodation listings visit - **www.worldsnowboardguide.com**

Tourist Risoul
Risoul F-05600 Guillestre, Hautes-Alpes
++33 (0) 4 92 46 02 60

Overall rating out of 10 **6** **Cool palce to ride**

St Lary

FRANCE

MOUNTAIN DATA

Top Lift at - 2450m

Ride Area
90km of piste

Bottom Lift at - 1600m
Vertical Drop - 850m
Number of Runs - 40
Longest - 2.5 miles (4km)

TERRAIN LEVELS

Easy	74%
Intermediate	14%
Advanced	12%
Expert =	

TERRAIN TO SUITE

Freeride	40%
Trees	No
Backcountry	Poor
Freestyle	5%
Halfpipe	Yes 1
Terrain Park	Yes 1
Carving	50%

SNOW DATA

Average Snowfall

Snowmaking
10% cover of the slopes
Winter Periods
Dec to April
Summer Riding
None

SLOPE ACCESS

Total Lifts = **32**
Uplift Rate - 25,000 people an hour.
2 Cable cars
9 Chair lifts - **22** Drag lifts
**Leashes Required*

Lift Times
8.30am to 4.30pm

Lift Pass Rates
1 Day pass 180 Fr
6 Day pass 790 Fr
Season pass

Travel Guide

Fly to **Tarbes** airport in Spain 2 hours away.

Train services go to Lannemezan, 20 minutes.

Route Planner: Via Tarbes, head south on the D935 and D929 towards the Spannish Border to Reach St Lary.
*Drive time from **Calais** is 12[1/4] hours
700 miles (1126 km)

pic - St Lary

The main village of **Saint Lary** lies at 630 metres in the Aure Valley; above here there are two smaller villages, **Saint Lary La Cabane** at **1,600** metres, and **Saint Lary Pla D'Adret** at 1,700 metres. All three are connected by a series of lifts, with the upper villages reachable by road, or from Saint Lary by the cable car which takes you to the slopes. This relatively small resort lies in the **French Pyranees** and goes back to the 1950's. If you think that French ski resorts are massive purpose-built shams, this place will make you think again. What you get is a resort that is very snowboard-friendly, with good terrain that can be tackled by any rider. However, this is also a popular resort which results in a number of long lift queues, especially at weekends.

Freeriders looking for vast powder bowls are not going to get them here. Advanced and hardcore riders wanting major long steeps are going to find this place a bit easy without too many challenges. The cluster of black runs off the **Tortes** chair offers some opportunities for freeriders to excel on fairly featureless terrain. Alternatively, the area known as **Bassia** is pretty cool, and will suit riders looking for trees to shred.

Carvers looking for fast, wide piste to lay out big turns on will find the few reds that are available are basic but okay. They should also provide novices who are getting to grips with a hard boot set up, some early learning opportunities.

Freestylers will find the snowboard park on **Vallon Du Portet** interesting, with its long boardercross circuit, a not-so-good pipe, and a series of hits.

Beginners will certainly find the easy blues spread out across the resort perfect for learning, with a mixture of chair lifts and drags to ferry you around. The short easy stuff reached from **Saint Lary Pla D'Adret** will sort you out, before taking the runs over on **Vallon Du Portet**. The **Corniche** is a long, easy blue that freeriding novices will soon be able to handle.

An old *Pyrennean* village, **St Lary** is laid out along a main street where you'll find chalets and hotels. Services are extremely good here, without the hustle and bustle of tourist traps. Although somewhat limited, most facilities are found in Saint Lary, rather than the other two villages. Eating and night-time hangouts are okay: quiet, tame but inexpensive.

For accommodation listings visit - www.worldsnowboardguide.com

Saint Lary Tourist Office
37 Rue Principale, St Lary Soulan. F-65170
++33 (0) 5 62 39 50 81

Overall rating out of 10 **6** **Okay resort but very basic**

Sainte-Foy

MOUNTAIN DATA

Top Lift at - 2620m

Ride Area
24km of piste

Bottom Lift at - 1550m
Vertical Drop - 1070m
Number of Runs -
Longest - 4.3 miles (7km)

TERRAIN LEVELS

Easy	23%
Intermediate	54%
Advanced	23%
Expert =	

TERRAIN TO SUITE

Freeride	**60%**
Trees	A few
Backcountry	Yes
Freestyle	**30%**
Halfpipe	No
Terrain Park	No
Carving	**10%**

SNOW DATA

Average Snowfall

Snowmaking
0% cover of the slopes
Winter Periods
Dec to April
Summer Riding
None

SLOPE ACCESS

Total Lifts = **5**
Uplift Rate - 12,000 people an hour.
5 Chair lifts

**Leashes Required*

Lift Times
8.30am to 4.30pm

Lift Pass Rates
1 Day pass 165 Fr
6 Day pass 780 Fr
Season pass

Travel Guide

Fly to **Geneva,** 2 1/2 hours transfer time.

Train services to Bourg-St-Maurice, 20 minutes away.

Route Planner: Via Bourg-St-Maurice take the N90 direction Tignes and Val d'Isere for Saint -Foy

*Drive time from **Calais** is 13 hours 568 miles (915 km)

pic - Soft Snapper

Sainte-Foy is a gem of a place and one that is still a bit of a secret. This natural, off-piste heaven is no match, in terms of ride area, to some of its near neighbours like Tignes. But so what the great thing here is that you don't have to run the gauntlet of ski-school upon ski-school lining every slope, or millions of package tour numpties wearing their finest holiday clothes, topped off with those sick headbands carrying the name of their favourite resort. No, this place is a purist's hangout; snowboarders come here because they want to snowboard, and therefore are prepared to put themselves out. The few runs are mostly unpisted trails that are well balanced, and both beginner and advanced riders will find a week's visit well worth the effort.

Freeriders Before you hit these slopes, note all the rules, since this quiet place is well known for avalanches. Don't head off without a guide, who can be hired on a daily basis. Once on the mountain, freeriders are furnished with some excellent, natural terrain that will make you wet yourself with excitment at the very sight. You can ride from top to bottom on pleasers such as **Crystal** and **Cret-Creu**, which offer marked descents that serve up a portion of powder, garnished with a side order of trees. After a short trek from the L'Aiguille, you will gain access to an orgasmic area of powder and long chutes.

Freestylers need to discover how to seek out natural hits, since that's all you're going to get - but that's all you're going to need! Why bother making pipes in a natural heaven - they're better left to the tourist traps. Riding will never be as free or as natural as in this place. There are a couple of drop ins and plenty of banked walls just waiting to be hit, but novice air heads must take care and ride only with a competent rider who can pre-spot for you.

Carvers carry on past this resort and pose in **Val d'Isere**, where you will fit in much better. This is not a hard boot resort at all.

Beginners have much to be pleased about with some nice gentle rollers to practise on.

Off the slopes, you will find nothing like a purpose-built resort; in fact, you'll find nothing other than a few barns and the odd cow at rest. There is lodging close by, but it's spread out with no connections to night-life or eateries. But then, if you ride this place as it should be ridden, you won't want for anything else.

For accommodation listings visit - **www.worldsnowboardguide.com**

Tourist office Sainte-Foy

++33 (0) 4 79 06 95 19 **www.**

Overall rating out of 10 — **6** — **Basic but great freeriding**

St Gervais

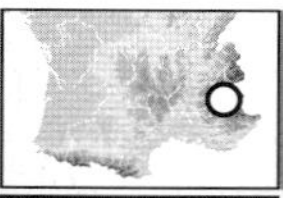

FRANCE

MOUNTAIN DATA

Top Lift at - 2353m
Ride Area
220km of piste
Bottom Lift at - 810m
Vertical Drop - 1542m
Number of Runs - 71
Longest - 1.9 miles (3km)

TERRAIN LEVELS

Easy	17%
Intermediate	70%
Advanced	13%
Expert =	

TERRAIN TO SUITE

Freeride	45%
Trees	A few
Backcountry	Yes
Freestyle	35%
Halfpipe	Yes 1
Terrain Park	Yes 1
Carving	20%

SNOW DATA

Average Snowfall

Snowmaking
20 snow cannons
Winter Periods
Dec to April
Summer Riding
None

SLOPE ACCESS

Total Lifts = **41**
Uplift Rate - 25,000 people an hour.
1 Tram - **2** Condolas
13 Chair lifts - **24** Drag lifts
**Leashes Required*

Lift Times
8.30am to 4.30pm

Lift Pass Rates

1 Day pass	188 Fr
3 Day pass	460 Fr
6 Day pass	880 Fr

Travel Guide

Fly to **Geneva** airport 50 minutes away.

Train services go to Le Fayet, 2minutes away.

Route Planner:
Via Paris, head down the A6 to Macon then take the A40 to St Gervais

*Drive time from **Calais** is 9 hours 544 miles (875 km)

pic - St Gervais

Despite its proximity to **Mont Blanc** and the ever popular **Chamonix**, **St Gervais** is not a very well known resort, probably due to the fact that no major tour operators go there. St Gervais itself is fairly small, but the lift pass **(Evasion Mont-Blanc)** covers 6 ski areas comprising of over 450km of slopes and some easily accessible off piste areas. It is also one of the areas covered on the *Ski Pass Mont Blanc* which allows access to the whole of the Mont Blanc region, (12 areas).

Freeriders should check out the huge wide open bowls at **Les Contamines,** where there is varied off piste riding almost everywhere you look. It's best when visibility and snow are good though, as if it is cloudy you will just get frustrated that you are missing all the best lines and hitting all the hidden cat-tracks. **Mont-Joy** has some good steep off-piste riding. It is possible to ride right down to Les Contamines, but taking a guide to avoid accidental cliff drops is highly recommended.

Freestylers have a fun park at **Mont Joux**, although it is not very impressive and seems to be rather neglected, particularly the halfpipe. The few jumps range from a small table top to a 30ft gap jump. It also gets very busy at times, especially weekends.

Carvers will find plenty of wide pistes, although some of them do tend to get chopped up by the end of the day. There are slalom courses at **Mont Joux** and across **Megeve** at **Rochebrune.**

Beginners can save money by getting a lift pass for just the **Bettex** area, which has a few nursery slopes, including one chair-lift. However, the slopes on the other side of the mountain tend to get more sun and are less icy. The areas around the **Mont d'Arbois** and **Ideal** lifts are recommended as there are a variety of easy runs as well as some easily reached harder ones for when you start feeling brave. The low point for beginners are the flat bits on the runs back down to **Bettex**.

Around the mountain there is a good choice of accommodation in **St. Gervais**, with over 30 hotels, chalets, lodges and apartments. A lot of these are located below the **St. Gervais-Bettex** gondola, so theoretically you can ride to your door, snow permitting. Local services are good and include ice skating, ice climbing, a cinema, loads of shops and a large number of restaurants. Night life, however, is tame and limited to one main club which is crap.

For accommodation listings visit - www.worldsnowboardguide.com

Tourist office St Gervais
115 av. du Mont-Paccard. F-74170 St Gervais
++33 (0) 450 47 76 08   E-mail: welcome@st-gervais.net

Overall rating out of 10 **6** **Cool but simple resort**

Serre Chevalier

MOUNTAIN DATA

Top Lift at - 3850m

Ride Area
200km of piste

Bottom Lift at - 1200m

Vertical Drop - 1630m
Number of Runs - 110
Longest - 6 miles (10km)

TERRAIN LEVELS

Easy	**42%**
Intermediate	**46%**
Advanced	**12%**
Expert =	

TERRAIN TO SUITE

Freeride	**60%**
Trees	Yes
Backcountry	Yes
Freestyle	**30%**
Halfpipe	Yes 1
Terrain Park	Yes 1
Carving	**10%**

SNOW DATA

Average Snowfall

Snowmaking
15% cover of the slopes
Winter Periods
Nov to April
Summer Riding

SLOPE ACCESS
Total Lifts = **74**
Uplift Rate - 68,000 people an hour.
6 Gondolas **3** Cables
18 Chair lifts - **47** Drag lifts
**Leashes Required*

Lift Times
8.30am to 8.30pm

Lift Pass Rates
1 Day pass 191 Fr
6 Day pass 970 Fr
Season pass

SLOPE ACTION

Snowboard Hire
Daily rates from 190 Fr
Kids from 185 Fr

Snowboard Tuition
Group lessons, from
from 620 Fr a day

Night Riding
Yes

Heli Boarding
Yes

Snowmobiles
Yes

Mountain Cafes
10

pic - Serre Chevalier

Serre Chevalier is one of the best places to ride in France. This great resort has heaps of major terrain, tight, open trees to weave, extreme drop offs to get the adrenaline going, big bowls with silly amounts of good powder, countless banks and gullies, super-fast flats to push the hair back, hits everywhere, and a giant, natural fun-park - all located next to an unassuming, old-fashioned French village (with a hint of the new here and there). As one local rider once put it 'who needs fun-parks, when this place is a complete fun-park at every level and distinction!' Serre Chevalier is suitable for everyone, with an area that links up with **Briancon** and **Le Monetier**, to provide 230km of terrain. Serre Chevalier is the largest of the three areas, and also the place for the best terrain and action. However, being a great resort does have its drawbacks as this is a major destination for package tour operators. This causes which has the result of causing some long lift lines first thing in the morning, but once up, things become a lot better.

Freeriders get to shred plenty of open, tight trees, gullies and deep bowls, as well as some long steeps, where advanced riders can busy themselves for weeks on end. Serre Chevalier is perfect soft boot territory, and those riders wanting wide expanses of powder without having to hike, should check out the stuff off the **Balme** chair lift.

Freestylers should basically session the whole mountain as there are too many hits to mention - it will take most riders at least a season to hit each jump only once. The place is a super-big, natural fun-park, with lots of logs to grind, and loads of big jumps everywhere. There's also a man-made pipe at the lower section of the **Yret** chair on **Le Monetier's** slopes should you need it.

Carvers are presented with as much alpine terrain as they could possibly need. If you have the bottle, the **Olympique** trail is a fast, black race run that bases out in the village of Chantemerle, and will certainly get the adrenaline pumping. You can get someserious speed down the Olympique trail, and although advanced riders and competent intermediate boarders will manage, novices should give this run a miss (unless they have a death wish).

Beginners should find the runs around **Frejus** more suited to their needs, with a number of long, easy runs that bring you back down the mountain into the village of **Villeneuve**, via some tree-lined trails. Serre Chevalier has a lot of drag lifts - some of which can be a nightmare, often travelling a long way at speeds suited to riding down, not up. Watch out for the sharp turns that some of the drag lifts make through the trees. If you can master Serre Chevalier's drag lifts, you shouldn't have any trouble in the rest of the world.

Serre Chevalier provides a number of options for lodging and other local services. These are situated along a stretched-out valley road, set back from the base lifts. **Briancon** is the largest place to stay, but is not so convenient for the main slopes, whereas the villages of **Chantemerle** and **Villeneuve** (a few miles apart, linked on the slopes and by road), offer the best facilities nearer the slopes. There are plenty of shops as well as good watering holes, but there is one small blip on Serre Chevalier's otherwise shining record: it's a tourist trap that attracts a number of British and Italian tour companies, who bring in far too many package groups.

Your dietary needs are well sorted here, with a vast selection of restaurants and fast-food outlets to choose from, including a number of creperies. *Le Frog* (please), is known for its French cuisine, as is the *Yeti*, *Nocthambule* and *Le Refuge*. For a decent fish meal, *La Bidulle* is highly recommended and is located in Villeneuve. *L'Amphore* is the place for a slab of pizza

Night-life is somewhat mixed here, with some happening and lively bars but also a few sad and very expensive disco's, Night life rocks until late in most bars so you don't need the clubs. Check out the likes of the *Iceberg* or *Yeti Bar,* where they often have live music. The *White Hare* is a cool hangout.

Accommodation: 30,000 visitors can be bedded around here. The choices range from a bunk house and modern apartment blocks for groups on the cheap, to classy hotels. *Handmade Holidays* offer excellent hotel and apartment style lodging only 100m from the slopes (they also own the Yeti and Underground bars that both rock until late tel +44 (0) 1453 885 599).

For accommodation listings visit - www.worldsnowboardguide.com

Summary: Without doubt, one of the best resort in France. Great freeriding with powder and full-on, freestyle terrain. The one bug is the hordes of skiers.
Money wise; Not the cheapest of resorts, but its worth every penny.

Overall rating out of 10 **10**

Tourist Office Serre Chevalier
BP 20-05240
La Salle Les Alpes
General info **++33 (0) 4 92 24 74 43**
Reservations **++33 (0) 4 92 24 74 43**
Avlanche info **++33 (0) 836 681 020**
www.serre-chevalier.com

pics - Serre Chevalier

Travel Guide

Fly to **Lyon** international
Transfer time to resort = **3** hours.
Local airport = Grenoble

Approximate global air travel times to **Lyon:**

from:		
	London	2 hours
	Los Angles	13 hours
	New York	9 hours

Bus services from Lyon airport, are available on a daily basis direct to Briancion.

Trains to **Briancion** (5 minutes)

Route Planner
Lyon

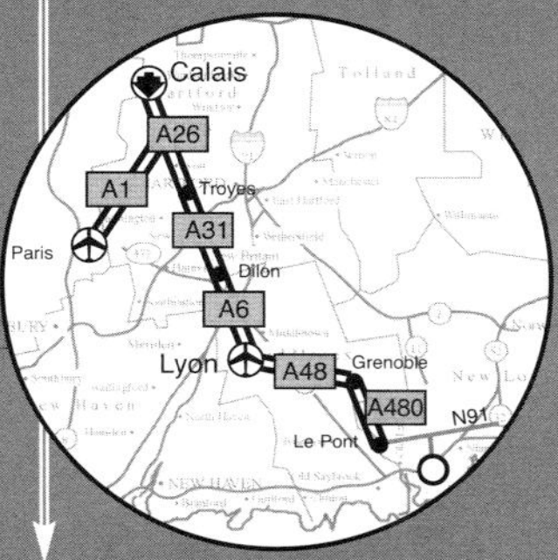

Serre Chevalier = **130** miles (209 km)
Drive time is about 3 hours

*From **Calais** 598 miles (962 Km)
Drive time is around **10½** hours.

Tignes

MOUNTAIN DATA

Top Lift at - 3450m

Ride Area
300km of piste

Bottom Lift at - 1550m

Vertical Drop - 1900m
Number of Runs - 65
Longest - 4 miles (6km)

TERRAIN LEVELS

Easy	**62%**
Intermediate	**29%**
Advanced	**9%**
Expert =	

TERRAIN TO SUITE

Freeride	**50%**
Trees	A few
Backcountry	Yes
Freestyle	**25%**
Halfpipe	Yes 2
Terrain Park	Yes 1
Carving	**25%**

SNOW DATA

Average Snowfall
500cm a season
Snowmaking
40% cover of the slopes
Winter Periods
Nov to April
Summer Riding
May to September

SLOPE ACCESS

Total Lifts = **74**
Uplift Rate 135,000 people an hour.
4 Trains-Gondolas-Cables
25 Chair lifts - **18** Drag lifts
**Leashes Required*

Lift Times
8.30am to 8.30pm

Lift Pass Rates

1 Day pass	228 Fr
6 Day pass	1070 Fr
Season pass	

SLOPE ACTION

Snowboard Hire
Daily rates from 200 Fr
Kids from 185 Fr

Snowboard Tuition
Group lessons, from from 170 Fr an hour

Night Riding
No

Heli Boarding
Yes

Snowmobiles
Yes

Mountain Cafes
10

pic - Tignes Tourism

If you happen to be one of the many millions of newcomers to snowboarding, then a little history is needed: **Tignes** is one of the major snowboard resorts in France, and has long been hosting national and international events. Throughout the year, snowboard teams and manufacturers host training camps and events, the most famous regular event to take place being the *Kebra Classic*, which has become the event of the early season. Tignes lies at 2,100m, and is found after a drive over an impressive dam, complete with a major piece of graffiti in its middle - sufferers of vertigo should keep their eyes closed going over as it's a long way down. Tignes links up with nearby **Val d'Isere** (a suberb of Kensington-snobsville) to offer an extensive 180 miles of all graded piste, and having been an Olympic host in the past, the runs are certainly up to scratch and will make any length of stay a memorable one.

Freeriders couldn't ask for anything better than what's on offer here. Advanced riders will be able to polish up their skills on a number of decent blacks and loads of red pisted runs. The *Surf Rider Snowboard Club* can take you off-piste to really experience what freeriding is all about, and if you have the cash, they can even arrange heli-board trips. An amazing off-piste area to check out with a guide, is situated off the **Tomeuse** chair lift at a section called **Vallee Perdue**. But take it easy (especially after a fresh dump), as it doesn't take much to trigger off avalanches in this area. There are many lines you can take, but one in particular is a 30m deep gorge, a bit like a giant boardercross course: at one point you have to take your board off and use a rope to drop through a hole to continue!

Freestylers should be well satisfied with the terrain as there are plenty of hits, cliffs, gullies and a few trees to shred. If the natural stuff is not enough to excite you, the 2400 metre terrain park located at **Combe de Palafour** should do the trick. The park has 500 metres of vert, and is loaded with spines and hits galore that can be ridden with a special lift pass, the **Plein Soleil pass** costing 173fr a day. Tignes well groomed halfpipe, which is often used for major competitions, can be reached off the Millonex drag lift with a pass costing just 63fr a day.

Carvers of all abilities are provided with dozens of pisted options. Runs like the **Grande Motte** are places to show off to onlookers as you lean right over.

Beginners will find the level of tuition excellent. It will help you explore some perfect novice slopes, without too many skiers disturbing your route. Kebra Surfing, which is Tignes oldest snowboard shop and school, offers a number of teaching programmes for freestyle or freeriding. A full weeks programme with hire, lift pass and video analysis costs from 3480fr.

Local services in **Tignes** are varied, extensive, and split between two main areas with a couple of satellite hamlets. The main happenings take place in **Tignes Le Lac**, the real hub of the resort. Le Lac packs in loads of apartment blocks for shared accommodation, along with a shopping centre, sports facilities and a number of places to eat and drink. Further up the main road lies the sprawling mass of **Val Claret**, which is similar to **Le Lac** and lies at the foot of the underground funicular train that takes you up to the highest slope areas. Wherever you choose to stay, prices are much the same - high. Tignes is an expensive resort whether you visit in winter, or come for summer snowboarding. Summer is actually a great time to visit as so much goes on, from snowboarding to watersports on the lake: there's even a skate park.

If you're on a diet when you arrive, then this place will kill it dead and you'll go home fatter than ever. Every type of fast-food is available along with a large selection of restaurants serving expensive French dishes with garlic overdose. Check out *The Wobbly Rabbit* if you're into Mexican food.

Night-life starts early and ends late - in fact, for some it never ends. This is a major party resort, but you will never have enough funds to keep going in the bars or clubs as beer prices are shocking. The best thing to do is tank up on supermarket carry-outs, then mine-sweep drinks from the hordes of aprés-skiers.

Accommodation: With over 28,000 visitor beds, this place has something for everyone, although there is not a wide selection of cheap accommodation. However, there are plenty of apartments for self-catering groups and scam merchants. Tour companies use this place big style, which means last minute package deals are always available at budget prices.

For accommodation listings visit - www.worldsnowboardguide.com

Summary: Great all-round resort with something for everyone, no matter what your ability is. However, watch out some for long lift queues and crowds.
Money wise: This is a very very expensive resort in all aspects but worth it.

Overall rating out of 10 **10**

Tourist Office Tignes Accueil
BP 51- F73321
Tignes Cedex

General info	**++33 (0) 4 79 40 04 40**
Reservations	**++33 (0) 4 79 40 03 03**
Avlanche info	**++33 (0) 836 681 020**

www.tignes.net

pic - A-Snowboards

pic - Tignes Tourism

Travel Guide

Fly to **Lyon** international
Transfer time to resort = **2½** *hours.*
Local airport = Chambery

Approximate global air travel times to **Lyon:**

from:		
	London	**2** hours
	Los Angles	**13** hours
	New York	**9** hours

Bus services from Lyon airport, are available on a daily basis direct to Tignes.

Trains to **Bourg-St-maurice** (15 minutes)

Route Planner
Lyon

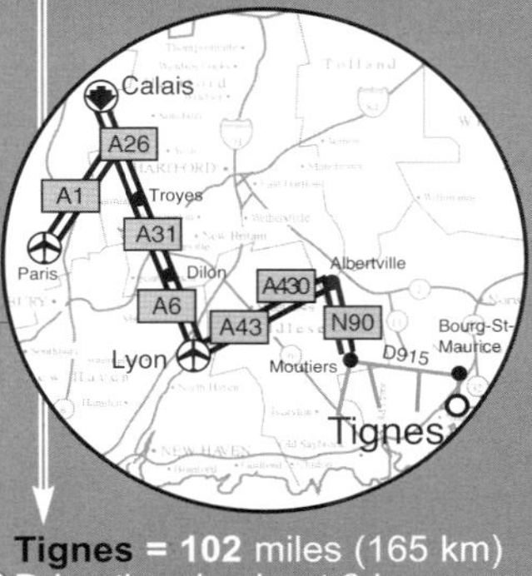

Tignes = **102** miles (165 km)
Drive time is about 2 hours

*From **Calais** 593 miles (995 Km)
Drive time is around **12** hours.

Val D'Isere

MOUNTAIN DATA

Top Lift at - 3450m

Ride Area
300km of piste

Bottom Lift at - 1550m

Vertical Drop - 1900m

Number of Runs - 129

Longest - 6 miles (10km)

TERRAIN LEVELS

Easy	**59%**
Intermediate	**33%**
Advanced	**8%**
Expert =	

TERRAIN TO SUITE

Freeride	**50%**
Trees	A few
Backcountry	Yes
Freestyle	**20%**
Halfpipe	Yes 2
Terrain Park	Yes 2
Carving	**30%**

SNOW DATA

Average Snowfall
100cm a season

Snowmaking
15% cover of the slopes

Winter Periods
Dec to April

Summer Riding
None

SLOPE ACCESS

Total Lifts = **74** + *Tignes*

Uplift Rate - 135,000 people an hour.

4 Trains-Gondolas-Cables

25 Chair lifts - **18** Drag lifts

**Leashes Required*

Lift Times
8.30am to 8.30pm

Lift Pass Rates

1 Day pass	228 Fr
6 Day pass	1070 Fr
Season pass	

Travel Guide

Fly to **Geneva,** $2^{1/2}$ hours transfer time.

Train services go to Bourg-St-Maurice, 20 mins.

Route Planner:
Via Bourg-St-Maurice take the N90 direction Tignes and then on to Val d'Isere
*Drive time from **Calais** is $10^{1/2}$ hours
597 miles (960 km)

Two things distinguish **Val d'Isere**, on the one hand you have a resort that has heaps of fantastic rideable terrain, (some of the best in France in fact), and on the other hand, this place is one of France's most stuck up resorts, full of scum bags mainly from the UK. Val d'Isere, largely colonised by yuppie pricks and pompous skiers, is way behind in terms of its attitude compared to other resorts more commonly associated with snowboarding. However, being linked with **Tignes,** this is one of the largest and best known resorts in France, with a massive 186 miles of piste (and even more off-piste), to suit all levels and forms of snowboarding. Numerous supplies of fresh snow arrive throughout the season, but beware, avalanches are a regular occurrence here.

Freeriders will find Val d'Isere an on and off-piste paradise, with piste-riding suited to all levels. Off-piste offers anything from couloirs and steeps, to some incredible powder and trees, with the best riding in areas like **Le Fornet** and **Solaise**.

Freestylers will probably prefer the fun-park in Tignes with its impressive halfpipe, although Val d'Isere does have its own park off the **Mont Blanc** lift, with a number of table-tops and quarter-pipes to session. The park can become overcrowded, but don't worry, Val d'Isere's has heaps of natural hits.

Carvers who can, will find this a great place to lay out some big arcs. For the idiots who insist on demeaning snowboarding by riding in one-piece ski-suits and matching headbands, you'll find enough sweeping runs to pose alongside Parisien, dickhead mono-boarders in the same sad ski-gear.

Beginners on their first ever day will find the two free slopes, loacted in the centre of the village, perfect. Once confident of putting together a few turns, there are plenty of easy slopes.

Off the slopes, **Val d'Isere** is a decent place in terms of appearance, having maintained a traditional French look whilst being very English-orientated. The big problem here is the bloody costs, with many pubs overpopulated with snooty bores. Drinking holes to try out are *Petit Danois* or *Cafe Face*, but avoid *Dick's T-Bar* - aptly named once you've encountered the management and staff. Overall, Val d'Isere is recommended for riding purposes, but give it a few years, until the town's atmosphere becomes a little less head-up-its-arse orientated.

For accommodation listings visit - **www.worldsnowboardguide.com**

Val d'Isere
Bp 228. F-73155. Val d'Isere
++33 (0) 4 79 06 06 06 www.val-disere.com.

Overall rating out of 10 **8** **Great mountain, crap town**

Valmorel

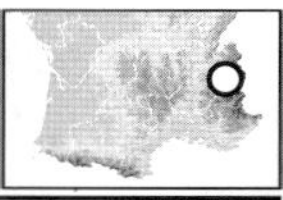

MOUNTAIN DATA

Top Lift at - 2550m

Ride Area 100km of piste

Bottom Lift at - 1250m

Vertical Drop - 1300m

Number of Runs - 50

Longest - 2.5 miles (4km)

TERRAIN LEVELS

Easy	**70%**
Intermediate	**20%**
Advanced	**10%**
Expert =	

TERRAIN TO SUITE

Freeride	**20%**
Trees	A few
Backcountry	Poor
Freestyle	**5%**
Halfpipe	Yes 1
Terrain Park	Yes 1
Carving	**75%**

SNOW DATA

Average Snowfall
400cm a season
Snowmaking
10% cover of the slopes
Winter Periods
Dec to April
Summer Riding
None

SLOPE ACCESS

Total Lifts = **54**
Uplift Rate - 27,500 people an hour.
2 Condolas
15 Chair lifts - **37** Drag lifts
**Leashes Required*

Lift Times
8.30am to 5.30pm

Lift Pass Rates

1 Day pass	187 Fr
3 Day pass	
6 Day pass	984 Fr

Travel Guide

Fly to **Geneva**, 2½ hours away.

Train services go to Moutiers, 10 minutes away.

Route Planner: Via Albertville, take the N90 and turn right on to the D95 to reach Valmore

*Drive time from **Calais** is 9½ hours 578 miles (930 km)

pic - Valmorel

As a relatively new resort, established around 20 years ago, **Valmorel** has grown into a family/group ski-centre. This is by no means an adventurous place - indeed it's best described as dull. Nevertheless, it is a well planned and well set out resort, with slopes that are ideal for simple piste-riding. Valmorel, on its own, boasts 50 or so trails which are not always that well maintained. When linked to **St Francois Longchamp**, the rideable terrain increases to a respectable 100 miles (160km). Getting around the slopes should pose no problems, although you might have to queue for lengthy periods of time with skiers who sing nursery rhymes to their offspring. Valmorel is not noted for having the best snow record, especially on the lower slopes. Still, once you do get away from the idiots in the lift lines and hit the slopes, things only get better. Keep an eye open, however, for ski-classes cluttering up certain slopes.

Freeriders are not going to get too excited with what's on offer here, but there is some alright off-piste riding around the **Mottet** area. Although Valmorel is a tame resort, some challenging riding is possible on a couple of black trails, though a good rider would rate them more as red runs.

Freestylers are going to be most disappointed. There is a so-called fun-park, but it's toss. By virtue of being a mountain, all resorts should have some natural freestyle terrain to catch some air, but this place doesn't. What there is, isn't up to much, so try mowing down ski families, and practice leaping over them as they lie on the ground screaming in fear (bliss).

Carvers who don't manage to hold an edge here, should give up snowboarding immediately and become a skier. Valmorel is a perfect resort for edging a board over at speed, or for general riding on intermediate trails.

Beginners, this area is littered with easy trails, but novices need to learn quickly to avoid sharing the same slopes with so many novice skiers.

Valmorel's village is dull, boring, expensive and full of some of the worst ski groups around (families). Accommodation options are good, but evenings aren't. Nothing happens, and there aren't any good bars of note, or come to that, places to eat. Well, there is *Pizzaria du Bourg* which serves up great slices, but overall the place is dull, crap, and comes at a price.

Tourist office Valmore
la maison de Valmore, Bourg-Morel, F-73260
++33 (0) 4 79 09 85 55 www.valmorel-la-belle.com

Overall rating out of 10 — **4** — **Incredibly dull resort**

Val Thorens

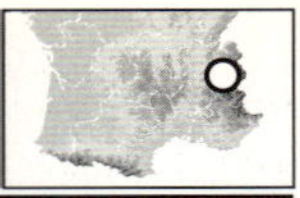

MOUNTAIN DATA

Top Lift at - 3200m

Ride Area 120km of piste

Bottom Lift at - 1800m

Vertical Drop - 1400m

Number of Runs - 67

Longest - 2 miles (3km)

TERRAIN LEVELS

Easy	**30%**
Intermediate	**52%**
Advanced	**18%**
Expert =	

TERRAIN TO SUITE

Freeride	**40%**
Trees	Yes
Backcountry	Yes
Freestyle	**20%**
Halfpipe	Yes 1
Terrain Park	Yes 1
Carving	**40%**

SNOW DATA

Average Snowfall
900cm a season

Snowmaking
25% cover of the slopes

Winter Periods
Nov to April

Summer Riding
Up to mid June

SLOPE ACCESS

Total Lifts = **47**

Uplift Rate - 125,000 people an hour.

3 Gondolas - **2** Cables

16 Chair lifts - **8** Drag lifts

**Leashes Required*

Lift Times
8.30am to 8.30pm

Lift Pass Rates

1 Day pass	235 Fr
6 Day pass	1160 Fr
Season pass	5000 Fr

SLOPE ACTION

Snowboard Hire
Daily rates from 210 Fr
Kids from 195 Fr

Snowboard Tuition
Group lessons, from
from 170 Fr an hour

Night Riding
No

Heli Boarding
Yes, from 365 a flight

Snowmobiles
Yes

Mountain Cafes
6

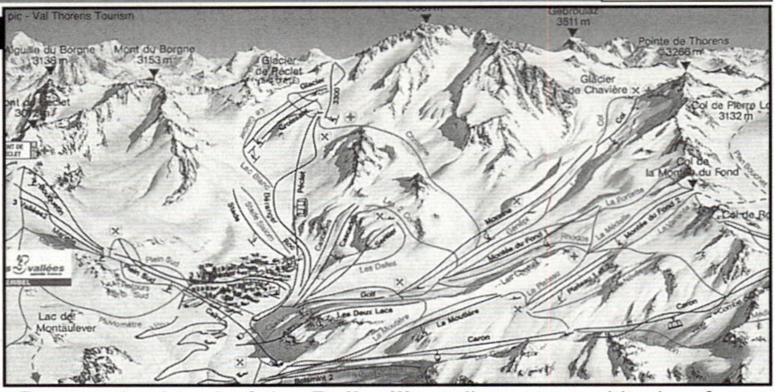

Set at the head of the **Belleville** valley, at an altitude of over 2,200 metres, **Val Thorens** is the highest resort in Europe and for some, one of the best. An extremely popular resort attracting millions of package tour groups, Val Thorens is a large, modern, purpose-built resort, carefully designed so that you never have far to go for the slopes. The lifts fan out in all directions, giving instant access to the entire **Trois Vallees** area and the chance to enjoy some of the most amazing snowboarding terrain in the world. It has to be said though, it would take years to sample this whole area, 400 miles (600 km) of terrain is a lot.

Here you'll find over 375 miles (**Trois Vallees**) of prepared piste, 40 mountain restaurants, 200 lifts and some truly great off-piste riding. Furthermore, although not noted as a summer resort, you can still ride here right up until early August. Not surprisingly, the altitude means this resort enjoys long hours of sunshine, an excellent snow record and good snowboarding for all grades. Don't be put off by the ugly appearance of Val Thorens, there are lots going on under its skin, to make this place great. Location is a key element here: if you're in the lower levels of one of the many apartment blocks, you may even be able to leap out of the nest, strap on your board, ollie over the balcony and land in a lift line, ready to be dragged up to the wide, open piste.

Freeriding intermediates should try the long, wide red runs around **Fond 1**, **Boismint** or the **Peclet Glacier**. The expert will relish the sheer volume of challenges on offer, from powder snow on the glaciers of **Peclet** and **Chaviere**, to world class, mogul-bashing on the long, steep **Cime de Caron** black run. If you have a head for heights, then visit **Le Plein Sud**, where you can cut some nice couloir descents.

Freestylers have a dedicated snowboard park near the **Funitel** lift, which has a boardercross circuit and a halfpipe. However, these are only kept in tip-top condition during a competition, rather than on a regular basis.

Carvers are as common here as the nappy-wearing ski groups, who often put a stop to a fast ride down, by falling over in the middle of one of the many excellent alpine trails. The Cime de Caron is a well-established black run that tests the best speed-freaks and race heads, who will also find that it's possible to have snowboard slalom training with poles.

Beginners have a variety of easy runs leading into the resort, which allow for easy access and steady progression. You don't have to travel far from the resort base before getting to a novice trail, but be advised, there are heaps of ski-classes that take up space. The local ski-school does a good job of turning milk-suckers into pint-swilling, piste gods within hours.

Val Thorens is a classic holiday camp on snow. The obvious remit when planning this place was, 'get them in, pile them high, and don't worry about how the place looks or feels'. The outcome is a place that looks dire, the perfect breeding ground for apres-ski groups, who flock here by the bucket load. This is not the cheapest resort in France, but it still has something for riders on a tight budget. Around the resort, you'll find a number of shopping complexes and places to eat. There is also a comprehensive sports centre, with a swimming pool and artificial climbing wall.

Job Seekers Contacts: Loads of work to be found in bars, hotels and chalets all season.

Food is plentiful here with a selection of more than 45 restaurants ranging from the normal selection of resort-style, expensive French restaurants, dodgy fast-food stands, to the normal offerings of a supermarket. For a cheap slap-up meal, try *El Gringo's,* or for something more classy, *Chalet Glaciers. The Scapin Pub* is also noted for its quick and affordable dishes which include pizza and garlic overdose food.

Night-life comes in the form of standard grade, aprés bull - they do so much of it here the place reeks. However, it's not all gloom as there are a number okay hangouts, and being a popular place, there's always plenty of mine-sweeping and talent to pick up. Check out *The Frog*, *The Malaysia*, or *The Underground.*

Accommodation: 20,000 visitors can sleep within spitting distance of the slopes. There are loads of self-catering apartment blocks with many actually on the slopes and next to a lift. *Pleisure Holidays* offer affordable and great snowboard trips with well equipped chalets on the slopes from £150 a week. Stay at *Chalet Trou* which sleeps up to 16 people from £150pp kitted out with tv, video, games console etc: tel ++44 02476 686835, info@pleisure.co.uk.

For accommodation listings visit - www.worldsnowboardguide.com

Summary: An average resort with excellent access to the slopes, offering good snowboarding. The low point is the tacky resort and large ski crowds.

Money wise: Overall this is an expensive resort but a good value one.

Overall rating out of 10 — **10**

Tourist Office Val Thorens
L'Eskival, F-3440
Val Thorens

General info	++33 (0) 4 79 00 08 08
Reservations	++33 (0) 4 79 00 08 08
Avlanche info	++33 (0) 836 681 020

www.valthorens.com

pics - Val Thorens Tourism

Travel Guide

Fly to **Lyon** international
Transfer time to resort = $2^{1/2}$ hours.
Local airport = none

Approximate global air travel times to **Geneva:**

from:		
	London	2 hours
	Los Angles	13 hours
	New York	9 hours

Bus services from Geneva airport, are available on a daily basis direct to Val Thorens.

Trains to **Moutiers** (15 minutes)

Route Planner
Lyon via Albertville

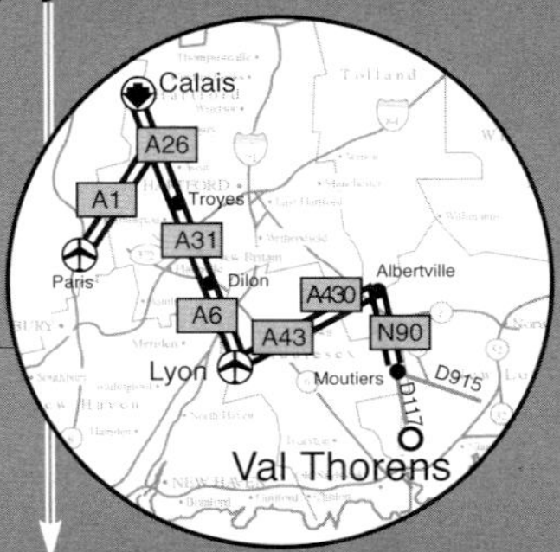

Val Thorens = 130 miles (209 km)
Drive time is about **2** hours

*From **Calais** 600 miles (965 Km)
Drive time is around **11** hours.

Abondance
Linked area with 200 Lifts & 280runs
50 minutes from Geneva airport.

Alpe du Grand Serre
Good riding here 20 Lifts & 35 runs
2 hours from Lyon airport.

Ala Foux d'Allos
2600m 112 km of piste 22 lifts
La Foux d'Allos, a purpose-built resort, is located way down in the southern section of the French Alps, 50 miles from the village of **Digne**. On its own, La Foux d'Allos offers a ride area of 70 miles, but linked with nearby resorts, the combined range gives freeriders of all levels 150 miles of terrain, with a good selection of advanced and novice runs.
Local services are slopeside and very affordable, if only a tad dull.
Fly to: **Nice** 2 hours away
tel- ++33 (0) 4 92 83 80 70

Auron
Some thick wood 28 Lifts & 36 runs
1 hour from Nice airport.

Bareges
Okay for novices 21 Lifts & 32 runs
45 minutes from Lourdes airport.

Bellevaux
Okay for carvers 24 Lifts & 32 runs
45 minutes from Geneva airport.

Briancon
Great linked area 72 Lifts & 250 runs
75 minutes from Turin airport (Italy).

Brides Les Bains
Super linked area 200 Lifts & 280 runs
120 minutes from Geneva airport.

Cauterets
Okay for carvers 16 Lifts & 42 runs
20 minutes from Lourdes airport.

Champagny en Vanoise
Terrain parks 110 Lifts & 121 runs
150 minutes from Geneva airport.

Chamrousse
Okay for novices 26 Lifts & 35 runs
1 hour from Lyon airport.

Combloux
Good all round 25 Lifts & 35 runs
45 minutes from Geneva airport.

Cordon
Good for novices 10 Lifts & 6 runs
50 minutes from Geneva airport.

Correncon en Vercors
Tiny novices haunt 11 Lifts & 35 runs
30 minutes from Grenoble airport.

Crest Voland Cohennoz
Good all-round 50 Lifts & 48 runs
60 minutes from Geneva airport.

Eaux-Bonnes Gourette
For slow carvers 26 Lifts & 40 runs
50 minutes from Geneva airport.

Font Romeu
Perfect for novices 35 Lifts & 40 runs
2 hours from Toulouse airport.

Gresse en Vercors
Very basic riding 16 Lifts & 20 runs
60 minutes from Geneva airport.

La Bresse Hohneck
Good for carvers 35 Lifts & 38 runs
70 minutes from Mulhouse airport.

La Chapelle d'Abondance
Big linked area 215 Lifts & 280 runs
50 minutes from Geneva airport.

La Grave
3568m 12 km of piste 4 lifts
La Grave is secretly stashed away in the **Oisans**. When the snow falls, this mountain has 7,100 vertical feet of drops, couloirs, cliffs, gullies, chutes, steeps, trees and crevices. This mountain isn't child's play so never ride alone. This is basically home to only die-hard extremists, with a few snowboarders who can hold their own. Still, the lack of skiing tourists simply quarantees 'no battle of the freshies' with untracked powder for days.

Freeriders will find above the only gondola, two T-bars that lead to the **Glacier de la Girose**. If La Grave hasn't seen snow in weeks, this mountain gets mogul madness. Therefore, the 15 minute hike over the top to **Les Deux Alpes** should entice the pipe and park enthusiast. If it does dump snow, cruise down the glacier, but be pre-warned of the numerous, unmarked crevasses. Contact the area's tourist office to find out about free guided tours. The community would like to put more safety into their terrain, where death by ignorance isn't an uncommon occurrence. Further down Glacier de la Girose, lies many steep cliffs and unavoidable gullies. Once past these gullies, stay on the traverse to the skier's right and keep an eye out for the gondola station at P1. Do not become bewitched by the untracked powder through the trees and river beds, or you will find yourself plummeting off 100m cliffs. **Ruillans**, spread out like curtains, are four couloirs to be explored. This gives you the chance to ride top to bottom. Further down, are some great natural quarter-pipes and tree runs. Take warning of the cliffs and the river near the bottom. This side of **La Meije** has held *The Derby* for the past ten years. In the world of snow racing, The Derby has the largest vertical drop of 2,150 metres on snowboard, ski, monoski or telemark.

Local facilities at La Grave are as basic as you can get. There are a few shops, and only a few lodging options to choose from (your neighbours will be cows and sheep). Riders spending a season here will find that rent and a season's lift pass is cheap. On the social scene, you will have to make your own. This isn't a beer swigging party hangout because the only pub closes early.
Fly to: **Grenoble** 2 hours away
tel- ++33 (0) 4 76 79 90 05

La Joue du Loup
2750m 97 km of piste 18 lifts
South of **Grenoble** and a stone's throw for the **Veynes**, lies the almost unheard of resort of **La Joue du Loup**, a tiny place place providing a mere half dozen trails. However, when linked with the resort of Superdevoluy, there's a more respectable 60+ miles to ride and explore. If you're an adventure seeker, nothing here is really that daunting. Great for first timers on a family outing. Slopeside lodging and services.
Fly to: **Lyon** 2 1/2 hours away
tel- ++33 (0) 4 92 58 83 57

La Norma
2750m 97 km of piste 18 lifts
La Norma is yet another unspoilt tourist spot, although it does get its fair share of weekenders. They who are attracted to the open trails that offer some steep and fast, although rather limited, riding with only a couple of black graded trails and nothing that will require many turns before you're back in a lift line. In truth this is a novices retreat where first timers can learn to ride without all the hassles associated with the big tourist resorts. Affordable slopeside services are available but are best described as dull.
Fly to: **Lyon** 21/2 hours away
tel- ++33 (0) 4 79 20 31 46

La Rosiere
2642m 55 km of piste 20 lifts
On its own, **La Rosiere** is a tiny outpost, with an even balance of terrain that any rider worth their salt will have licked in a day or two. However, as La Rosiere crosses the border with Italy and is lift linked to La Thuile, the 80+ miles poses a different question. Add the 900+ miles of the Aosta Valley, and suddenly we are into a whole new ball game, which will take the best of the best years to conquer. Okay slopeside lodging.
Fly to: **Geneva** 2 hours away
tel- ++33 (0) 4 79 68 05 1

La Tania
2738m 200 km of piste 70 lifts
La Tania offers access to a couple of very good steep runs ideal for freeriders and hardcore carvers. Freestylers will find a pipe, a park and enough natural hits, including the odd log to grind, to stay happy for a few days. Carvers who can, will love it here, with some great trails. Beginners will find the best slopes link with **Courchevel**. **La Tania** is a cool, relaxed place with good slopeside facilities and okay nightlife if just a bit dull.
Fly to: **Lyon** 2 hours away
tel- ++33 (0) 4 79 84 040

La Toussuire
Okay riding possible 20 Lifts & 26 runs
120 minutes from Grenoble airport.

Lans en Vercors
Basic carvers haunt 16 Lifts & 20 runs
35 minutes from Grenoble airport.

La Corber
For slow freeriders 18 Lifts & 24 runs
120 minutes from Grenoble airport.

La Grand Bornand
Okay overall riding 40 Lifts & 42 runs
55 minutes from Geneve airport.

Le Mont Dore
Good for all riders 20 Lifts & 30 runs
40 mins from Clermont Ferrand airport.

Le Sauze Super Sauze
Okay for carvers 24 Lifts & 45 runs
2 hours from Nice airport.

Les Angles
▲2400m 40 km of piste 20 lifts
Les Angles is definitely not one of your normal ski tourist traps. Located in the Pyranees, it shares a non-lift linked pass with a few neighbouring resorts, with 200 miles of average rideable terrain for all styles. It is, however, crowd-free, and an alternative to the massly populated areas further north. There's a pipe for air heads, but in truth most runs are for novices. There are plenty of slopeside services but most things around here are boring and dull and not the cheapest.
Fly to: **Perpigan** 1 1/2 hours away
tel- ++33 (0) 4 68 43 27 6

Les Carroz
Good pipe & parks 78 Lifts & 100 runs
2 hours from Geneva airport.

Les Contamines
All levels, all styles 26 Lifts & 44 runs
1 hour from Nice airport.

Les Gets
Good for all riders 60 Lifts & 61 runs
50 minutes from Geneva airport.

Les Houches
Good carving run 17 Lifts & 22 runs
55 minutes from Geneva airport.

Les Menuires
Big linked area 200 Lifts & 280 runs
140 minutes from Geneva airport.

Les Orres
Basic but okay 23 Lifts & 35 runs
140 minutes from Grenoble airport.

Les Sept Laux
Simple & laid back 30 Lifts & 42 runs
120 minutes from Grenoble airport.

Megeve
▲2350m 150 km of piste 41 lifts
Megeve on its own, is a very big resort with over 90 miles (or 150 km) of rideable area, but in sharing a joint lift and lift pass system with a number of other resorts, the area on offer increases to over 450 miles (720km) of piste making this place absolutely huge, and a joy for any type of snowboarder. The joint area offers lots of great freeriding for all levels which would take years to explore in depth. There is also some fantastic carving terrain plus lots of beginner slopes and various halfpipes for freestylers. Off the slopes there is good and affordable local services
Fly to: **Geneva** 1 hour away
tel- ++33 (0) 4 50 21 27 28

Metabief
▲1460m 40 km of piste 20 lifts
Metabief is slap bang on the border with Switzerland, which is probably why it is a cool and very friendly snowboard hangout. Although there are only 26 miles of piste and just a couple of black runs to entice hardcore freeriders, the place is still worth a visit. Laid back, unpopulated, with good slopes for all, and plenty of lodging and night-time action, although hangouts are some distance from the slopes.
Fly to: **Geneva** 1 hour away
tel- ++33 (0) 3 81 49 13 81

Molines en Queyras
Simple & laid back 15 Lifts & 35 runs
120 minutes from Grenoble airport.

Montchavin
▲3250m 200 km of piste 16 lifts
Linked to the tourist trap of **La Plagne**, this small resort suddenly seems a better option. On its own slopes, **Montchavin** has nothing to offer advanced riders, but plenty to entertain intermediate carvers and total beginners - they will find the place seemingly designed for them by Mother Nature. Freestylers are also presented with a park and pipe, but they are crap. Slopeside lodging is plentiful and okay.
Fly to: **Geneva** 2 hours away
tel- ++33 (0) 4 79 78 28 2

Morzine
▲2460m 140 km of piste 55 lifts
Morzine, as with the rest of the **Les Portes Du Soleil** area, it is highly rated due to its indirect access to over 400+ miles of terrain. Excellently graded runs and immaculate grooming separates **Morzine** from many of the region's resorts. Carvers will wet themselves. Beginners are presented with many good, easy slopes, the only bug is that they can often be the busy areas. Slopeside lodging is pricey.
Fly to: **Geneva** 2 hours away
tel- ++33 (0) 4 50 74 72 72

Peisey Nancroix Vallandry
Good for all riders 77Lifts & 115 runs
70 minutes from Geneva airport.

Peyragudes
Beginners haunt 16 Lifts & 35 runs
120 minutes from Toulouse airport.

Piau Engaly
Ok advanced runs 21 Lifts & 40 runs
2 hours from Toulouse airport.

Pra Loup
▲2500m 80 km of piste 31 lifts
Par Loup is more or less a beginner's and intermediate piste-lover's hangout. Advanced riders will want more than what's on offer. Spread over two areas, Par Loup and Molanes are not that bad to try, although being popular with weekenders and package tours, means clogged-up blues and busy lift lines. Accommodation is provided in a selection of affordable, tacky apartment blocks.
Fly to: **Toulouse** 21/2 hours away
tel- ++33 (0) 4 79 87 90 8

Pralognan La Vanoise
Super crap & Tiny 14 Lifts & 22 runs
1 hour from Chambery airport.

Praz de Lys
Basic but okay 22 Lifts & 44 runs
35 minutes from Geneva airport.

Praz sur Arly
Boring 14 Lifts & 20 runs
55 minutes from Geneva airport.

Puy St Vincent
Basic and dull 15 Lifts & 27 runs
120 minutes from Turin airport.

Saint Jean d"Arves
Total crap 6 Lifts & 12 runs
75 minutes from Lyon airport.

Saint Martin de Bellevill
Access to big area 200 Lifts & 300 runs
120 minutes from Geneva airport.

Saint Nicolas de Veroce
Access to big area 200 Lifts & 300 runs
50 minutes from Geneva airport.

Samoens
Good fun park 16 Lifts & 28 runs
30 minutes from Geneva airport.

St Francois Longchamp
Pipe and parks 54 Lifts & 75 runs
50 minutes from Chambery airport.

Superbagneres
Okay freeriding 16 Lifts & 30 runs
120 minutes from Toulouse airport.

Superdevoluy
Small halfpipe 31 Lifts & 61 runs
120 minutes from Lyon airport.

Thollon les Memises
Mainly for novices 18 Lifts & 15 runs
30 minutes from Geneva airport.

Val Cenis
Small and mixed 23 Lifts & 30 runs
50 minutes from Turin airport.

Val Louron
Small novice resort 12 Lifts & 25 runs
50 minutes from Tarbes airport.

Valfrejus
Small halfpipe 12 Lifts & 20 runs
110 minutes from Turin airport.

Valloire
Okay ride area 35 Lifts & 80 runs
120 minutes from Chambery airport.

Valmeinier
Good advanced runs 34 Lifts & 89 runs
120 minutes from Chambery airport.

Vars
Okay advanced runs 30 Lifts & 60 runs
140 minutes from Marseille airport.

Vaujany
Pipes and parks 81 Lifts & 110 runs
45 minutes from Grenoble airport.

Villard de lans
Okay advanced runs 27 Lifts & 34 runs
40 minutes from Grenoble airport.

Villard Reculas
Access to areas 82 Lifts & 110 runs
45 minutes from Grenoble airport.

GERMANY

GENERAL INFO AND FACTS

Capital - Berlin
Language - German
Currency - Deutschemark & Euro
Alcohol drinking age - 18
Drugs - Cannabis is illegal
Death Penalty - Doesn't exist
Age of consent for Sex - 16
Military Service - Compulsory
Electricity Supply - 240 Volts AC
International phone Code ++49
Highest Peak -

DUTY FREE
10 Litres of Alcohol
90 Litres of Wine - 110 of beer
800 Cigarettes
200 Cigars

GERMAN DRIVE GUIDE
All vehicles drive on the right hand side of the road
Speed Limits -
Motorways No Speed limit
Highways 81kph (62mph)
Towns 50kph (31mph)

German Snowboard Association
Zizelsbergerstrasse 3. 81476
Munchen
tel - ++49 (0) 89 7544 7320

TIME ZONES
Central European
GMT +1 Hour
Between March and October
GMT+2 Hours

INTERNATIONAL GATEWAY AIRPORTS
Munich
Innsbruck in Austria
Zurich in Switzerland

Not many people think of Germany as a snowboard destination and although it's no match for its close alpine neighbours, Germany can still boast plenty of rideable terrain. The dozen or so resorts are all located in the southern-most parts of the country, with some crossing over into Austria. The thing that seems to be consistent amongst about German resorts is the efficient way things are set out and how you're looked after. Most places are expensive and often stupidly overcrowded at weekends.

Travelling by car is a good idea, with resorts reached on one of the best road systems in the world. Unlike many other European destinations, there are no road tolls so you aren't hit with extra costs

Munich is the most convenient gateway airport for all the resorts with good onward travel facilities.

It is possible to take a train across Austrian, Swiss and French borders direct to many resorts making train travel a good option.

For those thinking about doing a season in Germany, work is possible but you will need to speak the language (or have a good grasp of it). EU nationals can stay as long as they want without a work permit.

Accommodation is similar to that in Austria, from affordable pensions to way overpriced hotels. It's often cheaper to stay in a nearby town. Night life in Germany is pretty cool, Germans like to party hard and the beer is pure nectar. Clubs and discos are not bad, although far too many bars allow Euro pop. Overall, Germany is not the cheapest place, but is highly recommended.

pic - bayerische Zugspitzbahn Tourism

Feldberg

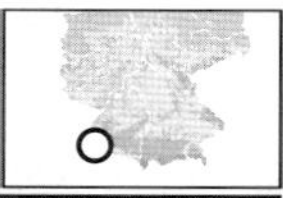

GERMANY

MOUNTAIN DATA

Top Lift at - 1448m

Ride Area
50km of piste

Bottom Lift at - 945m
Vertical Drop - 503m
Number of Runs - 50
Longest -1.7 miles (2.8km)

TERRAIN LEVELS

Easy	65%
Intermediate	15%
Advanced	20%
Expert =	

TERRAIN TO SUITE

Freeride	50%
Trees	A few
Backcountry	A bit
Freestyle	20%
Halfpipe	Yes 1
Terrain Park	Yes 1
Carving	30%

SNOW DATA
Average Snowfall

Snowmaking
10% cover of the slopes
Winter Periods
Dec to April
Summer Riding
None

SLOPE ACCESS
Total Lifts = **28**
Uplift Rate - 24,000 people an hour.
3 Chair lifts
25 Drag lifts
**Leashes Required*

Lift Times
8.30am to 4.30pm

Lift Pass Rates

1 Day pass	39 Dm
3 Day pass	99 Dm
6 Day pass	179 Dm

Travel Guide

Fly to **Zurich** in Switzerland 2 hours away.

Train services go direct to Feldberg.

Route Planner:
From Zurich head north along the B315 and travel via Schaffhausen to Feldberg

Feldberg is located in the south west of **Germany** in the **Black Forest** and a stone's throw from the **French** and **Swiss** borders. The town of Feldburg is a sprawling affair and offers its visitors a mass of attractions all year round. As a winter destination, this adequate resort is regarded by many in Germany as the country's number one resort even though in terms of terrain its 50 kms of piste are half of what is available over in **Garmisch,** which is south of Munich and Germany's most famous resort. **Felberg's** location means that if you are planning to visit by air then the easiest way to get here is to fly into Zurich in Switzerland and then hire a car and drive up or catch a bus. In terms of skiing and snowboarding, Felderg is a resort that attracts a lot of families as the two main mountain areas are made up largely of novice trails with a few intermediate slopes. All the runs are laid out over wide open spaces with a splattering of trees here and there namely on the **Grafenmatt-Hochst** mountain. This mountainis the one and only area that has anything difficult to ride with a few interesting black trails to check out. The runs on the **Seebuck** mountain are mostly intermediate trails while the **Gafenmatte** is home to the best novice slopes. Overall this is not a place that you would want to spend more than a few days at. The size and pace of what is going on here will make it a bore after three days, unless you are brain dead or a child in nappies.

Freeriders who want for a simple day's riding and are not too adventurous, will find **Feldberg** an ideal place to spend some time at. There is an okay mixture of terrain with the best and most challenging freeriding to be found off the letter **K** drag lift.

Freestylers should stick to riding in the terrain park located off the letter **E** drag lift. This is the only place to get any air time.

Carvers have a good resort for cruising with a number of well groomed trails to check out, especially those on the **Seebuck.**

Beginners have a mountain that is perfect for learning on with a number of easy blue trails that cover all the areas, but note that all the easy runs are served by drag lifts.

Feldburg is a large town with a very good choice of local services that include hotels, pension homes and chalets. There is also a good choice of bars and restaurants, the only draw back being that this is an expensive resort.

Feldberg Tourist Information
Kirchgasse 1, 79868 Feldberg.
++49 (0) 76 55 80 19 www.feldberg-schwarzwald.de

Overall rating out of 10 **5** **Okay beginners resort**

Garmisch

MOUNTAIN DATA

Top Lift at - 2830m

Ride Area
121km of piste

Bottom Lift at - 720m

Vertical Drop - 1350m

Number of Runs - 60

Longest -2.5 miles (3.2km)

TERRAIN LEVELS

Easy	**49%**
Intermediate	**49%**
Advanced	**2%**
Expert =	

TERRAIN TO SUITE

Freeride	**45%**
Trees	Yes
Backcountry	A bit
Freestyle	**15%**
Halfpipe	Yes 1
Terrain Park	Yes 1
Carving	**40%**

SNOW DATA

Average Snowfall

Snowmaking
15% cover of the slopes

Winter Periods
Nov to April

Summer Riding
None

SLOPE ACCESS

Total Lifts = **36**

Uplift Rate - 50,000 people an hour.

1 Gondolas - **6** Cables

4 Chair lifts - **25** Drag lifts

**Leashes Required*

Lift Times
8.30am to 8.30pm

Lift Pass Rates

1 Day pass	50 Dm
3 Day pass	141 Dm
6 Day pass	270 Dm

SLOPE ACTION

Snowboard Hire
Daily rates from 40 Dm
Kids from 35 Dm

Snowboard Tuition
Group lessons from
from 38Dm an hour

Night Riding
No

Heli Boarding

Snowmobiles
No

Mountain Cafes
12

Garmisch is **Germany's** most popular resort, although some say the resort of **Feldburg** has more claim to the favourite title award. What ever the merits of this, Garmisch certainly holds the title of being Germany's biggest and most famous resort which is located in the southernmost part of the country a short distance from **Munich** and within easy reach of **Stuttgart** and **Innsbruck** in **Austria**. This very German of German places is in fact an extremely popular all year round holiday destination that attracts thousands of visitors. The area offers loads of out-door sporting attractions as well as putting on lots of top sporting competitions. The ski world hosts all sorts of world ranking ski events here which includes ski jumping. Garmisch even played host to the **1936 Winter Olympics**, although to be fair, the world was a bit messed up during that period of time, so anyone boasting about such a role should be viewed with a bit of contempt. All said and done, this is a resort where you can have a good time, located beneath Germany's highest mountain, the **Zugspitze,** where a cable car goes to the rocky 2964m summit (no rideable descent is possible). The five resort centres dotted around the village are all connected by buses and trains. On the mountain, the slopes are divided into four areas and are serviced by around 50 lifts. The pistes will appeal mostly to intermediate riders looking for easy descents but expert riders will soon get bored.

Freeriders coming here for the first time may be a bit disappointed if they arrive thinking that they will find a mountain blessed with loads of hardcore freeride terrain. They will find a big mountain with a number of steep sheer unrideable faces, and a number of okay rideable slopes that will allow advanced riders to blast around at speed for at least two days, but bore them after three. Snowboarders in general favour the **Zugspitzplatt** slopes, which is the only area not directly linked on snow with the other sections. Although this is not an adventurous place, there are opportunities to ride through trees and on a good day a few stashes of powder can be cut.

Freestylers will find quite a few good natural hits as well as those built by local grommets. You'll also be able to grind a few downed logs around the tree areas, but in the main, this is not a great place for getting any serious air. However, there is a halfpipe but don't expect it to be maintained all the time.

Carvers who want to carve around on gentle, short slopes will favour the areas off the **Alpspitzbahn** cable car, but there is other carving to be found up on the Zugspitz slopes. Whatever area you ride, you'll have fun spotting how many mullets with head bands there are riding around with ski-boot set ups.

Beginners are well catered for with a number of spots ideally suited to novices. There is a number of easy options for riding up high and back down through the trees to the village and car parks.

The two linked towns of **Garmisch** and **Partenkirchen** are located just north of the **Austrian** border and are only a short distance from the base slopes. What you have here is an all year-round holiday destination which caters extremely well for it's visitors. There is a huge selection of places to stay with lodging spread out over a wide area, and other attractions set around the town. Numerous events are held in this town all year round, so not only is this place a very expensive town, it can also be very busy. The town has loads of sporting attractions and if you are feeling lucky there is a casino to try your hand in, but it's a mug game, you're better off saving your dosh for booze.

Restaurants are plentiful and cater for all tastes, if not all budgets. Most places serve up a variety of disgusting sausages and potato dishes. However, you can get some decent chicken and fish meals. Veggies should pay a visit to the *Grand Cafe* where they have a good menu including some normal dishes. If you do want to taste a local dish and don't mind sucking on bland pieces of horse meat, the check out the *Max Cafe*.

Nightlife here is pretty good and very lively set to a Bavarian theme. An excellent choice of German beers are available in a number of okay bars where the booze flows fast and well into the early morning hours, mind you, the music in most places is enough to make you want to leave. Check out the *Irish Bar* or the *Rose and Crown*.

The area can accommodate over 20,000 visitors with a number of places in the main town area or spread out into the countryside. Prices are not cheap and no real budget options exist even though there is a large number of pension's and self catering places. Still one thing is for sure, most places are of a very high standard and hotels come loaded with restaurants, bars, pools, and sporting centres.

For accommodation listings visit - www.worldsnowboardguide.com

Summary: An average resort with some decent intermediate and beginner terrain, but little for advanced riders to do. Local services are very good with lots to choose from.
Money wise: Overall this is an expensive resort that offers good value.

Overall rating out of 10 **6**

Tourist Office Garmisch
Richard Strauss-Platz 1a 1562. D-82455
Garmisch Partenkirchen

General info	**++49 (0) 88 21 180-0**
Reservations	**++49 (0) 88 21 180-0**
Avlanche info	

www.garmisch-partenkirchen.com

pics - Garmisch Tourism

Travel Guide

Fly to **Munich** international
Transfer time to resort = **1½** hours.
Local airport = none

Approximate global air travel times to **Munich:**

from:	London	1½ hours
	Los Angles	14 hours
	New York	9 hours

Bus services from Munich airport are available on a daily basis direct to Val Thorens.

Trains to the centre of Garmisch

Route Planner
Munich via Albertville

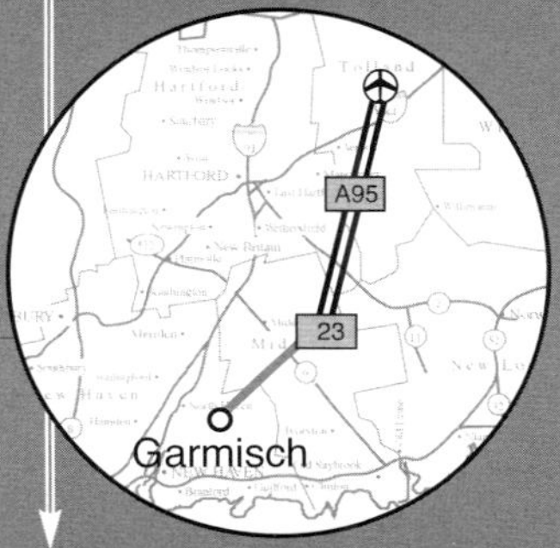

Garmisch = **87** miles (140 km)
Drive time is about **1½** hours

*From **Calais** 575 miles (925 Km)
Drive time is around **10** hours.

Schliersee

MOUNTAIN DATA

Top Lift at - 1700m

Ride Area
35km of piste

Bottom Lift at - 1175m

Vertical Drop - 525m

Number of Runs - 31

Longest - 2 miles (3.2km)

TERRAIN LEVELS

Easy	**24%**
Intermediate	**62%**
Advanced	**14%**
Expert =	

TERRAIN TO SUITE

Freeride	**40%**
Trees	A few
Backcountry	A bit
Freestyle	**20%**
Halfpipe	Yes 1
Terrain Park	Yes 1
Carving	**40%**

SNOW DATA

Average Snowfall
300cm a season

Snowmaking
0% cover of the slopes

Winter Periods
Dec to April

Summer Riding
None

SLOPE ACCESS

Total Lifts = **19**

Uplift Rate - 13,500 people an hour.

1 Gondola

2 Chair lifts - **16** Drag lifts

**Leashes Required*

Lift Times
8.30am to 8.30pm

Lift Pass Rates

1 Day pass	45 Dm
3 Day pass	80 Dm
6 Day pass	750 Dm

Travel Guide

Fly to **Munich** airport which is 1 1/2 hours away.

Train services are possible all the way to Schliersee.

Route Planner: Via Munich, go south on the A8/E45 Autobahn turning of at Kolbermoor to route 472 via the 307.
*Drive time from **Calais** is 10 3/4 hours
645 miles (1039 km)

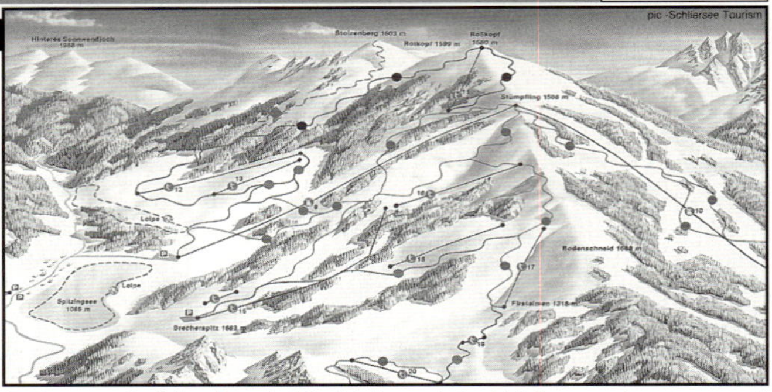

Frequented by **Munich's** high-society kiddies and some cool riders, **Schliersee** is also home to the living snowboard legend *Peter Bauer* (you still meet him riding here). What you get are two areas, interconnected by a free shuttle-bus: the **Taubenstein** is less crowded and is the place to be on a fresh powder day but you'll get bored pretty quickly in the days in-between! Most of the runs are intermediate and nothing will keep you excited for long. At the parking lot you jump on the shuttle that takes you to the **Stumpfling-an-Sutten** area at the other side of the **Spitzingsee**, where the whole area lies in front of you, waiting to be ridden.

Freeriders if there's enough snow, take the **Brecherspitz** lift, opposite the **Firstam,** to gain access to a freerider's paradise: long, steep tree-runs that remind you of **Canada**. On this mission you should follow the locals because there's a 25 metre cliff, with a flat and rocky landing hidden in the trees.

Freestylers have a good mountain to practice getting air at various points around the slopes. The **Osthanglift** T-bar takes you to a good freestyle area. If you stay on the slope-side of the lift on the way down, you'll find some good natural hits and spines decorated with some nice rollers. The **Firstalm** is where the funpark is but it doesn't get shaped too often.

Carvers have a very good mountain to ride, with well groomed runs that will intrigue the hopeless novice, but bore the tits off most advanced riders. However, the pistes are open enough to allow for some wide carves and to be fair, a decent amount of speed can be achieved. The longest run is the 3200m Sutten, which is good for screaming down in under 3 minutes.

Beginners have a cool first timer's resort, although there's a limited amount of slopes and a lot of weekend ski crowds cluttering up the place. Easy access is possible to all the beginner trails.

Local facilities are located in two areas, **Schliersee** in the east and **Rottach-Egern** in the west which has the best night-life and some cheap B & B's. Both places offer good local services but be prepared to pay for it because this is not a cheap hangout, no matter what you're after. Eating spots are good and evenings begin at the *Braustuberl Bar*, but watch out for the big waitresses who eat snowboarders for supper. Later, head for the *Moon-Club* where you are bound to find a nice fraulein.

For accommodation listings visit - www.worldsnowboardguide.com

Tourist Office Schliersee
Postfach 146 Bahnhofstr 11a. Germany
++49 (0) 8026 60650 e-mail:tourismus@schliersee.btz

Overall rating out of 10 **6** **Rather basic resort but okay**

Balderschwang
Intermediate's place 10 Lifts & 15 runs
Overall this is a boring place with a small and badly kept halfpipe.
120 minutes from Munich airport.

Bayerisch Eisenstein
Very dull place 7 Lifts & 8 runs
90 minutes from Munich airport.

Bayrischzell
Intermediate's place 22 Lifts & 37 runs
1 hour from Munich airport.

Berchtesgadener Land
Pipes and parks 21 Lifts & 20 runs.
Glitzy dump that thinks it's cool.
20 minutes from Salzburg airport.

Bischofsmais
Unbelievably dull 7 Lifts & 6 runs
1 hour from Munich airport.

Bolsterlang
Linked area resort 51 Lifts & 48 runs
There are worst places.Ok freeriding.
90 minutes from Munich airport.

Fellhorn
▲1967m 44 km of piste 30 lifts

Fellhorn is the mountain, **Obersdorf** is the town that serves it and together they are rated by many nationals as the best on offer in Germany. What you get is a mountain area that has a series of open trails with a few tree lines and a couple of decent steeps The I.S.F have found favour here and regularly stage top events in the competition standard halfpipe. Whereever you ride here, expect to bump into a lot of skiers as it's a popular hang out.

Freeriders, check out the Kanzelwand trail for a good ride.

Freeriders have a well maintained fun-park to play in.

Carvers, have a good series of pisted trails from top to bottom.

Beginners this place is perfect for all your needs.

There are good facilities 10 minutes from the slopes.

Fly to: **Munich** 1½ hours away

tel- ++49 (0) 8322 7000

Grainau
Intermediate places 12 Lifts & 12 runs
Okay for freeriders, but nothing to shout about. Dull pipe & park area.
90 minutes from Munich airport.

Jenner
Very easy going 5 Lifts & 8 runs
20 minutes from Salzburg airport.

Lenggries
Okay but basic 21 Lifts & 20 runs
40 minutes from Munich airport.

Mittenwald
▲2244m 22 km of piste 8 lifts

Mittenwald is located in the Isar Valley and is an okay freeriders destination. It is famous for its steep Dammkar run which is served by a cable car that climbs 1311 vertical metres with only one tower (sufferers of vertigo take note). Beginners have plenty of easy slopes while freestylers have a halfpipe. Local services are convenient but not cheap.

90 minutes from Munich airport.

Fly to: **Munich** 1½ hours away

tel- ++49 (0) 8823 33981

Oberammergau
▲1700m 10 km of piste 10 lifts

Oberammergau is a happy go lucky sort of place but certainly not the most adventurous of resorts. The west side of the valley, on the Kolben, is the place for novices and intermediate riders looking for gentle and simple terrain to shred. On the Laberjoch area the runs offer more testing and challenging terrain. For those freestylers wanting to get big air, the halfpipe is your best option, but it's not the best nor well kept. Okay expensive local services exist, but not near the slopes.

Fly to: **Munich** 1½ hours away

tel- ++49 (0) 8822 1021

pic - Garmisch Tourism

Oberaudorf
Utterly crap 4 Lifts & 8 runs
1 hour from Munich airport.

Oberjoch
Okay for beginners 14 Lifts & 22 runs
90 minutes from Munich airport.

Oberstaufen
▲1340m 20 km of piste 12 lifts

Oberstaufen is a collection of seven small rideable areas. The main offerings are to be found on the Hochgrat mountain which offers some good off-piste and challenging runs. Intermediate carvers will also find the slopes worth the effort while beginners have access to some okay areas. Off the slopes, this place is by no means cheap as it is a very popular German tourists town.

Fly to: **Munich** 2 hours away

tel- ++49 (0) 8386 9300

Pfronten
Good for all levels 16 Lifts & 68 runs
90 minutes from Munich airport.

Reit im Winkl
Super dull for all 21 Lifts & 30 runs
1 hour from Munich airport.

Rettenberg
Not a bad hangout with a halfpipe and fun park 14 Lifts & 40 kms of piste.
90 minutes from Munich airport.

Ruhpolding
They don't come much worst 8 Lifts
75 minutes from Munich airport.

Sankt Englmar
Okay for beginners 14 Lifts & 16 runs
90 minutes from Munich airport.

Schonau am Konigssee
Super boring 4 Lifts & 9 runs
20 minutes from Salzburg airport.

Schwangau
For beginners only 8 Lifts & 6 runs
70 minutes from Munich airport.

Oberjoch
Okay for beginners 14 Lifts & 22 runs
90 minutes from Munich airport.

Willingem
▲830m vert 240m 14 lifts

Willingen is a northern low key resort which is virtually unheard of. The area is spread over two large hills with mainly nursery slopes. The main hill has some decent runs with the option of cutting through the trees but lacks any great length. Note also that this place inhabited by lots of skiers (the older generation) and sledgers, so the few slopes that there are, are often very, very crowded, especially at weekends.

Freeriders have very little to keep them interested beyond an hour, but there are a few trees to drop through.

Freeriders, haven't got a chance here unless you dig your own hit.

Carvers will find the number **11** trail about the only thing of worth.

Beginners aged 1 or 100 will love it here as the slopes are so slow and easy you'll be able to change your nappy as you ride.

There are lots of small villages close by but they're all pricey.

Fly to: **Munich** 1 hour away

tel- ++49 (0) 05632 6715

Winterburg
▲809m 40 km of piste 55 lifts

Winterberg, is situated southwest of Dortmond in the **Sauerland** mountain range which not many snowusers have heard

The runs are spread over 5 hills with 25 slopes, but nothing too testing, the longest barely making 2 miles.

Freeriders have lots of trees to weave through and with many runs interlinking, there are a few nice freeride spots to check out.

Freestylers don't have a pipe or park but many of the runs have natural hits formed en route at the sides and there's also a number of ski jumps that you can air off.

Carvers could do worse, but if you know how to carve at speed then you won't want a week here.

Beginners, this place is great for you, however, only for a one off trip before going to Austria for your next snowboard holiday.

Very good and lively local facilities slope side or close by.

Fly to: **Dortmund** 1 hour away

tel- ++49 (0) 02981 24 64

GENERAL INFO AND FACTS

Capital - London
Language - English
Currency - UK Pound £
Alcohol drinking age - 18
Drugs - Cannabis is illegal
Death Penalty - Doesn't exist
Age of consent for Sex - 16
Military Service -Not Compulsory
Electricity Supply - 240 Volts AC
International phone Code ++44
Highest Peak - Ben Nevis

DUTY FREE
10 Litres of Alcohol
90 Litres of Wine - 110 of beer
800 Cigarettes
200 Cigars

UK DRIVE GUIDE
All vehicles drive on the left hand side of the road
Speed Limits -
Motorways 70mph (113kph)
Highways 60mph (97kph)
Towns 30mph (50kph)

British Snowboard Association
4 Trinity Square, Llandudno,
Conwy, LL30 2PY
tel - ++44 (0) 700 360 5

TIME ZONES
Central European
GMT +1 Hour

INTERNATIONAL GATEWAY AIRPORTS
Aberdeen
Edinburgh
Glasgow
London
Inverness

Your choice for riding in Britain is simple; you can choose one of the five real snow areas in Scotland, or the man made snow slopes in England. There is also the alternative of riding on one of the numerous and pointless artificial ski slopes dotted around the country.

Scotland's conditions are extremely poor, the wind can blow so hard that it hurts as it hits you at 70 miles an hour. All the resorts are similar: low level hills, with uneven trails that get stupidly crowded. Halfpipes are rare due to the weather conditions and you won't find any wide motorway runs. But the most notable point about Scotland, is the costs: lift tickets are a total rip off and offer very bad value for money, especially at **Cairngorm**. However getting to any of the areas should pose no problems with good air, rail and road links.

Season riders will find employment and lodging easily. If you want to teach snowboarding, you can do it legally without an instructor's certificate. However, it may help you get work. But whatever you do, don't bother with the *BASI* Ski/Snowboard course. It's utterly crap, bloody expensive and foreign countries are unlikely to accept a British qualification. UK winter sports (Skiing) are seen as a joke worldwide, plus *BASI* is a clueless group of nerds full of their own self importance and heads up their arses. What they teach you is different to the way it's done abroad. They really have no idea about snowboarding and if they can't get their own skiers recognised globally, what chance will snowboarders have? Go abroad and do either a **US, Canadian, European** or **New Zealand** course as they are all far better, more up to date and carry true global recognition.

In short, Scotland is a great country for its scenery, natural beauty and history, but not a destination for boarding or skiing. This is a place for purists not cheap gimmicks.

pic - San Tang - Rider Hamish McKnight riding at the British Championships

Glencoe

MOUNTAIN DATA

Top Lift at - 1108m

Ride Area: 11km of piste

Bottom Lift at - 300m

Vertical Drop - 800m

Number of Runs - 16

Longest - 1 mile (1.6km)

TERRAIN LEVELS

Easy	**60%**
Intermediate	**33%**
Advanced	**7%**
Expert =	

TERRAIN TO SUITE

Freeride	**60%**
Trees	None
Backcountry	None
Freestyle	**3%**
Halfpipe	No
Terrain Park	Occasionally
Carving	**10%**

SNOW DATA

Average Snowfall

Snowmaking
0% cover of the slopes

Winter Periods
Jan to April

Summer Riding
None

SLOPE ACCESS

Total Lifts = **7**

Uplift Rate - 4,300 people an hour.

2 Chair lifts

5 Drag lifts

**Leashes Required*

Lift Times
8.30am to 4.30pm

Lift Pass Rates
1 Day pass £17
6 Day pass £68
Season pass £195

Travel Guide

Fly to **Glasgow** airport 2 hours away.

Train services to the Fort William, 30 minutes away.

Route Planner: Via Glasgow, head north on the A82, via Dumbarton and Tyndrun to Glencoe From London, use the M1 M6, A74, to Glasgow.
*Drive time from **London** is about 10 hours.

pic - Sofr Snapper

Glencoe is **Scotland's** oldest resort and also boasts the longest vertical run (800m) in the country. This tiny outback is Scottish through and through, and the best place to ride in the country. Unlike other Scottish resorts, this is not a poor alpine imitation and okay, Glencoe may have very harsh weather patterns, but who cares, they do things the right way here and don't try and make out that they are something that they're not. This place is real and knows what it is about having kept a proper sense of proportion. This may not be a big place, but it is exactly what Scottish snowboarding should be about: simple, friendly and without an attitude. It also has the best natural terrain in the country making it a small natural fun park. In general, the runs will suit all levels, although not testing. However, Glencoe's remote location means it is far less crowded than other resorts. People who come here do so because they don't want the propaganda and bull of the other places.

Freeriders will find some good terrain in the main basin off either the top T-bar area or top button lift. Go right off the T-Bar to access sedate terrain (marked as intermediate), or go left off the top button lift to find a couple of reds and an interesting black trail that bases out into an easy green run.

Freestylers have a cool natural freestyle resort to ride, but the weather prevents the building or lasting of a pipe. However, ask the management and they'll happily do what they can to build you a decent big hit.

Carving is limited, but what there is, can be found on the **Etive Glades** run of the top T-bar.

Beginners should have no problems learning here as there are some excellent short runs to try out which are easily reached.

Local services can be found in the small village of **Glencoe**, a 6 mile drive away. It offers limited, but good, accommodation in a Scottish atmosphere with a number of excellent cheap B & B's and decent pubs. Alternatively, the village of **Onich** is 12 miles away and has a bigger selection of services, including a cool bunkhouse with a bar. **Fort William** is 30 miles away and has an even bigger offering. Wherever you stay, a car is a must. Glencoe is worth a visit, even if only to visit one of the most amazingly scenic areas of Europe and flavour some real Scottish culture without any hype.

Glencoe Mountain Area
Glencoe, Argyll PA39 4HZ
++44 (0) 1855 851 2266 **www.ski.scotland.net**

Overall rating out of 10 **4** **Limited riding, but very friendly**

Cairngorm

MOUNTAIN DATA

Top Lift at - 1080m

Ride Area
14km of piste

Bottom Lift at - 550m
Vertical Drop - 530m
Number of Runs - 28
Longest -1.8 miles (2.9km)

TERRAIN LEVELS

Easy	**34%**
Intermediate	**62%**
Advanced	**4%**
Expert =	

TERRAIN TO SUITE

Freeride	**30%**
Trees	None
Backcountry	None
Freestyle	**5%**
Halfpipe	Occasionally
Terrain Park	Occasionally
Carving	**65%**

SNOW DATA
Average Snowfall

Snowmaking
0% cover of the slopes
Winter Periods
Jan to April
Summer Riding
None

SLOPE ACCESS
Total Lifts = **16**
Uplift Rate - 12,000 people an hour.
1 Funicular train
1 Chair lift - **14** Drag lifts
**Leashes Required*

Lift Times
8.30am to 4.30pm

Lift Pass Rates
1 Day pass £20
7 Day pass £98
Season pass £300

SLOPE ACTION

Snowboard Hire
Daily rates from £8
Kids from £6

Snowboard Tuition
Group lessons, from
from £10 an hour

Night Riding
No

Heli Boarding
No

Snowmobiles
No

Mountain Cafes
3

pic - Paul Tomkins/STB?SMPC

It's all change on the **Cairngorms** in more ways than one. Firstly and most amazingly, it actually snowed and snowed a lot during last season (2001) going against the record of the previous ten or so years. But not only did it snow, it kept snowing all season, and as if that weren't enough, the snow stayed on the ground for a lengthy period of time that had the lifts still been running, it would have meant riding at the start of May. The other big change on the Cairngorms is the new funicular train. After years of countless arguments with environmental bodies, sad bird watchers and squares from various rambling associations, the *Cairngorm Mountain Company* finally got the go ahead to build the first ever funicular railway in **Great Britain** costing over £16 million (upgrading the old chair lifts and day lodge with money left over to build a new primary school down in **Aviemore** would have been a better way of spending that amount of cash). Still, the new train should greatly improve the up-lift capacity and time spent queuing for lifts. The funicular will also be a big relief to first timers as the beginner slopes are up at the top on the **Ciste**, which used to be reached by the old chair lift that often had to be shut down due to high winds. The train will be able to run in much greater winds and will travel a distance of 1200 metres from the top car park up to the new **Ptarmigan** restaurant in around six minutes. It won't be a cheap trip though as an adult return ticket is set to cost from £7.50 (the same money could buy two travel cards for a days unlimited train and bus travel around **London**). However, if the train works and the other new mountain facilities turn out to be good, then all the better. Let's hope that the attitude and standard of customer care by the **Cairngorm Mountain** company to its visitors, also changes for the better.

Freeriders who know how to ride, will find **Cairngorm** an almost complete waste of time, with no trees, no bowls or any real adventurous terrain to explore. Experienced riders used to long testing steeps will soon tire of Cairngom, with nothing to tackle apart from the West Wall, the only black run. The **White Lady** run can offer riders an okay time when it's not riddled with moguls.

Freestylers who like to go big off natural hits, forget it. However, in a more favourable light, there is a terrain park which has a series of big and small hits. The park which is sponsored by **Headworks**, also has its own boarder patrol. When snow permits there is also a half pipe which is used for local competitions.

Carvers turning up here expecting to find loads of wide open cruising slopes, will be very disappointed with what they find. On the best runs, you will be lucky to complete two big turns before you're back in a lift line. Nothing takes more than a minute.

Beginners, this place is definitely not for you. There are hardly any wide easy slopes, and the ones you do find are sandwiched between snow fences and constantly choked up with ski classes. Beginners are far better off going to '**The Lecht**', 40 minutes away.

There are no facilities such as accommodation or shops on the mountain. However, the **Spey Valley** is home to a number of good traditional local villages that serve an all year round tourist trade. **Aviemore**, which is only 9 miles from the slopes, is the nearest village and the main hangout, with places like **Kincraig, Kingussie Carrbridge and Grantown-on-Spey** all close by. Wherever you stay, local amenities are very good with each village offering something different. Aviemore is a cool place and attracts lots of visitors especially at weekends during the winter season. There are a number of places to hangout when the mountain is closed which includes an overkill in sports shops. There are also loads of out-door attractions to check out, such as 4x4 driving, go-karting, or climbing.

Aviemore has a good choice of eating outlets. *The Cairngorm Hotel* is very good where you can get great bar food at affordable prices (the soup and sandwiches are mega). *Harkais Chip Shop* does a mean fish supper, while the new *Einich Restaurant,* with its rather rounded chef, has an excellent choice of dishes. The *PH22* restaurant is the place for pizza. However, the number one place to dine in the whole valley has to be *The Ossian Hotel* in **Kincraig**, a total eating joy and great value.

Nightlife in Aviemore can be lively and thankfully there's no aprés ski rubbish, so beloved by skiers. *Chevvy's* and *Mambo's* are popular hangouts, while *Crofters* is the late place for a dance or to pick up a slapper.

The **Spey Valley** has a large selection of hotels, guest houses, bed and breakfast and self catering homes. Rates vary considerably, with the big hotels in and around **Aviemore** being the most expensive. The *Ossian Hotel* in **Kincraig** *tel 01540 651 242,* is the best in the valley with a top reputation for its services and its extremely affordable rates. *The Cairngorm Hotel* in Aviemore is also good value *tel 01479 810 233. Silverglades, 01479 810 165* is a top self-catering company in Aviemore as is *Pine Bank Chalets* on *01479 810 000.*

Summary: In general the Cairngorms are a shocking waste of time. However, when it does snow and you scam the lifts then the place is fine. Local services are very good.
Money wise: On the slopes prices are criminal, but elsewhere things can be very resonable.

Overall rating out of 10 — **3**

Tourist Office Aviemore
Grampian Rd, Aviemore, Inverness-shire

General info	**++44 (0) 1479 810 363**
Reservations	**++44 (0) 1479 810 363**
Cairngorm info	**++44 (0) 1479 861 261**

www.ski.scotland.net

pics - Aviemore Photographics

Travel Guide

Fly to **Glasgow** international
Transfer time to resort = **2½** hours.
Local airport = Inverness - 45 minutes away.

Approximate global air travel times to **Glasgow:**

from: London	**1**	hour
Los Angles	**10**	hours
New York	**9**	hours

Bus services from Glasgow airport are available on a daily basis to Aviemore.

Trains to the centre of Aviemore

Route Planner
Glasgow via Perth

Cairngorm = 134 miles (215 km)
Drive time is about **2½** hours

*From **London** 535 miles (806 Km)
Drive time is around **9** hours.

Nevis Range

MOUNTAIN DATA

Top Lift at - 1220m

Ride Area
15km of piste

Bottom Lift at - 100m
Vertical Drop - 580m
Number of Runs - 35
Longest - 1 mile (1.6km)

TERRAIN LEVELS

Easy	**65%**
Intermediate	**25%**
Advanced	**10%**
Expert =	

TERRAIN TO SUITE

Freeride	**60%**
Trees	None
Backcountry	A tiny bit
Freestyle	10%
Halfpipe	No
Terrain Park	No
Carving	**30%**

SNOW DATA

Average Snowfall

Snowmaking
0% cover of the slopes
Winter Riding
Jan to April
Summer Riding
None

SLOPE ACCESS

Total Lifts = **12**
Uplift Rate - 9,600 people an hour.
1 Gondola
3 Chair lifts - **8** Drag lifts
**Leashes Required*

Lift Times
8.30am to 4.30pm

Lift Pass Rates
1 Day pass £19.75
3 Day pass £48.00
Season pass £195 +

Travel Guide

Fly to **Glasgow** airport 2 hours away.

Train services to Fort William, 10 minutes away.

Route Planner: Via Glasgow, head north on the A82, via Dumbarton and Glencoe.
From London, use the M1, M6, A74, to Glasgow.
*Drive time from **London** is about 10 hours.

pic - Nevis Range

Nevis Range is **Scotland's** youngest resort having opened in 1989. The mountain has a modern gondola and T-bar lift system to rival anything in **Europe** (when it's working or T-bars are not falling off all the time). Where this place is no match for European resorts, is the weather. Scotland's draw back is the unpredictable weather patterns, which is often a mixture of high winds, driving sleet and rain or stupid blizzards. And Nevis gets its fair share of the lot, this place is also not helped by the fact that is is close to the west coast shore line. However, the people who run the place shrug off the problems related to the weather, and do their best to look after visitors. The modest array of mountain facilities cater well for those who do bother to check this place out, which can get busy at weekends but often deserted during week days apart from school holiday periods. Having hosted the **UK's** first 'British Snowboard Championships' way back in 1990, the resort has long been snowboard friendly, but don't expect too many things to be laid on such as terrain parks and halfpipes, the poor snow conditions don't allow for it. What they have managed to achieve on the slopes that lie in the shadow of **Ben Nevis**, Britain's highest mountain, is a fairly well balanced mixture of short runs that will mainly appeal to beginners even though most of the novice runs are serviced by drag lifts. Overall the terrain here is pretty unadventurous and an expert rider will tire of this mountain within an hour or two of being here.

Freeriders have a couple of good areas by **Scottish** standards to ride, namely the back bowl area which has a series of steeps.

Freestylers have to make do with either building their own hits to get air, or snow permitting, the gully under the main chairlift provides a small natural halfpipe for a bit of air time. The other thing to do is to ollie over the numerous downed skier pupils.

Carvers will find that the **Snowgoose Gully** is the area to lay some lines on. But overall Nevis is not a cruiser's resort.

Beginners have a number of easy slopes located at the lower areas not far from the top gondola station.

The town of **Fort William**, 6 miles away, has a big choice of accommodation and eating spots. There is some accommodation near the slopes but it's limited and isolated. Evenings are not hot but with plenty of pubs to try out, you can have a rowdy time.

For accommodation listings visit - www.worldsnowboardguide.com

Nevis Range
Torlundy, Fort William. Inverness-shire
++44 (0) 01397 705 825 www.ski.scotland.net

Overall rating out of 10 **3** **Expert riders won't enjoy it here**

REAL SNOW SLOPES

Glenshee

▲1060m 12 km of piste 24 lifts

Glenshee is Scotland's biggest resort, although not much different to the Country's smallest. This place was first to use snow cannons, but in truth, they haven't really helped to improve what largely is a disappointment. The 25 miles are spread out over varying slopes and on a good day, allow for bit of off-piste powder (there's never a good day though). The majority of runs are basic short novice trails with only two steep sections.

Freeriders have no trees, but a bit of powder on Glas Maol area.

Freestylers don't bother.

Carvers, can crank a it down the **Cairnwell** but not for long.

Beginners will hate the way the lifts are set out, however, the novice runs will provide some fun. Local facilities don't exist and what there is is, fairly dull.

Fly to: **Aberdeen** 1½ hours away

ⓘ **tel-** ++44 (0) 1339 741 320

The Lecht

▲823m 6 km of piste 12 lifts

The Lecht is by far the smallest resort in Scotland, however, this is also one of the friendliest and quite simply the best beginner's resort. This value for money area, only has a handful of runs that rise up from the car park allowing for good easy access by foot to the well maintained novice runs. This is not a place for those who want long testing steeps, (there are none) but being a place with a cool attitude towards snowboarding and a genuine and welcoming feel to it, its still okay, if only for an hour or two.

Freeriders could have the whole place licked in an hour or two.

Freestylers, they always try and build a park and pipe here, with locals from Aberdeen using this as a fun weekend hangout.

Carvers of beginner to basic intermediate only.

Beginners, this place is perfect for novices, the best in Scotland. Good affordable local facilities in Tomintoul, 15 minutes away.

Fly to: **Aberdeen** 2 hours away

ⓘ **tel-** ++44 (0) 1975 651 440

ARTIFICAL SNOW SLOPES

XCAPE Building SnowZone
Milton Keynes -tel - 01908 230 260.
New indoor centre with one main long sectioned slope and two lifts.
*Full details are not yet available at.

Tamworth Snowdome
Leisure Island, River Drive
Staffs. B79 7ND. tel - 0990 00 00 11.
1 Lift & 1 run. Bar and restaurant.
Tamworth has until reciently been the UK's number 1 indoor snow slope. Best suited to total beginners as the slope is rather short, the place has attracted a lot of freestylers with a series of man hits allowing for weekly freestyle sessions.

ARTIFICAL DRY SLOPES

Aberdeen Ski Centre
Aberdeen - tel - 01224 311 781.

Alford Ski Centre
Alford - tel - 01975 563 024.

Alpine Ski Centre
Aldershot - tel - 01272 25 889.

Ancrun
Dundee - tel - 01382 435 911.

Aviemore Centre
Aviemore - tel - 01479 810 624.

Avon Ski Centre
Churchill - tel - 01934 852 335.

Alston Training Centre
Alston - tel - 01434 381 886.

Bearsden Ski Club
Glasgow - tel - 0141 943 1500.

Beckton Alpine Centre
London - tel - 020 7511 0351.

Bishop Reindorp Ski Cnt
Guildford - tel - 01483 504 988.

Borowski Ski and Snowboard
Newhaven - tel - 01273 515 402.

Bowles Outdoor Center
Tunbridge Wells - tel - 01892 665 665.

Bromley Ski
Orpington - tel - 01689 876 812.

Brentwood Park Ski Cnt
Brentford - tel - 01277 211 994.

Cardiff Ski Cnt
Cardiff - tel - 01222 561 793.

Calshot Activities Centre
Southampton - tel - 01703 892 077.

Christchurch Ski Cnt
Alston - tel - 01434 381 886.

Craigendarroch Country Club
Ballater - tel - 01339 755 858.

Craigavon ski Centre
Lurgan - tel - 01762 326 606.

Crystal Place Sports Cnt
London - tel - 0181 778 9876.

Dan-yr-Ogof Ski Slopes
Swansea - tel - 01639 730 284.

Firpark Ski Centre
Tillycoultry - tel - 01259 751 772

Folkestone Ski Slope
Folkestone - tel - 01303 850 333

Glasgow Ski Centre
Glasgow - tel - 0141 427 4991.

Glenmore Lodge
Aviemore - tel - 01479 861 256.

Gloucester Ski/Board Cnt
Gloucester - tel - 01452 414 300.

Gosling Ski Centre
Welwyn Garden - tel - 01707 391 039.

Halifax Ski Centre
Uxbridge - tel - 01895 255 183

Harlow Ski School
Halifax - tel - 01422 340 760

Hemel Ski Centre
Hemel Hemstead - tel - 01442 241 321

Hillington Ski/Snowboard
Uxbridge - tel - 01895 255 183

John Nike Leisure Centre
Chatham - tel - 01634 827 979

Kendal Ski Club
Kendal - tel - 01539 733 031

Midlothian Ski Centre
Edinburgh - tel - 0131 445 4433

Ski Llandudno
Llandudno - tel - 0149 287 4707

Southampton Ski Centre
Southampton - tel - 01703 790 970

ITALY

GENERAL INFO AND FACTS

Capital - Rome
Language - Italian
Currency - Lire & Euros
Alcohol drinking age - 18
Drugs - Cannabis is illegal
Death Penalty - Doesn't exist
Age of consent for Sex - 16
Military Service -Compulsory
Electricity Supply - 240 Volts AC
International phone Code ++39
Highest Peak - Mont Blanc 4810m

DUTY FREE
10 Litres of Alcohol
90 Litres of Wine - 110 of beer
800 Cigarettes
200 Cigars

ITALIAN DRIVE GUIDE
All vehicles drive on the right hand side of the road
Speed Limits -
Motorways 113kph (70mph)
Highways 97kph (60mph)
Towns 50kph (30mph)

Italian Snowboard Association
Rosa Massimo. Via Maldonado 8
tel - ++39 (0) 45 834 1221
www.board-it.com/resorts
www.thomson-ski.co.uk

TIME ZONES
Central European
GMT +1 Hour
Between March and October
GMT+2 Hours

INTERNATIONAL GATEWAY AIRPORTS
Milan
Venice
Turin
Geneva *in Switzerland*

Italy is somewhat different from the rest of Europe, a little more temperamental it might be said. Rather sad mountain dress sense is quite obvious, with a love for the all in one day-glow colour ski suits That said, Italy is a great place to snowboard and one of the cheapest European countries to visit. Italian resorts (which vary more off the slopes than on) are stretched across the northern part of the country, with many linking with neighbouring countries.

If you're intending to drive in Italy, remember: Italians can't drive, the term 'giving way' refers more to bowel movements than it does to other road users! But due to the fact that Italy has loads of small, remote resorts tucked away off normal public transport routes, driving is often the only option. Italian resorts are not always well located for airports, most places require an average of three hours transfer.

Train services are not too convenient, but you can get fairly close to many places. Rail fares are cheap and so it's a good option. Bus fares are also cheap, but services are not very reliable and understanding the time tables is an art form in itself.

Riders looking to work, should have no real problems Lots of winter tour operators include Italy in their programmes and are always hiring catering staff and the normal array of tour reps etc. Italy is a member of the EU so normal visa rules apply

Accommodation is on the whole basic and cheap. Around resorts, facilities are not as intense as in France, but the over indulgence in aprés ski behaviour and stupid face painting is still the same. That aside, however, Italy is well worth a visit.

pic - Palmer Snowboards

Bormio

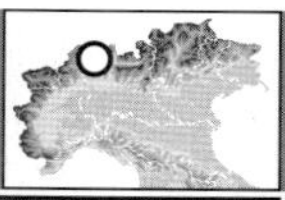

MOUNTAIN DATA

Top Lift at - 3012m

Ride Area: 28km of piste

Bottom Lift at - 1225m

Vertical Drop - 1787m

Number of Runs - 18

Longest - 8.7 mile (14km)

TERRAIN LEVELS

Easy	30%
Intermediate	50%
Advanced	20%
Expert =	

TERRAIN TO SUITE

Freeride	40%
Trees	Yes
Backcountry	Yes
Freestyle	20%
Halfpipe	No
Terrain Park	No
Carving	40%

SNOW DATA

Average Snowfall
300cm a season

Snowmaking
40% cover of the slopes

Winter Periods
Dec to April

Summer Riding
None

SLOPE ACCESS

Total Lifts = 17

Uplift Rate - 13,500 people an hour.

2 Cable cars - 1 Gondola

9 Chair lifts - 5 Drag lifts

**Leashes Required*

Lift Times
8.30am to 4.30pm

Lift Pass Rates

1 Day pass	50,000 Li
2 Day pass	95,500 Li
6 Day pass	260,000

Travel Guide

Fly to **Milan** airport, 4 hours away.

Train services are possible to Tirano 20 minutes away.

Route Planner:
Via Milan, head north via the towns of Lecco, Sondrio and Tirano, along the A38 to Bormio.
*Drive time from **Calais** is 12 hours 648 miles (1043 km)

pic - Bormio Tourism

Bormio dates back hundreds of years and it's quite possible that the *Romans* who built an ancient spa town near here could have actually been the first to shred the slopes in their tin hats. However, Bormio as we know it today is rated very highly in Italy, with it's modern roots going back to the early sixties when the resort started dragging punters up its mainly intermediate all-round terrain. Bormio is a fairly busy place, with an overkill in some very sad all in one ski suits. The ski world does a lot of racing on the slopes here; (Bormio hosted the 1985 World Championships) which suggests that there must be something on offer. Italian skiers like this place a lot, as do Germans and quite a lot of Brits. This means the slopes do become very clogged up at weekends and over holiday periods.

Freeriders have a mountain that is not extensive especially for advanced riders. There is some good off piste freeriding with powder bowls and trees to check out. The best stuff reached from the **Cima Bianca**, where the runs start off steep and mellow out to test the best. Don't bother hitting this stuff in hards, you'll regret it as this section is soft boot only terrain.

Freestylers wanting to get big air will not find a great deal, but there are plenty of natural hits. The resort doesn't have a pipe or park, the nearest is 10 minutes away at **Passo Dello Stelvio** (linked by a shuttle bus). The Stelvio glacier, the largest in Europe, offers the opportunity to snowboard during the summer.

Carvers will find that **Bormio** is an excellent place for any level and the 9 mile run from the top station down to the village provides plenty of time to get those big carves in. It's perfect for riders who want to see what it's like linking turns and by the time you hit the bottom, you'll know for sure.

Beginners will find the slopes at Bormio ideal for basics and excellent for progression. What's more, all the easy stuff can be reached without tackling a drag lift.

Bormio is a rather strange affair, but nevertheless a very rustic and Italian place. Accommodation is offered in a range of locations, with the choice of staying on or near the slopes. Around town, you soon notice how glitzy things are however, staying here can be done on a tight budget if you leave out dining in fancy restaurants: seek out one of the cheap pizza joints. Night-life is nothing to get excited about, in fact it's pretty dull but still boozey.

Tourist Office Bormio
Via Roma 131?B. Bormio 123032.
++39 (0) 349 903 300 **www.provincia.so.it/aptvaltellina**

Overall rating out of 10 — **5** — **Basic resort with simple slopes**

Cervinia

MOUNTAIN DATA

Top Lift at - 3488m

Ride Area
241km of piste

Bottom Lift at - 2050m
Vertical Drop - 1438m
Number of Runs - 129
Longest - 5 miles (8km)

TERRAIN LEVELS

Easy	**16%**
Intermediate	**65%**
Advanced	**19%**
Expert =	

TERRAIN TO SUITE

Freeride	**35%**
Trees	A few
Backcountry	A bit
Freestyle	**5%**
Halfpipe	Yes 1
Terrain Park	Yes 1
Carving	**30%**

SNOW DATA

Average Snowfall
990cm a season
Snowmaking
25% cover of the slopes
Winter Periods
Dec to April
Summer Riding
Yes

SLOPE ACCESS

Total Lifts = **33**
Uplift Rate - 28,500 people an hour.
3 Gondolas - **4** Cables
13 Chair lifts - **13** Drag lifts
**Leashes Required*

Lift Times
8.30am to 8.30pm

Lift Pass Rates

1 Day pass	53,000 Li
3 Day pass	97,000 Li
6 Day pass	270,000 Li

Travel Guide

Fly to **Geneva** airport
$2^{1/2}$ hours away.

Train services go to Chatillon, 20 minutes away.

Route Planner: Via Geneva, head south on the A40, via the Mont Blanc Tunnel. Then take the A5 and turn off on to 406.
*Drive time from **Calais** is $10^{1/2}$ hours
616 miles (991 km)

pic - Cervinia

Cervinia is something of a nothing and a place that you will either love or hate. This is Italy through and through: bland, no big deal and full of stupidly dressed skiers. Yet for all that, it's not a bad place to ride. Cervinia (which links the slopes with the big bucks **Swiss** resort of **Zermatt**) is a Eurocarver's paradise. The area has been attracting two plankers for years and in recent times more and more snowboarders have taken to the slopes and have been made welcome. It's fair to say that there's never been anything laid on for riders: no pipe, park or even a decent snowboard shop. Still, the terrain is the main thing and it's OK, suiting all levels with most emphasis favouring intermediates runs

Freeriders will find Cervinia a bit of a bore, although around the **Cieloalto** area some off-piste powder can be cut. However, the close proximity to **Zermatt** and the glacier means that there are good alternatives, which can be explored by going heli-boarding.

Freestylers won't find much here of interest: no pipe and no great natural hits. However, there is some fun to be had, even if it's just off the table tops around eating places (ask the Señor first if he minds Stalefish with his fresh pasta).

Carvers can test their skills on a variety of reds and some steep blacks which can be tricky if you're not giving it your all. However, the 22 km red run, Valtournenche, is the place to carve long and hard, while the blacks down into the village are cool.

Beginners, the place to get your first bruises is up at the Plan Maison, which is reached by a cable-car. Once up, be prepared to tackle some drag lifts in order to get to the easy flats, which also come with a heavy dose of ski schools. The runs rise up from the village at three main points and apart from a few areas, the lower sections are not beginner friendly, although there is a blue that leads down giving novices the chance to ride home.

Cervinia has plenty of affordable places to sleep and there's a number of cheap apartments and hotels to stay in, with easy access to the slopes a common feature. The resort has a host of activities going on, aimed at package holiday groups who can't think for themselves. The resort has a big choice of restaurants to choose from. Evenings come in the form of standard grade aprés ski bull in the likes of the *Dragon*, or the *Chimera* disco which pumps out bland Euro pop.

For accommodation listings visit - **www.worldsnowboardguide.com**

Cervina Tourist Office
Via Carrel 29, I11021, Breuil-Cervinia. Asota
++39 (0) 166 949 136 **www.cervinia**

Overall rating out of 10 **4** **Very bland and stuck up resort**

Cortina

ITALY

MOUNTAIN DATA

Top Lift at - 3243m

Ride Area 140km of piste

Bottom Lift at - 1224m

Vertical Drop - 2020m

Number of Runs - 52

Longest - 5.6 miles (9km)

TERRAIN LEVELS

Easy	**44%**
Intermediate	**45%**
Advanced	**11%**
Expert =	

TERRAIN TO SUITE

Freeride	**50%**
Trees	A few
Backcountry	A little
Freestyle	**20%**
Halfpipe	Yes 1
Terrain Park	No
Carving	**30%**

SNOW DATA

Average Snowfall
400cm a season

Snowmaking
10% cover of the slopes

Winter Periods
Dec to April

Summer Riding
None

SLOPE ACCESS

Total Lifts = **38**

Uplift Rate - 44,000 people an hour.

2 Cable cars

22 Chair lifts - **10** Drag lifts

**Leashes Required*

Lift Times
8.30am to 5.30pm

Lift Pass Rates

1 Day pass	63,000 Li
3 Day pass	
6 Day pass	313,000 Li

Travel Guide

Fly to **Venice** airport
2 hours away.

Train services go to
Calalzo Pieve (20 minutes)

Route Planner: Via Venice, head north on the A27 via Ponte Nelle Alpi. Then take the 51 via Tai di Cadore to Cortina.
*Drive time from **Calais** is 15 hours
752 miles (1210 km)

pic - Cortina Tourism

Every country has a place that the rich, famous and Royals head for, just to be seen 'on the piste' and to get a picture wearing sad clothing for the cover of Hello! Magazine. Enter **Cortina**, for this is one of those places, with so many balcony posers lieing around outside restaurants that the slopes are left quiet. This allows snowboarders space to roam and explore the terrain. Cortina, located in the northern reaches of the **Italian Dolomites,** is an ex-Olympic resort, whose area is made up of two large mountain plateaus that rise up around the village. On one side you have an area called **Faloria,** which connects up to **Forcella**, and rises to a height of 2950m. On the other side of the village lies the slopes of **Tofana.** *Tofana is* not connected by lift to the other areas, but can be reached via a cable car from the town or by the local bus to **Pocol.** The terrain here is pretty good and will suite all. Advanced riders get a mountain to challenge them to the limit and keep them interested for a week or even two, while intermediates will have ample opportunity to brush up on their skills and to progress nicely on a series of good slopes.

Freeriders will find that the most challenging runs are located down from the **Tofana,** which rises to 3243m and is accessed by cable car. From the summit you'll find plenty of stuff to check out.

Freestylers may not get man-made hits, but not to worry as there are plenty of natural ones with some cool drop offs and big banks to catch air from on both mountain sections. The **Tofana** area has the best stuff though.

Carvers; the **Sella Ronda** trail is definitely worth a visit, as is the **Canellone** which is a two planker's race run and the area to cut the snow in style, but not for wimps.

Beginners can progress here on good easy slopes, with the best stuff around the mid section of the **Tofana.** These can be reached by chair (rather than drag) lifts.

Cortina is a large place, with silly priced hotels and apartment style accommodation located mostly near or on the slopes. Around the village are various food joints offering the usual Italian fare. The evenings are pretty boring here and the rich only make it very glitzy. However, it s not all gloom as you can spend the evening mocking the rich and mine sweeping their drinks: they won't notice because they're too busy posing.

For accommodation listings visit - www.worldsnowboardguide.com

Cortina
Pizza San Francesso, 8 Cortina d"Ampezzo
++39 (0) 436 3231 www.

Overall rating out of 10 **5** **Incredibly dull resort**

Courmayeur

MOUNTAIN DATA

Top Lift at - 2775m

Ride Area
100km of piste

Bottom Lift at - 1225m
Vertical Drop - 1532m
Number of Runs - 28
Longest - 6 miles (10km)

TERRAIN LEVELS

Easy	44%
Intermediate	52%
Advanced	4%
Expert =	

TERRAIN TO SUITE

Freeride	40%
Trees	Yes
Backcountry	Yes
Freestyle	10%
Halfpipe	Yes 1
Terrain Park	Yes 1
Carving	50%

SNOW DATA

Average Snowfall
700cm a season
Snowmaking
15% cover of the slopes
Winter Periods
Dec to April
Summer Riding
Yes

SLOPE ACCESS

Total Lifts = **24**
Uplift Rate - 135,000 people an hour.
1 Cable car - **1** Gondola
8 Chair lifts - **8** Drag lifts
**Leashes Required*

Lift Times
8.30am to 4.30pm

Lift Pass Rates
1 Day pass 55,000
6 Day pass 276,000
Season pass 900,000

SLOPE ACTION

Snowboard Hire
Daily rates from 65,000 Li
Kids from 50,000 Li

Snowboard Tuition
Group lessons, from
from 240,000 Li an hour

Night Riding
No

Heli Boarding
No

Snowmobiles
No

Mountain Cafes
10

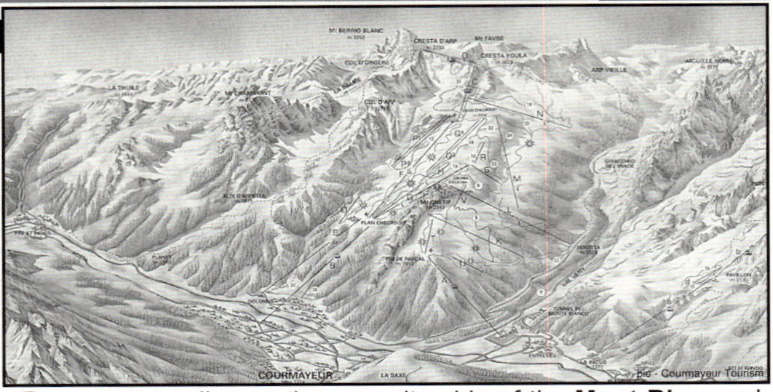

pic - Courmayeur Tourism

Courmayeur lies on the opposite side of the **Mont Blanc** valley and only a stone's throw away from the top **French** resort of **Chamonix** which is a short drive back up through the **Mont Blanc Tunnel**. Courmayeur, a high level resort gives access to slopes that can be ridden by all and generally, this is a good place to spend a week or two. However, with its mixture of traditional Italian architecture and its modern resort offerings, Courmayeur is a destination that attracts millions of British skiers and other foreign nationals every year. They then copy their Italian counterparts by cladding themselves in horrid expensive ski wear and cloging up the slopes to often bursting point. The village is well spread out, but there is no real chance of leaping out of the nest, ollieing over a balcony and landing in a lift queue: you are going to have to do a bit of walking in order to take the cable car up to the slopes. The terrain will please intermediate carvers, but bore advanced freeriders. Be warned, every man and his dog hits the slopes at weekends and holidays. The main thing you notice is the amount of plate bindings and ski boots that there are about, as this is a carver's pose place, although many don't know what to pose in (ski boots are a no-no people). Top Italian female pro *Martina Magenta* hails from Courmayeur and can often be seen carving up the slopes. If you ride here in summer, the best time to come is in May or June when the snow is still good and not too rutted or over slushy.

Freeriding here is pretty damn good, with some cool terrain to hit and the possibility of some trees to cut at the lower section. If it's powder and off piste riding you want, then Courmayeur is not the mega outlet like it's close French neighbour, but there is some good stuff to be had on steeps and trees down from the **Cresta D'Arp**. If you take the **Mont Blanc** cable car, you can gain access to the **Vallee Blanche** and ride into **Chamonix**. Although you will need to get the bus back, it'll be worth it.

Freestylers here make do with the natural hits as there is no park or pipe to ride. You can however, get big air and find enough to jib off, eg snow cannons, logs, stair rails, ski instructors, there's plenty. You'll also find plenty snow built up in lumps pushed to the side of runs or covering small trees and small mounts etc.

Carvers who like to stay on the pistes will find loads of well pisted runs to content themselves with, especially the areas under the **Bertolini** chair lift.

Beginners who decide to give **Courmayeur** a try won't be disappointed, it's a perfect place to learn, although the slopes can often be far too busy, leading to a few collisions. Novices should head for the runs off the **Checrouit** cable car, where you'll find some nice easy slopes to try out your first toe and heel side turns amongst the ski crowds, taking out the stragglers as you go.

Off the slopes, **Courmayeur** is a busy, stretched out place, with a lot going on. Most of the time the village plays host to package tour groups and although this helps to keep prices realistic, it does mean you have to rub shoulders with a lot of idiots. The village has a host of sporting attractions with the usual resort style swimming pools, ice rinks and fitness outlets. There is also an overdose of Italian style boutiques, selling expensive designer wear, but alas, there are no decent snowboard shops.

Job Seekers wishing to do a season here, should have no problem getting a job with one of the many tour operators or foreign ski schools that operate out of Courmayeur.

Food wise, Courmayeur does a good job fattening up its visitors with the usual option to pig out in a few pizza restaurants. There is also a number of basic holiday tourist style eateries offering funny sounding traditional Italian dishes. However, you can eat reasonably if you stick to the lower end pizza joints such as *La Boite,* but if you're feeling flush and want to dine, check out *Pierre Alexis.*

Night life in Courmayeur is late, loud and very boozy. Italians party hard here, but unfortunately so do a lot of aprés skiers, who give the place a rowdy and low life feel to it. Popular places to check out are the *Popas Pup*, *Bar Roma* or *The Red Lion*, all of which are lively watering holes with a young party style crowd.

Accommodation is very good here. The town can sleep 20,000 visitors with lodging close to the slopes and in the town centre. You can choose to bed down in one of the hotels, or stay in one of the self catering apartment blocks which can accommodate large groups of riders. There are also a number of very reasonably priced bed and breakfast homes to choose from.

For accommodation listings visit - www.worldsnowboardguide.com

Summary: Not a bad place, with some good carving but basic freeriding. Great for beginners apart from over crowded novice slopes. Good local services.
Money wise: Overall this is an expensive resort but also a good value.

Overall rating out of 10 — **7**

Tourist Office Courmayeur
Monte Bianco, Pizzale 3
Courmayeur. I11013
General info **++39 (0) 165 842 060**
Reservations **++39 (0) 165 842 060**
Avlanche info **++39 (0) 165 776 300**
www.courmayeur.net

pic - Michael Vechi

pic - Courmayeur Tourism

Travel Guide

Fly to **Geneva** international
Transfer time to resort = **1½** hours.
Local airport = none

Approximate global air travel times to **Geneva:**

from:		
	London	2 hours
	Los Angles	13 hours
	New York	9 hours

Bus services from Geneva airport are available on a daily basis as well as from Milan.

Trains to **Pre-St-Didier** (3 miles)

Route Planner
Geneva via Mont Blanc Tunnel

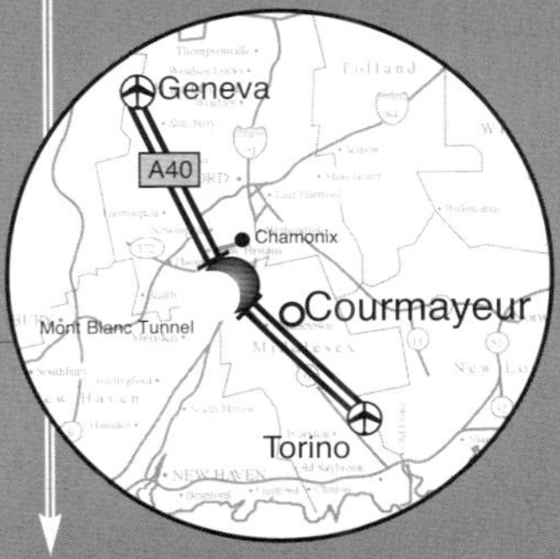

Courmayeur = 65 miles (104 km)
Drive time is about **2** hours

*From **Calais** 563 miles (905 Km)
Drive time is around **9½** hours.

La Thuile

MOUNTAIN DATA

Top Lift at - 2642m

Ride Area
85km of piste

Bottom Lift at - 1441m

Vertical Drop - 1200m

Number of Runs - 30

Longest - 7 miles (11km)

TERRAIN LEVELS

Easy	**44%**
Intermediate	**36%**
Advanced	**20%**
Expert =	

TERRAIN TO SUITE

Freeride	**30%**
Trees	Yes
Backcountry	Yes
Freestyle	**30%**
Halfpipe	Yes 1
Terrain Park	Yes 1
Carving	**40%**

SNOW DATA

Average Snowfall
500cm a season

Snowmaking
20% cover of the slopes

Winter Periods
Dec to April

Summer Riding
No

SLOPE ACCESS

Total Lifts = **15**

Uplift Rate - 16,000 people an hour.

9 Chair lifts -

6 Drag lifts

**Leashes Required*

Lift Times
8.30am to 4.30pm

Lift Pass Rates

1 Day pass	55,000
6 Day pass	280,000
Season pass	890,000

SLOPE ACTION

Snowboard Hire
Daily rates from 62,000 Li
Kids from 49,000 Li

Snowboard Tuition
Group lessons, from from 239,000 Li an hour

Night Riding
No

Heli Boarding
Yes, over the Rutor Glacier

Snowmobiles
No

Mountain Cafes
7

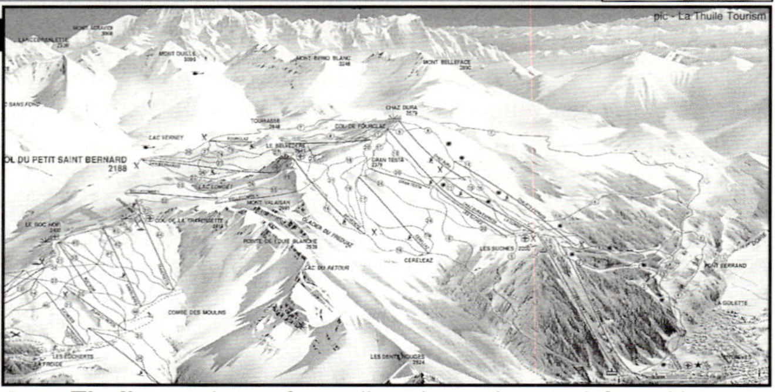

pic - La Thuile Tourism

La Thuile nestles a few miles down the road from it's more famous cousin **Courmayeur**, but unlike it's neighbour, it is a far quieter resort. This is despite the fact that it has a good 53 miles plus of piste and even more off piste for all snowboader styles and abilities. There is plenty to keep you occupied for a week or two. La Thuile is located in the **Aosta Valley** and links with **La Rosiere.** Collectively they provide over 100 miles (160km) of marked out and pisted terrain.

This is not just a hard boot carvers resort, the wide open pistes, steeps and trees are there for everyone. The terrain lies at a height that helps to ensure good snow conditions prevail all season, backed up by snowmaking facilities if it does get thin. For those who like powder, there can be fresh snow on the high, north facing slopes even in April. For those who like tree runs, you'll find perfect snow conditions throughout the season. An important aspect of the resort is that it is very well served by chairlifts, which makes waiting in line extremely rare. Most of all, it gives the rider the possibility of reaching the most remote parts of the resort (where skiers are few and the fresh snow is untouched) without having to hike steep slopes, with your board. La Thuile offers all snowboarders a vast range of possibilities that include long off-pistes in fresh powder, black runs with steep vertical drops, large perfectly prepared slopes for those who love carving and a variety of cliffs, natural jumps and virgin slopes.

Freeriders have some good black runs to try out: the **Diretta** (which runs through the trees) is full on and will test those who think they know it all. There's also some cool freeriding to be had on the **La Rosiere** side, while those looking for off-piste will find it off the **San Bernardo** chair. However the real off-piste is best tackled by going heli-boarding which is offered here.

Freestylers have a good pipe, which the local snowboard club help to look after. However, you may find that the abundance of natural hits dotted around both La Thuile and La Rosiere offer better air time.

Carvers have a variety of great pisted slopes for laying out big carves on and most can be tackled at speed without having to negotiate too many sightseeing skiers.

Beginners need to know that apart from a couple of small nursery slopes at the base, the main easy runs are located above the **Les Suches** area, which is served by chairlifts rather than all drags. However, slow learners will not be riding back into the village at the outset. To help get to grips with what snowboarding is about, why not take a few lessons with the local ski school? After all, they have been teaching snowboarding here for years and know their stuff. A two hour lesson cost from 239,000 Lira, you can alos take private lessons.

La Thuile is finally reached after a short drive up twisting and winding mountain road. On arrival, you are presented with a scenic and old Italian village with a hint of the new here and there. The main happenings are conveniently at the base of the slopes and straddle a large river. Visitors are made very welcome in La Thuile and local services cater very well for all your needs. Around the village you will find a few shops, places to pig out and one or two hotels with their own sporting facilities, such as a hotel swimming pool, gym and saunas. But other than that there is nothing major going on. Snowboard hire is best done from *Ornella Sports* +39 (0) 165 844 154.

As for eats, you can get all the usual Italian dishes here along with a selection of standard grade euro nosh. However, your choice of where to eat out is a bit limited on the whole. Still, that said, what is offered is good and you can eat very well here on a low budget. Restaurants of note are that of *La Rascards* for a choice of local dishes, or *La Grotta* which is known for its slices of pizza and pasta, although not the cheapest of places.

Night life in La Thuile is very tame by Italian standards, so if you're the sort that likes to party hard all night long, this is not your resort. La Thuile is a very relaxed place and there is nothing much going on. Any so called action seems to be as the lifts close when there is a flurry of apre nonsense. Still you can enjoy a beer in the *La Bricole* bar.

Accommodation, La Thuile is a relatively small resort with around 3000 beds, bunks or other things on which to kip on. However, what there is is quite sufficient for a weeks stay with the option to lieout horizontally in bed on the slopes or within a short walk of the first lifts. A number of tour operators offer full holiday packages here, so some good package deals are available.

For accommodation listings visit - www.worldsnowboardguide.com

Summary: An okay freeriders resort with some nice powder spots and trees to ride. Also good for carving but the slopes can be a bit tricky at the lower sections.
Money wise: Not cheap but overall an affordable resort to visit.

Overall rating out of 10 **7**

Tourist Office La Thule
Via Collomb, 4-11016
La Thule

General info	**++39 (0) 165 884 179**
Reservations	**++39 (0) 165 884 179**
Avlanche info	**++39 (0) 165 776 300**

pics - La Thuile Tourism

Travel Guide

Fly to **Geneva** international
Transfer time to resort = **2 1/4** *hours.*
Local airport = none

Approximate global air travel times to **Geneva:**

from:	London	2 hours
	Los Angles	13 hours
	New York	9 hours

Bus services from Geneva airport are available on a daily basis as well as from Milan.

Trains to **Pre-St-Didier** (3 miles)

Route Planner
Geneva via Mont Blanc Tunnel

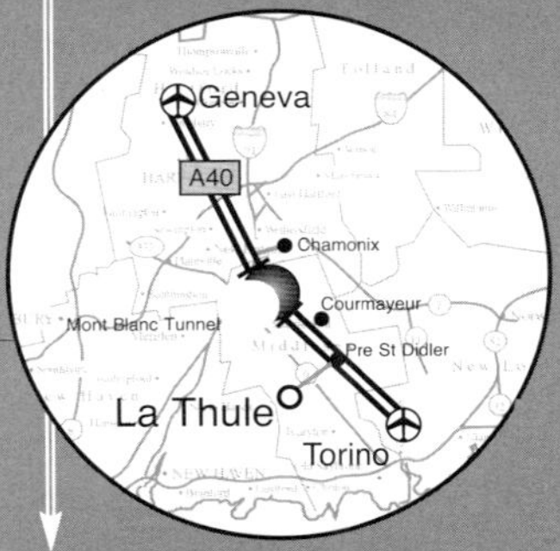

La Thule = 76 miles (122 km)
Drive time is about **2 1/4** hours

*From **Calais** 583 miles (939 Km)
Drive time is around **10** hours.

Limone

pic - Limone Tourism

MOUNTAIN DATA

Top Lift at - 2800

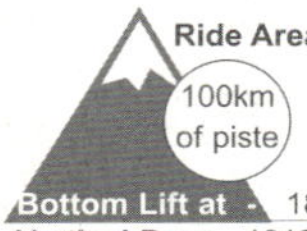

Bottom Lift at - 1861m

Vertical Drop - 1018m

Number of Runs - 46

Longest -

TERRAIN LEVELS

Easy	**30%**
Intermediate	**65%**
Advanced	**5%**
Expert =	

TERRAIN TO SUITE

Freeride	**60%**
Trees	A few
Backcountry	Yes
Freestyle	**15%**
Halfpipe	No
Terrain Park	Occasionally
Carving	**25%**

SNOW DATA

Average Snowfall

Snowmaking
15% cover of the slopes

Winter Periods
Dec to April

Summer Riding
None

SLOPE ACCESS

Total Lifts = **29**

Uplift Rate - 22,000 people an hour.

6 Chair lifts -

23 Drag lifts

**Leashes Required*

Lift Times
8.30am to 5.30pm

Lift Pass Rates

1 Day pass	51,000 Li
3 Day pass	124,000
6 Day pass	256,000 Li

Travel Guide

Fly to **Turin** airport $1^{1/2}$ hours away.

Train services are possible to Limone Piemonte.

Route Planner: from Turin (Torino) head south via Carmagnola, Cuneo, and Borgo S.Dalmazzo on the route 20 until you reach Limone.

Limone is located south of Turin and only a short distance from the **French** and Italian border. Limone is a traditional Italian town with a past that involves the railways. Today however, this relatively unknown holiday destination is a simple place that attracts summer and winter tourists all year round to sample its holiday attractions which include great mountains. The old sprawling town sits at the base of an impressive set of high peaks, with the 2344 metre summit of the **Cima Pepino** mountain well within sight. The place is not widely known as a ski or snowboard destination outside of **Italy** which can be a bit of a blessing as the place is not tainted with mass package ski tour groups. But on the down side, not being the most popular of places can often mean a lack of on-going resort development. Still, this may not be a big fancy resort boasting loads of steep challenging slopes, but you can nevertheless have a great time riding on slopes that can fill up with weekend visitors but are empty during the mid week periods. This is a simple resort that is suited to intermediate riders with very little to offer expert riders. Advanced riders will find some interesting terrain, but it won't take more than a few days to ride-out. The one big draw back about **Limone** is its annual snow record. Its fairly close proximity to the **Mediterranean** sea means that this is not a resort blessed with heaps of regular snow.

Freeriders have a cool mountain to explore and should find **Limone** a pleasant suprise. There is a good choice of areas to ride that offers, tree riding, lots of gullies and uneven trails to descend down. Expert riders will find the **Olimpica** run a pleaser.

Freestylers don't have any laid on facilities as such, the poor snow record prevents the annual building or maintaining of parks.

Carvers who usually prefer miles of perfect well groomed trails, may be a bit disappointed. Most of the main runs are a bit choppy and not great cruising trails, that said you can still carve here.

Beginners might well find that this resort is not for them. There are some good novice slopes but they are very limited and serviced by a host of drag lifts.

Limone is an old town located within easy reach of the slopes. The town offers basic but affordable facilities with a good choice of hotels, apartment blocks and some bed and breakfast homes.

For accommodation listings visit - **www.worldsnowboardguide.com**

Tourist Office Limone
Via Roma 30, Limone Piemonte, I 12015
++39 (0) 171 92319 www.limone.net

Overall rating out of 10 **4** **Rather basic but still good**

Livingo

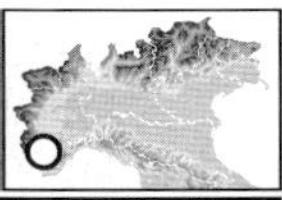

ITALY

MOUNTAIN DATA

Top Lift at - 2050m

Ride Area
80km of piste

Bottom Lift at - 1032m
Vertical Drop - 940m
Number of Runs - 55
Longest - 2.5 miles (4km)

TERRAIN LEVELS

Easy	44%
Intermediate	45%
Advanced	11%
Expert =	

TERRAIN TO SUITE

Freeride	35%
Trees	A few
Backcountry	A bit
Freestyle	10%
Halfpipe	Yes 1
Terrain Park	No
Carving	50%

SNOW DATA

Average Snowfall
250cm a season
Snowmaking
15% cover of the slopes
Winter Periods
Dec to April
Summer Riding
None

SLOPE ACCESS

Total Lifts = **30**
Uplift Rate 42,000 people an hour.
3 Gondolas
10 Chair lifts - **17** Drag lifts
**Leashes Required*

Lift Times
8.30am to 8.30pm

Lift Pass Rates

1 Day pass	52,000 Li
2 Day pass	69,000 Li
6 Day pass	265,000 Li

Travel Guide

Fly to **Milan** airport 3 1/2 hours away.

Train services goe Zernez in Switzerland. 20 minutes.

Route Planner: Via Milan, head north vai, Sondrio and then head up the A29 turning of left at La Rosa and on up to Livingo
*Drive time from **Calais** is 11 1/2 hours 628 miles (1010 km).

pic - Livingo Tourism

Something went wrong when **Livigno** was given the go ahead by the local planning committee as it's a badly laid out mess. Still, it's not totally crap and unlike many other Italian resorts, it rates low on the pretentious scale, although the sad one piece ski suits who shamefully ride in ski boots are still in evidence. As one of the cheaper resorts in Italy, the rich, sun tanning idiots are not so common, but it also has the effect of attracting lots of first time skiers, which makes it a very busy place. The height that Livigno is set at helps ensure a good snow record that lasts quite late into the season. The slopes are spread across both sides of the valley and offer loads of no-nonsense intermediate runs that will appeal to all rider styles. The way the area is set out means bussing around, with some notable bus queues. Once on the slopes, the runs are reached mainly by drag lifts which will annoy some first timers, but can be conquered.

Freeriders with some history are not going to be too tested here, although the black down from the Della Neve is worth a go and should appeal, unless you're a wimp. There's not much to shout about as far as off-piste is concerned. It is possible to find some, but it won't freak you out and some of the areas can be a pain in the arse for getting back to the resort. There are guiding services to help you find the best areas.

Freestylers are going to get the best fun by riding fakie in and out of the ski schools. There are some cool hits to get air off, but this is not a Freestylers paradise, even the pipe located on the **Mottolino** area is crap and rarely shaped.

Carvers get the chance to ride hard here on some OK carving runs. The **Vetta Blesaccia** is the slope to check out.

Beginners this resort is perfect for learning at with wide gentle runs located at lower sections which are easy to reach. Although slow learners will find the drags a real pain.

Livigno is cheap and cheerful, with lots of duty free shops. Accommodation is a mixture of hotels, B & B's and cheap apartments, which are easy to overload with extra bodies should you be visiting as a group on the cheap. There are numerous local amenities and a number of good restaurants, but the whole place has a cheesy feel to it and it can often be very crowded. Evenings are very boozy with a lot of throwing up in the streets.
For accommodation listings visit - www.worldsnowboardguide.com

Livingo Tourist Office
Via da La Gesa 65, 1-23030, Livingo, Sondiro.
++39 (0) 342 996 379 www.livingo.com.

Overall rating out of 10 - **4** **Not the most interesting place**

Madonna Di Campiglio

MOUNTAIN DATA

Top Lift at - 2580m

Ride Area
87km of piste

Bottom Lift at - 1520m
Vertical Drop - 985m
Number of Runs - 40
Longest - 2.5 miles (4km)

TERRAIN LEVELS

Easy	**54%**
Intermediate	**30%**
Advanced	**16%**
Expert =	

TERRAIN TO SUITE

Freeride	**50%**
Trees	A few
Backcountry	Yes
Freestyle	**25%**
Halfpipe	Yes 1
Terrain Park	Yes 1
Carving	**25%**

SNOW DATA

Average Snowfall

Snowmaking
35% cover of the slopes

Winter Periods
Dec to April

Summer Riding
None

SLOPE ACCESS

Total Lifts = **27**
Uplift Rate - 30,000 people an hour.
1 Cable car - **4** Gondolas
15 Chair lifts - **7** Drag lifts
**Leashes Required*

Lift Times
8.30am to 5.30pm

Lift Pass Rates

1 Day pass	52,000 Li
3 Day pass	120,000 Li
6 Day pass	265,000 Li

Travel Guide

Fly to **Verona** airport 2 1/2 hours away.

Train services are possible to Trento, 25 minutes away

Route Planner: Via Verona, go north on the A22 to the Mezzocorona Jct. Then take the A43 north and A42 south turning off at Dimaro and on to Madonna along the A239.

pic - Madonna Di Campiglio

Madonna Di Campiglio is one of the best resorts in the Dolomites and thankfully not tainted with too many cheap ski package tour groups, which helps to keep lift queues to almost zero. The pistes are relatively crowd free, although it should be said that Madonna does attract some of Italy's finest clientele. This well established ski haunt has now become a snowboarder's favourite, one that is trying really hard to satisfy boarders and it has to be said that it does a fairly good job. So much so, that the **International Snowboard Federation** has staged a number of top events in Madonna, attracting many top riders. It's not just the snowboarding they come for, the parties go off as well, with top bands and DJ's playing at the side of the half-pipe. The ride area, which rises up around the resort, is linked with **Folgarida** and **Marillea,** giving a combined coverage of over 100 miles of extremely well groomed trails and some good off-piste. Much of the terrain will suit riders who are just getting to grips with their style and ability, but advanced riders with a few years under their belts will find it a little unchallenging in places, but still okay.

Freeriders should check out the areas at **Spinale**, where you'll find some good powder spots and some nice tree sections to blast through lower down. **Fortini** also offers a testing time.

Freestylers like this place a lot and not just for the mega half-pipe (when an event is on) or the fun park and boardercross, located on **Groste** area. For those who like their hits natural, there are plenty of snow walls and steep hits to get air from.

Carvers, the race run normally set aside for ski races, is the place for competent riders who want to show skiers how a mountain should be tackled at speed and with only two edges.

Beginners, Madonna is one of the best first timers resorts around, with lots of well set out easy runs, allowing for easy access and quick progression to more difficult terrain.

The town has plenty of eating and sleeping options, with affordable places to sleep close to the slopes. Around the town, there are heaps of things to do with a whole manner of attractions such as ice speedway circuit and waterfall climbs. At night, things can get very lively, going off big style and lasting well into the early hours of the morning. There is a good choice of bars and clubs but they are all a bit pricey.

For accommodation listings visit - www.worldsnowboardguide.com

Madonna Di Campiglio
Madonna di Campiglio. I-38084
++39 (0) 465 442 000 **www.campiglio.net**

Overall rating out of 10 **4** **Good overall resort**

Prato Nevoso

ITALY

MOUNTAIN DATA

Top Lift at - 2100m

Ride Area
101km of piste

Bottom Lift at - 1490m
Vertical Drop - 550m
Number of Runs -
Longest -

TERRAIN LEVELS

Easy	50%
Intermediate	40%
Advanced	1%
Expert =	

TERRAIN TO SUITE

Freeride	20%
Trees	A few
Backcountry	Some
Freestyle	20%
Halfpipe	Yes 1
Terrain Park	Yes 1
Carving	60%

SNOW DATA

Average Snowfall
600cm a season
Snowmaking
7 snow cannons
Winter Periods
Dec to April
Summer Riding
None

SLOPE ACCESS

Total Lifts = **21**
Uplift Rate - 9,500 people an hour.
6 Chair lifts -
15 Drag lifts
**Leashes Required*

Lift Times
8.30am to 5.30pm

Lift Pass Rates

1 Day pass	45,000 Li
3 Day pass	
6 Day pass	255,000 Li

Travel Guide

Fly to **Turin** airport which is 1 hour away.

Train services to Mondovi which is 30 minutes away.

Route Planner: Via Turin, head south on the auto route A6 and turn off at signs for Mondovi. From here follow the signs to the resort. The distance from Turin is around 62 miles (100km).

pic - Soft Snapper

Prato Nevoso is a relatively unknown resort, yet this small and very friendly place has been operating as a ski resort since 1965, although not by any stretch of the imagination a big or adventurous hangout. Although Prato Nevoso is not a big or adventurous hangout, it is still good with some nice terrain that will please intermediate carvers and bring a smile to the face of all novices. Prato Nevoso is located close to the French border, only a pebbles throw from the **Mediterranean** sea in the southern part of the **Alps**. Despite its proximity to warm areas, this is an area with a good annual snow record with heavy snowfalls throughout the winter months. Since its birth the resort has constantly improved its facilities and is currently working on plans for new lifts which will greatly improve access and acreage of rideable snow. On its own, Prato Nevoso is tiny with only 30km of piste, however, being linked with the resort of **Aresina**, the rideable acreage rises to a respectable 100km plus. Lifts join to two resorts to form an area know as the '*Mondole Ski*' which offer a splattering of trees, some nice powder s wide open slopes.

Freeriders are presented with an area that will please those who like their mountains hassle free. There is option of going off piste by hiking with a pair of snow shoes and the resort publishes a '*Free Ride*' map to help you find the best spots. You can get further advice from the local snowboard club at *Surf Shop Prato.*

Freestylers are well catered for with a good flood-lit terrain park, which packs in not only a series of killer hits, but also a halfpipe and a permanent boardercross circuit.

Carvers will probably get the best out of the slopes here, with a selection of well maintained slopes. The runs are wide and sweeping free of any rocks and uneven obstacles.

Beginners have a resort that is perfect for them in every way with a good number of easy to reach novice runs.

Lodging and local services are based around the mountain with a number of hotels offering direct slope access. Overall, this is not an expensive resort unless you want it to be. You can bed down in the pricey *Hotel Galassia* or flake out in one of the inexpensive apartments. The village has an array of amenities from a pharmacy, to a mini golf course. There is also a number of okay restaurants, bars and night-clubs to check out.

For accommodation listings visit - www.worldsnowboardguide.com

Prato Nevoso Tourist Office
Piazza Mirtilli, 25-12083 Prato Nevoso
++39 (0) 174 334 130 www.pratonevoso.com

Overall rating out of 10 **5** **Good friendly resort**

Roccaraso

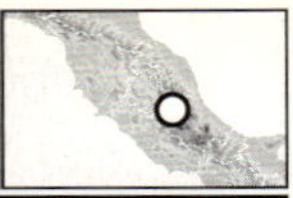

MOUNTAIN DATA

Top Lift at - 2142m

Ride Area
22km of piste

Bottom Lift at - 1280m
Vertical Drop - 862m
Number of Runs - 50
Longest - 2 miles (3km)

TERRAIN LEVELS

Easy	**48%**
Intermediate	**38%**
Advanced	**14%**
Expert =	

TERRAIN TO SUITE

Freeride	**40%**
Trees	Lots
Backcountry	No
Freestyle	**25%**
Halfpipe	Yes 1
Terrain Park	Yes 2
Carving	**35%**

SNOW DATA

Average Snowfall
100cm a season
Snowmaking
5% cover of the slopes
Winter Periods
Dec to March
Summer Riding
None

SLOPE ACCESS

Total Lifts = **31**
Uplift Rate - 30,940 people an hour.
2 Cable cars
12 Chair lifts - **7** Drag lifts
**Leashes Required*

Lift Times
8.00am to 5.30pm

Lift Pass Rates
1 Day pass 35,000 Li

Travel Guide

Fly to **Rome** airport, 2 hours away.

Train services are possible direct to Roccaraso from Rome.

Route Planner: Via Rome, take the A24 towards Aquila, then the A25 towards Sulmona. Once past Sulmona, follow the signs for Roccaraso. Journey time 2 hours.

pic - Burton Snowboards

East of **Rome,** in the region of **Abruzzo,** lies the mountain range of the **Apennines**. This range is home to a number of small areas collectively titled **Roccaraso** which was moulded into a ski resort in the 1950's and has been something of a national secret ever since. This place doesn't show up in your average travel brochure and due to this you don't find many foreigners here. In fact, during the week you might find it very quiet, but at the weekend, expect a deluge of **Romans** and **Neapolitans** sporting the most lurid all in one ski suits and large lift queues. There is nothing really challenging here, especially if the lack of altitude results in a lack of snow. However, the pistes are well maintained, and anyone who does find themselves in a lift queue can at least have fun mocking skiers in an array of sad outfits.

Freeriders will find a range of terrain to cover. Pistes are varied but will suffice more for those in the beginner or intermediate category than for advanced riders. There's little in the way of natural hits or off piste powder fields, but the low altitude means there are plenty of trees around (ie; **Monte Pratello**). Many of these are tightly packed though, and as such, inaccessible to many.

Freestylers are blessed with two parks (off lifts **1** and **22**) if there is enough snow out of which to build them or if the pisteurs can be arsed, whichever comes sooner. Otherwise take your shovel and build yourself a kicker or two.

Carvers will revel in the knowledge that the pistes are kept well groomed and that there's not a mogul in sight. There are a few steep runs available and many of these are pretty wide.

Beginners will find this a great place to get started. Plenty of easy runs on the lower slopes mean that you don't have to take the lift to the top to find what you need. There are gentle runs down from most of the lifts, however, the majority of the reds aren't over threatening so these will be handy as you progress.

The good news is that it is not over expensive here. There is lift-side accommodation at **Aremogna**, but the town of **Roccaraso**, a short drive down the hill, is where most of the visitors stay. This is also where the very limited nightlife occurs. Italians are not big drinkers and this reflects in the town's social scene. There are a couple of nightclubs, *Bilba* and *Jambo*, but most of the activity goes on within the confines of the hotels.

For accommodation listings visit - **www.worldsnowboardguide.com**

Roccaraso Tourist Board
67037 Roccaraso (L'Aquila) via C. Mori
++39 (0) 864 62210 www.roccaraso.com

Overall rating out of 10 **5** **Overall okay, but basic.**

Sauze D'Oulx

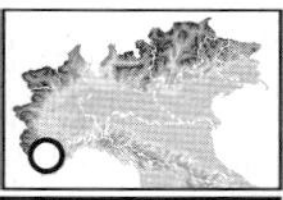

ITALY

MOUNTAIN DATA

Top Lift at - 2823m

Ride Area 120km of piste

Bottom Lift at - 1382m

Vertical Drop - 1441m

Number of Runs - 40

Longest - 2.5 miles (4km)

TERRAIN LEVELS

Easy	27%
Intermediate	61%
Advanced	12%
Expert =	

TERRAIN TO SUITE

Freeride	50%
Trees	Yes
Backcountry	Some
Freestyle	15%
Halfpipe	Yes 1
Terrain Park	No
Carving	60%

SNOW DATA

Average Snowfall

Snowmaking
5% cover of the slopes

Winter Periods
Dec to April

Summer Riding
None

SLOPE ACCESS

Total Lifts = **26**

Uplift Rate - 18,000 people an hour.

9 Chair lifts -

17 Drag lifts

**Leashes Required*

Lift Times
8.30am to 5.30pm

Lift Pass Rates

1 Day pass	49,000 Li
3 Day pass	130,000
6 Day pass	265,000 Li

Travel Guide

Fly to **Turin** airport, which is 1 hour away.

Train services are possible to Oulx, 5 minutes away.

Route Planner:
Via Turin, head north west on the A32 to Oulx and then on to Sauze d'Oulx.
*Drive time from **Calais** is 12 hours. 621 miles (1000 km)

pic - Sauze D'Oulx

Sauze d' Oulx is a resort that clubs together with a host of other areas to form one of the biggest rideable areas in Europe, known as the **Milky Way**. Located in the north west of **Italy,** Sauze doesn't have the greatest snow record, but does have a long history as a holiday camp style resort, the sort of place where certain low lifes come to get drunk near the snow. In truth, things aren't quite as bad as they sound and nowadays the place is inhabited by more Italians than package groups from afar. At one end of the **Milky way** is Sauze d' Oulx, perched at 1500m and at the other end is **Montgeneve** in **France**, which together offer over 285 miles of ridable terrain, linked by a hectic lift system covered by a single pass. This vast area that takes in the slopes of Sauze, **Sansicario**, **Borgata**, **Sestrieres, Claviere** and **Montgenevre** provides an area of mostly intermediate and beginner terrain, with enough stuff for advanced riders to take on. There are a few black graded knuckle rides up on the **Borgata** and **Sestrieres** area to test the best, particularly freeriders. The biggest cluster of runs are found on Sauze d' Oulx' own slopes, where intermediate freeriders will find loads of interconnecting red runs that weave through tight trees.

Freeriders looking for good off-piste won't be disappointed, with many runs leading through dense trees. The **Rio Nero** is a long favourite off piste trail that bases out at the road between **Oulx** and **Cesana**, but does entail a bus ride back to the lifts.

Freestylers have loads of natural hits to get air from, but you wouldn't call this a freestyler's hangout.

Carvers will find a staggering amount of good carving runs to ride in Sauze, making this a particularly good alpine resort.

Beginners will get on well, but note that there are dozens of drag lifts and instruction is nothing to shout about.

Resorts don't come much more basic than **Sauze**, although in a strange way, it all adds to the place and if you are out for a cheap time, this is where you'll get it. Lodging here is cheap in apartments and evenings are very lively, with pub upon pub and loads of good eating haunts making this place not so much a tacky hole but rather an okay place to visit. For a beer, check out the likes of *Paddy McGinty's* (full on Italian name or what!) or the *Banditos* disco for a late night drink, dance and some holiday skirt!

For accommodation listings visit - **www.worldsnowboardguide.com**

Tourist office Sauze d'Oulx
Piazza Assietta 18, I-10050, Sauze d'Oulx
++39 (0) 122 858 009 www.montagnedoc.it

Overall rating out of 10 — 7

Good friendly resort for all.

Val Gardena

MOUNTAIN DATA

Top Lift at - 2950m

Ride Area 965km of piste

Bottom Lift at - 1060m

Vertical Drop - 1890m

Number of Runs -

Longest -6.2 miles (10km)

TERRAIN LEVELS

Easy	**30%**
Intermediate	**60%**
Advanced	**10%**
Expert =	

TERRAIN TO SUITE

Freeride	**50%**
Trees	Lots
Backcountry	Yes
Freestyle	**20%**
Halfpipe	Yes various
Terrain Park	Yes
Carving	**30%**

SNOW DATA

Average Snowfall
250cm a season

Snowmaking
45% cover of the slopes

Winter Periods
Dec to April

Summer Riding
None

SLOPE ACCESS

Total Lifts = **27**

Uplift Rate - 27,000 people an hour.

5 Gondolas

14 Chair lifts - **8** Drag lifts

**Leashes Required*

Lift Times
8.30am to 4.30pm

Lift Pass Rates

1 Day pass	63,000 Li
3 Day pass	125,000 Li
6 Day pass	313,000 Li

Travel Guide

Fly to **Verona** airport 2 hours away.

Train services are possible to Bolzano which is 30 minutes away.

Route Planner:
From Bolzano, head north on the A22 and turn off at Bressanone taking the E66 towards Brunico and turning off on to the B244 to the resort area.

pic - Val Gardena

Val Gardena is located in the northern area of the **Dolomites** and forms a collection of resorts and mountain slopes that is said to be the largest snowboarding area in the world. There is a staggering 600 miles of marked trails and are serviced by some 460 lifts of all shapes and styles. Val Gardena has the unfortunate history of being the place where a particularly sad Brit with a Russian name achieved a so called top ski result (who gives a toss). However, this is not a sad place to snowboard, it's actually very good, with something for everyone. Val Gardena is a huge valley, housing three main villages and a handful of satellite hamlets. And truly, if you can't ride here and enjoy yourself, then you must be a closeted synchronised swimmer or worse, a downhill skier with a nice shiny medal! The main villages here are **Ortisei** (the biggest town in the area) and **St Christina**. Wherever you choose to stay, you can move around the resort via a regular shuttle bus service. The well set out mass of lifts don't connect up everywhere, but with a piste map you can get around a very large portion of it without too many problems. Try the circuit ride known as the **Sella Ronda**, which takes you around 15 miles of lift connected runs.

Freeriders on the whole find Val Gardena a cool place to ride, with a good mixture of terrain features from trees to banks and wind lips. The best off-piste riding can be had in areas like **Passo Pordoi**, but it's best tackled with the services of a local guide.

Freestylers will find that the fun park and half-pipe, located on the area known as the **Selda** which is the place to hang out and get some air.

Carvers of all levels will find millions of well pisted trails to get their fix from. Runs criss cross all over the area and no rider will see all of them in a week's trip, or even two.

Beginners who can't learn to snowboard here must be clueless idiots, this place is a first timers heaven. The runs up above **Ortisei** are full-on, perfect nappy territory.

Accommodation and evenings are very Italian, with loads of good options in the main villages or at one of the smaller hamlets, which will have cheaper places to sleep and hang out. Eating and other local happenings are much the same whereever you are: all are laid back and okay.

Accommodation: Visit www.worldsnowboardgiuide.

Val Gardena Tourist Office
Str Meisules 21a3, I-39048
++39 (0) 471 792 277 **www.val-gardena.com**

Overall rating out of 10 **8** **Great area with all round riding**

Abetone
Small simple area 25 Lifts & 24 runs
60 minutes from Firenze airport.

Bardonecchia
▲2750m 140 km of piste 24 lifts
Bardonecchia is one of Italy's oldest resorts, arranged around a residential town rather than a purpose built concrete jungle. Not much here for freestlylers, but carvers will get a bit more from the variation of long and wide slopes on offer at Colomion and Melezet (head to Jafferau for the steep stuff). There's some powder to be found, and a few trees. Freeriders with the funds can check out the backcountry behind Melezet via the heli-boarding option. Rookies should beware of the drag lifts.
Fly to: **Turin** 1½ hours away
ⓘ **tel-** ++39 (0) 122 99137

Chiesa
Novices & families 10 Lifts & 16 runs
110 minutes from Milan airport.

Cimone - Montecreto
Novices & families 28 Lifts & 30 runs
70 minutes from Bologna airport.

Claviere
Okay linked area 91 Lifts & 150 runs
90 minutes from Turin airport.

Corvara
Big linked area 460 Lifts & 532 runs
2 hours from Innsbruck airport.

Corno Alle Scale
This is not a resort that many people would have heard of, but its worth a mention and even a visit, especially if you fancy a night out in the nearby town of Bologna. Corno Alle Scale has plenty of terrain to suit all standards with some gnarly off-piste for freeriders to bury themselves in. But this is not a place for novices who like everything on hand, likewise freestylers looking for a host of man made hits will be disappointed. The only draw back about this place is that accommodation is located way back down the road (about 10 km) and with no local bus service, you must have your own transport. What is on offer is very basic but at least affordable. There is also a cheesy disco bar and a number of drinking holes.
Fly to: **Bologna** 1 hours away

Gressoney
▲2661m 200 km of piste 46 lifts
Located in the Aosta Valley, Gressony is the neighbour to nearby Champoluc, with heaps of pisted terrain between the two resorts. The large amount of off-piste terrain here, offers a lot of big drop-ins, gullies and wide open bowls to please all freeriders. For carvers, there are ample wide spaces and beginners have loads of easy flats to get hold off. Local facilities are very good and close to the slopes with some cheap options for lodging, eating and partying late at night.
Fly to: **Turin** 1 hour away
ⓘ **tel-** ++39 (0) 125 366 143

Kastelruth
Big linked area 460 Lifts & 532 runs
120 minutes from Verona airport.

Obereggen
Massive ride area 460 Lifts & 532 runs
90 minutes from Verona airport.

Passo Tonale
▲3025m 144 km of piste 30 lifts
Passo Tonale is a small resort offering some fine intermediate but limited expert terrain. Freeriders who like to go off piste and are prepared for a hike, the Pisgana trail is the one to check out. This run is over 9 miles long and runs down Presena Glacier. Freestylers have a small half-pipe while carvers will find the Bleis trail the one to put some lines on. Beginners have an excellent resort with fantastic easy slopes. Off slope services are basic.
Fly to: **Verona** 3 hours away
ⓘ **tel-** ++39 (0) 434 655 216

Pejo
Not a hot hangout 7 Lifts & 14 runs
85 minutes from Verona airport.

Piancavallo
▲1829m 24 km of piste 18 lifts
Piancavallo is a tiny purpose built resort and not unsightly. This is a cool place that will offer a day or twos relaxed riding. There is only a handful of runs that are split between beginner and intermediate level and nothing for advanced riders apart form a single graded black trail. Freestylers have a pipe but in the main this is a simple piste loving carvers place through and through. Chalet accommodation and good services are slope side.
Fly to: **Venice** 3 hours away
ⓘ **tel-** ++39 (0) 434 655 216

Pila
▲2750m 64 km of piste 14 lifts
Pila is fantastic resort located in the **Aosta Region**. What you will find here is a decent sized mountain with a series of pisted and unpisted trails that will keep any rider more than happy for a week. Although not extensive, the terrain offers advanced freeriders awesome off piste and trees areas. Freestylers have a pipe and novices have a great selection of easy runs. Local services are cheap, good and slope side.
Fly to: **Turin** 3 hours away
ⓘ **tel-** ++39 (0) 165 521 045

Pinzolz
Tiny boring resort 9 Lifts & 12 runs
130 minutes from Milan airport.

Pozza di Fassa
Within a big area 6 Lifts & 6 runs
2 hours from Milan airport.

Prato Nevoso
Tiny boring resort 13 Lifts & 15 runs
50 minutes from Turin airport.

San Cassiano
Big linked area 460 Lifts & 530 runs
120 minutes from Innsbruck airport.

San Martino Di Castrozza
Big linked area 460 Lifts & 530 runs
90 minutes from Venice airport.

San Sicario
Okay carving area 12 Lifts & 40 runs
75 minutes from Turin airport.

Sella Neva
▲1850m 29 km of piste 8 lifts
Sella Neva is a small resort in the north eastern corner of Italy bordering **Slovenia** and **Austria**. This is a popular carvers resort as well as offering some excellent freeridng and natural freestyle terrain. You can shred some trees at speed, go waste deep in powder or fly off endless cliffs. The fun park contains a half-pipe and is located of the Gilberti lift. This is also a good beginners resort. Sella Nevea is a good cheap resort with basic services.
Fly to: **Venice** 6 hours
ⓘ **tel-** ++39 (0) 428 330 18

Santa Caterina
▲2726m 40 km of piste 8 lifts
Santa Caterina is a resort that will appeal to sedate riders. Freeriders may be able to find some okay backcountry riding but its very limited and will only please intermediate riders. Freestylers have a half-pipe, but its not always looked after. Carvers just out for a simple day's piste riding will be at home, even granny could have a go. Fine for beginners but not a great choice of runs. Slope side services are good and affordable.
Fly to: **Verona** 4 hours away
ⓘ **tel-** ++39 (0) 342 935 598

Solda - Sulden
Very dull resort 11 Lifts & 13 runs
120 minutes from Verona airport.

Sestriere
▲2825m 400 km of piste 66 lifts
Sestriere offers the potential for some great advanced riding both on and off piste, with a vast amount of terrain to explore in this part of the Milky Way. Freeriders will find a good choice of challenging runs and some excellent off piste. Freestylers are not well catered for but you will still find some interesting natural hits. Carvers have acres of good terrain. Beginners should not want for much more than you get here. Off piste services are affordable and close to the slopes.
Fly to: **Turin** 2 hours away
ⓘ **tel-** ++39 (0) 122 755 444

St Ulrich
Big linked area 81 Lifts & 70 runs
90 minutes from Verona airport.

Trafoi
Super boring place 4 Lifts & 7 runs
120 minutes from Turin airport.

NORWAY

GENERAL INFO AND FACTS

Capital - Oslo
Language - Norweigan
Currency - Krone
Alcohol drinking age - 18 & 20
Drugs - Cannabis is illegal
Death Penalty - Doesn't exist
Age of consent for Sex - 16
Military Service -Compulsory
Electricity Supply - 240 Volts AC
International phone Code ++47
Highest Peak - Galdhopiggen 2472m

DUTY FREE
10 Litres of Alcohol
90 Litres of Wine - 110 of beer
800 Cigarettes
200 Cigars

NORWEIGAN DRIVE GUIDE
All vehicles drive on the right hand side of the road
Speed Limits -
Motorways 90kph (56mph)
Highways 80kph (50mph)
Towns 50kph (30mph)

Norweigan Snowboard Association
tel - ++47 (0) 67 154 825

www.board-it.com/resorts
www.thomson-ski.co.uk

TIME ZONES
Central European
GMT +1 Hour
Between March and October
GMT+2 Hours

Norway is famous for it's cross country skiing which is reflected in the fact that although there are over 160 resorts dotted around the country, 80% are simply not ridable. The terrain in the suitable areas is best for novices and intermediates, with little long term interest for advanced riders due to the lack of steep terrain.

Travelling around Norway is made easy by the country's excellent road and rail network, connecting well with international and domestic airports. The main gateway airport with regular international flights is **Oslo**, but onward travel usually means an extra 2 to 3 hours of travel.

If you're visiting Norway by car, you can take ferry crossings via ports in the UK, or short crossings from northern ports in Germany and Denmark. Driving in Norway is easy, but snow chains are a must in remote resorts.

The one common factor is Norway is its costs (super expensive in fact). Accommodation is pretty good with the most affordable type being cabins, which cater for groups. Hotels will burn a massive hole in your pocket. Beer prices are so high that evenings in the average bar are out of the question. The best advice is to bring heaps of duty free, or buy your drinks at the off licenses, but note, you have to be 18 to drink beer and 20 to buy or drink spirits.

Overall, Norway is really good but it does have some major drawbacks, like its total lack of music talent, stupidly expensive booze and the world's worst knitwear. On the other hand, the women in this part of the world are to die for.

pic - Stig

Main international Gateway Airport Oslo

Geilo

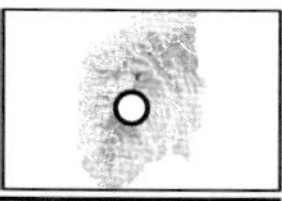

NORWAY

MOUNTAIN DATA

Top Lift at - 1173m

Ride Area 25km of piste

Bottom Lift at - 800m

Vertical Drop - 275m

Number of Runs - 32

Longest - 1.2 mile (2km)

TERRAIN LEVELS

Easy	22%
Intermediate	56%
Advanced	22%
Expert =	

TERRAIN TO SUITE

Freeride	30%
Trees	A few
Backcountry	No
Freestyle	30%
Halfpipe	Yes 2
Terrain Park	Yes 1
Carving	40%

SNOW DATA

Average Snowfall
125cm a season

Snowmaking
50% cover of the slopes

Winter Periods
Nov to May

Summer Riding
None

SLOPE ACCESS

Total Lifts = **18**

Uplift Rate - 21,000 people an hour.

4 Chair lifts -
14 Drag lifts

**Leashes Required*

Lift Times
8.30am to 20.30pm

Lift Pass Rates

2 Hour pass	140 Kr
1 Day pass	230 Kr
6 Day pass	870 Kr

Travel Guide

Fly to **Oslo** airport, which is 4 hours away.

Train services are possible direct to Geilo from Oslo and take around 2 hours.

Route Planner:
Via Oslo , head north on highway 7 via Honefos, Gol and Hol to reach Geilo. The distance is aound 150 miles (240 km) and will take 2 hours .

Located roughly 4 hours from **Oslo** and situated in the **Hallingdal Valley**, the largest mountain area in Europe, **Geilo** is the oldest resort in Norway. The well laid out town is easy to get around and lies close to the slopes, making for an easy attack of the runs first thing in the morning. The slopes rise up on two sides of the valley, with terrain that is well maintained, leaving lots of corduroy tracks to mess up in the early hours. Geilo's slopes will suit intermediate and novice riders mostly, with little to set the heart racing for advanced or even competent riders, although there are a few black graded runs. The two separate areas (which aren't connected) rise up to give a maximum lift height of 1173 metres. If you want to ride both places, you'll have to take a snow taxi, which is not included in your lift pass. The **Vestila** area, which is actually the smaller of the two, has the longer runs, with a mixture of blues, reds and a couple of blacks.

Freeriders who pick a resort for powder and fast long adventurous trails, will not be satisfied here. There is no great adrenaline rush if you re a competent rider, just a couple of challenging runs to tackle and only a small amount of good powder terrain to seek out, but there are some trees to shred off the **Heissen** lift.

Freestylers wanting air will find the 100 metre halfpipe, or the selection of hits in one of the two fun parks, the place to be. Night riding in the pipe is possible, so don t fret if you miss the morning because you slept in after scoring with a local the night before.

Carvers in shiny hard boots and race boards, give this place a miss, you ll stand out like a sore thumb and be loudly laughed at. Norwegians don t care too much for posing euro faggots. However, the number 14 trail has some nice carving spots.

Beginners are presented with an excellent choice of easy slopes to tackle, starting out at the base area with good flats higher up and easy runs back into the village.

Geilo is a sprawling affair with good accommodation, but nothing comes cheap. Geilo also offers loads of things to do, you can try ice climbing, snow rafting or if you fancy reducing your balls to the size of two peas, you can sign up for a night in a snow hole. Eating here is simple but even a basic pizza will set you back 70Kr. Night life will sting you if you plan to drink heavily or chat up a good looking Norwegian lass. *Hos John's, Laverb* and the *Bardola* are the places to try your luck.

Tourist office Geilo
Geilo. N-3580
++47 (0) 3209 5900

Overall rating out of 10 — **5** — **Basic resort with some good runs**

Hemsedal

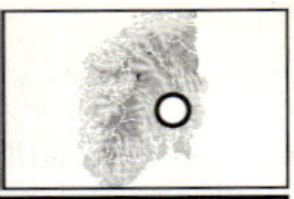

MOUNTAIN DATA

Top Lift at - 1405m

Ride Area
40km of piste

Bottom Lift at - 650m
Vertical Drop - 800m
Number of Runs - 30
Longest - 3.7 mile (6km)

TERRAIN LEVELS

Easy	**53%**
Intermediate	**27%**
Advanced	**20%**
Expert =	

TERRAIN TO SUITE

Freeride	**60%**
Trees	Yes
Backcountry	A bit
Freestyle	**25%**
Halfpipe	Yes 1
Terrain Park	Yes 1
Carving	**15%**

SNOW DATA

Average Snowfall
65cm a season
Snowmaking
15% cover of the slopes
Winter Periods
Nov to May
Summer Riding
None

SLOPE ACCESS

Total Lifts = **15**
Uplift Rate - 23,000 people an hour.
4 Chair lifts -
11 Drag lifts
**Leashes Required*

Lift Times
9.30am to 9.30pm

Lift Pass Rates

1 Hour pass	230 Kr
3 Day pass	560 Kr
6 Day pass	900 Kr

Travel Guide

Fly to **Oslo** airport, about 2 1/4 hours away.

Train services are possible to Gol from Oslo and take around 2 1/4 hours.

Route Planner:
Via Oslo, head north on highway 7 via Honefos and Gol and on to Hemsedal. **Oslo** to resort is **137** miles (220km).

pic - Hemsedal Tourism

Hemsedal's height, location and use of snow cannons all help to ensure a good snow record and a long season. This is a resort that has been attracting riders of all ages for years, especially freestylers. The slopes lie about 3 kilometres from the main town and are reached by a free shuttle bus. The terrain will appeal to all standards, with 40 kilometres of well prepared piste for freeriders to carve. The runs are serviced by a good lift system which, unlike some neighbouring resorts, is not all drag lifts.

Freeriders don't need to look too far to find some nice terrain. From the back of the **Totten Summit,** you're treated to some excellent cliffs and powder, which will test even the advanced rider. Make a bee-line for the run known locally as the **Annus,** a long, steep couloir that should be treated with respect. If it's trees you're after then you're in luck, there s are loads of them.

Freestylers looking for some hits, should take the **Holdeskarheisen** and **Roniheisen** chairs to reach some cool terrain, including a tight gully to pull air in. The pipe and park are very dependent on snow conditions, however when sufficient snow has fallen, they build things well and high.

Carvers in hard boots who dare grace the slopes will find the runs known as the **Hemsedalsloypa** and **Kuleloyas** the place to lay out turns. These may not be the longest runs in the world, but they're not for wimps. The **Sahaugloypa** is also a decent run on which to get some speed together. In many of Norway's resorts the runs are usually very short, so it comes as a big relief to find a trail that lasts more than two seconds. The **Turistloypa** is the longest descent and although it's easy (even for novices still in nappies), it's worth a blast if only to avoid being on a lift again.

Beginners seem to fare well wherever they go in Norway. Hemsedal is no exception, the only difference is that at least there is something worth progressing onto after mastering the easy flats at the base and those higher up.

If you plan to put **Hemsedal** on your calling card, only do so if you have a bank balance akin to that of Richard Branson. Put simply, Hemsedal is very expensive. Accommodation can be had near the slopes with the cheapest option being a cabin. The main snowboard hang out for evening madness is the *Hemsedal Café*, which is expensive, but cool.
Accommodation: Visit www.worldsnowboardgiuide.

Tourist Office Hemsedal
Po Box 3. Hemsedal
++47 (0) 32 06 01 56

Overall rating out of 10 **7** **A very good resort for all**

Narvik

NORWAY

MOUNTAIN DATA

Top Lift at - 1002m

Ride Area
16km of piste

Bottom Lift at - 125m
Vertical Drop - 886m
Number of Runs - 8
Longest - 3 mile (1.8km)

TERRAIN LEVELS

Easy	15%
Intermediate	30%
Advanced	55%
Expert =	

TERRAIN TO SUITE

Freeride	70%
Trees	A few
Backcountry	A bit
Freestyle	10%
Halfpipe	Yes 1
Terrain Park	Yes 1
Carving	20%

SNOW DATA

Average Snowfall

Snowmaking
30% cover of the slopes
Winter Periods
Nov to May
Summer Riding
None

SLOPE ACCESS

Total Lifts = **5**
Uplift Rate - 23,000 people an hour.
1 Gondola - **2** Chair lifts - **2** Drag lifts
**Leashes Required*

Lift Times
10.00am to 9.00pm

Lift Pass Rates

2 Hour pass	155 Kr
3 Day pass	430 Kr
6 Day pass	620 Kr

Travel Guide

Fly to **Oslo** airport and then to Evenes which is 50 miles on.

Train services are possible direct to Narvik from Oslo and will take 20 hours.

Route Planner:
Via Oslo , head north on E6 all the way up to Narvik, which is at least a 20 hour drive.

pic - Narvik Tourism

About 1 hour west of the **Swedish** resort of **Riksgransen** lies **Narvik**, a hidden treasure in snowboard circles. With only 5 lifts and a summit that only just gets over 1000 metres, Narvik isn't your typical holiday resort: it's a small-town situated at the foot of a superb mountain, with lifts only opening in the afternoons on weekdays and all day on weekends and holidays. The busiest times are in February and Easter, but other than that, lift lines are practically non-existent and being located so far north, tour groups have never heard of this place. This helps to keep the slopes free of sad two plank numpties.

Freeriders should get the most out of this area. Much of the riding terrain is above the tree-line, but the lack of tree runs is fully compensated by plenty of natural pipes, bowls, cornices and cliffs to fly off. For fat lazy riders or those who prefer not to exhaust themselves with hiking, you'll be able to have a good blast within the lift covered area. The area known as Fagernesfjellet is a paradise for relatively advanced freeriders. The lifts only cover a small percentage of actual terrain available and as heli-boarding is forbidden in Norway, heaven is waiting if you're prepared to hike. There are no rules regarding where you can board, but before you take off, it's advisable to hook up with one of the locals who will show you the secret spots. In addition to **Morkolla**, with its enormous amount of snow, Narvik's backcountry offers wicked extreme terrain.

Freestylers don't have a fun park, although one is planned for the future. There is, however, plenty of good natural terrain for getting air and the flat stuff allows for loads of ground spinning.

Carvers should check out the pistes of **Fagernesfjellet** which are steep, wavy and well suited to carvers. Mind you, hard booters are a rare thing here and to be honest, this place is far better challenged in a good pair of softs.

Beginners will probably have a better time in **Ankernes**, a resort which is 3 miles away, rater than the main slopes of Narvik.

Narvik is at the base of the slopes and everything is within walking distance. Expensive is the key word around here, but lodging in a cabin or a room at *Breidablikk Inn* is one of the easiest on the pocket. As for night life and partying, things happen at the *Fossestua* which has a pool table and is good for a beer and a late night session.

Narvik Tourist Office
Kongens 66 Box 318, 8500 Narvik
++47 (0) 471 795 122

Overall rating out of 10 **6** **A tad limited but still okay**

Oppdal

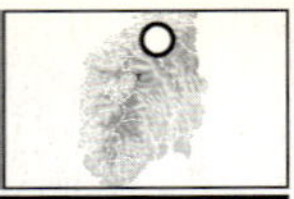

MOUNTAIN DATA

Top Lift at - 1260m

Ride Area
77km of piste

Bottom Lift at - 545m
Vertical Drop - 715m
Number of Runs - 28
Longest - 2.5 mile (4km)

TERRAIN LEVELS

Easy	**31%**
Intermediate	**43%**
Advanced	**26%**
Expert =	

TERRAIN TO SUITE

Freeride	**60%**
Trees	A few
Backcountry	Yes
Freestyle	**30%**
Halfpipe	Yes 1
Terrain Park	Yes 1
Carving	**10%**

SNOW DATA
Average Snowfall

Snowmaking
45% cover of the slopes
Winter Periods
Nov to May
Summer Riding
None

SLOPE ACCESS
Total Lifts = **16**
Uplift Rate - 15,000 people an hour.
2 Chair lifts -
14 Drag lifts
**Leashes Required*

Lift Times
9.30am to 9.00pm

Lift Pass Rates
1 Hour pass 200 Kr
3 Day pass
6 Day pass 830 Kr

Travel Guide

Fly to **Oslo** airport, about 4 hours away.

Train services go direct to Oppdal from Oslo, and take around 4hours.

Route Planner:
Via Oslo, head north on E6 all the way up to Oppdal.

pic - Oppdal Tourism

Oppdal is situated 93 miles south of the town of **Trondheim**, where three valleys (originating in different parts of the country) meet. The resort is divided into four main areas, providing something for all riders with some of the best off-piste Norway has to offer. The snowboard scene is expanding in Oppdal (as everywhere else in the world) and most weekends the place is 'invaded' by boarders from the city of Trondheim. During the usual winter holiday period, the population doubles, so if you're not particularly fond of lines and crowds, try to stay clear. As one of Norway's biggest areas, Oppdal will appeal (as with much of this country) to easy going, piste loving freeriders. The 80 km of piste are for beginners mainly as there's nothing for advanced riders to get too excited about, and even intermediates will soon tire of the place. At the top of **Vangslia** there's a black run, but the mountain flattens out at the bottom making it a short and uneventful trail, unless you're a beginner joining at the top of lift A, where it becomes an excellent easy area.

Freeriders are kept interested with some particularly good freeride terrain to explore that includes trees, steeps and powder. The stuff found in **Stolen Valley** is pretty good, but due to avalanche danger, the area is often closed. However, the runs on the Vangslia mountain offer the best time, with some nice terrain features to ride, including steeps.

Freestylers have a pipe (not a hot one, though) and a snowpark. The **Adalen** area is a natural snowpark which should keep air heads aroused for a day or two. Ground grommets will find the uneven slopes great for flatland tricks.

Carvers can experience what it's like to fly, by cutting some lines on the *Downhill World Cup* arena. What's more, Oppdal's longest run reaches a respectable 2.5 miles, offering a long ride.

Beginners are well catered for, with loads of novice trails stretched across the 4 connected areas all accessed with one lift pass. Snowboard instruction is also very good.

In the main, local services are varied but expensive. For a convenient place to sleep, stay at the *Hellaugstol* camp ground, about 100 metres from the slopes, or at *Landsbytorget* in Stolen where a group can share an apartment. At night, check out '*The Jaeger Pub*' or go skating.

For accommodation listings visit - **www.worldsnowboardguide.com**

Tourist Office Oppdal
Po Box 50 Oppdal - N7341
++47 (0) 72 42 17 60 **www.**

Overall rating out of 10 **5** **A nice small freeriders resort**

Stryn

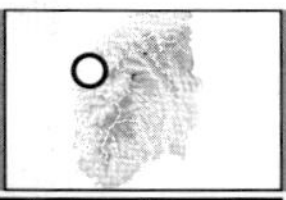

NORWAY

MOUNTAIN DATA

Top Lift at - 1580m

Ride Area 10km of piste

Bottom Lift at - 830m

Vertical Drop - 750m

Number of Runs - 8

Longest - 2.5 mile (3km)

TERRAIN LEVELS

Easy	25%
Intermediate	75%
Advanced	0%
Expert =	

TERRAIN TO SUITE

Freeride	55%
Trees	None
Backcountry	None
Freestyle	40%
Halfpipe	Yes 2
Terrain Park	Yes 1
Carving	5%

SNOW DATA

Average Snowfall
500cm a season

Snowmaking
30% cover of the slopes

Winter Periods
Feb to March

Summer Riding
April to June

SLOPE ACCESS

Total Lifts = **2**

Uplift Rate - 1,000 people an hour.

1 Chair lift -

1 Drag lifts

**Leashes Required*

Lift Times
9.00am to 9.30pm

Lift Pass Rates

2 Hour pass	210 Kr
3 Day pass	495 Kr
6 Day pass	890 Kr

Travel Guide

Fly to **Oslo** airport and then inland to Trondheim.

Train services are possible to Trondheim from Oslo.

Route Planner:
Via Oslo, head north on route 7 to Gol and then take the 52 to Signol onto the route 1 and route 60 via Olden to Stryn.

pic - Stig

Stryn is located at the base of the **Jostedalsbreen** glacier and is Norway's most famous summer resort (in fact the only one of note). The glacier gets so much snow during the winter (five metres plus), that the lifts are usually totally buried and as they couldn't run them even if they wanted to.

Although this is a popular snowboarders hangout, it should be pointed out that Stryn is also very popular with skiers, resulting in fairly long lift queues. What's more, a number of ski teams spend time on the slopes doing training sessions, swelling the numbers further. Still, leaving the two plankers aside, what you have is a small glacier mountain offering some interesting and steep riding on slopes where snow holds its condition all day. A lot of Norwegians simply come up to strip off and sunbathe (an often enjoyable sight). However, for those wanting to snowboard the 10 kilometres of terrain are serviced by just two lifts; a double chair and a drag lift. A lot of snowboard camps are held here each year with lots of pros on the teaching staff.

Freeriders coming here in search of big powder bowls, dense trees and limitless off piste should forget it; Stryn has none of that. In the main, you are presented with some steep, but featureless terrain.

Freestylers are the ones who are going to benefit from a trip to Stryn the most, apart from the natural hits and the famous road jumps (as seen in many a video), the man made kickers are superb. The camp's pipes are located on the higher sections, while lower down is a pipe that anyone can use.

Carvers in hard boots, get real and have the summer off, because this is not a carvers resort whatsoever. Two fat turns and you re down. This is a soft boot hangout only.

Beginners that are easily intimidated may find this place a little daunting as the slopes are steep, but there are some areas to play about on if you really want to ride here.

Stryn is located along a road that is littered with campsites offering cheap places to sleep. The main hangout is the village of **Hjelle**, 15 minutes from the slopes, where you can rent a shared cabin from 420 Kr. The main local pub is where the only action takes place with numerous late night drinking sessions happeningplace on a daily basis (although it costs)..

Stryn Tourist Office
Stryn
++47 (0) 57 87 5340 www.

Overall rating out of 10 **5** **Only good for summer freestyling**

Trysil

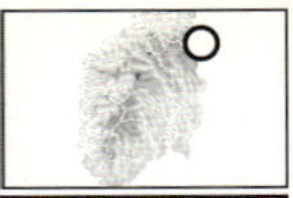

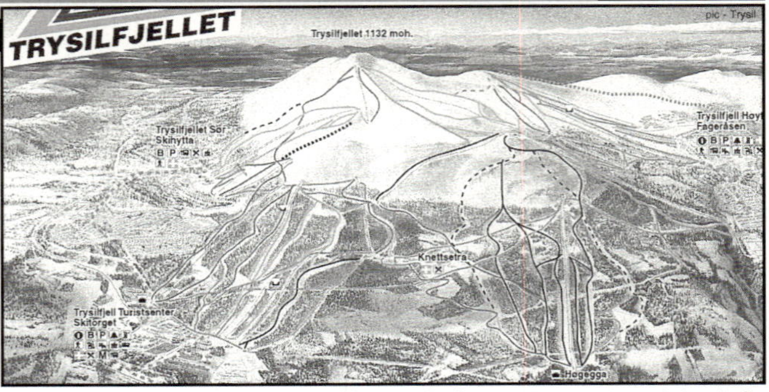

MOUNTAIN DATA

Top Lift at - 1100m

Ride Area
64km of piste

Bottom Lift at - 450m
Vertical Drop - 685m
Number of Runs - 62
Longest -3.4 miles (5.4km)

TERRAIN LEVELS

Easy	**60%**
Intermediate	**21%**
Advanced	**19%**
Expert =	

TERRAIN TO SUITE

Freeride	**45%**
Trees	A few
Backcountry	A bit
Freestyle	**35%**
Halfpipe	Yes 3
Terrain Park	Yes 1
Carving	**20%**

SNOW DATA

Average Snowfall
200cm a season
Snowmaking
10% cover of the slopes
Winter Periods
Nov to May
Summer Riding
None

SLOPE ACCESS

Total Lifts = **24**
Uplift Rate - 22,000 people an hour.
4 Chair lifts-
20 Drag lifts
**Leashes Required*

Lift Times
9.30am to 9.00pm

Lift Pass Rates

1 Day pass	200 Kr
3 Day pass	540 Kr
6 Day pass	920 Kr

Travel Guide

Fly to **Oslo** airport which is around 140 miles away.

Train services are possible to Zerenz, 20 minutes away.

Route Planner: Via Oslo, take the E6 to Hamar then the route 25.

Trysil is supposed to be Norway's largest resort and is definitely big by most Norwegian standards, and a very good place to snowboard. Situated just over two hours from **Oslo**, Trysil is a resort that caters well for its visitors, no matter what time of year. Snowboarding is possible here between the months of November and May, on slopes that cover a large percentage of the **Trysilfjellet** mountain, which is predominately suited to beginners and basic intermediate riders. There are runs for advanced riders which will keep them interested for some time. Strangely the higher you go, the easier things get, notably at the top section of the slopes, where a wide open and somewhat flat snow field opens up above the tree line.

Freeriders who venture here will find some okay tree riding and a bit of powder, but in the main the terrain is a bit dull and featureless. The runs up from **Hogegga** are the most challenging, with a series of black runs that snake through trees to the base.

Freestylers make up a large number of the riders seen ripping up Trysil. To keep the air heads happy the management have provided them with a decent fun park and three halfpipes that are dotted around at various locations. These are all very well maintained, although on occasions a bit of do it your self pipe shaping is called for though.

Carvers if you must strap on boots that are better suited to skiers and insist on posing over your edges at speed, then Trysil allows you ample opportunity to put in some extremely wide turns (especially on the higher sections) but don't come here expecting a mass of long, super fast trails.

Beginners. there are two types of orgasm, one with a good looking Norwegian chick and the other is learning to snowboard at Trysil. The place is learner heaven, with a mass of easy slopes that are well linked and well serviced by the lift system.

The village of **Trysil** is 2 km from the slopes and offers good local facilities, although what is on offer is stupidly expensive and would make a weeks stay a struggle with funds, and impossible on a low budget. Accommodation is offered in a huge number of cabins and hotels, (all will burn deep into the pocket). Still, a few beers will help dampen the shock of prices (once pissed, you no longer care what the next things costs).

For accommodation listings visit - **www.worldsnowboardguide.com**

Trysil Tourist Office
Trysil Ferie, Trysil 2420
++47 (0) 62 45 05 11

Overall rating out of 10 **6** **Not bad with some okay runs**

Ai
Super boring place 46 Lifts & 7 runs
2½ hours from Oslo airport.

Filefjell Skiheiser

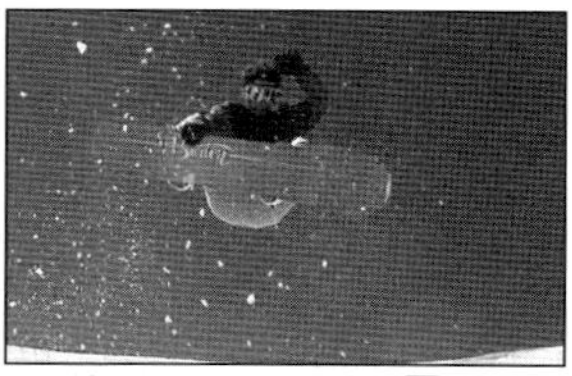

▲ 1125m 8 km of piste 3 lifts

This is one of Norways smallest resorts and also one of the most boring. There is very little on offer, other than a few over rated intermediate and beginner runs and a small terrain park with an equally small halfpipe. In its defense its well looked after by local riders. The nearby village offers very basic lodging and other services all of which come at a high price.

Fly to: **Fagerness** 2 hours away
ⓘ **tel-** ++47 (0) 613 6 7247

Gausdal
A bit dull but okay 9 Lifts & 20 runs
2½ hours hours from Oslo airport.

Gaustablikk
A few okay runs 5 Lifts & 8 runs
2 hours from Oslo airport.

Gol
Total waste of time 7 Lifts & 6 runs
2 hours from Oslo airport.

Grong
Forget it altogether 6 Lifts & 10 runs
15 hours from Oslo airport.

Hoven
Okay night riding 4 Lifts & 12 runs
2½ hours hours from Oslo airport.

Kvitfjell
2 good halfpipes 7 Lifts & 20 runs
60 minutes from Oslo airport.

Lilliehammer / Hafjejj
▲ 1050m 25 km of piste 8 lifts

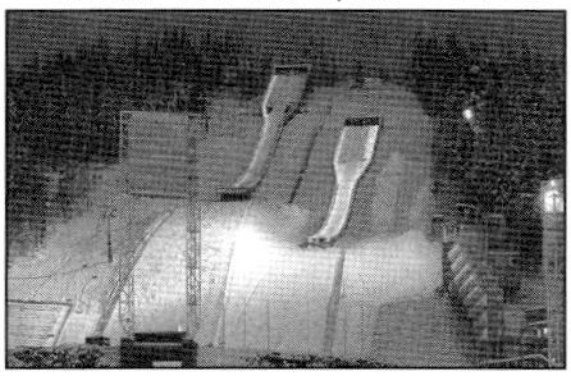

This is Norway s famous resort if for know other reason other than it once hosted the winter Olympics. However, just because they flew the 5 rings , doesn t mean that its a good measure of what s on offer. What you get here is a narrow cluster of runs with an okay mixture of all ability terrain that includes a long black run from almost the top to the bottom. Freestylers have an okay halfpipe for catching air while beginners a few easy to reach novice slopes although crowded.

Fly to: **Oslo** 2 hours away
ⓘ **tel-** ++47 (0) 612 77950

Nordseter
Forget it altogether 3 Lifts & 4 runs
3 hours from Oslo airport.

Norefjell
Overall not bad 10 Lifts & 15 runs
60 minutes from Oslo airport.

Rustadhogda
Small pipe nothing else 3 Lifts
3 hours from Oslo airport.

Sjusjoen
Only good for no hoper's 1 Lift
80 minutes from Oslo airport.

Stranda
Okay for slow beginners 5 Lifts
120 minutes from Oslo airport.

Tromso
Pipe and park only 6 Lifts
2 hours from Oslo airport.

Uvdal Alpinsenter
Boring to the extreme 4 Lifts
2 hours from Oslo airport.

Valdres

▲ 1580m 10 km of piste 4 lifts

Valdres is a small unassuming typical Norwegian resort with a good reputation amongst Norway s snowboard population. The tree lined runs will suit intermediate freeriders and air heads. Carvers looking for lots of wide open flats will be disappointed, as will advanced riders looking for major hits or deep gullies. Still, there is some extreme terrain with trees to check out that should keep the average freerider happy for a day or two. Grommets will find enough logs to slide down. The fun park and pipe are also good and offer the best chance of pulling some good air. First timers should have no problem here, the flats at the base area are full-on for collecting the first bruises with ease.
Lodging is the usual Norwegian offerings, with a number of decent chalets or apartments to choose from. Night wise, simply crank up the walkman and down your duty free booze.

Fly to: **Oslo** 2 hours away
ⓘ **tel-** ++47 (0) 61 360 400

Voss

▲ 945m 40 km of piste 10 lifts

Voss is a very popular resort with over 40km of well groomed trails that will please carvers and basic freeriders. The limited off-piste on offer is not bad and allows the chance to go steep and deep above and below the tree line in a number of spots. Freestylers should avoid trying to catch air out of the permanent ski jump here, as you re not allowed too. Instead check out the pipe or the numerous natural hits dotted around the whole area.

Fly to: **Bergen** 2½ hours hours away
ⓘ **tel-** ++47 (0) 56 510 051

Vassfjellet

▲ 670m 9 km of piste 5 lifts

Vassfjellet is not a tourist resort perched way up high on a mountain and boasting millions of square miles of ridabe piste backed up with a modern base complex decked out with purpose built hotels and other tourist traps. No, this is a locals place and serves the masses from neighbouring towns and the city of **Trondheim** a few miles away. If you re on a road trip and fancy something different then check this place out, it s pretty cool and very snowboard friendly, with a large number of student riders from Trondheim s University. They are given student concessions on lift passes, so if you re doing the college or Uni number, be sure to carry your student card. The terrain is fairly well matched in terms of level and styles and although the slopes here can be described as dull, most riders will find something to keep them content for an hour. By most standards this is a very small resort with only around 6 miles of piste (half of which is flood lit for night riding). This place is by no means going to hold the attention of advanced riders for too long, especially if you re looking for big powder bowls and large cliff drops. Still there is a 2 mile run to keep you occupied for a few minutes, (which offers the opportunity to ride at speed and take out a few skiers en route). If you really want to find out where the best ride areas are, contact the guys at the local snowboard club, there are no guides here but they will give you a few pointers.
Freeriders have a few wooded sections to cut through, but they won t take long to ride through.
Freestylers roaming around will find some banked walls to check out, as well as a pipe and park.
Carvers who can will have the whole area done in five minutes.
Beginners will find this place more than adequate with a good selection of easy runs.

At the end of the day, every one heads off back to Trondheim by a regular bus service. There s a good selection of places to sleep, eat and drink at almost affordable prices. Night-life is also pretty good but booze will cost you dearly.

Fly to: **Oslo** 3 hours away
ⓘ **tel-** ++47 (0) 7283 1270

SPAIN

GENERAL INFO AND FACTS

Capital - Madrid
Language - Spanish & Catalan
Currency - Peseta & Euros
Alcohol drinking age - 18
Drugs - Cannabis is illegal
Death Penalty - Doesn't exist
Age of consent for Sex - 16
Military Service -Not Compulsory
Electricity Supply - 240 Volts AC
International phone Code ++34
Highest Peak - Mulhachen 3478m

DUTY FREE
10 Litres of Alcohol
90 Litres of Wine - 110 of beer
800 Cigarettes
200 Cigars

SPANNISH DRIVE GUIDE
All vehicles drive on the right hand side of the road
Speed Limits -
Motorways 120kph (74mph)
Highways 90kph (56mph)
Towns 50kph (30mph)

Spanish Snowboard Association
Gran Via 29, 800 Oficina 4,
Madrid.
tel - ++34 (0) 1 5222 803

www.board-it.com/resorts
www.thomson-ski.co.uk
TIME ZONES
Central European
GMT +1 Hour
Between March and October
GMT+2 Hours

Main international Gateway Airport

Barcelona
Madrid
Malaga

NorIf you thought **Spain** was only about bull fighting and tacky seaside resorts inhabited by Europe's finest villains, then think again. Spain is also about snowboarding and while it's not as intense as other parts of Europe, it's certainly worth more than a mention as well as a visit.

Spain has some thirty resorts offering every type of terrain possible and to suit all style's of riding and abilities.

Spain hasn't always had the greatest snow record and with many of the resorts not being the most up to date, there's very little artificial snowmaking to help out when the real stuff is lacking. Resort facilities are not the greatest either, with little or no snowboard facilities, poor options for places to sleep and limited snowboard hire options.
However, this is generalising because the big areas like **Sierra Nevada** are an easy match for the rest of Europe, indeed it will put a lot of northern places to shame.

The Spanish tend to be a bit like their Italian cousins, they love to pose and in doing so end up looking stupid in designer ski suits. Snowboarding is, however, fairly well received throughout the country.

The majority of the resorts are situated in the north of the country and can prove tricky to reach with a hit and miss public transport service. Your best bet is to hire a car at airport and drive, this way you can leave quickly if you dislike a place.

One last point, Spanish snowboarding is not as cheap as you may think. Don't think of it as just a cheap alternative to **France** or **Austria**, although Spain is certainly cheaper than **Switzerland**.

pic - K2 Snowboards

Alto Campoo

▲2175m 10 Lifts & 11 runs

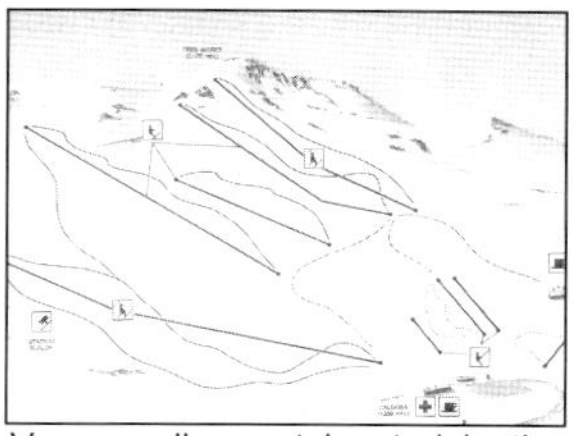

Very small resort located in the **Cantabrian Mountain**s, in the far north of Spain. The area has a series of short trails mainly of intermediate level with nothing challenging for advanced riders. Overall, this is a simple retreat that will please carvers, bore freestylers but suit novices.

Off the slopes there is a couple of small hotels and limited basic local services near the base area.

Fly to: **Madrid** 3 hours away

ⓘ **tel-** ++34 (0) 9-42 75 40 01

Astun

▲2324m 14 Lifts & 28 runs

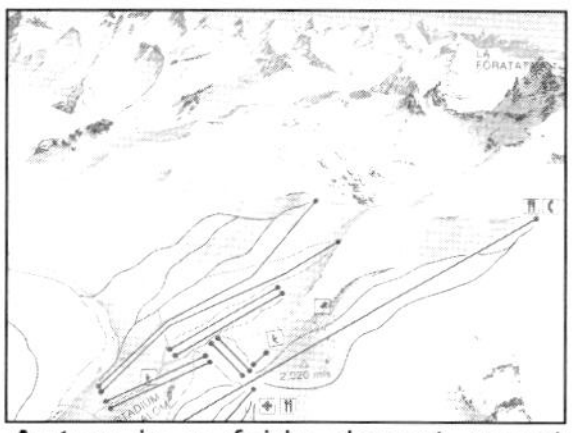

Astun is a fairly decent resort which lies in the **Astun Valley** in the north of Spain. Although a rather featureless resort, Astun nevertheless has some interesting terrain that will keep freeriders of all levels happy for a few days and intermediates content for a week. Carvers have a number of long sweeping trails to do their thing on and beginners have a good series of easy slopes.

Local services at the base area are basic and affordable.

Fly to: **Pamplona** 1-1/2 hours away

ⓘ **tel-** ++34 (0) 9-74 373 034

Boi Taull

▲2030m 8 Lifts & 17 runs

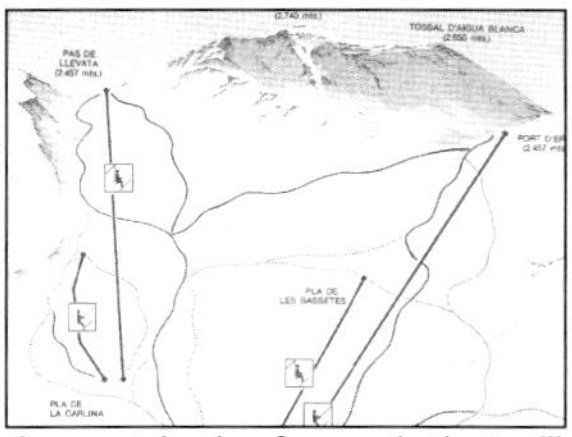

A resort in the far north that will bore the tits off you if you know how to ride and spend more than two days here. Not to say this place is no good, its just that its a bit limited unless you re a total beginner. However, that said, there is still a couple of fast blacks for carvers to try out and the odd natural hit for freestylers to gain some air off.

No convenient local services.

Fly to: **Barcelona** 1 hour away

ⓘ **tel-** ++34 (0) 9-3 414 66 60

Candanchu

▲2400m 24 Lifts & 22 runs

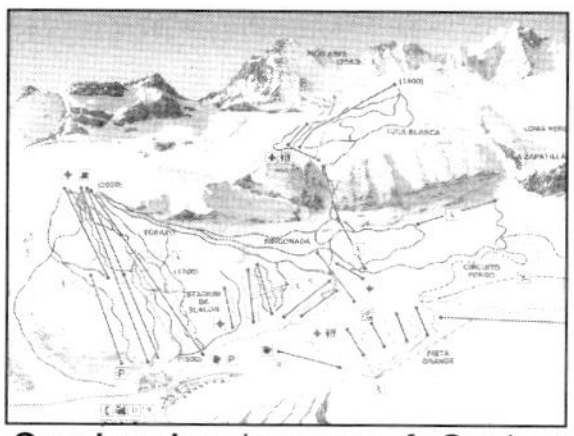

Candanchu is one of Spain s better resorts and is located close to the French border. What you get here is a resort that offers every level and style of rider a good time. Riders who have made the grade will certainly be tested here with a series of fast black trails and a number of very good red runs. Freeriders will find much to keep them amused with a number of nice off piste areas that on occasions provides deep powder stashes. Freestylers are occasionally provided with a half-pipe and fun park as well as there being a lot of good natural terrain to get air from. First timers will find this place perfect for learning at.

Local facilities are close the base slopes, offering a number of hotels a selection of restaurants, shops and a few bars. Although not a cheap place, its still affordable and worth a visit.

Fly to: **Barcelona** 4 hours away

ⓘ **tel-** ++34 (0) 9-74 373 034

Cerler

▲2364m 13 Lifts & 21 runs

Although not a very big resort, with only 30km of marked piste, **Cerler** is one of Spain s best natural freeride/freestyle resorts. it is laid out above the ancient village of **Benasque** up in the **Pinneos Mountains** in the north of Spain. On the slopes, freeriders will find an abundance of fast trails both on and off the piste with numerous areas where its possible to shred through some tight trees and down some deep powder. Most of the runs are graded red and will appeal to intermediate riders, however advanced riders wanting an easy time with a bit of a challenge, will also like it here especially on the runs that descend from the **Cogulla** peak. Freestylers will find some nice hits while beginners will find this place is perfect .

Good local facilities are provided a short distance from the main base area, with hotels and shops.

Fly to: **Barcelona** 2 hours away

ⓘ **tel-** ++34 (0) 9-74 55 10 12

El Formigal

▲2200m 18 Lifts & 27 runs

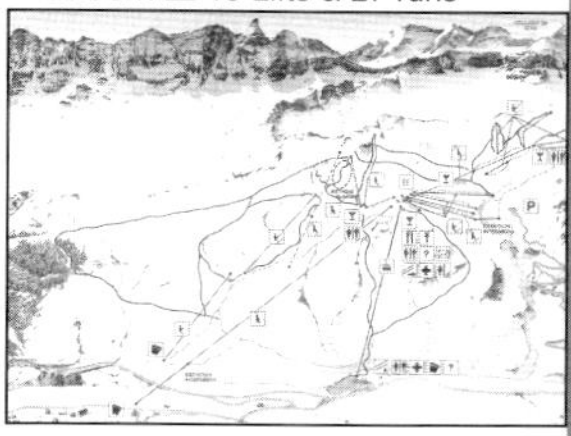

Located way up in the north of the country on the French border, **El Formigal** is a modern purpose built affair. It offers some very good snowboarding on its wide open crowd frees slope that will appeal to piste loving carvers and beginners mostly. Fast riding freeriders and hard core freestylers are not going to be tested too much. There is no pipe or park but there is a lot of good natural freestyle terrain to get air from. Off the slopes you will find a good selection of affordable slopeside services.

Fly to: **Barcelona** 3 hours away

ⓘ **tel-** ++34 (0) 9-42 48 81 25

La Pinilla
Good for freeriders 12 Lifts & 16 runs
1 1/2 hours from Madrid airport.

Lunda
Tiny place for novices 7 Lifts & 7 runs
4 1/2 hours from Madrid airport.

Manzaneda
Basic for freeriders 6 Lifts & 13 runs
6 hours from Madrid airport.

Masella
Excellent riding 10 Lifts & 42 runs
2 hours from Barcelona airport.

Navacerrada
Good for carving 11 Lifts & 12 runs
1hour from Madrid airport.

Port Aine
Basic freeriding area 6 Lifts &16 runs
2 1/2 hours from Barcelona airport.

Port del Comte
Lots of thick trees 15 Lifts & 29 runs
1 1/2 hours from Barcelona airport.

Rasos De Peguera
Small novice area 5 Lifts & 14 runs
1 1/2 hours from Barcelona airport.

San Isidro
Good all round area 13 Lifts & 20 runs
3 hours from Bilbao airport.

Super Esport
Good area with trees 7 Lifts & 20 runs
120 minutes from Oslo airport.

Vall de Nura
Small pipe nothing else 3 Lifts
3 hours from Barcelona airport.

Vallter 2000
Good for carvers 7 Lifts & 12 runs
2 hours from Barcelona airport.

Valgrande Pajares
Best for novices 14Lifts & 15 runs
6 hours from Madrid airport.

Valdezcarry
Basic but okay 11 Lifts & 17 runs
3 1/2 hours from Madrid airport.

Valcotos
A bit on the dull side 8 Lifts & 7 runs
2 1/2 hours from Madrid airport.

Valdesqui
Very boring terrain 10 Lifts & 11 runs
2 hours from Madrid airport.

Valdelinares
Very small and boring 5 Lifts & 7 runs
4 hours from Madrid airport.

Baqueria Beret

MOUNTAIN DATA

Top Lift at - 2510m

Ride Area 77km of piste

Bottom Lift at - 1500m
Vertical Drop - 1010m
Number of Runs - 46
Longest - 3 miles (5km)

TERRAIN LEVELS

Easy	**44%**
Intermediate	**46%**
Advanced	**10%**
Expert =	

TERRAIN TO SUITE

Freeride	**40%**
Trees	A few
Backcountry	A bit
Freestyle	**15%**
Halfpipe	Yes 1
Terrain Park	Yes 1
Carving	**45%**

SNOW DATA
Average Snowfall

Snowmaking
50% cover of the slopes
Winter Periods
Dec to April
Summer Riding
None

SLOPE ACCESS
Total Lifts = **25**
Uplift Rate - 29,000 people an hour.
17 Chair lifts
8 Drag lifts
**Leashes Required*

Lift Times
8.30am to 9.00pm

Lift Pass Rates

1 Day pass	3200 Pts
3 Day pass	8600 Pts
6 Day pass	15,300 Pts

Travel Guide

Fly to **Barcelona** airport, 4 hours away.

Train services via a transfer by bus from the French town of Montrejea.

Route Planner: Via Barcelona, head west on the N11 via Marrtorell and Lleida at which point take the N230 north to the resort.

pic - Edd Seymour

Baqueria Beret is Spain's biggest and possibly most glamorous resort, but don't let that put you off because when the snow is good (which it usually is) this purpose built haunt is not too bad to ride. This hasn't been missed by the *International Snowboard Federation*, who have held both slalom and halfpipe events here on numerous occasions, which is an indication that the place has something to offer. The terrain is spread out over four connecting areas, all of which are easy to reach and will largely appeal to intermediate piste loving carvers.

Freeriders looking for some cool off-piste to ride will be pleasantly surprised, with some great powder riding to be had well away from the chicken sticks in bad suits. Check out the areas on the **Tuc De Dossal** that are reached by chair lift, or hit the stuff up at **La Bonaiqua**. Advanced riders are the ones who will be most disappointed, apart from two black graded runs there's not a great deal of testing stuff.

Freestylers have a rather limited amount of good natural freestyle terrain, but there is the odd good hit to get air from, plus a few drop offs to try out. The half-pipe is off the **Mirador** chair, but you may find it an advantage to borrow a shovel from the lift hut to do a bit of pipe shaping yourself, the resort doesn't look after itself.

Carvers take over on the slopes here with terrain that is ideal for hard alpine riding. The resort is mainly suited to intermediates with some nice red runs but not many expert trails. For the less talented edge merchants, there are some easy blue runs.

Beginners will take kindly to this place as this is a good resort to start out on and progress steadily with. Much of the terrain is easily reached by chair lifts and if you don't like Pomas or T-Bars then you'll be happy to know that you can get around the whole area without having to use them.

Accommodation is close to the slopes, but eating and entertainment is not of a snowboard related nature. Still there is a supermarket for food and loads of **Tapas** (bar snacks). Evenings are OK and drinks are cheap (well compared to say drinks in France) apart from in the clubs where drinks are a flat rate of 1,000 pesetas each). Check out *Lobo* first, then *Tiffany's,* where the music is as crap and old as the name, but when you're drunk at four in the morning, who cares?

Tourist Office Baqueria Beret
SA Apartado 60, Viela, E25530
++34 (0) 973 644455 www.baqueira.es

Overall rating out of 10 **4** **A bit of a dull place really**

La Molina

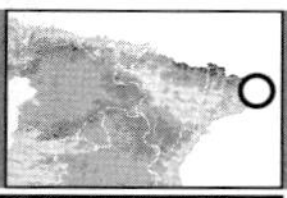

SPAIN

MOUNTAIN DATA

Top Lift at - 2540m

Ride Area 40km of piste

Bottom Lift at - 1600m

Vertical Drop - 875m

Number of Runs - 25

Longest - 2.5 miles (4km)

TERRAIN LEVELS

Easy	52%
Intermediate	37%
Advanced	11%
Expert =	

TERRAIN TO SUITE

Freeride	40%
Trees	Some
Backcountry	A bit
Freestyle	20%
Halfpipe	Yes 2
Terrain Park	Yes 1
Carving	40%

SNOW DATA

Average Snowfall

Snowmaking
25% cover of the slopes

Winter Periods
Dec to April

Summer Riding
None

SLOPE ACCESS

Total Lifts = **15**

Uplift Rate - 20,000 people an hour.

2 Chair lifts

13 Drag lifts

**Leashes Required*

Lift Times
8.30am to 4.30pm

Lift Pass Rates

1 Day pass	2800 Pts
3 Day pass	76000 Pts
6 Day pass	67,600 Pts

Travel Guide

Fly to **Barcelona** airport which has about a 2 1/2 hour transfer time.

Train services are possible direct to La Molina.

Route Planner:
Via Barcelona, head north on the N152 via Granollers, Ripoli and Ribes de Freser

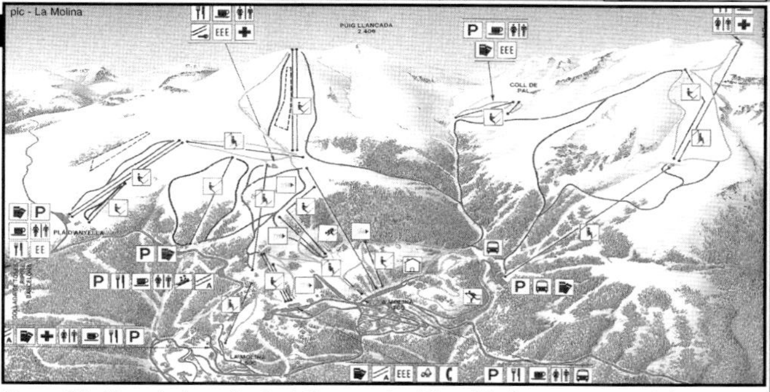

La Molina is located at the end of the **Moixero** mountain range in the **Pyrenees.** Its slopes descend from the summit of the **Tosa de Alp** peak and connect by a short bus ride to the neighbouring and slightly larger resort of **Masella**. These are both welcome alternatives to big resorts scattered around the northern alps simply because mid-week, lift queues don't exist and the slopes are blissfully crowd free. The people of La Molina make you feel very welcome and coupled with neighbouring Masella, both areas have great terrain to shred, with slopes that are covered by trees up to the midway point and then clear pistes up to the summit. The terrain will capture the imagination of most intermediate riders, no matter what their style is, but advanced riders may feel a little left out.

Freeriders in search of extremes that require helmets should forget it, but for the rest, there's ample to search out. Off-piste opportunities present you with loads of trees, with some nice back bowls and good powder stashes on the **Marsella**.

Freestylers get treated better here than in many other so called snowboard-friendly resorts. When snow allows, they provide a pipe and plenty of kickers on **La Molina**, while over on **Marsella,** there's a complete snowboard area called the **Radical Bosc** with hits galore, all of which are marked out on a rider's piste map.

Carvers get the chance to polish up their skills on well groomed pistes and because this place isn't busy, you can go completely balls out without the worry of running over small children.

Beginners in La Molina or Marsella will find that the nursery slopes are wide and spacious. Instruction services are excellent, with foreign speaking instructors available (which helps).

Off the slopes, this is not a resort designed for package groups of clueless skiers without manners. No, **La Molina** is a laid back place with a simple appeal offering affordable accommodation with the chance of staying close to the slopes. Local services are very basic, however, there are enough good facilities to keep you amused with a further selection of amenitiesdown in the village of **Puigcerda**, which is only 10 minutes. The *El Bodegon* restaurant is the place to check out if you want to try some local dishes while night life in La Molina is what you make of it. There s no great action here but you can have a good time in the *Sommy Bar*.

For accommodation listings visit - **www.worldsnowboardguide.com**

La Molina Tourist Office
Estacion de Montana La Molina, E 17573
++34 (0) 72 892 031

Overall rating out of 10 **5** **Not bad for a few dasy fun.**

Sierra Nevada

MOUNTAIN DATA

Top Lift at - 3300m

Ride Area
64km of piste

Bottom Lift at - 2102m

Vertical Drop - 1198m

Number of Runs - 40

Longest - 3.7 miles (6km)

TERRAIN LEVELS

Easy	**55%**
Intermediate	**31%**
Advanced	**14%**
Expert =	

TERRAIN TO SUITE

Freeride	**45%**
Trees	No
Backcountry	A bit
Freestyle	**20%**
Halfpipe	Yes 1
Terrain Park	No
Carving	**20%**

SNOW DATA

Average Snowfall

Snowmaking
35% cover of the slopes

Winter Periods
Dec to April

Summer Riding
None

SLOPE ACCESS

Total Lifts = **19**

Uplift Rate - 32,000 people an hour.

2 Cable Cars, **8** Chairs

9 Drag lifts

**Leashes Required*

Lift Times
8.30am to 4.30pm

Lift Pass Rates

1 Day pass	3500 Pts
3 Day pass	8800 Pts
6 Day pass	17,300 Pts

SLOPE ACTION

Snowboard Hire
Daily rates from 3000 Pts
Kids from 2350 Pts

Snowboard Tuition
Group lessons, from from 3450 Pts

Night Riding
Yes in the pipe

Heli Boarding
No

Snowmobiles
No

Mountain Cafes
2

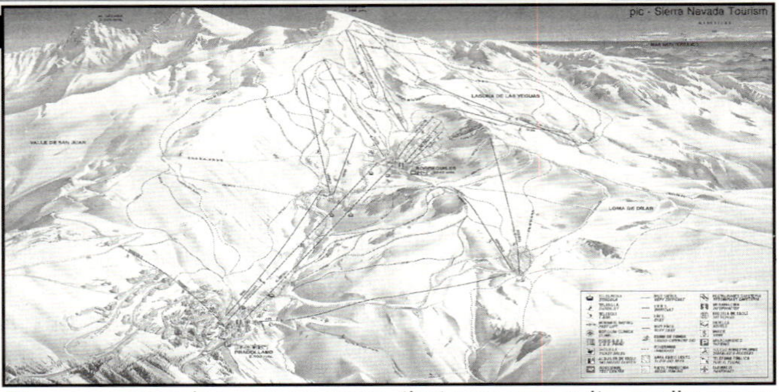

It seems amazing, wrong even, that you can quite easily snowboard in the morning in deep powder snow, then pop down to the beach just over an hour away for a huge seafood meal, a swim in the Mediterranean sea and a relax on a sun soaked coast, but that's exactly what you can do from here in this most southern resort of **Sierra Nevada**, located a short distance form the town of **Granada**.

It's possible from the high point of **Veleta** to see the **Atlas Mountains** of **Morocco** across the **Mediterranean**. Sierra Nevada is an OK place to ride and is particularly well suited to beginners and hard boot carvers, as well as offering some cool off-piste freeriding in powder bowls. The purpose built resort is well located for the slopes. These are first accessed by the main gondola which deposits you in **Borreguilles,** directly onto fantastic beginner s piste. Go up higher and you will be on slopes whose angles are great for free carving - just that perfect angle to really lay 'em out in perfect control. Night-riding is done on the **Rio** slope, a 2 mile run that provides one of the best lit night trails anywhere. However, there are no set days or times for night-riding, you will need to check at the lift ticket office on a daily basis to get details.

Freeriders should check out the stuff just below the peak of **Veleta** at 3398m. To do this, traverse to the **Olimpica** and where this crosses the **Diagonal,** kick hard to your left and travel off piste on an itinerary known as **Tajos de la Virgen**. The view above you is truly stunning, (a bowl edged with dramatic cliffs). The **Dilar** chair takes you towards the **Radio Telescope**, where after a walk along the ridge you can see below a huge expanse of off-piste which you have just travelled over on the chair. Take any line, the slope is a good safe angle with an easy traverse back to the **Solana** piste and the **Dilar** chair.

Freestylers have to make do most of the time, with an array of unusual natural hits. They do build a pipe when snow conditions permit it. However, if you ride over to **Tajos de la Virgen** run, you'll find rolling jumps verging into vertical kickers. Kick back again towards the **Cartujo** piste and make use of the piste edge with it's many varied banked sides to gain more air time.

Carvers are much in evidence here as the slopes lend themselves really well to edging a board over at speed, especially on the fast black trails. Particular good blacks for this are down from the **Borreguilles**.

Beginners; the **Borreguilles** area is full on for learning the art of hurtling down a mountain on a board, but not the only place to go. Much of this resort is excellent for novices with good snowboard instruction facilities.

Off the slopes, **Sierra Nevada** is a cool place with a lot going on. Getting around the village, which is extremely steep, is pretty tough on foot though (especially once you have had a few beers). There is a bus service that runs until midnight, or alternatively, a chair lift that links the various levels to the centre of the village, for which you will need a valid lift pass to get on. The main set back for this place is the high cost of everything, which may have something to with the fact that the Sierra Nevada attracts a lot of the Spanish elite, and all the baggage that clings on to them. However, what is on offer is of a high standard with locals making you welcome.

If you don t like Spanish food then don t fret, this place serves up all kinds of affordable grub from **Chinese** to **Mexican**. The main thing to watch out for, is that because this is a busy place, restaurants fill up early on in the evening and so a lot of waiting for a table is common place. Still, a meal, at a price, can be had in the likes of the *Ruta del Veleta*, (very posh and expensive but good). *Tito Luigi* is good for a cheap meal.

If you like hard, fast and drunken action, there is plenty of it here but nothing happens until late. Bars and clubs don't get going until at least midnight, then it rocks and you'll have no trouble staying out late, drinking until you drop at 5 in the morning. The *Soho Bar* and *La Chicle* are your main late hangouts, where Senorita s are in plentiful supply all night long.

Accommodation comes in all manner of styles and prices starting at super expensive. Most of the accommodation is located within easy reach of the base lifts and is pretty good, with some accommodation options at affordable prices. For budget riders, there's a hostel offering cheap beds with joint lift pass package rates.

For accommodation listings visit - www.worldsnowboardguide.com

Summary: Not bad for some no frills riding, with okay terrain for carvers and easy going freeriders but little for freestylers. Very good choice of local services.
Money wise: Overall, this is a very affordable resort offering good value.

Overall rating out of 10 **7**

Tourist Office Sierra Nevada
Pl Marina Pineda, 10-2
Granada.

General info	**++34 (0) 958 24 91 11**
Reservations	**++34 (0) 958 24 91 22**
Avlanche info	**++39 (0) 93 325 6391**

www.

pic - Trey Tomsik /Dufone Snowboards

pic - Sierra Nevada

Travel Guide

Fly to **Madrid** international
Transfer time to resort = **3**$^{1/2}$ *hours.*
Local airport = Malaga 1$^{1/2}$ hours

Approximate global air travel times to **Madrid:**

from:	London	**3** hours
	Los Angles	**14** hours
	New York	**10** hours

Bus services from Madrid via a change over at Granada, on a daily basis.

Trains to **Granada** (20 miles)

Route Planner
Madrid

Sierra Nevada = **270** miles (435km)
Drive time is about **6**$^{1/2}$ hours

*From **Calais** 1257 miles (2022Km)
Drive time is around **24** hours.

SWEDEN

GENERAL INFO AND FACTS

Capital - Stockholm
Language - Swedish & Lapp
Currency - Krona
Alcohol drinking age - 18 & 20
Drugs - Cannabis is illegal
Death Penalty - Doesn t exist
Age of consent for Sex - 16
Military Service -Not Compulsory
Electricity Supply - 240 Volts AC
International phone Code ++46
Highest Peak -

DUTY FREE
10 Litres of Alcohol
90 Litres of Wine - 110 of beer
800 Cigarettes
200 Cigars

SWEDISH DRIVE GUIDE
All vehicles drive on the right hand side of the road
Speed Limits -
Motorways 110kph (68mph)
Highways 90kph (56mph)
Towns 50kph (31mph)

Contacts and general info

Swedish Snowboard Association
Raetteli Sirpa, Idrottens Hus. S-12387 Farsta
tel - ++46 (0) 8 605 6000

TIME ZONES
Central European
GMT +1 Hour
Between March and October
GMT+2 Hours

Main international Gateway Airport
Stockholm

AustSweden emulates its neighbouring cousin **Norway** in almost every aspect; cold climate, short winter days and expensive beer. Like Norway, Sweden has a lot of listed resorts - approximately 150. However, 80% or so cater just for cross country skiing, so a lot Swedes head down to **France** and **Austria** to ride, leaving their own resorts generally crowd free, which helps when you see the size of some of the areas (tiny).

In general, 99.9% of all resorts are small and at a low level. Terrain will suit mainly intermediate freeriders and freestylers with treeriding and excellent off piste opportunities. Fast carvers won t be too impressed and advanced boarders may find things a bit limiting, but novices will have a good time on loads of easy slopes.

Getting around the country is easy, although you may have to do some travelling to reach some of the far flung resorts. Air, bus and rail services are damn good ,but all are very expensive.

Sweden has the reputation of being very expensive, especially booze. Resort facilities and services are of a high standard. Accommodation in the form of hotels, little wooden cabins or hostels. A basic Bed and Breakfast home costs from 350kr per night while a bunk in a hostel is around 150kr or a cabin from 170Kr a night.

Over all, **Sweden** may not be the most adventurous country in which to ride, but it s worth a road trip in June when you can still ride in T-shirts: What s more, Swedes are cool people and the girls are gorgeous and absolutely stunning.

pic - Stig

Are

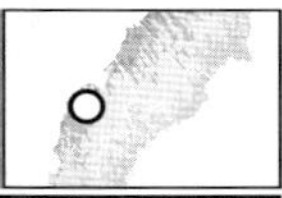

MOUNTAIN DATA

Top Lift at - 1274m

Ride Area

90km of piste

Bottom Lift at - 400m

Vertical Drop - 880m

Number of Runs - 102

Longest - 4 miles (6.6km)

TERRAIN LEVELS

Easy	40%
Intermediate	50%
Advanced	10%
Expert =	

TERRAIN TO SUITE

Freeride	50%
Trees	Yes
Backcountry	Yes
Freestyle	35%
Halfpipe	Yes 2
Terrain Park	Yes 1
Carving	15%

SNOW DATA

Average Snowfall

Snowmaking
50% cover of the slopes

Winter Periods
Dec to April

Summer Riding
None

SLOPE ACCESS

Total Lifts = **48**

Uplift Rate - 50,000 people an hour.

2 Cable cars - **1** Gondola

6 Chair lifts - **39** Drag lifts

**Leashes Required*

Lift Times
8.30am to 4.30pm

Lift Pass Rates

1 Day pass	250 Kr
6 Day pass	1250 Kr

Travel Guide

Fly to **Stockholm** and then inland to Ostersund airport.

Train services are possible to Are from Stockholm which takes around 10 hours.

Route Planner:
Via Stockholm, take the E4 north to Gavle and then to Bergby at which point you head north west along the E14 via Ostersund to Are.

pic - Are Tourism

Are is the biggest and most developed resort in the whole of Scandinavia and unlike many Swedish resorts, this isn t a poxy little hill — it s a good sized mountain that will give all rider levels a good time. It is situated in the middle of Sweden, near the town of **Ostershund**. The runs here cover three main mountains all accessed by one lift pass, although the lifts themselves don t link up. Are is the largest area with the most challenging terrain while runs on **Duved** and **Bjornange** are a lot shorter and will appeal to novices and intermediates mostly.

Freeriders will find a lot of varied terrain , from cornices and wind lips to steeps, as well as some cool tree runs. If you can afford it, you can also explore the off-piste by helicopter (but it s not cheap). However, if you can t afford a heli-trip, by paying the fee, you can catch a lift on a piste basher up to the top of Are s **Areskuten** 1400m summit. This allows you to descend some excellent terrain that goes off in different directions but still allows you to get back to the base (study a lift map first).

Freestylers have a great funpark known as **The Snowboard Land Park,** which is on the **Brackemyren** run and comes loaded with a number of big hits to gain maximum air from. There are also two pipes, one in the park and the other at the base of lift **10**. The pipe has 3 metre plus walls and is regularly used to host international competitions that attract the worlds top pros.

Carvers who like laying out big arcs will find the well groomed pistes ideal for leaving a signature in the snow. The long red run from the top of the **Kabinbanan** cable car that eventually takes you home via some wood, is perfect for this.

Beginners should not feel left out here, there are plenty of easy slopes which run from the top lift to the base area. The of runs on the **Duvedsomradet** area are cool with varying terrain features.

Off the slopes, what you get here is similar to what you would find in any top resort in the **Alps**. However, hurts the wallet and you shouldn t bother trying to do a week here on a tight budget, you won t last. Still, you won t be disappointed with the level of services and convenience of the accommodation. For food check out *Broken Dreams* for a burger and local grub or *Bykrogens* for a pizza. Night-life is very pricey, but don t hold back, spend and be merry in places like the *Sundial* or the *Diplomats*.

For accommodation listings visit - www.worldsnowboardguide.com

Tourist office Are
Arefjall AB, Box 53. S-830 ARE
++46 (0) 46 647177 50

Overall rating out of 10 **7** **Very good laid back resort**

Riksgransen

pic -Stig

MOUNTAIN DATA

Top Lift at - 900m

Ride Area: 24km of piste

Bottom Lift at - 500m

Vertical Drop - 400m

Number of Runs - 20

Longest - 1 mile (1.6km)

TERRAIN LEVELS

Easy	**44%**
Intermediate	**50%**
Advanced	**10%**
Expert =	

TERRAIN TO SUITE

Freeride	**60%**
Trees	No
Backcountry	Yest
Freestyle	**35%**
Halfpipe	Yes 3
Terrain Park	Yes 1
Carving	**5%**

SNOW DATA

Average Snowfall
500cm a season

Snowmaking
0% cover of the slopes

Winter Periods
Dec to April

Summer Riding
None

SLOPE ACCESS

Total Lifts = **6**

Uplift Rate - 7,500 people an hour.

2 Chair lifts

4 Drag lifts

**Leashes Required*

Lift Times
8.30am to Mid-night

Lift Pass Rates

1 Day pass	250 Kr
3 Day pass	475 Kr
6 Day pass	1100 Kr

Travel Guide

Fly to **Stockholm** and then inland to Riksgransen.

Train services go direct to Riksgransen a 20 hour journey from Stockholm.

Route Planner:
Riksgransen is near the Swedish/Norweigan border east of the Norweigan town town of Narvik off the E6 and E10 routes.

In the far north of **Sweden** and close to the Norwegian border lies the remote resort of **Riksgansen**. A place with one of the most unusual seasons in Europe and one that has become a snowboarder s favourite for summer road trips and snowboard camps. **Riksgransen** is located just 125 miles from the Arctic circle which would suggest that this is a cold place, but because of its proximity to the **Gulf Stream** and the **Atlantic Ocean**, riding in a T-shirt is quite normal in the latter months of the season. Un-like most resorts in Europe, Riksgransen doesn't open until mid February and stays open until late June, or as long as the snow allows the lifts to be used. You can ride all day in a T-shirt, and strangely enough you can still snowboard right up until midnight when there is still bright natural day light. Although no one tends to hang out here for more than a week to ten days, you won t be too disappointed if you re a no-nonsense freerider, or a full on freestyler.

Freeriders will find some good off piste with steeps, windlips, and cool hits for getting air born. If you sign up for heli-boarding, you get the chance to see the best of **Lapland's** backcountry terrain, but is not cheap whatsoever.

Freestylers are attracted to Riksgransen in big numbers. They hold the *Swedish Snowboard Cup* here and Swedes like their hits big and laid on. So apart from loads of really good natural freestyle terrain to check out, they also build and maintain a damn good halfpipe and fun park (mainly for the camps), with loads of hits for pulling air off, this includes an awesome quarter pipe for those who know what it s about.

Carvers will feel out of place here and to be honest, the terrain is not really that good for laying out big turns on. However, via the **Ovre** lift you do get access to a decent red that joins up to a black.

Beginners do make it up here, but in truth, it s a long way to come just for a couple of small easy flats.

Riksgransen Hotel is where it all happens off the slopes. Beds and food are offered at reasonable prices. You can also pig out at Lappis cafe. There s no night-life as such here, in fact there is none at all, However, you can have a very good drinking session in the *Riksgransen Hotel* which often last all night. Summer up here is for riders in a van, equipped with a tent, loads of duty free booze and a copy of Penthouse.

Riksgransen Tourist Office
S-980 28 Riksgransen
++46 (0) 980 400 80 **www.baqueira.es**

Overall rating out of 10 — **5** — **Okay but only for a few days**

Bjorkliden
▲960m 22 km of piste 5 lifts
By any stretch of the imagination, Bjorkliden is a small resort with a mixture of basic beginner terrain to simple intermediate carving slopes. Still, overall it s not a bad resort and offers a lot of interesting opportunities, just not of a very advanced level. However, freeriders who find the marked out runs a bit of a bore could sign up for a heli-board trip and enjoy some cool backcountry riding. While freestylers can make do with a decent sized terrain park with a good halfpipe and hits.
Nothing local near the slopes but what is available a few miles away is okay but pricey.
Fly to: **Kiruna** 59 miles (95km) away
ⓘ **tel-** ++46 (0) 647 17700

Bjornrike
▲950m 15 km of piste 7 lifts
Small resort that offers the average rider an afternoons okay carving on a number of trails which include a couple of fast blacks. But in the main, this is a resort to please beginners with a low IQ.
Slope side lodging and accommodation and other resort facilities are expensive but okay.
Fly to: **Stockholm** 5 hours away
ⓘ **tel-** ++46 (0) 684 3200

Bydalen
▲1010m 50 km of piste 11 lifts
Overall, this is not a bad place to spend a few days if you are beginner wanting nice and easy runs or a freerider looking for easy to negotiate tree runs. Riders who rate themselves can see if it s justified with a good selection of black runs to try out. Freestylers don t have too much to test them, but as with most Swedish resorts, locals build their own hits and session them all day long. There is also some fast carving runs to suit the carvers.
Fly to: **Stockholm** 5¼ hours away
ⓘ **tel-** ++46 (0) 643 32011

Funasdalen
▲1200m 90 km of piste 34 lifts
Fundasdalen is rated by many as one of Sweden s best resorts, offering a good level of varied terrain and with plenty to keep expert and beginner riders happy for a good few days. Riders who like to go fast can do so here on a series of black runs and a great selection of red intermediate trails. If back country riding without the hiking is your thing, heli-boarding is available to those with sufficient means. Freestylers don t need to go heli-boarding as they are provided with 2 halfpipes and a number of terrain parks that all house some mighty big hits with spines, gaps and quarter pipes. Beginners have an equally good number of basic trails.
Okay slope side lodging and services.
Reach **Funasdalen** via **Roros** airport in Norway 1 hour away.
tel- ++46 (0) 684 21420

Hemavan

▲1135m 30 km of piste 7 lifts
Hemavan is a rather unusual resort that has a reasonable marked out ride area and an even bigger unmarked backcountry terrain accessible by helicopter. For those freeriders who can t fly off to secret powder bowls, there are some nice areas close to the lifts including lots of trees at the lower section of the slopes. This is not a resort noted for its advanced terrain, indeed there is only a couple of advanced graded runs, but for intermediates and first timers, this is a fine place to check out and spend a few days.
If you do decide to visit this place then be prepared to put yourself out as there are no local facilities on the slopes and although accommodation and other amenities are not too far away, it s very spread out and will require a car.
Fly to: **Stockholm** 12 hours away
ⓘ **tel-** ++46 (0) 954 104 50

Hovfjallett
▲595m 9 km of piste 6 lifts
Hovfjallett is basically a waste of time unless you are aged 80, wearing a hearing aid and excel at speeds of one mile an hour. Although the area has a few black runs and half a dozen red trails, all can be licked by an average rider in the time it takes to have a curry induced crap. However, the place is friendly and provides a good halfpipe for air heads.
Fly to: **Torsby** 15 minutes hours away
ⓘ **tel-** ++46 (0) 560 10550

Idre Fjall
▲890m 60 km of piste 30 lifts
In the top ten ranking of Sweden s resorts **Idre Fjall** is a place that will suit all levels and rider styles. The area has a combination of easy runs and a number of testing black runs. Nothing here is all that long, indeed the longest trail measures just under 3km, however, this is a place that can take a good few days to explore, especially if you sign up for a heli-board trip. Freestylers have a terrain park and a halfpipe which the locals take great pride in and keep in good condition.
Off the slopes you will find a good choice of slope side lodging and places to eat and drink in.
Fly to: **Mora** 40 minutes hours away
ⓘ **tel-** ++46 (0) 253 41000

Lofsdalen
Good night riding 8 Lifts & 30 runs
2½ hours from Stockholm airport.

Nya Dundret
Super boring place 3 Lifts & 13 runs
2 hours from Stockholm airport.

Salen

▲890m 155 km of piste 100 lifts
Salem is about as big as they get in **Sweden,** with over 155 km of marked rideable terrain spread out over four areas offering every thing you could want both on the slopes and off. The terrain is split evenly between all levels and with a host of advanced runs that will have the hardest of riders tested to the limits and needing a week to conquer what is on offer. Freeriders will be pleased to find lots of cool areas to get a fix with deep powder stashes and fast steeps off-piste. And for those wanting to go high off man made hits, then there is a host of terrain parks and halfpipes to satisfy your needs. As for beginners, **Salem** is absolutely perfect for getting to grips with the basics of snowboarding on a series of easy to reach novice slopes.
Resort services are extreme with literally dozens of hotels, restaurants and night time hangouts much of which is either on the slopes or very close to them.
Fly to: **Mora** 1 hour away
ⓘ **tel-** ++46 (0) 280 20250

Strolien
▲830m 5 km of piste 7 lifts

Strolien is a small affair with nothing great to shout about unless you are a novice or intermediate rider who looks for simple slopes. There is nothing much here to please advanced riders, with only a couple of black runs. Freeriders will find that this place has some nice off-piste areas although very limited, while freestylers have numerous natural hits to get air from and a pipe. Basic lodging is available but none of it is that cheap.
Fly to: **Trondheim** 1 hour away
ⓘ **tel-** ++47 (0) 647 70 170

Sundsvall
Super boring place 2 Lifts & 4 runs
2 hours from Stockholm airport.

Sunne
Small carvers resort 8 Lifts & 16 runs
2½ hours from Oslo airport.

Tarnaby
Super boring place 46 Lifts & 7 runs
3 hours from Stockholm airport.

Vemdalsskalet
Basic riding for all 8 Lifts & 18 runs
Stockholm is 5 hours away.

GENERAL INFO AND FACTS

Capital - Bern
Language - German/French
Currency - Swiss Francs & Euros
Alcohol drinking age - 18
Drugs - Cannabis is illegal
Death Penalty - Doesn t exist
Age of consent for Sex - 16
Military Service - Compulsory
Electricity Supply - 240 Volts AC
International phone Code ++41
Highest Peak - Mont Rosa 4634m

DUTY FREE
10 Litres of Alcohol
90 Litres of Wine - 110 of beer
800 Cigarettes
200 Cigars

SWISS DRIVE GUIDE
All vehicles drive on the right hand side of the road
Speed Limits -
Motorways 120kph (74mph)
Highways 800kph (50mph)
Towns 50kph (31mph)

Contacts and general info

Swiss Snowboard Association
Po Box 371. CH-8029. Zurich
+41 (0) 1 388 5070

TIME ZONES
Central European
GMT +1 Hour
Between March and October
GMT+2 Hours

Main international Gateway Airports

Innsbruck
Salzburg
Munich *in Germany*
Zurich *in Switzerland*

The Swiss have gained their riches by shrewdness and getting in on the act early. So it's no wonder their resorts have been welcoming snowboarders for some time and providing them with a huge variety of services. It's never been a big deal for Swiss areas to build halfpipes and fun parks.

What you find in Switzerland is a decent mixture of the old and new. Many resorts are made up of old chalets that look the part, while others are sprawling modern affairs. Verbier is a huge and very impressive place, spoilt only by the fact that it s damn expensive and that it attracts Royalty and idiots on Big Foot skis.

Travelling around the country is made easy with a good road network that links up well with the rest of Europe. To drive on Swiss motorways you need to buy a road tax called the Vignette, which costs around Sfr 30 and can be purchased from Automobile Associations or at border crossings. The tax disc must be shown in the window and fines are payable if you are caught without it.

Flying options are excellent in Switzerland, with most resorts reachable within a 3 hour transfer from the main gateway airports. For such a small country with so many high mountainous areas, it's amazing how good and how many direct train routes there are to resorts. Trains wind their way up to some of the smallest places, travelling up such steep inclines that you're left wondering just how good the brakes are! Few resorts don't have their own train station, or one more than 15 km from away. Bus services are also good, especially from airports, but although they're cheaper than the trains, the buses are slower and less frequent.

Switzerland is not a member of the EU, so all foreign nationals need a passport. However, visas are not required for many nationals, but you must obtain proper permits if you want to work, even as a kitchen porter. You can get cash in hand work with no questions asked, so long as you don't draw attention to yourself.

When it comes to money, Switzerland is costly - budget riders be warned nothing is cheap, and this is not a country where you can scam your way around easily, although thankfully a lot of resorts have bunk houses and youth hostels that help to keep costs down.

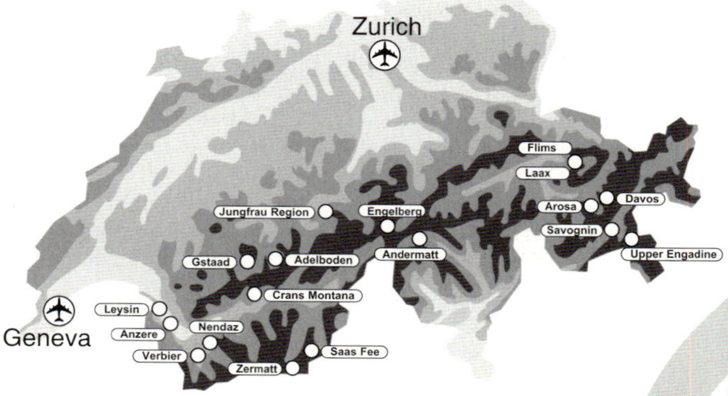

pic - Andrew Hourmont - Rider Gilbert Wager at Les Diablarets

Adelboden

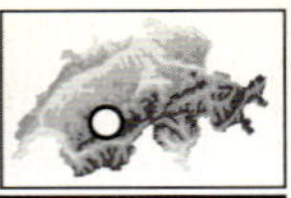

MOUNTAIN DATA

Top Lift at - 2350m

Ride Area
97km of piste

Bottom Lift at - 1356m

Vertical Drop - 994m
Number of Runs - 87
Longest - 4 miles (7km)

TERRAIN LEVELS

Easy	**48%**
Intermediate	**44%**
Advanced	**8%**
Expert =	

TERRAIN TO SUITE

Freeride	**40%**
Trees	A few
Backcountry	A bit
Freestyle	**20%**
Halfpipe	Yes 2
Terrain Park	Yes 2
Carving	**40%**

SNOW DATA

Average Snowfall

Snowmaking
5% cover of the slopes
Winter Periods
Nov to May
Summer Riding
None

SLOPE ACCESS

Total Lifts = **29**
Uplift Rate - 33,000 people an hour.
2 Cable Cars - **5** Chair lifts
22 Drag lifts
**Leashes Required*

Lift Times
8.30am to 4.30pm

Lift Pass Rates

1 Day pass	50 Sfr
3 Day pass	126 Sfr
6 Day pass	204 Sfr

Travel Guide

Fly to **Geneva** airport, 3 hours away.

Train services to Frutigen station (15 minutes).

Route Planner: Via Geneva, take the N1 to Lausanne, the N9 to Aiglg and the B11 before taking the B73 to the resort.
*Drive time from **Calais** is 9½ hours
550 miles (885 km)

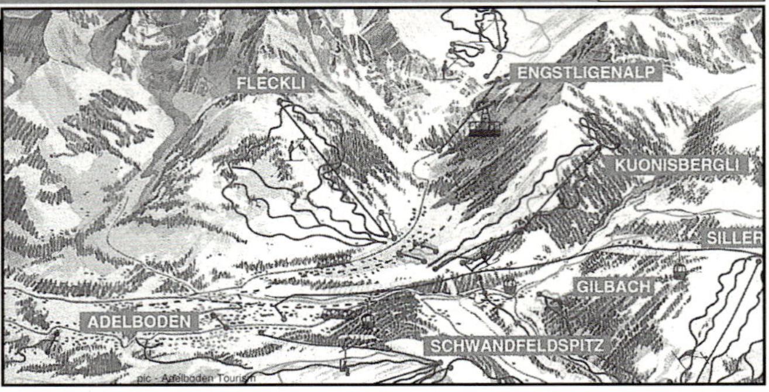

pic - Adelboden Tourism

Adelboden, which links with Lenk, is a decent sized picture postcard swiss resort, located a short distance from the resort of **Gstaad** and close to the glitzy resorts of **Wengen Grindelwald** and **Murren**. However, unlike its neighbours, this is a less popular place making it that bit quieter with crowd free slopes. This is also not a resort favoured by tour operators, although a few do bus in the two plankers to mess things up. What you get to ride here is split into 6 areas all linked by lifts. Collectively, all the areas provide terrain that will keep novices and intermediates happy for a week, while expert riders will have things sorted in a few days after tackling the blacks on the **Geils** area. The mountain has some nice diverse terrain that will bring a smile to most freeriders. It also has some okay backcountry riding offering a few powder stashes and some fun pisted areas.

Freeriders will find plenty to keep themselves occupied with here. The **Geils** area offers some good off-piste riding coupled with a series of black runs that will test the best and draw tears if you fail to respect the terrain.

Freestylers are spoilt for choice here, with the option to ride two funparks, one at Sillerenbuhl and the other on the Hahnenmoos area. Both parks come equipped with a good selection of gaps and some nice kickers. There s also a cool man made half-pipe and as various naturally formed pipes with big walls for getting maximum air. Locals here like to ride the natural hits and have a number of secret spring boards that are tucked away, so hitch up with a local and go big.

Carvers will find that **Adelboden** will suit their needs perfectly, especially competent intermediate hard-booters who like to leave a signature in the snow on wide open trails.

Beginners have a mountain that caters for them in every aspect, good novice areas with easy access from the village, excellent snowboard tuition at the local snowboard school and runs serviced by easy to use lifts, although many are drag lifts.

Off the slopes, **Adelboden** offers plenty of slope side accommodation with various hotels and a number of chalets to choose from, all in a relaxed setting. Eating out is mixed with some affordable options. Night life is also okay, but on the whole, not rocking.Check out such bars as the *Alpenrosli* and *Lohner.*

For accommodation listings visit - www.worldsnowboardguide.com

Tourist Office Adelboden
Adelboden, CH-3715
++41 (0) 33 673 8080 **www.adelboden.ch**

Overall rating out of 10 **6** **An okay crowd free resort**

Andermatt

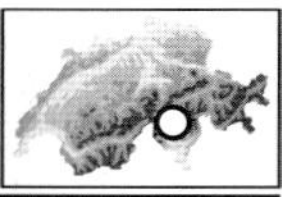

MOUNTAIN DATA

Top Lift at - 2963m
Ride Area 56km of piste
Bottom Lift at - 1436m
Vertical Drop - 1527m
Number of Runs - 24
Longest - 3 miles (5km)

TERRAIN LEVELS

Easy	30%
Intermediate	42%
Advanced	26%
Expert =	

TERRAIN TO SUITE

Freeride	70%
Trees	Some
Backcountry	Yes
Freestyle	20%
Halfpipe	Yes 1
Terrain Park	Yes 1
Carving	20%

SNOW DATA

Average Snowfall
850cm a season
Snowmaking
0% cover of the slopes
Winter Periods
Dec to April
Summer Riding
None

SLOPE ACCESS

Total Lifts = **12**
Uplift Rate - 30,000 people an hour.
2 Cable Cars - **4** Chair lifts
6 Drag lifts
**Leashes Required*

Lift Times
8.30am to 4.30pm

Lift Pass Rates

1 Day pass	52 Sfr
3 Day pass	136 Sfr
6 Day pass	190 Sfr

Travel Guide

Fly to **Zurich** airport 2 hours away.

Train services are possible direct in to Andermatt.

Route Planner: Via Zurich, head south on the N3 and turn of at signs for Schwyz onto the A8 and N2 to Andermatt.
Zurich
to resort = 72 miles

pic - Andermatt Tourism

Andermatt is a very small resort, located close to the **St.Gotthard Pass** tunnel with a reputation for excellent powder snow that other resorts can only dream about. This may not be a massive resort, but what it does have is a respectable 1500 metres of vertical with some damn fine steeps, lots of off-piste and crowd-free slopes that are generally also skier free (apart from major holiday times) making **Andermatt** a great place to snowboard There is excellent terrain for advanced riders in soft boots and is noted for its testing runs that also appeal to intermediates who are beginning to sort out their riding. The area is split into four areas with the most testing terrain to be found on the **Gemsstock** slopes, easily reached from Andermatt by a two stage cable ride. From the top, you get to ride down some serious open steep bowls that eventually make their way to the base. However, to guarantee that you do get back to the base, you are well advised to use the services of a local guide.

Freeriders have an excellent resort to explore, with great off-piste riding in big powder areas. If your thing is fast steeps and banked walls, **Andermatt** is a resort that will serve your needs well and will easily keep you interested for a week or so.

Freestylers are provided with a fun park and half-pipe on the Gemsstock area, but they're not particularly hot. However, there is plenty of good natural terrain to get from with big naturally formed banks and some cool drop offs.

Carvers who like to perform will be pleased to find that there's plenty of fast sections to really crank some big turns on. The **Sonnenpiste** is a decent run to try out before hitting some of the blacks on the **Gemsstock** area.

Beginners usually head for the **Natschen** area, but if you're a slow learner this may not be your resort The slope graduation goes quickly from easy to very hard.

Good accommodation can be found in chalets or in one of the hotels, with access to the slopes very easy by foot. The old village is as Swiss as they come: somewhat boring and somewhat basic. However, it's not as expensive as some other Swiss resorts and as you can ride hard all day, who needs major night-life? A few beers in a bar free of moaning package tour apr s numpties should do the trick.

For accommodation listings visit - www.worldsnowboardguide.com

Andermatt Tourist Office
Po Box 247, Bahnhofplatz, Andermatt. CH-6490
++41 (0) 41 887 1454 www.andermatt.com

Overall rating out of 10 **7** **A very good all round resort**

Anzere

MOUNTAIN DATA

Top Lift at - 2362m

Ride Area
40km of piste

Bottom Lift at - 1423m
Vertical Drop - 939m
Number of Runs - 24
Longest - 3 miles (4km)

TERRAIN LEVELS

Easy	**40%**
Intermediate	**50%**
Advanced	**10%**
Expert =	

TERRAIN TO SUITE

Freeride	**45%**
Trees	A few
Backcountry	A bit
Freestyle	**10%**
Halfpipe	Yes 1
Terrain Park	Yes 1
Carving	**45%**

SNOW DATA

Average Snowfall
800cm a season
Snowmaking
5% cover of the slopes
Winter Periods
Nov to April
Summer Riding
None

SLOPE ACCESS

Total Lifts = **12**
Uplift Rate - 33,000 people an hour.
1 Gondola - **4** Chair lifts
7 Drag lifts
**Leashes Required*

Lift Times
8.30am to 4.30pm

Lift Pass Rates

1 Day pass	46 Sfr
3 Day pass	125 Sfr
6 Day pass	180 Sfr

Travel Guide

Fly to **Geneva** airport, 3 hours away.

Train services are possible to Sion station (15 minutes).

Route Planner:
Via Geneva, east on the N1 and N9 to Sion and turn left and then drive up the steep road to Anzere.

pic -Anzere Tourism

Anzere is one of Switzerland's custom built resorts that dates back to the sixties. This small resort with a modest 25 miles of piste, sits at an altitude of 1500m. This has helped to ensure a good annual snow record of over 800 centimetres a season on slopes that get a lot of sun. This allows for plenty of tanning as you ride the slopes or sip a beer at a mountain bar. Overall, Anzere is a fun, happy-go-lucky place that will appeal to the laid back snowboarder. A lot of families and older skiers hang out here, but snowboarders can mingle with ease with both and riders are not ignored or snubbed. The 25 miles of runs are simple and all styles will find something to keep them happy, but it appeals mostly to novices and riders just getting things dialled. Anzere would be worth a visit for a few days if you're on a road trip, but a two week trip will prove to be a bit of a bore for those riders who rate themselves at an advanced level.

Freeriders in soft boots will fair well on the areas found off the **Les Rousses** and **Le Bate** chair lifts. The trees at the lower parts although not extensive, do offer some pine shredding. The Swiss don't particularly like the woods being cut up, so beware, you may encounter a few sharp tongues from the locals.

Freestylers can spin off a number of natural hits and there are ample areas for practising your switch stance, especially on the runs frequented by the oldies who are leisurely sliding around on their two wooden planks.

Carvers are much in evidence here, with the terrain lending itself well to some good edge-to-edge riding. Competent riders will find the black under the **Pas-de-Maimbre** gondola worth a visit. It should be said that this run could be a red, but it's OK and allows for a few quick turns.

Beginners should achieve the most on the well matched and easy slopes which can be tackled by taking the **Pralan-Tsalan** chair lift and then by using the drags (hold on tight, wimps).

Anzere is a well laid out village, with a good choice of accommodation (mostly expensive) but budget snowboarders will find affordable beds in a selection of apartments and chalets. *Village Camp* offers decent priced lodgings while the *Avenir* does the best pizza. For evenings, it's best to check out *La Grange* or the *Rendezvous*. *Central Sports* is the place to rent snowboard gear.
For accommodation listings visit - www.worldsnowboardguide.com

Tourist Office Anzere
Ch-01972 Anzere.
++41 (0) 27 399 28 05 **www.**

Overall rating out of 10 **6** **A good but basic beginners place**

Arosa

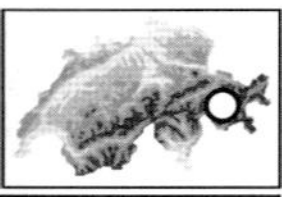

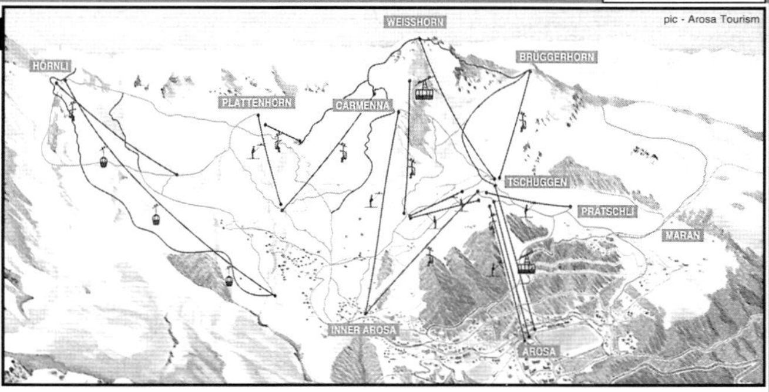

pic - Arosa Tourism

MOUNTAIN DATA

Top Lift at - 2653m

Ride Area
64km of piste

Bottom Lift at - 1740m
Vertical Drop - 914m
Number of Runs - 55
Longest - 3 miles (5km)

TERRAIN LEVELS

Easy	38%
Intermediate	56%
Advanced	6%
Expert =	

TERRAIN TO SUITE

Freeride	50%
Trees	A few
Backcountry	Yes
Freestyle	20%
Halfpipe	Yes 1
Terrain Park	Yes 1
Carving	30%

SNOW DATA

Average Snowfall
n/a
Snowmaking
10% cover of the slopes
Winter Periods
Dec to April
Summer Riding
None

SLOPE ACCESS

Total Lifts = **16**
Uplift Rate - 22,000 people an hour.
3 Cable Cars - **7** Chair lifts
6 Drag lifts
**Leashes Required*

Lift Times
8.30am to 4.30pm

Lift Pass Rates

1 Day pass	55 Sfr
3 Day pass	
6 Day pass	220 Sfr

Travel Guide

Fly to **Zurich** airport about 3 hours away.

Train services are possible direct into Arosa via Chur.

Route Planner: Via Zurich, head south on the N3 to Chur and then take the winding road up to Arosa, a distance of around 100 miles (160km).

Arosa is all Swiss, and a place that fits in perfectly in with how the Swiss marketing chiefs would have you see it. This is one of those cosy Swiss hamlets perched high above the tree drenched valley floor. The resort sits above 1800 metres and is located in the east of the country not far from the town of **Chur** and the better known resort of **Davos**. However, unlike Davos, this is not a massive sprawling mountain town, Arosa is a quiet traditional swiss village loaded with all the charm you could hope for, although spoilt slightly by its glitzy stuck up image. Still, the area offers some good snowboarding opportunities and will make a week s trip a good one if you re a novice or intermediate rider. Advanced riders have very little to keep them interested beyond a day or so. The 40 plus miles of open wide trails are serviced by a modern and well appointed lift system that can shift over 22,000 people an hour uphill with just 16 lifts Although Arosa is not on the calling card of every tour operator, the few that do use this place help to cause a few lift lines and the odd bottle neck on certain slopes. The runs are spread out over two areas, that of **Hornli** and **Weisshorn** where the most challenging terrain is located.

Freeriders who want to sample some tracks at speed, should check out the black on the **Weisshorn**. If you want to get into some freshies then take the off-piste track to the resort **Lenzerheide** via the **Hornli** slopes, but do so only with a guide.

Freestylers have a good half-pipe located at **Carmennahue.** This is also the location for the fun park which is equipped with a standard series of hits including one or two nice kickers. However, this is also a place that offers some good natural freestyling, but you have to look for it.

Carvers who like to slide around on gentle well prepared slopes and without any surprises, will find Arosa ideal for their needs.

Beginners in Arosa could do a lot worse. The slopes here provide novices an easy time and allow for some quick progression.

Off the slopes you will find a limited selection of facilities, but enough to get by with. Accommodation is well stationed for the lifts and comes in the standard grade swiss hotel format. Warm, cosy, charming and costly. Eating out and night time action is not hot at all, but if you re only out for a quiettime away from the crowds, this place will do nicely..

For accommodation listings visit - www.worldsnowboardguide.com

Arosa Tourist Office
Arosa. Ch-7050
++41 (0) 81 378 70 21 **www.arosa.ch**

Overall rating out of 10 **6** **Good place for freeriders**

Crans Montana

MOUNTAIN DATA

Top Lift at - 3000m

Ride Area
160km of piste

Bottom Lift at - 1484m

Vertical Drop - 1500m
Number of Runs - 60
Longest -7.5 miles (12km)

TERRAIN LEVELS

Easy	**38%**
Intermediate	**50%**
Advanced	**12%**
Expert =	

TERRAIN TO SUITE

Freeride	**40%**
Trees	Yes
Backcountry	Yes
Freestyle	**25%**
Halfpipe	Yes 1
Terrain Park	Yes 1
Carving	**35%**

SNOW DATA

Average Snowfall
700cm a season
Snowmaking
10% cover of the slopes
Winter Periods
Nov to April
Summer Riding
April to October

SLOPE ACCESS

Total Lifts = **42**
Uplift Rate - 32,000 people an hour.
2 Cable Cars - **2** Gondolas
8 Chairs lifts - **9** Drag lifts
**Leashes Required*

Lift Times
8.30am to 8.00pm

Lift Pass Rates
1 Day pass 52 Sfr
3 Day pass
6 Day pass 239 Sfr

SLOPE ACTION

Snowboard Hire
Daily rates 28 Sfr
Kids from 22 Sfr

Snowboard Tuition
Group lessons, from from 40 Sfr

Night Riding
Yes

Heli Boarding
Yes

Snowmobiles
No

Mountain Cafes
12

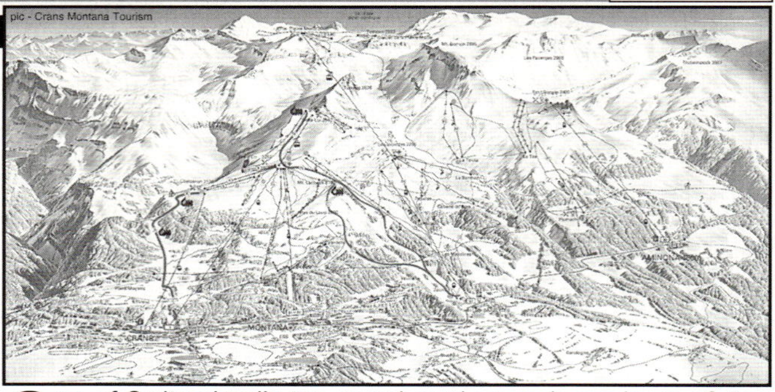

pic - Crans Montana Tourism

One of Switzerland's top snowboard areas is made up of two linking towns, that of **Crans** and **Montana.** Both of which are pretty outstanding and make a totally full-on place with plenty of interest for all. Both areas fuse together to provide over 100 miles (160km) of all-level and all-rider style terrain. Snowboarders have been cutting up these slopes for years, which has lead to a resort with some of the best snowboard instruction and facilities anywhere in Europe. Unfortunately the popularity of this area does mean some stupidly long lift queues with skier cluttered slopes. A lot of tour operators throughout Europe come here with package groups (especially from the UK) and so there's a lot of idiots messing up early morning runs.

Still, for all the area has to offer, advanced riders are not always tested, with the terrain largely covering intermediate or novice levels. The hardest listed run is the black that runs down from the **Toula** chair, which is best tackled in softs as the unevenness in parts is better ridden in something where you can easily absorb the bumps at speed.

Freeriders in search of off-piste and fresh powder, need to hook up with a guide and set off to areas around the **Plaine Morte Glacier**, where you can make your way to nearby **Anzere**. The route goes through some tunnels, which makes it well worth the effort. The area known as the **Faverges** is cool and for riders with some idea of what they're doing, there are some decent steeps to tackle - but watch out for the thigh burning traverse on the way back. For those who can afford it, you can do some cool heli-boarding on some major terrain.

Freestylers are well catered for, with a good pipe on **Pas du Loup,** which can be reached by the **Montana-Arnouvaz** gondola. The fun park at **Aminona** is loaded with rails spines and gaps, so new schoolers will love it and for those who want to find out how to ride a pipe correctly or to get big air, there is a number of schools that will help out, all of which offer some of the highest levels of snowboard tuition in Europe (they practically invented snowboard instruction here).

Carvers have plenty of long reds to check out. In particular the red run that drops away from the **Plaine Morte** down to the village of **Les Barzettes,** is perfect to lay out some big lines and with a length of 7.5 miles, you have plenty of time to get it right.

Beginners are treated to a variety of no nonsense blues which may require some navigation to avoid drag lifts. That said, this is a good novices resort, apart from the sometimes busy slopes. What really stands out is the superb level of snowboard tuition available, with a 3 hour group lesson costing from 40 Sfr. The guys at the *Pacific Snowboard Shop* will sort out any instruction you may need from beginners to freestylers.

As well as supposedly having the largest linked resort in **Switzerland, Crans-Montana** also said to have the largest number of hotels and accommodation options of any mountain resort in the country. However, you could actually be forgiven for not classing this place as resort at all, but rather a large bustling town which in effect is what it is. The whole area is serviced by a regular bus service which is the best way to get around if you don't have a car (taxi prices are criminal). There are loads of sporting outlets, dozens of shops, (check out *The Avalanche* ++41 (0) 402 2424 for snowboard hire) a cinema and if you are feeling realy lucky, a casino.

Around town you are spoilt for choice when it comes to restaurants with a selection of over 80 eateries no one need starve here. This place is blessed with simply loads of places to get a meal and even though this is an expensive resort, there are affordable joints such *San Nick's,* which offers some good pub grub or *Mamamias* for a slice of pizza or a bowl of pasta at just about affordable prices. If you wish to splash out, try *Le Sporting's.*

Night life is pretty damn good here and well in tune with snowboard lifestyle, although it is carried out along side some very sad Swiss style apr s ski nonsense (simply to please holiday crowds who don t know how to have a good time). Cool hangouts to have a beer in include The *Amadeus Bar* and *Constellation,* both with a party mood and loud music. The *Memphis Bar* is a good bar.

Accommodation: The 40,000 plus tourist beds are spread throughout a large area with the option to stay in either **Crans** or **Montana.** Lodging options are fairly extensive with a good choice of slope side hotels or a large selection of self catering apartment blocks for groups, but on the whole nothing comes cheap whereever you stay.

For accommodation listings visit - www.worldsnowboardguide.com

Summary: A big snowboarders resort offering something for everyone. Great carving and excellent freeriding areas. Lots of local services but a very busy place.
Money wise: Overall, a very expensive resort but well worth the costs.

Overall rating out of 10 **8**

Tourist Office Crans Montana
Avenue de La Gare
Montana CH-3962
General info **++41 (0) 27 485 04 04**
Reservations **++41 (0) 27 485 04 04**
Avlanche info **++41 (0) 1 187**
www.crans-montana.ch

pics - Crans Montana

Travel Guide

Fly to **Geneva** international
Transfer time to resort = **3** hours.
Local airport = none

Approximate global air travel times to **Geneva:**

from:		
	London	**2** hours
	Los Angles	**13** hours
	New York	**9** hours

Buse services from **Geneva** take around 3 hours direct to the centre of the resort.

Trains to **Sierre** (10 minutes)

Route Planner
Geneva

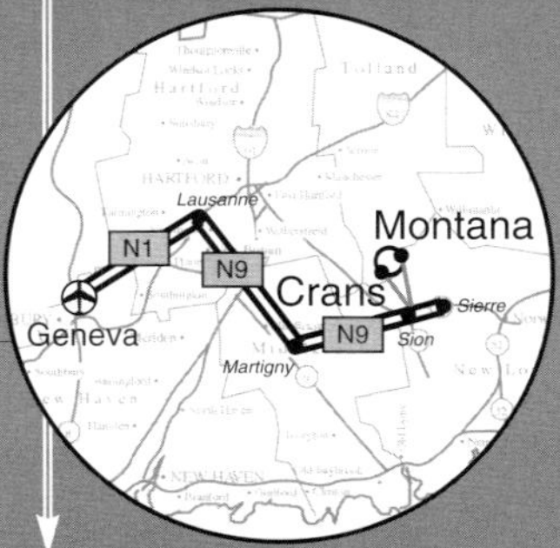

Crans Montana = 118 miles (190km)
Drive time is about **3** hours

*From **Calais** 625 (1005 Km)
Drive time is around **12** hours.

Davos

MOUNTAIN DATA

Top Lift at - 2850m

Ride Area
320km of piste

Bottom Lift at - 1560m

Vertical Drop - 2000m
Number of Runs - 75
Longest - 6 miles (9.5km)

TERRAIN LEVELS

Easy	**38%**
Intermediate	**50%**
Advanced	**12%**
Expert =	

TERRAIN TO SUITE

Freeride	**60%**
Trees	Yes
Backcountry	Yes
Freestyle	**30%**
Halfpipe	Yes 2
Terrain Park	Yes 1
Carving	**10%**

SNOW DATA

Average Snowfall
550cm a season
Snowmaking
5% cover of the slopes
Winter Periods
Nov to April
Summer Riding
No

SLOPE ACCESS

Total Lifts = **53**
Uplift Rate - 36,500 people an hour.
14 Funiculars, Cable & Gondolas - **9** Chairs lifts - **30** Drag lifts.
**Leashes Required*

Lift Times
8.30am to 8.00pm

Lift Pass Rates

1 Day pass	55 Sfr
3 Day pass	150 Sfr
6 Day pass	273 Sfr

SLOPE ACTION

Snowboard Hire
Daily rates 28 Sfr
Kids from 22 Sfr

Snowboard Tuition
Group lessons, from from 40 Sfr

Night Riding
Yes

Heli Boarding
Yes

Snowmobiles
Hire and tours

Mountain Cafes
15

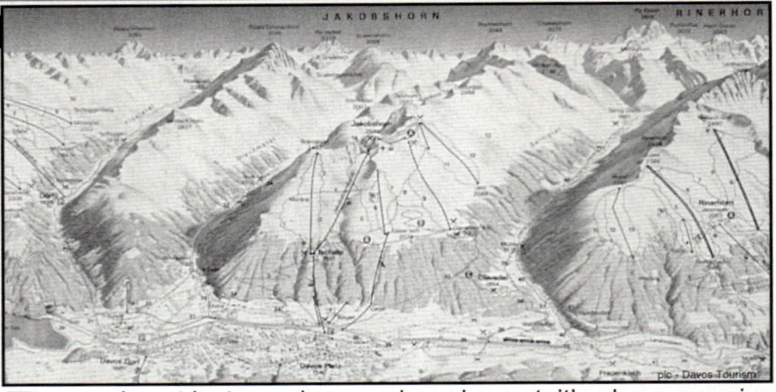

plc - Davos Tourism

Davos is not just a major snowboard resort, it's also a massive town that offers just about all you need to have a cool time. This very happening place offers the lot; tons of deep powder, loads of trees, big natural hits, half-pipes, fun parks, a boarder-cross circuit and night riding. All this on 200 miles (320km) of fantastic snowboard terrain, on slopes that hold the snow well.

Davos is located in an area that makes it ideal to check out many other resorts, including the famous retreat of **Klosters** (*the place where Prince Charles and Prince Harry first tried snowboarding Points for Harry, yer he has the makings of a rider, but dad, stick to skis Sir. As for William, well see)*. However, back to Davos which is a resort that needs to be visited a number of times if one is to ride the whole area. Davos itself, has a bit of an attitude when it comes to money, but it's a working town and so far less snobby than other similar places. More importantly, Davos offers access to some major snowboarding terrain - there's enough stuff here to keep any rider busy for a long time. There are two main areas and most snowboarders head for the runs on the **Jakobshorn**, which can be reached with ease.

Freeriders will wet themselves when they see the off-piste opportunities, which are mega and best checked out with the services of a guide. The run down to **Teufi** from **Jakobshorn** is pretty cool, but you will have to bus back to Davos. From the top station (which is well above the tree lines), advanced or intermediate freeriders will find a number of testing blacks which mellow out into reds as they lead straight back down to the **Ischalp** mid-section. From here you could carry on down through the trees to the base or if you want an easy final descent, there's an easy blue that snakes it's way home, ideal for novice freeriders.

Freestylers have long been provided with a good pipe and park area, however, they weren't always well maintained, apart from at competition times. Now that has changed and the new park, with its two pipes on the **Parsenn** slopes, is excellent as is the abundance of natural freestyle terrain.

Carvers won't be disappointed here, the 6 mile red run into the village of **Serneus** is full-on and you should be carving big style at the end of this one.

Beginners wanting to get to grips with things should go see the guys at the '*Top Secret* snowboard school', the instructors really know how to turn you from a side standing fool into a powder hound. At the top station of **Jackobshorn**, novices are treated to wide open easy flats which are serviced by drag lifts or a short cable car ride. Alternatively, there are plenty of very easy runs lower down on the Parsenn slopes.

If you re the sort of individual that wants to be housed, fed and watered in a charming sweet little village with cow bells hanging from rickety old sheds, don t bother with this place. Despite its some- what glitzy image, off the slopes, **Davos** doesn t muck around, lacks style, doesn t come cheap nor is this a visually pleasing joint. What you have here is a massive drab mountain town offering a huge choice of everything. Although this is a super expensive place that attracts international conferences and all that goes with them, you still get a large slice of snowboard lifestyle. Local facilities include sports centres, lots of shops, and even a Casino (don t bother though, it s a mugs game).

Two words that don t go together in Davos, cheap and eating out, but if you have the cash then the options for dining high on the hog are excellent. There is a good choice of restaurants offering every type of cuisine, ranging from local dishes to Chinese. You will also find a few fast food joints serving cardboard burgers and horrid euro style fries (chips should be fat and greasy UK style).

Night life in **Davos** rocks despite being so damn expensive. There is a good choice of bars and late night clubs, with live bands and artists playing seven nights a week. Most places pump out modern music but a few play sickening euro pop to please the apr s skiing nerds. The *Bolgenschanze Hotel* is one of the best hangouts, providing the full snowboard lifestyle package and gets packed out with loads of chicks gagging for it.

Accommodation in Davos is second to none. On top of there being loads of expensive hotels, Davos also has an affordable snowboarders hostel come hotel called the *The Bolgenschanze'* which offers a number of *ride and stay'* packages at reasonable prices (++41 81 43 70 01). The town also boast a host of bed and breakfast joints.

For accommodation listings visit - www.worldsnowboardguide.com

Summary: A big snowboarders resort offering something for everyone. Great carving and excellent freeriding areas. Lots of local services but very busy.
Money wise: The biggest let down here are the prices. **V**-EXPENSIVE

Overall rating out of 10 **10**

Tourist Office Davos
Promenade 67.
CH-7270 Davos
General info **++41 (0) 81 415 21 21**
Reservations **++41 (0) 81 415 21 21**
Avlanche info **++41 (0) 1 187**
www.davos.ch

pic - Davos Tourism

Travel Guide

Fly to **Zurich** international
Transfer time to resort = **2 1/2** hours.
Local airport = none

Approximate global air travel times to **Zurich:**

from:	London	**2 1/2** hours
	Los Angles	**13 1/2** hours
	New York	**10** hours

Bus services from **Zurich** take around 2 1/2 hours direct to the centre of the Davos.

Trains to **Davos** centre.

Route Planner
Zurich via Klosters

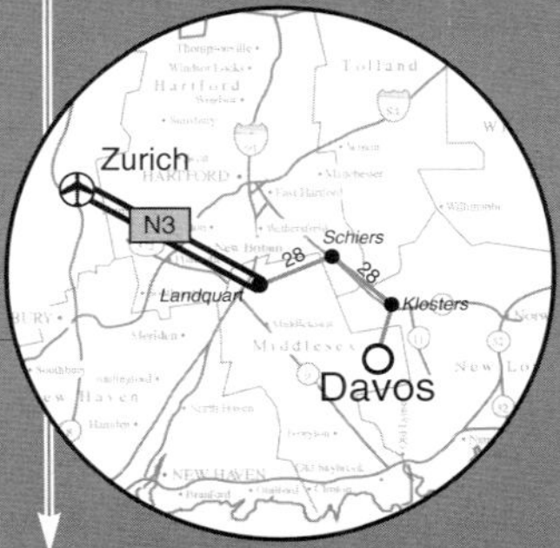

Davos = 95 miles (159km)
Drive time is about **2 1/2** hours

*From **Calais** 620 (997 Km)
Drive time is around **13** hours

Engelberg

MOUNTAIN DATA

Top Lift at - 3020m

Ride Area 80km of piste

Bottom Lift at - 1050m

Vertical Drop - 1970m

Number of Runs - 44

Longest - 2.5 miles (4km)

TERRAIN LEVELS

Easy	**30%**
Intermediate	**60%**
Advanced	**10%**
Expert =	

TERRAIN TO SUITE

Freeride	**45%**
Trees	A few
Backcountry	Yes
Freestyle	**15%**
Halfpipe	Yes 1
Terrain Park	Yes 1
Carving	**40%**

SNOW DATA

Average Snowfall
200cm a season

Snowmaking
5% cover of the slopes

Winter Periods
Nov to April

Summer Riding
Yes

SLOPE ACCESS

Total Lifts = **25**

Uplift Rate - 23,000 people an hour.

6 Gondolas & **1** Funicular

4 Chair lifts - **13** Drag lifts

**Leashes Required*

Lift Times
8.30am to 4.30pm

Lift Pass Rates

1 Day pass	50 Sfr
3 Day pass	130 Sfr
6 Day pass	214 Sfr

Travel Guide

Fly to **Zurich** airport, about 2 hours away.

Train services are possible to Lucerne (45 minutes).

Route Planner:
Via Zurich, head south on the routes 123/N4a/N14/N2 to Stans and turn off at signs for Engelberg

pic -Engelberg Tourism

Engelberg is a cool resort located slap bang in the middle of the country, not far from the town of **Lucerne** or the resort of **Andermatt**. By any standards, **Engelberg** has a very impressive rideable vertical drop which is said to be the longest in Switzerland. The beauty of this place is that it s left alone by mass ski crowds so the place has a cool laid back feel about it, without the hype. The ride area is a bit unusual and spread out from the village area. This is a resort noted for its avalanches so lots of attention is called for before trying out any of the slopes. The main happenings are offered on the **Titlis** area noted for its intermediate terrain but somewhat lacking for those who like to shine. The **Gerschnialp** area is for those sucking on a dummy (beginners).

Freeriders have a very good mountain here with some great off-piste to check out, but be warned, avalanches are common here. Some of the best off-piste terrain can be found having taken the **Jochstock** drag lift to reach the slopes on the **Alpstublii**, where you will find some amazing runs. Another easy to reach gem is the **Laub** area, which bases out conveniently to allow you to do it again. But this pleaser should not be tried out unless you know the score and can handle fast steeps, because this one will wipe your lights out for good if you balls up. Guide services are available here so use them, and stay alive.

Freestylers who like it done for them will find the pipe and park on the **Jochpass** area the place to head for, but it has to be said that this is not a resort that s hot on pipe shaping. Still, who cares, the area has plenty of good natural hits to check out.

Carvers have a fair selection of well looked after pisted runs or some fine unpisted slopes. Check out the **Jochpass** trails for a burner, but the best advice is leave your hard boots at home and do some soft boot carving, this place is good for it.

Beginners, 30% of the slopes are said to be easy terrain, but in truth if you re a fast learner, then you soon get to ride a further 60% of slopes which are rated intermediate.

Local services at the base area are of a high standard located in a traditional Swiss setting. The village offers some affordable accommodation but don t expect cheap digs near the slopes. There is a number of restaurants here which are all simular in style and price, but as for night life, its a bit dull.

For accommodation listings visit - www.worldsnowboardguide.com

Tourist Office Engelberg
CH- 6390 Engelberg.
++41 (0) 81 4 10 20 20 **www.engelbergtourism.ch**

Overall rating out of 10 **6** **Good for a weeks holiday**

Flims

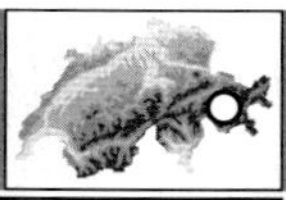

MOUNTAIN DATA

Top Lift at - 2813m

Ride Area 80km of piste

Bottom Lift at - 1100m

Vertical Drop - 1763m

Number of Runs - 32

Longest -8.7 miles (14km)

TERRAIN LEVELS

Easy	**45%**
Intermediate	**39%**
Advanced	**16%**
Expert =	

TERRAIN TO SUITE

Freeride	**45%**
Trees	Yes
Backcountry	Yes
Freestyle	**20%**
Halfpipe	Yes 2
Terrain Park	Yes 2
Carving	**35%**

SNOW DATA

Average Snowfall
720cm a season

Snowmaking
20% cover of the slopes

Winter Periods
Nov to April

Summer Riding
May to October

SLOPE ACCESS

Total Lifts = **14**

Uplift Rate - 12,000 people an hour.

3 Gondolas - **5** Chair lifts

6 Drag lifts

**Leashes Required*

Lift Times
8.30am to 4.30pm

Lift Pass Rates

1 Day pass	54 Sfr
3 Day pass	150 Sfr
6 Day pass	296 Sfr

Travel Guide

Fly to **Zurich**, airport, about 3 hours away.

Train services are possible to Chur 40 minute transfer.

Route Planner: Via Zurich, head south on the E3 to Chur and then head west on the route 19 to Flims via Laax.

Zurich
to resorts = **88** miles

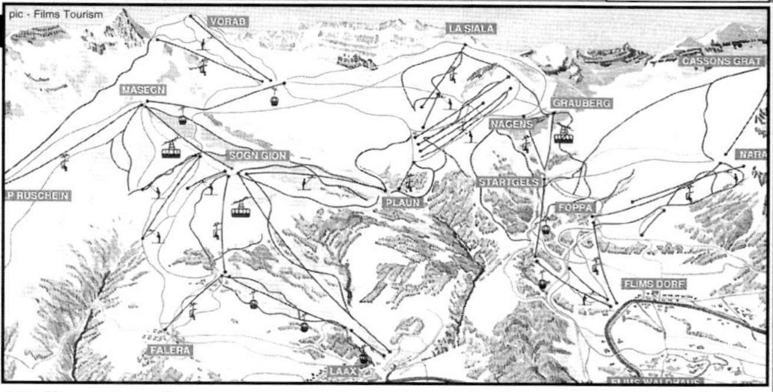

Flims is often over shadowed by its bigger brother, **Laax**. However, this gem of a place deserves to be given a platform of its own and although Laax is far bigger, Flims can hold its own. What's more, being the junior partner, Flims tends to be a little less crowded even though the two resorts link up on the slopes by lifts and share a joint lift pass. Flims sits at a slightly higher altitude than Laax but on the whole, the slopes are the same in both areas. Indeed on the mountain you would be forgiven for thinking that this was two resorts although in many ways it s not. Both places share a lift pass and the series of pisted runs connect well with each other. The trails above Flims are well prepared and offer a mixture ranging from gentle blues, to a fast black trail running down the **Cassons** slopes which falls away sharply.

Freeriders have for years been aware of what is on offer here whether up on Flims or over on the Laax slopes. For a nice long freeride trail that's not over testing, try out the **Segnes** trail which is a red run that shoots down from the **Cassons** and arrives to connect up with the **Grauberg** trail.

Freestylers wanting a fix from a well shaped half-pipe wall, will need to make their way up to the **Crap Sogn** area above Laax. Here you find an extremely well maintained pipe and park shaped by a pipe dragon. There is another pipe open during the summer months further up on the **Vorab Glacier**.

Carvers sticking to Flims will not have themselves overtaxed, but there is a nice series of good red runs below **Narus** that will make for a few good lines at a controlled speed. The **Heini** is a long red that starts out as a black down from the **Cassons** and will sort out the boys from the men (or birds from the skirt).

Beginners have a well set out series of novice trails from the base area of **Flims Dorf.** The easy blues start out from the **Narus** and allow first timers a good choice of easy to negotiate descents back down to the base area.

Flims offers a good choice of slope side accommodation and places to eat. Riders on a budget, book in at *Gliders* which is a cool backpackers place where a bed will cost around 45 Sfr a night with breakfast available for an extra fee. Night life in Flims is not too hot, but what s on offer is okay in the likes of the *Albana* bar which has a good vibe about it.

For accommodation listings visit - www.worldsnowboardguide.com

Tourist Office Flims
Kur-und Verkehsveren Flims, Waldhaus. CH 7018
++41 (0) 81 920 92 00   www.laax.ch/

Overall rating out of 10 — 9 — Excellent riding area

Grindelwald - Jungfrau

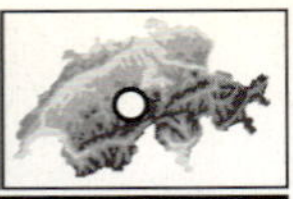

MOUNTAIN DATA

Top Lift at - 2971m

Ride Area
200km of piste

Bottom Lift at - 943m
Vertical Drop - 1467m
Number of Runs - 195
Longest - 9 miles (15km)

TERRAIN LEVELS

Easy	**28%**
Intermediate	**57%**
Advanced	**15%**
Expert =	

TERRAIN TO SUITE

Freeride	**50%**
Trees	Yes
Backcountry	Yes
Freestyle	**25%**
Halfpipe	Yes 2
Terrain Park	Yes 2
Carving	**25%**

SNOW DATA

Average Snowfall
530cm a season
Snowmaking
15% cover of the slopes
Winter Periods
Nov to April
Summer Riding
Yes

SLOPE ACCESS

Total Lifts = **43**
Uplift Rate - 40,000 people an hour.
11 Gondolas & Funiculars
20 Chair lifts - **12** Drag lifts
**Leashes Required*

Lift Times
8.30am to 4.30pm

Lift Pass Rates

1 Day pass	52 Sfr
3 Day pass	
6 Day pass	254 Sfr

Travel Guide

Fly to **Zurich** airport, about 2 hours away.

Train services are possible to Interlaken (10 minutes).

Route Planner:
Via Zurich, head south on the E41, N4a/N14 via Hergiswil and then the N8 to Interlaken. From here follow the signs for Grindelwald.

Grindelwald is one of the resorts that helps form the area more commonly known as the **Jungfrau Region**. The other resorts that make up this sector are **Wengen** (very posh and super up its arse attitude), and **Murren** the most laid back and snowboard friendly of the three. Grindelwald sits up at an altitude of some 1034 metres and scenically, is an impressive place. However, the same can t be said of the rideable terrain that is immediately on offer from the base village, for this is not an adventurous mountain resort and freeriders will soon get bored of the place, although it is a very good carvers resort. The 200 plus kilometres of marked piste stretch out across two large wide open plateaus that stretch up from both sides of the village, with the slopes on the **Mannlichen** and **Kl.Scheidegg** side linking up with the runs that descend back down into Wengen. You can also reach **Murren** via the slopes but in truth, it can be a bit of a pain the arse. Grindelwald is a large sprawling resort that attracts a lot of visitors, there is no such thing as a good time to visit to avoid crowds, the place is always packed. The main access lifts are not only slow but the queues for them can be hellish and can often mean a 50 minute wait in line. Still, once you do get up on the slopes and the conditions prove to be favourable, provided you are not wanting to be tested, you will be able to have a good time.

Freeriders who stick to **Grindelwald** are not going to find a great deal to keep them entertained, not because it s crap, there s just not that much to appeal. The best freeriding terrain is in **Murren**

Freestylers don t tend to head here on mass, as this is a dull freestylers resort, with little to get air from. There is a pipe and park up on the **Oberjoch** area, but they are not up to much.

Carvers should fair well here. The slopes may be busy, but there is still plenty of piste to lay out lots of wide linked turns on.

Beginners have a host of nice gentle open slopes to learn on, the only draw back being that the access to them is not convenient.

The village at the base of the slopes has a number of hotels and chalets to choose from, but nothing comes cheap as this place is stupidly expensive. Not all the accommodation is close to the slopes so expect to do some hiking to and from the base lifts. The resort has a host of sporting attractions, a lot of hotel restaurants but little or no cheap fast food, the night-life also sucks.

For accommodation listings visit - **www.worldsnowboardguide.com**

Tourist Office Grindelwald
Po Box CH 3818
++41 (0) 33 854 1212 **www.grindelwald.ch**

Overall rating out of 10 **6** **This is not an adventrious place**

Gstaad

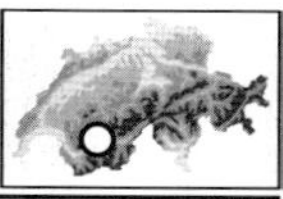

SWITZERLAND

MOUNTAIN DATA

Top Lift at - 2005m
Ride Area
241km of piste
Bottom Lift at - 995m
Vertical Drop - 840m
Number of Runs - 60
Longest -2.2 miles (3.5km)

TERRAIN LEVELS

Easy	60%
Intermediate	30%
Advanced	10%
Expert =	

TERRAIN TO SUITE

Freeride	50%
Trees	Yes
Backcountry	Yes
Freestyle	20%
Halfpipe	Yes 1
Terrain Park	Yes 1
Carving	30%

SNOW DATA

Average Snowfall

Snowmaking
5% cover of the slopes
Winter Periods
Nov to April
Summer Riding
May to Sept

SLOPE ACCESS

Total Lifts = **69**
Uplift Rate not available an hour.
3 Cable cars -**14** Gondolas
38 Chair lifts - **14** Drag lifts
**Leashes Required*

Lift Times
8.30am to 4.30pm

Lift Pass Rates

1 Day pass	50 Sfr
3 Day pass	130 Sfr
6 Day pass	235 Sfr

Travel Guide

Fly to **Geneva** airport 2 1/2 hours away.

Train services to Gstaad/ Vevey station.

Route Planner:
From Geneva, take the N1/N9 via Lusanne to Aigle at which point turn of on to the A11 to Gstaad just after the village of Saanen.

pic - Soft Snapper

Gstaad is part of a massive slope linked area void of the mass holiday groups. What you get here is crowd free snowboarding with miles of backcountry adventures and over 150 well prepared pistes covered by a single lift pass. Welcome to **Gstaad,** a place where snowboarding comes as second nature and a place that despite its appeal for attracting far too many poncy image junkies with designer eye-wear, is a place that has a good snowboard feel to it and one where you can ride hard. Despite the sad gits that flock here, the area has long allowed snowboarders freedom to roam its slopes, which are split between a number of areas with **Gstaad** sitting mid-way between them. The areas most favoured by snowboarders are **Saanenmoser** and **Schonried** which can be reached without any hassle from Gstaad. Further afield is **Les Diablerets** which is a glacier that s open in the summer months.

Freeriders are somewhat spoilt for choice here with some notable freeriding terrain over on the **Saanen** area where with aid of a guide, you can ride out some great powder fields. Alternatively, for something a little more testing you should head up to the **Les Diablerets** glacier.

Freestylers have a number of half-pipes to choose from, with the best offering of park and pipe on the **Sanserloch** area. However, constructed half-pipes are not always necessary here as there is a lot of diverse natural terrain with some notable cliffs and big wind lips. Check out the cliffs up at **Huhnerspiel**.

Carvers who like to lay a board over at speed on super steeps, have few options on where to do it. Much of what is levelled out here can be tackled by a competent intermediate rider. However, don t be put off as overall this is a good carvers area with some nice red trails to blast on the **Lauenen** slopes.

Beginners have the biggest percentage of easy slopes around here much of which is not linked and spread out between the areas with some of the best runs on the **Saanenmoser** slopes.

Gstaad is not for those with a weak stomach as on the poncy, snobbish, fur clad scale, this joint rates high and therefore is very expensive. However, good affordable lodging can be had in places like the *Snoeb Hotel*, a specialist riders hangout. Night life here can also be good with an okay selection of bars.

For accommodation listings visit - **www.worldsnowboardguide.com**

Tourist Office Gstaad
CH-3780
++41 (0) 33 748 81 81 **www.gstaad.ch**

Overall rating out of 10 **7** **Cool hang out with good riding.**

Laax

MOUNTAIN DATA

Top Lift at - 3018m

Ride Area
241km of piste

Bottom Lift at - 1020m

Vertical Drop - 1998m

Number of Runs - 60

Longest - 9 miles (15km)

TERRAIN LEVELS

Easy	**45%**
Intermediate	**39%**
Advanced	**16%**
Expert =	

TERRAIN TO SUITE

Freeride	**45%**
Trees	Yes
Backcountry	Yes
Freestyle	**20%**
Halfpipe	Yes 2
Terrain Park	Yes 1
Carving	**35%**

SNOW DATA

Average Snowfall
720cm a season

Snowmaking
20% cover of the slopes

Winter Periods
Nov to April

Summer Riding
May to Sept

SLOPE ACCESS

Total Lifts = **32**

Uplift Rate - 18,000 people an hour.

6 Gondolas - **4** Cable cars

10 Chairs lifts -**12** Drag lifts

**Leashes Required*

Lift Times
8.30am to 4.30pm

Lift Pass Rates

1 Day pass	56 Sfr
3 Day pass	150 Sfr
6 Day pass	280 Sfr

SLOPE ACTION

Snowboard Hire
Daily rates 28 Sfr
Kids from 22 Sfr

Snowboard Tuition
Group lessons, from from 40 Sfr

Night Riding
No

Heli Boarding
No

Snowmobiles
No

Mountain Cafes
17

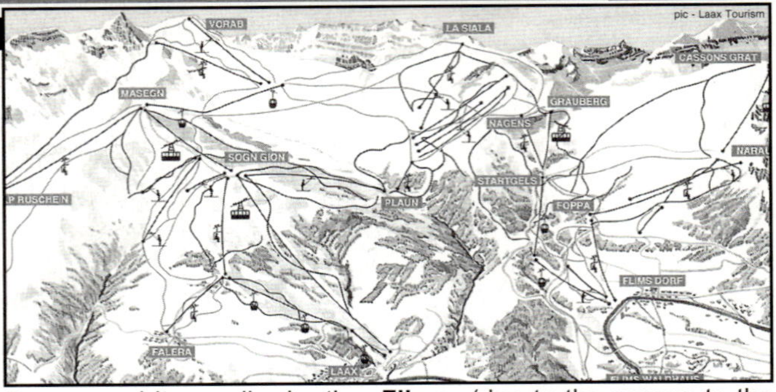

Laax and its smaller brother **Flims** (due to the access to the slopes on the **Vorab** glacier) are all year round Swiss treasures and pure snowboard heaven. This place is highly regarded by those snowboarders who know about it and what you have here is a full on snowboarder's resort that links up with **Flims/Dorf** (a more sedate skier's hangout). Together they form an area regarded as one of the most snowboard friendly places in Switzerland. The resort bosses go out of their way to help snowboarders and it's no wonder that when the ISF pus on events, the world pro's all seem to make it here. The resort now plays host to a Boardercross competition that is growing in stature season by season. When events are held here, it's not just the top riders that come to perform, some big name pop stars and DJ s also put in an appearance (mind you, such pop stars and over paid DJ s with crap ego s who want to be pop stars, do so only to boost record sales, not because they care about snowboarding. Scum the lot of them). It is also notable that not many tour operators (the dreaded Brits in particular) plague these slopes. If ever there was a mountain meant for snowboarders free of two plankers, this is it. Every level of snowboarder will be able to enjoy it here. The initial access to the slopes is at **Murschetg**, where a cable car whisks you up to the slopes on the area known as **Crap Sogn Gion**. It's here you'll find one of the halfpipes, but if it's freeriding terrain you're after, check out the offerings on the **Vorab** area.

Freeriders are tempted by some amazing off-piste opportunities with some cool tree riding and full-on powder. The ride down from **La Siala** summit, off lift **15,** is a real pleasure and can be tackled by most intermediates. Alternatively, for some easy to reach, classic off-piste riding, check out the **Cassons** area, which is on the slopes above **Flims** and forms the top area, but it's not for the faint-hearted.

Freestylers are coaxed here with the choice of two halfpipes, which incidentally are shaped with the first Pipe Dragon in Europe. To tempt you further there s also an absolutely awesome fun park which is packed with an array of hits to test all level of air heads. The main pipe is the one located on the **Crap Sogn Gion** off lift number **10** or **2**, while the other pipe is up at the V**orab Glacier** and is open in the summer months.

Carvers can cut most of the slopes here in style as they piste the runs regularly (and to perfection), making it a great place for laying big turns. It's not the most testing carvers resort, but those with balls should try out the long black race run, **Crap Sogn,** back down to the base station of **Murschetg**.

Beginners have a great mountain where learning the basics is a joy on simple, hassle free slopes, which are easy to reach from all parts of the resort.

Both the villages of **Laax** and **Flims** (which are 10 minutes apart by road) sit at different levels and offer a host of good local facilities that will make a two weeks stay well worth the effort. Mind you, neither come cheaply and two weeks will burn a big hole in your wallet. Laax is the smaller of the two villages and has more of a ski outlook and attitude, but nevertheless, Laax has a good choice of apartments or hotels, if you shop around you will find budget options. The village has a host of attractions from squash courts to an outdoor ice rink.
Job Seekers, will find that this is not an easy place to get a job, especially if you can t speak German or even have a good grasp of it.

Food is much the same as in any other high mountain retreat, that is lots of hotel restaurants all serving up generally bland, traditional Swiss meals at very high prices. Still, there is a number of notable places to get a good meal including the odd pizza joint such as *Pomodoro* in **Flims**. If you fancy a fish meal then look no further than *Crap Ner* restaurant in Laax, which is noted for its food (and its prices).

Night-life in either **Laax** or **Flims** is very good and fairly well suited to snowboard lifestyle (apart form the cost of a beer). Nothing here is of mega status but the bars on offer are good for getting messy in while listening to some good tunes. But do remember, this is **Switzerland,** so tank up on supermarket or your duty free supplies beer before going out, all the bars are expensive.

Accommodation: Some 6000 visitors are offered somewhere to sleep here, and although the choice of lodging, and the prices are good, most places are a little spread out and for most, may entail a walk to the slopes. For those on a tight budget, the bunk house, *Gliders Paradise,* is the place to check into.

For accommodation listings visit - www.worldsnowboardguide.com

Summary: Excellent resort that can be ridden all year round. The slopes are great for freeriders and freestylers as well as suiting beginners. Good local services.
Money wise: Top value resort but also a very, very expensive place

Overall rating out of 10 **9**

Tourist Office Laax
Laax. Ch-7031
General info ++41 (0) 81 921 4343
Reservations ++41 (0) 81 921 4343
Avlanche info ++41 (0) 1 187
www.laax.ch/

pics - Laax Tourism

Travel Guide

Fly to **Zurich** international
Transfer time to resort = **2½** *hours.*
Local airport = none

Approximate global air travel times to **Zurich:**

from:		
	London	**2½** hours
	Los Angles	**13½** hours
	New York	**10** hours

Buss services from **Zurich** take around 2½ hours direct to **Laax** via **Chur.**

Trains to **Chur,** 40 mins away.

Route Planner
Zurich via Chur

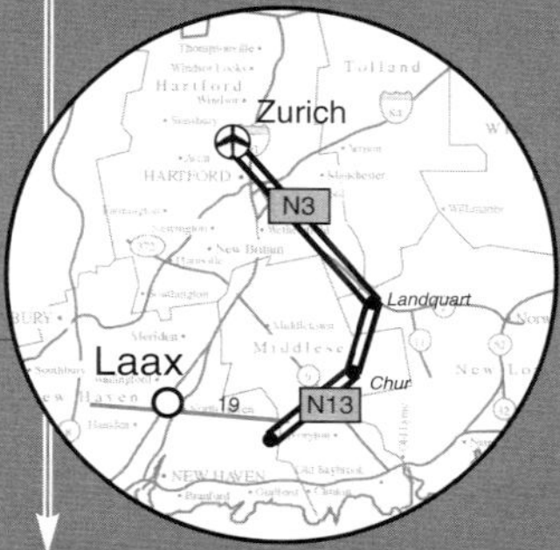

Laax = 90 miles (145 km)
Drive time is about **2½** hours

*From **Calais** 585 (941 Km)
Drive time is around **10** hours.

Leysin

MOUNTAIN DATA

Top Lift at - 2200m

Ride Area
120km of piste

Bottom Lift at - 1300m

Vertical Drop - 900m
Number of Runs - 30
Longest - 4 miles (6km)

TERRAIN LEVELS

Easy	**30%**
Intermediate	**50%**
Advanced	**20%**
Expert =	

TERRAIN TO SUITE

Freeride	**50%**
Trees	Yes
Backcountry	Yes
Freestyle	**30%**
Halfpipe	Yes 1
Terrain Park	Yes 1
Carving	**20%**

SNOW DATA

Average Snowfall

Snowmaking
20% cover of the slopes
Winter Periods
Nov to April
Summer Riding
At Les Diablerets (5km)

SLOPE ACCESS

Total Lifts = **19**
Uplift Rate - 18,000 people an hour.
2 Gondolas - **7** Chairs lifts
10 Drag lifts.
**Leashes Required*

Lift Times
8.30am to 4.30pm

Lift Pass Rates

1 Day pass	55 Sfr
3 Day pass	140 Sfr
6 Day pass	250 Sfr

SLOPE ACTION

Snowboard Hire
Daily rates 28 Sfr
Kids from 22 Sfr

Snowboard Tuition
Group lessons, from from 40 Sfr

Night Riding
No

Heli Boarding
Yes

Snowmobiles
No

Mountain Cafes
6

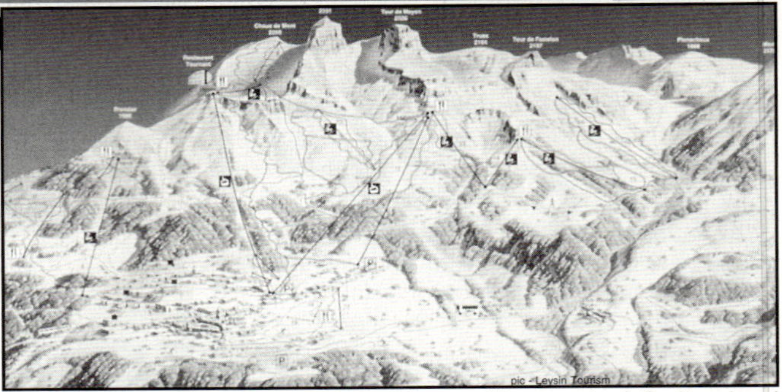

pic - Leysin Tourism

Leysin is located in the French speaking part of Switzerland and has become one of the best and most happening snowboard haunts in the country. Unlike many more popular ski resorts, this place isn't really known for its skiing which has allowed it to be adopted by snowboarders This has helped to ensure that the place has a low key friendly appeal about it with- out any bull or hype (singing star Gabrielle, had her first snowboard lesson here and she loved the place).

The resort goes out of its way to be snowboard friendly and since 1992 has been playing host to the *International Snowboard Federation World Pro Tour* event. This event is attended by the world s top riders and you can see the whole place turned into a festival occasion lasting for at least a week. Leysin is in fact an old and rather large sprawling mountain town and not a modern purpose built resort like some found nearby. What you get here is a high up mountain that in a good winter, offers everything to keep adventure seeking advanced riders happy, while also appealing to first timers who don't want to use a drag lift straight away. A notable point about Leysin is that it s not a popular resort with holiday companies, which is a good thing as the slopes don t get clogged up although weekends can still be a bit busy with locals and punters from Geneva. However, once you do get up on the slopes, you can roam freely over acres of great terrain without seeing another soul for hours.

Freeriders have plenty of great terrain to explore, with tree runs down to the village, or extreme terrain with bowls and cliffs which you can reach by dropping in to your right on the **Berneuse**. You should also check out the official off-piste runs that give you the feeling of backcountry riding, for example try the route behind **Tour D' Ai,** starting at the top of **Chaux de Mont**.

Freestylers will be able to spin huge airs in the *ISF* pro tour pipe, which is normally maintained, but don't be shy to ask for a shovel at the nearby lift hut. As well as the pipe, the fun park (located between **Berneuse** and **Mayen**) has quarter pipes and gaps to ride. Mind you, it's not usually built until the end of February.

Carvers with only hard boots and alpine boards are the ones who are going to be disappointed. There is some good carving to be had, but overall, this is a soft boot resort. The **Berneuse** is a good place to lay out some big turns.

Beginners can get going at the nursery slopes which have easy to use rope tows, before venturing up to slopes on the **Berneuse.** The drag lift at the **Chaux de Mont** will be difficult for first timer and beginners should not use this lift, even for the lower section, as the exit point is on a very steep piece of terrain. The local ski schools handle all the snowboard tuition here.

Being such a spread out place means that depending on where you re booked into, you could end up doing a lot of hard walking, unless you have a car. Around the town, life is very easy going with a lot of Americans hanging around due to the American colleges based here. Local services are basic but acceptable, offering a well located sports centre equipped with a swimming pool and indoor tennis and squash courts. If you happen to speak the language (French and German) you could even while away your evening at the cinema. Anyone who fancies a skate can check out the ramps down in **Aigle,** about 40 minutes away,however, there s plenty of street in Leysin which the locals will happily share with you.

Plenty of restaurants to choose from, but a few of them are tucked away so you will need to study your tourist guide to search them all out. Generally, prices are in the middle to high bracket but affordable food is available, especially if you check out the offerings at the cool bunk house called *Club Vagabound* which is located away up on the back road. The town also has a couple of cheap pizza restaurants.

Night-life in Leysin is just as it should be, nothing major but plenty going down with a lively crowd that s always ready to party. The partying is aided by a lot of young American students (none of whom can drink anything like the amounts the Europeans sup). The main spots are *Club Vagabound*, although on Saturday nights it gets way too busy, and *Top Pub* which is much quieter.

Accommodation: The options for a bed range from a classy hotel to the normal array of pensions along the main high street. One of the best options is the really cool bunk house called *The Vagabond,* which offers cheap nightly rates and has a cool bar. Alternatively, *Chalet Ermina* is a really good bed and breakfast place and great value.

For accommodation listings visit - www.worldsnowboardguide.com

Summary: First class ultra friendly snowboard resort with terrain to suit all levels and styles. Great freestyle terrain and okay for novices. Great local services.
Money wise: Generally an expensive resort, however, lots of budget options.

Overall rating out of 10 **10**

Tourist Office Leysin
Po Box 100,
CH-1854 Leysin

General info	**++41 (0) 24 494 2244**
Reservations	**++41 (0) 24 494 2244**
Avlanche info	**++41 (0) 1 187**

www.leysin.ch

pic - San Tang - Rider - Tommy Marsh

pic - Leysin Tourism

Travel Guide

Fly to **Geneva** international
Transfer time to resort = **$2^{3/4}$** hours.
Local airport = none

Approximate global air travel times to **Geneva:**

from:		
	London	2 hours
	Los Angles	13 hours
	New York	9 hours

Bus services from **Geneva** take around 2 hours direct to **Leysin** via **Aigle.**

Trains to **Leysin** central.

Route Planner
Geneva via Aigle

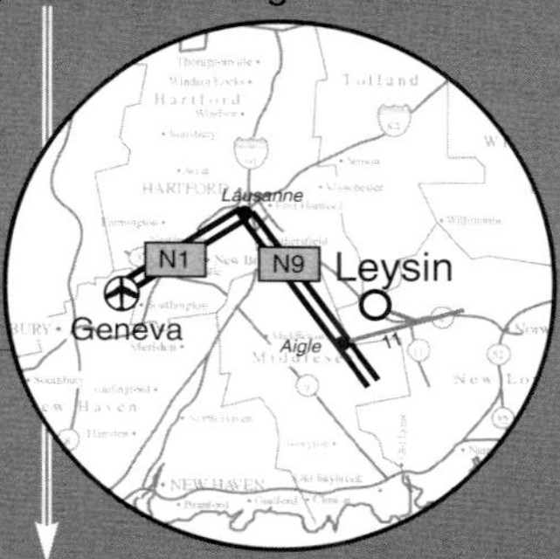

Leysin = **151** miles (241 km)
Drive time is about **$2^{3/4}$** hours

*From **Calais** 518 (833 Km)
Drive time is around **$9^{1/4}$** hours.

Nendaz

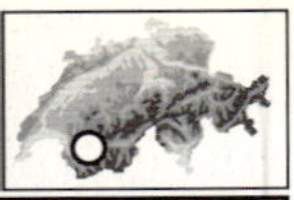

MOUNTAIN DATA

Top Lift at - 3300m

Ride Area
177km of piste

Bottom Lift at - 1365m
Vertical Drop - 1935m
Number of Runs - 195
Longest - 9 miles (15km)

TERRAIN LEVELS

Easy	**37%**
Intermediate	**57%**
Advanced	**6%**
Expert =	

TERRAIN TO SUITE

Freeride	**45%**
Trees	Yes
Backcountry	Yes
Freestyle	**20%**
Halfpipe	Yes 3
Terrain Park	Yes 2
Carving	**35%**

SNOW DATA
Average Snowfall

Snowmaking
5% cover of the slopes
Winter Periods
Nov to April
Summer Riding
At Verbier

SLOPE ACCESS
Total Lifts = **41**
Uplift Rate - 25,000 people an hour.
3 Gondolas - **1** Cable car
9 Chair lifts - **28** Drag lifts
**Leashes Required*

Lift Times
8.30am to 4.30pm

Lift Pass Rates

1 Day pass	50 Sfr
3 Day pass	130 Sfr
6 Day pass	230 Sfr

Travel Guide

Fly to **Geneva** airport, about $2^{1/2}$ hours away.

Train services are possible to Sion (15 minutes).

Route Planner: From Geneva, take the N1 via Lausanne to Sion and then the N9 via Val d Herens and Haute Nendaz.
*Drive time from **Calais** is $9^{1/2}$ hours 544 miles (875 km)

pic - Nendaz Tourism

Being in the shadow of a big brother can often have its drawbacks, and the little guy may get left out and dismissed as not worth the effort. Not in this case. **Nendaz** is the lesser known relation of **Verbier** and along with a number of other resorts, forms the collective **'Les 4 Vallees',** located $2^{1/2}$ hours east of **Geneva** just up from the town of **Sion.** Although linked by lift with **Verbier, Nendaz** offers an entirely different experience and is a lot less formal and populated. What you have here is a resort with a selection of runs starting from the base and which connect up with the neighbouring hamlets and slopes of **Veysonnaz**, **Thyon** and **Siviez.** What s more, with the **Mont Fort** area offering some great summer snowboarding, this place becomes a bit of an all year round treasure. Apart from Nendaz s unique piste markings and the fact that they have installed snowmaking facilities all the way to the top, this place is one only a few locations in Europe to offer Heli-boarding with passenger collection and mountain guides. You can fly to the heart of the **Rosablanche** glacier to ride major backcountry powder spots.

Freeriders will be pleasantly surprised when they arrive and see what this area has to offer both on and off-piste. Both advanced and timed riders will find a weeks stay a pleasure while thrill seekers can test themselves to the limits.

Freestylers are provided with loads of possibilities for gaining air (and not just in a helicopter).There are numerous fun parks and half-pipes around here, the closest to Nendaz being the park up on the Veysonnaz slopes. If it s natural hits that you favour, you will find loads of banks, gullies and cool areas with logs to grind.

Carvers have as much here as any other style of rider, particularly on the series of red trails above Siviez and on Veysonnaz slopes where you can shine on your edges at speed.

Beginners should leave after a week s visit at a new level. The gentle slopes directly above Nendaz will suit you re every need.

Off the slopes, **Nendaz** offers a quality selection of places to sleep, eat and drink in at prices to suit everyone, not just the elite, as is often the case in many resorts. Furthermore, basic local services are well appointed and you can sleep close to the slopes. Locals make you very welcome which helps to give this place a good vibe. There are some good night spots to check out.
For accommodation listings visit - **www.worldsnowboardguide.com**

Tourist Office Nendaz
Haute-Nendaz, CH 1997
++41 (0) 27 88 1444 **www.**

Overall rating out of 10 **7** **Some good freeriding to be had**

Savognin

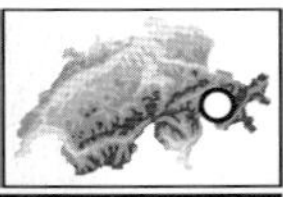

SWITZERLAND

pic - Savognin Tourism

MOUNTAIN DATA

Top Lift at - 2713m

Ride Area
80km of piste

Bottom Lift at - 1210m
Vertical Drop - 1513m
Number of Runs - 27
Longest - 4 miles (7km)

TERRAIN LEVELS

Easy	35%
Intermediate	63%
Advanced	2%
Expert =	

TERRAIN TO SUITE

Freeride	20%
Trees	Yes
Backcountry	Yes
Freestyle	15%
Halfpipe	Yes 1
Terrain Park	Yes 1
Carving	65%

SNOW DATA

Average Snowfall
400cm a season
Snowmaking
10% cover of the slopes
Winter Periods
Nov to April
Summer Riding
No

SLOPE ACCESS

Total Lifts = **17**
Uplift Rate - 16,000 people an hour.
2 Cable cars
3 Chair lifts - **12** Drag lifts
**Leashes Required*

Lift Times
8.30am to 4.30pm

Lift Pass Rates

1 Day pass	50 Sfr
3 Day pass	130 Sfr
6 Day pass	2320 Sfr

Travel Guide

Fly to **Zurich** airport, 2 hours away.

Train services to the town of Tiefencastelt (5 minutes)

Route Planner: Via Zurich, head south on the N3 to Chur and take the A3 via Tiefencastelt to Savognin.
*Drive time from **Calais** is 10[1/2] hours 603 miles (970 km)

Two hours south of **Zurich** lies the relatively unknown resort of **Savognin** that is fast becoming a magnet for snowboarders out for a good time and for riders who want to steer clear of the big resorts because they don t want to get caught up in the hustle and bustle of large ski crowds. Fortunately the ski press don t mention **Savognin,** which helps to keep this gem a small secret for snowboraders to do as they please with. The natives are super friendly and happy to have snowboarders on their slopes. The local snowboard scene is cool with its own riders club where you can find out all there is to know about this place, such as the best hits or runs and where to get messy in the evenings when the lifts are closed.

Freeriders of an advanced level are going to be disappointed if its testing stuff you crave for, there is none really. You can have a bit of excitement on the black run known as the **Pro Spinatsch**, running down from the **Tiggignas** chair lift, it is also the location of Savognin s fun park. It doesn t take too long to conquer if you know what you re doing on your edges.

Freestylers will find the best air to be had is either off the nicely shaped walls in the half-pipe or in the fun park which is tooled up with fun boxes, gaps, spines, rails and a quarter pipe. For some natural hits there are a few cliff drops and some air to be had on the area called *Tiem.*

Carvers have some particularly well groomed runs for arcing over on in full view of the lifts, allowing those clad in *Oxbow* gear to show off their latest designer jumpers and sad flower patterned yellow pants. A good piste to suit all levels whether you re in soft or hard boots, is the **Cresta Ota**, which runs down from the **Piz Cartas** summit and makes for a good time.

Beginners are looked after with a number of easy blues and the option of being able to slide back to base at the end of the day on easy to handle runs. However, uplift is mainly via drag lifts.

Savognin is a small village with nothing major going on, although it s affordable and doesn t come infested with apr s ski crowds. Accommodation is a mixture of Swiss pensions and hotels, all of which are well located for the slopes. There are one or two good evening haunts, with the best place to get a beer being the *Zerbratent Paulin.*

For accommodation listings visit - www.worldsnowboardguide.com

Tourist Office Savognin
Kur-und Verkehrsverein. Savognin. CH 7460
++41 (0) 81 684 2222 www.graubuenden.ch/savognin

Overall rating out of 10 **6** **Okay for a few days**

Saas Fee

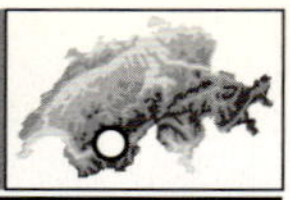

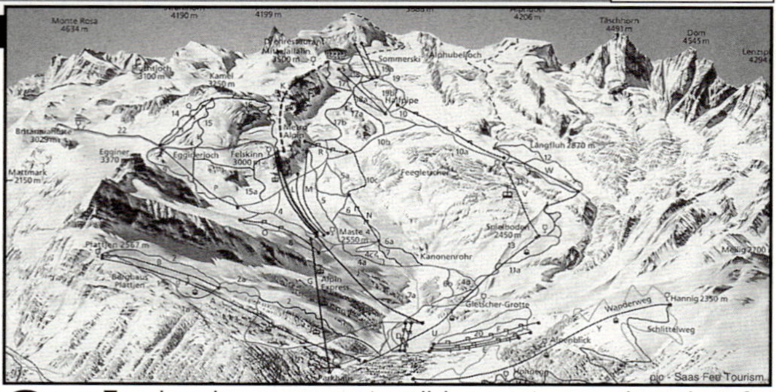

MOUNTAIN DATA

Top Lift at - 3500m

Ride Area
100km of piste

Bottom Lift at - 1800m

Vertical Drop - 1700m
Number of Runs - 40
Longest - 5.6 miles (9km)

TERRAIN LEVELS

Easy	**40%**
Intermediate	**50%**
Advanced	**10%**
Expert =	

TERRAIN TO SUITE

Freeride	**25%**
Trees	Yes
Backcountry	Yes
Freestyle	**25%**
Halfpipe	Yes 3
Terrain Park	Yes 1
Carving	**50%**

SNOW DATA

Average Snowfall

Snowmaking
5% cover of the slopes
Winter Periods
Nov to April
Summer Riding
None

SLOPE ACCESS

Total Lifts = **19**
Uplift Rate - 18,000 people an hour.
8 Gondolas & Funiculars
18 Chair lifts & Drag lifts
**Leashes Required*

Lift Times
8.30am to 4.30pm

Lift Pass Rates

1 Day pass	58 Sfr
3 Day pass	160 Sfr
6 Day pass	270 Sfr

SLOPE ACTION

Snowboard Hire
Daily rates 28 Sfr
Kids from 22 Sfr

Snowboard Tuition
Group lessons, from from 40 Sfr

Night Riding
Thursdays

Heli Boarding
Yes

Snowmobiles
No

Mountain Cafes
10

Saas-Fee has been a resort well known to snowboarders for many years. They have been building half-pipes, parks and other obstacles since way back and before many others areas had even heard of snowboarding. With its high altitude glacier, Saas-Fee also provides a mountain where you can ride fast and hard in the summer months, indeed for some, this is the only time worth visiting. Winter or summer, this is still a cool place that stages numerous competitions in both seasons and snowboard manufactures do a lot of product testing. Saas Fee is a resort with two faces. In summer the small glacier area has a snowboard park which boasts three half pipes, a boardercross course, and various hits. However, in winter the snowboard park shuts down and the resort focuses itself on family skiers. They do maintain a half-pipe, but that's the nearest you'll get to specialist snowboard terrain. Most of the mountain is geared to skiers and possibly hard-booters. There's a variety of red and black runs, as well as nursery slopes and top to bottom blue runs, but nothing to really test you (although the runs off the **Hinterallalin** - when open - are supposed to be more challenging). Pisting is somewhat haphazard away from the main stations at the mid point and top glacier, so expect moguls on red and black runs.

Freeriders will be disappointed to find that the off-piste is limited by crevasse danger around the glacier - but there are some nice tree runs off **Platjen**. Alternatively, the runs off the **Hinterallalin** drag lift will sort out the wimps, with some cool freeriding to be had and some fast steep sections to try out.

Freestylers could be excused for thinking something is amiss as the natural hits are few and far between - locals tend to build their own hits and session them. Still, you may find some hits off the **Mittaghorn** and **Langfluh** lifts. There s also a few drop offs to be enjoyed near the **Langfluh** and **Platjen** areas.

Carvers will favour **Saas Fee** the most, with a host of pisted runs on which to lay out some wide tracks. No matter what your level, you'll soon be carving in and out of the two plankers in style on graded runs from steep blacks to tame blues. The runs under the **Mittelallalin** restaurant is a great area for carvers.

Beginners are not left out, **Saas Fee** has plenty of novice runs, but some of the blue pistes have long flat sections to catch you out, resulting in a fair bit of skating along. You'll also get really used to T-bars by the time you leave this place. The lower runs have a reputation for rocks and worn patches, so take care when you first head out. However, the best way to find out what s what, is to call in on the boys at the *Paradise Snowboard School*, they'll show you how to get around any obstructions.

Saas Fee is a car-free place where you get around by either electric vehicles or on foot. However, everything is located close to each other and the slopes. The town is a cool place, with options to sleep close to the slopes in hotels or chalets. Money wise, Saas-Fee can be very expensive if you're staying in a hotel and eating out in restaurants, but on the other hand, you can do things cheaply by staying in an apartment and feasting on supermarket produce. The resort crams in loads of amenities, from swimming pools, a cinema, a museum, an ice rink to heaps of shops, including a couple of cool snowboard shops centrally located; *Popcorn* ++41 (0) 958 19 14 and *Powder Tools* ++41 (0) 89 220 7792.

Being a modern and popular resort, Saas Fee is well equipped to feed all its visitors no matter what their chosen diet is. There are well over 50 restaurants here many based in hotels but also a good number of independent ones. Notable places to pig out in are the *Boccalino* for pizza or the *Lavern* for traditional Swiss food. *Hotel Allalin* is a good restaurant with affordable meals set in a rustic style.

Night life is very good here despite there being a few places offering the ski apr s crap. Snowboard life-style centres around the *Popcorn* bar and snowboard shop, but the *Happy* bar is cheaper (especially at happy hour 7:30 - 8:30 daily). There are a few other bars worth checking out. If you decide to stay in and party, watch out for the 'hush police' - too much noise after 10pm and you'll get fined around 120 Sfr.

Accommodation: 7500 visitors can be housed here. Hotels come as one would expect, standard Swiss and expensive. However, with this place comes a good number of affordable bed and breakfast places apartment and chalets for those wanting to go self catering. Whereever you stay, nothing is too far from the slopes.

For accommodation listings visit - **www.worldsnowboardguide.com**

Summary: Sass-Fee is a great summer snowboard destination, but it s not as hot in winter, but still worth a visit. Local services are great with a good vibe.
Money wise: Very expensive resort but budget riders can get by.

Overall rating out of 10 — **7**

Tourist Office Saas-Fee
CH-3906
Saas Fee.

General info	**++41 (0) 27 958 1858**
Reservations	**++41 (0) 27 958 1858**
Avlanche info	**++41 (0) 1 187**

www.saas-fee.ch

pic - Nitro Snowboards

pic - Saas-Fee Tourism

Travel Guide

Fly to **Geneva** international
Transfer time to resort = **2** hours.
Local airport = none

Approximate global air travel times to **Geneva:**

from:	
London	2 hours
Los Angles	13 hours
New York	9 hours

Bus services from **Geneva** take around 3 hours direct to **Saas-Fee** via **Brigg.**

Trains to **Brigg** (20 minutes).

Route Planner
Geneva via Visp

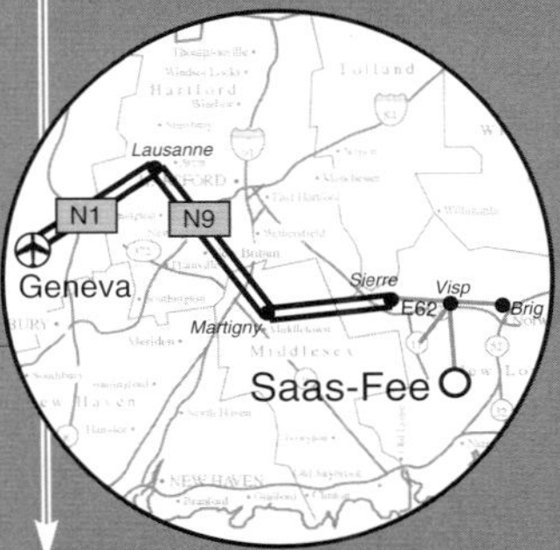

Saas Fee = 145 miles (235 km)
Drive time is about 3 hours

*From **Calais** 582 (936 Km)
Drive time is around **10½** hours.

Verbier

MOUNTAIN DATA

Top Lift at - 3505m

Ride Area
241km of piste

Bottom Lift at - 1500m

Vertical Drop - 1830m

Number of Runs - 77

Longest - 9 miles (15km)

TERRAIN LEVELS

Easy	**40%**
Intermediate	**40%**
Advanced	**20%**
Expert =	

TERRAIN TO SUITE

Freeride	**60%**
Trees	Yes
Backcountry	Yes
Freestyle	**20%**
Halfpipe	Yes 2
Terrain Park	Yes 2
Carving	**20%**

SNOW DATA

Average Snowfall
350cm a season

Snowmaking
5% cover of the slopes

Winter Periods
Nov to April

Summer Riding
May to October

SLOPE ACCESS

Total Lifts = **100**

Uplift Rate - 26,000 people an hour.

3 Gondolas - **1** Cable car

9 Chair lifts - **28** Drag lifts

**Leashes Required*

Lift Times
8.30am to 4.30pm

Lift Pass Rates

1 Day pass	58 Sfr
3 Day pass	170 Sfr
6 Day pass	292 Sfr

SLOPE ACTION

Snowboard Hire
Daily rates 28 Sfr
Kids from 22 Sfr

Snowboard Tuition
Group lessons, from
from 40 Sfr

Night Riding
No

Heli Boarding
Yes

Snowmobiles
No

Mountain Cafes
10

Verbier is a big resort in more ways than one: Big slope area, big mountain and big on extreme terrain. However, Verbier is also big on the stuck and poncy scale being a resort that goes out of its way to attract the rich, the stuck up elite, disposed European royals and their side kicks. Despite its great terrain and summer snowboarding opportunities, this is also a resort where snowboarding is still fairly small (less than 5% of slope users) but don't fret, the attitude is pretty cool and snowboarders are welcome everywhere, although you have to share the slopes with a lot of scum bags in fur hats poncing around the mountain on their stupid *Big Foot* skis. Still, on the plus side of things Verbier offers all year round snowboarding up on the **Mont Fort Glacier,** although you won't be riding down to the village in June. The snow record here is good and even in a poor season, it's still possible to ride to the resort in April. Generally, the terrain gives over to all levels, offering every rider something to get their teeth into. However, Verbier is essentially a freerider's resort, with easily accessible powder, trees, hard-pack, cliffs, hits and extremes, some of which necessitate a hike first.

Freeriders who know just what snowboarding is all about will be very impressed with Verbier. The *Verbier Extreme* competition is now regularly held here which should give you an idea of what awesome terrain is on offer. The **Mont Gele** cable car serves no piste, just a series of off-piste runs and couloirs of varying extremity; tuck your balls (or equivalent) away before you get up here. The less squeamish should check out the areas round the back of **Lac des Vaux** — the **Col des Mines**, and **Vallon d' Arbi** routes steer you towards wide open powder fields with the words 'session me' written all over them. If trees are your thing, Verbier has loads of them, especially in the **Bruson** area, but remember, Switzerland is the one country that protects its forests, so shredding the spruce is not always appreciated.

Freestylers have a park and pipe to ride all year round, located up on **Mont-Fort,** although pipe bashing is not Verbier's strong point. Anyway, the natural stuff around **La Chaux** and **Lac des Vaux** lifts, are the places to get air.

Carvers in hard boots will enjoy several different runs, but the best is undoubtedly the long, wide red piste that goes from the top of **Attelas** all the way back to the **Medran** lifts. There's also some cool stuff at **Savoleyres** and **Ruinettes**.

Beginners will find that the main areas are actually closed to snowboarders, which means that first timers are faced with steeper slopes. The best option is the runs at **Savoleyres**, where you are certain to be end up doing a few 180 butt spins. Some lifts can be tricky, so keep to the slower chair lifts. Lift pass checking is slack, so think on, but don't get caught as they jail you here.

Off the slopes, **Verbier** is a Royals, city slickers & lottery winners only place, with prices that exclude everyone else. There's no such thing as a cool scene unless you can pay for it. The place is over populated with farts and their spoilt off spring (rich kids with attitude but no brains). Bedding down is costly and if you get caught scamming on someone's floor, you could face a 200 Swiss Franc fine. However, the resort is well set out and can sleep over 15,000 rich skiers. Overall, Verbier simply is not a place to visit on a tight budget, unless you have a degree in scamming. To get the information on Verbier, check with the guys at '*No Bounds*' or '*Extreme*' snowboard shops.

Bring stacks of tins of baked beans with you and a cooker, as unless your name is Princess Lucky, you simply won t be able to afford any of the restaurants or even the supermarkets. Food in a town that attracts the super rich, is not easy to come by cheaply, although there are loads of restaurants to choose from with a cross the board range of menus from Chinese to bland Swiss fondues.

Night life, take a fork lift truck and ram in through the doors of the main bank, then take you re spoils to any one of the bars and if your lucky, you may just have enough francs to get a fruit juice. Night-time costs the earth here unless you can scam your way into a club pretending that you re Sara Fergusions lap dog. The clubs are not only costly but play crap music to please the lame heads who don t know any better.

Accommodation: There are 15,000 beds on offer in Verbier. But as with but at a high price, but thats not to say you won t be able to get a bed somewhere. The best two options open to you are 1) take a package tour, or 2) hook up with a local bird, no matter how ugly, and promise her the earth in order to get in her bed.

For accommodation listings visit - www.worldsnowboardguide.com

Summary: Extremely good resort with some of the best extreme in Switzerland and some great summer riding, but this place is hellish in terms of being stuck up.
Money wise: Criminally expensive, makeing the place attractive to the rich

Overall rating out of 10 **9**

Tourist Office Verbier
Valais,Verbier
CH-1936

General info	**++41 (0) 27 775 38 88**
Reservations	**++41 (0) 27 775 38 88**
Avlanche info	**++41 (0) 1 187**

www.verbier.ch

pics - Verbier Tourism

Travel Guide

Fly to **Geneva** international
Transfer time to resort = **2** hours.
Local airport = none

Approximate global air travel times to **Geneva:**

from:		
	London	2 hours
	Los Angles	13 hours
	New York	9 hours

Bus services from **Geneva** take around $2^{1/2}$ hours direct to **Verbier** via **Martigny.**

Trains to **Le Chable** (10 minutes).

Route Planner
Geneva via Martigny

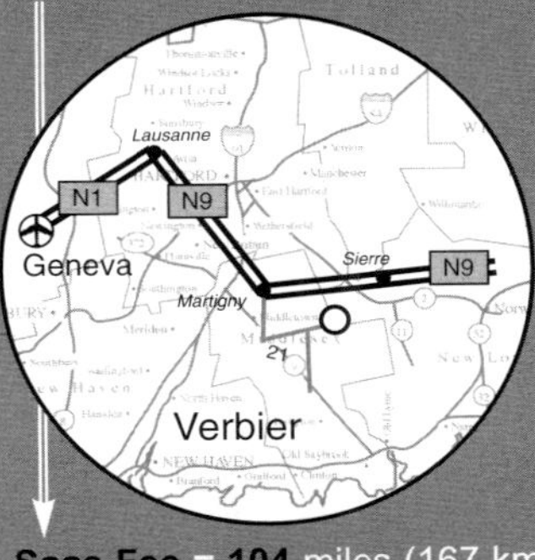

Saas Fee = 104 miles (167 km)
Drive time is about **2** hours

*From **Calais** 540 (869 Km)
Drive time is around $9^{1/2}$ hours.

Villars

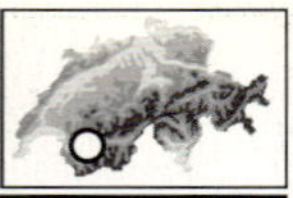

pic -Villars

MOUNTAIN DATA

Top Lift at - 3300m

Ride Area
99km of piste

Bottom Lift at - 1200m
Vertical Drop - 913m
Number of Runs - 52
Longest - 3 miles (5km)

TERRAIN LEVELS

Easy	**35%**
Intermediate	**55%**
Advanced	**10%**
Expert =	

TERRAIN TO SUITE

Freeride	**30%**
Trees	A few
Backcountry	Yes
Freestyle	**10%**
Halfpipe	Yes 1
Terrain Park	Yes 1
Carving	**60%**

SNOW DATA

Average Snowfall

Snowmaking
5% cover of the slopes
Winter Periods
Nov to April
Summer Riding
At Les Diablets

SLOPE ACCESS

Total Lifts = **45**
Uplift Rate - 16,000 people an hour.
8 Gondolas & Funiculars
5 Chair lifts - **36** Drag lifts
**Leashes Required*

Lift Times
8.30am to 4.30pm

Lift Pass Rates

1 Day pass	45 Sfr
3 Day pass	120 Sfr
6 Day pass	230 Sfr

Travel Guide

Fly to **Geneva** airport, 2 hours away.

Train services are possible to Ollon (10 minutes).

Route Planner: From Geneva, head along the N1 and N9 and turn off at Aigle on route 9 towards Monthey turning left for Villars. *Drive time from **Calais** is 9 1/2 hours 516 miles (830 km)

Villars, in the French speaking part of Switzerland, is a simple place that sits in view of the high peaks of the **Les Diablerets Glacier,** where you can snowboard winter and summer. Villars is a popular place that get its fair share of visitors throughout the season. The slopes are well spread out covering the **Les Chaux** and **Bretaye** areas and linked after some careful navigation, with the base area at Les Diablerets. Overall the place is not noted for being a hardcore destination, in fact, it s true to say that this is a resort that favours piste loving hard boot carvers and family ski groups. However, the resort has a good attitude towards snowboarding and regularly allows its slopes to be used for various competitions. If you get a bit tired of it here and fancy something a more challenging, you can easily head up to **Les Diablerets.**

Freeriders are not known for flocking to this place because although there is some okay freeriding terrain, it s not that extensive in terms of steep blacks on or off-piste. That said, the black trail running down from **Les Chaux** is a real pleaser which if you stick to the left, can also be tackled by intermediates as it mellows out the further it spreads across the slope. The place for some great freeriding is up on the **Les Diablerets** slopes.

Freestylers can either decide to ride the pipe and park areas that are split between the **Bretaye** slopes and **Les Chaux** slopes. However, this is not one of those resorts where one can get too excited about the man made frills, and coupled with the fact that this place is not as snow sure as the slopes up on **Les Diablerets**, sculptured hits are not always guaranteed.

Carvers have the best of the slopes here from the long gentle blues and a couple of steep blacks on the **Les Chaux** area, to the excellent pisted reds on the **Bretaye** area.

Beginners' slopes are out numbered by intermediate ones, but don t be put off, this is a good first time resort although the place has a lot of drag lifts.

Local services and accommodation options are comfortably provided in the setting of a traditional Swiss village located close to the slopes. The amenities on offer are some what basic but perfectly adequate for a weeks family fun holiday!. In general an affordable week can be had, Night-lift is on the dull side with only a few bars and the odd disco.

For accommodation listings visit - www.worldsnowboardguide.com

Tourist Office Villars
Villars Sur Ollon. CH-1884
++41 (0) 24 495 32 32 www.

Overall rating out of 10 **6** **Very basic resort but okay**

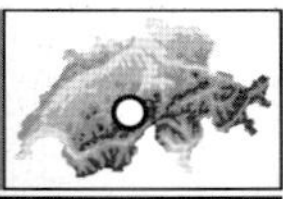

Wengen - Jungfrau

MOUNTAIN DATA

Top Lift at - 2971m

Ride Area
200km of piste

Bottom Lift at - 943m
Vertical Drop - 1050m
Number of Runs - 53
Longest - 4 miles (7km)

TERRAIN LEVELS

Easy	28%
Intermediate	57%
Advanced	15%
Expert =	

TERRAIN TO SUITE

Freeride	50%
Trees	Yes
Backcountry	Yes
Freestyle	25%
Halfpipe	Yes 1
Terrain Park	Some times
Carving	25%

SNOW DATA

Average Snowfall
530cm a season
Snowmaking
15% cover of the slopes
Winter Periods
Nov to April
Summer Riding
No

SLOPE ACCESS

Total Lifts = **43**
Uplift Rate - 40,000 people an hour.
21 Gondolas & Funiculars
22 Chair lifts - **12** Drag lifts
**Leashes Required*

Lift Times
8.30am to 4.30pm

Lift Pass Rates

1 Day pass	52 Sfr
3 Day pass	
6 Day pass	254 Sfr

Travel Guide

Fly to **Zurich** airport, about 2 hours away.

Train services are possible to Interlaken (10 minutes).

Route Planner:
Via Zurich, head south on the E41, N4a/N14 via Hergiswil and then the N8 to Interlaken. From here follow the Lauterbrunnen and then signs for Wengen.

pic - Interlarken Tourism

Wengen, which is part of the **Jungfrau Region**, is one of **Switzerland's** more famous resorts, but the reason for this is a mystery really. It can t just be for the terrain on offer, which although not bad, is not major, nor can it be for the welcome you get here. No Wengen has simply become well known because the idle rich, certain deposed European royals and a certain class of scum bag skier from Britain frequent this resort en-masse. The place reeks of snobbery, which is a bit of a shame because this is not a crap resort, far from it. With the slopes on offer here and at **Grindelwald** and at neighbouring **Murren**, a rider can have a good weeks riding on terrain that has something for all, although not a great deal for expert riders. Wengen, which shares direct slope access with Grindelwald, lies at an altitude of 1274 metres and is reached via the village of **Lauterbrunnen**, which is also the main access point for Murren. Wengen and Grindelwald are much the same, with Wengen having a few more interesting spots to try out. You can also descents from a height of 2971 metres, which is higher than Grindelwald, but in truth there is not much to separate the two places. However, Murren, the least crowded of the three resorts, offers the most challenging terrain and out of the three areas, it is also the most snowboard friendly. Wengen hasn t got a clue what its policy is towards snowboarding. A couple of seasons ago, the management set up a really good terrain park with loads of features, then the following year they decided not to build a thing for freestylers preferring to make a euro carvers (faggots in hard boots and head bands) area.

Freeriders are best off on the runs at **Murren**, off the **Schilthon.** Great powder stashes can be found in a number of spots.

Freestylers have pipe and park up on the **Oberjoch** area via Grindewald. **Wengen** also has some natural hits.

Carvers will blend in well here as there's a lot of Euro's with head bands and one piece suits posing on **Wengen's** slopes.

Beginners will only be put off by the crowds of skiers falling around on the gentle slopes. **Wengen** has the best novice terrain, while **Murren** has the worst.

Wengen offers a lot of local facilities with lodging close to the slopes. However, if you decide to stay here, it's going to cost you dearly with nightlife totally geared around apr s-ski rich gits.

For accommodation listings visit - www.worldsnowboardguide.com

Tourist Wengen
Po Boz CH 3823
++41 (0) 33 855 1414 **www.wengen-muerren.ch**

Overall rating out of 10 **6** **Spoilt by the stuck up attitude**

Zermatt

MOUNTAIN DATA

Top Lift at - 3885m

Ride Area
230km of piste

Bottom Lift at - 1620m
Vertical Drop - 2200m
Number of Runs - 77
Longest - 9 miles (15km)

TERRAIN LEVELS

Easy	**33%**
Intermediate	**45%**
Advanced	**22%**
Expert =	

TERRAIN TO SUITE

Freeride	**50%**
Trees	Yes
Backcountry	Yes
Freestyle	**20%**
Halfpipe	Yes 1
Terrain Park	Yes 1
Carving	**30%**

SNOW DATA

Average Snowfall
300cm a season
Snowmaking
25% cover of the slopes
Winter Periods
Nov to April
Summer Riding
May to September

SLOPE ACCESS

Total Lifts = **73**
Uplift Rate - 39,800 people an hour.
25 Gondolas & Funiculars
14 Chair lifts - **34** Drag lifts
**Leashes Required*

Lift Times
8.30am to 4.30pm

Lift Pass Rates

1 Day pass	62 Sfr
3 Day pass	170 Sfr
6 Day pass	306 Sfr

SLOPE ACTION

Snowboard Hire
Daily rates 28 Sfr
Kids from 22 Sfr

Snowboard Tuition
Group lessons, from from 40 Sfr

Night Riding
No

Heli Boarding
Yes, flights to Monte Rosa

Snowmobiles
No

Mountain Cafes
36

pic - Zermatt Tourism

Zermatt is an impressive resort and sits in the direct shadow of the mighty **Matterhorn.** Zermatt is money mountain and not on the calling card of many snowboarders because it s so damn expensive. To be fair however, things seem to have got easier and more and more riders on a budget are managing to get by here, this is despite the fact that it is one of the most famous resorts in Europe, although it could be questioned why. Maybe it s to do with its very elitist status, but what the heck, this is a place that can be ridden in the summer up on **Theodul Glacier** when all the fur clad posers have gone home, so it's not all bad news. Zermatt, with its 230 kilometres of marked piste and countless acres of backcountry terrain is a very impressive place with a great mountain to ride. Extensive heli-boarding opportunities are on offer with trips up to the **Monte Rosa** at 4250 metres, the **Alphubeljoch** at 3782 metres and up to the **Plateau Rosa** at 3479 metres. Not though, heli-boarding is not cheap at Zermatt with trips costing from 450 Sfr. Still, you don t need to take a helicopter in order to explore Zermatts fantastic terrain. Once you have made the hike to the first lifts from the main town, or in some cases taken the bus, and hit the slopes, the array off lifts will whisk you up the mountain to numerous start of points. The mountain layout is a bit confusing and will take some piste map navigating before you can ride all the areas with ease, but stick in there because it s worth getting it right in order to not get lost or not miss out on the best trails. On the slopes you will notice a lot of Italian posers as your lift pass also covers the neighbouring Italian resort of **Cervinia**.

Freeriders on the lookout for open powder bowls and couloirs to ride will be kept busy in a number of areas. **Zermatt** offers a lot of advanced off-piste riding, with some excellent runs on the **Stockhorn** or over at the **Schwarzsee** areas. If riding trees is your thing, note that Zermatt totally restricts riding through the forest areas. For a nice buzz, you should get off the main cable car at the middle station and ride back in to town along a small road. If you have the money, you can also take a day's heli-boarding with *Air Zermatt*, but it is very expensive: two flights over the **Monte Rosa** will cost you around 450 SFr.

Freestylers are provided with an ever improving half-pipe, but as there is so much good natural terrain, it s not that important.

Carvers are much in evidence here, preferring to cut up the number of good and long testing runs that descend en-route to the village via some extremely crowded lower novice trails.

Beginners may find **Zermatt** a bit tricky but not a big problem, just a bit tainted with too many first timers on skis clogging up the easy trails. However, you can ride easily higher up the mountain, making for some long, easy runs to progress on. Local snowboard instruction is notably good here with lessons for all levels.

Off the slopes, **Zermatt** is a large, car free town that is also stupidly pricey which may call for some major scamming to get by. A useful tip when travelling here from abroad is, if you fly into **Geneva** and plan to take the train down to **Zermatt**, buy your train ticket at a Swiss Tourist office in youe home country before you enter Switzerland, it can work out a lot cheaper. Around the town you are presented with loads of shops, various sporting centres and other visitor attractions. However, the town also comes with an abundance of snooty ski punters many of which will be on over-priced ski tours. Not that getting around the main part of town is not much of a problem, but in parts you will find that a lot of walking is required. cars are banned here and only local taxis and buses are available to shuttle you around at a price.

Any snotty resort that overcharges for lifts and accommodation, also means getting a reasonable meal is beyond the budget of most. There is however, a *Macdonalds* for a cheap Mac attack (you have to forget Macdonalds disgusting ethics when you re staving). The supermarket near the train station offers cheap eateries and for many a diet of crisps, mars bars and cheap beer is enough.

Nightlife is spoilt by the rich apr s ski scene and the costs of everything, but that s not so say you can t have a good time here, you can. There is a cool snowboarder s bar located on the bridge en-route to the Matterhorn lift in the **Swartzee** area. Around town there is a large selection of bars offering different themes and some being quite lively. There are also a number of late night discos such as the *Pink Elephant* or *Le Broken*, but all have shockingly expensive booze.

Accommodation can be super expensive and beyond the budget of most snow-boarders. However, there is a youth hostel located about 400 metres from the main lifts in the centre of town, which is cheap and offers half board accommodation.

For accommodation listings visit - www.worldsnowboardguide.com

Summary: Zermatt is an extremely good resort with terrain for all styles and levels. The resort has a lot of good facilities, but do note, this is a very, very snobbish place.

Money wise: Prices at this resort are simply criminal and not justified.

Overall rating out of 10 **8**

Tourist Office Zermatt
bahnhofplatz, Ch 3920.
Zermatt

General info	**++41 (0) 27 967 0181**
Reservations	**++41 (0) 27 967 0181**
Avlanche info	**++41 (0) 1 187**

www.zermatt.ch

pics - Zermatt Tourism

Travel Guide

Fly to **Geneva** international
Transfer time to resort = **3½** hours.
Local airport = none

Approximate global air travel times to **Geneva:**

from:	London	2 hours
	Los Angles	13 hours
	New York	9 hours

Bus services from **Geneva** take around 4½ to 5 hours direct to **Zermatt.**

Trains go direct to **Zermatt**.

Route Planner
Geneva via Visp

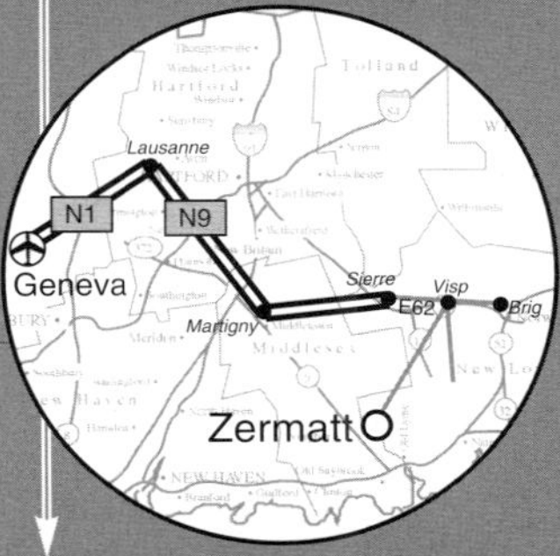

Zermatt = 160 miles (257 km)
Drive time is about **3½** hours

*From **Calais** 665 (1070 Km)
Drive time is around **10½** hours.

St Moritz - Upper Engadine

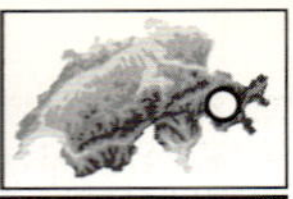

MOUNTAIN DATA

Top Lift at - 3025m

Ride Area
354km of piste

Bottom Lift at - 1856m
Vertical Drop - 1169m
Number of Runs - 47
Longest - 3 miles (5km)

TERRAIN LEVELS

Easy	10%
Intermediate	70%
Advanced	20%
Expert =	

TERRAIN TO SUITE

Freeride	50%
Trees	A few
Backcountry	Yes lots
Freestyle	20%
Halfpipe	Yes 1
Terrain Park	Yes 1
Carving	30%

SNOW DATA

Average Snowfall
300cm a season
Snowmaking
15% cover of the slopes
Winter Periods
Nov to April
Summer Riding
At Diavolezza

SLOPE ACCESS

Total Lifts = **54**
Uplift Rate - 62,000 people an hour.
11 Gondolas & Funiculars
29 Chair lifts - **14** Drag lifts
**Leashes Required*

Lift Times
8.30am to 4.30pm

Lift Pass Rates
1 Day pass 60 Sfr
3 Day pass
6 Day pass 282 Sfr

Travel Guide

Fly to **Zurich** airport, 4 hours away.

Train services are possible to St Moritz.

Route Planner: From Zurich, head south on the N3. Turn off at Landquart onto the route 28 to Zernez and then take the R-28 down to St Moritz.
Calais is 9 1/2 hours 516 miles (830 km)

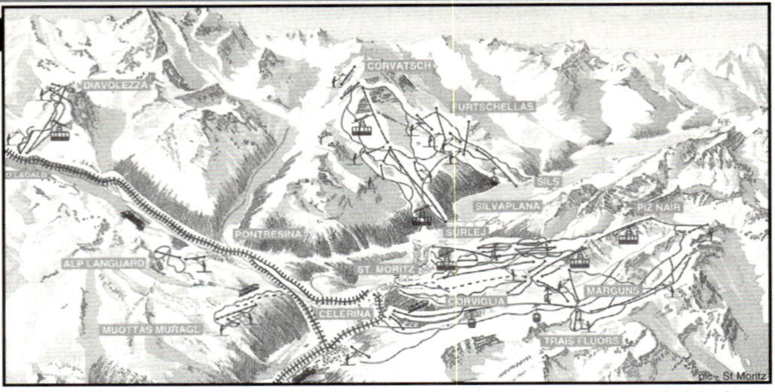

St Moritz has two classic distinctions, on the one hand this has to be one of the finest natural backcountry freeride places to ride in **Switzerland**, but on the other hand, St Moritz happens to be top of the league when it comes to snobbery. Without doubt this is one of the most expensive resorts on the planet, and not with-standing the outrageous costs here, the place attracts so many stuck-up rich idiots, that you can smell the fur clad sods a mile away. St Moritz is a high altitude resort that along with the areas of **Pontresina** and **Diavolezza,** form the **Upper Engadine** region. Diavolezza is a glacier mountain that hosts summer snowboarding allowing for all year round riding. St Moritz, which gives access to the slopes on the **Corviglia** and **Marguns,** is an area that is largely made up of intermediate pisted runs which get stupidly busy on most days and unfortunately there are not too many expert pisted trails to escape the hordes of learning skiers. However, there is heaps of adventurous off piste terrain to check out, but only do so with the advice and services of a local guide.

Freeriders have a huge amount of great backcountry terrain taht will blow your mind beyond, with lots of steeps, gullies, cliffs and virgin powder to seek out. Some of the best freeriding can be found up on the **Diavolezza** glacier, which is for serious riders only. On the **St Moritz's** area the slope to check out is the steep that drops that drops down from the **Piz Nair** summit.

Freestylers have a park and pipe but neither are that well looked after. The mega heaps of natural terrain is far better for getting air.

Carvers will find lots of fairly easy and ordinary well pisted runs to cruise down. But really you should freeride only at this place.

Beginners may not have the best selection of novice trails to start out with, but what is on offer is superb if only too busy.

Off the slopes **St Moritz** can easily be summed up as an over priced, over hyped ugly sham that rips you off big style for everything and attracts some very sad gits in designer wear and fur hats. Accommodations which is provided in an array of hotels and chalets, is available in a spread out area while the town boasts a lot of poncy shops and places to get a meal, but you have to look hard to find an inexpensive burger bar. As for having a good night out and a few beers, unless you re a brain dead mutant who owns a gold credit card, forget it, it sucks big style.

For accommodation listings visit - www.worldsnowboardguide.com

Tourist Office St Moritz
Po Box CH 7500
++41 (0) 81 837 333 **www.stmoritz.com**

Overall rating out of 10 **8** **Way too poncy but great riding**

Beatenberg

▲1905m 16 km of piste 5 lifts

Beatenberg is a blip of a place not far from **Interlarken** and above **Lake Thun**. The 10 miles of beginner friendly, intermediate dull and advanced crap terrain is spread out over a slope area unspoilt by mass crowds. In truth this is not a snowboarders destination unless you re recovering from piles and need somewhere out of the way to convalesce in peace. Local services are very basic but at the same time offer more than what is on the slopes.

Fly to: **Zurich** 2 hours away

ⓘ **tel-** ++41 (0) 33 841 1818

Bettmeralp

▲2710m 32 km of piste 12 lifts

On its own, **Bettmeralp** offers a mere 20 miles of basic carving terrain, but by linking with the **Aletsch** area, you suddenly have a more respectable 60 plus miles of okay freeride terrain in an area that also has a number half-pipes and a couple of fun parks for big air possibilities. Generally, the slopes here will suit beginners and mid way merchants as well as giving advanced riders something to look forward too. Okay local services but costly.

Fly to: **Zurich** 2½ hours away

ⓘ **tel-** ++41 (0) 27 927 1291

Braunwald

▲1900m 24 km of piste 8 lifts

Braunwald is located two hours from **Zurich**. This small place has gained a reputation as a friendly freestyle outpost where locals and those in the know spend the weekend getting air. They regularly build decent half-pipes and parks here for which they stage various events in. The terrain itself is nothing to shout about but is still cool and rarely attracts more than a 5 minute lift queue. Off the slopes things are laid back, good but basic.

Fly to: **Zurich** 1 hours away

ⓘ **tel-** ++41 (0) 55 643 1108

Champrey

▲2277m 99 km of piste 35 lifts

Champrey is a resort that forms part of the massive **Portes du Soleil** area, which boast a lift linked area of over 400 miles. **Champery** it self has 62 miles of terrain, with something for all but nothing that outstanding. They have a park and half-pipe here, but are not known for their upkeep. However, an intermediate freerider will like this place although the slopes do get busy. Local services are very good in a village full of character .

Fly to: **Geneva** 1½ hours away

ⓘ **tel-** ++41 (0) 24 479 2020

Champoussin

▲2150m 24 km of piste 8 lifts

Champoussin is yet another resort that helps to make up the **Portes du Soleil** area. This is a major plus because you would by no means want to get stuck with what's on offer here. A rider who knows what's will have this place done and dusted in an hour, even a quick learning novice could lick the place in a day or two. This a resort that old timers wanting to find their youth will like, but anyone else will find it dull.

Local services near the slopes.

Fly to: **Geneva** 1½ hours away

ⓘ **tel-** ++41 (0) 24 477 2977

Chateau d'Oex

▲1800m 48 km of piste 10 lifts

Chateau d'Oex is a place that is relatively unknown by the masses. When you see what s on offer its soon clear to see why. Famed more for balloon races, the slopes here are very ordinary and won t take a good rider that long to conquer. However with a further 150 miles of terrain in the area to check out, a week s visit here will be worth the effort. Freestylers get to ride a pipe and beginners have some good slopes.

Good slope side services.

Fly to: **Geneva** 2 hours away

ⓘ **tel-** ++41 (0) 26 924 7788

Klosters

▲2844m 160 km of piste 12 lifts

Forget the reason for **Klosters** fame, this resort offers any rider a challenging time with good off-piste that will please freeriders. Carvers have some excellent runs to try out and freestylers have a fun park (not hot mind, better to use the one at nearby Davos). Great also for beginners. The biggest let down here is the brown nosed ski snobs from the UK, hoping to be seen with a royal. Okay local services but pricey.

Fly to: **Zurich** 2 hours away

ⓘ **tel-** ++41 (0) 410 2020

Lenzerheide

▲2865m 152 km of piste 36 lifts

Lenzerheide is a big place that covers two mountain slopes, offering some really nice open riding with tree line trails to the base area. Intermediate freeriders and carvers are in for a treat here, with the biggest cluster of runs to be found on the **Statzerhorn** slopes while freestylers have an okay half-pipe and park on the **Rothorn** slopes. Beginners should love this place with easy trails all over the place high and low. Good laid back local services slope side.

Fly to: **Zurich** 2 hours away

ⓘ **tel-** ++41 (0) 81 384 3434

Les Diablets

▲3000m 64 km of piste 28 lifts

Les Diablets is a cool snowboarders hangout that offers sum-

mer riding on the glacier. However, this is not a place for piste loving carvers, no, this is a freeriders retreat offering some great backcountry riding in deep powder, but not for the faintheart-ed, some of this stuff will take you out quick style if you balls up. Although not a big place, this is a good unspoilt haunt that caters well for freestylers and novices. Good slope side services.

Fly to: Geneva 1½ hours away

ⓘ **tel-** ++41 (0) 24 492 2358

Meiringen-Hasliberg

▲3000m 64 km of piste 28 lifts

Meiringen-Hasliberg has a history related to *Sherlock Holmes,* but today what you have is great snowboarders out back close to the **Jungfrau Region.** There s no hype here, no mass holiday crowds, just a cool mountain with something for everyone. There are wide powder fields, gullies and big cliffs on a mountain that is majorly snowboard friendly providing a decent pipe and park and good beginner areas. Good lodging and local services close by.

Fly to: **Zurich** 1½ hours away

ⓘ **tel-** ++41 (0) 33 972 5151

Morgins

▲2000m 67 km of piste 16 lifts

Morgins, on the Swiss side, is yet another resort that forms part of the massive **Portes du Soleil** area which crosses into France. On the Swiss side, Morgins is the highest resort and not a modern imitation of some of its cousins. What this place has to offer is easy access to over 40 miles of direct terrain and a further 360 miles of linked terrain. Collectively, there is something for everyone.

Good slope side local services

Fly to: **Geneva** 1½ hours away

ⓘ **tel-** ++41 (0) 24 4777 2361

Rougemont

▲2156m 19 km of piste 3 lifts

Rougemont is a tiny place that links indirectly with its bigger and more famous cousin **Gstaad**. This helps boost the 12 miles of terrain on offer here to a respectable 150 miles plus. Rougemont on its own is not a place that you would book a week's holiday at, indeed only a rider so stoned that an inch seems like a mile will enjoy this place. However, there is a small half-pipe and an 80 year old beginner will fair well. There are slope side facilities, but over all, this place is very dull.

Fly to: **Geneva** 2½ hours away

ⓘ **tel-** ++41 (0) 26 925 8333

Throughout Eastern Europe there are loads of amazing snowboard destinations located in high mountain areas. However, the biggest problem in this part of the world, is who s shooting who in order to play president. One minute you have a top resort and the next it s a battle ground. Still if you decide to try out the east then remember that on the whole, travel can be a nightmare and most places have bugger all services with undeveloped resorts. But the big plus for this part of Europe are the costs, cheap to the extreme is the easiest way to put it, with prices so low it s worth ducking and diving from the odd stray bullet.

Freeriders will enjoy the unpredictable and uneven terrain features found in most rideable places but freestylers will be left a little disappointed if big pipes and man made terrain parks are your thing. Such things are almost none existent however lots of natural freestyle terrain is available along with some very big cliff jump areas.

Overall, resort s services are very basic with low key primitive accommodation, restaurants and amenities. Locals in many parts of the east have never seen westerners and on the whole are very friendly and will look after you, especially if you flash a few dollars.

The best way of travelling in Eastern europe, is to hire a car or bring your own reliable vehicle.

Always check with the national embassy to get the latest facts about travel to any part of Eastern Europe.

Bulgaria

Time - Zone
GMT +1 Hour (GMT +2 March -April)

Capital - Sofia
Language - Bulgarian
Currency - Lev

Bulgaria is ahead of its neighbours in attracting westerners to sample its winter hospitality with a number of resorts which provide a very good and a far cheaper alternative to the resorts in the Alps.

Traveling to Bulgaria should pose no real problems with international flights arriving at the capital of **Sofia.** Note for entering Bulgaria visitors from EU member countries don t need a visa Another point, forget about credit cards, although there are not widely accepted, you re better off with hard cash, *US Dollars* are the best currency for changing into Lev s.

On the slopes, piste preparation is not hot and mountain facilities are primitive but prices are very low and the pistes are un-crowded. Accommodation, on the whole, is very basic and eating out is not up to much along with very basic night life styled in 70 s discos theme. However, lodging, food and booze are stupidly cheap.

A number of tour operators offer package tours to Bulgaria with great budget deals available.

Bansko

▲1762m 20 km of piste 8 lifts

Banasko is situated in the Pirin Mountains some 160km south of the capital. This tiny place is actually okay although it won't keep an advanced ride interested for too long. The one black rated trail is not that long. However, carvers of an intermediate level will find the trails perfectly good. Local services are provided in a traditional Bulgarian style. There are a number of good hotels and bed and breakfast homes to choose from, all at very reasonable rates. Bansko also has a number of simple restaurants serving up local dishes such as Banski Staretz. the night life is very simple with a selection of taverns selling cheap local brews.

Fly to: **Sofia** 3 hours away

ⓘ **tel-** ++359 (0) 2 43331

Pamporovo

▲1930m 25 km of piste 15 lifts

Pamporovo is a purpose-built resort, located in a thick pine forest with claims of being Europe's sunniest resort. However, the selection of easy slopes will please first timers, entertain intermediate freeriders and carvers, but bore the heck out of advanced riders, especially those looking for big natural air. Still Pamporovo now has a halfpipe which freestylers can gain some air time from, but it has to be said that it s not always a well maintained pipe. Local facilities include a selection of hotels well equipped to look after winter visitors. There is a shopping complex, hotel swimming pool, sauna, a number of bars and the odd disco all within easy reach of the slopes and all with a common theme, cheap. Every thing is affordable and booze is almost a give away.

Fly to: **Sofia** 2^2 hours away

ⓘ **tel-** ++359 (0) 2 43331

Vitosha

▲1926m 22 km of piste 19 lifts

Close to the Bulgarian capital of **Sofia**, lies the resort of **Vitosha.** A gondola takes riders from the city limits up to Aleko at 1810 meters. The slopes get an average snow base of around 3 metres a season along with plenty of sunshine making riding here a pleasant experience on empty slopes, that offer trees for freeriders, but no halfpipe for freestylers. However carvers have a few good flats to ride. Beginners can ride with ease from top to bottom. The village offers a number cheap hotels. The best night spot is the *Hotel Prostor*

Fly to: **Plovdiv** 1 hour away

ⓘ **tel-** ++359 (0) 2 43331

Borovets - Bulgaria

MOUNTAIN DATA

Top Lift at - 2543m

Ride Area
40km of piste

Bottom Lift at - 1317m
Vertical Drop - 193m
Number of Runs - 20
Longest - 3 miles (5km)

TERRAIN LEVELS

Easy	32%
Intermediate	64%
Advanced	4%
Expert =	

TERRAIN TO SUITE

Freeride	45%
Trees	A few
Backcountry	None
Freestyle	5%
Halfpipe	Yes 1
Terrain Park	Some times
Carving	50%

SNOW DATA

Average Snowfall

Snowmaking
Zero

Winter Periods
Nov to April

Summer Riding
No

SLOPE ACCESS

Total Lifts = 8
Uplift Rate - 9,700 people an hour.
1 Gondolas
2 Chair lifts - 5 Drag lifts
**Leashes Required*

Lift Times
8.30am to 4.30pm

Lift Pass Rates in UK £

1 Day pass	£12
3 Day pass	£20
6 Day pass	£60

Travel Guide

Fly to **Plovdiv** airport 71 miles (115 km.)

Bus services from Sofia are possible direct to Borvets with a transfer time of around $2^{1/2}$ hours.

Route Planner: Via Sofia, take the route 82 south out of the city via the town of Pancharevo and Samokov to reach Borovets.

pic - Borovets

Borovets is the best known of the **Bulgarian** Resorts, with a wide range of facilities and on one of the highest rideable areas in Eastern Europe. Locals say that the season comes late in Borovets: mid-February often sees only half the runs open, but riders in the know say that April has the best snow. The terrain is mainly suited to intermediate carvers, with nothing too challenging for the experienced. The 23 miles of piste is split into three areas, offering open runs and lines through trees. Hard packed snow and ice frequently make the runs tough work and with small rocks sticking out when there's poor snow cover, a little vigilance is essential. Some of the best riding can be found on the runs above the 2500m point. The 6 person gondola ride to the top station takes about 25 minutes and to avoid queues avoid the period between 9am and 11am. A tip for those on a package trip is to buy your lift ticket before you arrive, it could save you £20.

Freerider's favourite spot is an off-piste run down under the gondola pylons. This takes you from the top station down between a red run to the left and a black run on the right.

Freestylers will be glad to know that it s not frowned upon if you want to build kickers to catch some air from, but expect everyone else to be launching themselves off any hits you do build.

Carvers will find enough wide areas to put in a few turns, but overall this is not a very good carving resort.

Beginners have only one official blue marked run, but you should soon master some of the reds. Take note, the French designed lift system caters well for skiers, but it's not hot for novice boarders. The main problem is some of the lift take-offs are quick with deep rutted tracks that will throw you off with ease. One particular lift is so bad that it's not uncommon to see bodies dropping like flies.

Off the slopes, the purpose built village of **Borovets** is a small place set around 1400 metres. The main hotels are the *Rila, Samokov* and the *Olympic*. Everything here is cheap. Food is basic, filling and mainly based on pork and chicken. Evenings are okay and go on until the early hours of the morning and with booze so cheap be prepared for serious drinking and wicked hangovers. It's worth noting that having strong foreign currencies such as Dollars, is a good idea as most places don't accept credit cards or travellers cheques. Inflation is also rampant, so don't change too much money at once.

For accommodation listings visit - **www.worldsnowboardguide.com**

Tourist office Borovets
Balkantourist, Borovets 2010, Bulgaria
++359 (0) 2 835 219 www.

Overall rating out of 10 **4**

Slopes can be ridden in a day

CZECH REPUBLIC

Time - Zone
GMT +1 Hour (GMT +2 March -April)
Capital - Prague
Language - Czech
Currency - Koruna

The Czech Republic is not really noted as a hot destination for either skiers or snowboarders. The are about half a dozen semi - developed resorts but none are that good with little to offer in terms of exciting riding on generally small mountains with short trails, serviced by antique lift systems and almost no piste preparation. Still, if you do give CZ a visit the country is cheap and the people are very friendly. Entry into the country is easy but visas are required for certain nationals.

Harrachov
▲1020m 8 km of piste 15 lifts
Harrachov is a popular resort with nationals and provides a few okay runs to suit beginners mostly with only one black trail.
Local facilities are based close to the slopes and are very cheap.
Fly to: **Prague** 2 hours away
ⓘ **tel-** ++42 (0) 432 929 248

Janske Lanze
▲1275m 6 km of piste 11 lifts
Janske Lanz'e only notable point is that it has the longest run in the country at 1.7 miles (2.7km) but there is little else here of interest. Cheap convenient local services.
Fly to: **Prague** 2[1/4] hours away
ⓘ **tel-** ++42 (0) 439 94661

Pec Pod Snezkou
▲1600m 12 km of piste 45 lifts
Pec Pod Snezkou has lots of lifts but bugger all decent terrain.
Cheap convenient local services.
Fly to: **Prague** 2[1/2] hours away
ⓘ **tel-** ++42 (0) 439 962 475

Spindleruv Myn
▲1310m 25 km of piste 31 lifts
Spindleruv Mlyn has several rideable areas and snow cover is usually good until late April. The best runs can be found on **Medvedin** and around **Svaty Petr**. These areas have snowmaking and night riding and an interchangeable lift ticket is offered. A chairlift ascends **Snezka** (1602 m), the Czech Republic's highest mountain, but no runs lead down to the valley. Overall this is a basic freerider's haunt, but by no means testing.

Off the slopes. **Spindleruv** is a scattered community based around the old village of **St. Peters,** which dates back as far as the 1800's. Locals services are cheap and very basic, don t expect heaps of things laid on because they aren t.
Fly to: **Prague** 2hours away
ⓘ **tel-** ++42 (0) 438 93656

Zelezen Ruda

▲1200m 15 km of piste 26 lifts
Zelezen Ruda is one of the largest ski centres in the Czech Republic centred on a 16th century mining settlement. The **Spicak** snow area with its 9 lifts is popular with advanced riders, but it should be pointed out that the advanced terrain is limited to one difficult run. **Spicak** is linked by a shuttle bus to the other slopes (but the lift ticket is only valid on **Spicak**). **Pancir**, the other main rideable area, is served by a long chair and offers very easy trails. Prices throughout the area are low, but still slightly higher than in the rest of the Czech Republic.
Off the slopes things are low key and extremely affordable, with beds on and near the slopes.
Fly to: **Munich** (Germany) 2[1/2] hours away
ⓘ **tel-** ++42 (0) 186 97132

GEORGIA

Time - Zone
GMT +4 Hours
Capital - Tbilsi
Language - Georgian
Currency - Lari

Although there are a couple of resorts that, in the past, have been promoted by the state tourist bureau, but theses days the country is so war torn that the only advice is forget it, the place is too dangerous.

Georgian Winter Sports Fed
ⓘ **tel-** ++995 (0) 8832 942 151

HUNGARY

Time - Zone
GMT +1 Hour (GMT +2 March -April)
Capital - Budapest
Language - Hungarian
Currency - Forint

There are about two dozen known resorts in Hungary located mainly in the Matra region. Overall Hungary is not up too much in terms of terrain and facilities. None of the resorts offer any real hardcore freeriding or adventurous carving. But most areas will suit beginners not looking for much. There is a healthy attitude towards snowboarding with a few halfpipes.

Hungarian Ski Association
ⓘ **tel-** ++36 (0) 1 114 868

KYRGHYZSTAN

Time - Zone
GMT +1 Hour (GMT +2 March -April)
Capital - Bishkek
Language - Kyrgyz
Currency - Som

Kyrghyzstan is not noted for its developed ski resorts with only two on offer. However, what Kyrghyzstan is noted for is heli-ski operations giving access to loads of virgin slope to please good freeriders, what s more its cheap.

Tie-Shan Heli-Ski Company
ⓘ **tel-** ++7 (0) 3312 429 825

MACEDONIA

Time - Zone
GMT +1 Hour (GMT +2 March -April)
Capital - Skopjet
Language -Macedonian
Currency - Macedonian Denar

Macedonia, which was the former **Republic** of **Yugoslav,** has five or so recognised ski resorts. Although equipped with rather old fashioned lift systems they have terrain that will suit all levels and are a match for a many western alpine resort.
Macedonian Ski Association
ⓘ **tel-** ++389 (0) 228 360

LATAVIA

Time - Zone
GMT +2 Hour (GMT +3 March -April)
Capital - Riga
Language - Latvian
Currency - Lat

Latavia hasn t really got what one would call high snow capped mountains that allow easily accessible, fast and hard snowboarding. Instead what you have here are low level hills and a cool bunch of eager snowboarders trying to get things done.

Valmiera is the main snowboarders hangout in Latavia, and is located 80 miles (130km) north of the Latvian capital Riga. What you get here are two slopes, with longest measuring a mere 170 metres and serviced by two basic lifts and one snow-cannon the (only one in Latvia). You couldn t split this place into styles and levels, suffice to say that novices alone will have half an hours fun. The winter allows for some limited riding on real snow while the summer sees an influx of boarders to ride the only sliding carpet, (better known as a *Dry Slope*), in the **Balkans.** During the summer a lot of BMX riders also turn up to ride the BMX dirt track, while others simply come to chill out and take the occasional boat trip on the river **Gaujañ**.

Valmiera is happy to have snowboarders try out its hill, but as yet they haven t been able to provide a halfpipe or fun-park However, plans are being put forward and it s hoped that for this coming season some kickers will be built for air heads to get high.

Snowboarding has been quite slow to catch on here, but at last you can now get snowboards and boots for hire at the base and snowboard instruction is also now available on request.

Lodging and other local services at the slopes are not for wimps or for those looking for all the creature comforts of an Alpine resort. You can choose to to stay in one of the small camping style houses located behind the slopes, which use old wood stoves for heating. Alternatively in the town of **Valmiera** you will find hotels and other basic cheap lodgings. For night-life, it s do it yourself with a *Walkman.* Or check out, *Multi Klubs, Tirgus iela 5, ph 42 32114* for a party.

The only way to get to the place, with piece of mind, is to hire a car and drive yourself. However, youcan also get here by either bus or train from **Riga**.

Fly to Riga International airport 80 miles away.
Bus: transfers takes 2 1/2 hours.
Trains: via Riga take 2 1/2 hours.
Driving: via Riga, head north on the A2 for 50 miles travelling via Sigulda and turning north via Cesis to reach Valmiera.

ⓘ Any information concerning opportunities in Latvia
can be communicated through email address:
HYPERLINK
mailto:skramba@hotmail.com
skramba@hotmail.com

HYPERLINK
http://www.valmiera.lanet.lv/~baili
www.valmiera.lanet.lv/~baili

POLAND

Time - Zone
GMT +1 Hour (GMT +2 March -April)
Capital - Warsaw
Language - Polish
Currency - Zloty

Poland has a long history in building ski resorts which date back decades, and in many cases a lot earlier than some western alpine nations. The main difference being much of what has been built in Poland over the years was neither that good, nor long term and in most cases hideous in design and layout. Today the country has around 30 resorts but many are more or less defunct and in truth there are only a couple of decent and well developed areas. Still Poland is friendly country and what it may lack in terms of slope facilities it more than makes up for with it s helpful and cool attitude. The International Snowboard Federation has seen the merits of Poland s enthusiasm to snowboarding and has staged a number of major tournaments in the country which once included the *World Youth Championships*.

Gubalowka
in the Tatras region ▲1120m 11 lifts..

Jaworzna Ktynicka
in the Tatras region ▲1114m 1 lift.

Karpacz
in the Tatras region ▲1340m 10 lifts.

Kasina Wielka
in the Snieznica Tatras region ▲1000m.

Koziejowka
in the Tatras region ▲520m 1 lift.

Krynica Czarny
in the Tatras region ▲620m 1 lift.

Limanowa Lysa Gora
in the Tatras region ▲785m 1 lift.

Lubomierz
in the Tatras region ▲960m 1 lift.

Nosal
in the Tatras region ▲1170m 4 lifts.

Nowy Tard Kowaniec
in the Tatras region ▲700m 1 lift.

Piwniczma Sucha Dolina
in the Tatras region ▲1025m 4 lifts.

Poreba Wielka Koninki
in the Tatras region ▲965m 4 lifts.

Poreonin Galicowa Grapa
in the Tatras region ▲980m 1 lift.

Prehyba Lysa Gora
in the Tatras region ▲1175m 1 lift.

Stare
in the Tatras region ▲970m 1 lift.

Szczawnik
in the Tatras region ▲520m 1 lift.

Szcawnina
in the Tatras region ▲740m 2 lifts.

Tylicz
in the Tatras region ▲795m 1 lift.

Zakopane

▲1960m 27 km of piste 20 lifts.
Zakopane, once a seventeenth century forestry settlement, is now a small, and **Poland's** best known resort, made up of a number of non-linked areas where you can snowboard. In general the whole area will give intermediates and advanced riders a good time and something to get their teeth into. At **Kasprow Wierch**, you will find some fine freeriding to be had in two treeless bowls. Freestylers have had a halfpipe in the past but it s not permanent. Beginners don t fair too well either here and to cap it all, 16 of the 18 lifts are very old and dodgy drag lifts.
Lodging and local facilities are surprisingly very good, offering affordable places to sleep, eat and party close to the slopes.
Fly to: **Kracow** 2 hours away
ⓘ **tel-** ++48 (0) 165 14614

ROMANIA

Time - Zone
GMT +2 Hour (GMT +3 March -April)
Capital - Bucharest
Language - Romanian
Currency - Leu

There has been skiing in some form or another in Romania for almost a hundred years in a country with major mountainous areas. there are about a dozen resorts, some of which are very good and offer excellent riding terrain.
Romanian Ski Association
ⓘ **tel-** ++68 (0) 262 320

Poiana Brasov

▲1770m 14 km of piste 11 lifts
Poiana Brasov is a small resort with just 9 miles of marked out terrain offering some limited advanced carving on the **Valea Lupului** trail to basic freeriding through trees up on the **Postavarul** area. Although the slopes are not noted for having long lift queues, some of the runs can be very busy, especially the beginner areas. Freestylers will have to make do with getting air by building hits and then hiking them as there is no halfpipe here or any good natural kickers.
Off the slopes the purpose built resort is suitable for a few days hangingout with a few cheap hotels and lots of cheap night-life.
Fly to: **Bucharest** 3 hours away
ⓘ **tel-** ++40 (0) 68 262 320

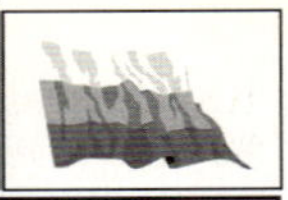

pic - Chris Homer

GENERAL INFO

Capital Moscow
Language - Russian
Currency - Rouble
The Rouble is the official currency. There is an array of coins from 1, 5, 10, 50, and 100 Rouble coins. The best foreign currencies to carry are, US Dollars, German Marks or UK Sterling. Credit cards are widely useable in Moscow, but not in the rest of Russia.

Drugs - Cannabis is illegal
Death Penalty - Doesn t exist
Age of consent for Sex - 16
Military Service - Compulsory
Electricity Supply - 240 Volts AC
International phone Code ++95
Codes from:
Britain - 007
USA - 0117
Canada - 0117
New Zealand - 00117

Visas
All visitors to Russia must have a passport and a valid visa. The maximum visa time for a tourist is 30 days, however, various other visas are available. Such as a business visa which can last for up to 60 days. A transit visa only lasts for 24 hours and is used for individuals who intend only to pass through the country en -route to another. There is a charge for visas and delays brought about due to too much bureaucracy. Contact national embassies for full details.

Medical Services
Euromedical Emergency
tel: 432 1616
European Medical Cnt
tel: 251 6099

A helpful point to note is that most visitors can get free emergency medical care provided the individual has a valid passport.

Time wise
GMT +2 hours

The West s influence has taken over and **Russia** is not the place it used to be. Although snowboarding is now on the scene it s still very much in its infancy here.

The capital city **Moscow**, where everything is freely available at the right price, has a few snowboarding areas. **'Moscow's 3 Hills'** are all within half an hour of the city centre via the extremely efficient Metro. Alternatively get on a suburban *elektrichka* train, pay less than a buck, and head out of the city for more resorts and enter a whole new Russia. The people are friendly and everything is dirt cheap. Okay you get basic lifts, food and accommodation, but you ll see the real Russia and snowboard on uncrowded slopes. The **Caucasus Range** to the south of Russia is home to Europe s highest mountain in **Elbrus**. At 5642m it s larger than the west s best by a few hundred metres.

Snowboarding is possible from mid-November to late April but be prepared for temperatures as low as -25c in mid February. At the resorts equipment hire is occasionally available but it is highly recommended to take your own. English is spoken by some Russians in Moscow, but very few in the southern mountains so learning a few words of Russian will make things a lot easier.

Kant

Kant is located within an industrial estate to the south of Moscow, 20 minutes from **Red Square**, this is Moscow s most accessible hill. From the metro it s only a five minute walk. Generally it is regarded as a club field, with hourly rates of $3 US, available to non-members. One of the most bizarre hills ridden, it has 270 degree views of drab old apartment blocks. It started life as a dump and is classed as an artificial hill. The disused dump was filled with earth, had grass planted on it, and to increase its gradient and length, rubbish was transported from surrounding building sites. This can cause problems with your base when there is limited snow coverage so to counteract this, management often sprinkle sawdust over the thin areas.

The *Kant Sports Club* has four lighted slopes with four *Russian* type Boogie System lifts to serve them. This system requires the rider to hire a boogie and regardless of whether you are goofy or regular the lifts are equally difficult.

The runs are generally about 200 metres long and suited to beginners or intermediates who want to mess around. There are some hits available but the landings are pretty sketchy. Still there is plenty of fun to be had and three piste bashers do their best to keep the slopes in good condition. Near the slopes there is also a cheap cafe and a few shops.

The nearest metro is Nagornaya (on the Grey Line)
Resort for info tel ++ 95 316 9577

Krylatskoye

Krylatskoye is **Moscow's** best local resort with 12 lifts located on two hills and is very small. Runs are 250 to 350 metres long and uncrowded. The slopes are gentle and can be taken at an easy pace for beginners or flat out by intermediate riders. There are also some small natural drop offs and a few hits available.

The lifts, which is an assortment of a boogie system, button lifts and water ski type pullies. are operated by three different companies. A pay as you ride token system operates with tickets being purchased from the kiosk at about 29US cents a go. Piste bashers are not used on the slopes but the runs are often to be found in good condition. The resort, as most things in Russia, is old fashioned and outdated, but has a real fun feel about it. At the bottom of the slopes is a red London bus which has been converted into a cafe.

Krylatskoye slopes are a 20 minute walk, from the Metro station and well worth a visit.
The nearest metro is at Krylatskoye (on the Blue Line).
Resort for info tel ++ 95 480 4308

Sparrow Hills

Sparrow Hills is situated in the south-west of Moscow on the only high ground near the city, it is the smallest of the **Moscow's 3 Hills**. There are two simple slopes, about 250 metres in length, which form a backdrop to the very impressive ski jumps located here. Two boogie lifts serve the runs. The resort is close to the New Moscow State Circus so you can double up on your day with a bit of fun.

Paramonovo

Paramonovo, from Savyolovsky train station in Moscow, is a one hour journey north on an *elektrichka* surban train to the Tourist Station. From the desolate station platform take a 10 minute walk back down the railway line from the direction the train has just come to the main road. From here a taxi can take you the remaining 7km to the Paramonovo slopes. The fare will be about $5US, but be prepared to wait a while as there are few cars around. The resort, a local hunt for the rich Moscovites, is set amongst pine trees in the fresh air and countryside. The advertising literature boasts 10 boogie lift systems covering 10km of piste . This may actually be true but generally as few as 3 lifts operate intermittently which can cause queues at weekends. The runs are similar length to the Moscow s 3 Hills but provide a lot more possibilities for tree riding and sizeable hits. They even have spotters on the main jumps. Boogies cost around $5US (or £3UK) to hire for a day and then all lifts are free. Cheap accommodation is available near the slopes.

Resort for info tel ++ 95 165 90 81

pics - Chris Homer

Travel Guide

Gateway international airport is, **Moscow** (Sheremetevo). The airport is 18 miles out of the city.

Approximate global air travel times to **Moscow:**

from: London 5½ hours
Los Angles 17½ hours
New York 14 hours

Buses services in Russia are cheap and on the whole good but they are also notoriously slow and time tables are a myth.

Train services around the country are okay and very affordable. The metro trains in Moscow are superb with stations that are a work of art. It is also possible to take trains from the west to the east, but you will need to change trains on route as Russia uses a different rail gauge.

Dombai – Russia

MOUNTAIN DATA

Top Lift at - 3051m

Ride Area ?km of piste

Bottom Lift at - 1650m

Vertical Drop - 1450m

Number of Runs - 22

Longest - 3 miles (5km)

TERRAIN LEVELS

Easy	**35%**
Intermediate	**40%**
Advanced	**25%**
Expert =	

TERRAIN TO SUITE

Freeride	**50%**
Trees	Lots
Backcountry	Yes
Freestyle	**15%**
Halfpipe	No
Terrain Park	No
Carving	**5%**

SNOW DATA

Average Snowfall

Snowmaking
Zero

Winter Periods
Nov to May

Summer Riding

SLOPE ACCESS

Total Lifts = **11**

Uplift Rate not available

1 Gondolas
4 Chair lifts - **6** Drag lifts
**Leashes Required*

Lift Times
8.30am to 4.30pm

Lift Pass Rates - *Rouples*

1 Gondola trip	25 Rouples
Cost per lift	2 Rouples
Cat Rides	20 Rouples

Travel Guide

Fly to **Moscow** and then fly inland to Mineral nye Vody which is 62km from Dombai.

Trains, not possible.

Route Planner: Via Mineral nye, you need to head south for a few km s along the M29, cutting off at Essentuki on to the A157 and the A155 via Teberda and to Dombi.

pic - Chris Horner

Set amongst the **Caucasus Mountains** near the **Georgian** border is **Dombai** with its unique atmosphere and visited by your average Russian tourist, many of whom are from the surrounding towns and villages, who tend to go up the mountain to eat, view the peaks and drink Vodka as opposed to boarding. The riding is good with plenty to suite all. The lower slopes provide some runs through the trees which are gentle and ideal for beginners. Even though the mountain has three piste bashers grooming is infrequent and piste markings generally range from poor to non-existent. There are lots of hiking options available although Russians are not big on going off-piste.

The chair lifts and cable cars are from the bygone era and nothing is new. You will see some of the most ingenious repair work undertaken. Take for instance the broken perspex windows of the gondola car, they ve had drilled holes either side of the crack and then sewn it together. The lifts are interesting with a pay as you ride system. When lifts are down, some of the piste basher drivers charge each person to ride on a Cat Track tour. Safety is not high on the list of priorities, but it has to be remembered that this is Russia and anything goes.

Freeriders will find that this is mainly their destination. Due to the limited number of snowboarders (about 5%) when the powder falls it can be ridden for days with no chance of being tracked out.

Off the slopes accommodation is basic, cheap and widely available. Food is filling, service of a Russian standard and don t expect to see a menu when you are here! Try the **Georgian** hot cheeseboard called **Khachapuri.** To get the very most out of a trip would require a translator as foreign languages are generally not spoken. The locals are friendly and are very pleased to meet foreigners, especially English speakers, as they like to practice their language skills and love to share their drink with you. Night time madness is best sampled in the *Hotel Vershiny*. There are two disco/bars and a few places to eat. The ground floor disco is generally more locals with a mixture of European and old Russian *"Pop"*. Snowboard videos are shown behind the DJ s stand and the place has a distinct 70 s feel purely by accident. A swimming pool and a sauna is also available in the hotel but you may need a health card to get in. Overall the place is very interesting and has a very pioneering feel to it. If you are planning a trip to Russia bring your snowboard with you and have an adventure in the **Caucussus**.

Tourist Office Dombai
Dombai
++95 (0) 86522 78168 **Accommodation ++95 (0) 865 58 279**

Overall rating out of 10 — **7** — **A unique experence**

Slovenia

Slovenia is a small European country, surrounded by **Italy, Austria, Hungary** and **Croatia**, which at first seems hard to find, then difficult to leave. Though not one of the famous ski countries it's said to be the land with the oldest known ski-history, and home the longest flood-lit run in Europe. All the resorts are rather small, family oriented and located in the north of Slovenia.

Don't expect well-maintained halfpipes or parks, their snowboard evolution has not quite reached European standards yet. The resorts usually offer decent on slope side accommodation and local services are a lot cheaper than Austrian and other alpine areas. The notable point about Sloveinia s resorts are the cat walk style walk ways connecting lifts. However, at least the lifts don t suffer long queues.

Locals are a friendly bunch and although the main language is Slovene, people speak enough English or German to help you get by.

Riders travelling by car from other parts of Europe will be pleased to find that fuel is only two thirds the price of the **German/Austrian** price, but for using the freeways you have to pay road tolls. Most shops take credit cards but you might have problems finding cash machines for instant cash so make sure you bring enough cash with you.

Public transport around the country is good, but you are really better of having your own transport or a car hire

Pohorje and Areh:

Vertical 325m to 1347m
Park/pipe: None but two jumps no Dragon
No. of lifts:: 1 Gondola, 3 Chairs, 12 Drag lifts
Lift prices : 1 day Adult: 3.700sit Youth: 3.200sit
Lift times Open: 9am to 4pm and 5pm to 9pm
Night riding: yes, with the longest run in Europe
Winter season: Dec- Mar
Tourist information:
+386-62-211262 Sports centre: +386-62-2208841
Snow-report: +386-62-9821. internet: www.sk-branik.si

The **Pohorje Mountains**, lie south of **Maribor**, which is one of the biggest cities in Slovenia. The town has its own airport and is easy to reach by car or train and is only 12 miles from the Austrian border. The snow fall is rather unpredictable, although there is a lot of snowmaking. The whole resort is within the treeline and there's often some amazing freeriding.

Pohorje and **Areh** are separate summits, the top lift stations are interconnected with a free shuttle bus running every hour. There's also catwalks connecting the different lifts but they're very flat and can be a pain in the arse. The **Areh** area is higher so there's better snow and no snowmaking necessary, unfortunately there's only a few drag-lifts. **Pohorje** on the opposite has excessive snow-making, longer runs, the gondola and chair lifts, night riding, and it takes you down all the way to the city.

There's no pipe and the park consists of two hits, which are too icy to be fun. There are some rollers and the catwalks give you something to jump off, but nothing really big. Although this is not a place for advanced riders, it s perfectly okay for beginners and slow intermediate carvers.

To get to the mountain by car from Maribor, just follow the **Pohorje** signs. The car park is only ten minutes from **Maribor.** You can also drive up to **Areh**, taking the highway **E59** to **Ljubiljana**. By bus take the number 6, direction Vzpenjaca .
Accommodation: The hotel *Bellevue*, in the middle of the resort, is now a youth hostel costing from 2.000 sit a night but you'll need to reserve in advance.

ROGLA

Vertical: 1050m to 1517m
Park/Pipe: yes and a pipe Dragon
No. of lifts:: 2 Chairs, 9 Drag lifts
Lift prices : 1 day Adult: 3.400sit, 6 day 14.000sit
Tourist information:
+386-63-7681110. internet: www.unior.siprices:

Rogla is 25 miles from Ljubiljana, Slovenia's capital and is easy to reach by car, taking the E59 highway, exit at Slov.Konjice, from there on you just follow the signs to the summit.

Although **Rogla** recently hosted the *Youth Snowboard World Championships,* this is a very flat resort and not at all challenging. It's laid back and a family hang-out with only a few steep runs which still don't make it worth spending a whole day here. What does make you wanna come back though is the excellent good and cheap pizza place at the summit and the chance to go snowmobiling.

Tourist information: +386-41-508-881

Japan

GENERAL INFO

Capital Tokyo
Language - Japanese
Currency - Yen

Drugs - Cannabis is illegal
Death Penalty - Doesn t exist
Age of consent for Sex - 16
Military Service - Compulsory for males
Electricity Supply - 100 Volts AC 2 pin plugs
International phone Code ++81
English Information Tokyo Tel. 03 3201 3331

Japanese slope levels
Green = Nursery
Red = Intermediate
Blue = Advanced

Language Guide
(Greetings)
Good morning
ohayo gozaimasu
Good afternoon
konnichiwa
Good evening
konbanwa
Excuse me
sumimasen ga
Goodbye
sayonara
Goodnight
oyasumi nasai
Thank you
arigatou
Yes **Hai**
No **Iie**

(Useful Phrases)
Do you speak English?
Eigoga hanasemasu ka
I don't speak Japanese
Watashi wanihon-go ga hanasemasen
Where is____station?
eki wa doko desu ka
A return ticket please
ofuku onegaishimasu
One way
kata michi onegaishi masu
Does this train stop at
kono densha wa -----ni tomarimasu ka
How much is it?
ikura desu ka
Can you tell me the name of a good hotel?
ii hoteru wo shoukai shite kudasai
What is the (hotel's) telephone number?
(hoteru no) denwa bango wa nan ban desu ka

Continued down page

pic - San Tang

Snowboarding has hit **Japan**, *tsunami* -like, and swept away a lot of the discriminatory ski only policies. Every year the situation improves and with the huge number of riders now around there are very few places that can afford to turn away their custom. Some places even cater specifically for riders, notably some of the smaller ones who have developed their terrain parks to attract freestylers. **Oze Tokura** and **Minakami Tenjindaira** are two such examples. Snowboarding in Japan has been greatly influenced by the European scene. Most lift systems are Swiss or Austrian in make and the term ski area is known as the **Ski Gelande** (taken from German). A lot of resorts, restaurants and shops also take French or German names. Night-riding is big in Japan and almost all resorts offer some kind of flood-lit runs. One of the reasons for the popularity of night riding must be the lack of a party scene.

Japanese snowboarders seem to have a lack of experience, a mix of intense reserve and a desire to be noticed by the opposite sex. You will see a lot of riders on their knees looking up-slope in semi-pose mode while wearing the latest gear. The majority of those you meet will be ready to try out their conversational English on you and most can say a few words although whether they can understand you is a different matter.

If you want to buy a snowboard in Japan there's an area of **Tokyo** totally dedicated to sports shops, which from October to March is full of all the gear you could imagine. *Ochanomizu/Kanda* is the place to go for a board. Prices tend to be cheaper than the UK but higher than in the US. The main sports department stores, are **Victoria, Mizuno,** and **Minami**, each with six floors of gear,

Travelling around:
Train - If you're planning on visiting a few different resorts the Japan Rail Pass must be the way to go. Japan's train service is excellent (frequent, clean, on time) but expensive if you buy your tickets in Japan. The Rail Pass can be bought for 7, 14 or 21 day periods from your local tour operator before you travel to Japan. Prices are approximately £150, £220, £280. This is one of the best deals you will get so seriously consider this option. The pass includes unlimited travel on the world renowned bullet trains (shinkansen) which slash hours off your journey.

Bus - If you're staying in Tokyo and want to visit a couple of resorts, most Japanese tour companies run one, two or three day tours to resorts all over **Honshu**. These packages work out much cheaper than doing it alone. *Big Holiday* has 50 buses leaving every night from **Sunshine City** bus terminal near **Lkebukuro** station in Tokyo. The buses all leave around 23.00 and time their journey so that you arrive in your resort by 07.30.

Car - If you want to hire a car out here you'll have to bring your International Driver's License - without which there is no way you are going to be able to climb into the driver's seat. One difficulty will be the language, because working out the insurance terms will be a nightmare. If you have a friend who speaks the language then you stand a far better chance. The cheapest cars can be hired from large companies such as **Toyota**, **Nippon** and **ORIX** from 6000 yen a day but these are dinky toys big enough for only two (at a push!) A reasonably sized saloon car like the Honda Civic will set you back 10,000 yen for 24 hours,

Plane: To get to **Hokkaido** a return airfare works out the same as the train if you don t have a Rail Pass. If you re thinking of flying, it s best to book a whole package tour. Internal flights here are more expensive than short international ones.

Japan Travel: tel (03-3502-1461 (00 88 22-2800 from the UK) is an excellent English language phone service that can tell you anything you want to know concerning transport (fares and timetables) or accommodation. It will even help with language problems.

Japan, especially the north island of **Hokkaido** gets plenty of snow. It s location puts it in the path of the cold air stream that comes off Hokkaido. Before reaching Japan this air stream picks up its moisture over the Japan Sea. It then dumps when it hits the Japan Alps running up the west coast. From January through till March you can expect to have 3m base in most of the serious resorts. Several of the **Honshu** resorts boast a season from October till May, but it s only really in Hokkaido where you can expect to find any decent conditions as late as this. In fact none of the resorts are seriously running until mid-December but a few, in the name of good publicity, spend their money on creating a long strip of snow on a shallow slope and declare themselves open at the end of October. At this time it s still pretty hot and humid.

Basically you have a good 3-4 month period to check things out although you are seriously advised to avoid the slopes at the beginning of January. During the first week of the year the Japanese have a long national holiday granted by most companies - it s as crowded as hell.

Riding off-piste: There are certain resorts, maybe a majority, in Japan where snowboarding is mainly a fashion statement and Tokyoites go for their one day on the slopes every year. These places tend to be pretty strict in the way they control boarding. Often some lifts are still (the number gets fewer every year) closed to boarders and any off piste will be fenced off and patrolled. On the other hand there are a few

pic - Palmer Snowboards

Travel Guide

Gateway international airport is, **Tokyo** which is located on the Honsuu Island

Approximate global air travel times to **Tokyo:**

from: London	$11^{3/4}$	hours
New York	$13^{3/4}$	hours
Zurich	$11^{3/4}$	hours

Language guide continued

A half-day lift pass, please
han nichi ken one gaishimasu
A one-day lift pass, please
ichi nichi ken onegaishimasu
A two-day lift pass, please
futsuka ken onegaishimasu
Where is the lift/pipe/gondola/ski area?
lift/pipe/gondola/ski joÖ wa doko ni ari masu ka
Is all the area open to boarders?
snowboard wa dokodemo dekimasu ka

Typical meals

Menrui (noodles):
Ramen - Chines noodles which are served in steaming hot soy sauce soup with pork Japanese spring onion, fish paste and seaweed. Many varieties of this exist - find your favourite.

Soba - Noodles - buckwheat noodles often served in a hot soup with vegetables and seaweed, fried tofu or tempura (green peppers/pumppkin/shrimp/squid deep-fried in batter).

Udon - Noodles a thicker variety of noodles served in a hot soup as above.

Donburi (rice dishes)

Katsu don - pork cutlet with egg and onions in sweet soy sauce on rice.

Gyudon - Thin strips of beef on rice

Oden - Eggs/giant radish/fish paste/thick seaweed stewed in fish stock and served hot.

Man - Soft Chinese filled rolls with meat, curry, pizza or sweet red bean.

Onigiri - Rice balls wrapped in seaweed paper often with different fillings. The tuna-mayonnaise rice-ball is well adapted to western palettes. Umeboshi (pickled plum) is a little more difficult to stomach.

pic - Mark Elle

areas where the resorts really do cater for the more hardened rider and ski/board patrol will even tell you which backcountry areas are good/safe, and you may meet some locals to ride off with.

Wherever you go, those of you always looking to cut the fresh will be pleased to know that you'll probably find yourself alone, carving the ivory. Japanese are very compliant, so 99% wouldn't dream of leaving the slopes for a little off-piste. There are ski-patrols of course but they are fairly inconspicuous, so the chances of you being whistled at are really slim.

Accommodation in Japan doesn't boast any great deals when it comes to somewhere to put your head for the night. Resort hotels are very popular with the Japanese, who will pay through the nose for a room with a view. The advise is to avoid the western style hotels and go for a traditional Japanese inn (**Ryokan**) or a family-run hotel (**Minshuku**). Both are usually reasonably priced (nice tatami-mat rooms for 7000 yen including evening meal and breakfast are possible) and you get the added feel of authenticity. Normally very small, these hotels are typically very Japanese in style-tatami-mat floors, table heaters, futon, yukata (traditional bath robe) and slippers all make up what can be a very pleasant cultural experience when you're off the slope. The Japanese are quiet lot and for the most part you'll find the staff are extremely welcoming and helpful.

The food in Japanese inns is great and usually traditional, but you ll sometimes even find some western foods on your plate - omelette and ham often appear at breakfast time. If you can stomach fish, rice and natto (curdled soy beans) in the morning, all power to you- it's a great way to prepare the body for the day's onslaught on the slopes.

Resort food, is usually pretty varied although there seems to be a 'standard' menu which you'll find at pretty much every resort. Meals range from western snacks like hotdogs and fries to Japanese noodle and rice dishes. Recommended is the quintessentially Japanese ski lunch of curry, pork cutlet and rice, washed down with a can of Asahi Superdry, Japan's premium beer. All for about 1500 yen, usually obtained by exchanging a ticket bought at a vending machine (jidoo hanbaiki). Look lost and forlorn if confused - someone will help you! For those you like to pig out big style, will find that some resorts offer all-you-can-eat (viking) deals for around 1500-2000 yen, which allows you to stuuf down various strange fish and traditional noodle dishes.

pic - Mark Elle

There are hundreds of slopes in Japan, and, contrary to what you may have heard it is possible to have an excellent time riding here. But don t expect to find resorts on a large European scale. Japan has 4 main islands with snowboarding mainly limited to Honshu, the biggest island and home to the majority of the population. The northern island of Hokkaido is the other resort destination.

Lift passes generally cost between 4,000 yen (£20) and 5,000 yen (£25) per day and are only slightly discounted if you purchase more than a days worth. Passes can be bought with cash at the resort, or just as easily at convenience stores all over country. (Lawson, AM-PM, 7-Eleven and Family Mart are the main ones). These stores usually produce a pamphlet listing the resorts they offer passes for. Their prices, which include 1,500 yen or so worth of lunch vouchers, are better value than buying at the resorts themselves.

Tokyo - indoor slopes

SSAWS (pronounced **'zaus'**) stands for Spring, Summer, Autumn, Winter, Snow, and is the biggest indoor slope in the world. Despite the expense (it costs as much as a "real" resort) it's worth a visit mainly for the novelty. It even has two chair-lifts inside as well as a travellator. The dome itself is huge and contains two slopes of different gradients. Both give 80m vert and are 490m long although one starts off steeper (20 degrees). They're cool for mucking around on and just about long enough to keep you happy for a morning. There's also a small hit but overall it s best for beginners.

With snowboarding being so hugely popular, the dome is very busy all year round, especially at weekends and evening times when you could queue a long while for a run which you can flat all the way down in seconds. Everything is automated so at busy periods they restrict your slope time to ensure the runs don't start to resemble the streets of Tokyo.

A day pass cost from 5,400 yen (about £28!). With the pass you could use the slope all day (switching from board to skis) but only if you have skis. Rentals are available but will push the price up.

SSAWS is a 30min-train journey on the **Chuo Line** running east from **Tokyo** station. Get off at **Minami-Funabashi** station from where it s only a five-minute walk. You can't miss the huge dome. By car it's also easily accessible and visible from the **Higashi Kanto Expressway** , half way between **Tokyo** and **Narita.**

Coolval Tokyo (03-5392-9006), an indoor boarder's only slope, in Tokyo, is a lot smaller than SSAWS but does have a pipe. The slope's is 65m long and open 10.00 - 23.30 all year round and costs around £12-14 for 90 minutes use. To get here, it s a 5 min walk from **Ukimahunado** station on the **Saikyo** line, 20 mins north from **Ikebukuro** and **Shinjuku**.

On the Hokkaido Island,

Niseko

pic - Mark Elle

Top lift 1175m. 38 Runs 22 Lifts

Niseko is the best of the Japanese resorts and compares well with resorts in North America and Europe. Niseko is mostly a freeriders resort and the main attraction has to be its big mountain terrain. During the months of January and February you can expect regular and major dumps of snow which you can quite often still be ridden in mid-April. continued over

Niseko is essentially one mountain although it is divided up into three linked areas covered by one mountain pass. This area does have avalanches so check with the ski patrols to get the latest info.

Niseko-Hirafu (0136-22-0109) 1200m. If you have to choose just one resort to ride at Niseko, it should be **Hirafu**. For freestylers there is a well maintained half-pipe at the top of lift 4 as well as a small park near the bottom of the **Alpen Course**. It is also possible to shred some trees to the right of lift 7 and on the hillside across to the left of the **Alpen** chair lift.

Niseko-Higashiyama (0136-44-1111) 1170m-320m. **The Prince Hotel Group** runs Higashiyama and also the only hotel at the base on this side of the mountain. There are tree runs. On the piste, the green *Down hill/Family* course from top to bottom of the **Prince Gondola** is a long cat track with a few cool air points.

Niseko Annupuri Kokusai (0136-58-2080) 1156m-400m. Annupuri is the most exposed to high winds and on a bad day the top runs may be closed. This can be a problem if you want to link the three resorts although a bus also runs around the base of the mountain. There is more beginner and intermediate terrain here, although the runs at the very top are the best on the hill for carvers who can.

The tops of **Annupuri, Higashiyama**, and **Hirafu** are all within a few hundred metres hike of the top of the mountain (1308m). From here you can ride down backcountry to **Goshiki Onsen** (hot springs) on the opposite side of the mountain. To get back you ll need a taxi or the infrequent bus.

Niseko Kokusai Moiwa 0136-58-2016) 930m-420m, is a cheaper and much smaller resort on a lower peak just to the west of the main mountain. It is probably only worth a trip if you have more than 3 or 4 days in the area, but it is reputed to offer some great backcountry riding.

Backcountry tours can be organised through the *Niseko Outdoor Adventure Sports Club* (0136-23-1688), which has a shop and office near the Hirafu base. One day will set you back 9500 yen.

Getting here is easy, you can fly to **Sapporro Chitose International Airport** and catch a direct (4 hour) bus, or take a train from **Sapporo** which will take slightly less time, at around 3 hours.

For accommodation, it is often best to book a package deal. This way your accommodation will be arranged for you. If you want to plan everything yourself; either call the tourist office (0136-22-5151 (Hirafu), or try the **Alpen** (0136-22-1105) or **Prince Hotels** (0136-44-1111). Both are large and located at the foot of the slopes. They offer both Western and Japanese style services. Expect to pay upwards of £50 a night unless you hit on a deal, usually for five or more people.

Other **Hokkaido** Hills, are **Asahidake** (0166-97-2234) and its located in the centre of Hokkaido with two lifts and where you're free to make your own route down (a major draw point in regulated Japan). There are plenty of trees and with Hokkaido's excellent snow record there is usually plenty of powder.

Furano

Furano (0167-22-1111) is a major summer and winter resort. It is run by the **Prince Hotels Group**, which offers the largest hotel slopeside. There is also plenty of accommodation to be had in the town. It can be reached by bus from either **Sapporo** or **Asahikawa** (the nearest airport). This place is one of Japan's most famous ski areas and has hosted World Cup ski events. There's a big night skiing area, plenty of trees and natural hits for freeriders and also long groomed runs for carvers. In the centre of Hokkaido it is known to get very cold in January which means the powder usually remains fine.

pic - Furano Resort

Sapporo Kokusai (011-598-4511) is 30 minutes from Sapporo, is well set up for boarders with both a park and pipe. You can find good freeriding and some excellent riders. Japanese who decide to do a season but don't want to move to a resort itself, often take a part time job in Sapporo and spend their free time riding here. Sapporo was one of the first in Japan to actively encourage riders. The run below the gondola is fun, while a hike to the top gives access to some backcountry.

On the Honshu Island,

Hachimantai (0195-78-2212) 1450m. Hachimantai in the **Tohoku** region could be done as a "day" trip with the overnight bus from Tokyo, but really it's pretty far north on the way to **Hokkaido**. There are plenty of good natural hits, an excellent halfpipe and some decent backcountry.

Appi Kohgen (0195-73-5111) 1300m-502m. A large modern resort with runs which are cut out through trees.

Zao

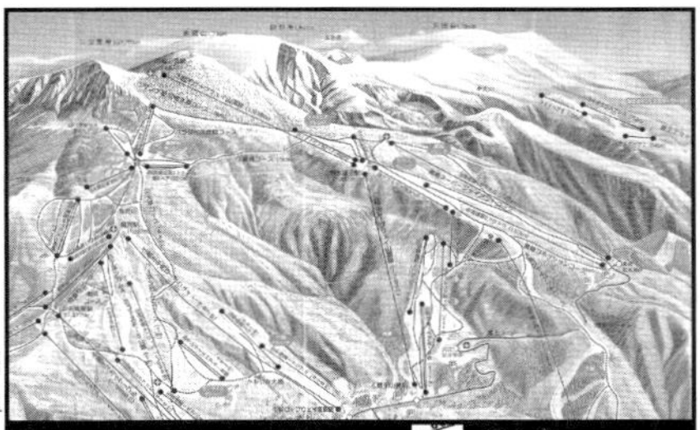

pic - Zao

Top lift 1660m. 60 Runs 42 Lifts

Zao (0236-94-9328) is a major winter resort. The runs are long and well suited to carving or freeriding but with only a limited amount of off-piste and tree runs.

Getting here; take the bullet train ($2^{1/2}$ hours) from **Tokyo** to **Yamagata** from where it is a 40 minute bus ride up to the mountain (18000 yen return). A cheaper option is to catch a night bus (12000 yen return) but this means 7 hours on a coach.

Manza Onsen (0279-97-3117) is a high resort by Japanese standards but also pretty small. Just down the road from Manza Onsen is **Omote Manza** which is a more popular resort with boarders.

Oze Tokura (0278-58-7511) 1420m-1080m, is a small resort within 3 hours drive of Tokyo. It has become well known by dedicating itself to snowboarders and organising regular events. The mountain itself is nothing special, but freestylers should enjoy the funpark and halfpipe.

Tanigawadake Tenjindaira (0278-72-3575) is a small ski area and if you stick to the marked courses you'll soon get bored. Despite this it's popular with local riders because of the large backcountry area that it gives access to. It's also a high level resort by Japanese standards and is open with natural snow from December to May. Located just above **Minakami** in **Gunma Prefecture**, this is a place where you have to be careful not to be caught by the ski patrol if you decide to ride off into the unknown. The Japanese call such patrols urusai, which means loud or "noisy". There are quite a few riders who base themselves here for a season partly because of the cheaper season pass. The best time to visit is between mid-January and the beginning of March, when there is enough snow to ride down to the base of the gondola giving the resort an extra 300metres of vertical. The only problem is that your day lift pass doesn't cover the gondola so if you try a longer run you should do it late in the day or make sure that you can afford the £5 a time gondola charge. There's loads of accommodation in **Minakami** town. There's a tourist office opposite the station that will help you out.

Minakami Okutone (0278-72-8101) 1083m-650m is a small resort popular with riders because of the easy road access and relatively cheap lift pass. The main attraction is the halfpipe.

Iwappara (0257-87-3211) 985m-400m. 10 minutes from EY station, is mainly suited to beginners and intermediates and has some wide open runs for carving.

Kandatsu Kohgen (0257-85-5111) 1000m-460m. On a good snow day this is the pick of the resorts near to the station and offers some steep terrain and tree runs below the lifts. The black runs aren t groomed so leaving plenty to shred.

GALA Yuzawa (0257-85-6543) 1181m-800m. Conveniently located, it even has its own bullet train stop, (one along from **Echigo Yuzawa**) this is a modern set-up, especially popular with the younger day trippers. Here you don t have to endure a 10-minute bus journey but you will have to put up with higher prices and unfriendly staff (even a single locker costs £5).

Maiko Kohgen Korakuen (0257-83-3211) 920m-260m. 15 minutes by bus from **Echigo Yuzawa** this resort offers all types of riding. There is a pipe, a tiny park and plenty of terrain to keep freeriders happy. Out of the resorts, near to EY station it s perhaps the only one where freeriders could enjoy consecutive days and actually find something different.

Joetsu Kokusai (0257-82-2745) 1017m-200m, is a little further afield (30-mins by bus). It has one of the largest terrain parks (i.e. more than 4 jumps) in Japan and two good pipes. These are both in front of the Edwardian looking hotel. For freeriders the Osawa slopes are best. This is a good resort for boarders, although some of the lifts are old and slow. It is not worth visiting the peak.

Muikamachi Hakkaisan (0257-75-3311) 1170m-355m can be a powder paradise in January and February. It is an hour further west from Echigo Yuzawa (30-mins by local train to Muikamachi, then 30-mins by bus). Because of this it is usually less busy but still managable in a day trip from Tokyo. The resort is especially popular with skiers out to enjoy the moguls, so there is usually plenty of terrain left for freeriding. Below the gondola is a 3km downhill course that will take it out of you. The No. 3 chairlift lets you enjoy a shorter workout. The **Raku** (easy) course allows you to cut through the thick forest and offers plenty of air points but there is no pipe or park. The area itself is one of the most famous in Japan for sake (rice wine) which you will no doubt get to taste if you stay here. In the winter **'Atsukan'** (hot rice wine) is good for warming you up, it s available here and in all other resorts.

pic - Mark Elte

Top lift 1065m. 44 Runs 17 Lifts

Naeba

Naeba (0257-89-2211) 1789m-900m. Naeba is perhaps the most famous resort in Honshu and more like a western one in terms of the number of hotels and other things going on. It is a 45-mins bus journey from Echigo Yuzawa station. Snowboarding has been allowed all across the hill since the 98/99 season and they have now built their own mini park and regularly host air contests. However, there is no pipe and the resort is best for freeriders. Similarly to Niseko and Zao, you can happily enjoy three or four days here without getting bored. There are some excellent tree runs if you duck the ropes and because of the lack of Japanese who do this you're always able to make your own tracks. The best spots for doing this are below the No. 1 gondola, and of the No. 2 gondola.

Accommodation in Naeba is operated by the Prince Group, which offers a variety of modern slopeside accommodation (0257-89-2311). Prices start from £45 per person unless you are in a group of more than four. Although if you call in advance there are usually special deals going, including lift pass. **Oji Pension** (0257-89-3675) is just 5 minutes walk behind the Prince Hotel, and is run by the friendly Mr. Sakamoto. He has a stock of new rental boards and a Brazil shirt signed by Pele. A futon, breakfast and evening meal should cost around 7500 yen, and he can sort you out with lift pass discounts.

Shin-Etsu - Nagano

pic - Mark Elte

Shiga Kohgen (0269-3402404) includes about 10 separate resorts, among which is **Yakebitaiyama** where the first Olympic snowboarding gold medal was won.

Kitashinshu Kijimadaira is home to regular snowboard contests and good for both freeriding and freestyling.

Nozawa Onsen (0269-85-2068) is a major ski resort in **Nagano** with a big area and beautiful views. Riders were banned up till '98 and were only allowed on a few green runs in '99. Rumours have it that the whole area will be opened up from 2000, which should give excellent back-country possibilities. Check with the local tourist office however before you commit. It's famous for its hot springs and thus has plenty of accommodation on offer.

Myoko Kohgen (0255-86-3911) **Seki Onsen** is a resort, which understands the needs of the powder hounds. Near the west coast in **Niigata Prefecture** it has a great snow record, often with 1m plus dumps overnight in Jan/Feb. There's a decent pipe and some good natural hits and kickers. Locals or the patrol will advise you on back country riding - they'll also tell you that you have to take responsibility for yourself, although in the land of group culture it's cool to find somewhere that lets you do this. Seki Onsen is the home resort for **Masanori Takeuchi**, a well-known Japanese rider.

Hakuba 47 (0261-75-3533) 1620m-820m, and **Happo-one** (0261-72-3066) 1831m-760m are both major winter hang-outs although up until now they have not been totally snowboarder friendly. Both would be worth a visit if they open up all their area to riders. Check in advance.

Arai Mountain & Snow Park

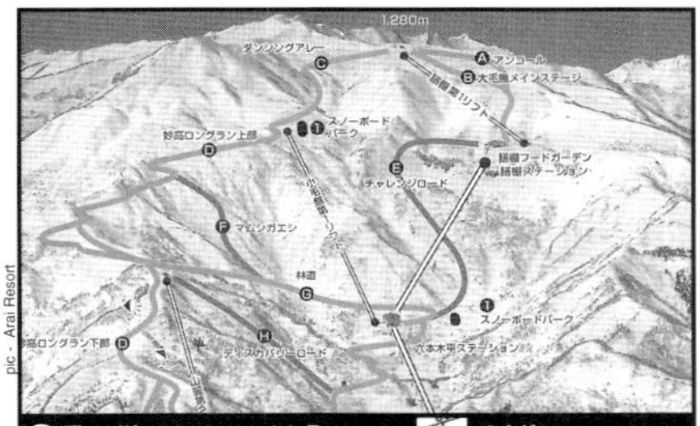

pic - Arai Resort

Top lift 1280m. 14 Runs 6 Lifts

Arai Mountain & Snow Park (0255-70-1111) 1280m-329m. Arai Mountain Resort has been running for less than 10 years and was developed by the *Sony Corporation*. As a result the facilities are quality, and unlike a lot of other Japanese resorts the lifts are all new and fast. It's definitely one of the best resorts on **Honshu** and attracts some very good riders. It often hosts rider camps in the spring and international contests. The terrain is in a bowl and even allows for a little hiking (unfortunately banned by most resorts here). There are two very well kept pipes but the main attraction is the powder resulting from the big dumps because of its location in the first mountain range west of the Japan Sea. This could also be seen as its main drawback as it is a long way from **Tokyo.**

To get to **Arai.** take the bullet train to **Nagano** (2 hours from Tokyo) then a local train (1hr 40mins) then a free shuttle bus (15-mins) to the slopes. All this will set you back about £90 in train fares, so it may be worth looking into bus tours if you don t have a rail pass.

The Club Hotel

Tel ++81 (0) 255 70 1500

Westwoods Hotel

Tel ++81 (0) 255 70 1100

pic - Mark Eite

JAPANESE ROUND UP

Appi
▲1290m 55km of piste with 40 trails 30 lifts
Fly to: **Hanamaki**
ⓘ **tel-** ++81 (0) 195 735011

Hunter Mountain
▲1638m 12km of piste with 12 trails 8 lifts
Fly to: **Tokyo**
ⓘ **tel-** ++81 (0) 287 324 580

Mitsumata Kagura
▲1845m 35km of piste with 38 trails 25 lifts
Fly to: **Tokyo** 40 minutes away.
ⓘ **tel-** ++81 (0) 257 889 006

Oze Iwakura
▲1703m 20km of piste with 20 trails 15 lifts
Fly to: **Tokyo** 2 hours away.
ⓘ **tel-** ++81 (0) 278 583 222

Rusutsu
▲995m 40km of piste with 35 trails 18 lifts
Fly to: **Sapporo Chitose**
ⓘ **tel-** ++81 (0) 136 463 111

Sahoro
▲1030m 20km of piste with 25 trails 10 lifts
Fly to: **Sapporo Chitose** 1-1/2 hours away.
ⓘ **tel-** ++81 (0) 1566 4667

Shiga Yakebitaiyama
▲2000m 80km of piste with 114 trails 24 lifts
Fly to: **Matsumoto**
ⓘ **tel-** ++81 (0) 269 342 404

Shizukushi
▲1356m 33km of piste with 28 trails 18 lifts
Fly to: **Hanamaki**
ⓘ **tel-** ++81 (0) 196 932 520

Togari
▲1050m 20km of piste with 26 trails 12 lifts
Fly to: **Nagano**
ⓘ **tel-** ++81 (0) 269 653 161

Togari
▲1050m 20km of piste with 26 trails 12 lifts
Fly to: **Nagano**
ⓘ **tel-** ++81 (0) 269 653 161

GENERAL INFO AND FACTS

Capital - Canberra
Language - English
Currency - Australian Dollar A$
Alcohol drinking age - 18
Drugs - Cannabis is illegal
Death Penalty - Doesn t exist
Age of consent for Sex - 16
Military Service -Not Compulsory
Electricity Supply - 240 Volts AC
International phone Code ++61
Highest Peak -

AUSSIE DRIVE GUIDE
All vehicles drive on the left hand side of the road
Speed Limits -
Motorways 110kph (68mph)

TIME ZONES
Australia & Pacific
GMT +8 and 10 Hours

Main international Gateway Airport

Sydney
Melbourne

pic -Mt Buller Resort

Australia has some nine resorts located on the eastern mountain ranges on the state boarders of **New South Wales** and **Victoria**. There are also places to ride on the separate southern based island of **Tasmania.** All the main land resorts are easy to reach from the two major ports of entry, **Melbourne** and **Sydney**.

Overall Australian snowboarding opportunities are no where near as good as what is available in **Europe**, **North America** or in near by **New Zealand**. Still, to make up for dull mountains with below average slopes, Aussie's have a reputation for being party animals (better described as drunken louts with no culture really).

Road travel in Australia is good but with the draw back of having to pay high toll charges at the entry gates to mountain ski resort areas. Once through the entrance gate, snow chains must be carried at all times. It s illegal not to have them and could result in a A$200 fine.

Melbourne and **Sydney** both offer airborne answers to your inland travel problems, although they are not recommended due to high cost. Melbourne even has a domestic helicopter service for getting around.

If a train ride through the countryside is what you seek enroute to a resort, then central station in **Sydney** or **Spencer Street** in Melbourne is where you should head for. Melbourne doesn t have a direct train line going to any of the alpine regions, however, Sydney on the other hand has a direct train line to **Jindabyne** which is a central location for the resorts in **New South Wales.**

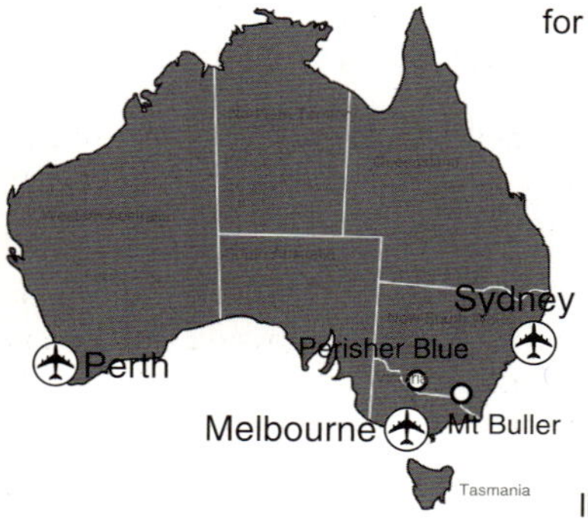

Bus companies run daily trips from major cities to the better resorts. Cost varies depending on which mountain you are going to visit. For around A$55 single you can let some one else drive while you kick back and watch a video.

Accommodation will vary depending on your budget. Five star chalets lodges, club lodges and hostels can all be found above the snowline but it may be cheaper if a bed is sought in a nearby town.

If you want to spend a season in Australia it would be best to get here in late April, because this is when resorts start advertising job in daily papers etc. The normal Australian winter season is between June and mid September.

Mount Buller

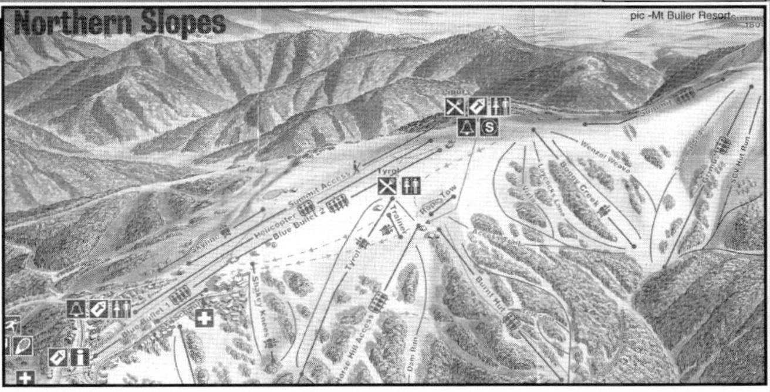

MOUNTAIN DATA

Top Lift at - 1790m

Ride Area
80m of piste

Bottom Lift at - 1390m

Vertical Drop - 400m

Number of Runs -

Longest -1.6miles (2.5km)

TERRAIN LEVELS

Easy	**25%**
Intermediate	**45%**
Advanced	**30%**
Expert =	

TERRAIN TO SUITE

Freeride	**60%**
Trees	Yes
Backcountry	Yes
Freestyle	**20%**
Halfpipe	Yes 1
Terrain Park	Yes 1
Carving	**20%**

SNOW DATA

Average Snowfall
1.5 metres

Snowmaking
15% cover of the slopes

Winter Periods
June to October

Summer Riding
None

SLOPE ACCESS

Total Lifts = **27**

Uplift Rate - 40,000 people an hour.

13 Chair lifts -

14 Drag lifts

**Leashes Required*

Lift Times
8.30am to 4.30pm

Lift Pass Rates

1 Day pass	A$55
3 Day pass	A$170
7 Day pass	A$385

Travel Guide

Fly to **Melbourne** international airport which is 248 miles away and will take 5 hours by bus to reach.

Route Planner:
Via Melbourne, take the Maroondah highway route 153 north to Mansfield and then follow signs for Mt Buller.

Mt. Buller is 400 acres of riding pleasure, with 26 lifts that would, in a perfect world, whisk 39,500 snowboarders per hour up the 400m vertical rise so they could make the best of Victoria s largest trail system. **Buller** as it is affectionately known is the closest major resort to **Melbourne** so weekend riding is not recommended, unless you enjoy lift lines and busy slopes. The terrain mix at Buller will keep all levels of rider amused for sometime, with an even spread between all levels.

Freeriders who like their terrain with a side serve of steeps, should head for the summit and try to tame **Fannys Finnish** or **Fast One** which are Bullers most notorious black diamond runs. If you have conquered Fannys then it must be time to head backcountry with the best reached by hiking out past the fire hut on the summit to a place known as **Buller Bowls**. The bowl is serious terrain that will avalanche if given the chance, so it is best to check conditions with the ski patrol. If tree runs take your fancy then slip off the side of **Standard** and make tracks between the snowgums. If you are early it is possible to get fresh tracks in the powder stashes in this area.

Freestylers have an abundance of natural hits which makes the trails resemble a spread out fun-park. Buller has a snowcat with a halfpipe blade mounted on the back to shape the pipe which is located on the **Summit Ridge**.

Carvers, the runs can often be a bit rutted, but with some good early morning grooming, speed freaks can cut some nice fast tracks down a number of well spaced trails to suit all levels.

Beginners will manage perfectly well at Buller, with a good selection of easy slopes that are crowd free on weekdays but crowd drenched on weekends. Rookies should go and get a lesson from one of the professional instructors at the ski school, which also offers a *'Discover Boarding'* lift ticket.

Off the slopes Mt Buller is a equipped resort with great options for doorstep riding. Buller has the most on-mountain accommodation in Victoria, so guests can stay above the snowline and take full advantage of the fact that Buller has the largest number of alpine restaurants and night-spots in the state with partying up here going on until day light hours. But note this is an expensive resort that attracts Aussie s finest.

For accommodation listings visit - **www.worldsnowboardguide.com**

Tourist office Mt Buller
Buller Ski Lifts.
++61 (0) 3 5777 6052 **www.skibuller.com**

Overall rating out of 10 **6** **A cool resort with a good vibe**

Perisher Blue

MOUNTAIN DATA

Top Lift at - 2034m

Ride Area 3008 acres

Bottom Lift at - 1650m

Vertical Drop - 350m

Number of Runs - 95

Longest - 2 miles (3km)

TERRAIN LEVELS

Easy	**30%**
Intermediate	**50%**
Advanced	**20%**
Expert =	

TERRAIN TO SUITE

Freeride	**50%**
Trees	Yes
Backcountry	Yes
Freestyle	**25%**
Halfpipe	Yes 1
Terrain Park	Yes 1
Carving	**25%**

SNOW DATA

Average Snowfall
250cm a season

Snowmaking
Over 85 acres

Winter Periods
June to October

Summer Riding
None

SLOPE ACCESS

Total Lifts = **51**

Uplift Rate - 62,000 people an hour.

12 Chair lifts -

39 Drag lifts

**Leashes Required*

Lift Times
8.30am to 4.30pm

Lift Pass Rates

1 Day pass	A$73
3 Day pass	A$205
7 Day pass	A$315

Travel Guide

Fly to **Sydney** airport with a 6 hour transfer time.

Train services are possible to Jindabyne which is 45 minutes away.

Route Planner: From Sydney, head south to Jindabyne and then take the Kosciuszko road to reach Perisher Blue. Jindabyne to Perisher is 20 mile (33km).

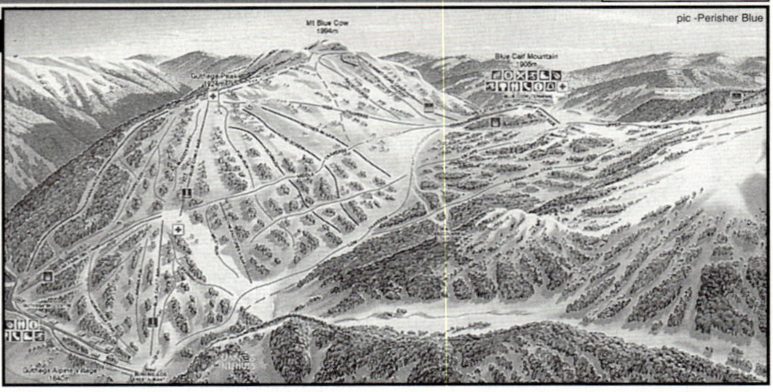

pic -Perisher Blue

Perisher Blue is in the **Kosciusko** National park in the **Snowy Mountains**. **Mt Kosciusko**, the highest point in the country is called Australia s *'Super Resort* as it has come about through the amalgamation of a number of resorts including, **Perisher**, **Blue Cow**, **Guthega** and **Smiggins.** There are 1250 hectares of ride-able terrain with an elevation to 2054m. However the vertical descent is only about 350m. Nevertheless they have installed over 50 lifts and the Australians make the most of the terrain available. Another plus is the huge amount of encouragement for snowboarders. There is a fun-park, a separate *Board Riders* school a woman s snowboard programme, a Board rider s guide and the *Addiction Snowboard* store where they will tune and groom your stuff. The mountain itself has a good range of difficulties but unfortunately the black runs are few and far between. Also if you stick too much to pisted areas you will find little to challenge riders above intermediate standard. Most of the black runs are accessible by T-bar only and it really is a drag.

Freeriders should check out the **Guthega** and **Blue Cow** areas. There are winding creek beds and some nice little rock drop offs. For powder try out the **Burnum**, **Eyre** and **Leichhardt** runs, thought don t bother in September as it s all gone.

Freestylers, the fun-park has the potential to be fantastic but by the end of the season (Sep-Oct) the lack of maintenance begins to show. Talking to the locals the park is over rated in the guides but they are obviously happy that any provision was made at all. It runs the full gammet of toys from a boardercross style series of quarter pipes to plastic picnic tables, barrels and rails.

Beginners there are plenty of open easy slopes. However, although there are over 50 lifts most of these are T-bars and J-bars which are slow and not very snowboarder friendly.

Hotels in the resort cost at least $130-A a night. However you can stay just outside the resort for around $65 for bed, brekie and a huge supper. Don t worry about getting around because there is a free bus service between **Perisher** and **Smiggins** every ten minutes. There are no hostels or lodges for riders on a tight budget but if you ask around you could secure some floor space with a local rider. Night life here comes as standard grade Australian, very boozy and with Ozzy girls flashing their tits.

For accommodation listings visit - **www.worldsnowboardguide.com**

Pershier Blue Tourist Office
Po Box 42, Pershier Valley. NSW
++61 (02) 64 59 44 21 **www.perisherblue.com**

Overall rating out of 10 **6** **Not bad for some simple riding**

New South Wales resorts

Charlotte Pass

▲ 1920m ⊠ 4 lifts.
Charlotte Pass is located some 310 miles (500 km) south of Sydney. The resort is the highest in New South Wales and provides a rather small amount of rideable terrain with only five access lifts. Overall the area will suit slow learning beginners and carvers without a brain. Still the slopes are crowd free and will do for an afternoons fun. But forget about staying for more than a day or two (dull is the word).

Accommodation is conveniently located near the slopes at the Kosciusko Chalet, which offers mid priced beds, eating and a bar.
Fly to: **Canberra.**
ⓘ **tel-** ++61 (0) 575 211

Mount Selwyn

◊ 12 km of piste ⊠ 12 lifts.
Mount Selwyn is a small resort that is the ideal family ski resort but totally dull for any advanced snowboarder. The small amount of terrain on offer is best suited to piste loving slow going carvers.

The nearest accommodation and local facilities are to be found in the town of Adaminaby.
Fly to: **Sydney** 5 hours away.
ⓘ **tel-** ++61 (0) 549 488

Thredbo Alpine Village

▲ 2037m ◊ 70 km of piste ⊠ 12 lifts.
Thredbo is a large resort that has the highest lift access slopes and longest trail in Australia. Extensive use of snowmaking and good piste grooming make this a cool place for a weeks stay. The terrain here is equally matched for all levels and styles of riding with much of the mountain suited to intermediates. Although there are a number of steep advanced runs to keep hardcore freeriders happy for a good few days. Freestylers will also be pleased to find that there are a number of places to gain air from some big natural hits. There is also a good halfpipe and terrain park which has a series of man made jumps. Carvers have some really nice runs to excel on including a rather long trail that measures almost 6km (the longest trail in Australia0. The beginner slopes here are ideal for first timers with easy runs on the upper sections as well as on the lower areas making the whole mountain accessible.

The nearest accommodation and local facilities are located at the base of the slopes with a selection of hotels restaurants, sporting attractions and shopping. Nightlife is very lively but basic.
Fly to: **Sydney** 5 hours away.
ⓘ **tel-** ++61 (0) 64 594 100

Victoria resorts

Mount Baw Baw

Mt Baw Baw is a small resort and the closest to the city of Melbourne. Overall nothing grabs you about this place unless you are a total beginner with a few hours to kill. The eight lifts cover a mixture of uneven terrain with a splattering of trees and gentle pistes that will suite carvers.

Local facilities are basic but very good with a choice of lodges and holiday apartments although not all that affordable apart from the Youth Hostel ++64 (0) 65 1129
Fly to: **Melbourne** 1 1/2 hours away.
ⓘ **tel-** ++64 (0) 3 764 9939

Mount Buffalo

Mount Buffalo is not only a well established resort with a long history as a ski resort, but also a dull boring novices hangout that will bore the tits off any advanced freerider within an hour of being here.
Fly to: **Melbourne** 2 1/2 hours away.
ⓘ **tel-** ++64 (0) 3 764 9939

Mount Butler

▲ 1790m ◊ 80 km of piste ⊠ 26 lifts.
Big resort with a lot of terrain to suit all levels and all rider styles. The resort has a healthy attitude towards snowboarding and allows riders on all the slopes as well as provide two halfpipes and a fun park to please halfpipes.
Fly to: **Melbourne** 2 hours away.
ⓘ **tel-** ++64 (0) 357 776 077

Falls Creek

▲ 1780m ◊ 75km of piste ⊠ 22 lifts.
Falls Creek is a well developed modern resort that will make a weeks stay well worth it but any longer a bit tedious. The 90 or so marked out trails are evenly split between beginner and advanced level, but although there are a lot of runs none are that long. Still the terrain is good and expert riders will find a selection off steep runs of the Ruined Castle chairlift which also gives access to some open sections as well as a route down to the terrain park. Carvers, who like to go fast, will be able to down the fast, blacks of the International T-bar , while beginners will find the Eagle chair gives access to good nursery slopes.

Lots of good accommodation exists at the base of the slopes in Falls Creek village where you will shops, bars and restaurants.
Fly to: **Albury** 1 hour away.
ⓘ **tel-** ++61 (0) 357 583 224

Mount Hottam

▲ 1850m ◊ 245 hectares ⊠ 13 lifts.
Mount Hottam is Australia s highest resort and thus is the most snow sure area. The slopes area is a mixture of easy to negotiate beginners runs to tricky fast steeps that often cross between the more gentle slopes, so novice beware, one minute you could be riding down a simple blue and the next minute hurtling down a steep black trail (study your piste map). Generally this is a resort that will suit intermediate freeriders with a number of very good trails that take you off the piste and in and out of open bowls and wide snow fields. Some of the best freeride trails can be found off the Heavenly Valley chair lift which will give you access to some short but steep blacks that although may not take too long to do, they will however, test you to the limits. Over the last few years the resort has expanded its terrain cover which now includes some double diamond runs that are seriously steep and not for wimps. They are reached by the Gotcha chair lift which also takes you over to some nice blue out back trails. Carvers will love this place as it will suite your style of riding with twisting fast trails that take you over the whole area. Total Beginners only have a couple of green trails which are located right up at the top of the Summit chair, however quick learners will soon be able to tackle the array of blue trails with some of the most interesting to be found off the Village quad chair lift. Freestylers who like fly high off natural hits will find loads of cool drop offs and lots of natural lips to gain air from. There is also a cool halfpipe and okay terrain park to check out.

Generally this is an expensive resort but it offers lots of things to do, all of which are well appointed for both on the slopes and the slope side village. Off the slopes visitors will find an abundance of resort facilities with a large selection of well placed hotels, lodges and other accommodation outlets that collectively can sleep over 4000 holiday makers. The village has a good selection of places to get a meal in and a number of good late night drinking outlets.
Fly to: **Melbourne** 2 hours away.
ⓘ **tel-** ++61 (0) 357 593 550

NEW ZEALAND

New Zealand (NZ) is located in the south western **Pacific** and consists of two main islands, North and South, and several smaller ones. There are around twelve public snowboarding resorts and a dozen or so areas operated by private clubs know as **Club Fields** .

The international gateway airports are, **Auckland** and **Wellington** for North Island resorts, with **Christchurch** and **Queenstowns** serving South Island areas. The average journey time from London is 21 hours with a few stop overs.

Driving in NZ is an economical way to get around. Car hire services are available at all the airports, when hiring you should ask about deals for road trips to the mountains, these can include discounts on accommodation and lift passes. Campervans are a cheap hire option with a five day hire costing from $460.

Bus travel in **NZ** is cheap and convenient, either with a local bus company or one of the majors with most resorts covered. You can travel from **Queenstown** to **Christchurch** for around $40.

Most resorts can be reached by train which is not that expensive. However, you need to transfer by local bus, in most cases this will be under 12 miles.

Taking a Snowboard Tour is a good idea if you re visiting **NZ** for a short time, as it would help maximise your time on the mountain. There are a number of companies offering all inclusive boarding tours for **New Zealand,** shop around because prices are competitive.

New Zealand resorts tend to have very limited on-mountain accommodation, so you will be most likely staying in some nearby town. Naturally, these vary in size as does the night-life from the busy, party towns to the quieter club fields. For example, **Queenstown** has some 20 bars and clubs and is often referred to as the action and adventure capital of **NZ**. **Wanaka** or **Methven**, on the other hand, are much quieter and more relaxed with only 2 or 3 bars. Choose according to your tastes and desires, but don t worry the snowboarding scene in NZ is excellent.

Snowboarding aside, New Zealand offers a huge selection of other outdoor activities. White-water rafting, river surfing, jet boating etc, and of course NZ is the birth place for bungee jumping. So if you like the flow of adventure and have money to burn, then NZ is a must destination.

GENERAL INFO AND FACTS

Capital - Wellington
Language - English
Currency - New Zealand Dollar NZ$
Alcohol drinking age - 18
Drugs - Cannabis is illegal
Death Penalty - Doesn t exist
Age of consent for Sex - 16
Military Service -Not Compulsory
Electricity Supply - 240 Volts AC
International phone Code ++64
Highest Peak -

NZ DRIVE GUIDE
All vehicles drive on the left hand side of the road
Speed Limits -
Motorways 100kph (60mph)

TIME ZONES
Pacific
GMT +12 Hours

Main international Gateway Airport

Christchurch
Queenstown
Wellington

INFORMATION SOURCE

Brown Bear New Zealand Ski & Snowboard Guide
This is a cool and free publication listing all the latest facts regarding New Zealands resorts.
Contact them at the address below for details.

Po Box 31 207, Ilam
Christchurch 8030
New Zealand
tel: =64 3 358 0935
e-mail:info@brownbear.co.nz
web: www.snow.co.nz

Cardrona

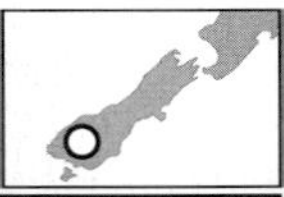

NEW ZEALAND

MOUNTAIN DATA

Top Lift at - 1894m

Ride Area 320 hectares

Bottom Lift at - 1504m

Vertical Drop - 390m

Number of Runs - 25

Longest -1miles (1.6km)

TERRAIN LEVELS

Easy	**25%**
Intermediate	**55%**
Advanced	**20%**
Expert =	

TERRAIN TO SUITE

Freeride	**50%**
Trees	No
Backcountry	Yes
Freestyle	**30%**
Halfpipe	Yes 4
Terrain Park	Yes 1
Carving	**20%**

SNOW DATA

Average Snowfall
240cm a season
Snowmaking

Winter Periods
June to October
Summer Riding
None

SLOPE ACCESS

Total Lifts = **8**
Uplift Rate - 7,000 people an hour.
3 Chair lifts
5 Drag lifts
**Leashes Required*

Lift Times
9.00am to 4.00pm

Lift Pass Rates
1 Day Adult NZ$59
1 Day Child NZ$29
1 Day Student NZ$30

Travel Guide

Fly to **Christchurch** is 3½ hours away. **Queenstown** is 60 minutes from Cardrona.

Route Planner: From Christchurch, take routes 1,8,8A and 89. The drive time is around 3½ hours **277 miles (446km)**

Queenstown is: **36 miles (58km)**

pic - Cardrona

Cardrona lies off the **Crown Range** road between **Wanaka** and **Queensland.** Shuttle bus services operate from both towns, so it is accessible wherever you choose to base yourself. With just 5 lifts serving three wide basins, Cardrona offers some of the best and driest snow in New Zealand. They regularly hold national snowboard competitions here such as the *New Zealand Nationals* which includes a boardercross event. Although this may not be in the super league of big resorts, the humble offerings here are never the less acceptable and will appeal to all levels and style of rider. If you are moved by the steep and deep then you won t be disappointed with such areas known as **Powder Keg** and **Arcadia Chutes** reached off the **La Franch** chair.

Freeriders will love it here. There is a fantastic variety of snow-gathering gullies and plenty of rocks to throw yourself off. **Keg** and **Arcadia** are the areas where **Cardrona** holds it s *National Extreme Championships*. Records have been set by dropping down the 30 metre plus **Eagle Rock** in **Captain's Basin**, so if you re feeling suicidal this one is for you. If the runs within the boundary don t satisfy you, you could go heli-boarding in Cardrona s expansive back bowls.

Freestylers are provided with a cool funpark that comes with a large table top and spines. There are also two halfpipes, reached off the **Macdougall** quad chair lift with one built to *ISF* competition standards and shaped with a special blade attachment fitted to the grommers.

Carvers will find either of the two main faces ideal for laying out some big turns on. The **Sluce Box** is a great carvers run.

Beginners may find the novice slopes a bit overcrowded on weekends and during holidays. However, persevere as this is a resort that should appeal to first timers with nice beginners runs of the **Macdougall** quad, which allows for easy progression.

Off the slopes life goes on in the town of **Wanaka** about 20 miles away, or in Queenstown 35 miles away. Wanaka is the quieter of the two and more relaxed place with a number of cool bars and plenty of cafes. If you get to know the right people you ll be able to join in on the popular past time s of Keg parties. Overall, prices for accommodation are good and affordable.

For accommodation listings visit - **www.worldsnowboardguide.com**

Tourist office Cardrona
Po Box 117, Wanaka.
++64 (0) 3 443 7341 **www.cardrona.com**

Overall rating out of 10 **6** **A good intermediates resort**

Cornet Peak

MOUNTAIN DATA

Top Lift at - 1649m

Ride Area 280 hectares

Bottom Lift at - 1200m

Vertical Drop - 420m

Number of Runs - 25

Longest -1.6 miles (2.5km)

TERRAIN LEVELS

Easy	**20%**
Intermediate	**45%**
Advanced	**35%**
Expert =	

TERRAIN TO SUITE

Freeride	**55%**
Trees	
Backcountry	Yes
Freestyle	**30%**
Halfpipe	Yes 1
Terrain Park	Yes 1
Carving	**15%**

SNOW DATA

Average Snowfall
1000cm a season

Snowmaking
10% cover of the slopes

Winter Periods
June to October

Summer Riding
None

SLOPE ACCESS

Total Lifts = **7**

Uplift Rate - 7,000 people an hour.

3 Chair lifts -

4 Drag lifts

**Leashes Required*

Lift Times
8.30am to 4.30pm

Lift Pass Rates
1 Day Adult NZ$62
1 Day Child NZ$31
1 Day Student NZ$54

SLOPE ACTION

Snowboard Hire
Daily rates NZ$40
Kids from NZ$30

Snowboard Tuition
Group lessons, from from NZ$60

Night Riding
From 4pm to 9pm

Heli Boarding
Yes, flights from NZ$600

Snowmobiles
No

Mountain Cafes
3

pic - Cornet Peak

Located amid the southern alps and lakes of the **South Island**, **Cornet Peak, on the shores of Lake Wakatipu,** is only 30 minutes from the hustle and bustle of the town to **Queenstown**.

Cornet, which has a shared lift pass with the neighbouring resort of **The Remarkables** , has terrain suitable for snowboarders of all abilities, with slopes that offer a combination of wide open pistes and well groomed trails that drop to a vert of 428 metres. The ride area is serviced by six well set out lifts and to ensure good snow cover at all times, Cornet has a multi-million dollar snowmaking system that covers from top to bottom. The low altitude here gives Cornet natural, undulating terrain with great spines and gullies for some of the best-riding available. The **Cornet Express** high-speed, detachable quad takes you to the summit where you gain access to some hot back bowls so loved by hard core freeriders. Check they are open though, because if you catch an avalanche and survive, it could be a long hike out when there is powder. However, it is worth it and make sure you ride the **Rocky Gully** T-bar.

Freeriders will find the runs down from the summit pretty cool, especially the **M1**. Advanced riders should try out the series of blacks from the summit known as the **Exchange Drop**, which if you don t treat with respect will make your eyes water as you do *DROP.* Powder hounds looking for some steep, deep, fluffy stuff need to check out the back bowls or the terrain around the **Sarah Sue** run, but note riding down this area does entail a hike back up to the resort to get on the lifts again.

Freestylers should try out **Sara Sue** off **Greengates** for some big spine jumps, banks and natural quarter-pipes. **Cornet** is continually developing its terrain parks with table tops and rails built into various strategic fun-parks all over the mountain. But beware, Cornet gets pretty crowded so be careful. The patrollers, including some on snowboards, are serious about using look outs on blind jumps, especially down **Exchange Drop**, where you would do well to obey the *No-Hit/No Jump* and slow down zones to avoid any trouble.

Carvers will enjoy the long blue trail known as the **M1** as well as the runs known as **Greengates** and **Million Dollar**, which are pisted to perfection and great for leaving some nice long lines on.

Beginners will find the best stuff is off the **Meadows** chair and alongside the learners poma. But there isn t a mass of novice trails here, although what is available is still good. The local ski school offers a *Snowboard Starter'* package for $60 and is well worth the money as instructors know their stuff.

After a hard days riding, the next best thing is to be able to hang out in a place that offers you a good choice of accommodation, plenty of restaurants and loads of bars with varying price ranges to suite all pockets. And that is exactly what you get in **Queenstown**, a big town full of all the joys and spoils to make a week a month or even a year an eventful one. Queenstown has every possible holiday services you could want and a vast array of outdoor sport activities. You can take part in paragliding, rock climbing, go jet skiing or even have a game of golf (if you re sad enough) or really bored.

For job seekers, **Cornet Peak** employs 340 seasonal staff, so provided you apply at the correct time, work should be no drama.

Being a big town, as one would expect, there is a massive choice of restaurants and cheap cafes in Queenstown. Every type of food is available with lots of options to eat cheaply. Notable places for a feed are; *The Cow*, which offers moderately priced pizza and spaghetti. *Berkels Gourmet* frys up a good burger, while *Gourmet* is good for breakfast.

Night life, in Queenstown rocks hard and late. Locals here like and know how to party hard, and if there s nothing laid on then guaranteed something will happen to set the evening off. The choice of bars is great with some good boozers, such as the *Red Rock Cafe* which also serves good bar food. The *World Bar* is also cool hangout.

Accommodation around here is very impressive, but forget about any beds slopeside. **Queenstown** has the biggest selection and best budget options, its also close to all the off-slope action. Motels are a common form of accommodation around here as are bed and breakfast homes. *Bungy Backpackers* is a cheap hangout tel ++64 03 442 8725. *Melbourne Motor Lodge* is an affordable choice tel ++64 03 442 8431.

For accommodation listings visit - www.worldsnowboardguide.com

Summary: Good freeriding resort offering some very nice powder areas. The resort management has a healthy attitude towards snowboarding making this a cool place.

Money wise; Overall this is an expensive resort but offers good value.

Overall rating out of 10 **7**

Tourist Office Cornet Peak
Mt Cook Line, Po Box 359.
Queensland

General info	**++64 (0) 03 442 4620**
Reservations	**++64 (0) 03 442 4620**
Snowphone	**++64 (0) 0900 99766**

www.
www.MOUNTCOOK.CO.NZ

pic - Scott Needham

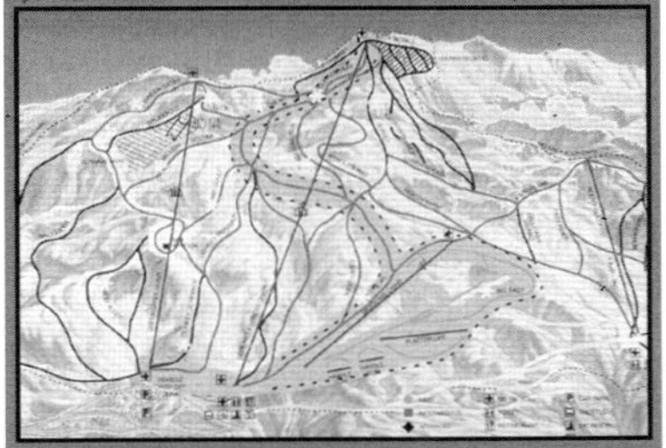

pic - Cornet

Travel Guide

Fly to **Christchurch** international
Transfer time to resort = **5½** *hours.*
Local airport = Queensland, 10 miles away

Approximate global air travel times to **Christchurch:**
includes change overs from: London **26¾** hours
Los Angles **15½** hours

A bus from **Queensland will** take around 20 minutes.
From Christchurch, its 6 hours.

Trains to **Queensland** only.

Route Planner
Queensland - Christchurch

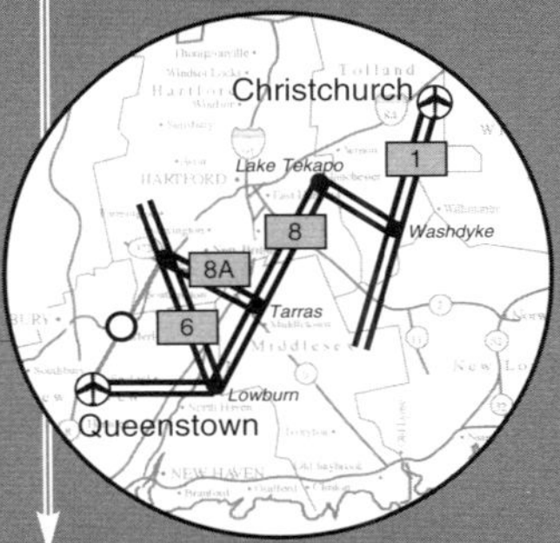

Cornet Peak = 10 miles (18 km)
Drive time is about 20 minutes

Mt Hutt

MOUNTAIN DATA

Top Lift at - 2075m

Ride Area
280 hectares

Bottom Lift at - 1585m
Vertical Drop - 655m
Number of Runs -
Longest - 1.2 miles (2km)

TERRAIN LEVELS

Easy	**25%**
Intermediate	**50%**
Advanced	**25%**
Expert =	

TERRAIN TO SUITE

Freeride	**50%**
Trees	No
Backcountry	Yes
Freestyle	**25%**
Halfpipe	Yes 1
Terrain Park	Yes No
Carving	**20%**

SNOW DATA

Average Snowfall
180cm a season
Snowmaking
10% cover of the slopes
Winter Periods
June to October
Summer Riding
None

SLOPE ACCESS

Total Lifts = **10**
Uplift Rate - 9,200 people an hour.
2 Chair lifts -
8 Drag lifts
**Leashes Required*

Lift Times
9.00am to 4.30pm

Lift Pass Rates
1 Day Adult NZ$58
1 Day Child NZ$28
1 Day Student NZ$46

Travel Guide

Fly to **Christchurch** airport 90 mins away.

Bus services from Metven to Mt Hutt take 30 minutes.

Route Planner:
From Christchurch, take highways 73 & 72 trrough Tardhurst and Homebush to Metven and then on up to Mt Hutt.

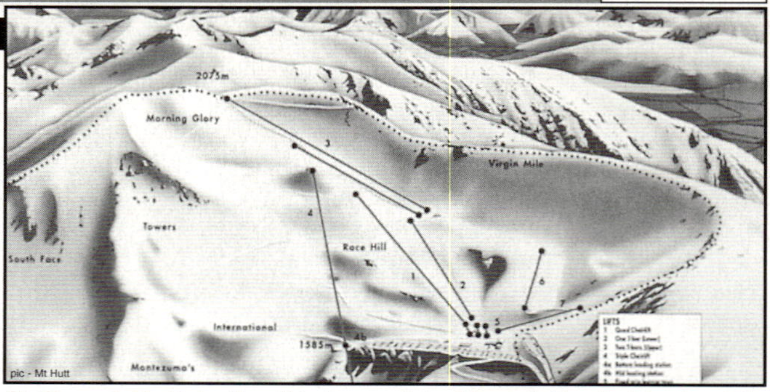

pic - Mt Hutt

Mount Hutt is the third resort in **Mount Cook Line's** *Big Three* , located 30 minutes from **Methven**. This is an early opening resort mainly thanks to its snowmaking facilities as well as the high altitude. You can enjoy some of the best snow cover for the longest season in the South Island. The 9 lifts service an excellent expanse of terrain for everybody to take advantage off. Being one NZ s biggest commercial resorts means that Mt Hutt can become very busy, attracting alot of family ski groups. However, don t let that stop you, the resort is very snowboard friendly and there are plenty of good areas to ride with out crashing into two plankers all day.

Freeriders who like the challenge of steep and extreme terrain, then the **South Face** is covered with double black diamond runs to test the most cockiest of all riders. Other great runs to check out, especially for ungroomed and touched powder, are **Towers** and **Virgin Mile**. Here you can ride free of crowds but remember that **Mt Hutt** is a very popular resort so move fast on powder mornings to get the best uncut stuff which there is plenty off on offer with no need to hike to.

Freestylers and park specialists, there is to be a new ISF standard halfpipe and accompanying terrain park under the triple chair above the mid-station. With a dedicated crew of snowboarding staff and locals you can expect a high level of maintenance and plenty of people to ride with. You will find plenty to jump and launch off down **Exhibition Bowl**, **Morning Glory** and through **Race Hill**, although exercise some caution on these blind jumps. If possible have someone spotting if possible especially if there are races or training in the area.

Carvers gracing the slopes in hard boots will find some nice corduroy terrain around **Broadway** to carve up.

Beginners, Mt Hutt is considered one of the best learning resorts in NZ with novice trails serviced by fixed grip tows.

Off the slopes you can base your self in Methven, **Christchurch** or **Ashburton**, all offering a variety of accommodation, food and nighlife. Methven is the closest, just 30 minutes away. Budget accommodation is limited so try to book ahead. There are plenty of restaurants and cafes serving a variety on dishes at varying rates. Night lifts is okay in the bars but avoid the cheesy disco s.
Accommodation: Visit www.worldsnowboardgiuide.

Tourist Office Mt Hutt
Po Box 14 Metven 8353
++64 (0) 3 302 8811 **www.**

Overall rating out of 10 **5** **Very basic but okay for a day**

Mt Lyford

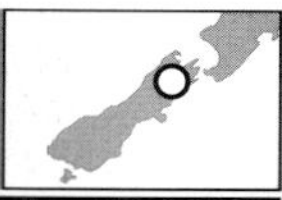

NEW ZEALAND

MOUNTAIN DATA

Top Lift at - 1555m

Ride Area 305 hectares

Bottom Lift at - 1249m

Vertical Drop - 1527m

Number of Runs - 25

Longest - 1.2 miles (2km)

TERRAIN LEVELS

Easy	45%
Intermediate	40%
Advanced	15%
Expert =	

TERRAIN TO SUITE

Freeride	60%
Trees	No
Backcountry	Yes
Freestyle	20%
Halfpipe	Yes 1
Terrain Park	Yes 1
Carving	20%

SNOW DATA

Average Snowfall
260cm a season
Snowmaking

Winter Periods
June to October
Summer Riding
None

SLOPE ACCESS

Total Lifts = 6
Uplift Rate not available

6 Drag lifts
**Leashes Required*

Lift Times
9.00am to 4.30pm

Lift Pass Rates
1 Day Adult NZ$35
1 Day Child NZ$10
1 Day Student NZ$20

Travel Guide

Fly to **Christchurch** airport 2 hours away.

Bus services from Christchurch with changes at Culverden and Waiau

Route Planner:
From Christchurch, take highway 7 north and highway 70 via Culverden and Waiau to reach My Lyford.

pic - Burton Snowboards

Located just hours from **Christchurch** and only 18 miles from the town of **Kailoura,** is the small and commercial resort of **Mount Lyford**. This totally privately owned mountain, may not be the biggest resort in **New Zealand**, but by the same token it s not the smallest and unlike some of the other commercial resorts, Mt Lyford is far more affordable and offers great value for money for any rider who can handle a few days. Mt Lyford is a very snowboard friendly hangout and on occasions, has snowboarders out-numbering skiers. Figures show that there is often 70% riders to 30% two plankers. Still whoever is here, the slopes can be best described as overall dull for any more than a few days if you stick to the marked slopes but great if you go heli-boarding into the backcountry areas. The area gets a good annual snowcover that is spread out over two areas which are somewhat different to each other. The **Lake Stella** area, a short drive around the mountain, is the advanced riders spot while beginners and intermediates will find the best slopes on the **Terako field**.

Freeriders should make their way to the top of **Mt Terako** via the Terako lift for some uneven terrain. From the top and after a short hike, you can either ride down the series of steep blacks such as **Die Hard**, or you can elect to take the slightly easier runs such as the **Triller**. Riders who can afford it and want to ride some backcountry powder, will be able to experience the best stuff by taking a heli-board trip with *Hanmer Helicopters.*

Freestylers may find Mt Lyford a little non-happening but still worth a visit to wile away a day with out the crowds. The slopes are not blessed with an abundance of natural hits. However, you will find a few rocks to leap over and one or two windlips.

Carvers will find the least to do here if your only desire is corduroy trails. However, an hour here will allow for some fun.

Beginners will love Mt Lyford because you can practice your thing on some very tame slopes, which are free of large ski groups. The only thing is that all the lifts are drags.

Off the slopes the by word is, very basic and dull . There is chalet accommodation along the access road but little else. *Keiths Cafe* is the place for breakfast while the *Lodge Hotel* will provide some evening madness.

For accommodation listings visit - www.worldsnowboardguide.com

Tourist Office Mt Lyford
Private Bag, Waiau. North Canterbury
++64 (0) 3 315 6178 www.mtyford.co.nz

Overall rating out of 10 **4** **This place can be a bit boring**

Mt Dobson

MOUNTAIN DATA

Top Lift at - 2046m

Ride Area 400 hectares

Bottom Lift at - 1690m

Vertical Drop - 655m

Number of Runs -

Longest - 1.2 miles (2km)

TERRAIN LEVELS

Easy	**20%**
Intermediate	**40%**
Advanced	**40%**
Expert =	

TERRAIN TO SUITE

Freeride	**50%**
Trees	
Backcountry	Yes
Freestyle	**20%**
Halfpipe	Yes 1
Terrain Park	Yes 1
Carving	**30%**

SNOW DATA

Average Snowfall
200cm a season

Snowmaking

Winter Periods
June to October

Summer Riding
None

SLOPE ACCESS

Total Lifts = **4**

Uplift Rate - 3,200 people an hour.

4 Drag lifts

**Leashes Required*

Lift Times
9.00am to 4.30pm

Lift Pass Rates
1 Day Adult NZ$40
1 Day Child NZ$14
1 Day Student NZ$30

Travel Guide

Fly to **Christchurch** airport 90 mins away.

Bus services with change overs at the town Fairlie.

Train services to Timaru, 8 miles from the resort.

Route Planner: From Christchurch, take highway 1 south and highway 8 to Fairlie and then on to Mt Dobson.

pic - NZ Tourism

Mount Dobson is a small commercial resort located in the **Southern Canterbury** region of the country on the South Island. With a mere nine miles or so of rideable marked piste, Dobson boasts at having the largest beginners slopes in New Zealand. Whatever the merits of such a claim are, Mt Dobson is a laid back place and has far less hassle about it compared to some of the bigger commercial resorts. The slopes here attract family groups and those out for a simple afternoons sliding around. Even though lift prices are a lot cheaper than other resorts, the slopes are not over populated with budget minded skiers. The terrain offers a mixture of easy gentle slopes and a number of short fast tracks which are all serviced by drag lifts.

Freeriders, of an intermediate level, will find a day riding the slopes here is not a bad way to pass some time. The best of which will be the trails on the main face of the T-bar and runs off the **West** and **East** trails. Riders who like something to get stuck into and need a few challenges, may find **Dobson** a little repetitive and lacking in general interest. However, there is some nice challenging riding in the back bowls and the series of short blacks that drop down from the West and East runs, will give you something to think about. The **Bluff** is not a bad run and has a few humps en-route to the bottom of the **Platter 2** drag lift.

Freestylers are presented with a halfpipe and a park above the West Valley slope area. To reach the pipe, you need to ride the T-bar and head off around the **West Trail**, which is a blue graded run. You couldn t call this place a natural freestyle retreat, but like most resorts, there s always something to leap off.

Carvers who like to do big wide turns but don t like to do them for too long, will find Mt Dobson perfectly in tune with their thinking and liking. Nothing here takes that long to carve up, with only a couple of fast pisted tracks to choose from.

Beginners will find the whole place a joy and even though a number of the runs graded Difficult and Intermediate are a bit over rated and can be challenged after a short time by most.

Off the slopes, accommodation and other local facilities are offered in the towns of **Fairlie** or **Kimbell**. What you get in either, is very basic, affordable and sufficient for a few days stay. Night life is very tame and not up to much.

For accommodation listings visit - www.worldsnowboardguide.com

Tourist Office Mt Dobson
30 Alloway Street. Fairlie.
++64 (0) 3 685 8039 **www.dobson.co.nz**

Overall rating out of 10 **4** **Some very good beginner runs**

Ohau

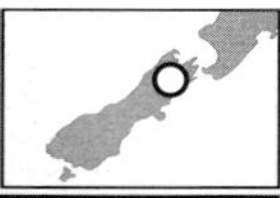

NEW ZEALAND

MOUNTAIN DATA

Top Lift at - 1925m

Ride Area 400 hectares

Bottom Lift at - 1400m
Vertical Drop - 655m
Number of Runs -
Longest - 1.2 miles (2km)

TERRAIN LEVELS

Easy	**20%**
Intermediate	**50%**
Advanced	**30%**
Expert =	

TERRAIN TO SUITE

Freeride	**50%**
Trees	No
Backcountry	Yes
Freestyle	**30%**
Halfpipe	Yes 1
Terrain Park	Planned
Carving	**20%**

SNOW DATA

Average Snowfall
180cm a season
Snowmaking
Zero
Winter Periods
June to October
Summer Riding
None

SLOPE ACCESS

Total Lifts = **3**
Uplift Rate - 7,000 people an hour.
3 Drag lifts
**Leashes Required*

Lift Times
9.00am to 4.30pm

Lift Pass Rates
1 Day Adult NZ$40
1 Day Child NZ$13
1 Day Student NZ$28

Travel Guide

Fly to **Christchurch** airport 2 hours away.

Bus services from Christchurch with changes at Twizel or Omarama

Route Planner:
From Christchurch, take highways 1 and 8 via Twizel.

pic - Regis

Some would say that you haven t truly snowboarded in **New Zealand** until you have spent a day at **Ohau Ski Area** and a night at the **Ohau Lodge.** Seemingly in the middle of nowhere, about half way between Queensland and Christchurch, most people make the mistake of only visiting Ohau for a day en-route between other resorts. The views alone here are amazing with Mount Cook, NZ s highest mountain, in sight all around the area. This internationally renowned snowboarders resort offers some excellent riding for all levels on amazingly crowd free slopes with a fair share of good powder days. Riders come here because they know that this place cuts it, without any hype of bull shit, just a damn fine mountain that will please hardcore freeriders with a good choice of steeps.

Freeriders are most at home here. Apart from the two learner areas at the base and the wide groomed Boulevard Run, the terrain is generally steep. Left of the T-bar, is the steepest part of the area with the **Escalator** trail being the steepest run on the mountain. The strong-nerved should consider traversing further than Escalator, past the **Rock Bluff** and ride down to the **Platter** lift. The face above the day lodge, offers some steep runs and because it gets sun early in the day, it s often the best place to ride in the morning. On the other face, the **Exhibition** and **Escalator** runs, remain in the shade until late in the day.

Freestylers will have to make do with natural hits, if getting high on a board is you re type of fix, nothing is laid on here.

Carvers may at first feel left out, however after some close examination, you will soon see that there is enough pisted carving trails to shine on, with runs like the **Shirt Front**, where you can give some style at speed.

Beginners tend to hang out on the **Boulevard** run although it does get a little steep in places (below **Top Flat**). Boulevard does give less confident riders a good reign of the mountain and a few ski areas have such an easy run from there highest point.

The **Ohau** experience is best enjoyed by staying at the *Ohau Lodge*, situated at the base of the mountain. Food and booze are available in the Lodge on back down in the town of Twizel. Wherever you decide to chill out, theres a good choice of cool hangouts with resonable prices for booze.

For accommodation listings visit - **www.worldsnowboardguide.com**

Tourist Office Ohau
Po Box 51, Twizel. South Island
++64 (0) 3 438 9885

Overall rating out of 10 **7** **A decent freeriders resort**

Porters Heights

MOUNTAIN DATA

Top Lift at - 1950m

Ride Area 365 hectares

Bottom Lift at - 1340m

Vertical Drop - 610m

Number of Runs - 17

Longest - 720m

TERRAIN LEVELS

Easy	**20%**
Intermediate	**40%**
Advanced	**40%**
Expert =	

TERRAIN TO SUITE

Freeride	**50%**
Trees	
Backcountry	Yes
Freestyle	**30%**
Halfpipe	Yes 1
Terrain Park	Yes 1
Carving	**20%**

SNOW DATA

Average Snowfall
290cm a season

Snowmaking
10% cover of the slopes

Winter Periods
June to October

Summer Riding
None

SLOPE ACCESS

Total Lifts = **5**

Uplift Rate - 3,000 people an hour.

5 Drag lifts

**Leashes Required*

Lift Times
9.00am to 4.30pm

Lift Pass Rates

1 Day Adult	NZ$45
1 Day Child	free
1 Day Student	NZ$38

Travel Guide

Fly to **Christchurch** airport 1 hour away.

Bus services with change overs at Springfield.

Trains to Springfield, 12 miles from the resort.

Route Planner:
From Christchurch, take highway 73 via Yardhurst, Kirwee and Sheffield.

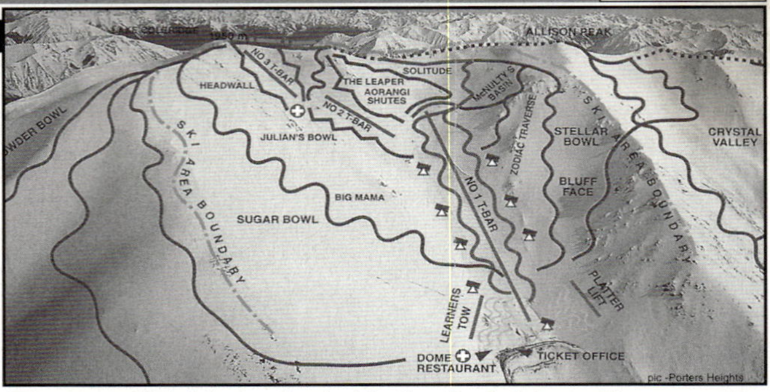

Porters Heights is situated in the **Craigieburn Range** and is the closest boarding area to **Christchurch**. The whole area is likened to a large terrain park with heaps of runs that can t be beaten on a powder day with cool challenging chutes and hits. Legendary runs like Big Mama (one of the largest in the Southern Hemisphere) and **Bluff Face** (NZ s steepest) help to make this an extremely interesting and challenging resort for any snowboarder.

Freeriders should go to the top of the **No 3** T-bar, because from here the mountain is yours. The view of **Lake Coleridge** and surrounding mountain ranges is spectacular. Don t hang around sightseeing for too long though - the first tracks on **Big Mama** aren t available all day. It is a reasonably easy traverse (with a little climbing) along a ridge line to the top of Big Mama, but it s not until you re standing at the top of the slope that you realise just how long the run is. It is a huge 620 vertical metres from top to bottom - one of the largest vertical drops in a lift accessed area in NZ. If you re fit enough to enjoy long powder runs, Big Mama is heaven. If you prefer chutes, traverse to the left from the top of lift No 3 T-bar to **Aorangi Chute**s and the **Leapers,** where the terrain is steep and the chutes are narrow. **Bluff Face** is another cool place to ride reached via a traverse down to **McNulty's** cat-track and hike up to the summit of **Allison Peak**. The **Powder Bowl** and **Crystal Valley** runs are both outside the ski boundary. There is a great boarding to be had on both, but the hike can be a mission. For reasons of safety, inform the ski patrol if you intend to go into any of these areas.

Freestylers have a lot here to check out. There s an international size halfpipe in **McNulty's Basin** and heaps of good natural hits dotted around the whole area.

Carvers will find the runs down either side of the **No 1** T-bar have a reasonably consistent gradient and make excellent cruising runs for intermediate boarders.

Beginners will find the runs limited to a few short flats at the base area which are serviced by a couple of easy to use lifts.

Off the slopes the best place to stay is in nearby **Springfield,** where there s some good lodging options, good eating out and great night time happenings shared with friendly locals.

For accommodation listings visit - www.worldsnowboardguide.com

Tourist Office Porters Heights
Po Box 15, Springfiled.
++64 (0) 3 318 4008 **e-mail: ski@portersheights.co.nz**

Overall rating out of 10 **7** **Good place to ride for all**

Treble Cone

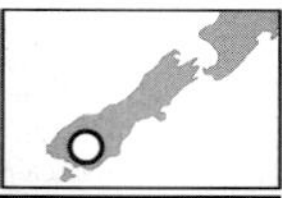

pic - Treble Cone

MOUNTAIN DATA

Top Lift at - 1860m

Ride Area 550 hectares

Bottom Lift at - 1250m

Vertical Drop - 610m

Number of Runs - 25

Longest - 1 mile (1.6km)

TERRAIN LEVELS

Easy	**15%**
Intermediate	**45%**
Advanced	**40%**
Expert =	

TERRAIN TO SUITE

Freeride	**60%**
Trees	No
Backcountry	Yes
Freestyle	**15%**
Halfpipe	Yes 1
Terrain Park	Yes 1
Carving	**25%**

SNOW DATA

Average Snowfall
250cm a season

Snowmaking
12% cover of the slopes

Winter Periods
June to October

Summer Riding
None

SLOPE ACCESS

Total Lifts = **5**

Uplift Rate - 7,000 people an hour.

2 Chair lifts

3 Drag lifts

**Leashes Required*

Lift Times
9.00am to 4.30pm

Lift Pass Rates
1 Day Adult NZ$59
1 Day Child NZ$29
1 Day Student NZ$49

Travel Guide

Fly to **Christchurch** or **Queensland**.

Bus services from Queensland to the resort are available hourly.

Route Planner: From Christchurch, take highways 1, 8, 8A and 89. The drive time is around 6 hours.

Treble Cone provides some incredible terrain, on and off piste in a major scenic place. Some would say that Treble Cone gets more than its fair share of dry southern snow as well as the resort boasting a vert un-matched in the rest of the country. With 40% advanced terrain, Treble is known as one of New Zealands more testing and challenging resorts that competent freeriders and freestylers should love and be able to go home with a few stories to tell after tackling some major steeps, long chutes and deep powder bowls on some gnarly black faces.

Freeriders will like it here especially when there has been some fresh snow. A particular good area to drop into is **Powder Bowl.** A wide open slope leading into the lower gullies for some big powder turns and super floating glides. For the more adventurous the off-piste in the **Matukituki Basin** is the place to check out.

Freestylers should head to the top and from the summit, drop into the **Saddle Basin** alongside the **Saddle** double chair, to take advantage of loads of natural hits and halfpipes to gain maximum air time. The **Gun Barrel**, which is also reached from the summit, is another legendary, long natural halfpipe where banked slalom events are regularly held. The terrain park is loaded with hits and the halfpipe is serviced by a lift. And if you re still not satisfied and in need of an adrenaline rush, there are loads of big drops offs and rocks of all sizes dotted all over the mountain.

Carvers need not feel left out as Treble Cone has done lots of work developing a series of well groomed runs down the face of the mountain which are ideal for laying down some big wide arcs.

Beginners may note that although Treble Cone is not known as a beginners mountain don t be put off, as there is still enough to try out without killing yourself on the first day. Its skiers who can t handle it here, not fast learning boarders.

Away from the slopes local services are provided down in Wanaka, a quiet and relaxed place that provides good places to kip and a few bars popular with snowboarders. For some decent food why not try *Kai Whaka Pai* for a tasty treat and great coffee. *The Pot Belly Stove* also serves up decent local food. Places to check out for a beer are the likes of the *Barrows,* which is the locals haunt, or the *Outback Bar* which has a pool table and serves booze until late.

For accommodation listings visit - www.worldsnowboardguide.com

Tourist Office Treble Cone
Po Box 206 Wanaka
++64 (0) 3 443 7443 **e-mail: tcinfo@treblecone.co.nz**

Overall rating out of 10 **7** **Some gnarly terrain to cherck out**

The Remarkables

MOUNTAIN DATA

Top Lift at - 1934m

Ride Area 220 hectares

Bottom Lift at - 1703m

Vertical Drop - 357m

Number of Runs -

Longest - 1 mile (1.6km)

TERRAIN LEVELS

Easy	**25%**
Intermediate	**30%**
Advanced	**30%**
Expert =	

TERRAIN TO SUITE

Freeride	**70%**
Trees	No
Backcountry	Yes
Freestyle	**20%**
Halfpipe	Yes 1
Terrain Park	Yes 1
Carving	**10%**

SNOW DATA

Average Snowfall
290cm a season

Snowmaking
10% cover of the slopes

Winter Periods
June to October

Summer Riding
None

SLOPE ACCESS

Total Lifts = **5**

Uplift Rate - 3,000 people an hour.

3 Chair lifts

5 Drag lifts

**Leashes Required*

Lift Times
9.00am to 4.30pm

Lift Pass Rates
1 Day Adult NZ$58
1 Day Child Free
1 Day Student NZ$46

Travel Guide

Fly to **Christchurch** or **Queensland**.

Buses from Queensland to the resort are available on an hourly basis.

Route Planner: From Christchurch, take highways 1, 8, 8A and 89. The drive time is around 6 hours.

The Remarkables lies within sight of the **Cornet Peak** resort. Higher in altitude, the car park is the same level as Cornet s summit, with the result being that the mountain is very craggy and rocky. The **Remarkables** tends to be alot quieter than **Cornet Peak** with less skiers. It also gets some incredible powder days and offers terrain for every style and grade of rider. The area is some what sheltered but still gives out plenty of sun and loads of natural snow. The **Homeward** runs are the place to shred some deep powder where you can ride some long floating turns with an amazing back drop. The **Homewards** take you right down to the access road to catch the shuttle bus back to the base building in order to do the whole thing again. The runs here are accessed by three chairlifts, the **Alta** double chair, services the best intermediate terrain to suit carvers or freeriders. The **Sugar** quad is the lift to take if you have a bit of go in you. Where you can get access to some good advance terrain and competent intermediate stuff. However, advanced riders looking to cut it in style and be pushed to the fore should check out the runs found off **Shadow** lift.

Freeriders if you are prepared to do some hiking, then after checking the snow conditions with the patrol, you can reach some major dogs bollocks terrain with big chutes and scary steeps. Turn left off the **Shadow** and hike 20 minutes up to the ridge to access the area known as **Esclator** and **Elevator** above Lake Alta. If you continue up along the ridge then the chutes get narrower and more extreme, so be bloody careful if you don t want this to be your last ever run. Go left off **Sugar** for the **Toilet Bowl** a freeriders heaven, which again takes you to the access road and the shuttle bus.

Freestylers tend to prefer **Cornet** to **Remarkables** even though there is no park or pipe here. Riders will find plenty of cliff and rock drops to get air from, especially in areas around **Sugar** and **Alta**. There are also plenty of cat-tracks to drop off.

Carvers will find a number of runs to laying out big super G turns on but in truth this is not a groomed piste lovers home.

Beginners have two superb learner areas with fixed grip tows and an excellent snowboard school that will soon get you sorted out and cutting the mountain up in style.

Off slopes services in **Queenstown** (*section on Cornet Peak*).
For accommodation listings visit - **www.worldsnowboardguide.com**

Tourist Office The Remarkables
Mount Cook Group. Po Box 359 Queenstown.
++64 (0) 3 442 4615 www.

Overall rating out of 10 **7** **Some cool expert terrain to ride**

Turoa

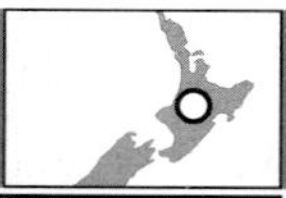

NEW ZEALAND

MOUNTAIN DATA

Top Lift at - 2322m

Ride Area
1000 acres

Bottom Lift at - 1600m
Vertical Drop - 720m
Number of Runs - 43
Longest - 1 mile (6km)

TERRAIN LEVELS

Easy	25%
Intermediate	50%
Advanced	25%
Expert =	

TERRAIN TO SUITE

Freeride	40%
Trees	No
Backcountry	Yes
Freestyle	30%
Halfpipe	Yes 1
Terrain Park	Yes 1
Carving	30%

SNOW DATA

Average Snowfall
200cm a season
Snowmaking
5% cover of the slopes
Winter Periods
June to November
Summer Riding
None

SLOPE ACCESS

Total Lifts = **11**
Uplift Rate - 10,400 people an hour.
4 Chair lifts
7 Drag lifts
**Leashes Required*

Lift Times
9.00am to 4.30pm

Lift Pass Rates
1 Day Adult NZ$54
5 Day Adult NZ$234
1 Day Youth NZ$29

Travel Guide

Fly to **Auckland** and inland to Palmerston.

Bus services with a change over at Ohakune.

Train services to Ohakune.

Route Planner: From Auckland, head south on highways 1,3 and 4 to Ohakune and then on to the resort.

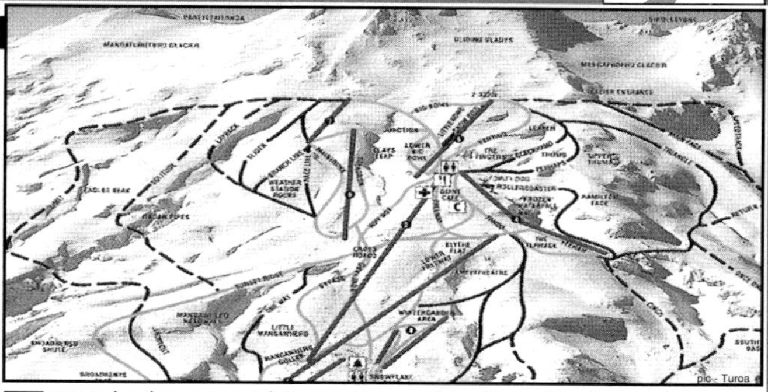

Turoa is the second largest resort in New Zealand. It is covered with gullies, bowls, walls and wide slopes: the type of terrain only found on a volcano. This can vary incredibly from year to year, depending on the amount of snow cover. Because the area is so large and conditions can vary so much as well, it is worthwhile spending time in the bars down in **Okakune**, meeting the locals to find out where the best spots are. The runs marked on the trail map are of little more than aesthetics value. There are countless possible routes and like **Whakapapa** on the other side of the mountain, the fun of riding at Turoa is finding them.

Freeriders, of an advanced level, should get to the top of the **Bacardi** T-bar. From here you can appreciate the scope of the place and get an idea of where you d like to ride. The runs out to your right (**Limit, Solitude** and **Layback**) are long runs in wide open spaces, where the thrill of riding down an active volcano can be fully realised. The runs way out to your left (S**peedtrack, Main Face** and **Triangle**) are a little steeper. There is nowhere on Turoa where the urge to climb **Ruapehu's Peak** is stronger than when viewing **Mangaheuheu Glacier**, from the **Glacier Entrance** run. If you want to hike to the top, check with the ski patrol on the best route and do not go without telling them. They ll also appreciate it if you can report to them on your return. It doesn t matter which route you take from the peak back to the ski area, they are 475 of the most unforgettable vertical metres in New Zealand.

Freestylers have a decent park, however on a powder day, which don t occur with great frequency in the North Island, Turoa s walls and gullies beckon you to charge hard. There s nothing like launching off **Clays Leap** or the **Mangawhero Headwall** and landing in the safe hands of powder.

Carvers learn to freeride and get real!

Beginners will find the **Alpine Meadows** area beside the car park the place to start out on. The cafeteria is right beside it so its never too far to go for a bit of a warm up .

There is an abundance of local facilities in **Ohakume**, only 10 miles away. Accommodation is provided as cheap B&B s, inexpensive motels and pricey hotels. Food and drinking is plentiful, *Clinches Cafe* is the place for breakfast.
For accommodation listings visit - **www.worldsnowboardguide.com**

Tourist Office Turora
Po Box 846, Ohakume
++64 (0) 3 385 8456 **e-mail: information@turoa.co.nz**

Overall rating out of 10 **6** **A simple resort but still okay**

Whakapapa

MOUNTAIN DATA

Top Lift at - 2300m

Ride Area 220 hectares

Bottom Lift at - 1625m

Vertical Drop - 675m

Number of Runs - 40

Longest -1.7 miles (2.8km)

TERRAIN LEVELS

Easy	30%
Intermediate	45%
Advanced	25%
Expert =	

TERRAIN TO SUITE

Freeride	50%
Trees	No
Backcountry	Yes
Freestyle	25%
Halfpipe	Yes 1
Terrain Park	Yes 1
Carving	25%

SNOW DATA

Average Snowfall
300cm a season

Snowmaking
10% cover of the slopes

Winter Periods
June to November

Summer Riding
None

SLOPE ACCESS

Total Lifts = **23**

Uplift Rate - 23,000 people an hour.

6 Chair lifts -

17 Drag lifts

**Leashes Required*

Lift Times
9.00am to 4.30pm

Lift Pass Rates

1 Day Adult NZ$54
5 Day Adult NZ$216
1 Day Youth NZ$27

Travel Guide

Fly to **Auckland** airport and inland to Taupo airport.

Train services are possible to National Park, which is 12 miles away.

Route Planner:
From Auckland, head south on highways 1 to Taupo and then on to Whakapapa.

pic - Whakapapa

Whakapapa is located near **Tuora,** on the slopes of **Mount Rauapehu.** The diversity of the terrain here is caused by the way the underlying volcano has formed over millions of years. As the largest recognised ski resort in the country, Whakapapa has something for everyone, with steeps, cliffs, fast chutes gullies and big natural banks allowing for some big air.

Freeriders who know what s what, will be aware of the awesome area known as the **Pinnacles**. Simply put, if you re not a damn good advanced rider, then stay away. The Pinnacles are a series of cliff runs, that will wipe the lights out for good if any rider mucks up!!!!!

Freestylers will be pleased to learn that management have, in the last few years, splashed out thousands of big bucks on a new *Pipemaster*. Having now learned how to turn it on, the halfpipe can boast perfectly groomed walls with a nice big vert and good transitions allowing for great smooth take offs.

Carvers can carve away for days on well groomed trails and take a week to do them all a few times over, with a number to test the best of the edge merchants

Heaps of good locals facilities exist in varying villages all in easy reach of the slopes. Prices vary, but on the whole well affordable and worth the effort of a weeks stay.

For accommodation listings visit - **www.worldsnowboardguide.com**

Whakapapa Tourist Office
Private bag, Mount Ruapehu.
++64 (0) 7 892 3738 **e-mail:snow@whakapapa.co.nz**

Overall rating out of 10 **6** **Some awesome freeride areas**

New Zealand Club Field resorts

There are 25 ski areas in New Zealand, 13 of these are commercially owned and operated. The other 12 are known as Club fields as they are non-profit organisations run by club committees. Small, social and New Zealand made, they are a classic piece of Kiwiana and well worth while checking out. In recent years many people have rediscovered the charms and attractions of Club Fields. They are lured by the uncrowded slopes, with the spectacular setting of the Southern Alps, spread out as a back drop.

Facilities at the club fields tend to be quite modest and basic, There are no club fields with chairlifts, but some do have T-bars or platter lifts. The most common lift is the rope tow. If you contact the club offices in advance and tell them the day you wish to come, they can help arrange a ride for you by putting you in touch with someone else who is driving there. Local Ski or Snowboard Shops will sometimes have booking sheets of people who are going or want to go to a clubfield.

ACCOMMODATION:

All the club fields have on-mountain lodging available. This can range from dormitory cabin style to double rooms with ensuite. If you are planning on staying overnight on the mountain, ring ahead to check there are vacancies because often they have large groups and clubs booked in or staying and may be full up, depending on bed numbers. There are package deals available which can include accommodation, an evening meal and breakfast, and discounted day passes (and sometimes transport too). There are cheaper prices for staying mid-week and for a week. This is a great time to go because there is usually not many other people to share the slopes with.

For day visitors, there is a cafeteria or snack shop for food. It is a good idea to bring a few of your own munchies too. There is usually a communal dining and kitchen area where you can prepare and eat food.

At some clubfields you can buy alcohol (mainly beer), but supplies can run out, so if you are staying a night or more it would be wise to bring your own, if you are one of those people who need a couple of cold one to finish the day off.
Check with the ski area first about their policy on alcohol.

CLUB FIELD DIRECTORY ~
NORTH ISLAND:

MANGANUI - Mount Taranaki
Stratford Mountain Club
PO Box 3271. New Plymouth
Tel: 06 765 7669 - Office
Tel: 06 765 5493 -Lodge in winter

TUKINO - Mt Ruapehu
Aorangi Ski Club, PO Box 1945
Wellington
Tel: 04 478 0116 - Office
Tel: 06 387 6294 -Lodge in winter

SOUTH ISLAND:

CENTRAL CANTERBURY:
All the clubfields listed below, except Erewhon, are located in the Craigieburn Mountain Range. To get there take highway 73, which goes from Christchurch to Greymouth via Arthurs Pass.
Mt Cheesman, Broken River, Temple Basin, Porter Heights (commercial field) and Mt Olympus, have a combined season pass deal.

AMURI SKI AREA
Mount Saint Patrick
PO Box 129, Hanmer Springs
North Canterbury
Tel: 025 341 806

BROKEN RIVER SKI CLUB
PO Box 2718, Christchurch
Tel: 03 366 6644

CRAIGIEBURN VALLEY SKI CLUB
PO BOX 2152, Christchurch
Tel: 03 365 2514

EREWHON SKI CLUB
c/o 20 Morley Street,
Christchurch
Tel: 03 351 8196

MOUNT CHEESMAN
PO Box 22-178, Christchurch
Tel: 03 379 5315

MOUNT ROBERT
Nelson Lakes National Park
Nelson Ski Club, PO Box 344
Nelson
Tel: 03 548 8336

MOUNT OLYMPUS
Windwhistle Sports Club
PO Box 25055, Christchurch
Tel: 03 366 6644

TEMPLE BASIN SKI CLUB
PO Box 1228, Christchurch
Tel: 03 377 7788

AWAKINO, Saint Mary's Range,
North Otago, Waitaki Ski Club Inc
PO Box 191, Oamaru
Tel: 03 434 5110
Snowphone: 03 436 0771

FOX PEAK SKI CLUB
PO Box 368, Timaru
South Canterbury
Tel: 03 685 8539
Snow Report: 03 688 0044

JOB SEEKERS CONTACTS:
If you are looking to find work for the winter at a New Zealand Ski Area, make sure you have arranged an appropriate work visa for the duration of your stay. Contact the office of the ski field where you wish to work as early as you can. Ask to speak to or write to the attention of the Personnel Manager and enquire about their application procedures and deadlines.

Below is a list of areas and their recruitment procedures.

Whakapapa, Turoa, Porter Heights, Coronet Peak and The Remarkables ski areas, do their recruiting through the New Zealand Employment Service, to which you have to be registered as available and looking for work. This services is available to non residents of New Zealand, providing that they are eligible.

Application forms are available from the beginning of March and are open for two months, usually closing by the 23 of April. Find out which branch of the NZES is processing applications for the ski area where you wish to work and contact them directly.

Other commercial and club fields advertise their job vacancies in local and national newspapers, usually during February and March. Mount Hutt ski-field accepts applications as early as November for some positions, until March 31.

Whakapapa ski area run their own Ski Industry Training Course ($277 for nine days) designed to give new and potential employees a foundational insight and knowledge into what s involved in the industry. Other ski areas have their own induction programs for new employees, usually run a few weeks before the ski-field is scheduled to open for the season.

For any further information contact any of the below addresses:.

New Zealand Ski Industries
Federation Inc
PO Box 27501, Wellington.

New Zealand Ski Patrol
Association Inc
PO Box 889. Christchurch

New Zealand Snowboard
Association
PO Box 27501, Wellington

New Zealand Snowboard
Instructors Association.
PO Box 22239, Christchurch

Argentina and **Chile** are two countries that are split by an the awesome Andes Mountain range which is home to a vast array of ski resorts, from large internationally acclaimed chic areas to small and humble locals hills . Take your pick: they re relatively easy to get to and can be pretty cheap when you re there.

The **Chilean** and **Argentinean** resorts are mainly located in two regions along the Andes; the **High Andes** between **Santiago** (Chile) and **Mendoza** (Arg), and the **Lake District/Patagonia** further south. The regions differ in many aspects, the High Andes region contains a bunch of resorts in the area around S.America s highest peak, **Aconcagua.** These include **Portillo, Valle Nevado, Farellones, La Parva** and **El Colorado** (all in Chile) and **Los Penitentes** and **Las Lenas** (in Argentina). The resorts are high, much above the treeline, and receive good light snow due to their high altitude. They are also considered to be top notch resorts and this is reflected in their prices of accommodation it s steep.

The Lake District/Patagonia region is an area of lower peaks in the Andes about 1000 miles further south. Several resorts on both sides of the border dot the slopes of different peaks, many of them on live or extinct volcanoes. These include **Pucon** (Chile), and **Chapelco**, **Catedral** and **Cerro Bayo** (Arg). The resort of **Termas de Chillan** (Chile) lies midway between the two regions. The resorts occupy lower elevations and so have slightly less reliable and wetter snowfall. They are however situated within an easy hitch of towns and so make for cheaper accommodation and eating. There are also several small rope tow areas occupying the slopes of many volcanoes in the Chilean Lake District, eg. **Osorno.**

Flights from London into either **Buenos Aries** (Arg) or **Santiago** (Ch) cost from £600 return, and take about 14 hours. As airports are well out of town, taxis into city centres ~~cost about~~ $15 into Santiago and $30 into Buenos Aires, but try bargaining as it works. Coaches run into Santiago for $2 and into B.A. for $12. Don t bother trying local buses, they take hours and probably won t let you take your board bag on.

Car hire is expensive; $300 a week plus mileage in Argentina and $250 in Chile. Both countries are serviced by an exhaustive network of long distance buses which aren t your stereotype *latin America* affair. Distances are long but the buses are comfy, and due to the heavy competition are often half empty. If you can spare the extra few dollars go for a coche cama which means bed coach or reclining seat.

Tip: Chile is about a third cheaper than Argentina for almost everything, including accommodation, food, booze and travel. Inflation rates are relatively low and the economies and political situations are fairly stable, however, both Latin American countries have rather dodgy political and financial histories, so things may change overnight.

Travellers cheques may be cashed at banks and large hotels but with dire rates of commission being taken in Argentina.

Better to bring plastic and use the abundant ATM s to withdraw cash when you need to, you get a better rate and less commission charged. If you take cash, make sure it s U.S. $.

Food is good and relatively cheap (steak, pizza and pasta in Argentina), beer about $1.50 (Chile) and $3 (Arg) per litre in bars. Snowboard gear is available in Argentina in B.A and at resorts. In fact the next season s stuff hits the shops 5 months before it gets to the UK. Gear is harder to find in Chile especially outside the few specialist shops in Santiago.

Night clubs in Argentina usually do not start until midnight. All common drugs (dope etc) are illegal in both countries with heavy penalties if caught. Paperwork, if you are rumbled, takes forever to sort out and you can bank on being inside for a long time before it s sorted. Dope is however popular and widely used. The people are among the most friendly and welcoming in the World. Spanish (castillano) is the main language, though many people in the tourism industry and local boarders often can speak English.

pic - Random Snowboards (pic dose not denote area)

In Brief

Mountain Data

Antuco *Chile*
Summit 1850m **Vertical** 450m
Lifts 2 **Runs** 2

Antillanca *Chile*
Summit 1535m **Vertical** 464m
Lifts 3 **Runs** 7

Cerro Bayo *Argentina*
Summit 1730m **Vertical** 720m
Lifts 5 **Runs** 8

Cerro Mirador *Chile*
Summit 450m **Vertical** 350m
Lifts 1 **Runs** 20

Chapelco *Argentina*
Summit 1970m **Vertical** 720m
Lifts 10 **Runs** 35

El Colorado *Chile*
Summit 3333m **Vertical** 900m
Lifts 16 **Runs** 25

El Fraile *Chile*
Summit 1825m **Vertical** 800m
Lifts 2 **Runs** 4

Gran Catedral *Argentina*
Summit 2050m **Vertical** 1000m
Lifts 32 **Runs** 50

Lagunillas *Chile*
Summit 2480m **Vertical** 350m
Lifts 3 **Runs** 12

La Burbuja *Chile*
Summit 1620m **Vertical** 320m
Lifts 2 **Runs** 3

La Hoya *Argentina*
Summit 3340m **Vertical** 1100m
Lifts 12 **Runs** 40

Las Lenas *Argentina*
Summit 1850m **Vertical** 450m
Lifts 14 **Runs** 46

La Parva *Chile*
Summit 3630m **Vertical** 960m
Lifts 14 **Runs** 20

Llaima *Chile*
Summit 1800m **Vertical** 300m
Lifts 5 **Runs** 5

Lonquimay *Chile*
Summit 1850m **Vertical** 200m
Lifts 2 **Runs** 2

Los Penitentes *Chile*
Summit 3190m **Vertical** 614m
Lifts 7 **Runs** 25

Perito Moreno *Argentina*
Summit 1450m **Vertical** 450m
Lifts 5 **Runs** 2

Portillo *Chile*
Summit 3340m **Vertical** 750m
Lifts 11 **Runs** 22

Pucon *Chile*
Summit 2400m **Vertical** 960m
Lifts 9 **Runs** 22

Las Lenas *Argentina*
Summit 1850m **Vertical** 450m
Lifts 14 **Runs** 46

Termas de Chillan *Chile*
Summit 2500m **Vertical** 700m
Lifts 6 **Runs** 15

Valdelen *Argentina*
Summit 830m **Vertical** 250m
Lifts 2 **Runs** 2

Capital - Buenos Aires
Language - Spanish
Currency - Peso
Alcohol drinking age - 18
Drugs - Cannabis is illegal
Age of consent for Sex - 16
Electricity Supply - 240 Volts AC
International phone Code ++54

ARGENTINA DRIVE GUIDE
All vehicles drive on the Right hand side of the road
Speed Limits -
Motorways 120kph (62mph)

TIME ZONES
GMT +4 Hours

Argentinian Snowboard Association
Zabala Street 2679 8*
ARG 1426 Buenos Aires
Tel++54 (0) 1 796 1951

Asociacion Argentina de Turismo
Viamonte 640, 10, 1053 Buenos Aires, Argentina
Tel++54 (0) 1 322 2804

Chapelo

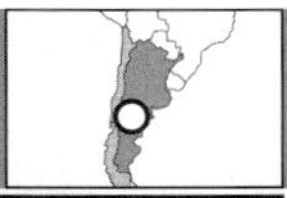

ARGENTINA

MOUNTAIN DATA

Top Lift at - 1970m

Ride Area
32km of piste

Bottom Lift at - 1250m

Vertical Drop - 720m

Number of Runs - 35

Longest - 4.3 miles (7km)

TERRAIN LEVELS

Easy	40%
Intermediate	30%
Advanced	30%
Expert =	

TERRAIN TO SUITE

Freeride	50%
Trees	Yes
Backcountry	Yes
Freestyle	30%
Halfpipe	Yes 1
Terrain Park	Yes 1
Carving	20%

SNOW DATA

Average Snowfall
Data not available

Snowmaking
Data not available

Winter Periods
June to September

Summer Riding
None

SLOPE ACCESS

Total Lifts = **10**

Uplift Rate - 11,600 people an hour.

6 Chair lifts

4 Drag lifts

**Leashes Required*

Lift Times
9.00am to 4.30pm

Lift Pass Rates *in US $*
1 Day Adult US$25
6 Day Adult US$230

Travel Guide

Fly to **Buenos Aires** and then inland to Bariloche.

Trains to Bariloche with a two hour transfer time.

Route Planner: Via Bariloche, head north to San Martin de Los Andes on highway 234 and then take the bumpy dirt road Hwy 19 to reach the resort.

Just above the town of **San Martin De Los Andes** lies the resort of **Chapelco** which despite being a small resort still offers a big variety of terrain for all types and levels of rider. The arrival of a new resort director has led to the development of a number of snowboard friendly policies on the mountain, including the construction of a permanent halfpipe accessed from the **Palito** drag lift, and a programme of snowboard demos and freestyle classes. A low elevation means unreliable snow cover at the base area but up at the mid station things are usually fine. The resort has a good reputation among Argentine boarders, but due to its North facing aspect suffers unreliable snow conditions at times. The slopes are equipped with a modern lift system and a number of mountain cafes. But note, food and drink on the mountain is expensive.

Freeriders will find, that when the lower section has snow cover, it offers a rolling terrain of fast cruising dotted with cat track hits.The moss shrouded Lenga trees are well spaced for excellent tree riding off the sides of the mid and lower pistes, but lack pitch in places. Steeps are found on the faces of **Cerro Teta** and the **La Pala** face (40 degree) which remain unpisted and are fed by a speedy quad and poma drag respectively. Although short these faces provide the buzz that the freerider is looking for with 3-10m cliff bands laying down the gauntlet between the **Teta** and the **La Puma** areas. The back bowl offers superb powder if you re willing to do the one hour hike back out.

Freeriders have a permanent halfpipe accessed from the **Palito** drag lift which the locals session all day long.

Carvers may find that due to the lack of good piste grooming, the runs are bumpy and rutted, making this place not so ideal.

Beginners have an mountain with 40% of the terrain graded to suite their needs, but its not all ideal or super easy.

Accommodation can be found in **San Martin** 18 miles from the base. The *Poste del Caminero' Hostel* has bunks from $10 a night. There is a helpful tourist office to get you sorted. The town is small enough to be able to walk everywhere. Check out the *'Deli* by the lake for cheap snacks and the best priced beer in town. There are also a couple nighclubs and laid back bars.

For accommodation listings visit - www.worldsnowboardguide.com

Tourist office Chapelco
Cumbres de Chapelco. 233 Suipacha LOC 20.
++54 (0) 1 350 021 www.

Overall rating out of 10 — **5** — **A simple resort but still okay**

Cerro Bayo

Top lift at	1730m
Max Vert	720m
Ride area	12 miles of piste
Beginner	***20%***
Intermediate	***50%***
Advanced	***30%***
Lifts	8

Cerro Bayo is a resort with a local hill feel and some wicked scenery across the lakes of **Patagonia**. The area has 5 lifts giving access to an assortment of treelined pistes with an upper T-bar extending the last 300m above the trees to the summit. Freeriders can ride a 720m vertical off piste bowl before heading back into the trees to pick up a chair or continue to the base.

Lodging and eating can be found in the village of **Villa La Angostura**, which is a small and very friendly place. Services are limited and not really geared towards winter holiday makers. However, it s a cool place with a few restaurants and places to kip in. Access to and from the slopes is made easy by either driving up yourself or taking the shuttle bus or even taxi (pricey).

Fly to **Buenos Aires** and then **Bariloche** 2 hours away.

Resort Information;
tel ++54 (0) 1 3256 922

Gran Catedral

Top lift at	2050m
Max Vert	1000m
Ride area	45 miles of piste
Beginner	***15%***
Intermediate	***60%***
Advanced	***25%***
Lifts	5

Gran Catedral lies west of **San Carlos de Bariloche**. The resort is spread across three peaks and gives rise to the second most extensive resort in S.America. Although a low elevation prevents snow cover to the base for the whole season, cover is usually good higher up with a variety of terrain. Best freeriding areas include the off piste from the Piedra del Condor peak.

Accommodation is available at the base, but expensive. Cheaper and better for nightlife and eating is to stay in Bariloche.

Fly to **Buenos Aires** and then **Bariloche** 20 miles away.

Resort Information;
tel ++54 (0) 1 312 242

La Hoya

Top lift at	2050m
Max Vert	1000m
Ride area	45 miles of piste
Beginner	***15%***
Intermediate	***60%***
Advanced	***25%***
Lifts	5

La Hoya is decent size resort, by **South American** standards, located a short distance from the town of **Esquel**. The notable point about this place is the amount of advanced level terrain on offer that will suite hard core freeriders 100%. Although some of which will entail hiking and a few thigh burning traverse sections. The area has good intermediate trails as well as okay novice runs at the lower sections, but no halfpipe for freestylers.

Accommodation and other facilities are available at the base area.

Fly to **Buenos Aires** and then **Bariloche** 40 minutes away.

Resort Information;
tel ++54 (0) 1 3256 922

Perito Moreno

Top lift at	3340m
Max Vert	1100m
Ride area	2 runs
Beginner	***20%***
Intermediate	***60%***
Advanced	***20%***
Lifts	5

Perito Moreno is a tiny resort with more lifts than runs. This tiny outpost is located about 16 miles from the town **El Bolson**. On the slopes what you have is a mountain area covered with densely spaced trees with the piste cut out in a straight trail with a thin stretch of wood in the centre of the main Pista de Mario. Freeriders will find that although the piste is limited there is good backcountry with great powder, but be prepared to hike.

Basic lodging at the base, and down in **El Bolson**.

Fly to **Buenos Aires** and then **Bariloche** 2 1/2 hours away.

Resort Information;
tel ++54 (0) 1 944 92 600

Primeros Pinos

Top lift at	1500m
Max Vert	50m
Ride area	5 runs
Beginner	***90%***
Intermediate	***10%***
Advanced	***0%***
Lifts	3

Primeros Pinos is not really a resort as such. What you have here is a mountain area operated by a local company equipped with a few portable lifts which are placed wherever the best snow is, which on occasions is non existant. However, when the place is able to tow punters up, the decents are for one style and one level of ride only. Beginners, nothing else. Truly if you can ride and have two hours experisence don t bother with this place.

Some beds at the base, but main services down in **Zapala**.

Fly to **Buenos Aires** and then **Bariloche** 1 1/2 hours away.

Resort Information;
tel ++54 (0) 1 3256 922

Valden

Top lift at	830m
Max Vert	250m
Ride area	3 runs
Beginner	***35%***
Intermediate	***65%***
Advanced	***0%***
Lifts	2

Valden is located way down in the southern tip of the country and the bottom of the Andes. As well as being Argentina s smallest resort, it is also one of the busiest ,attracting large numbers of skiers on a regular basis. It s a bit hard to see why because there is naff all here, no decent piste or off-piste just a few intermediate and beginner areas. There is little else here to please especially if you re an advanced rider or freestyler.

All local services are found down in the town of **Rio Turbio**.

Fly to **Buenos Aires** and then **Rio Gallegos** 1 1/2 hours away.

Resort Information;
tel ++54

Las Lenas

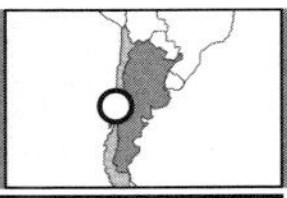

MOUNTAIN DATA

Top Lift at - 1850m

Ride Area
64km of piste

Bottom Lift at - 1050m
Vertical Drop - 450m
Number of Runs - 46
Longest - 4 miles (6km)

TERRAIN LEVELS

Easy	**25%**
Intermediate	**40%**
Advanced	**35%**
Expert =	

TERRAIN TO SUITE

Freeride	**70%**
Trees	Yes
Backcountry	Yes
Freestyle	**20%**
Halfpipe	Yes 1
Terrain Park	Yes 1
Carving	**10%**

SNOW DATA

Average Snowfall
Data not available
Snowmaking
Data not available
Winter Periods
June to October
Summer Riding
None

SLOPE ACCESS

Total Lifts = **14**
Uplift Rate - 9,000 people an hour.
7 Chair lifts
7 Drag lifts
**Leashes Required*

Lift Times
9.00am to 4.30pm

Lift Pass Rates *in US $*
1 Day Adult US$35
6 Day Adult US$275

Travel Guide

Fly to **Buenos Aires** and then inland to Mendozas.

Trains to **Malargue**, 40 miles from Las Lenas and will take 1 hour to reach.

Route Planner:
Via Mendozas, head south on highway 40.

Las Lenas has become a major destination for pro-riders, be they a sponsored rider doing some race training, or an air head getting the latest action with a film crew for a new video which we will have seen all before. You know the thing, over paid riders jumping off massive cliffs into deep powder fields and then shots of them getting drunk, being sick, and unconscious as a mate shoves a pole up an arse while another one cuts their hair very short, (*please spare us this crap from now on)*. Still on a positive note, it s no wonder that those in the know, and those with the money, (this place is mega bucks) come here when you look at what the resort has to offer. It s steep, above treeline and offers the rider big mountain terrain. It s high elevation usually ensures good deep fluff, while the 14 lifts (7 chairs) access 40 miles of piste and an abundance of challenging off piste terrain. But although this is easily the most challenging area in S.America (the *S.American Extremes* are held here) **Las Lenas** also has its bad points. Its high altitude renders it totally above tree line and the mountain is hit by major winds that close operations frequently during September

Freeriders willing to do the short hikes can get to 50 degree faces and as big ball cliff drops helping to make this placea freerider s dream. **The Marte** chair delivers you to terrain that is possibly the best that the S**outhern Hemisphere** has to offer.

Freestylers have a good pipe and park at the base which is the setting for the Reef big air comps.

Carvers can have a great time here with some well groomed fast trails and some great steep un-groomed runs.

Beginners have a really good mountain to learn on with slopes that are easy to reach and don t all mean having to use a drag lift. You can get snowboard tuition here but the instructors all speak **Spanish**, so bring your phrase book with you.

Lodging in **Las Lenas** is pricey (4 star hotels), though it is often easy to get a bed in the workers dormitory for $10 per night. Otherwise the nearest affordable beds are in **Malargue**, a small town down the valley. Transport to the resort is by bus from Buenos Aires (14 hours) or from **Mendoza** ($12 one way and 6 hours). The resort offers professional services and plush hotels as well as late night discos. In short, this place is a must if you can work out a way of affording to stay here.

Tourist office Las Lenas
Valle de Las Lensas, Malargue-Mendoza 5613
++54 (0) 1 627 71100

Overall rating out of 10 **7** **A really good place to ride**

CHILE

Capital - Santiago
Language - Spanish
Currency - Peso
Alcohol drinking age - 18
Drugs - Cannabis is illegal
Age of consent for Sex - 16
Electricity Supply - 240 Volts AC
International phone Code ++56

CHILE DRIVE GUIDE
All vehicles drive on the Right hand side of the road
Speed Limits -
Motorways 120kph (62mph)

TIME ZONES
GMT +4 Hours

pic -Scott Needham

Argentinian Snowboard Association
Zabala Street 2679 8*
ARG 1426 Buenos Aires
Tel++54 (0) 1 796 1951

Asociacion Argentina de Turismo
Viamonte 640, 10, 1053 Buenos Aires, Argentina
Tel++54 (0) 1 322 2804

Pucon

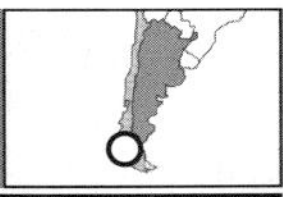

CHILE

MOUNTAIN DATA

Top Lift at - 2400m

Ride Area 1000 acres

Bottom Lift at -

Vertical Drop - 960m

Number of Runs - 22

Longest -

TERRAIN LEVELS

Easy	30%
Intermediate	40%
Advanced	25%
Expert =	

TERRAIN TO SUITE

Freeride	50%
Trees	
Backcountry	Yes
Freestyle	20%
Halfpipe	Yes 1
Terrain Park	No
Carving	30%

SNOW DATA

Average Snowfall
Data not available

Snowmaking
Data not available

Winter Periods
June to September

Summer Riding
None

SLOPE ACCESS

Total Lifts = **9**

Uplift Rate - 11,600 people an hour.

3 Chair lifts

6 Drag lifts

**Leashes Required*

Lift Times
9.00am to 4.00pm

Lift Pass Rates in US $
1 Day Adult US$22
6 Day Adult US$199

Travel Guide

Fly to **Santiago,** which is 492 miles from Pucon.

Bus services from Santiago are possible with a change over, and will take around 12 hours.

Route Planner: Via Santiago, head south on highways 5 and 119 via Temuco and Villarrica and then on up to Pucon.

pic -Soft Snapper

Pucon is a friendly and laid back place situated on the slopes of the **Villarica Volcano** in the **Lake District** region. It provides the rider with a perfect natural funpark for freestylers and cool freeriding destination. It should keep all snowboarders no matter what your ability, busy and content for a good seven days or more, although the volcano is still live and smoking. The resort is made up of four old creaking chairlifts and three drags, all but one of which are above treeline. Plans are afoot to install a further lift above the long left hand chair to access the steeper higher terrain. The feeling of riding the mountain is unique. The previous volcanic eruptions and lava flows have left behind a terrain of rollers and deep gullies. While the lift-accessed area is not particularly large and the lift positioning unimaginative, it contains some excellent freeriding/freestyle terrain with neverending hits, corniches and huge natural halfpipes that easily compensate for the lack of steeps. In short it s a playground. Snow quality varies due to the lower elevation and local climate factors. Storms roll in from the Pacific and drop their load, or the mountain may become fogged in. Winds quite often affect the operation of the old lifts.

Freeriders should check out the gullies on the left, and the cliff banks on the far right of the area. Steeper freeriding can be found by hiking from the tops of lifts, and guides (essential) can be hired in town to hike to the crater if you long to stare into the fiery bowels of Earth before riding back to the base for a coco.

Freestylers are now presented with an okay halfpipe, when conditions permit. However, whether there is a pipe or not, the area has so much natural terrain for getting air, that it s not really needed. There are some major cliff jumps and big banks here.

Carvers don t bother, piste bashing it s not the thing here.

Beginners will manage here but in truth there are better places.

The nearest accommodation is found in **Pucon** 1 mile away where you can get a cheap bed from as low as $8 a night. Access to the resort is by hitching at the foot of the access road or by minibus taxi ($6 per person return) from agencies in town. Adventure tourism is big in Pucon. Rafting ($20-35) is a buzz, take the upper trip as the lower one is for wusses. Good night time hangouts include *Mamas and Tapas* where local girls strutt their stuff, and *Piscola.*

Tourist office Pucon
Pucon. Villarica
++56 (0) 1 350 021

Overall rating out of 10 **5** **An interesting place to ride**

Antuco

Top lift at	1850m
Max Vert	450m
Ride area	2 runs
Beginner	***20%***
Intermediate	***50%***
Advanced	***30%***
Lifts	2

Antuco is one of Chile s resorts that can easily be over looked, simply because there is not much to look at. Located on a volcano (like so many other resorts in this part of the world). Antuco is a place best left to locals in the area. It s certainly not worth going out of you re way to visit. The two runs wouldn t hold the attention of a nat beyond 30 seconds. Beginners can have fun, but freestylers forget it as should piste loving carvers.

Best lodging are local and local services can be found at Los Angeles (not the US city), 40 minutes away.

Fly to **Santiago**, then bus via **Los Angeles** 40 mins away.

Resort Information;
tel ++56 (0) 2 332 651

Antillanca

Top lift at	1534m
Max Vert	465m
Ride area	2 runs
Beginner	***40%***
Intermediate	***30%***
Advanced	***30%***
Lifts	3

Antillanca is yet another volcano based resort. However, unlike simular hangouts there is at least some good backcountry tours you can take and without too much hiking or traversing, though you d better be tooled up incase you get lost on one of the many other volcanos in the area. The pisted areas provide some basic freeriding above and amid trees. Nothing is laid on for freestylers but there are rocks to get air from.

Good facilities are available at Antillanca s base area.

Fly to Santiago, then bus which will take over 10 hours.

Resort Information;
tel ++56 (0) 64 2 322 97

El Colorado

Top lift at	3333m
Max Vert	903m
Ride area	7 runs
Beginner	***40%***
Intermediate	***20%***
Advanced	***40%***
Lifts	16

30 miles, or 40 minutes from the capital is El Colorado, Chile's biggest resort. Being so close to Santiago has its draw backs as the slopes can often get very busy with Chile s high earning city dwellers who have been coming to the resort for skiing, since the thirties. The 25 marked out trails cater for everyone s needs especially advanced riders although the off-piste is a bit naff. However, this is a good resort for piste carvers and novices.

Expensive lodging, restaurants and bars are all slopeside.

Fly to **Santiago**, then bus, which will take 40 minutes.

Resort Information;
tel ++56 (0) 2 246 3344

La Parva

Top lift at	3630m
Max Vert	960m
Ride area	20 runs
Beginner	***15%***
Intermediate	***55%***
Advanced	***30%***
Lifts	13

La Parva is another resort in the throws of Santiago, and another popular modern affair loaded with all the razzmatazz and trappings found at many big foreign resorts. However, this is not big resort, but rather a good two days and its an all done sort of place. Still what is available is extensive, well set out and caters well for piste lovers and fast riding freeriders with some nice blacks and expert trails to try out. Good for beginners as well.

Lots of good local facilities are provided at the base area of the slopes, but nothing comes cheaply.

Fly to Santiago, then bus, which will take 50 minutes.

Resort Information;
tel ++56 (0) 233 2467

Llaima

Top lift at	1800m
Max Vert	300m
Ride area	7 runs
Beginner	**70%**
Intermediate	**30%**
Advanced	**0%**
Lifts	7

Visitors could be excused for getting a bit confused when they arrive here. Nothing to do with the slopes, but more to with the fact that there two Llaima s here with both using name and both similar in character with much the same terrain, number of runs and lifts serve them. Another common feature about this place is that for any fast riding thrill seekers, pick somewhere else, as this place is very flat and basically boring.

Best lodging and local facilities in Temco, 5 minutes away.

Fly to **Santiago** and then to **Ladeco** 55 minutes away.

Resort Information;
tel ++56 (0)

Portillo

Top lift at	3348m
Max Vert	750m
Ride area	22 runs
Beginner	***20%***
Intermediate	***30%***
Advanced	***50%***
Lifts	12

Portillo is a world renowned American run resort located at the foot of Aconcagua. Its high elevation provides it with plenty of dry snow making for good powder. 11 lifts access some 22 pistes and an abundance of steep off piste faces. Heli operations will take those with flexible enough plastic to higher elevations and descents.

The resort is distinctly up-market offering expensive accommodation and eating in its ugly complex of posh hotels, condos and slightly cheaper dormitories . Access Portillo by hitching from Los Andes, via the access road

Fly to Santiago and then bus 2 hours away.

Resort Information;
tel ++56 (0)

Termas De Chillan

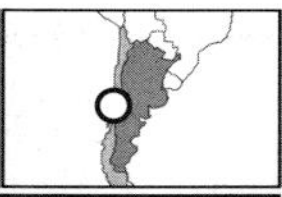

CHILE

MOUNTAIN DATA

Top Lift at - 2500m

Ride Area
40km of piste

Bottom Lift at - 1680m
Vertical Drop - 890m
Number of Runs - 40
Longest - 4 miles (6km)

TERRAIN LEVELS

Easy	**40%**
Intermediate	**40%**
Advanced	**20%**
Expert =	

TERRAIN TO SUITE

Freeride	**70%**
Trees	Yes
Backcountry	Yes
Freestyle	**20%**
Halfpipe	Yes 1
Terrain Park	Yes 1
Carving	**10%**

SNOW DATA

Average Snowfall
Data not available
Snowmaking
Zero
Winter Periods
May to October
Summer Riding
None

SLOPE ACCESS

Total Lifts = **3**
Uplift Rate - 6,500 people an hour.
1 Chair lift
2 Drag lifts
**Leashes Required*

Lift Times
9.00am to 4.00pm

Lift Pass Rates *in US $*
1 Day Adult US$38
6 Day Adult US$265

Travel Guide

Fly to **Santiago** which is over 350 miles away.

Trains to **Chillan** which is only 30 miles away from the resort.

Route Planner:
From Santiago, head south on highway 5 to Chillan and then turn off to Termas via Pinto.

pic- Scott Needham

Termas De Chillan is a small resort positioned on the south facing slopes of a dormant volcano and boasts the longest season of any of the S. American resorts. Despite a good snow record the resort has done little to make the most of it and offers only three ageing chairlifts and three drags. Most of the terrain is above treeline with the lower chair retrieving adventurous boarders from the trees and depositing them back at the base. The upper chair, **Don Otto,** not only accesses the best freeriding terrain on the mountain, but also holds the record for being the longest chairlift in S. America (2.5 Km). It is also one of the oldest and slowest and its frequent closure whenever the wind blows, means it s long overdue for replacement. The alternative when this chair is down is to ride a succession of three drags, (the middle poma holding the record for most blokes rendered infertile) to access some neat gullies with big banks. Plans have been made to extend the top drag further into the higher terrain which otherwise is rewarding but the hike-to country.

Freeriders will find what is regarded by locals as the best on offer, is accessed via a 10 minute hike from the top of the temperamental **Don Otto** chair. Hiking right from the top of this the rider is rewarded with 890 vertical meters of open bowls that exit into a series of 35-45 degree chutes back into the base. With pisting operations seemingly unheard of here the area is a freeriders dream. Beware though, avalanche control is also almost unknown of and you d be lucky to ever see the ski patrol.

Freestylers have a well constructed snowboard park and pipe reached off the middle poma.

Carvers who require pisted corduroy tracks, Mickey Mouse is really an Elephant, get the picture!

Beginners, if it were not for the way the lifts are laid out, then this would be an ideal novices haunt, but it s not.

With the nearest town being 50 miles away the resort has developed a complex of hotel and condo s below the base, mainly catering for affluent **Chile**an and visiting westerner. This accommodation is far out of reach of the average boarders pocket making finding somewhere to sleep nearby a problem. Four bed apartments ($25 per-person) can be rented at **Las Tranoas** 10 km from the base. Without your own transport access to the base is dependant on either hitching (relatively easy) or if you re staying in Chillan, taking the early bus.

Tourist office Termas de Chillan Resort
Providencia, Loc P41
++56 (0) 2 252 5776

Overall rating out of 10 **7** **Some gnarly ares to drop in to**

IRAN

pic - Trip

Capital - Tehran
Language - Persian & Arabic
Currency - Iranian Rial (IR)
Drugs - Cannabis is illegal
Electricity Supply - 220 Volts AC
International phone Code ++98
IRANIAN DRIVE GUIDE
All vehicles drive on the Right hand side of the road
Highest Peak:
Mount Damavand 5186m
Flight time from the UK
5 hours direct

TIME ZONES
GMT +3½ Hours

Dispel all the myths you have heard of this mighty country. Iran is safe for tourists, it is cheap, the food is excellent, you can drink the tap water, and most importantly there are some excellent snowboard resorts.

It may be surprising to hear that 30% of all people on Iranian slopes are snowboarders.

The ski lifts are well maintained and there have been no accidents in the past twenty years.

Iran has two big ski resorts, Shemshak and Dizin. Both resorts are within 2 hours drive from the capital, Tehran. There is also a resort called Towchal that has just opened.

Shemshak - 4000m (12000ft)
This resort is only a 45-minute drive from Tehran. The route is stunning, there are interesting towns to stop at on the way, and if you are hungry try out the amazing kebabs. Shemshak is well known as a resort for advanced skiers and snowboarders. The slopes are steep and funnily enough, have names such as The Wall . There are approximately eight extremely long runs with access to off piste slopes. Iranian slopes are generally long, wide, interconnect and there are no trees. This resort is undulating so it is hard to see all the different slopes. This is the most popular resort. There are cafes on the slopes and hotels and chalets at the bottom of the slope. It is extremely easy to find accommodation since a lot of people come here for the day or they stay at their own chalets. A one day ski-pass costs a measly $12 for an adult. It is also very easy to hire snowboard and ski equipment. A whole set up per day costs approximately $15 and don't worry it is not second hand stuff from Russia - a lot of the equipment is brand new.
If you want to have good apres-snowboard sessions this is the place to be. A lot of the Persians who come here are young, rich students studying in America or Europe and are probably on holiday seeing their parents. So practically all of them speak English, they are very western in their outlook and they are up for a damn good party. Shemshak is known as the party resort. So, look out for a group of snowboarders that look friendly and go up and chat, mention that you have heard that this is the party resort and they are sure to tell you what's going on.

Dizin - 4300m (12900ft)
If you continue along the road for another 30mins after Shemshak you will reach Dizin. At an altitude of 12,900 feet this is the highest snow resort in Iran and attracts the most amount of snow. Iran gets powder snow by the bucket loads. It is not uncommon for 50cm to land overnight every night during a dump in Shemshak. And more lands in Dizin. However, because of this huge amount of snow, there are a lot of avalanches, and the Iranians just let them happen naturally. There is no dynamite bombing. Therefore, there is the risk that the road to Dizin might be blocked with snow.

However, in the past three years the road has been open most of the time. To be on the safe side check at Shemshak before driving along.
Dizin is a completely different resort to Shemshak. The views are amazing. You can see unending mountain ranges and there is a clear view of the highest mountain in Iran, the semi-active volcano, Mount Damavand. Also, it is possible in this larger resort to see all the nine runs. Like Shemshak, the runs are wide, long and interconnecting and there are no trees. However, the slopes are not as steep attracting beginners through to advanced riders. The price for ski pass and hired equipment is the same as in Shemshak. It is also easy to find accommodation here in the hotels.
Towchal - 3500m (10,500ft)
This resort can be reached directly from Tehran City. There is a gondola that you can take from the north of the city up the mountain directly to the resort. The gondola, which was built during the 1970s when the Shah was in power, had been closed for over twenty years. However, it has recently been refurbished and opened again. Costs of gondola tickets and ski passes for next season are not yet known, therefore, it is best to contact the Iranian tourist board when you go to find out the newly released prices.

How to get to these resorts:
Contact 'Persian Voyages' in London (details at end of article) to get a competitive airline ticket to Iran.
You will have no problems arriving at Tehran airport with your own snowboard equipment, however, make sure it is in a snowboard bag. It is best to get a taxi from the airport into Tehran - it will cost you $6 maximum and will take half an hour.
You cannot rent cars in Iran so it is best to organise a bus tour from Tehran up to the ski resort you want to go to. This only costs $6-$7. Either you can go up for the day or you can leave the tour and stay in the resort for the week then catch a tour bus back down. Go to one of the many sports/ski shops in Tehran to organise a tour.

General information about all resorts:
The season is from the beginning of December to the end of March. You can easily go off piste, and there are vast fields of powder. However, there are no ski patrols recording the avalanche risks and triggering off avalanches where needed to reduce the risk. It is possible to hire a guide to go off piste for approximately $5-6 per day. The guides are extremely reliable and are usually trained in Switzerland and Austria. There are also reliable mountain rescue teams. There are no heli-boarding facilities.
Most of the time weather is reliable. You are sure to get a good week of riding in whenever you go.

There are a variety of lifts in these resorts ranging from gondolas and chairlifts to buttonlifts.
Also, it is wise to take your own food to the resorts. Look out for a town called Fasham on the way to Shemshak - you can buy all your basics there.

Accommodation
The concept of bed and breakfast accommodation is non-existent in Iran. However, because accommodation is so cheap why not stay in a 4 star hotel for $50 per night for a double room. Head for the north of the city: this is the safest area and has upmarket hotels such as the Hilton and the Sheraton. You can also contact the Iranian tourist board and ask them to organise accommodation for you in Iran.

What to wear:
On the slopes it is fine to wear your normal snowboard gear. However, if you are a girl make sure you are wearing a beanie. If it is sunny and you are boiling it is not advisable to strip off to your t-shirt on the slopes, if you are male or female. At all other times, women have to cover their hair and body but you do not need to wear a black cloak or chador . Instead it is fine to wear a colourful thin silk scarf tied under your neck and wear loose trousers, shirts with long sleeves, and a loose thin jacket that reaches down to your knees. It is fine to smoke anywhere except while walking along the street. Guys should not wear shorts and it is best to wear long sleeved shirts.

The food:
The food is unbelievably tasty - with fresh kebabs, amazing rice based dishes, fresh cheese, a lot of vegetarian dishes, amazing sweets and an array of fruit to choose from. Things you have to be careful about are eating salads and herbs that may not have been washed properly. However, keep in mind that it is absolutely safe to drink tap water. Also, check out Arak - Iranian vodka made from raisins and dried apples containing 35-45% alcohol. It is illegal for the Muslims to drink Arak but it is not illegal for Armenian Christians to drink it. Therefore, as tourists, you can buy Arak from the Armenians for approximately $3 for 2 litres.

Iranian Tourist Board
0098 21 643 210026
The tourist board can organise accommodation for you, work out an itinerary, give advice on prices and give telephone numbers for places and it s OK, they speak English.

The Persian Voyages
Info@persianvoyages.com
London based travel agency dealing with flights to Iran

ALGERIA
Reportedly has **2** resorts.
Capital: Algiers.
Travel: Very dodgy. The flight time from London is 2 1/4 hours.
Top peak- Mt Tahat 2918m.
Time Zone - GMT + 1 hour

ARMENIA
Reportedly has **2** resorts.
Capital: Yerevan
Travel: restricted.
Time Zone - GMT + 3 hours

BELGIUM
Reportedly has **12** slope centres where you can snowboard.
Capital: Brussels
Travel: no problems. The flight time from London is 1 hour.
Top peak- Botrange 694m
Time Zone - GMT + 1 & 2 hours

BOLIVIA
Reportedly has **1** resort which is the worlds highest.
Capital: La Paz
Travel: not great. The flight time from London is 17 hours.
Top peak- Mt. Tocoputi 2918m.
Time Zone - GMT - 4 hours

BOSNIA
Reportedly had **15** resorts, but since are all are now discarded battle grounds, don t bother.
Capital: Sarajevo
Travel: dangerous.
Top peak- Triglab 2864m.
Time Zone - GMT + 1 & 2 hours

BRAZIL
Has no known resorts.
Capital: Brasilia
Travel: cheap, but slow. Flight time from London is 10 hours.
Top peak- Mt. Pico de Banderia 2890m.
Time Zone - GMT - 5 hours

CHINA
Reportedly has **5** resorts.
Capital: Beijing
Travel: is restricted and note, this is a very oppressive country so be careful. The flight time from London is 10 hours.
Top peak- Mt Everest 8848m.
Time Zone - GMT + 8 hours

CROATIA
Reportedly has **2** resorts.
Capital: Zagreb
Travel: hit and miss! The flight time from London is 2 1/2 hours.
Time Zone - GMT + 1 & 2 hours

DENMARK
Reportedly has **2** ride areas.
Capital: Copenhagen
Travel: no problem. The flight time from London is 1 3/4 hours.
Time Zone - GMT + 1 & 2 hours

GREECE

Get this, **Greece** the hot spot where bodies bare all on countless sun drenched beaches scattered around numerous islands, also has a winter sports industry. Not well known, and come to think of it not even thought of by most. Never the less you can snowboard at any one of **15** recognised ski centres, though some are very dubious. However there are a number of mountain ranges where snow falls on an annual basis allowing the chance to shred it. Athens may be the historic home of the Olympics but just 2 1/2 hours away is the resort of Parnassos, where you can ride some 20 runs. Although the Greeks allow snowboarders on the slopes they re not totally sure about the whole scene yet and may at times seem a bit stand-offish but they re cool enough. Greece is definitely not a freestylers playground, forget about halfpipes or fun-parks. Some of the areas may have stupidly short runs and be equipped with an antique single lift system located along side the resort s only building, and true the terrain is not that great, it s generally flat, not well groomed and not very adventurous, but what the heck your riding in Greece.

If you fancy giving Greek snowboarding a go remember to contact the resort prior to leaving to see if the place is actually open and check on the latest conditions. The resorts are unbelievably basic, many without any facilities. You won t find dozens of places to eat sleep or drink in and as for hard core partying at night, forget it, this is Walkman and your duty free booze territory. Be well advised to take your own snowboard because hiring options are zero. Getting to the resorts is best done by self driving as the public transport is poor.
Travel: okay but slow
Capital: Athens
Travel: okay. The flight time from London is 3 hours.
Top peak- Mt. Olympus 2917m
Time Zone - GMT + 2 & 3 hours

GEORGIA
Reportedly has **2** resorts.
Capital: Tbilisi
Travel: is dangerous in this war torn country.
Top peak- Pik Konnunizma 7494m.
Time Zone - GMT + 4 hours

HOLLAND
Reportedly has **51** dry slopes to snowboard at.
Capital: Amsterdam
Travel: okay. The flight time from London is 1 3/4 hours.
Top peak- Vaalserberg 321m.
Time Zone - GMT + 1 & 2 hours

HUNGARY
Reportedly has **19** resorts.
Capital: Budapest
Travel: is not slow. The flight time from London is 2 1/2 hours.
Top peak- Mt. Kekes 1015m.
Time Zone - GMT + 1 & 2 hours

ICELAND
Reportedly has **12** resorts which allow snowboarding both in the winter and summer months. None of the resorts are big or offer extensive mountain services. What you have are basic low level mountains with poor road access to them. On the slopes runs tend to be short and not that well kept. However, Iceland is a very friendly snowboard country and resorts are more than happy to provide hits for freestylers to get air off. Visitors to Iceland will notice that apart from the short day light hours, that this is a very expensive country. Visa requirements for entry in to the country are very liberal but you will need to have return flight tickets on arrival.
Capital: Reykjavik
Travel: no problems
Top peak- Oraefajokull 2119m.
Time Zone - GMT

Resort file;

Blafjoll
20 runs with 11 lifts located 20 minutes from Reykjavik.
Info tel: ++354 (0) 1-52600

Hlidarfjall
Top lift 1000m with 4 lifts located 5 minutes from Akureyri.
Info tel: ++354 (0) 6-27733

Kerlingarfjoll
10 runs with 5 lifts located 3 hours from Reykjavik.
Info tel: ++354 (0) 525 4461

Skidastadir
9 runs with 4 lifts located 2 hours from Reykjavik.
Info tel: ++354 (0) 46 22280

INDIA

Capital: New Delhi

Travel: is slow. The flight time from London is 10 hours.
Top peak- Nanda Devi 7817m.
Time Zone - GMT + 5½ hours

Reportedly has **5** resorts. One of the best areas to ride is said to be at the resort known as **Auli,** near **Joshimath** in the **Garhwal Himalaya's,** where snowboarding expeditions have taken place. **Manali** is a place that offers some major heli-boarding while the areas known as **Narkanda** and **Kufri** are only suitable for total beginners and as they have very little in terms of facilities they are not recommended. The Indian season is best from mid-December to the end of March. All the areas offer a variety of terrain with a lot of treeriding and backcountry hikes possible, although you should only go backcountry riding in India with a knowledgeable mountain guide.

Resort locations guide:
Gulmarg - is in the Kashmir region 32 miles from Srinagar and has 5 lifts and heli-boarding.

Auli - is in the Uttar Pradesh region 10 miles from Joshimath with 12 miles of wooded piste.

Kufri - is in the Himachal region 9 miles from Shimla and is a flat place to suite beginners.

Narkanda - is in the Himachal region 40 miles from Shimla with the top lift at 3143m.

Manali - is in the Himachal region just 35 miles from Kullu.

Rohtang - is in the Himachal region just 30 miles from Manali.

All the Indian resorts provide very basic local facilities but are very cheap indeed.

For more details contact:
The Indian Winter Games Ass.
Western Naval Command
Shaheed Bhagar, Singh Rd
Bombay.

Indian Government Tourism
7 Cork Street,
London, W1X 2AB
tel: ++44 (0) 437 3677/8

IRAN

Reportedly has **12** resorts dotted around the country. However, most have been left to waste away as Iran is noted for skiing.

Capital: Tehran

Travel: very risky. The flight time from London is 6 hours.
Top peak- Qolle-Ye 5604m.
Time Zone - GMT + 3½ hours

ISRAEL

Reportedly has **1** resort.
Capital: Jerusalem.

Travel: is okay but girls should not hitch around alone. The flight time from London is 4½ hours.
Top peak- Mt Atzmon 1208m.
Time Zone - GMT + 2 hours

JORDAN

Reportedly has **1** dry slope that is privately owned by the King.
Capital: Amman

Travel: is not easy. The flight time from London is 5 hours.
Time Zone - GMT + 2 hours

KYRGYZSTAN

Reportedly has **1** resort.
Capital: Bishkek

Travel: is very dodgy.
Time Zone - GMT + 5 hours

LEBANON

Capital: Beirut

Travel: is not easy. The flight time from London is 4½ hours.
Time Zone - GMT + 2 hours

Reportedly has **6** resorts. There are more than 300 snowboarders in **Lebanon** who can ride at a number of high snow capped mountains spread along a stretch of the country. The Lebanese Snowboard Association (LSA) was founded back in 1993. Lebanon s most famous resorts are **Cedars** and **Faraya**. Cedars is located in the northern half of the country about 80 miles from Beirut. The slopes are small with only a couple of runs and five lifts. Faraya, which only 30 miles from Beirut, is the biggest of Lebanons resorts, although it is still relatively small compared to european destinations. Faraya has a dozen lifts with about as many runs that are rated mainly as intermediate standard with a couple of advanced runs and some very basic beginners trails. Entry in to Lebanon by foreign nationals is allowed but be careful as it wasn t that long ago when the country was at civil war with its self. All visitors need a passport and a visa to entry the country. The country is made up of Muslims and Christians, which was the main cause of the civil war. People are very friendly but don t take things for granted and don t stray off in to known areas.

LIECHTENSTEIN

Capital: Valduz

Travel: okay. The flight time from London to Zurich in Switzerland is 1½ hours.
Highest peak: Grauspitze 2599m
Time Zone - GMT + 1 & 2 hours

Liechtenstein is located between the boarders of Switzerland and Austria. The main resort is that of **Malbun** which is located 2 hours from Zurich airport. The resort is not big with only 20 km of piste and 8 lifts. The slopes are mainly rated intermediate but there are few steep blacks. The resort also provides a terrain park.
Off the slopes there are a number of hotels, bars, and restaurants close to the lifts. But this is a very expensive place.

LITHUANIA

Reportedly has **5** resorts.

Capital: Vilnius

Travel: Dodgy. The flight time from London is 3 hours.
Time Zone - GMT + 2 & 3 hours

MACEDONIA

Reportedly has **3** resorts.

Capital: Skopje

Travel: Dodgy. The flight time from London is 4 hours.
Highest peak: Solunska 2540m.
Time Zone - GMT + 1 & 2 hours

MOROCCO

Capital: Rabat

Travel: is not easy. The flight time from London is 3 hours.
Time Zone - GMT
Top peak: Mt. Toubkal 4165m.
Morocco has a number of resorts located in the **Atlas Mountains**. Most foreign nationals can enter the country with a valid passport without a visa, but you will need to have a return ticket when you enter the country.
The resort of **Oukaimeden,** which is half an hour from **Marrakech,** is the largest resort on Morocco with eight lifts and 12 miles of piste. At the base are a small number of hotels.
Local transport services are plentiful, but beware taxi and bus drivers will rip you off at every opportunity. If you have the time and means you could do a big road trip and enter Morocco from Europe via a ferry crossing from Spain.

NEPAL
Reportedly has **1** resort.
Capital: Kathmandu
Travel: okay but slow.
Top peak- Mt. Everest 8843m.
Time Zone - GMT + 5¾ hours

PAKISTAN
Reportedly has **1** resort.
Travel: Can very dodgy. The flight time from London is 11 hours.
Capital: Islamabad
Top peak- K2 8611m.
Time Zone - GMT + 5 hours

PERU
Reportedly has **1** resort but no lifts, it s a hike up only area.
Capital: Lima
Travel: not convenient. The flight time from London is 20 hours.
Top peak- Mt. Huascaran 6272m.
Time Zone - GMT - 5 hours

PORTUGAL

Capital: Lisbon
Travel: fine. The flight time from London is 2½ hours.
Top peak- Estrela 1991m.
Time Zone - GMT + 1 & 2 hours

Portugal, believe it or not, has a mountain winter sports resort where you can snowboard, complete with uphill lift services. Although Sierra de Estrela is no match for the main European Alps it's still real snow and cheap to visit. It's worth noting that the summit manages over 2000m, higher than anything in Scotland and higher than many Scandinavian resorts. Portugal has a good snowboard following that stems from it's influences and links with the big surf scene here. The Portuguese snowboard association was set up 1996 and is independent of any skiing group and fully supports the International Snowboard Federation. There are around 2000 snowboarders in Portugal and they are backed up by 4 snowboard clubs. The riding style favour mostly freeride and freestyle with only a few Alpine/Carvers around.

The people are really friendly and if you do decide to do a road trip for a two day visit in winter, remember that even if this snow is miserable, at least the people are not: They are warm and friendly and will show you a cool time, partying and chasing gorgeous women, while waiting for the white stuff to fall. Getting around in winter is best done with your own vehicle, local transport is not good.

Sierra de Estrela,

Portugal's only resort is that of **Sierra de Estrela,** located in the mid-northern region of the country. Despite the area's altitude, conditions are not always that favourable. The warm winds that blow in from the Atlantic coast also make it impossible to have snowmaking facilities. Most riders only check the place out at weekends and if the locals want to ride any longer they tend to visit Sierra Nevada in **Spain** and **Val D'Isere** or **Isola 2000** in **France**. Fortunately the 1996/97 season saw good snow falls of around 8 metres in depth, which allowed the *Portuguese Snowboard Federation* to hold their first ever national snowboard championship. The resort is planning new lift facilities for the coming seasons to allow more access to a greater area. At present it only gives 10 hectares of lift serviced terrain, though there is more to explore if your willing to do some hiking.

Freeriders will find some amazing off piste, that will appeal as much to intermediate riders as it will to advanced. If you take the lengthy hike over to the area called **Covado de Boi** at the opposite side of the main area, you'll gain access to a good share of couloirs to ride and some big hits to fly off. The only real drawback is that once at the bottom, if you have someone waiting with a car to take you back to the main area, you'll have to hike back. Still work hard, play hard! The other good place to check out is **Lagoa Escura**, a big slope where the best powder is to be had on a totally crowd free area that bases out at an amazing lake.

Freestylers should also check out the Covado de Boi area, where there's a 300 metre natural half pipe, which on occasions has 3 metre walls banked up.

Carvers who like to ride only long wide runs, forget it. This place is not for you. That said though, there are some open areas that allow for a few signatures in the snow with your edges.

Beginners this place is absolutely perfect for you, although hopelessly limited.

Because **Sierra de Estrela** is an ecological natural park, there are a lot of development restrictions on and around the mountain. Although some accommodation is available close by, the best option is in **Covilha**, 12 miles away where you'll find hotels, restaurants, shops to hire snowboards, bars, discos and places to simply hang out, all at affordable prices.

SERBIA
Reportedly has **25** resorts, which are now battle grounds and arms dumps since the country (which is full of psychopathic bigots) went to war on with its own.
Travel: very dangerous.
Top peak- Gerlachovsky 2655m.
Time Zone - GMT + 1 & 2 hours

SOUTH AFRICA
Reportedly has **1** resort called **Tiffindell** and is the only place in **South Africa** with snow making facilities.
Capital: Pretoria - CapeTown
Travel: is not the most convenient and be carefull, crime is rampant, the worst in the world. The flight time from London to Cape Town is 12 ½ hours.
Time Zone - GMT + 2 hours
Top peak-Mt. Aux Sources 4165m.

SOUTH KOREA

Reportedly has **19** resorts which include the worlds largest indoor snow slope owned by Daewoo.
Capital: Seoul
Travel: okay.
Top peak- Halla-San 1950m.
Time Zone - GMT + 9 hours

Korean resort guide:

Alps Resort
8 runs with 5 lifts located 40 minutes from Seoul.
Info tel: ++82 (0) 392 681 5030/9

Bears Town Resort
12 runs with 9 lifts located 40 minutes from Seoul.
Info tel: ++82 (0) 357 32-2534

Chonmasan Resort
4 runs with 7 lifts located 40 minutes from Seoul.
Info tel: ++82 (0) 346 594 1211

Hyundai Sungwoo Resort
21 runs with 8 lifts located $2^{1/2}$ hours from Seoul.
Info tel: ++82 (0) 372 40-3000

Daemyung Hongchon
13 runs with 12 lifts located 2 hours from Seoul.
Info tel: ++82 (0) 366 434 8311

Korea Condo Resort
3 runs with 2 lifts located 50 minutes from Seoul.
Info tel: ++82 (0) 374 35 0454

Muju resort
30 runs with 13 lifts located 3 and a half hours from Seoul.
Info tel: ++82 (0) 657 322 9000

Phoenix Park Resort
12 runs with 7 lifts located 50 minutes from Seoul.
Info tel: ++82 (0) 374 33-6000

Seoul Resort Resort
3 runs with 1 lift located 30 minutes from Seoul's centre.
Info tel: ++82 (0) 346 591 1230

Suanbo Sajo Maeul Resort
7 runs with 5 lifts located 2 and a half hours from Seoul.
Info tel: ++82 (0) 441 846 0750/5

Yangji Pine Resort
8 runs with 7 lifts located 40 minutes from Seoul.
Info tel: ++82 (0) 335 38-2001

Yong Pyeong Ski Resort
18 runs with 16 lifts located 40 minutes from Seoul.
Info tel: ++82 (0) 374 35 5757

TAIWAN

Reportedly has **1** resort.

Capital: Taipei

Travel: okay. The flight time from London is 14 hours.
Top peak. Yu Shan 3997m.
Time Zone - GMT + 8 hours

TURKEY

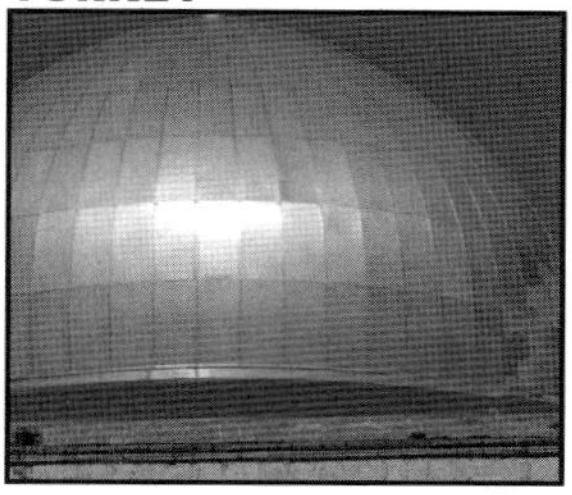

Capital: Ankara

Travel: okay. The flight time from London is 4 hours.
Time Zone - GMT + 2 & 3 hours

If **Turkey's** human rights record wasn't as bad as it is, it would be far easier to recommend a visit to this little talked of winter sports destination. Most people who visit this massive country do so only in the summer months, and most never venture from the main tourist destinations. Outside the normal tourist traps Turkey can be a hostile place. However, Turkey is an amazing country with spectacular mountains.

What you will experience in Turkey is a mixture of good freeriding on mountain slopes that will offer all levels something to take on. Advanced riders will need to find out from locals where the best off piste is and see if you can hire the services of a local mountain guide. Like all mountains, Turkeys peaks can be very dangerous so extreme caution should be taken. Ski or snowboard patrols are not common and especially not in remote areas. Still for those who can afford it, there are options to go heli-boarding with a guide. Turkey's resorts, which although they're great value for money are also very primitive and not big with only a few marked out trails and poor mountain facilities

Off the slopes resorts services are very basic. Where there are slope services, they are surprisingly very good with hotels, restaurants, and bars on the slopes allowing for plenty of doorstep snowboarding. The one big feature about Turkey and what it has to offer is the cost of things, 'Cheap', making Turkey better than many parts of Europe.

Travel to Turkey should pose no real problems. It would be a good idea to check with your local travel centre to see which companies offer winter package deals. Onward travel from airports and train stations may prove to be the trickiest of all your tasks. But give it a go as Turkey, despite its well documented faults, is well worth a visit for a snowboard holiday.

ULUDAG

Uludag, located south east of the **Istanbul**, is the biggest resort in **Turkey** boasting high altitude riding, heli-boarding and a good lift system. This small resort, is also the playground for Turkeys rich. The 16 miles of pistes are well located to the resort with a number of hotels on the slopes allowing for convenient doorstep riding on a daily basis. In general this is a resort that offers mainly intermediate easy going freeriders a simple time. And although there are a number of black steeps up on the **Zivre Peak** area, Uludag will not hold the attention of adrenaline seekers for too long.

Freeriders are presented with a mountain that offers the chance of riding some okay off piste on the **Kusaklikaya** area, reached off the Kusaklikaya chair lift. There's also the chance to shred through trees and ride some decent red runs at speed especially the trail that descents from the **Zirve** summit. Here the runs start out as a fast open black before descending into a red and tamer blue to the base, but be prepared for a 400 metre hike.

Freestylers will have to make do with getting air from the natural hits, as no permanent pipe exists. However, there are some really good gully to ride up. Log freaks will also find some wood to grind.

Carvers will be able to stretch themselves on wide open pisted runs which offer a mixture of fast reds on the **Kusaklikaya** area and blues on the **Beluv** area.

Beginners are best staying on the **Beluv** area, which has some good novice runs reached by either chair or drag lift. Note, that the easy slopes can get busy at weekends but like the rest of the mountain, are crowd free on week days.

Uludag is a match for many foreign resorts, boasting good slope side hotels and a number of okay places to eat and drink. Although this is a place that caters for **Turkeys** high earner's, it's still a very affordable place that has a lively night scene and is well worth a visit.

FREDRIK SARVELL
SCOTT ARNOLD
AMY JOHNSON
TINA BASICH*
TERO AINONEN
ROGER HJELMSTADSTUEN
TOM GILLES
© 2001 Tarē 7. all rights reserved. Photography: Espen Lystad (portrait) Stan Evans (action) Falun, Sweden *Boots only www.airwalk.com

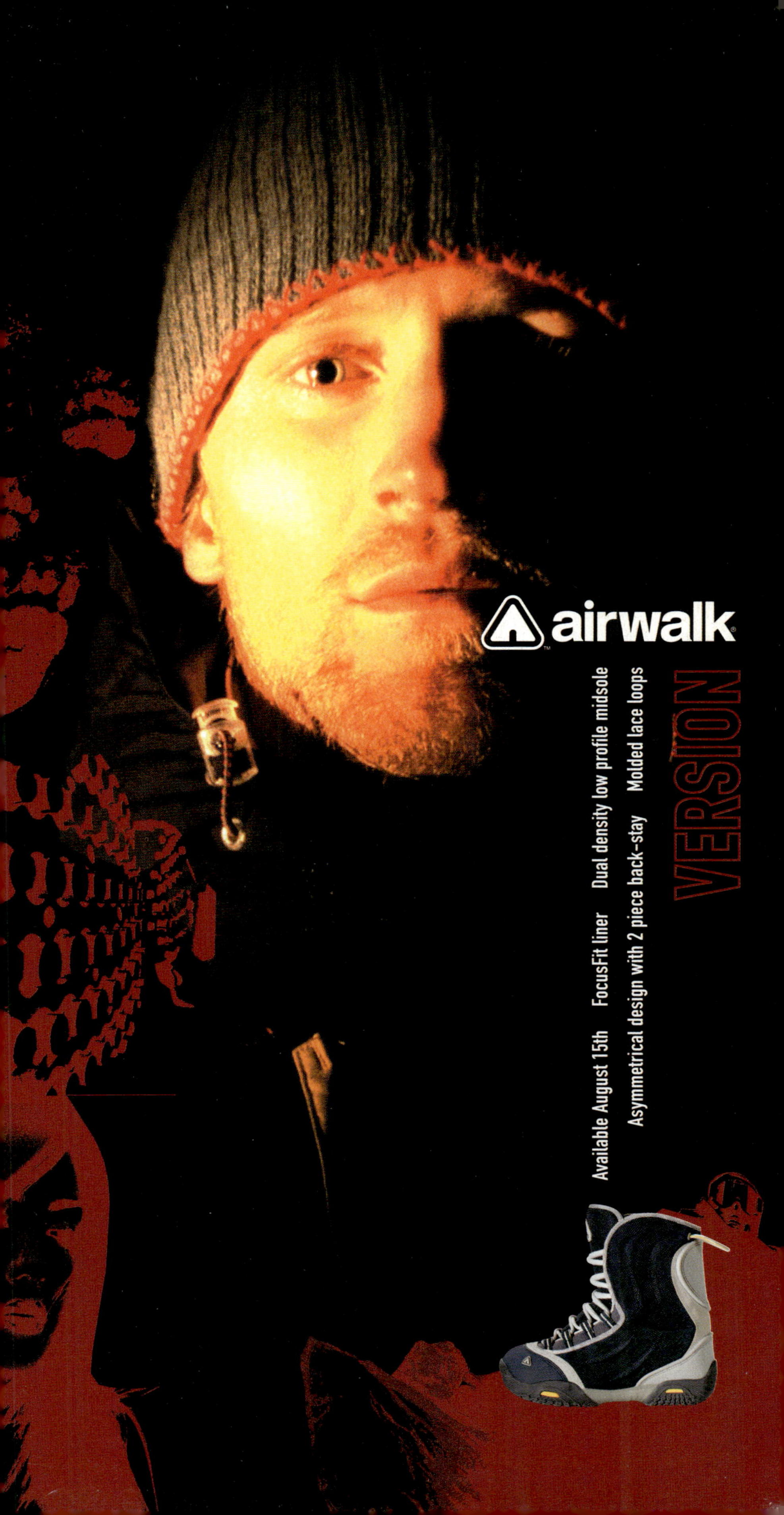
airwalk
Available August 15th FocusFit liner Dual density low profile midsole
Asymmetrical design with 2 piece back-stay Molded lace loops
VERSION

FLOW Flow and the Flow device are the registered trademarks of Goodwell International Ltd. and are exclusively licenced to Neil Pryde Ltd. PowerTriangle® is a registered trademark of Goodwell International Ltd.
tune into www.flow.com
for more product info and the latest news

pic by scalp, rider: stefan karlsson
flowsystem
rider
stefan
karlsson
FL_19+Morphan
FLOW
Custom Performance Boots & Bindings

A to Z Country Index

PALMER
SNOWBOARDS
Check out Shaun's new video game from Activision, "Shaun Palmer's Pro Snowboarder", coming this fall.
SHAUN PALMER'S PRO SNOWBOARDER
CHRIS WHO?
Mammoth has a big pipe and Chris Nelson smokes it everyday.
palmerusa.com
SHAUN WHO?
Shaun Palmer dropped out of high school during the 1986 season to become a pro snowboarder. He was 17.
1986
SESSIONS SNOWBOARD SHOP
Ultra sport
Ultra Sport (UK) Ltd
Acton House, Long Eaton, Nottingham NG10 1FY
T: 0115 973 1001 F: 0115 946 1067
E-mail: palmer@ultra.sportuk.com
Website: www.ultrasportuk.com
photography by Chris Carnel, Bud Fawcett, JVC

CHECK ANDREW OUT IN OPTIGRAB TB10 THIS FALL

FIG.05-08

PHOTO
RUBEN SANCHEZ
STANDARD FILMS
04
08
12
16
NW.TM.
RDR.
ANDREW CRAWFORD
#01.AD.#02.CRFD
KEVIN JONES . DANIEL SAPPA . MIKEY LeBLANC . GIAN SIMMEN
JACOB SODERQVIST . ANDREW CRAWFORD . MARTIN CERNIKPAULINE RICHON
DARIUS HERISTCHIAN . LUKAS HUFFMAN . TRISTAN PICOT
JAKOB WILHELMSON . DANNY KASS
FRONTSIDE
360°
MDL.LGND LEGEND
FTRS.HB.SYS
DUAL-DENSITY THERMOFORMED UPPER
TOE WEB SYSTEM
CALF COMPRESSION WINDOW
HEEL BRACE SYSTEM
3-D MOLDED TONGUE
INTEGRATED HIGHBACK SUPPORT
SPEED LACING
Anterior support with a comfortable and natural flex, this system is modeled after our upper web system. An ergonomic design built to imitate the toes' natural form and flex.
Ultra Sport (UK) Ltd
Acton House, Long Eaton, Nottingham NG10 1FY
T: 0115 973 1001 F: 0115 946 1067
E-mail: northwave@ultra.sportuk.com
Web: www.ultrasportuk.com
Ultra sport
northwave
snowboard boots
NORTHWAVE EUROPE TEL: 39.0423.2884
PIVA S.R.L. VIA FERRARIS, 54
31044 MONTEBELLUNA (TV)
WWW.NORTHWAVE.COM